PageMaker 4

an

easy

desk

reference

Robin Williams

Peachpit Press
Berkeley ▾ California

I would suggest that Apple Computer purchase the rights to this book and package it, labeled "Open Me First," with every purchase of a new Mac.
—JIM GAREY, *MacPac Printout*

The Little Mac Book should be required reading for all beginning Mac'ers.
—BILL DRENNEN, *VMEG Connection*

This handy-dandy little reference book will become as useful as your dictionary.
—BUD KAMENISH, *LCS Access*

If I had it all to do over again, and I just bought a Macintosh, this book would be my most important purchase, next to the Mac itself. Peachpit Press, you done good!
—PHILIP C. RUSSELL, *Mouse Droppings*

The Mac is not a typewriter

Buy this book, read it, follow its advice. Rarely had I been as impressed with a book as I am with this one.
—JERRY WHITING, *Aldus Magazine*

If you create pages on the Mac, you need this book!
—BMUG *Newsletter*

It is rare that we will say a book is must reading, but *The Mac is not a typewriter* definitely qualifies.
—CBT *Directions*

What a superlative book!
—WILL SCHER-GRODNER, *The Mac Street Journal*

Delightful!
—ALLAN HALEY, *International Typeface Corporation*

Lets the reader in on some of the secrets that have been used for centuries to make type pleasing, beautiful, readable, and artistic.
—BUD KAMINISH, *LCS Access*

A great little book for novice and expert alike.
—*MacUser*

Short, elegantly laid out, and delightfully unpretentious in tone.
—GUY KAWASAKI, *MacUser*

An excellent resource manual.
—LORRAINE CZOLBA, *GATFWorld*

This slim volume packs a wonderfully engaging introduction to basic typography.
—*Personal Publishing*

Filled with useful down-to-earth counsel.
—RICHARD D. JOHNSON, *Small Press*

Her section on hanging the punctuation alone is worth the price of the volume.
—*Computers in Libraries*

This book should be required reading for every newly-dubbed desktop publisher, regardless of hardware platform.
—C.J. METCHSKE, *From the Desktop*

I plan to keep a copy beside my Mac and refer to it often.
—MAJIE ALLEY, *The Mac Monitor*

The perfect book to help you learn the differences between what you may have learned as a typist and what you need to learn to make the best use of your Macintosh.
—GEOFFREY FLETCHER, *Australian MACWORLD*

Buy it, and keep it next to your computer.
—SARAH BROOKS, *UAUG News*

A book I've been searching for for a long time.
—ANDY BAIRD, *MUG News Service*

Gathers all the Macintosh typographic lore into one small, easily digested package.
—BOB LeVITUS, *MacUser*

An essential guide to getting the most from your Mac.
—*U&lc Magazine*

Williams runs through subtle matters which nonetheless have an important part in professional-quality typesetting. . . familiar subjects which the author treats simply and clearly, using helpful illustrations.
—HENRY BERRY, *COSMEP Newsletter*

Peachpit Press
2414 Sixth Street
Berkeley ▾ California ▾ 94710
415.527.8555
800.283.9444
415.524.9775 fax

Notice of liability
The information in this book is distributed on an "As is" basis, without warranty.
While every precaution has been taken in the preparation of this book, neither
the author nor Peachpit Press, Inc., shall have any liability to any person or entity
with respect to any liability, loss, or damage caused or alleged to be caused
directly or indirectly by the instructions contained in this book or by the
computer software and hardware products described herein.

Trademarks
Throughout this book trademarked names are used. Rather than put a trademark
symbol in every occurrence of a trademarked name, we state we are using the
names only in an editorial fashion and to the benefit of the trademark owner
with no intention of infringement of the trademark.

Library of Congress Cataloging-in-Publication Data
Williams, Robin
    PageMaker 4: an easy desk reference/Robin Williams.
        p.   cm.
    Includes index.
    1. Desktop publishing.   2. PageMaker (Computer program)
I. Title.   II. Title: PageMaker four.
Z286.D47W5382   1991
686.2'2544536–dc20   90-49587
                                           CIP
ISBN 0-938151-28-2   : $29.95

0 9 8 7 6 5 4 3 2
Printed and bound in the United States of America

Used with permission
etaoin shrdlu, by Herb Caen. First printed in the San Francisco Chronicle in 1979.

beginnings, by Carl Dair. From his most wonderful book, *Designing with Type*.
Published by University of Toronto Press, 1967.

A passage by Jan White, printed in another of my favorite books, *How to Spec Type*,
by Alex White. Published by Watson-Guptill Publications, 1987.

A quote from Sean Morrison in his great little book, *A Guide to Type Design*.
Published by Prentice-Hall, Inc., 1986.

This book is dedicated, with so much love and respect,

To **Ryan,** age 12, who asked, "When you finish this book, are you going to spend time with us again?"

And to **Jimmy,** age 8, who mused, "I can't figure out whether you're diurnal or nocturnal; you work all day and you work all night."

And to **Scarlett,** age 4, who kept reminding me, "That's the way it is in Life, Mom."

Overview of Contents

CONTENTS

247   SECTION 5 ▾ INDENTS & TABS

411   SECTION 10 ▾ **LINKING TEXT & GRAPHICS**

429   SECTION 11 ▾ **TEXT WRAPPING**

443   SECTION 12 ▾ **TEMPLATES**

SECTION 13 ▾ **BOOK PUBLICATIONS**
477   (INCLUDING TABLE OF CONTENTS AND INDEXING)

533   SECTION 14 ▾ **COLOR**

559   SECTION 15 ▾ **IMPORTING & EXPORTING**

575   SECTION 16 ▾ **SAVING & REVERTING**

583   SECTION 17 ▾ **TABLE EDITOR**

Acknowledgments

I first thank my editor, **Mary Grady,** for the incredible amount of work she put into this book. In my arrangement with Peachpit Press, I hire my own editor and provide Peachpit with camera-ready pages. Mary tested, edited, copy-edited, and indexed each section, penciling in the thousands of cross-references along the way. Oh my gosh it was a lot of work. I thank you, Mary, for the strength and value you added to this book. And I thank you for your friendship.

I must thank **Beverly Scherf** for doing a final proofreading of this book (yes, she read it from cover to cover). Beverly caught a number of details that slipped past Mary and me, even though we each read it at least thirty times. It never ceases to amaze me how that can happen. Thank you, Beverly!

Another great bundle of thanks to **Harrah Argentine,** who designed four of the almost-irrelevant articles included in this book. Harrah spent an enormous amount of time researching and illustrating images for the stories, and then designing the pages. She did a much more beautiful job than I ever could have done, and has added a touch of beauty to the book. Thank you, Harrah.

I send a huge thank you to **Janet Butcher,** with her technical expertise as a service bureau manager, for a great deal of input on the printing and color sections, for all her meticulous care in nursing all these pages out of the lino, as well as for her wonderful moral support and general sweetness;

And I thank **Kimberly Scott,** for her incredible generosity with technical support and information;

Ronni Madrid and **Barbara Sikora,** for adjusting the text on 400 pages when the page size changed halfway through the book;

Olav Martin Kvern and **Steve Roth,** truly nice guys and authors of *Real World Page-Maker* (a high-powered book that every advanced user of PageMaker should read), for their cheerful willingness to share their expertise and for allowing me to expand some of their great tips into step-by-step tasks in this book;

Jerry Whiting and **Craig Danuloff** of Aldus Corporation, for keeping me abreast of the most current developments in PageMaker;

Dan Burke, of Stickney-Burke Printers, for sharing his time, his hot type, and his Linotype machine;

Marjorie Cerletti, for her loving care of my littlest one and her valiant attempts at keeping my house in some semblance of order (a most overwhelming task);

Ellen Geohegan, for bringing me such delicious meals on those days when she knew I wasn't going to take time out to cook for myself;

And **Jim Hampson,** whom I have never actually met, but who taught me of Matters of Great Consequence, none of which had anything to do with PageMaker.

An enormous thank you to **Ted Nace,** publisher of Peachpit Press and a most wonderful person, who was so patient with me as this book got bigger and bigger and farther and farther behind deadline. The entire staff at Peachpit is an incredibly special group of people, and I feel very proud and lucky to be a Peachpit author.

Including philosophical reflections,
the like not to be found in any
Ordinary manual.

Don't read this book from cover to cover!

This book is definitely not meant to be read from cover to cover. It would be stupid of me to write a software reference manual this large that had to be read from one end to the other because nobody would read it.

This book is not a tutorial. It does not take you through lesson plans to teach you how to use PageMaker. There are already good books like that. This is strictly a reference book. But an interesting reference book.

In the first part of each section, you'll find background information on one particular topic. For instance, in the Indents and Tabs section, there is information on the logic behind indents and tabs (yes, there really is logic), along with lots of examples and suggestions. Then each section breaks into a list of tasks: for instance, how to create a tab, move a tab, delete a tab, make tabs with leaders, etc. Every possible thing you could ever think of to do in PageMaker has a separate task with step-by-step directions for accomplishing that task.

So you can choose to read the preliminary information to understand the whole picture, or you can skip it and jump directly to the task you want to accomplish. Find the task you need by skimming through the appropriate section, looking it up in the index, or finding the exact reference number in the list of tasks in Appendix B. Or you *could,* of course, read from cover to cover.

I repeat myself a lot in this book. I tried never to assume that you previously read any other part of the book. Although everything is extensively cross-referenced, many times I repeat information so you don't have to waste time flipping to another section for important info.

I feel it is my obligation to make this book as useful as possible to you. If you have any suggestions, comments, or useful tidbits of information, please let me know as I'd be happy to incorporate them into future editions.

Robin

Please note:

- Numbers in parentheses—like so: (3.102–3.107)—mean you will find relevant, interrelated information in those paragraphs. You don't *have to* read the relevant information; the references are just there for your convenience.

- A thick bar along the side of a column indicates that the information next to it is of particular importance or interest.

- A short quotation separate from the main body of information indicates an educative statement or comic relief.

- Here and there throughout the book are short articles of vaguely relevant interest, stories of Aldus Manutius, Johannes Gutenberg, or some historical curiosity relating to type and printing (like the story on the next page). These exist simply because this is my book and I wanted to put them in. The articles may make for interesting reading while you wait for your work to come out of the printer.

beginnings

The use of written or printed symbols as a basic element of design is not a discovery of our era; it is not even a result of the invention of movable type by Gutenberg. It reaches back into the dawn of civilization, to wherever and whenever man took up a tool and attempted to inscribe on a receptive surface a message to be preserved. It would seem that there was something of an instinctive urge in the dark recesses of the pre-civilized mind towards an orderliness and a pattern in the grouping of the symbols which were to convey this message.

As far back in the history of man's effort to write as you care to go, this innate sense of orderliness has dominated his graphic art. The clay tablets of Mesopotamia and the hieroglyphs of Egypt, the circular tables of Crete and the precise geometry of the Greek letters, the careful alignment of the flowing characters of the Chinese and the musical lilt of Persian script, the solemnity of the Roman inscriptions and the decorated pages of the Book of Kells—need one go on?—all these attest the desire of the hand that recorded to please the eye that would read. The forms of these patterns were many, and they arose out of the whole composite of the art and the culture from which they stemmed.

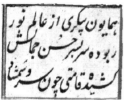

The invention of movable type did not change this urge towards the beautiful in graphic presentation; it simply provided the means, denied to the ancients, of reproducing the original work and so widening the public who would see and read. The early printers of Mainz and Basle and Venice were not indifferent to the obligation this freedom imposed on them, and so they sought, with meticulous care and craftsmanship, to make each letter, each line, each page as beautiful as they had been in the manuscripts which had sired the art of printing. The typecutter put all his skill and sense of form into the creation of beautiful individual letters; the typesetter sought to combine these characters into pages of dignity; and the pressman took painstaking care to reproduce the whole uniformly, with just the right amount of ink, so that none of this elegance might escape making its timeless imprint upon paper.

Each in his own time, often with crude tools poised against resisting surfaces, tried to make the written record the epitome of the art and culture of his own period. Bone against clay, chisel against stone, brush against silk, quill against parchment, lead against paper, each tool made its characteristic mark, and each surface received the impression in its characteristic way. The hand of the artist accepted his materials and made the most of them. The tradition is long and the urge is deep.

The speed of reproduction of the written word by machines in a modern printing plant would astound the ancients. But if they could see it, they might wonder why, with the labour of writing so eased by mechanical devices, we are not able to put even greater thought into the design of our printing.

No doubt these same ancients would also not understand the cost sheet we would show them; they would find the urgency of deadlines as an excuse for shoddiness incomprehensible; they would be bewildered by the complex relationships of individual specialists involved in doing the work they once did single-handed. And they would probably return to their primitive tools shaking their heads with awe at the accomplishments of twentieth-century printing technology, but yet distressed that all the art and loving care they had lavished on the written and printed word counted for so little. They might well conclude that, while we can produce more and faster, they could give a better product.

Carl Dair

DESIGNING WITH TYPE

Never bother to remember anything
you can look up in a book.

— *Albert Einstein*

1 ▾ Basics

This section covers just the basics of working in PageMaker, with some of the basic Macintosh functions explained as well, as they are related to creating publications in PageMaker.

Although the rest of the book assumes you understand the features discussed here, you will always find cross-references directing you to the specific details that can be found in this section.

Remember, this book is not meant to be read from cover to cover (see the introduction on page xvii). If you are just beginning with PageMaker, you may want to skip the first segment on defaults and return to it later when the terms make more sense.

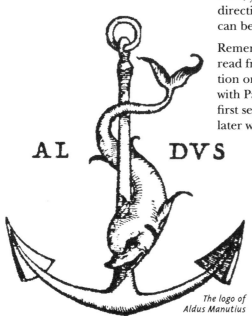

AL DVS

*The logo of
Aldus Manutius*

A few definitions

1.1   Press

With the mouse, *pressing* is very different than *clicking*—a *click* is when you give a short tap on the button, while a *press* is when you *hold the button down*. They accomplish very different objectives.

1.2   Press-and-drag

Whenever you see the term *press-and-drag*, it means to *press* the mouse button down, *hold it down*, and *drag* the mouse across the table.

1.3   Keyboard vs. Keypad

When you read the word *keyboard*, it is referring to the normal keyboard you see in front of you with all the characters on it. The word *keypad* is referring to the numeric section on the right of the keyboard. The *keypad* looks like calculator keys.

1.4   Pasteboard

The *pasteboard* is the area in the window that is outside of the page outline. It acts just like a drafting table: a page you are working on in PageMaker is comparable to a paste-up board on your drafting table; as you change paste-up boards, your drafting table stays the same, right? Same with this pasteboard—anything you place on it at any time will still be there when you change pages. This comes in very handy. Also, you have more room than you see—hold down the Shift key and choose "Fit in window" from the Page menu and you will see the boundaries of the pasteboard that you have available to work within (called the *mini-view* or *Fit in World;* 1.108).

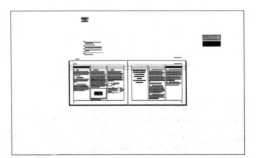

The outer border shown here appears in the mini-view, defining the limits of the pasteboard.

1.5   Handles

In an object-oriented program such as PageMaker, every object is a separate entity. Every object—text blocks, imported graphic files, clip art, PageMaker graphic shapes, lines—has its outer edges defined by *handles*. The handles appear on the object when you click on it with the pointer tool. *Once handles are showing,* the object can then be manipulated (deleted, resized, copied, cut, etc.).

The eight handles that appear on a graphic image.

This text block has been selected with the pointer tool. Notice the four handles on the corners. Text blocks also have window shade loops, seen at the top and bottom. See 3.95–3.102.

The four handles and two loops that appear on a text block.

T ✦ Y ✦ P ✦ E

gives body and voice

to silent thought.

The speaking page

carries it

through the centuries.

Friedrich Schiller

✦

1.6 A **default** is a pre-set option that PageMaker automatically reverts to if nothing else is chosen. For instance, with the standard defaults, every time you begin a new text block the text comes up with Times, 12 point, auto leading, with no indent. When you draw a line, the pre-set option is 1 point. When you draw a box, the border is 1 point and the fill inside is None. You can adjust these so the pre-set options, or *defaults,* are exactly what *you* need to work with.

You can set two different sorts of defaults: *application* and *publication.*

1.7 **Application defaults.** You can change the defaults for the entire Page-Maker application so every time you open the program and create a *new* publication, it is already set to your specifications. This is very handy if you create a lot of one particular kind of publication, perhaps tabloid newsletters. See 1.11, Scenario #1.

1.8 **Application defaults** will not affect any publications you have already created. The application defaults *you* set will override the original PageMaker defaults (to restore the original ones, see 1.15).

1.9 **Publication defaults.** You can set the defaults for just the particular *publication* you are working on at the moment (1.14). These are temporary defaults that will *not* be carried over into the next publication you open or create, but they will be saved along with this one. You can change them over and over again, depending on what part of the project you are working on. See 1.11, Scenario #1. *Publication defaults override any application defaults.*

1.10 Be careful! It is possible to set reverse text or a reverse line as the default, so every time you type or draw a line or shape, it shows up invisible. It's also possible to set a default text wrap so every object you draw or paste forces the text away from itself (text wrapping is discussed in Section 11). *Whenever something happens over and over again, it is because there is a default somewhere.* Reset it.

1.11 Scenario #1: Setting defaults

The key to recognizing defaults and knowing when it is time for you to change them is this: if something occurs regularly, it is a default. If you want something different to occur regularly, it is time for you to change the defaults.

For instance, if a box fills itself with a solid shade every time you draw with the rectangle tool, there is a default; if you want to draw boxes with a 10% shade, change the default. If the insertion point jumps to the middle of the column every time you click the I-beam, there is a default of a center alignment; if you want a regular left alignment, change the default. If you get extra space between the paragraphs every time you hit a Return, there is a default. If the text appears in some strange font every time you type, there is a default.

Sometimes things change and you don't know why. I'll tell you why: it's because you are *accidentally changing the default.* **If there is nothing selected when you choose anything from the menu or any dialog box, you are setting a default.** It happens all the time: we forget to select before we try to change something. Whenever we do that, we set a new publication default.

Let's say your department regularly produces tabloid publications—every morning you have to create a new publication and you change the Page Setup to your tabloid specs. Well, rather than reset the Page Setup and all the other specs each time you begin a new publication, you can set the **application defaults** to those specifications you regularly need; e.g., tabloid-sized paper, eight pages, one-inch margins all around, double-sided with facing pages, autoflow text, wrap all graphics with a 1-pica standoff, all boxes with a thin double border and a solid fill. Set up your style sheets (Section 6)—from which of course you may deviate on the various publications. Then, every morning when you begin a new publication, these specs are already set up!

This scenario gets more complex, but if you're ready for it, read on: Let's say you typically bring in your stories from a word processor, but you always type the heads directly into PageMaker because you want to override the columns. In your style sheet, before you open any publication, select the style Headline as an application default; whenever you start a new text block, you will automatically type in the Headline style.

Let's say you've created your publication, placed all your stories, positioned all your graphics, typed all the heads, and now you need to draw a series of 8-point lines. But remember, you previously set an application default to a thin double line. So now you can set a temporary (**publication**) default: with nothing on the page selected, choose the 8-point line. Now all your lines will automatically draw in 8 point.

You are ready to put captions under all the photos. You previously set your **application** default for text as Headline, so every time you start to type, the text shows up in the Headline font. But that's not what you want now! So override the application default with a **publication** default: with *nothing* selected, choose your Caption style from your style sheet (or choose *No Style* and select the font, size, and style from the menus); now everything you type will be in the Caption formatting, so you don't have to go back and change it after each time you type.

Next time you begin a *new* publication, you will again have the *application* defaults, but not these temporary ones you created in this publication.

If you want to do this:	**Then follow these steps:**	**Shortcuts ▾ Notes ▾ Hints**
1.12 Set the **application** defaults *(1.7–1.8)* for the entire PageMaker program	■ From the PageMaker desktop, *when you can see the PageMaker menu but no publication is open,* use the **pointer** to choose any menu item that is not gray, or change any item in any dialog box you can call up.	■ Anything you change at this point will become an *application* default. ■ To change the printer type and the paper size in the "Print to" dialog box, see 1.13.
1.13 Set **application** defaults in the Aldus printer dialog box for Printer type and Paper size **Printer:** ⌷ LaserWriter II NT ⌷ **Paper:** ⌷ Letter ⌷	■ Open PageMaker and create a New, untitled publication. ■ Save and name the publication. ■ Draw at least one line or type at least one character so it is not a blank page. ■ From the File menu choose "Print...." ■ Change the Printer and the Paper size to your preference. ■ Print the one-page publication. ■ Save it again (Command S).	■ Unfortunately, you can't change the default for anything else in the Print dialog box. Wouldn't it be nice to default the crop marks? ■ You *can* print a blank page for this, if you choose, as long as you make sure to check that dialog box option before printing. ■ After setting this default, you can throw away the one-page publication. ■ (Actually, you know what? The last paper size you chose to print in any publication, if you saved, becomes the new "default.")
1.14 Set **publication** defaults for the current open publication	■ Your publication must be open. ■ Click once on the **pointer tool,** *even if the pointer tool is already selected.* ■ Choose any menu item that is not gray, or change any item in any dialog box that you can call up.	■ You can really click on *any* tool to ensure that nothing in the window is selected. ■ Anything you change at this point will become a *publication* default. ■ *Publication* defaults will override *application* defaults just for this publication.

If you want to do this:

1.15 Revert back to the original
PageMaker defaults

PM4 Defaults

Then follow these steps:

- At the Finder/Desktop (before starting
  or after quitting PageMaker), open your
  System Folder.
- In the System Folder you will find a
  document titled "PM4 Defaults." This file
  now contains the current application
  defaults that you have set.
- Throw that file in the trash; when you
  restart PageMaker, the original default
  settings built into the program will be
  returned.

Shortcuts ▾ Notes ▾ Hints

- Really, this is OK! If you take a peek into
  your System Folder the next time you
  quit PageMaker, you will find that the
  "PM4 Defaults" file came back, containing the original application defaults!

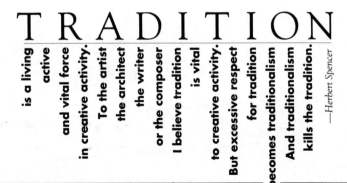

TRADITION is a living active and vital force in creative activity. To the artist the architect the writer or the composer I believe tradition is vital to creative activity. But excessive respect for tradition becomes traditionalism And traditionalism kills the tradition. —*Herbert Spencer*

1.16 The Defaults

The following is a list of the specifications you can adjust—some items from the menu, some from the appropriate dialog box.

FILE MENU	YOU CAN SET:
Page setup	Page size
	Orientation
	The page number to start numbering with
	The number of pages in the publication
	Whether the publication is single- or double-sided
	Whether to show facing pages for double-sided publications
	Margins
	Style of numbers for automatic page numbering
	Prefix to use for Table of Contents and Index
	4.01: Restart page numbering
Print	Printer type
	Page size

EDIT MENU	YOU CAN SET:
Preferences	Measurement system
	Vertical ruler measure
	Whether the guides are on the front layer or on the back layer
	Size of type to show as "greek" text in the smaller window views
	Screen resolution of detailed graphics
	Whether to let you know if word spacing is too tight or too loose
	Whether to let you know if text lines are violating the paragraph "keeps" controls
	What size and what font to show in the Story Editor
	4.01: Save option of Faster or Smaller

OPTIONS MENU	YOU CAN SET:
Rulers	To show or to hide
Snap to rulers	On or off
Zero lock	Locked or unlocked *(if Rulers is on)*
Guides	To show or to hide
Snap to guides	On or off *(if Guides is on)*
Lock guides	On or off *(if Guides is on)*
Column guides	Number of columns and space between *(if Guides is on)*
Autoflow	On or off

PAGE MENU	YOU CAN CHOOSE:
No defaults can be set from this menu.	

—continued

Defaults *—continued*

TYPE MENU	YOU CAN SET:				
Font	Any font	Type options:	Small cap size	Spacing:	Word spacing
Size	Any "graphic art" size listed		Super/subscript size		Letter spacing
Leading	Any leading listed		Superscript position		Pair kerning on or off; above the point size of your choice
Set width	Condensed (70%) to **Expanded (130%)** or anywhere between 5% and 250%	**Paragraph**	Subscript position		
			Indents		
			Paragraph space *(the amount of leading before and/or after a Return)*		Whether leading is proportional or not
Track	Very loose letterspacing to very tight letterspacing				Percentage of the point size for auto leading
			Text alignment *(same as if chosen from the Alignment command in the Type menu)*	**Indents/Tabs**	Left indent
Type style	Any style listed				Right indent
Type specs	Font				First-line indent
	Size		Dictionary		Tabs
	Leading	Rules:	Rules (lines) above and below paragraphs	**Hyphenation**	On or off
	Set width				Manual with dictionary, or Manual with algorithm
	Color		Grid size *(under Options…)*		
	Position: whether to set normal (hello), in superscript (^{hello}), or in subscript ($_{goodbye}$)		Grid alignment *(under Options…)*		Limit number of consecutive hyphens
		(Options)	"Keeps" controls		
			Widow and orphan control		Hyphenation zone
	Case: whether to set in ALL CAPS, lower case, or Small Caps		Column and page break controls	**Alignment**	Any paragraph alignment
				Style	Which of the styles in the style sheet to type with
	Track (any setting)		Inclusion of Table of Contents label		
	Type style of your choice				

Defaults —*continued*

ELEMENT MENU	YOU CAN SET:
Line	Any line or border
Fill	Any fill or shade
Text wrap	Wrap option and standoff
Rounded corners	Any corner
Define colors	Text color
Link options	Options for updating and storing links for text and graphics

WINDOWS MENU	YOU CAN SET:
Toolbox	To show or to hide
Scroll bars	To show or to hide
Style palette	To show or to hide
Color palette	To show or to hide

*M*ore matter is being printed and published today than ever before, and every publisher of an advertisement, pamphlet or book expects his material to be read. Publishers and, even more so, readers want what is important to be clearly laid out. They will not read anything that is troublesome to read, but are pleased with what looks clear and well-arranged, for it will make their task of understanding easier. For this reason, the important part must stand out and the unimportant must be subdued . . .

The technique of modern typography must also adapt itself to the speed of our times. Today, we cannot spend as much time on a letter heading or other piece of jobbing as was possible even in the nineties.

—*Jan Tschichold, 1935*

Page setup

1.17 Minimums and maximums:

Item	Minimum	Maximum
Page size	.01" x .01"	17 x 22 inches
No. pages	1	999
Numbering sequence	1	9999
Margins	0	Total not to exceed page size

1.18 Page sizes are as follows

Letter size:	8.5 x 11 inches
Legal size:	8.5 x 14 inches
Tabloid size:	11 x 17 inches
Custom size:	Any size from the minimum to maximum (1.17)

1.19 In PageMaker when you choose to create a *New* publication, the first thing you see is the **"Page setup" dialog box,** (1.21) because in PageMaker you can have control over *everything*. This is the place to set up the size and number of your pages, the orientation of the screen, the number with which to begin paginating, the parameters of the outer margins, and the format of your automatic numbering.

1.20 At any point in the creation of your document you can come back to "Page setup" and change any of the specifications *except* the number of pages (you need to do that from the Page menu; 1.27). Just remember, though, if you have several pages already created and you decide to change the size or the orientation of the page, the text and graphics already placed on the pages *will not* adapt themselves to the new specifications—they will sit very patiently right where you left them, and you will have to adjust them all manually.

The "Page setup" dialog boxes   *(from the File menu, choose "Page setup...")*

1.21
The "Page setup"
dialog box

This submenu contains
pre-set page sizes;
see 1.23; 1.24

You can customize the size of
any page; see 1.23; 1.24

See 1.24; 1.25

This is for automatic page
numbering; see 1.28; 1.29

See 1.33; 1.34

This is only in version 4.01. Use it
when you print a Book List with
automatic renumbering; see 13.27

This sets non-printing margin
guidelines on the page; see 1.36

Hit Return to
shortcut OK

You can press
Command Period

Page setup

| OK |
| Cancel |

Page: **Letter**

Page dimensions: **8.5** by **11** inches

| Numbers... |

Orientation: ● Tall   ○ Wide

Start page #: **1**   # of pages: **1**

See 1.26

Options: ☒ Double-sided   ☒ Facing pages

See 1.35

☐ Restart page numbering

Margin in inches: Inside **1**   Outside **0.75**

Top **0.75**   Bottom **0.75**

1.22
Click on the button "Numbers..." in the "Page setup"
dialog box to get the "Page numbering" options. These
options allow you to customize the automatic *page*
numbering (1.30; 1.139a,b).

When you are ready to create a table of contents or an index,
you can use this option to customize the page numbers that
appear within the table or the index; see 1.31

See 1.30

Page numbering

| OK |
| Cancel |

Style: ● Arabic numeral   1, 2, 3, ...
      ○ Upper Roman   I, II, III, ...
      ○ Lower Roman   i, ii, iii, ...
      ○ Upper alphabetic   A, B, C, ... AA, BB, CC, ...
      ○ Lower alphabetic   a, b, c, ... aa, bb, cc, ...

TOC and index prefix: [   ]

If you want to do this:	**Then follow these steps:**	**Shortcuts ▾ Notes ▾ Hints**
1.23 Change the page size	■ From the File menu choose "Page setup." ■ Press on the box next to "Page" to see the pop-up menu of sizes; select the size of your choice. Its measurements will appear in the "Page dimensions" boxes.	■ The maximum page size is 17 x 22. If you use a printer that cannot supply paper large enough to print your full page on one piece, you can **tile** when you print (18.90–18.91) and use the tiles to paste up. ■ If the publication *page* size is smaller than the printer's *paper* size, your job will print centered on the paper. Choose to print crop marks (18.82–18.83) to show the outer dimensions of your publication page.
1.24 Create a custom page size	■ From the File menu choose "Page setup." ■ Press on the box next to "Page" to see the pop-up menu of sizes; select Custom. ■ Type in the size of your choice in the boxes next to "Page dimensions" (the first box is the horizontal measurement; the second is the vertical measurement.)	■ If you type the dimensions for a wide format (say, 10 x 7) but leave the orientation on "Tall," the orientation command will take precedence and you will get a 7 x 10 page.
1.25 Change the orientation	■ From the File menu choose "Page setup." ■ Choose "Tall" for a vertical format; choose "Wide" for a horizontal format.	■ If you return to Page Setup later and switch orientations, all customized columns will recenter between the new margins.
1.26 Establish the number of pages	■ From the File menu choose "Page setup." ■ Type in the number of pages you want in the "# of pages:" box, up to 999.	■ Obviously, don't put more pages in one publication than you can easily back up. ■ Pages cannot be added here *after* OK has been clicked the very first time; you *can* add them from the Page menu (1.118).

If you want to do this:	**Then follow these steps:**	**Shortcuts ▾ Notes ▾ Hints**
1.27 Add or delete pages	▪ You can't go back to add or delete pages from the Page Setup dialog box *after* you once click the OK button.	▪ You *can* add or delete pages from the Page menu at any time your publication is on the screen (1.118–1.120).
1.28 Start numbering pages with a number other than 1 Start page #: 2	▪ From the File menu choose "Page setup." ▪ Type in the number you wish to begin the document with in the "Start page #" edit box.	▪ The page icons (1.30; 1.96) will reflect these numbers, as well as the automatic page-numbering feature (1.138–1.140). ▪ Standard procedure worldwide is that odd-numbered pages are right-hand; even-numbered pages left-hand. ▪ In double-sided publications, the first page (as it is usually an odd number) is never shown as part of a two-page spread. If you want to see it as such, start the numbering with an even number. ▪ Pages can be *numbered* up through 9,999; that is, if you have 20 pages in your publication and you start numbering them with 468, your publication will have pages 468 through 487.
1.29 Renumber the pages, starting with a different number Start page #: 453	▪ From the File menu choose "Page setup." ▪ Change the number in the "Start page #" edit box.	▪ Pages can be *numbered* up through 9,999 (see the note just above).

If you want to do this:	**Then follow these steps:**	**Shortcuts ▾ Notes ▾ Hints**

1.30   Format the page numbers

Style: ○ **Arabic numeral**   1, 2, 3, ...
      ○ **Upper Roman**   I, II, III, ...
      ◉ **Lower Roman**   i, ii, iii, ...
      ○ **Upper alphabetic**   A, B, C, ... AA,
      ○ **Lower alphabetic**   a, b, c, ... aa,

[1 | 2 | 3]   *The page icons that appear in the bottom left portion of the screen, indicating how many pages are in the publication, will always be Arabic no matter what format you choose.*

- From the File menu choose "Page setup."
- Click on the button "Numbers...."
- Click in the button to choose your style. *(Be sure to read the notes in the next column)* ☞

- Your choice here will only affect how the *automatic* page numbers (1.139a/b) are displayed. It will have no effect on any page number you type without using the auto feature.
- Roman numeral styles, both upper- and lowercase, can only number as high as 4,999; 5,000 through 9,999 appear as regular Arabic numbers.
- Alphabetic style, both upper- and lowercase, can only number as high as ZZ (52); 53 through 9,999 appear as Arabic numbers.
- No matter what format you choose, the page icons appear as normal (Arabic) numbers.

1.31   Create a prefix for Index and Table of Contents entries

TOC and index prefix: [**Section 1:**]

- From the File menu choose "Page setup."
- Click on the button "Numbers...."
- Type a prefix of up to 15 characters.

- This prefix will appear in the Table of Contents and in the Index you create (see Sections 12 and 13). For instance, if you are creating a multi-volume reference with one index, this prefix could define in which volume an item is found, as well as the page number. Or perhaps you want to specify items that are found in the Appendix.
- This prefix is specific only to the *publication* it is created in; that is, since you will typically create each chapter of a book as a separate publication, each one can have its own prefix; e.g., Chapter One: p.14; Appendix B: p. 4.

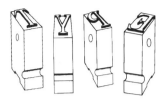

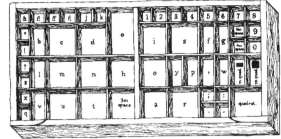

lower case

When type was first being used to print words, each letter was cast on a separate little piece of metal (backwards, of course, so when it printed it would be facing the right direction). These tiny pieces of metal were kept in large, flat, wooden cases, with separate little compartments in each case for each letter. There was one case for the capital letters, and one case for the small letters. To make life easy, all type was stored in the same cabinet, the case for capital letters always above the corresponding case for small letters; thus capitals became known as "uppercase," and small letters became known as "lowercase."

Now, when a printer wanted to create a publication, he would take letters out of their compartments, one by one, and place them in a composing stick until he had enough letters for a whole line, then place that entire line in a chase. When all the lines for the entire page were in, he would lock the chase up tight. If he didn't lock it up tight, the letters might spill all over the floor and it would take a very long time to pick up all those tiny little pieces of type and the boss would probably be angry. Can you imagine each one of the letters, the spaces, and the punctuation marks in this paragraph being each on a separate tiny piece of lead? Can you imagine spilling all those letters on the floor and having to pick them all up and put them back into their special compartments in their case? Can you imagine doing that to backwards letters?

composing stick

Even if the letters didn't get spilled all over the floor, when that page was completed the movable type had to be broken down anyway and placed back into the little cubbies. Some letters are difficult to distinguish when they're backwards (let alone upside down if you dropped them on the floor), such as b's and d's, or p's and q's. That's where the phrase "Mind your p's and q's" originated—a printer's admonition to his apprentice to make sure things were put back into their proper places. It was probably on a placard placed over the washbasin as a precursor to the ubiquitous "Wash your hands before returning to work."   *—rw*

15

If you want to do this:	**Then follow these steps:**	**Shortcuts ▾ Notes ▾ Hints**

1.33 Create a single-sided publication

Single-sided with margin guides

- From the File menu choose "Page setup."
- Make sure there is no X in the checkbox next to "Double-sided." If there is, click once in the box to remove it.

- Choosing single-sided will leave your margins exactly the same on every page, as opposed to double-sided (see below). Single-sided assumes the final version of your publication will be copied onto only one side of the paper.

1.34 Create a double-sided publication

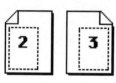

Double-sided with same margin guides

Options: ☒ **Double-sided**

- From the File menu choose "Page setup."
- Make sure there is an X in the checkbox next to "Double-sided."

- "Double-sided" assumes the final version of your publication will be copied onto two sides, which usually means they will be bound in the inner margin. When you have selected double-sided, notice the margins in the Page Setup do not state Left or Right, but Inside and Outside. When you choose Double-sided, the margins flip-flop, so the inner margin (where you typically leave more space) is always at the bound edge.
- **This does not make your printer print on two sides of the paper**—it only means when you take these originals down to your copy center and have them copied and bound, the layout will have allowed for the binding edge.
- Nor does it automatically create a wider inside margin! That's your responsibility.

The way to simplicity is hard labor, but it must never seem like hard labor.
—*Arthur Rubinstein*

If you want to do this:	Then follow these steps:	Shortcuts ▾ Notes ▾ Hints

1.35 Show facing pages

Facing pages

Options: ⊠ Double-sided ⊠ Facing pages

- From the File menu choose "Page setup."
- **If** the Double-Sided option is checked (1.34), **then** you can check this box to show the two-page spreads.

- Right-hand pages are always odd-numbered; left-hand pages are always even-numbered.
- Even with Facing Pages checked, the first page (as it is usually an odd number) will stand alone. If you want to see the first two pages of your publication as a two-page spread, put an even number in the "Start page #" box (1.28).

1.36 Set or change the margin

Margin in inches: Left 1   Right 0.75
Top 0.75   Bottom 0.75

- From the File menu choose "Page setup."
- Select the numbers in the margin boxes and type in your own specifications (press the Tab key to move from edit box to edit box).

- **These margins are only *guidelines* for your text and graphic placements—** anything placed outside of these margins will also print, limited only by the printing area of your printer.
- Margin guides, unlike ruler guides, cannot be changed from the publication page; you must return to "Page setup" (File menu).
- If you later return to Page Setup and change the margins, any *columns* you have customized will be re-centered within the new margins. *And then* if you redo the master page columns, the new columns will not appear on pages that you previously customized (1.60).
- Margins can be set anywhere from 0 to the numbers that add up to the total width or depth of the page.
- If you want to override the measurement system currently in use, see 1.221.

Rulers and Ruler Guides

1.37 Minimums and maximums:

Item	Minimum	Maximum
Ruler guides	0	40 per page

The maximum of 40 per page includes any master guides. If facing pages are showing, the limit refers to 40 total on the *two* pages.

1.38 Horizontal measurement options:

Standard inches

Decimal inches

Millimeters

Picas (⅙ inch [.167 inch];
12 points per pica)

Ciceros (4.55 mm)

1.39 Vertical measurement options:

Standard inches

Decimal inches

Millimeters

Picas (⅙ inch [.167];
12 points per pica)

Ciceros (4.55 mm [.177 inch];
12 cicero points per cicero)

Custom (4 to 256 points)

1.40　PageMaker provides a vertical and a horizontal **ruler** for each publication. The measurements in each of these rulers can be customized to your particular preference (e.g., picas instead of inches), and can be re-customized at any time.

1.41　The **ruler guides** are *non-printing,* dotted guidelines that act as a T-square or a non-photo blue pen. They allow you to measure and place objects or text precisely, yet they do not restrict the flow of the text.

1.42
- The horizontal ruler can be set to a different measurement than the vertical ruler.
- Ruler guides can be placed on master pages to show up on every page.
- Ruler guides can be added, moved, or deleted at any time.
- Guides and objects can be made to snap to the ruler measurements.
- You can create an invisible grid and easily align all text and graphics on the grid.
- The zero point can be moved.
- On a color monitor, the guides are opaque and can hide thin lines that are underneath them. See 1.65a to send the guides to the back.

The rulers and ruler guides

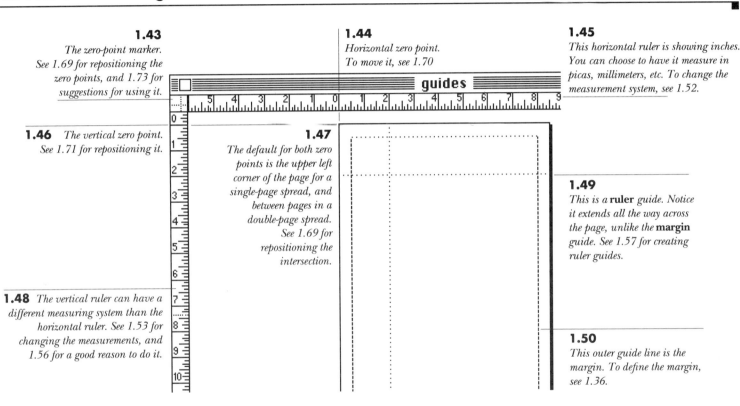

1.43
The zero-point marker.
See 1.69 for repositioning the
zero points, and 1.73 for
suggestions for using it.

1.44
Horizontal zero point.
To move it, see 1.70

1.45
This horizontal ruler is showing inches.
You can choose to have it measure in
picas, millimeters, etc. To change the
measurement system, see 1.52.

1.46 *The vertical zero point.*
See 1.71 for repositioning it.

1.47
The default for both zero
points is the upper left
corner of the page for a
single-page spread, and
between pages in a
double-page spread.
See 1.69 for
repositioning the
intersection.

1.49
*This is a **ruler** guide. Notice*
it extends all the way across
*the page, unlike the **margin***
guide. See 1.57 for creating
ruler guides.

1.48 *The vertical ruler can have a*
different measuring system than the
horizontal ruler. See 1.53 for
changing the measurements, and
1.56 for a good reason to do it.

1.50
This outer guide line is the
margin. To define the margin,
see 1.36.

If you want to do this:	Then follow these steps:	Shortcuts ▾ Notes ▾ Hints
1.51a Show the rulers	▪ From the Options menu choose "Rulers"; a checkmark will appear next to the item to indicate they are showing (called "on").	▪ Press Command R.
1.51b Hide the rulers	▪ From the Options menu choose "Rulers"; the checkmark will disappear, indicating the Rulers are not showing ("off").	▪ Press Command R. ▪ While the rulers are hiding, the "Zero lock" command cannot work.
1.52 Change the horizontal ruler measurements 	▪ From the Edit menu choose "Preferences.... " ▪ Press on the box next to "Measurement system" to get the pop-up menu; select the measurement of your choice.	▪ Changing the measuring system here will cause all other measurements in all other dialog boxes to follow the same system; e.g., column guides, paragraph spacing, hyphenation, etc. ▪ Measurements are accurate to $\frac{1}{2880}^{\text{th}}$ of an inch, supposedly at any size. ▪ Any measuring system can be temporarily overridden in any dialog box (1.221).
1.53 Change the vertical ruler measurements Vertical ruler: ✓Inches / Inches decimal / Millimeters / Picas / Ciceros / Custom	▪ From the Edit menu choose "Preferences...." ▪ Press on the box next to "Vertical ruler" to get the pop-up menu; select the measurement of your choice (to work with "Custom," see 1.54).	▪ The vertical ruler measurements choice allows you to have different units of measure in each ruler. ▪ The *vertical measure* applies *only* to the vertical ruler; whereas the *measuring system* applies to every dialog box that uses measures, *as well as* to the horizontal ruler.

If you want to do this:	Then follow these steps:	Shortcuts ▾ Notes ▾ Hints
1.54 Use a custom measurement in the vertical ruler	■ From the Edit menu choose "Preferences." ■ Press on the box next to "Vertical measure" to see the pop-up menu; choose "Custom." ■ Now in the box to the right there is a "12"; this is the default. Type in any number of points from 4 to 256.	■ If you type in a point value that is the same as your leading, then it will be very easy to align the baselines of your type across the columns (which you really should be doing, you know; see 1.56). ■ Use this in conjunction with "Snap to rulers" (1.55) to create an underlying grid that will make it remarkably easy to align all text and graphics at any size view. ■ Just remember that when you change measurements, the text and graphics that were already on the page don't move to match the new measurements.
1.55 Use "Snap to rulers"	■ Press on the Options menu; if there is a checkmark next to "Snap to rulers," it is already on. ■ If there is no checkmark, choose "Snap to rulers" *or* press Command [.	■ With this command, all graphic tools, ruler guides, text blocks, and objects will snap to the tick marks on the rulers, rather than be able to be placed between exact increments. Notice the tick marks get more precise as the view gets larger (at 400% the inch ruler easily shows 32^{nds} of an inch). ■ Used in conjunction with the vertical ruler set in the point increments of your leading (1.54), this allows you to align the baselines of type across the columns very easily and precisely. In fact, it just does it for you—so take advantage of it (1.56). ■ "Snap to rulers" works even if the rulers themselves are not showing.

1.56 Scenario #2: Aligning Baselines

A baseline, of course, is the invisible line that type sits on. When there is text in more than one column on a page, it is very important, if the piece is to look unified and professional, that the baselines across the columns be aligned. The bottom of photos and graphics should also align with a baseline. PageMaker makes this very easy for you.

Mrs. Malaprop

The baseline, the imaginary line the type sits on.

- Simply follow the steps in 1.54 to customize the *vertical* ruler—in the "points" box, type the point size of the *leading* of your body text. (If your leading is "Auto," multiply the size of the type by 1.2—that is your leading; 4.52.) Your vertical ruler will now have tick marks in those point increments.
- From the Options menu, choose "Snap to rulers" if it isn't already on (the checkmark indicates it is on).
- From the Options menu, choose "Snap to guides" if it isn't already on (the checkmark indicates it is on).
- Now as you place ruler guides, text blocks, and graphic objects, they will automatically snap into position, following the ruler increments, and the baselines will be neatly aligned. You'll notice that even the tools (except the pointer and the text tool) will jump across the page, rather than move smoothly—they are jumping from tick mark to tick mark on the rulers.
- If you *do* want to place something *between* tick marks on the rulers, simply turn off the "Snap to rulers" command in the Options menu and you will have control over the tools again.

If you have added a few extra points of space after paragraphs, or if you have subheads tucked into your body copy, this will throw off the consistency of your baseline alignments. They may align at the top of the page, or at the bottom of the page, but sometimes it is not possible to make them align all the way down, unless you have a thorough working knowledge of grid theory and are using it. If not, you do need to make a conscious decision to align those baselines either at the top or at the bottom, and follow your decision consistently throughout your publication.

There is another option you could use to align the baselines, even if headings and subheads throw them off alignment: the "Grid size" and "Align to grid" features (nested in the Paragraph command from the Type menu; 4.89–4.99). But this method creates uneven gaps, because it forces extra space between paragraphs or after headlines. This "Align to grid" feature does work effectively with inline graphics in many cases, though (4.62; 4.100–4.101).

If you want to do this:	Then follow these steps:	Shortcuts ▾ Notes ▾ Hints
1.57 Add a ruler guide, either on a master page (1.122–1.127) **or** on any publication page	▪ Make sure the rulers are showing; if they are not, from the Options menu choose "Rulers" *or* press Command R. ▪ Using any tool, point in either ruler; the cursor will become an arrow. ▪ *Press* in the ruler; the cursor will become the two-headed arrow. This means you have picked up a ruler guide. Press-and-drag the two-headed arrow onto the screen; the dotted ruler guide will come along with it. Wherever you let go of the mouse button, there you will place the guide.	▪ Guides placed on the master pages will show up on every page. *They can be moved or deleted from any single page, though,* unlike other master page objects, such as text or graphics. ▪ Remember, these ruler guides will not print. You can have 40 per page, including any from the master pages. (This 40 per page actually means 40 per screen—if you have facing pages showing, you can only get 40 for both pages.)
1.58 Reposition any ruler guide either on a master page (1.122–1.127) **or** on any publication page	▪ You must use the **pointer tool** to reposition a guide. ▪ *Press* on the guide (you should see the two-headed arrow) and drag it to its new position.	▪ *If you don't see the two-headed arrow, you have not picked up the ruler guide!* ▪ If you can't pick up a guide, you may have previously set the guides to stay in the **back** (1.65). If so, find a spot on the guide where nothing is overlapping it (no text block or graphic) and pick it up from there.
1.59 Delete a ruler guide either on a master page (1.122–1.127) **or** on any publication page	▪ You must use the **pointer tool** to remove a guide. ▪ *Press* on the guide (you should see the two-headed arrow) and drag it off any edge of the screen, whether the rulers are showing or not, and let go. If the edge of the page is showing, you can just drop it off the edge.	▪ Another possibility for not being able to pick up the guides is that you have *locked* them. Check the Options menu (1.66). ▪ Repositioning or deleting master guides while on a *publication page* will not change them on any other page or on the master page.

If you want to do this:	Then follow these steps:	Shortcuts ▾ Notes ▾ Hints
1.60 Show the master page guide changes on a publication page where they're not showing up	▪ On the publication page, from the Page menu choose "Copy master guides." If the command is gray, it means the current page is already displaying the master guides. If you can't see the guides, maybe they are hidden; see 1.63b.	▪ You see, if you go back to the *master page* and change any ruler or column guide, that change *will not appear* on any publication page you have *customized;* that is, on any page where you added or moved or deleted a ruler or a column guide.
1.61 Delete all ruler guides at once, except the master guides	▪ From the Page menu, choose "Copy master guides."	▪ Rather than drag each guide back to its ruler one by one, you can choose this command to delete them all (except, of course, the master guides).
1.62 Delete all master page ruler guides	▪ On a master page (1.122–1.127), *press* on a guide with the **pointer tool** (you should see the two-headed arrow) and drag the guide off the edge of the page, or off any edge of the screen. ▪ Repeat for each ruler guide.	▪ Unfortunately, it is not possible to remove all the guides at once. It would be nice to be able to do that, wouldn't it? You can temporarily hide them, though (1.63a).
1.63a Hide all guides	▪ If you can see the guides, then the Options menu has "Guides" with a checkmark next to it. Choose "Guides" again to take the checkmark off (or press Command J).	▪ This is nice to do regularly to view your work without all the stuff in the way. ▪ This gets rid of *all* guides, not just ruler guides. ▪ When the guides are not showing, "Snap to guides" from the Options menu will not function, nor can you create new column guides.
1.63b Show all guides	▪ If you cannot see the guides, then the Options menu has no checkmark next to "Guides." Choose "Guides" again to show them (or press Command J).	

If you want to do this:	Then follow these steps:	Shortcuts • Notes • Hints
1.64a Use "Snap to guides"	■ From the Options menu choose "Snap to guides" *or* press Command U. (When in effect, there will be a checkmark by the command.)	■ This command causes any tool (except the pointer and the text tool) and anything you move, be it text or graphics, to snap to any guideline—ruler or column or margin—it gets close to. This doesn't mean you cannot place it *away* from a guide—it just means that if you get close to one, PageMaker will make sure it's placed right on it.
1.64b Turn off "Snap to guides"	■ From the Options menu choose "Snap to guides" *or* press Command U.	
1.65a Send all guides to the back layer	■ From the Edit menu choose "Preferences...." ■ Under "Guides," click on "Back."	■ All objects in PageMaker are on separate *layers,* including the guides. The default setting is for the guides to be the top layer. (See 1.151–1.157 for more info on layers.)
1.65b Bring all guides to the front layer	■ From the Edit menu choose "Preferences...." ■ Under "Guides," click on "Front."	■ Sending the guides to front and back sends *all* guides—rulers, columns, and margins.
1.66a Lock all guides	■ From the Options menu choose "Lock guides." This will put a checkmark by it.	■ Locking the guides keeps them in their place so they can't be accidentally moved. This also helps prevent them from getting in the way when trying to pick up something from another layer.
1.66b Unlock all guides	■ From the Options menu choose "Lock guides." This will take the checkmark off.	

1.67   Important note re: locking guides or sending them to the back: at first this seems like a good idea when you find yourself picking up ruler guides instead of drawn lines or objects. The problem is that the guides are so handy and so often used that it becomes more awkward to have them locked or behind. If a guide is in the way of an object, just **hold down the Command key** and you will be able to select the object (1.173). But when the *guides* are *behind,* you cannot grab them without moving the entire overlaying object.

If you want to do this:

Then follow these steps:

Shortcuts ▾ Notes ▾ Hints

1.68 Reposition margin guides

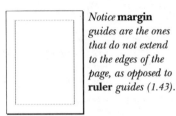

*Notice **margin** guides are the ones that do not extend to the edges of the page, as opposed to **ruler** guides (1.43).*

- You can't. Not from the page, anyway.
- But you *can* from the Edit menu: choose "Page setup."
- Change the values for the margins (1.36).

- Margin guides are the ones that *do not* extend the width/depth of the page.
- They cannot be picked up with any tool.
- When you reposition the margin guides, text that has already been placed *will not* adjust to the new margins—you'll have to do that yourself.
- The left and right *column guide defaults* are directly on top of the left and right *margins*. You *can* press-and-drag to move the *column* edges; you cannot move the margins.

1.69 Reposition the zero point, both horizontally and vertically

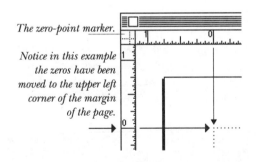

The zero-point marker.

Notice in this example the zeros have been moved to the upper left corner of the margin of the page.

- Check the Options menu to make sure "Zero lock" has no checkmark by it; if it does, choose "Zero lock" again to unlock.
- There is a white box in the upper left corner where the two rulers intersect, called the *zero-point marker.*
- Press in the zero-point marker, using any tool. Press-and-drag onto your page; intersecting guidelines will follow the mouse movement. The *intersection* is the zero point.
- When the intersection is where you want it, let go of the mouse button; the intersecting guides will disappear and the zeros will align at that point.

- Whenever you want to reposition the zero point, **you must start from the zero point marker again.**
- Changing the zero point is very handy for measuring column widths, measuring sizes of shapes and graphics, comparing items, centering zero on the page, etc.
- See Scenario #3: Using the zero point (1.73).

If you want to do this:	**Then follow these steps:**	**Shortcuts ▾ Notes ▾ Hints**
1.70 Reposition just the horizontal zero point *(1.38)*	▪ Follow the steps in 1.69, but just drag *straight across* the horizontal ruler.	▪ This leaves the vertical zero point intact.
1.71 Reposition just the vertical zero point *(1.39)*	▪ Follow the steps in 1.69, but just drag *straight down* the vertical ruler.	▪ This leaves the horizontal zero point intact.
1.72a Lock the zero point	▪ From the Options menu choose "Zero lock." Zero lock now has a checkmark next to it on the menu and is "on."	▪ Obviously, this locks the zero point in position so you don't accidentally move it.
When the zero point is locked, the zero point marker is blank		
1.72b Unlock the zero point	▪ From the Options menu choose "Zero lock." This removes the checkmark on the menu and turns it "off."	▪ You must unlock the zero point before you can move it.
When the zero point is unlocked, the zero point marker has little guidelines		

GEOMETRY
can produce legible letters,

*but Art alone
makes them beautiful.*

Paul Standard

1.73 **Scenario #3: Using the Zero Point**

The default for the zero point is the upper left corner of the page on a single page, or the center of a double-page spread. Perhaps you are customizing your columns and you want the first column to be exactly two inches wide—you can move the zero point over to the left *margin* edge and measure from there.

Perhaps you need to draw a keyline or a box the width of the column and 4⅜6" deep. So bring down the *vertical* zero point to the place where the top of the box will start; measure down from there.

To center a short rule (line) in the horizontal middle of an 8.5" page, bring the horizontal zero marker over to 4.25 (the center of 8.5). Follow the guidelines in the ruler as you draw the line; you can draw it precisely the same distance on either side of the centered zero.

The ruler reflects where one edge of the column gutter is—the edge the pointer is pressing on.

I moved the zero point to the upper left corner of the margin. I moved the column in to measure exactly two inches across.

I moved the vertical zero point down so I could draw the box to measure.

Notice the ruler reflects the outer dimension of the box as it is drawn.

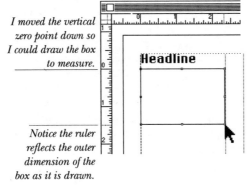

I moved the zero point to the center of the page. Then I drew the rule equidistant from the zero, starting at -1.25 and ending at +1.25. Notice the ruler reflects the ends of the line.

Columns and Column Guides

1.74 Minimums and maximums:

Item	Minimum	Maximum
Columns	1	20 per page
Column width	.167 (=⅙") (=1 pica) (=12 pts.)	Page width
Space between columns	0	Width between margins

1.75 Column guides vs. margin guides

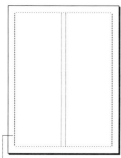

Text will flow between column guides. Margin guides (the outer border) do nothing but provide a visual reference. But remember, what you see here is a **column** *guide directly on top of the outer* **margin** *guide!*

1.76   With column guides you can control the flow of text onto the page—when you *place* text, it pours into the columns. You cannot *place* text (3.27–3.28) into the space between the columns, although you can *manually* insert type into it.

1.77   In PageMaker you can set up to 20 columns per page (typically they are kept within the margins that were determined in the Page Setup (1.36), but they *can* be dragged beyond, out to the edge of the paper).

1.78   After you specify columns, Page-Maker automatically places them on the page in equal widths, centered between the margins. You can customize them at any time to the width and placement of your choice. The column *widths* can all be different, but it is not possible to create columns with differing amounts of space *between* them on one single page.

1.79   It *is* possible, though, to set up a certain number of columns and place text in them, then change the number or width or placement of the columns without disturbing the type already set, and then pour more text into the new columns. The

Aldus manual likens it to wax being poured into a mold—after the mold is removed the wax stays put. This is one way to arrange multiple columns of text on a page.

1.80   If you want the same columns on every page in your publication, set the columns up on your master pages (1.82–1.85; 1.129). Even master columns, though, can always be customized on any single page, so you are not ever stuck with anything.

1.81   When you type directly into Page-Maker, the insertion point will always create a text block across the *column* it is placed in, anchoring itself to either edge. Of course, this also can always be overridden if you choose (1.208; 3.58). Isn't it nice how PageMaker always lets *you* have control?

If you want to do this:

1.82   Create equal columns

Then follow these steps:

- From the Options menu, choose "Column guides…."
- If your publication is double-sided and shows facing pages, there is a box that gives you the choice of setting a different number and size of columns for the left and the right pages; check that box if you want to do so.
- Type in a number from 1 to 20 in the box labeled "Number of columns."
- Type in the amount of space you want between the columns in the box labeled "Space between columns."
  - If you want no space, type 0;
  - If you want to override the current measurement (perhaps you want the space in picas rather than inches), see 1.221.

Shortcuts ▾ Notes ▾ Hints

- If "Column guides…" is gray, it is probably because "Guides" is off. Choose "Guides" again to turn them back on, and "Column guides…" will then be available.
- There is usually a default of at least one column already on the page; it is not possible to have less than one column.
- Notice you can press on either margin edge, get the two-headed arrow, and drag the far outer left and right *column* guide edges anywhere you like (notice the *margin* guides stay put, though; 1.36; 1.75).
- Remember, in the dialog box you can press the Tab key to move from edit box to edit box. Actually, you can do this in any dialog box on the Mac, thus avoiding that reach for the mouse.
- You can create columns on one or both master pages (1.122–1.127) or on each separate publication page. Even if you create columns on a master page, you can still customize, add, or remove them on any publication page.

If you want to do this:	**Then follow these steps:**	**Shortcuts ▾ Notes ▾ Hints**
1.83 Create unequal columns 	▪ Create columns as in 1.82; click "OK," and then: ▪ On your page, choose the **pointer tool.** ▪ Press on a column guide (you will see the two-headed arrow) and drag the column to the desired position. Let go when it is whcrc you want it to be placed.	▪ The far outer left and right column guide edges sit right on the margin guides (1.75). You can also press-and-drag *those* column guides wherever you like, even outside of the margins. Text will align with the *column edges,* not with the *margin edges* (see 3.19). ▪ Notice as you move an inner column guide that has space between, both edges of that space come with you. ▪ When you move a column edge, the dotted line in the horizontal ruler moves *with the column edge the pointer is pressing on.* This allows you to place your column in the exact, measured position you want. ▪ Use the rulers in conjunction with the larger page views and repositioning with the zero point to measure columns and position them (see 1.69–1.71; 1.73).
1.84 Widen or narrow a column	▪ With the **pointer tool,** simply press on one edge of the column and drag it.	▪ Notice the ruler keeps track of the edge that is being dragged. ▪ From the page you can change the *width* of the columns, but not the *space between.* To change the space between columns, see 1.85.

If you want to do this:	Then follow these steps:	Shortcuts ▾ Notes ▾ Hints
1.85 Widen or narrow the space between columns	▪ From the Options menu choose "Column guides...." ▪ If there is a *number* in the "Number of columns" box, then just type a new measurement in the "Space between columns" box. ▪ If it says *Custom* in the "Number of columns" box, you cannot change the space between. You will have to first replace *Custom* with a number, then you can change the space between.	▪ Remember, you can override the current measurement system if you prefer; for instance, if the dialog box is asking for inches, you could use picas instead (1.221). ▪ It says *Custom* because you moved a column on that page. Replacing *Custom* with a number will center that number of columns between the margins again.
1.86 Revert the columns to equal widths	▪ From the Options menu choose "Column guides...." ▪ If you have moved any column edge, the "Number of columns" box now says "Custom." Simply type in a number here and PageMaker will reset the columns.	▪ The columns will be reset to their original formation: centered between the margin guides.
1.87 Change a master page column guide on one publication page	▪ With the **pointer tool,** simply press-and-drag any column edge to its new position.	▪ Even though it may be a column that was originally placed on a master page, you can pick it up and move it just like any other guide. *This will not affect the master page columns or columns on any other page.*
1.88 Revert any customized columns back to the master page columns	▪ On the publication page, from the Page menu choose "Copy master guides."	▪ Doing this will replace *all* guides (column and ruler guides) with the master guides.

If you want to do this:	**Then follow these steps:**	**Shortcuts ▾ Notes ▾ Hints**
1.89 Delete all columns	▪ From the Options menu choose "Column Guides…." ▪ In the "Number of columns" box type in the number 1 (you cannot have fewer than one column).	▪ If you do this on your master pages, it will delete all columns from all the pages *where you did not customize them.* Any customized columns will stay the same. ▪ To delete any customized columns after deleting the master columns, from the Page menu choose "Copy master guides" on each relevant page.
1.90a Hide the column guides	▪ From the Options menu choose "Guides." This will take the checkmark off the command.	▪ Doing this will hide or show *all* the guides—rulers, columns, and margins. ▪ When the guides are hidden, the "Snap to guides" function doesn't work, nor can you create columns.
1.90b Show the column guides	▪ From the Options menu choose "Guides." This will put a checkmark on the command.	
1.91a Send the column guides to the back	▪ From the Edit menu choose "Preferences…." ▪ Under "Guides," click in the button "Back" to send the guides to the back.	▪ Column guides, like all guides, are on the top layer (layers: 1.151–1.157). If you find this irritating because they get in the way when you're trying to grab other objects, send them to the back.
1.91b Bring the column guides to the front	▪ From the Edit menu choose "Preferences…." ▪ Under "Guides," click in the button "Front" to bring the guides to the front.	▪ *You can select an object under a guide* by pressing the Command key and clicking on the object you want. ▪ When guides are at the back, though, there is no way to reach them if they are under any other layer, not even with Command-clicking.

If you want to do this:

1.92a Lock the column guides in place

1.92b Unlock the column guides

Then follow these steps:

- From the Options menu choose "Lock guides." This places a checkmark next to the command.

- From the Options menu choose "Lock guides." This removes the checkmark from the command.

Shortcuts ▾ Notes ▾ Hints

- This command locks *all* guides—rulers, columns, margins. It locks guides that are currently on the page, as well as any new ones that are created.
- This is another solution to the problem of the guides being on the top layer. If they are locked, they cannot be moved and thus their layer does not get in the way of selecting objects.
- Actually, though, in general practice it is much easier to Command-click (1.172; 1.173) to get beneath guides than it is to keep locking and unlocking them (or sending them to the back).

Passion without reason is blind; reason without passion is dead. *—Will Durant, paraphrasing Spinoza*

Pages and Page Views

1.93 A publication in PageMaker can be up to 999 pages long (limited, of course, by your disk storage space). Each page is represented by a page icon. If there are more than 15 or so pages in the publication (depending on the size of your screen), scroll arrows will appear on either end of the line of icons. This subsection details all the ways of moving from one page to another.

1.94 PageMaker provides seven different sizes with which to view your document. From mini-view (where you can see the entire pasteboard) to 400% (where precision alignment is remarkable), each view has its own advantages.

1.95 In "Page setup" you determined how many pages were to be in your publication. At any time, though, you can add or delete pages. As you do this, the page icons come and go also, and pages are renumbered to adjust for it.

1.96

In a double-sided publication, the page icon indicates whether it is a right-hand page (odd-numbered) or a left-hand page (even-numbered). In a single-sided publication, all pages are right-hand.

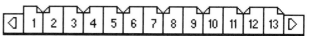

This arrangement indicates that there are more than 13 pages in this publication, and it is set up double-sided with facing pages. Notice the scroll arrows at either end.

If you want to do this:	Then follow these steps:	Shortcuts ▾ Notes ▾ Hints
1.97 Go to the next page	■ Click on the icon of the next page.	■ Press Command Tab.
1.98 Go to the previous page	■ Click on the icon of the previous page.	■ Press Command Shift Tab.
1.99 Go several pages next	■ Press Command Tab Tab Tab, pressing a quick Tab for each page you want to pass; e.g., three Tabs will take you three pages over.	■ You won't see the pages in-between— you will go directly to the page. ■ If your pages are double-sided, each Tab takes you over one double-page spread.
1.100 Go several pages previous	■ Press Command Shift Tab Tab Tab, pressing a quick Tab for each page you want to go back; e.g., three Shift-Tabs will take you three pages previous.	■ You won't see the pages in-between— you will go directly to the page. ■ If your pages are double-sided, each Tab takes you over one double-page spread.
1.101 Go to any page, if there are fewer than about 15 pages *(meaning all page icons are visible)*	■ Click on the icon of the page.	
1.102 Go to any page, if there are more than about 15 pages *(page icon scroll arrows are visible)*	■ With any tool, press on the scroll arrow at either end of the page icons to find the page number you want; then click on the page icon. • **OR** from the Page menu choose "Go to page…"; type in the number; click OK.	■ No matter which tool you are using, the cursor will become the arrow when it is on a page icon. ■ Press Command G; type the page number; hit Return.

If you want to do this:	**Then follow these steps:**	**Shortcuts ▾ Notes ▾ Hints**
1.103a Show the last page **icon** in the publication	▪ Hold down the Command key. ▪ Click on the right arrow at the *end* of the page icons.	 *Page icon scroll arrows*
1.103b Show the first page **icon** in the publication	▪ Hold down the Command key. ▪ Click on the left arrow at the *beginning* of the page icons.	▪ This trick doesn't take you to the *page;* it just makes the page icon visible so you can click on it.
1.104 Jump past half-a-dozen page icons	▪ Hold down the Shift key. ▪ Click on one of the page icon arrows.	
1.105 Pan through all the pages	▪ Hold down the Shift key. ▪ From the Page menu choose "Go to page..."; let go of the Shift key. ▪ Click the mouse when you want the cycle to stop.	▪ Starting at the first page, PageMaker will cycle through all the pages in the publication. When the last page is reached, the cycle will begin again, skipping the master pages.
1.106 From a master page, return to the page you were last working on	▪ Press Command Tab.	
1.107 Change the view of the page you are *going to* into "Fit in Window" size	▪ Hold down the Shift key while clicking on the page icon.	▪ When that page appears, it will be in "Fit in Window" size.
1.108 View the entire pasteboard (1.4) *(the mini-view; also known as "Fit in World")*	▪ Hold down the Shift key *before you press the mouse button.* ▪ From the Page menu, choose "Fit in window."	▪ In this view you can see the entire pasteboard, which comes in very handy when you're looking for things you placed off to one side earlier. On a large screen you may not notice a big difference between this and the 25% view.

If you want to do this:	Then follow these steps:	Shortcuts ▾ Notes ▾ Hints
1.109 View the page at 25%	■ From the Page menu choose "25%" **or** press Command 0 (zero).	■ 25% depends, of course, on the page size of your document.
1.110 View the entire page in the window *("Fit in window")*	■ Press Command W (W for Window); **or** hold the Shift key down and click on the current page icon; **or** while at Actual Size, hold down the Command and Option keys and click anywhere in the window.	■ Command W is a good shortcut to keep in mind even if you are already in that view; sometimes at "Fit in window" you move the pages so they are off-center—Command W will place them right back in the middle of the window instantly.
1.111 View the page at 50%	■ From the Page menu choose "50%" **or** press Command 5 (5 for 50%).	■ 50% is a good view for placing rules and text blocks. If your "Snap to rulers" and "Snap to guides" from the Options menu are on, your placements will be extremely precise.
1.112 View the page at 75%	■ From the Page menu choose "75%" **or** press Command 7 (7 for 75%).	■ 75% and 50% are great for drawing lines between columns or across the page.
1.113 View the page at Actual Size	■ While in any view and with any tool, **point** to the area you wish to see at Actual Size. ■ Hold down the Command and Option keys. ■ Click.	■ Of course, it is possible to get to Actual Size by choosing that command from the Page menu *or* by pressing Command 1 (one), but those methods don't always take you where you want to go, and you often have to scroll around looking for your work. This method takes you directly to what you want to see.

If you want to do this:	**Then follow these steps:**	**Shortcuts ▾ Notes ▾ Hints**
1.114 View the page at 200% (*twice Actual Size*)	▪ While in any view and with any tool, **point** to the area you wish to see at 200%. ▪ Hold down the Command, Option, and Shift keys. ▪ Click where you are pointing.	▪ Of course, it is possible to get to 200% by choosing that command from the Page menu *or* by pressing Command 2, but those methods don't always take you where you want to go, and you have to scroll around looking for your work. This method takes you directly to what you want to see. ▪ If something is selected, that item will be centered when the view changes to 200% from the menu. ▪ 200% view is great for precise alignment!
1.115 View the page at 400%	▪ From the Page menu, choose "400%," **or** press Command 4 (4 for 400%). ▪ If something is selected, that item will be centered when the view changes to 400%.	▪ 400% *seems* like the place to go for incredibly precise alignment; if your ruler is in picas, each tick mark is 2 points ($\frac{1}{36}$ of an inch). Unfortunately, what you see is not always what you get— you'll notice things look different in Actual Size, in 200%, and in 400%. What you see in 200% seems to be the most accurate.
1.116 Change the view of *all* the pages in the publication	▪ Hold down the Option key while choosing a view from the menu.	▪ This will change every page to the view of your choice, so the next time you go to any page, it's set the way you want. ▪ You can also use this in conjunction with the Shift key to get the mini-view for all pages.

If you want to do this:

Then follow these steps:

Shortcuts ▾ Notes ▾ Hints

1.117 Move the page in any direction without using scroll bars

 The grabber hand cursor

- With any tool selected, hold down the Option key.
- *When you press the mouse,* the tool cursor will become the grabber hand.
- Press-and-drag; the hand will move the page around in any direction for you.
  - ▫ If you hold the Shift key down in addition to the Option key, you will restrain the movement of the hand to just vertical or just horizontal, whichever direction you move first.

- Using the grabber hand allows you to move more freely and with more control than with the scroll bars, as you can move diagonally.

- Using the Shift key makes the grabber hand act just like a scroll bar, but you have more control over the speed.

1.118 Add or insert pages

- Pages are always inserted *before, after,* or *between* the page(s) you are viewing, so go to the appropriate page (1.101–1.102).
- From the Page menu choose "Insert pages...."
- Choose whether to insert the page *before* the page you are viewing, *after* it, or— if you have facing pages—*between.*
- Click OK.

- You can Undo the insert if you do it *before you click the mouse or switch tools:* from the Edit menu choose "Remove insert pages," or press Command Z.
- If the publication is double-sided, be aware that if you add or delete an *odd* number of pages, all the left-hand pages will become right-hand pages and vice versa; your placed objects will adjust to the switched left and right *margins,* but if there are any differences in column widths or placements, they will all have to be adjusted manually.
- Inserting pages automatically creates new page icons and renumbers any automatically-numbered pages.

If you want to do this:

Then follow these steps:

Shortcuts ▾ Notes ▾ Hints

1.119 Remove or delete pages

- From the Page menu choose "Remove pages...."
- Type in the page number(s) of the page(s) you wish to remove. If you want to remove only one page, type the same page number in both boxes.
- Click OK; you will get a warning box thoughtfully checking to make sure you really want to do this. If you do, click OK.

- If you decide you want those pages back, *don't touch a thing!* See 1.120 below.
- Deleting pages automatically deletes their page icons.
- If pages have been auto-numbered with Command Option P (1.139a,b), all those numbers will automatically adjust.
- Be forewarned: in a double-sided publication, if you add or delete an *odd* number of pages, all the left-hand pages will become right-hand pages and vice versa; objects will adjust to the new left and right *margins,* but you will have to make any other adjustments manually.

1.120 Replace pages that were deleted

- If you haven't made any move since you deleted the pages (screaming is okay), you can use the Edit menu to choose "Undo delete pages."

- Really, Undo won't work if you do *anything* before you choose to Undo—don't even click the mouse or change tools!
- You do have one safety catch: Revert or mini-Revert.
  - If you choose "Revert" from the File menu, the publication will revert to the way it was last time you saved, which is why you should save very often, like every three minutes.
  - If you hold the Shift key down while you choose "Revert," the publication will revert to the last *mini-save* (the last time you added or deleted a page, etc.; 16.3).

If you want to do this:	**Then follow these steps:**	**Shortcuts ▾ Notes ▾ Hints**

1.121 Find out what page you're on when there are more than 999 pages

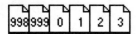

- From the Page menu choose "Remove pages…"; it will tell you what page(s) you are viewing; then you can just Cancel it.
- **OR** this is a good trick:
  - With the *text tool,* create a small text block (1.206) that has all four handles on the pasteboard.
  - Type **Page**, spacebar, and press Command Option P. It should look like this: **Page PB** (PB for pasteboard).
  - Size this text large enough that you can read it at "Fit in window" size.
  - With the **pointer tool,** drag any edge of the text block onto any page; the **PB** will turn into the number of that page. Then move the text block back onto the pasteboard to use on another page.

- After page 999, the page icons start over again at 0. So when you're on page 1783, the page icon says 83—you don't know if it's page 1783 or 4583 or 9883. *(Yes, you're right; this is a trick you probably won't need very often. One never knows, though.)*
- The automatic page numbers will *print* correctly—it's just the icons that have trouble.

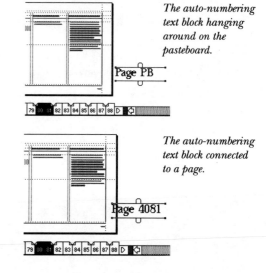

The auto-numbering text block hanging around on the pasteboard.

The auto-numbering text block connected to a page.

Master Pages

1.122 You can create a PageMaker publication with up to 999 pages. If every page in a publication of this length had an 8-point rule (line) across the top of the page, it would take a long time just to set that up. And then if you changed your mind and wanted a 4-point rule instead, it would take just as long to change it all.

1.123 Well, thank goodness PageMaker has **master pages.** Anything you place on a master page will show up on every page in the publication (which I call *publication pages,* to distinguish them). You can draw that 8-point rule on *one* master page and it will show up on all 999 pages. If you change your mind later, you can change the line to a 4-point rule on that one master page and it is instantly changed on all 999 pages.

1.124 Text, graphics, column guides, ruler guides, text-wrapping attributes, and automatic page numbers can all be placed on a master page. Even though they appear on all pages, you do have the option of ignoring all master elements on any page, hiding any of them, and modifying any master *guides*. You cannot *alter* any master page item (except guides) while you are on a *publication page;* that is, if you want to change or edit objects or text, you must return to the master page.

1.125 Master pages are identified in the bottom left corner of the screen by the pages with the L and R (Left-hand and Right-hand). If your publication is not double-sided, you will see only a right-hand page.

Master page icons for a double-sided document.

Master page icon for a single-sided document.

1.126 *Master pages themselves cannot be printed.* It is possible to ask for 0 (zero) pages in Page Setup, and you will still have master pages. But no matter what you put on them, they won't print.

1.127 If you want hard copy of the master page, you must create at least one page (1.118) for a single-sided publication, and two for a double-sided; then you can print those new pages.

If you want to do this:	**Then follow these steps:**	**Shortcuts ▾ Notes ▾ Hints**
1.128 Go to a master page	• In the bottom left corner of the window is a page icon marked **R**; if the page setup specifies *double-sided*, then there are two page icons, one **L** and one **R**—these are page icons for the **master pages**. • Click on one of the master page icons to go to that page. • **OR** use the "Go to page…" command from the Page menu (Command G).	• If the publication is *not* double-sided, then anything you place on the one master page will show up on every page. • If the publication *is* double-sided, then you can set up items to appear only on left- or right-hand pages separately. • To return to the publication page you were working on, press Command Tab.
1.129 Set up guides on a master page	• Set up margin guides (1.36), ruler guides (1.57), and column guides (1.82–1.83) just as you would on any other page.	• These guides will show up on every page, but unlike the graphics or text on a master page, guides can be moved or removed from any publication page with the pointer tool (except, of course, for the margin guides). • If you go back to your master page and change the guides, those changes *will not appear* on any publication page where you have customized (added, removed, or moved) any guides. See 1.130.
1.130 Show newly-created master guides on a previously-created or customized publication page	• While viewing the publication page, from the Page menu choose "Copy master guides."	• If you create pages first, then go back and create a master page, you will have to follow this step in order to see the *guides*.
1.131 Place text on a master page	• Create text in PageMaker (3.5–3.26) or place text (3.27–3.58) on a master page just as you would on any publication page.	• Any text you place on a master page will show up on every page, *but you will not be able to edit or move it on the publication pages.*

If you want to do this:	Then follow these steps:	Shortcuts • Notes • Hints
1.132 Place a graphic on a master page	• Create graphics in PageMaker (Section 2) or place graphics (9.92) on a master page just as you would on any publication page.	• Any graphic placed on a master page will show up on every page, *but you will not be able to edit or move it on the publication pages.*
1.133 Set up a graphic to text wrap on a master page	• Follow the same procedure as you would on any publication page (Section 11).	• Text on the master page will wrap around the graphic, as will text on every publication page! Finally. See 11.38.
1.134 Modify or delete master page items from the master page	• You must **return** to the master page in order to modify it; click on the **L** or **R** page icon. • Modify or delete text (Section 3), graphics (Section 9), or guides (Section 1) just as you would from any other page.	• You can go back to a master page at any time and modify any element; it will instantly change every publication page—*except* guides (see 1.130).
1.135 *Remove* master page items from any single page in the publication	• While viewing any publication page, from the Page menu choose "Display master items." This will remove the checkmark from the menu command and remove all master page text and graphics from that one page; guidelines will remain.	• Unfortunately, if you have facing pages showing it is not possible to delete master items from one side and not the other. See 1.136 for a trick to hide some of the objects. See the tip in 19.5 for using the power-paste feature to display specific master page items.

If you want to do this:	Then follow these steps:	Shortcuts ▾ Notes ▾ Hints

1.136 Hide just *some* of the master page objects so they don't appear on the publication page *(and thus will not print)*

- With the drawing tools (Section 2), create opaque boxes ("None" line and "Paper" fill) and cover the items you don't want to see or print. Also see 19.5 for another trick along these same lines: hiding all the master page items, but power-pasting the ones you *do* want on the page.

- Hiding a master page object that has a text wrap attached to it will not prevent text from wrapping around it on the publication page. Only turning off "Display master items" from the Page menu will stop text wrap on a master object.

1.137 View (display) the master page items on the publication page *(if for some reason they're not visible)*

- While viewing the publication page, choose "Display master items" from the Page menu. This will place a checkmark next to the command and will show all text and graphics from the master pages.

- If there is already a checkmark next to "Display master items," it means they are already visible. If you don't see anything, check your master page to make sure they are there.
- Also check to make sure there are no opaque boxes covering the master items (with the pointer tool, choose "Select all" from the Edit menu; all handles will show up. Now, are there handles covering the areas where there are supposed to be master items? If so, click once to remove all handles, but remember where the ones are that border the objects you want to get rid of. Then select and remove those opaque boxes; 1.175).

If you want to do this:

Then follow these steps:

Shortcuts ▾ Notes ▾ Hints

1.138 There are three ways to number your pages in PageMaker:

- Type the number **manually** on any page. This number will never change until you retype it.
- Type an **automatic placeholder** on a *master page*. This number will change as pages are added or deleted. It will appear in the same place on every page (1.139a).
- Type an **automatic placeholder** on the *individual pages*. This number will also change as pages are added or deleted. It can be placed on each page individually (1.139b).

1.139a Automatically number the pages *from the master page* so every page number will be in the same place

- Go to a master page; view at Actual Size (1.113) the spot where you want to place the number.
- Choose the **text tool** (the **A**; 3.10).
- Click to set the insertion point at the approximate placement for the number, **or** create a bounding box to hold it (1.206).
- Press **Command Option P**; this will create an **LM** or an **RM** which is the *placeholder,* standing for Left Master or Right Master. (Don't worry—on every *publication page* LM or RM will turn into the actual number of that page.)
- Select the text with the **text tool** and change the font, style, size, and alignment to suit your fancy (Section 3).
- With the **pointer tool,** reposition the page number text block (press-and-drag it; 3.108) wherever you like.

- You can also type any other text with the page number to create composite numbers, such as *Page 0* or *– 0–* or *4–0* or anything else you like; simply type in the text, then press Command Option P where you want the number to appear.
- If your pages are double-sided, you will have to create one placeholder on *each* of the two master pages, left and right.
- Right-hand pages are *always* even; left-hand pages are *always* odd.
- The page will be numbered with the number that is on its page icon.
- The numbering starts with the number that is entered in the "Page setup" dialog box (1.28), found under the File menu (1.17).
- All pages will automatically renumber when you change the number in the "Start page #" box in the "Page setup" dialog box, or when you add or delete pages.
- See 1.140 for formatting the numbers as Arabic, Roman, or alphabetic.

If you want to do this:	**Then follow these steps:**	**Shortcuts ▾ Notes ▾ Hints**

1.139b Automatically number the pages individually

- Follow the steps in 1.139a, but do it on any publication page.

- Well, you might ask, why should you bother using the auto feature on individual pages rather than manually typing each page number? Because auto numbers will automatically change if you insert or delete pages or change the page number you started the publication with. Any page number you type manually will simply stay that very number.
- Numbering the pages individually allows you to vary the placement and choose which pages are to be numbered.
- Sometimes you may need to hide the master page items (1.135). You can still set an automatic, individual page number.

1.140 Format the *automatic* page numbers, whether on the master page or on individual pages

Style: ⦿ **Arabic numeral**   1, 2, 3, ...
        ○ **Upper Roman**   I, II, III, ...
        ○ **Lower Roman**   i, ii, iii, ...
        ○ **Upper alphabetic** A, B, C, ... AA,
        ○ **Lower alphabetic** a, b, c, ... aa,

- From the File menu choose "Page setup."
- Click on the button "Numbers...."
- Click in the button to choose your style.
  Be sure to read the notes in the next column ☛

- Roman numeral styles, both upper- and lowercase, can only number as high as 4,999; 5,000 through 9,999 appear as regular Arabic numbers (1, 2, 3...).
- Alphabetic style, both upper- and lowercase, can only number as high as ZZ (52); 53 through 9,999 appear as Arabic numbers.
- No matter what format you have, the page icons appear as normal (Arabic) numbers.
- See 1.141 for the few instances where you can override the format.

If you want to do this:

Then follow these steps:

Shortcuts ▾ Notes ▾ Hints

1.141 Override the automatic page number **formatting** on pages you have automatically numbered individually

- Read the column to the right.
- With the **text tool,** on the publication page double-click on the page number to select it.
- Press Command Shift K (that's the keyboard shortcut to turn lowercase letters into uppercase letters; you could, of course, go into "Type specs..." from the Type menu and change the "Case").
- To change the numbers back to lower-case again, repeat the process (you can turn lowercase into uppercase and back again, but you can't turn text that has been *typed* as uppercase into lowercase).

- The only overriding you can do is to change lowercase Roman or lowercase alphabetic into uppercase (i.e., iii into III, or bb into BB).
- You can only override pages that you numbered individually. Well, you *can* override it on the master page, but why bother—if you're going to do that, it makes more sense to just change the formatting style from the "Page setup" dialog box.

1.142 Quick tip for auto-numbering individual pages

- Create an automatic page number (type Command Option P) on the pasteboard; it will display **PB** (for pasteboard).
- Format it with the font, style, alignment, size, etc., that you want. Size the text block conveniently.
- Leave it on the pasteboard, completely off the publication page. Whenever you need it, select it with the **pointer tool,** copy it, and paste it on. Whichever page you paste it onto, the PB will turn into that page number.

- Selecting it with the pointer tool rather than the text tool will retain the text block form. If you select it with the text tool and paste it, the text block will conform to the column, as usual.

AN ILLEGITIMATE, HOMELESS MAN, DYING IN abject poverty, changes the course of history and his name goes down through the ages as a household word. There's hope for us all. Johannes Gensfleisch zur Laden zum Gutenberg is generally credited with inventing the printing process. Actually, there was already printing of a sort, but Gutenberg perfected the craft with the invention of movable type. (Kind of like there were already computers in the world, then the Mac was invented.) However, back in the 9th century the Chinese were already carving wooden blocks to print prayer scrolls; in the 11th century they

developed movable type of clay and metal. In the 13th century the Koreans were casting metal type in sand molds. Movable type is the key thing here—rather than having to carve each page as a separate block, movable type allows one to put together a page of characters, print it, take those characters apart and put them

a 14th century copyist

back together in another order for another page. Now, the Chinese and Koreans had an obvious problem—their languages have too many billions of characters to make this process practical. Plus there was no ink invented that could stick to metal. Besides, these Far Easterners just plain preferred calligraphy anyway. Well, the Europeans in the 15th century didn't know anything about what the Chinese and Koreans had done, so they had to re-invent movable type. Gutenberg was in luck. By the time he came along, the process of papermaking was well-developed; punch-important step in of metal, was al-the gold- and silver-which Gutenberg was metalcasting was well coins and medals; used for cheese, processing, and those industrious Van Eycks, had

Herr Gutenberg

making, which is an creating letters out ready developed in smithing trades (of a practitioner); under way, creating presses were being wine, textile weaponsmithing. And Dutch painters, the invented an oil-based ink that would adhere to metal. Now isn't it an interesting thought to ponder what might have happened if Johann had been born a hundred years earlier, before the world was ready for him? Or if the boys in the garage had been born fifty years earlier? Eventually someone would have gotten the printing process together, but would we ever have had Macintoshes?

(continued on page 73)

Selecting, Layering, and Moving

For small erections
may be finished
by their first architects;
grand ones,
true ones,
ever leave the copestone
to posterity.
God keep me
from ever
completing anything.
O, Time,
Strength,
Cash,
and Patience!

Herman Melville,
Moby Dick

1.143 In PageMaker every *object* is on a separate *layer*. Understanding this and using it to your advantage is a key skill in working with this program. Once you know what the layers are and how to select them, move them, group them, and manipulate them, all the rest of PageMaker will make much more sense. In fact, all the other sections in this book assume you understand selecting, layering, and moving objects. So you'd better read this.

Selecting

1.144 *The pointer tool, used for selecting objects.*

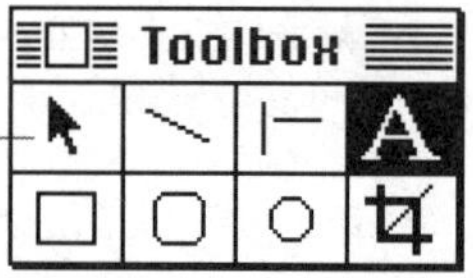

1.145 PageMaker is an "object-oriented" program; that is, each and every item you put on the screen is a separate **object**—each graphic, text block, and line. **Selecting** is the simple process that tells the Mac you are about to do something to an object.

1.146 You *must* select objects before you manipulate them. If you are going to stretch or condense a graphic, make a line longer, delete an object, resize a text block—the basic Macintosh rule is always **select first, then manipulate**.

1.147 **Always select objects with the pointer tool.** While you use the drawing tools to *create* the objects, you use the **pointer tool** to **select** the objects, such as the entire text block or the separate graphic elements.

1.148 To **de**select anything, just click in any blank space or on any tool in the Toolbox.

1.149 There are two exceptions to the rule that you always select with the pointer tool:

1) **to modify text** (not to remove or stretch the text *block*, but to modify the *characters* themselves, such as when you change font or size or style), you must use the **text tool** to select the particular characters you wish to modify (Section 3);

2) **to crop a graphic,** you must select it with the **cropping tool** (9.104).

1.150 And remember, no matter how hard you try, you cannot select any master page objects if you are not viewing the master page itself! (You *can* manipulate master page *guides,* though, on any separate publication page.)

Layering

1.151 In object-oriented programs, you can pick up and move each item, modify it, or delete it. You can also *stack* the objects one on top of the other and then change the order of their stacking. It is this stacking, or **layering,** that is often the cause for great consternation.

1.152 It is important to consciously think of every object on the screen as being on a separate layer, as if each were on its own little piece of clear acetate. You can see the outer dimensions of these little pieces of clear acetate when you use the **pointer tool** and click on any item—two to eight *handles* will appear (1.157), depending on whether it is a line or a graphic or a block of text. **An object will show handles when it is ready for moving, modifying, or deleting.**

1.153 When objects overlap, one item may get "lost" behind the other. Don't worry—unless you actually deleted it, *it is still there* and you can easily retrieve it (1.172–1.176) or adjust its layering order (1.177–1.178).

1.154 Unfortunately, it is very simple to inadvertently create an *invisible* layer that gets in your way and causes confusion because you don't know it's there (see 1.175 for finding and deleting it).

1.155 Guides are *always* the top layer, unless you specifically choose to keep them as the back layer (use "Preferences..." from the Edit menu to send them to the back; see 1.65–1.67, 1.215).

1.156 Once the idea of layering is clear to you, all of PageMaker makes much more sense. You will find it easy to overlay items, send them to the back or bring them to the front to suit your arrangement, temporarily group them together to move them as a unit, dig underneath other layers to find a missing item, remove items from the bottom layer without touching the top, and generally make life easier.

1.157a *This graphic, created in PageMaker, is selected. Notice the eight handles.*

b) *This graphic was also created in PageMaker and is selected, showing its handles. It is on a layer separate from the white box above.*

c) *This text block was created in PageMaker and is selected. Notice its four corner handles and two windowshade loops. It is also on a separate layer.*

d) *In this image, all three of the layers have been stacked. They are still three separate layers, as shown in e) below.*

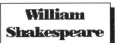

e) *This image shows all three layers with all of their handles.*

Moving Objects

1.158 Once an object is *selected,* you can **move** it by pressing-and-dragging on it. If there are complex graphics or a block of formatted text to move, PageMaker has to gather everything up before it can move it. To accommodate you, there are two ways to move objects: a **fast move** and a **slow move.**

FAST MOVE

1.159 A **fast move** picks up just the *outline* of the information—it looks like a blank box. This is much faster and easier for PageMaker to deal with, and thus faster for you. To do a fast move, press on a selected object or a group of selected objects *and move the mouse instantly;* you will get just the outline. Wherever you let go of the mouse, the outline will stop there and redisplay the objects in their new position. This works well, combined with "Snap to guides," to quickly and precisely align objects in place, even while in the small window view.

In a fast move, you see just an outline of the image.

SLOW MOVE

1.160 A **slow move** picks up the actual visual image of everything selected. This takes longer, but for aligning baselines of text or the border of a graphic, it is indispensable. To do a slow move, with the pointer tool *press* on a selected object or group of selected objects. Hold the mouse button down; at first you will see a watch, which means PageMaker is gathering everything up. After a second or two, depending on how complex the object is, you will see the four-headed arrow. Still holding the mouse button down, drag the objects—you will see every particle of every object as it moves along. This is particularly handy for precise alignments at the larger views.

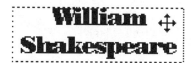

In a slow move, you see the entire visual image.

BE CAREFUL

1.161 Be careful about moving a group of selected objects, especially in the small views. If there is a text block in the group, your safest bet to move *everything* successfully is to press on that text block to drag the entire group. Avoid pressing on one of the *lines* in a group move; you can easily end up stretching one line instead of moving the whole selected group. **Whenever you are about to move a group, make sure you see the four-headed arrow before you drag, and not a two-headed arrow or a crosshair!**

1.162 If you accidentally stretch or move something out of position, *immediately* press Command Z to Undo, **or** from the Edit menu choose "Undo stretch/move"!! Then try again.

If you want to do this:	**Then follow these steps:**	**Shortcuts ▾ Notes ▾ Hints**
1.163 Select a text block 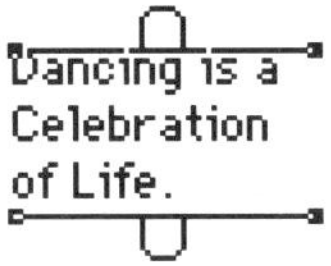 Dancing is a Celebration of Life.	■ With the **pointer tool,** click anywhere in the block of text. You will see handles on all four corners (if all four corners are visible at the view you are in).	■ Also read Section 3 on Text (3.107).
1.164 Select a graphic 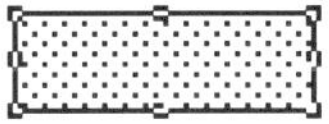	■ With the **pointer tool,** click anywhere on the graphic. You will see eight handles.	■ Also read Section 2 on Drawing Tools (2.23) and Section 9 on Graphics.
1.165 Select a line	■ With the **pointer tool,** click anywhere on the line. If you can see the *ends* of the lines, you will see a handle on each end.	■ If you pick up a guide when you try to select a line, hold down the Command key while you click on the line.
1.166 Deselect an object *(text blocks, graphics, lines, etc.)*	■ Select a different object; ■ **OR** click in any clear area outside of any object, including outside any text block; ■ **OR** click on any tool in the toolbox.	
1.167 Deselect *all* objects	■ Click in any clear area outside of any object, including outside any space within a text block; ■ **OR** click on any tool in the toolbox.	

What we need is Progress
with an escape hatch.
—John Updike

If you want to do this:

Then follow these steps:

Shortcuts ▾ Notes ▾ Hints

1.168 Select more than one object using the Shift-click method
(See 1.169 to use the marquee method)

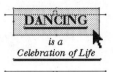

- With the **pointer tool,** select the first object by clicking once on it.
- Hold down the Shift key and click on all other objects you want to add to the group.
- To **de**select an object from the group, hold down the Shift key and click on the object again.

- You can use Shift-clicking in combination with Command-clicking (1.172) to pick up objects that are under other layers.

1.169 Select more than one object using the marquee method
(See 1.168 to use the Shift-click method)

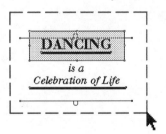

- Position the **pointer tool** in any clear area outside of any object; *make sure you click outside any text block.*
- Press-and-drag to draw the *marquee* (selection rectangle) around all objects to be selected. When they are enclosed within the dotted rectangle, let go.

- The marquee will select only those objects that have *every one of their handles* enclosed in its space (e.g., if your text block has handles that run across the page, you will need to draw the marquee large enough to encompass them). Or just Shift-click if you miss something, as noted in 1.168.
- Because the marquee will select only objects with all handles enclosed in its space, you can use it to select smaller objects that are under a larger layer (1.176).
- To *deselect* an object from the group, hold down the Shift key and click once on the object.

If you want to do this:	Then follow these steps:	Shortcuts ▾ Notes ▾ Hints
1.170 Add objects to those already selected	■ With the **pointer tool,** hold the Shift key down while you click on other objects.	■ If you change your mind about selecting an object, keep the Shift key down and just click on the object *again* to deselect it.
1.171 Deselect an object or two from a group of selected objects	■ Hold down the Shift key. ■ With the **pointer tool,** click on any object you want to deselect from the group.	■ If you change your mind about deselecting an object, keep the Shift key down and click on the object again to re-select it.
1.172 Select an object that is underneath another object	■ Hold down the Command key. ■ With the **pointer tool,** click on the top object; it will show handles. ■ Click again to select the next layer. ■ Repeat until the desired object is selected.	■ Used in conjunction with the Shift key (1.168), you can dig down through layers and select them into a group along the way. ■ Remember, a graphic with a Fill of "None" must be selected by clicking on its black border, so you may have to hunt around to find it (also see 1.174–1.175).
1.173 Select an object that is under a guide	■ With the **pointer tool,** hold down the Command key and click on the object.	■ Guides are always on the top layer, unless you choose to "Lock guides" from the Options menu or send them to the back through "Preferences" in the Edit menu (1.65–1.67; 1.215).

If you want to do this:	**Then follow these steps:**	**Shortcuts ▾ Notes ▾ Hints**
1.174 Select *all* objects on the screen, no matter what layer they are on	■ From the Page menu choose "Fit in window" *or* press Command W (you don't *have* to be in this view, but it allows you to see everything on the page). ■ Choose the **pointer tool.** ■ From the Edit menu choose "Select all" *or* press Command A; handles will appear on every object.	■ This picks up everything on the *screen* (whether you can see it or not), not just the *page;* that is, any items on the pasteboard will also be selected. ■ This is a good way to find any invisible graphics or text blocks that may be getting in your way, or to find objects hidden under other opaque objects. ■ When you have selected all objects, you can move, delete, or copy them all at once. ■ If, at this point, you see any objects that do not have handles on them, they must be from the master page (1.122–1.127).
1.175 Select an object that seems to be invisible	■ Select all objects (1.174). ■ Look for any handles that have nothing inside them. ■ Once you find the troublesome item, **de**select all objects by clicking in any blank area, or by clicking on the pointer tool in the Toolbox. ■ With the **pointer tool,** click on the spot where you saw the handles of the invisible object. If you get handles belonging to an object on *top* of the one you want, hold down the Command key and click once at a time until handles appear on the invisible object of your choice.	■ If the object you want does not show handles, perhaps your screen view is too large to see the handles on either end. Go to "Fit in window" view (press Command W). If you still don't see the handles, the object you want must be on a master page (1.122–1.127). ■ Once the object is selected, you can delete it by pressing the Backspace/Delete key. ■ **OR** you can now copy it, cut it, stretch it, modify it, or do anything else your little heart desires.

If you want to do this:	**Then follow these steps:**	**Shortcuts ▾ Notes ▾ Hints**
1.176 Select an object that is hidden or trapped under another, including a line or border that is under a guide	▪ Hold down the Command key and click with the **pointer tool** to dig down through the layers; with each click you will select the next layer down, then cycle through the layers again; ▪ **OR** with the **pointer tool,** press in a clear area *(make sure you are also outside of any text block)* and drag to produce the *marquee,* or selection rectangle. You'll select anything that is *entirely* enclosed within this marquee. *So,* if you want to select a smaller item under a larger item, draw the marquee too small to capture the entire larger object; you'll select just the smaller object(s) underneath.	▪ This first method will pick up any object under a guide, also. ▪ If you can see little objects under a text block, use this second method: 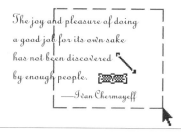
1.177 Bring an object in front of another	▪ With the **pointer tool,** select the object you want to bring forward to the top layer (click once on it). You may need to Command-click (1.176). ▪ From the Element menu choose "Bring to front" *or* press Command F (F for Front).	▪ When you send an object to the back, you send it *all the way to the back,* not just behind the top layer. So be conscious about what you are sending where. Oftentimes what you need is to bring something else forward, not send the top item back. And conversely, items brought forward are brought all the way forward.
1.178 Send an object behind another	▪ With the **pointer tool,** select the object you want to send behind all the others (click once on it). ▪ From the Element menu choose "Send to back" *or* press Command B (B for Back).	▪ You can select more than one item at a time and send them back or bring them forward. They will stay in their same order.

If you want to do this:	Then follow these steps:	Shortcuts ▾ Notes ▾ Hints
1.179 Select text to modify	■ With the **text tool:** □ Double-click on a word to select the word and the space after it; □ **Or** triple-click to select an entire paragraph; □ **Or** press-and-drag over the characters you want to modify.	■ Be sure to read Section 3 on Text, especially 3.123–3.138. ■ You might also want to check out 1.223–1.224, on how to select text using the numeric keypad.
1.180 Select rotated text to move or modify as a graphic	■ With the **pointer tool,** click once on the rotated text (3.180–3.190).	■ Detailed text information is in Section 3.
1.181 Select rotated text to edit as text	■ With the **pointer tool,** triple-click on the rotated text; this will give you the Story Editor for editing (8.42).	■ Story Editor information is in Section 8.
1.182 Select an imported graphic to crop	■ With the **cropping tool,** click on a graphic (9.104).	■ Graphic information is in Section 9.

1.183 This miscellaneous subsection covers some last tidbits of useful information. Some of this information is particular to PageMaker, some to basic Macintosh functions that are especially indispensable adjuncts to PageMaker.

a) Cut/Copy/Paste and the Clipboard
These commands work exactly the same in PageMaker as they do in any other Macintosh program, allowing you to remove or copy objects or text and paste them in elsewhere. This section clarifies which tool to use to cut or copy different parts of the publication.

b) Scrapbook
The Scrapbook works exactly the same as in any other program on the Mac, enabling you to permanently save graphics or text (from PageMaker or from any other program) for use at any time in any publication. This subsection will just clarify The Scrapbook for those who have never used it before, or those who don't feel quite comfortable with it yet.

c) Bounding box, or drag-placing
Create a *bounding box* or *drag-place* to control precisely the space that text or a graphic initially occupies—great for placing a lot of things on the pasteboard to have them handy for working on later.

d) Preferences
The Preferences command (found in the Edit menu) holds some handy but hidden goodies. You'll also find several practical applications for changing your Preferences in the Rulers and Ruler Guides subsection (1.145–1.173).

e) Overriding the measurement system
PageMaker, consistent with its philosophy of letting you have control over everything, allows you to override the ruler specifications for any little particular measurement you happen to need at the moment, without changing the rulers; e.g., even though your measurement system may be in inches, you can set your paragraph spacing in points.

f) Numeric keypad
You can use the numeric keypad to type numbers, move the insertion point through the text, or cut and paste. Combined with the Shift key, you can use the keypad to select text for editing.

g) Key Caps
Key Caps is where you find all of the characters the Mac provides to make your type look truly professional.

h) Find File
Don't forget about this great desk accessory for finding 'lost' files on your desktop, or for finding files to Open or folders to Save into while working inside PageMaker.

i) Creating more space in the publication window
This section is simply a tip on how to maximize your viewing area, especially if you are working on the small screen of a Mac Plus, SE, or Classic.

Clipboard

1.184 The **Clipboard** is a temporary storage place for text or graphics. Whenever you cut or copy an object or text, it is placed on the Clipboard. It will stay on the Clipboard until you turn off the computer. Whenever you choose to **paste,** PageMaker (and all other Mac programs, actually) pastes a copy of whatever is on the Clipboard. You can paste the item an infinite number of times. *(Deleting or clearing an object or text* does not *place it on the Clipboard.)*

1.185 An important thing to remember about the Clipboard is that *it holds only one selection at a time;* as soon as you cut or copy another item, the new item replaces anything previously on the Clipboard.

1.186 Since the Clipboard is a System tool and not just a PageMaker function, you can put an item into the Clipboard from another program (such as a graphic from SuperPaint), and then paste it into PageMaker.

1.187 The Clipboard has a limit of 64K as the largest amount of text that you can cut or copy into it. If you try to paste more than that, it will yell at you.

1.188 The Clipboard treats text in two different ways, depending on whether you select the text with the **pointer tool** or with the **text tool.**

1.189 With the **pointer tool:**

a If you select an entire text block *with the pointer tool,* it will paste into the Clipboard with all the formatting intact (size, style, line length, etc.). If you were to view the Clipboard (1.197), you would see the exact text block you copied or cut.

b If you select an entire text block *with the pointer tool* and then paste it into your publication *with no insertion point flashing and no text selected,* it will still be the exact same text block. It will not be threaded to any other text block.

1.190 With the **text tool:**

a If you select text *with the text tool,* it will appear in the Clipboard as 12-point Geneva, no matter what the specifications are. But if you choose to paste that 12-point Geneva text into your publication, all the original formatting and specifications are returned, *except for the line length.*

b When you paste, if there is *no insertion point flashing, or if the insertion point is on the pasteboard or outside of any column,* the text will create its own text block, with the line length being the width of your page margins. All other formatting will stay the same. It will not be threaded to any other text block.

c With **either tool:** If, however, *an insertion point is flashing or text is selected* when you paste, the newly-pasted text will keep its original *character* formatting (font, size, style, etc.), but will adapt to the *paragraph* formatting (line length, tabs and indents, etc.) of the paragraph it is pasted into. (*Selected* text will be *replaced.*)

For more info on cutting, copying, and pasting *text,* see 3.118–3.121.
For more info on cutting, copying, and pasting *graphics,* see 9.97; 9.99.

If you want to do this:	**Then follow these steps:**	**Shortcuts ▼ Notes ▼ Hints**
1.191 Cut	■ To select *an object,* click once on it with the **pointer tool** (1.163–1.182); **or** to select *characters,* press-and-drag over them with the **text tool** (3.137–3.138). ■ Then from the Edit menu choose "Cut," or press Command X.	■ **Cut** will **remove** the selected item from the screen and place it on the Clipboard, ready for pasting. If you press the Back-space/Delete key or choose "Clear" from the Edit menu, the item will be removed, but *not* placed on the Clipboard.
1.192 Copy	■ To select *an object,* click once on it with the **pointer tool** (1.163–1.182); **or** to select *characters,* press-and-drag over them with the **text tool** (3.137–3.138). ■ From the Edit menu choose "Copy," or press Command C.	■ **Copy** will **leave** the selected object or text on the screen and place a **copy** of it on the Clipboard, ready for pasting.

1.193 Paste
(graphics or text)
	■ To **paste a graphic or text,** from the Edit menu, simply choose "Paste," or press Command V.
	■ Basically:
	  □ If there is an *insertion point* flashing when you "Paste," text and graphics will be inserted beginning at that insertion point; text will pick up the existing paragraph formatting (1.190c), and graphics will become *inline graphics* (9.91).
	  □ If the *pointer tool* is chosen when you paste, text will create a separate text block (1.190c) and graphics will be independent (9.90).
		■ If "Paste" on the Edit menu is dimmed, it means the Clipboard is empty.
		■ If you cut or copy a text block or a graphic and paste it back onto the same page, it shows up on the page slightly shifted from the original it was copied from (if it is visible), or if the original is not there, it pastes into the center of the page.
		■ To paste into the exact position it was cut or copied from, *power-paste with the pointer tool:* **Command Option V** (see 1.194).
		■ When you paste a graphic, if you do not want it to be an *inline graphic* (9.91) connected to a text block, then make sure there is no insertion point flashing!

If you want to do this:	**Then follow these steps:**	**Shortcuts ▾ Notes ▾ Hints**
1.194 Power-paste a text block or a graphic into the exact position it was cut or copied from	▪ With the **pointer tool,** select and cut or copy a text block or graphic as usual (1.191–1.192). ▪ Paste the object by pressing Command Option V. ▪ Read the column to the right.	▪ If you copied an object and it is still visible on the screen, the power-pasted item will land directly on top of the original, which may make you think it didn't happen. It did. ▪ Power-pasting like this will work even if you change page views, turn pages, or open another publication before you paste! ▪ If the original location is no longer visible, the object will be pasted into the center of the screen.
1.195 Power-paste multiples *(Step-and-repeat)* 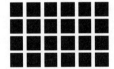 *First the top left block was power-pasted across in a row. Then the entire first row was copied and power-pasted down.*	▪ With the **pointer tool,** select and cut or copy a graphic or text block as usual (1.191–1.192). ▪ Paste the object with Command Option V; *it will be pasted directly on top of the original,* which makes it look like it didn't happen, but it did. ▪ With the **pointer tool,** move the pasted object any distance from the first one, keeping in mind that all other objects that will be power-pasted will be that same distance from the one before it. *Do not let go until the object is exactly where you want it! If you let go, then move it again, you cannot power-paste.* ▪ Press Command Option V as many times as you want to repeat the object.	▪ In step-and-repeat power-pasting, you move the pasted object a certain distance from the original. As you power-paste, each object will be placed that same relative distance from the one before it. ▪ You can select more than one object, as long as you move them all as a unit after you paste them. ▪ You can move the screen, even change the view, and it will still work, as long as there is space *visible.* If it runs out of room, it can't continue the pattern. ▪ Don't move objects during power-pasting! ▪ You can't power-paste text that has been cut or copied with the *text tool,* nor can you power-paste anything while the text tool is selected.

If you want to do this:	Then follow these steps:	Shortcuts ▾ Notes ▾ Hints
1.196 **Clear,** from the Edit menu, or **Backspace/Delete**	▪ Select an object or text (1.163–1.176). ▪ From the Edit menu choose "Clear" *or* press the Backspace/Delete key.	▪ Both **Clear** and the **Backspace/Delete** key will **remove** the selected object or text from the screen, but *will not* place it on the Clipboard—it's just gone. ▪ These commands come in very handy when there is something on the Clipboard you wish to keep, since cutting would replace the Clipboard item. ▪ Undo (from the Edit menu, *or* press Command Z) will undo this action, *if* you Undo *before you do anything else.*
1.197 View the contents of the Clipboard	▪ With any tool, choose "Show clipboard" from the Edit menu. ▪ To close it, click in its close box (upper left corner of its window); **or** from the File menu choose "Close"; **or** simply click on the publication page that you see behind the Clipboard.	▪ Text in the Clipboard is not editable. ▪ Text sent to the Clipboard with the text tool is displayed in 12-point Geneva; when you paste it back into the publication, though, all its formatting reappears. ▪ Read 1.188–1.190 for further clarification of what the Clipboard does to text.

If you want to do this:	Then follow these steps:	Shortcuts ▾ Notes ▾ Hints

1.198 Undo

- From the Edit menu choose "Undo ____" **or** press Command Z.

- As you do different things in your publication, the Undo command will change, telling you what action will be undone. If the action cannot be undone, "Cannot undo" appears dimmed in the menu.

1.199a You *can* Undo:

You can undo these actions:
- Moving ruler guides and column guides
- Adding or deleting ruler guides
- Creating columns
- Moving or resizing graphics or text blocks, including stretching PageMaker draw graphics
- Cropping imported graphics
- Editing text

And you can undo these commands:
- "Cut," "Copy," and "Clear" commands from the Edit menu or keyboard
- "Paste" command from the Edit menu or keyboard, *if* it was pasted using the *text tool*
- "Copy master guides" from the Page menu
- "Insert pages..." and "Remove pages..." from the Page menu
- "Page setup..." changes

1.199b You *cannot* Undo:

- Pasting while using the pointer tool
- Page view changes or scrolling
- Movement of text tool insertion point, using the mouse or keyboard
- Selecting or canceling selections
- Any changes to line widths, line patterns, and fill patterns
- Text rotation
- "Bring to front/back" commands
- Any commands from the Windows or Type menus
- Changes using the "Style" or "Color" palettes
- Any command from the File menu, except "Page setup..."

- You can only Undo *the very last thing you did!* So if you do something you don't like, or if you do something that makes you want to scream, first try Undo. Then scream if necessary.
- Often you can cancel what you just did by doing the opposite; that is, if you pasted a graphic, then while it is still selected just hit the Backspace/Delete key rather than try to Undo it. Or if you accidentally turned text upside down, select it again and turn it right side up. It really would be nice if we could undo line widths or fill patterns, wouldn't it.
- See Section 16 on Reverting and mini-Reverting for serious undoing.

If you want to do this:

Then follow these steps:

Shortcuts ▾ Notes ▾ Hints

Scrapbook

1.200   Put a graphic into the Scrapbook

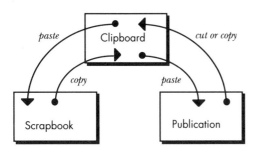

- Select the graphic. If it has more than one layer, be sure to get all the layers. (If you have trouble, read the subsection on Selecting and Layering: 1.143–1.182).
- Copy it (from the Edit menu choose "Copy," *or* press Command C); the graphic is now on the Clipboard (1.184–1.190; 1.192).
- From the Apple menu, choose "Scrapbook."
- While viewing the Scrapbook, from the Edit menu choose "Paste," *or* press Command V.
- Close the Scrapbook window (click in its close box in the upper left corner) to get back to your publication, *or* just click on the PageMaker window under the Scrapbook.

- The Scrapbook is a standard Macintosh desk accessory that permanently stores graphics or text for you. The only way into or out of it is through the Clipboard.
- You could also use the "Cut" command (1.191) to put an object in the Scrapbook.
- You can group together as many objects as you like and paste them all into the Scrapbook at once.

- When you paste any image into the Scrapbook, the current ones move over to make room for it; you're not *replacing* anything.

If you want to do this:	**Then follow these steps:**	**Shortcuts ▾ Notes ▾ Hints**
1.201 Put text into the Scrapbook	▪ Select text with the **text tool** by pressing-and-dragging over it; **OR** select text with the **pointer tool** by clicking on the text block. ▪ From the Edit menu choose "Copy," *or* press Command C. ▪ From the Apple menu, choose "Scrapbook." ▪ While viewing the Scrapbook, from the Edit menu choose "Paste," *or* press Command V. ▪ Close the Scrapbook window (click in its close box) to get back to your publication, *or* just click on the PageMaker window under the Scrapbook.	▪ There is an important difference between copying text that has been selected with the *text tool* and copying text that has been selected with the *pointer tool*—the Scrapbook does different things to them, just like the Clipboard (1.188–1.190): ▫ If you select an entire text block with the **pointer tool,** it will paste into the Scrapbook with all the formatting intact (size, style, line length, etc.), and it will come back exactly the same. ▫ If you select text by highlighting it with the **text tool,** it will paste into the Scrapbook as 12-point Geneva, no matter what the specifications were. But if you choose to paste that 12-point Geneva text back into your publication again from the Scrapbook, all the formatting and specifications are returned (except line length)! ▪ If there is no insertion point flashing when you paste into the *publication,* the text will create its own text block, which will be the width between the page margins.
1.202 Delete any image from the Scrapbook	▪ From the Apple menu choose "Scrapbook." ▪ In the open Scrapbook, find the image you want to delete. ▪ From the Edit menu choose "Clear."	▪ You could, of course, use "Cut" instead, but keep in mind that "Clear" does not put the item on the Clipboard.

If you want to do this:	**Then follow these steps:**	**Shortcuts • Notes • Hints**
1.203 Paste an *object* from the Scrapbook onto a page	■ From the Apple menu choose "Scrapbook." ■ Scroll to the image you want to copy onto your page. ■ While viewing the image, from the Edit menu choose "Copy," *or* press Command C. ■ Return to your publication (either click in the close box of the Scrapbook window *or* click on the PageMaker window). ■ From the Edit menu choose "Paste." ■ *Don't click anywhere!* While the handles are still on the object(s), press on a solid part or directly on text and drag it to its place. ■ If you change your mind or if you blew it, you can Undo the paste (Command Z) immediately.	■ You could also choose "Cut," of course, but that would delete it from the Scrapbook. ■ If the *pointer tool* was chosen before you opened the Scrapbook, the pasted objects will be set right in the middle of the page. ■ If *any other tool* besides the pointer tool is chosen, and there is no flashing insertion point, when you paste objects they will be set right in the middle of the page and the pointer tool will be chosen for you automatically. ■ If *an insertion point is flashing,* which means the *text tool* is chosen, the object will be pasted into the text as an *inline graphic* (9.91). Be careful! You'll probably accidentally paste objects as inline graphics at least 23 times before you finally start to remember to watch for that insertion point.
1.204 Paste *text* from the Scrapbook onto a page	■ Follow the steps in 1.203 above to copy the text and return to the publication. ■ Using the **text tool,** click to set an insertion point where you want the text to begin (see note to the right ☞). ■ From the Edit menu choose "Paste," *or* press Command V.	■ If an insertion point is set *within* an existing text block, the type will flow into that text block. ■ If an insertion point is set *outside* of any existing text block, the type will create a new text block. ■ If no insertion point is set, the type will create a new text block. ■ Also read 1.190–1.193 on cutting and pasting, as well as 3.121.

69

If you want to do this:

1.205 Place Scrapbook items as graphics

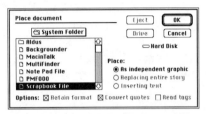

Find the Scrapbook File in the System folder.

 The Scrapbook place icon

Then follow these steps:

- Choose the **pointer tool.**
- From the File menu choose "Place...."
- Find your way to the contents of the System Folder (navigate by clicking on "Drive" if necessary to access another disk, and double-clicking on folders to open them; see *The Little Mac Book* if you're not clear on finding your way around).
- In the Place dialog box, while viewing the contents of the System Folder, click once on the file called "Scrapbook File."
- Click in the radio button (on the right) to place this as an **independent graphic** (*this is very important—if you don't click that button and there happens to be an insertion point flashing somewhere, the entire contents of your Scrapbook will pour into that text block*).
- Click OK; in your publication, you will see a new cursor with a number on it; the number indicates how many items are loaded into that cursor—the number of items in your Scrapbook.
- Each click of the mouse will place one of the items on the publication page, and the number on the cursor will reduce.
- To evaporate the rest of the items without placing them, click on the pointer tool.

Shortcuts ▾ Notes ▾ Hints

- All objects that are placed this way drop in as PICTs (9.14–9.21).
- This is one way to turn a large cap letter into a graphic that you can apply a text wrap to (see Section 11 on text wrapping). Create the letter as a separate text block and copy it into the Scrapbook *using the pointer tool.* If it is the first item in the Scrapbook, it will be the first item placed.
- Of course, if you have created several different Scrapbook files, you can open the one that you know holds the image you want; it may not necessarily be in the System Folder.
- You don't *really* need to choose the pointer tool first; the crucial thing is that you don't leave a flashing insertion point lying around somewhere. By clicking on the pointer tool, that's just not possible.
- If you are positive there is no insertion point anywhere, then you can shortcut the OK button by simply double-clicking on the file name. Without an insertion point, your only option is an independent graphic anyway.
- If you accidentally placed the entire Scrapbook in a text block, Undo immediately (Command Z). If it's too late to Undo, see 9.198.

If you want to do this:

Then follow these steps:

Shortcuts ▾ Notes ▾ Hints

Bounding Box (or drag-placing)

1.206 Create a bounding box to **type** into

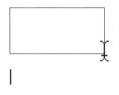

Press-and-drag with the text tool to create a bounding box like this.

When you let go, the box becomes invisible, but it's still there; the insertion point waits.

This text has been typed into an invisible bounding box. The depth will expand as you type, but not the width.

As you type or paste text, it will fill the bounding box.

- Choose the **text tool.**
- Anywhere *outside of any existing text block,* press-and-drag; this will create a *bounding box,* as shown on the left.
- When you let go of the mouse, the box *seems* to disappear, but it is actually just invisible; that perimeter you created is still there!
- The insertion point is flashing in the upper left of this invisible box; type and you will see the text word-wrap as it reaches the outer limits of the bounding box; the depth will expand to accommodate the text.

- This is a particularly useful technique to use when you want to type a headline across two columns—just set up a bounding box across the two and the text will override the column guides. Or when you wish to set page numbers or any other little bit of text, create a tiny little bounding box just big enough to hold your input.

1.207 **Paste** text into a bounding box

- When you are ready to paste text, create a bounding box as above (1.206).
- From the Edit menu choose "Paste," *or* press Command V.
- The text will paste into the bounding box, and the depth will expand to fit.

If you want to do this:	**Then follow these steps:**	**Shortcuts ▾ Notes ▾ Hints**

1.208 Drag-place text into a bounding box

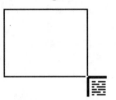

This is the image you will see as you drag a loaded text icon.

- When you are ready to **place** text, get the file as usual (from the File menu choose "Place..."; select the text file to place into PageMaker; see 3.51–3.52; **or** pick up text from a window loop; 3.89; 3.102).
- On your publication page, you should have a loaded text icon (3.82–3.83). With that icon, *don't click!* Instead, press-and-drag to create the bounding box (1.206); when you let up on the mouse, the text will flow into that space.

- Unlike when pasting or typing into a bounding box, *when you place text, the depth does not expand.* The text will flow into *just* that space you created.
- This is a great technique for placing a bunch of stories all over the pasteboard to see what you have to work with— drag-place just a few lines of each story. Even though only a few lines are visible, the text block contains the entire file.

1.209 Drag-place a graphic into a bounding box

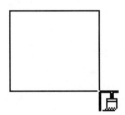

This is the image you will see as you drag a loaded graphic icon. (The icon itself may be different, depending on what type of graphic file you are placing; 9.92).

- When you are ready to **place** a graphic, click on the **pointer tool.** Get the file (from the File menu choose "Place..."; and select the graphic file you wish to place into your publication; see 9.92).
- On your publication page, you should see a loaded graphic icon (9.92). With that icon, press-and-drag to create the bounding box (as shown at left); when you let up on the mouse, *the graphic will flow into that space, meaning it will squeeze into whatever shape that space is, which may not be proportional!* Note that it is not cropped or necessarily resized, but has simply filled the space you gave it.

- Using the pointer tool ensures you will not inadvertently place it as an *inline graphic* (9.91).

- If you drag-place a graphic and it is out of proportion, position the tip of the **pointer tool** directly on a handle; hold down the Shift key and *press* the mouse button on that handle. Hold to the count of three; the image will snap back into its original proportions (not necessarily its original *size,* but its original *proportions*).

(continued from page 50)

NYWAY, GUTENBERG (BORN IN 1399 IN MAINZ, Germany) was getting into political trouble with the goldsmithing guilds in the city. So he ran off to Strasbourg, where it seems he began developing his printing equipment in the strictest secrecy. The history books are always wondering why he was so secretive, but is that so unusual? Aren't we still trying to keep PostScript hints and unbreakable codes secrets? **W**ell, the man was obsessive. Driven. An artist. Broke. He went back to Mainz with his perfected system, and in 1450 (at 49 years of age) talked a local financier, Johann Fust, into lending him money – 800 guilders, with the press equipment as security. But Gutenberg was a perfectionist. Besides, he didn't have PageMaker. He couldn't just change his leading with the click of a mouse to make those forty-two lines of type fit on the page. He couldn't press Command-Shift-J and make everything justify. No, he had to have every letter carved and molded backwards out of a separate tiny piece of lead; create other separate letters for the initial caps; take all these backwards letters and arrange them backwards in a wooden flat; insert varying amounts of lead space between each word to justify the text; insert slugs of lead between the lines; ink it up and run it through the press; check for typos, which obviously meant quite a bit of readjusting; then after getting a hundred or so good proofs, take all the letters out of that wooden flat and put them back into their cases (that's movable type) and start all over again with the next page. Whew. And just the thought of keyboarding the Bible is overwhelming. **G**utenberg worked on his project for two years, and Fust got a bit impatient at the lack of progress. Give the guy a break, Fust, he didn't have a Mac IIfx. He didn't even have a typewriter. Fust loaned him 800 more guilders and insisted on becoming a partner. **I**n 1457 Fust had really had it. Seven years. So he took Gutenberg to court and sued for the 1600 guilders he had loaned him, all the type, all the presses and other equipment, all the completed work on the 200 Bibles, plus an extra 426 guilders as interest on his loan. With the judge being another member of the Fust family, Gutenberg didn't stand a chance. **B**ut Fust was a banker – what did he know about printing Bibles? Certainly Gutenberg's most skilled foreman, Peter Schoeffer, wouldn't desert him and traitorously decamp to the buttered side of the press? Alas, Peter was in love with Fust's daughter. Fust and Peter Schoeffer went on to publish what has become known as the first printed piece of work in the world, the 42-line Mazarin Bible. And Peter married the boss's daughter.

(continued on page 88)

1.210 **The "Preferences" dialog box** *(from the Edit menu, choose "Preferences...")*

This measurement system choice affects the horizontal ruler and any dialog box that uses measurements; see 1.211 or 1.52.

The vertical ruler measurements can be different than the horizontal ruler; see 1.212 or 1.53

This determines how text displays in the smaller views; see 1.214

You can choose on which layer you want the guides; see 1.215, 1.65, or 1.67

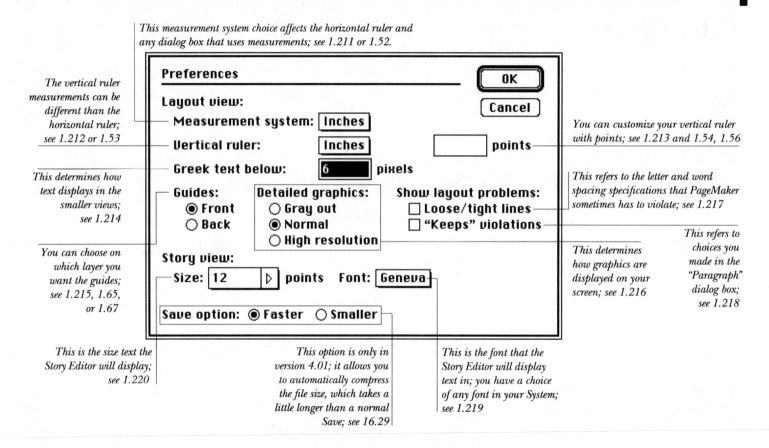

Preferences

Layout view:

Measurement system: `Inches`

Vertical ruler: `Inches`

Greek text below: `6` **pixels**

Guides:
- ● **Front**
- ○ **Back**

Detailed graphics:
- ○ **Gray out**
- ● **Normal**
- ○ **High resolution**

Show layout problems:
- ☐ **Loose/tight lines**
- ☐ **"Keeps" violations**

Story view:

Size: `12` ▷ **points** **Font:** `Geneva`

Save option: ● **Faster** ○ **Smaller**

`OK`

`Cancel`

`____` **points**

You can customize your vertical ruler with points; see 1.213 and 1.54, 1.56

This refers to the letter and word spacing specifications that PageMaker sometimes has to violate; see 1.217

This determines how graphics are displayed on your screen; see 1.216

This refers to choices you made in the "Paragraph" dialog box; see 1.218

This is the size text the Story Editor will display; see 1.220

This option is only in version 4.01; it allows you to automatically compress the file size, which takes a little longer than a normal Save; see 16.29

This is the font that the Story Editor will display text in; you have a choice of any font in your System; see 1.219

If you want to do this:	Then follow these steps:	Shortcuts ▾ Notes ▾ Hints

Preferences

1.211 Change the unit of measure on the horizontal ruler *and* in the dialog boxes

Layout view:
Measurement system: ✓Inches
Inches decimal
Millimeters
Picas
Ciceros

- From the Edit menu choose "Preferences."
- Under "Layout view: Measurement system:" press on the shadowed box; this will show the pop-up menu of choices; choose one.

- All measurements in all dialog boxes, such as Page Setup, Column Guides, Paragraph, Indents/tabs, etc., will follow the measurement system you chose here.
- You can temporarily override any measurement system in any dialog box (1.221).
- Measurements are accurate to $\frac{1}{2880}^{th}$ of an inch, supposedly at any page view size.

1.212 Change the unit of measure for the vertical ruler

Layout view:
Measurement system: Inches
Vertical ruler: ✓Inches
Inches decimal
Millimeters
Picas
Ciceros
Custom

- From the Edit menu choose "Preferences."
- Under "Layout view: Vertical ruler:" press on the shadowed box; this will show the pop-up menu of choices; choose one (for "Custom," see 1.213).

- You can, of course, set the vertical and horizontal measures to the same unit. Or perhaps you really like to measure your column widths and line lengths in picas, but want inches vertically. The greatest thing about the vertical ruler measurement is that you can customize it to your leading value, thus making it so easy to align baselines across columns (1.213).

1.213 Customize the measurement of the vertical ruler

Vertical ruler: Custom 12 points

- From the Edit menu choose "Preferences."
- Under "Layout view: Vertical ruler:" press on the shadowed box; choose "Custom."
- In the points box, type in the number of points you want the vertical ruler divided into, from 4 to 256. Each tick mark will represent that number of points, numbered in groups of fives (not picas!).

- If you set the Custom box to the point size of your leading and use "Snap to rulers" from the Options menu, you can make sure the baselines of your text align (see Scenario #2, 1.56).
- You can't override the points to use any other unit of measure (e.g., you can't customize the vertical ruler to half inches).

If you want to do this:

Then follow these steps:

Shortcuts ▾ Notes ▾ Hints

1.214 Change the number of pixels for showing "greek" text

Greek text below: pixels

        "Greek" text

- From the Edit menu choose "Preferences."
- Type in a value here from 0 to 32,767 (but don't type the comma!); any type smaller than that number of pixels at any view *smaller than Actual Size* will display as "greek."

- A *pixel* is one of the dots *(picture elements)* on the screen—all the images you see are created from these dots. The Mac screen has 72 dots per inch.
- "Greek" text is much easier for PageMaker to draw, thus it can display the screen much more quickly. The default is set at 6 pixels, since type below that size is too difficult to read anyway. If you want your 75% and 50% views to draw more quickly, set the greek text number higher.

1.215 Send the guides to the *front* or to the *back*

Guides:
◉ Front
○ Back

- From the Edit menu choose "Preferences."
- Under "Guides" choose "Front" or "Back."

- The standard default puts the guides in *front,* which means guides (*all* guides) are always the top layer (see 1.151–1.157 re: layering). This can be irritating when you are trying to pick up a line or other object that is directly under a guide. The easiest solution is to hold down the Command key and click on the object to select it. See 1.65–1.67.
- When guides are at the *back,* though, you cannot dig down through the layers with the Command key to pick them up— whatever is on top of the guides must be physically moved, or you must find someplace to grab the guide where there is nothing overlying it. It's worse than having them in front.

If you want to do this:

1.216 Adjust the resolution of detailed, non-PageMaker graphics

Detailed graphics:
○ Gray out
◉ Normal
○ High resolution

 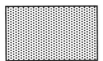

Normal　　　*Same image grayed out*

1.217 Show loosely-spaced and tightly-spaced lines

Show layout problems:
☒ Loose/tight lines

Generally, only justified text can be forced into tight or loose spacing.

A gray area delineates the text with problems

Then follow these steps:

- From the Edit menu choose "Preferences."
- Under "Detailed graphics" choose one of the following:
  - **Gray out:** This provides the fastest screen display; graphics are shown as gray rectangular forms.
  - **Normal:** graphics, including TIFFs, are shown as low-resolution screen images. PICTs over 64K in size are shown as monochrome TIFF images.
  - **High-resolution:** graphics, including color images, are shown at full resolution.

- From the Edit menu choose "Preferences."
- Under "Show layout problems" click on "Loose/tight lines."

Shortcuts ▾ Notes ▾ Hints

- This command affects just the screen display—images will print as usual.
- When placing graphics larger than 256K, PageMaker gives you the option of storing a complete copy of the graphic in the publication itself, as opposed to just providing a low-res screen version linked to the original for printing purposes (see 9.82–9.88). Even if you *don't* store the complete copy, choosing high-rcs will give you a high-res image if you want it.
- With "Gray out" or "Normal" setting, you can choose to view any TIFF at high-res, temporarily, by holding down the Control key as the screen redraws; e.g., when turning pages, changing views, scrolling.

- This command is directly connected to the spacing limits set in the "Spacing attributes" dialog box (4.10–4.11).
- When a line of text or an inline graphic has more spacing (loose lines) or less spacing (tight lines) than the specified limits, a gray or colored bar shades the text (the bar won't print). It is up to you to fix the problem lines yourself by changing spacing, line length, words, etc.
- Generally, only justified text can be forced into tight or loose spacing.

If you want to do this:	Then follow these steps:	Shortcuts ▾ Notes ▾ Hints
1.218 Show lines that violate the "keeps" commands established in the Paragraph dialog box **Show layout problems:** ☐ **Loose/tight lines** ☒ **"Keeps" violations**	■ From the Edit menu choose "Preferences." ■ Under "Show layout problems" click on "'Keeps' violations."	■ This command is directly connected to the widow, orphan, or keep-with-next specifications you set in the "Paragraph specifications" dialog box (3.191–3.202). ■ Lines of text or inline graphics that violate the commands you set are indicated with a gray or colored bar. It is up to you to fix them yourself by manually bumping lines down, rearranging the lengths of text blocks, changing type specifications, etc.
1.219 Change the font displayed in the Story Editor **Font:**	**New York**		■ From the Edit menu choose "Preferences." ■ Under "Story view," press on the shadowed box next to "Font" to display the pop-up menu of fonts; choose one.	■ It's a good idea to choose only those fonts with a city name, as they are bit-mapped and designed for the resolution of the screen. They will be clearer and will display faster than non-city-named (which are generally *outline*) fonts.
1.220 Change the font size displayed in the Story Editor **Story view:** **Size:**	12	▷ **points**	■ From the Edit menu choose "Preferences." ■ Under "Story view," press on the arrow in the box next to "Size" to display the pop-up menu of font sizes; choose a size; **or** type the size of your choice into the edit box.	■ The clearest size to read will be the font size that is shown in outline format, as that bitmapped size is installed in your System and can be reproduced most efficiently on the screen. (Different fonts have different screen sizes installed.) 9 10 11 12 14 *The 9 and 12 point sizes of this particular font will be the easiest to read on the screen.*

If you want to do this: Then follow these steps: Shortcuts ▾ Notes ▾ Hints

Overriding ruler measurements

1.221 Override the current ruler measurement in any dialog box that asks for measures

inches
millimeters
picas
points
ciceros
cicero points

After [0p5] inches

Example of overriding the inches with points to add extra space between paragraphs.

- No matter what the current measurement system, you can override it with the following abbreviations:

  Inches: type **i** after the value.
  e.g., *2.75 inches = 2.75i*

  Millimeters: type **m** after the value.
  e.g., *3 millimeters = 3m*

  Picas: type **p** after the value.
  e.g., *3 picas = 3p*

  Points: type **0p** before the value
  (that's a *zero* and a *p*).
  e.g., *6 points = 0p6*

  Picas and points: type a value for picas, type **p**, type the value for points.
  e.g., *2 picas & 6 points = 2p6*

  Ciceros: type **c** after the value.
  e.g., *5 ciceros = 5c*

  Cicero points: type **0c** before the value
  (that's a *zero* and a *c*).
  e.g., *4 cicero points = 0c4*

  Ciceros and points: type a value for ciceros, type **c**, type the value for points.
  e.g., *5 ciceros & 4 points = 5c4*

- This will leave your rulers intact, but allow you to specify in other measures.
- This is extremely useful, for example, when the measurements are in inches, but you want to specify the space between paragraphs in points, or perhaps the space between columns in picas.
- You can override the measurement, but when you come back to that dialog box you will find that PageMaker has translated the overriden value into the equivalent measure for the system it's currently working in; that is, if you type **1p** to override the inches, the next time you see that dialog box it will no longer say **1p,** but **0.167,** which is the equivalent in inches. I wish it wouldn't do that.
- Just for your information:
  □ 1 pica = .167 inch
  □ 1 cicero = .177 inch (4.5 mm)
  □ Picas and ciceros are both divided into 12 points.
  □ In traditional type, 6 picas equals .996 of an inch; in Macintosh type, 6 picas (72 points) is exactly one inch.

If you want to do this:	Then follow these steps:	Shortcuts ▾ Notes ▾ Hints

Numeric keypad

1.222 Type numbers with the keypad

- Press Caps Lock down.

- You can also press the Clear key instead of Caps Lock to toggle between using the keypad for numbers or for arrow keys (1.223). But there is no visual clue that tells you which mode you are currently in—you just have to type and see what comes up, then decide if you need to press Clear or not.

1.223 Use the keypad as arrow keys

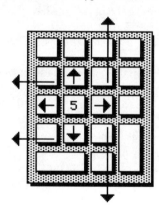

- The insertion point must first be somewhere in the story.
- Make sure Caps Lock is **not** down.

- If you examine the diagram on the left, you'll see that it's pretty logical, really:

  8 takes you up a line
  2 takes you down a line

  7 takes you to the beginning of the line
  1 takes you to the end of a line

  9 takes you up a screen
  3 takes you down a screen

  4 takes you left one character
  6 takes you right one character

  5 always types a 5

- If you get numbers and Caps Lock is not down, press the Clear key.
- When you hold the Command key down in addition, you move in the same direction, but in bigger chunks.

Command *plus:*
  8 takes you up a paragraph
  2 takes you down a paragraph
  7 takes you to the beginning of the sentence
  1 takes you to the end of a sentence
  9 takes you to the top of a story
    (if it's on the same page or facing page)
  3 takes you to the bottom of a story
    (if it's on the same page or facing page)
  4 takes you left one word
  6 takes you right one word
  5 always types a 5

If you want to do this:	Then follow these steps:	Shortcuts • Notes • Hints
1.224 Select text with the keypad	■ Hold down the Shift key. ■ With the Shift key down, use any of the keypad shortcuts in 1.223 or 1.226; as the cursor moves, the text will be selected.	■ This is particularly great for picking up those little bits that you miss at the end of a selection, or for removing a few characters at the end of a selection: just hold down that Shift key and use the arrow keys (1.226) or keypad keys (1.223) to add to or delete from it.
1.225 Cut and paste with the keypad *(see 1.191–1.193 for more specific info regarding the basic cut-and-paste concept)*	■ Make sure the keypad is giving you arrow keys; if it is giving you numbers, then press the Clear key before you try this. ■ To **Cut:** select the text or graphic as usual; press the decimal point on the keypad. ■ To **Paste:** press the zero on the keypad.	■ Read 1.163–1.176 if you need help selecting text or graphics. Also read 1.224 right above this. ■ See 1.189–1.190 to understand where it will paste.
1.226 Use other keyboard shortcuts to move the insertion point	Left one character: LeftArrow Right one character: RightArrow Left one word: Option LeftArrow Right one word: Option RightArrow Up one line: UpArrow Down one line: DownArrow Up one paragraph: Command UpArrow Down one paragraph: Command DownArrow For the extended keyboards: Up a screen: PageUp Down a screen PageDown To top of story: Home To bottom of story: End	■ If you press the Shift key in addition to the arrow keys, you will *select* the text as the insertion point moves.

If you want to do this:	Then follow these steps:	Shortcuts ▾ Notes ▾ Hints

Key Caps

1.227 View the Key Caps keyboard layout

- From the Apple menu, choose "Key Caps."

- The Keyboard Layout icon must be in your System Folder. This desk accessory is just to show you where all those special typographic characters are hiding.

1.228 View all four of the keyboard layouts

- From the Apple menu, choose "Key Caps."
- From the Key Caps menu item that now appears on the far right of the menu, choose the name of the font whose keys you want to see (if you are experimenting right now, choose an outline font; that is, a font without a city name).
- You are looking at all the characters that are accessible in that font without pressing any extra keys (you already know those characters).
- Hold down the Shift key; you are looking at all the Shift characters (you already know those, too).
- Hold down the Option key; you are looking at some of the accent marks and alternate characters available.
- Hold down both the Option and the Shift keys; you see more alternate characters.
- To hide the Key Caps layout, simply click in its close box in the upper left.

- Different fonts sometimes have different characters available. Most of them, though, hide the same characters under the same keys; for instance, ¢ in all fonts is Option 4. City-named (bitmapped/ QuickDraw) fonts have fewer characters than non-city-named (which are usually outline/PostScript) fonts. See 18.29–18.42 for more information of fonts in general.

If you want to do this:

1.229 Use alternate characters in
your publication
(*for accent marks, see 1.231*)

Then follow these steps:

- From the Apple menu, choose Key Caps.
- Choose your font from the menu item that
  now appears on the far right: Key Caps.
- Find the character you want to use by
  holding the keys mentioned in 1.228
  (Shift, Option, or Shift-Option); then
  press to find the key your character is
  hiding beneath (e.g., if you hold Option
  while you press 7, 8, or 9, you see that the
  bullet is hiding under the 8).
- Once you know where that character is,
  close up Key Caps (click in its close box)
  to return to your publication.
- With the **text tool,** click to set the insertion point where you want the character
  to appear.
- Press the combination of characters;
  e.g., hold the Option key down while you
  press the 8 and you will get a bullet: •.

Shortcuts ▾ Notes ▾ Hints

- Accessing alternate characters is exactly
  the same as accessing the characters on
  the keyboards that are above the numbers. For instance, just as you hold the
  Shift key and press 8 to get an asterisk,
  you can hold the *Option* key and press 8
  to get a bullet: • .
- Don't forget about the chart at the end
  of this book that lists the most common
  alternate characters.

If you want to do this:	**Then follow these steps:**	**Shortcuts ▾ Notes ▾ Hints**

1.230 Insert an alternate character from another font

- Follow the steps in 1.228 to find the key that holds the character you want; say you need to use this character, ❏, which is only found in the font Zapf Dingbats.
- On your page, type the appropriate keys in your current font that, if you *were* in Zapf Dingbats, would give you the character you want. Then type the word after it; go back to that character, select it, and change the font to Zapf Dingbats (3.140);
- **OR** type *up to* that character; change the font; type that character; then change the font back to what you were working with (3.140).

- Using the first method noted here, the character that initially appears is not what you want; in this case you will type an 'o.' When you change the font, however, it will *become* the character you saw in the Zapf Dingbats keyboard layout.
- You may find that the character you want is only in another font. Then simply use that font, even in the middle of your current font. (That is sometimes called a "visiting" font.)
- See 8.73 for a trick to enter a character that you can later find and change automatically throughout the entire publication.

1.231 Use accent marks, as in the word **piñata**

The most common accent marks:

- ´ Option e
- ` Option ~ (tilde)
- ¨ Option u
- ~ Option n
- ^ Option i

- Follow the steps in 1.228 to find the key that holds the accent mark you need.
- On your page, type the word that has the accent mark, *but stop right before typing the character that needs the mark over it.*
- Use the character combination that will create the accent mark—nothing should show up on your page!
- Now *let go of all keys* and type just the letter to be under the mark—it will appear with the accent mark above it.

Example
- The mark ~ is accessed by holding down the Option key and pressing **n**, as you discovered by looking at Key Caps (or perhaps you used the chart at the end of this book).
- Type **p i**.
- Hold down the Option key and press **n**; nothing will appear.
- Now let go of the Option key and press **n** again.
- The accent mark will appear *over* the letter: **ñ**.
- Type the rest of the word: **p i ñ a t a** .

If you want to do this: ▪   Then follow these steps: ▪   Shortcuts ▾ Notes ▾ Hints ▪

Find File

1.232 Use Find File to locate a file while at your Desktop, *before* opening PageMaker

The Find File window

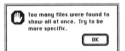

You'll get yelled at if you give him too few letters to work with.

- From the Apple menu, choose Find File.
- Type in a few letters of the name of the file you want; the more letters, the more specific and the quicker the search (If you have too few letters, the little man on the right will yell at you).
- Click on the little man (or press Return); he will find all the files that have those characters in their names, and will list them in the box in the middle of the window.
- If the file you want is listed, click once on it (notice the scroll bars; if the scroll bars turn gray, press an arrow to see more of the list).
- In the list box on the bottom right, Mr. Find File will tell you exactly where you can find that file. Either remember where it is, or tell him to get it for you: From the Find File menu (now appearing at the far right of the menu bar), choose "Move to desktop." He will usually place it on the Desktop for you.

- Even if you can't remember the entire name, he will look for any file that has the sequence of characters you specify.
- You can tell the little man to look only in certain places, such as in a particular folder or disk, by choosing "Search Here..." from the menu item that appears on the top right of your menu bar; **or** tell him to search a different disk (if you have more than one disk available) by clicking on the name of the disk that appears in the upper left of the Find File window.
- If you see your file listed before the stop sign turns dark, you can tell him to stop looking by clicking on that stop sign yourself. Even though you don't see the typical watch cursor to remind you to wait, he is looking until the Stop sign turns dark.
- It's all too possible to move a file to the Desktop and later forget where it came from. If this happens, click once on the file icon while you're at the Desktop; from the File menu choose "Put Away." Mr. Find File will come get it and put it right back where it belongs. What a guy.

If you want to do this:

1.233 Use Find File to locate a file while you are working inside PageMaker

(Perhaps you want to "Save as..." into a particular folder or you want to "Open" a file and you can't quite remember where it is, or maybe you're just too lazy to go find it)

Then follow these steps:

- From the Apple menu choose "Find File."
- Type in the name or part of the name of the file you wish to locate; click once on the little man.
- When he gives you the list of files he's found, click on the one you want; now close Find File (click in the close box in the upper left of its window).
- Back at your publication, when you go now to the "Save as..." dialog box or to the "Open..." dialog box, that file (or at least the folder that contains it) will be waiting for you.

Shortcuts ▾ Notes ▾ Hints

- If the file you want is on another disk, you can use the Find File menu (that now appears at the far right of your menu). From that Find File menu, choose "Search here..." and tell him which disk or folder to search.
  Or simply click on the name of the disk that appears in the upper left corner of the Find File window—it will switch him to another disk.

If you want to do this:	Then follow these steps:	Shortcuts • Notes • Hints

Create more window space

1.234 On a small screen, open up more space in the window

Do any or all of the following:
- If the rulers are showing, hide them by choosing "Rulers" from the Options menu; *or* by pressing Command R.
- If the scroll bars are showing, hide them by choosing "Scroll bars" from the Windows menu.
- If the Style palette is showing, hide it by choosing "Style palette" from the Windows menu; *or* by pressing Command Y; *or* by clicking in its little close box.
- If the Color palette is showing, hide it by choosing "Color palette" from the Windows menu; *or* by pressing Command K; *or* by clicking in its little close box.
- If the Toolbox is showing, hide it by choosing "Toolbox" from the Windows menu; *or* by pressing Command 6; *or* by clicking in its close box.

- Obviously, hiding all these things can make it awkward to work—it's your choice.
- Without scroll bars, you can still use the grabber hand to move around: while the Option key is down, any tool will turn into the grabber *when the mouse is pressed;* press-and-drag to move the page (1.117).
- When scroll bars are missing, the page icons will be missing too. Use the "Go to page..." command from the Page menu to navigate; *or* press Command Tab to go to the next page; Command Shift Tab to go to the previous page (1.97–1.107).
- The Style list is always available under the Type menu.
- The Color palette can always be brought back with Command K.

(continued from page 73)

JOHANNES GUTENBERG ENDED UP HOMELESS IN THE street at the age of 56. Like any obsessive personality, he managed to find some way to carry on his printing in some manner, but he grew increasingly blind. Looking at tiny little pieces of lead all day isn't any better for your eyes than staring at a computer screen, it seems. He never did really get it together again; eventually a local bishop took pity on this destitute inventor and put him on welfare, providing him with a yearly allowance of grain, cloth, and wine. **B**ut what goes around comes around, doesn't it? Even though Fust took over and went on to become rich and to proclaim himself as the publisher of this history-making product, who do we remember? That's right, that impecunious blind old inventor who spent his life struggling for something he believed in. Fust isn't even in the dictionary. **D**evelopers took to the printing press like developers took to the Mac. In less than forty years there were more than a thousand presses operating all over Europe. By 1500 there were 150 presses in Venice alone! More than two million books had been printed. How many people were there in Europe in 1498, anyway? **I**t caught on quickly, but the technology didn't advance very rapidly. Until the early 1970s, everything you saw printed was created using Gutenberg's technique—tiny little movable pieces of lead type. The only significant advancement had been Otto Mergenthaler's Linotype machine in 1882—it could very noisily produce a whole line of type at a time, rather than one character at a time! Wow! **I**n the early '70s a revolution began in the graphic and type world with the advent of electronic type. (The New York Times was printed for the last time by linotype in 1979.) Now things are really moving fast. But, as on a roller coaster, the speed is exhilarating—who cares if you get a little dizzy? — *rw*

"No one can say today how electronics will affect printing. We cannot for the present foresee a complete suppression of book printing with individual movable metal types as discovered by Gutenberg."
Elizabeth Geck, 1968

a 20th century author, designer, typesetter, & publisher

2 ▾ DRAWING TOOLS

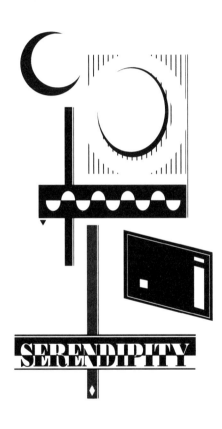

2.1 PageMaker provides several tools for creating simple graphics directly in your publication. They all work in a similar manner; they are all object-oriented and can layer, as explained in Section 1; and you can manipulate their size, shape, and fill pattern at any time.

2.2 You can set the defaults for the lines and fills for all the tools so they automatically draw with whichever line or border width and fill you most regularly use. This way you don't have to select and change them each time. These defaults can be set for the entire PageMaker application or for just the publication you are working on. For instance, you'll find this very handy when you are about to draw several boxes with identical borders and fills; set a publication (temporary) default and you're ready to go. (See 1.6–1.16 for greater detail on defaults.)

2.3 This section first gives instructions that are common to all the tools, then breaks down into tasks particular to each tool.

The drawing tools

2.4   **To choose any draw tool,** simply click on it while the Toolbox is showing (if the Toolbox is not showing, choose "Toolbox" from the Windows menu, or press Command 6). Don't press-and-drag to select a tool—just click on it. Your cursor will change (2.11) when you move it away from the Toolbox.

2.5   **Diagonal-line tool** draws lines at any angle. If you press the Shift key while you draw, you will restrain its movements to only 45° and 90° lines. When you draw vertical and horizontal lines, you can flip the line to draw on either side of the crossbar cursor (see the example in 2.6).

2.6   **Perpendicular-line tool** draws only 45° and 90° lines; you can flip 90° lines to draw on either side of the crossbar cursor.

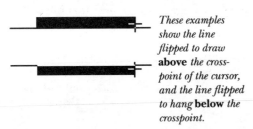

These examples show the line flipped to draw **above** *the crosspoint of the cursor, and the line flipped to hang* **below** *the crosspoint.*

2.7   **Square-corner, or rectangle tool** draws rectangles with square corners (although you *can* select the shape and turn it into a rounded-corner rectangle). The rectangle begins drawing from a corner, with the beginning point anchored to the page. If you press the Shift key while you draw, you will restrain its shape to a square.

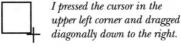

I pressed the cursor in the upper left corner and dragged diagonally down to the right.

2.8   **Rounded-corner, or rounded-rectangle tool** draws rectangles with rounded corners (although you *can* select the shape and turn it into a square-cornered rectangle). The rectangle begins drawing from a corner, with the beginning point anchored to the page. If you press the Shift key while you draw, you will restrain its shape to a square. Examples of corners are in 2.14.

2.9   **Oval/circle tool** draws ovals. Pressing the Shift key restrains its shape to a circle. It begins drawing at a "corner" (as opposed to drawing from the center of the circle).

2.10   **Cropping tool.** This is not a draw tool—it is used for cropping imported graphics. Cropping tool information is found in Section 9 on Graphics, 9.104.

2.11   **The draw tool cursor.** This is the crossbar icon that appears when you choose a draw tool. The "hot spot," or the point of the tool where the action happens, is right in the center where the two bars meet—that is the point from which lines and boxes will begin drawing. For your convenience, the crossbar will automatically turn back into a pointer when it is in a scroll bar, the Toolbox, the menu, the rulers, or on the page icons.

2.12   **The basic rule,** when using draw tools, is that the tool itself is only used for creating the inital shape; if you want to do anything to that shape (move it, stretch it, delete it, etc.), *you must use the* **pointer tool.**

The drawing tools

2.13
The Toolbox

You can press anywhere in the title bar and drag the Toolbox around on the screen.

Diagonal-line tool (2.5)

Perpendicular-line tool; also known as the Straight-line tool (2.6)

Click in the close box to hide the Toolbox. Press Command 6 to show it again.

Use the pointer tool to manipulate the objects you draw (2.12)

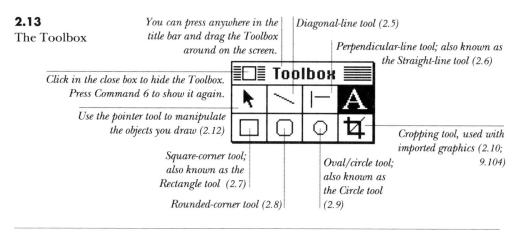

Cropping tool, used with imported graphics (2.10; 9.104)

Square-corner tool; also known as the Rectangle tool (2.7)

Oval/circle tool; also known as the Circle tool (2.9)

Rounded-corner tool (2.8)

2.14 The available corner styles
(from the Element menu, choose "Rounded corners...")

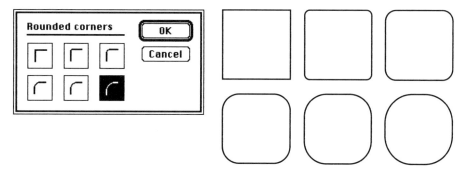

2.15 On a publication page, you can select more than one shape or line together, and then change all their line widths, borders, corners, and fill patterns with the same click.

2.16 You can use the line widths in the "Line" submenu for any kind of line, as well as for the borders of any rectangle, square, oval, or circle. You can also make any one of those lines "Reverse," where the white part of the line turns black and the black part turns white. Take a look at the examples on the following page.

2.17 The line widths shown on the screen are actual size, except "None," "Hairline," and ".5 pt." Depending on the resolution of your screen, what you see using those fine lines may not be exactly what prints. Check the examples on the following page for actual printed examples.

2.18 A "fill" is the "color" that fills a shape. The patterns from the Fill submenu are all opaque (except "None") and so will hide anything behind them. As with the line widths, the resolution of your screen does not always show exactly what will print; check the examples on the following page.

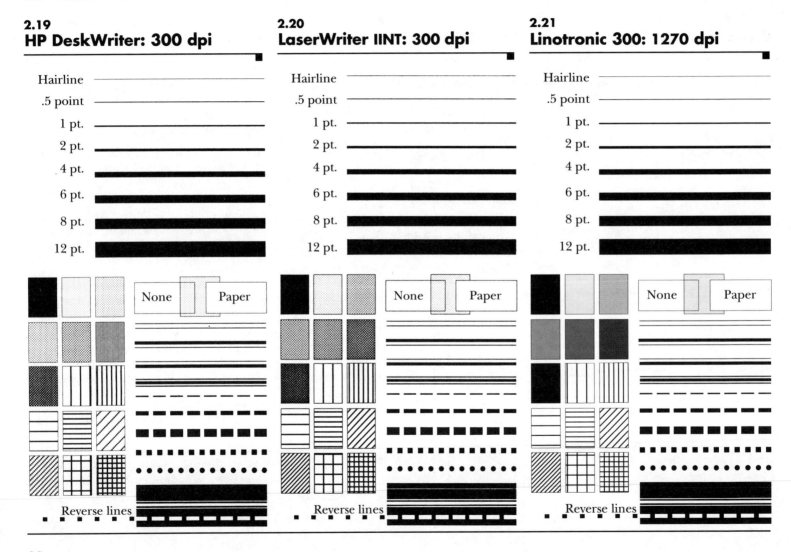

2.19
HP DeskWriter: 300 dpi

Hairline
.5 point
1 pt.
2 pt.
4 pt.
6 pt.
8 pt.
12 pt.

None   Paper

Reverse lines

2.20
LaserWriter IINT: 300 dpi

Hairline
.5 point
1 pt.
2 pt.
4 pt.
6 pt.
8 pt.
12 pt.

None   Paper

Reverse lines

2.21
Linotronic 300: 1270 dpi

Hairline
.5 point
1 pt.
2 pt.
4 pt.
6 pt.
8 pt.
12 pt.

None   Paper

Reverse lines

If you want to do this:	Then follow these steps:	Shortcuts ▾ Notes ▾ Hints
2.22 Draw an object 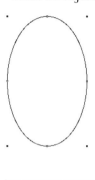 *Notice the eight selection handles on this object— one at each corner and one on each side.* *Lines have only two handles—one at each end.*	■ In the **Toolbox,** click once on the tool of your choice; the cursor will automatically become a crossbar when you leave the Toolbox (2.11). ■ Position the center of the crossbar where you want the object to begin. ■ Press-and-drag until the object is the size you want it; release the mouse button. (If you want to move or resize the object, you must use the *pointer tool.*)	■ As soon as you let go of the mouse button, the object is drawn and will show its selection handles. If you immediately decide you don't want what you've just drawn, **now** is a good time to press the Backspace/Delete key to get rid of it. Or if you want to change its line or border width or inside fill pattern, go up to the Element menu and choose whichever one you want (2.15–2.21). ■ If you click anywhere outside the object, the selection handles disappear. To select it again, see 2.23. The object must be selected before it can be manipulated.
2.23 Select one or more drawn objects (**Important:** *read the section on Selecting: 1.144–1.176. It covers selecting more than one object at a time, as well as selecting hidden or lost objects, invisible objects, objects under other layers, etc.)*	■ With the **pointer tool,** click anywhere on the object (if the object has a fill of "None," you must be sure to click on the border itself, as there is literally nothing inside the border; see the example of "None" in 2.21). ■ To select more than one object, hold the Shift key down while clicking on each one (1.168); **Or** with the **pointer tool,** press in a blank area and drag to draw a marquee around the objects (1.169).	■ If handles don't show up when you click on the object, it may be under another *layer* (1.151–1.156 re: layers). Hold down the Command key and click on the object; with each click you dig down through the layers. You should see handles appear on each layer, including the object you're looking for. ■ If you still can't get handles, the object is probably on a master page. You must go to the master page to change any objects that were placed there (1.122–1.127; 1.134).

If you want to do this:	Then follow these steps:	Shortcuts ▾ Notes ▾ Hints
2.24 Delete a drawn object	▪ With the **pointer tool,** click anywhere on the object to select it (you should see handles). ▪ Hit the Backspace/Delete key, *or* from the Edit menu choose "Clear."	▪ If you have trouble selecting the object, see 2.23, as well as 1.164–1.176. ▪ You can Undo a delete—from the Edit menu choose "Undo delete." Remember, you must Undo *before you do anything else, even before you click again.* If the menu doesn't say "Undo delete," you're too late.
2.25 Delete lots of objects	▪ With the **pointer tool,** hold down the Shift key and click once on each of the objects you want to delete (you should see handles on all of them). ▪ Hit the Backspace/Delete key, *or* from the Edit menu choose "Clear."	▪ The point is, you can select any number of objects and then delete them with the Backspace/Delete key. See 2.23 for a few more hints on selecting. ▪ See 1.164–1.176 for *detailed* information on selecting.
2.26 Move one or more objects ⬦ *When moving objects, you should see this four-headed arrow,* not *a two-headed arrow.*	▪ With the **pointer tool,** click on the object you want to move. For moving more than one, hold down the Shift key and click once on each of the objects (you should see handles on all of them). ▪ Position the very tip of the pointer on a solid part of one of the objects—*not on any handle!* ▪ Press-and-drag to move the object(s); if you have selected more than one, they will all move together. *You should see the four-headed arrow; if you see a two-headed arrow, then let go, Undo (Command Z), and try again.*	▪ You can also use the marquee from the pointer tool to select more than one object; see 1.164–1.176 for detailed information on selecting. ▪ You can Undo a move—if you don't like where you've placed it and want to put it back, from the Edit menu choose "Undo move" (Command Z). ▪ PageMaker has a fast move (press and move quickly—you'll see just the outline) and a slow move (press, wait, then move—you'll see the actual objects). See 1.159, 1.160.

If you want to do this:	**Then follow these steps:**	**Shortcuts ▾ Notes ▾ Hints**
2.27 Move one or more objects to another page	▪ Follow the steps in 2.23 to select the objects to be moved. Then either: ▪ Cut the objects, go to the page you want to move them to, and paste them onto the new page (see 1.184–1.193 for detailed information about cutting and pasting); ▪ **Or** simply move the objects out to the pasteboard, making sure no handles are connected to the page; then go to the new page and put them on (you will have to re-select the objects after you get to the other page).	▪ You can power-paste objects into exactly the same position as on the page they came from by pressing Command Option V (see 1.194 for more details on power-pasting). ▪ One of the great features of PageMaker: anything placed on the pasteboard (the area outside the page; see 1.4) will stay there, just as if you were working on your drafting table.
2.28 Move a tiny little object (*when it's so little that the cursor obscures it and you can't see where it's going*)	▪ Create a larger object about an inch away from the one you need to reposition. ▪ Select both objects (Shift-click or use the marquee; 2.23). ▪ With the **pointer tool,** press on the larger object; as you drag the larger one, the smaller one comes along too. ▪ After repositioning the small object, click anywhere outside the objects to deselect them both; then select the larger one (click once on it) and delete it (hit the Backspace/Delete key).	▪ This works great. It'll look like this: *The two objects selected. You can see that if I were to press on the little square, the four-headed cursor would completely cover it.* *The two objects moving. By moving the larger object, I can easily place the smaller one precisely.*

If you want to do this:	Then follow these steps:	Shortcuts ▾ Notes ▾ Hints
2.29 Move objects in a straight line	■ With the **pointer tool,** select the object(s), as in 2.23. ■ Hold the Shift key while you press-and-drag the objects; the movement will be restrained to just the vertical or horizontal, whichever direction you first move.	■ You can keep the mouse button down, but re-press the Shift key to change direction.
2.30 Draw or move objects in perfect alignment with guide lines	■ In the Options menu, make sure "Snap to guides" has a checkmark next to it (meaning it's on); if not, choose it to turn it on. ■ As you draw or move, you'll notice that when the cursor gets close to a guideline, it jumps onto it.	■ The "Snap to guides" feature allows you to draw and move objects very precisely, even while in a reduced page view.
2.31 Draw or move objects in perfect alignment with the ruler tick marks	■ In the Options menu, make sure "Snap to rulers" has a checkmark next to it (meaning it's on); if not, choose it to turn it on. ■ You'll notice that with "Snap to rulers" on, the cursor kind of jumps around the screen rather than moves smoothly. As you draw with the tools or move objects, they jump from tick mark to tick mark on the ruler—in fact, you cannot position anything *between* the marks.	■ Using "Snap to rulers" makes it so easy, for instance, to place lines every half inch or copy a one-inch box every two inches—objects just get right on those ruler marks. ■ You can customize your vertical ruler in your choice of point increments (1.212; 1.213), thus further enhancing the precision.

If you want to do this:	Then follow these steps:	Shortcuts ▾ Notes ▾ Hints
2.32 Stop the cursor or the objects you are moving from jerking around on the screen	■ Check the Options menu: if there is a checkmark next to either "Snap to rulers" or "Snap to guides," choose them again (one at a time, of course) to turn them off.	■ Read 2.30 and 2.31.
2.33 Change a line width or a border	■ With the **pointer tool,** select the objects that have a line width or border you wish to change. ■ From the Element menu, choose the submenu "Line"; choose any one of those 18 lines. You can choose "Reverse" *in addition* to any line.	■ See 2.23 and 1.164–1.176 if you need info on selecting. ■ Examples of all the line widths and styles on three kinds of printers are found in 2.19–2.21. ■ The white space between double and dotted lines is always opaque. ■ Design jargon for "lines" is "rules."
2.34 Change the line width or the border of a *group* of lines or drawn shapes	■ Just follow the directions above (2.33), first selecting *all* the objects to be changed.	■ Don't neglect this trick—it's a great timesaver.
2.35 Reverse a line width or border	■ Select one or more drawn objects, as explained in 2.23. ■ From the Element menu choose the submenu "Line." ■ Choose "Reverse."	■ Reverse can be used *in combination with* any other line. ■ All double, triple, dotted, or dashed lines are opaque in the white area; when reversed, that white area becomes black. See 2.19–2.21. ■ Make sure there is an object selected before you choose "Reverse"; otherwise you will set a default (1.6–1.11) and everything you draw will have a reverse line.

If you want to do this:

2.36 Find an invisible or "lost" object

Then follow these steps:

- Reduce the view to Fit in Window size, or at least some size where you can see most of the page where the object is lost.
- With the **pointer tool,** from the Edit menu choose "Select all."
- You will see handles on every object, no matter how many layers (1.151–1.157) they may be under.
- If the object you're looking for is there, you will see its handles; take note of its location.
- Click once in any blank area or on the pointer tool to release all the handles, then go back and select the lost object. You may need to click around until you hit upon it, or draw a marquee around the area (1.176), or Command-click to find it under another layer (1.172, 1.175) and Bring it to the Front (Element menu; 1.177).

Shortcuts ▾ Notes ▾ Hints

- Can you find the invisible object and the "lost" object in this melee?

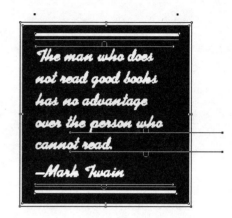

If you want to do this:	Then follow these steps:	Shortcuts · Notes · Hints

Lines

2.37 Lengthen or shorten a line

When you press directly on the handle, the pointer will turn into the crossbar cursor again. The part of the crossbar that overlaps the line will turn white.

- With the **pointer tool,** click anywhere on the line to select it; handles will appear.
- Position the very *tip* of the pointer on an end handle.
- Press on the handle; you should see the *crossbar* cursor again. *If you see the four-headed arrow, you are not pressing in the handle; let go and press Command Z to undo any change you may have just made.*
- When you see the crossbar cursor, press-and-drag to the length of your choice.

- If you have trouble selecting the line, read 2.23, as well as 1.164–1.176.
- **Important:** if the line is perfectly straight (vertically, horizontally, or diagonally 45°) and you want to keep it so, hold the Shift key down while dragging.
- You cannot change the length of more than one line at a time, even if many are selected.

2.38 Straighten a crooked line

- With the **pointer tool,** click anywhere on the line to select it; handles will appear.
- Hold down the Shift key; position the very *tip* of the pointer on an end handle.
- Press on that handle and count to three.

- Any line from either line tool can be straightened after it has been drawn. This trick will anchor the end you are *not* pressing, and *your* end will snap out perfectly perpendicular to the anchor.
- If you have trouble selecting the line, read 2.23, as well as 1.164–1.176.

If you want to do this:	Then follow these steps:	Shortcuts ▾ Notes ▾ Hints
2.39 Change the direction of a line	▪ With the **pointer tool,** click anywhere on the line to select it; handles will appear. ▪ Position the very *tip* of the pointer on an end handle. ▪ Press on the handle; you should see the *crossbar* cursor again. *If you see the four-headed arrow, you are not pressing the handle; let go and press Command Z to undo any change you may have just made.* Try again. ▪ When you see the crossbar cursor, press-and-drag in any direction.	▪ If you have trouble selecting the line, read 2.23, as well as 1.164–1.176. ▪ The *other* end of the line will anchor itself to the page and you can move *your* end in whichever direction you choose, even if the line was originally drawn with the perpendicular-line tool. ▪ You cannot change the direction of more than one line at a time, even if many are selected.

Rectangles (with and without rounded corners) and Squares

2.40 Draw a perfect square	▪ From the Toolbox, click on either of the **rectangle tools.** ▪ Position the center of the crossbar where you want the *corner* of the box to begin. ▪ Hold down the Shift key while you press-and-drag to draw the box.	
2.41 Change a drawn rectangle into a perfect square 	▪ With the **pointer tool,** select the rectangle to be changed. ▪ Hold down the Shift key. ▪ With the **pointer tool,** press on any handle and count to three.	▪ The opposite side or corner will anchor to the page, and the side or corner you press on will snap into the square. ▪ If you have trouble selecting the rectangle, read 2.23, as well as 1.164–1.176.

If you want to do this:	Then follow these steps:	Shortcuts ▾ Notes ▾ Hints
2.42 Change the corners of one or more rectangles to a different corner 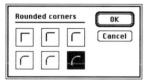	■ With the **pointer tool,** select all the rectangles or squares you want to change—either hold down the Shift key and click on each shape, **or** draw the marquee with the pointer tool (1.169). ■ From the Element menu choose "Rounded corners...." ■ Click on the corner you want; click OK.	■ You can do this to any rectangle or square, regardless of whether it was drawn by the square-corner or rounded-corner tool. ■ You can set a corner as a default (2.49–2.50) for the rounded-corner tool by choosing a corner *while no object is selected.* ■ If you have trouble selecting the object, read 2.23, as well as 1.164–1.176.
2.43 Resize a rectangle or square ■ *Vertically only* ■ *Horizontally only* ■ *In both directions* 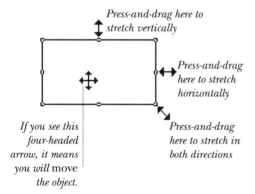	■ With the **pointer tool,** select one rectangle you want to resize by clicking on it. ■ To resize **vertically,** use the pointer tool to press-and-drag on a handle in the *middle* of the top or bottom edge; the cursor will become a double-headed, *vertical* arrow. ■ To resize **horizontally,** use the pointer tool to press-and-drag on a handle located in the *middle* of the left or right side of the shape; the cursor will become a double-headed, *horizontal* arrow. ■ To resize in **both directions,** use the pointer tool to press-and-drag on a *corner* handle; the cursor will become a double-headed, *diagonal* arrow. ■ If you see the *four-headed arrow,* you will not resize the object—you will *move* it.	■ If you decide you don't like what you just did, press Command Z to undo the stretch. ■ *Do not press the Shift key* when resizing any shape drawn in PageMaker! Although the Shift key will resize *imported* graphics proportionally (9.101), trying it on any rectangle or oval you've drawn in this program will instantly turn it into a square or a circle, respectively. *If that happens accidentally, immediately press Command Z (or choose "Undo Stretch" from the Edit menu).* ■ When resizing a *square,* though, keep the Shift key down to retain the shape.

If you want to do this:	Then follow these steps:	Shortcuts ▾ Notes ▾ Hints

2.44   Change the fill pattern

A double-line Reverse border with a 10% fill, placed on top of a black-filled background.

- With the **pointer tool,** select all the rectangles and squares you want to change—either hold down the Shift key and click on each one, **or** enclose them in the marquee using the pointer tool (1.169).
- From the Element menu press on "Fill" to pop out that submenu.
- Choose any one of the 17 patterns as a fill.

- See the examples of available fills in 2.19–2.21. Notice the difference between None and Paper.
- If you have trouble selecting the line, read 2.23, as well as 1.164–1.176.

Ovals and Circles

2.45   Draw a perfect circle

- From the Toolbox, choose the **oval/circle tool.**
- Hold down the Shift key while you press-and-drag to draw.

2.46   Change a drawn oval into a perfect circle

- With the **pointer tool,** select the oval.
- Hold down the Shift key.
- With the **pointer tool,** press on any handle and count to three.

- If you have trouble selecting the oval, read 2.23, as well as 1.164–1.176.
- The opposite side will anchor itself to the page; the corner you press will snap into a circle.

2.47   Change the fill pattern of one or more ovals or circles

This is a double-line Reverse border with a 10% fill, placed on top of a black-filled background.

- With the **pointer tool,** select all the ovals and circles you want to change—either hold down the Shift key and click on each one, **or** enclose them in the marquee using the pointer tool (1.169).
- From the Element menu press on "Fill" to pop out that submenu.
- Choose any one of the 17 patterns as a fill.

- If you have trouble selecting the shape, read 2.23, as well as 1.164–1.176.

If you want to do this:

2.48 Change the shape of the oval or circle
- *Vertically only*
- *Horizontally only*
- *In both directions*

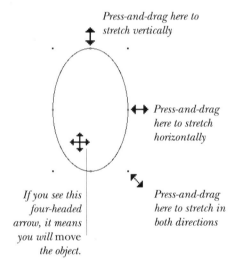

Press-and-drag here to stretch vertically

Press-and-drag here to stretch horizontally

If you see this four-headed arrow, it means you will move the object.

Press-and-drag here to stretch in both directions

Then follow these steps:

- To resize the oval, first select it by clicking on it once with the **pointer tool.**
- To resize **vertically,** use the pointer tool to press-and-drag on a handle in the *middle* of the top or bottom curve; the cursor will become a double-headed, *vertical* arrow.
- To resize **horizontally,** use the pointer tool to press-and-drag on a handle located in the *middle* of the left or right curve of the shape; the cursor will become a double-headed, *horizontal* arrow.
- To resize in **both directions,** use the pointer tool to press-and-drag on a *corner* handle; the cursor will become a double-headed, *diagonal* arrow.
- If you see the *four-headed arrow,* you will not resize the object—you will *move* it.

Shortcuts ▾ Notes ▾ Hints

- If you have trouble selecting the oval or circle, read 2.23, as well as 1.164–1.176.
- No matter how many objects you select, you can only resize one at a time.
- *Do not press the Shift key* when resizing any shape drawn in PageMaker! Although the Shift key will resize *imported* graphics proportionally, trying it on any rectangle or oval you've drawn in this program will instantly turn it into a square or a circle, respectively. If that happens accidentally, press Command Z immediately (or from the Edit menu choose "Undo Stretch").
- When resizing a *circle,* though, keep the Shift key down to retain the shape.

If you want to do this:	Then follow these steps:	Shortcuts ▾ Notes ▾ Hints
Set drawing tool defaults	*(also see Section 1: Setting Defaults 1.6–1.16)*	
2.49 Set defaults for any of the lines, fills, or corners *for the current publication*	■ Click on the **pointer tool,** even if it's already chosen. ■ From the Element menu, pop out the Lines submenu and choose any line. ■ From the Element menu, pop out the Fill submenu and choose any fill pattern. ■ From the Element menu, choose "Rounded corners..."; choose any corner, and click OK.	■ You can actually set the default with any of the other tools, but it is imperative that *no object is selected.* Clicking on the pointer tool ensures nothing is selected. ■ Setting the defaults, as explained in 1.6–1.16, enables you to draw the objects in the style of your choice, rather than having to select and change them afterward.
2.50 Set defaults for any of the lines, fills, or corners *for the entire PageMaker application*	■ Open PageMaker from its icon on the Desktop; **OR** close any publication you currently have open. ■ Follow the steps above, but do it when there is nothing on your screen but the menu bar.	■ Even though you set an *application default,* of course you can change any line or fill or corner or anything else you choose at any time in the open publication.
2.51 Set a text wrap default for drawn objects *(be sure to read Section 11 on Text Wrapping)*	■ With nothing selected *(for a publication default)* or with no publication open *(for an application default),* choose "Text wrap..." from the Element menu. ■ Select the center wrap option, set the standoff, and choose the flow (11.10–11.19). ■ Click OK.	■ Setting a default text wrap means every object you draw in PageMaker, place from the File menu, or paste from the Scrapbook or Clipboard will automatically have a text wrap around it. This might not be what you want. Be sure to read Section 11 on Text Wrapping.

3 ▾ Text

3.1　Minimums and maximums:

Item	Minimum	Maximum
Type size	4 pt.	650 pt.
	(tenth-point increments; .1)	
Leading	.1 pt.	1300 pt.
	(tenth-point increments; .1)	
Replacing text		64K
		(about 25 pages, in one text block)
Small caps size	1% or 1 pt.	200%
	(tenth-percent increments; .1%)	
Super/subscript size	1%	200%
	(tenth-percent increments; .1%)	
Super/subscript position	0%	500%
	(tenth-percent increments; .1%)	

3.2　This section covers all the different ways to work with text directly on the publication page in PageMaker, from creating to formatting. PageMaker gives you incredible control and flexibility in working with type. It's so much fun and so satisfying to perfect it right in front of your very eyes!

3.3　As you can see on the right, this section is broken down into specific aspects of working with the text. You deal with all these aspects at once while you work. But, unlike our brains, books function in a linear fashion, so you may have to do some crossing over between subsections in order to get all your questions answered.

3.4　One of the most important concepts in PageMaker is the **text block.** It is critical that you understand what a text block is and how it operates—if you are new to PageMaker, it would be a good idea to read that part of this section very carefully　(3.95–3.122).

Creating text directly on the page

3.5 PageMaker does not pretend to be a word processor (and word processors should stop pretending to be page layout programs). PageMaker does have the Story Editor, which is discussed at length in Section 8. The Story Editor contains the most important features of a word processor. It's great for writing lengthy text without leaving PageMaker, and has a terrific find-and-change feature that has saved me hundreds of hours. Literally.

3.6 If you have more than a small amount of copy, it is best to use the Story Editor or an outside word processing application to write, proof, and edit the text—and then drop it into PageMaker for formatting and layout.

3.7 However, PageMaker is fully capable of creating and editing text right on the screen, so for small amounts of text—such as an advertisement, small package design, flyer, announcement, invitation, etc.—it is usually more efficient to create it directly on the page. It's slower than a word processor because PageMaker uses more complex typographic information to dispay the text on the screen (letter spacing, word spacing, hyphenation, etc.).

3.8 Text is always contained in a **text block**—it cannot be on a page without being in a text block. If you take the pointer tool and click once on any text, you will see the boundaries of the text block and the *handles* at the four corners (this works most visibly at Fit in Window view).

Notice the little square *handles* at each of the four corners of this *text block.*

3.9 It's a good idea to make sure you understand **text blocks** (3.95–3.122) before you start creating text on the page. In some jobs you may want to have the differcnt parts of the text in separate, unconnected text blocks for easier manipulation, as text blocks can be picked up and moved around on the screen. In other jobs, you may want a lengthy story divided into several text blocks that are linked, or *threaded* together.

3.10 The **text tool** (3.11) is used to type or edit text in PageMaker. Click on the **A** in the Toolbox to get the text tool; when you move off of the Toolbox, the cursor becomes the **I-beam** (pronounced eye-beam), as shown in 3.12.

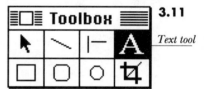

3.11

Text tool

3.12
Text tool cursor: the I-beam ⎯⎯ ‖
The little crossbar indicates the baseline (1.56) of the text.

3.13 This I-beam cursor is indicating that you are now in the typing mode—*it is just a pointer,* like any other cursor; it is not the I-beam that tells you where the type will begin.

3.14 When you have the I-beam and click the mouse button once, it sets down a flashing **insertion point.** It is the insertion point that allows you to type. It looks like this: | but it flashes.

Watch that insertion point!

3.15   As you type, the text will *begin* at the insertion point, and the insertion point will move along with the characters. If you press the Backspace/Delete key, the insertion point will backspace (and thus delete text) from wherever it is. PageMaker uses the standard Macintosh word-processing techniques, so most of this is probably already familiar to you.

3.16   To move the insertion point to another place in the text in order to edit or to start new text, simply use the mouse to position the I-beam where you want to type, and **click once.** The insertion point will move to wherever you click. (You can then move the *I-beam* out of the way, since it has served its purpose.)

3.17   You can also use the arrow keys to move the insertion point. The arrow keys, used in combination with the Shift, Option, and Command keys, can be used to *select* portions of text for editing (3.138; 1.226). The numeric keypad can also function as arrow keys and for selecting text, as well as for typing numbers (1.222–1.225).

3.18   When you click inside a text block, the insertion point lands right where you clicked, unless you clicked in the space at the end of a paragraph or between tabs, in which case it jumps over to the last character in that row.

Note: If you try to click or select text and the insertion point acts funny and won't go where you want it to, there is probably an invisible text block on top of the one you want. See 1.175–1.176 for finding and removing it.

3.19   When you click *within* the margins on the page, but *not* inside any existing text block, the insertion point will jump to the nearest left column guide (even if *you* think you have no columns on the page—PageMaker always provides at least one column; see 1.75).

If the insertion point does not align on the left when you click, it probably has a *default setting* of either a paragraph indent *or* a centered alignment (3.26). You can reset the default (3.20–3.22) *or* you can just reset the specs for the moment.

Also see the note in 3.18.

Formatting the insertion point

3.20 When you set the insertion point to begin a *new* text block, it will type with the *defaults* that have been chosen (1.6–1.10). You can check to see what the defaults are:

- Click once on the **pointer tool,** even if it is already selected.

- From the Type menu, press on "Style" (not "Type style"!).

- The "Style" submenu should have a checkmark next to *"No style."* (If there is a checkmark next to anything else, see 3.21).

- Now check out any of the other submenus from the Type menu. Anything that has a checkmark next to it, plus all the specifications in every dialog box, is what PageMaker is using for defaults; that is, that's what the insertion point is automatically formatted with for typing.

- Text you *place* will be formatted with the checked specifications if you choose not to "Retain the format" (3.52).

- You can change the defaults whenever you like (see 1.6–1.16 and 3.242–3.247).

3.21 Now if, when you checked the "Style" submenu, there was a checkmark next to any other style than *"No style,"* then *that style* is the default (see Section 7 on Style Sheets). You will type with *those* specifications, and when you place text without retaining the format or reading tags (3.52), it will pour in with those specifications.

To change the Style default to "No style," first click once on the pointer tool. Then choose "No style" from the Style submenu.

3.22 Anytime the insertion point is inserted into existing text, it picks up the formatting *from the character to its left* (unless it is before the first character in a paragraph; then it takes the formatting of the first character). This means it will type in whatever font, style, size, alignment, paragraph specs, style name, etc. of that left character, even if that left character is a blank space! (Blank spaces are formatted just like characters.) Pressing Return pushes the insertion point along, and the insertion point carries all that formatting along with it.

3.23 Now, while that insertion point is *flashing* (whether it is in existing text or beginning a new text block), if you go to any of the menus and change the formatting (specifications), the new formatting *will be poured into the insertion point,* and you will type with those new specifications. You are not setting a default in this case—you are **loading the insertion point.** *If you click anywhere else,* the insertion point again picks up the formatting from the character to its left, or from the existing defaults.

If you want to do this: ■	**Then follow these steps:** ■	**Shortcuts ▾ Notes ▾ Hints** ■

3.24 Type onto the page

- Choose the **text tool** (the **A**); the cursor will turn into the **I-beam** when you move away from the Toolbox.
- With the **I-beam,** point to where you want your text to begin; click the mouse to set down a flashing insertion point.
- While it is flashing, simply type.

- If you click on the page outside of any existing text block, the insertion point will jump to the nearest column guide. So, if you click and don't see the insertion point, you may need to move your page over so the column guide is visible.
- If you click outside of any column guides, the insertion point will stay where you click (unless it is not left-aligned; 3.19; 3.26).

3.25 Restrain the size of the text block
*(create a **bounding box** to type in so the handles don't run across the whole page)*

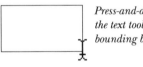

Press-and-drag with the text tool to create a bounding box like this.

When you let go, the box becomes invisible, but it's still there; the insertion point waits.

This text has been typed into an invisible bounding box. The depth will expand as you type, but not the width.

As you type or paste text, it will fill the bounding box.

- Choose the **text tool** from the Toolbox.
- Outside of any existing text block, *point* to where you want the text to begin.
- Press-and-drag in any direction; this will create a rectangle on the screen. Draw the rectangle the length of the line you need. When you let go of the mouse button, this rectangle will disappear, but the invisible form of it is still there! The insertion point will be flashing in the upper left of the invisible box.
- Type your text; it will fit into the line length of the rectangle you created. The depth will increase or decrease as necessary.

- When you click the I-beam outside of any column guides (such as outside the margin boundary or anywhere on the pasteboard), you create a text block that is the width of your margins. This means the handles go shooting across the screen and can be hard to find, sometimes causing problems. Creating a bounding box solves these.
- If the insertion point does not flash in the upper left of the bounding box (and you want it to do so), see 3.26.
- Creating a bounding box is definitely the best way to create text on the page and control the line length (and thus the handles) of the text block!

If you want to do this:

Then follow these steps:

Shortcuts ▾ Notes ▾ Hints

3.26 Make the insertion point align on the left

Indents:
Left   [0]   picas
First [1.5] picas
Right [0]   picas

The 1.5 entered in the "First" edit box indicates that the first line of each paragraph will be indented 1.5 picas.

Alignment: [✓Left / Center / Right / Justify / Force justify]

The alignment also determines where the insertion point flashes.

- With the **insertion point flashing,** from the Type menu choose "Paragraph...."
- In the "Paragraph specifications" dialog box, look under "Indents" at the box next to "First."
- If "First" has any number other than 0 (zero), then change that number to 0 (zero, not the letter O).
- Also check the "Alignment" box; if it says anything besides "Left" in that little box, press on the box to get the pop-up menu. Choose "Left" as the alignment.

- Of course, these directions will also apply if you want to make the insertion point align on the right, or centered, or any other way: instead of choosing "Left," choose the alignment of your choice (3.153–1.158). And instead of typing 0 in the First-line indent box (3.205), type the number of your choice.
- If you follow these directions *while the insertion point is flashing,* you will change the specifications for just this one time. If you want to change the specs more permanently, like every time you start a new text block, then before you follow these directions, choose the pointer tool. This ensures there is *no insertion point flashing.* What you are actually doing, then, is setting a new *publication default* (3.247; 3.242–3.244).

*L*etters are beautiful in themselves.
    Just like the faces of human beings,
some letters are intricately complex
while others are blank and simple.

—Kiyoshi Awazu

Placing text into PageMaker

3.27   This subsection deals with **placing text** into PageMaker that has been created in an outside word processor (such as Microsoft Word or Works, MacWrite, WriteNow, FullWrite, etc.). For information on placing text that you created in PageMaker's own Story Editor, see Section 8 (8.79). For info on placing stories from another PageMaker publication, see the subsection immediately following this one (3.59–3.80).

3.28   Placing text that has been created elsewhere is one of PageMaker's specialties. Rather than typing a lot of text directly on the page in PageMaker, type it into your word processor where you can edit, spell-check, and proof. Don't bother to format anything; don't space twice between paragraphs; don't spec headlines or captions; don't set up and indents—just type in straight text (of course hitting Return for each new paragraph). It is much more efficient to then drop your text into PageMaker and use style sheets (Section 7) to format everything. (Style sheets are the most valuable feature in PageMaker. You really must spend the time to learn to use them.)

3.29   Use your word processor (or the Story Editor) for what it does best—word processing. Use PageMaker for what it does best—page layout and text formatting. For this reason, it is not necessary to use a high-powered word-processing application (you don't need a helicopter to cross the street). If you are placing the text into PageMaker, a lot of the high-end word processing power is wasted—the multiple columns, headers and footers, indexing, outlining, tables of contents, etc., from an outside word processor cannot be used by Page-Maker. You don't even need to waste your time setting up style sheets in the word processor, since PageMaker can read simple little tags you set (3.36–3.39; 3.56) and automatically style the finished product to your specifications with PageMaker's own style sheets.

3.30   When you place a file, PageMaker calls that file a **story.** The story is the *entire file,* which you may break up into as many separate *text blocks* (3.95–3.102) as necessary. It is important to remember this distinction between a story and a text block.

3.31   Be sure to read the following subsection that goes hand-in-hand with placing text: **Text Flow** (3.81 to 3.88). Text flow controls how the text is poured onto the page—whether it just keeps pouring until it's finished, whether it stops and waits for you to tell it what to do next, or whether it stops and loads itself back up again. Oh, it's great to be in control.

The Options for placing text

3.32 When you place text that has been created in an outside word processor, you have three options of how that text will format when it pours into PageMaker. You can:

- Retain the format
- Ignore the format
- Read the tags

3.33 When you **retain the format,** PageMaker will hold most of the specifications you set up *in the original file,* but not all:

- Most character formatting will hold, such as font (if that font is in the System that is running PageMaker), type size, type style, paragraph spacing, alignment, etc.
- Tabs, indents, and returns are always held, and their ruler placement in PageMaker will match the original's.
- Line lengths will always adjust to the columns in PageMaker.
- Some formatting—such as multiple columns, headers and footers, hidden text, page numbers—are ignored.
- Footnotes from the word processing application will appear at the end of the story in PageMaker.

Basically, any kind of formatting that PageMaker can't do, it will not recognize.

3.34 When you **ignore the format,** (which is simply choosing *not* to "Retain the format"; 3.52) PageMaker will ignore *any formatting you applied when you created the file in your word processor* (except tabs, indents, and returns— you usually can't get rid of those). The file will be placed into PageMaker following the *default type specifications.* Please read 3.20 and 3.21 for an explanation of how to find out what the current defaults are.

3.35 Take note of the fact that the specifications are actually taken from the *Style* (as in Style Sheets; Section 7). Typically, the default style is "No style," *but you can set the default to any style you choose.* For instance, if you have set up a style sheet and want the files you place to pour in as your defined "Body text," then set "Body text" as your publication default (simply by using the *pointer tool* to choose "Body text" from the "Style" submenu in the Type menu). Then you won't have to select the text later to apply the style. Again, you really should read 3.20 and 3.21.

3.36 Tabs and indents from the original file will align themselves to the default tabs and indents in PageMaker, which may not be at all what you want. To prevent insanity, be sure to read Section 5 on Indents and Tabs.

3.36 **Reading tags** works hand-in-hand with Style Sheets (Section 7), so this will probably make more sense if you understand that great feature of PageMaker. Be sure to read Section 7 for a detailed explanation of style sheets, as well as directions on how to create tags (7.64). Briefly, what it will do for you is this:

3.37 In your word processor (or in the Story Editor in a slightly different fashion; see 7.63) you can type *tags.* Tags look like this: **<style name>.** Those are just angle brackets, found above the comma and the period. Between the angle brackets is the name of the style from your style sheet that you want to apply to that paragraph. After you type the tag, type the paragraph. Every time you change the style of a paragraph, you type a new tag in front of it.

3.38 When you place a file with tags into PageMaker and choose "Read tags," PageMaker will read the tag, *eliminate it from the text,* and apply the formatting you specified for that style. It's really incredible.

3.39 Be sure to read Scenarios #8 and #9 (7.69; 7.70–7.71) on using tags and style sheets in your publication!

The "Place..." dialog box for text   *(from the File menu, choose "Place...")*

3.40 *This **label** indicates which folder or which disk you are viewing the contents of.*

3.41 *If the file you want is not on this disk, click here to switch to another drive.*

3.42 *If you are viewing a floppy disk and it doesn't contain what you need, click here to eject it so you can insert another.*

3.43 *The **list box** shows the documents contained in the folder or on the disk named in the label (3.40).*

3.44 *If the icon looks like a little page, you can place it by double-clicking on it.*

3.45 *If the icon looks like a folder, it indicates there may be a file inside that you can place.*

Double-click on a folder to open it and view the contents.

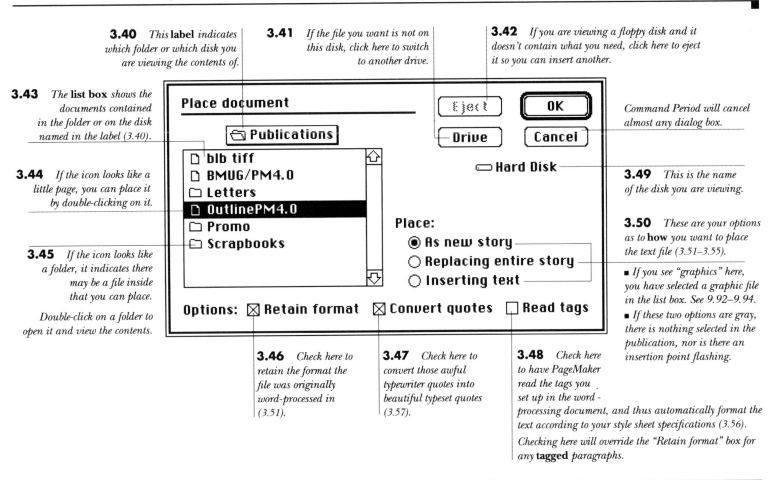

Command Period will cancel almost any dialog box.

3.49 *This is the name of the disk you are viewing.*

3.50 *These are your options as to **how** you want to place the text file (3.51–3.55).*

■ *If you see "graphics" here, you have selected a graphic file in the list box. See 9.92–9.94.*

■ *If these two options are gray, there is nothing selected in the publication, nor is there an insertion point flashing.*

3.46 *Check here to retain the format the file was originally word-processed in (3.51).*

3.47 *Check here to convert those awful typewriter quotes into beautiful typeset quotes (3.57).*

3.48 *Check here to have PageMaker read the tags you set up in the word-processing document, and thus automatically format the text according to your style sheet specifications (3.56). Checking here will override the "Retain format" box for any **tagged** paragraphs.*

If you want to do this:

3.51 Place text *as a new story* while *retaining* the format of the original document

Then follow these steps:

- From the File menu choose "Place...," *or* press Command D.
- In the list box (3.43), find the name of the document you wish to place into PageMaker (you may need to switch drives [3.41] or open folders [3.45] to find it).
- Click *once* on the name of the file you want to place.
- There should be an X in the "Retain format" checkbox (3.46); if there isn't, click once on it to put one there.
- If the document was typed using typewriter quotation marks instead of real quote marks (3.57), then by all means make sure "Convert quotes" has a check in it (3.47).
- "Read tags" (3.48) should *not* have a check.
- To place the selected file *as a new story* make sure the button "As new story" is chosen. (If you want to *replace an entire story* see 3.53; for *inserting text* or to *replace a portion* of a story, see 3.54–3.55.)
- Now, either click the OK button *or* double-click on the name of the file you wish to place.

—continued

Shortcuts ▾ Notes ▾ Hints

- Be sure to read 3.32–3.35 for a discussion on exactly what it means to retain the format. Basically, you are asking to retain the the type specifications in which you originally typed the file.

TEACHER
TEACHER
TEACHER
TEACHER

(a gift for me from Mary Boston)

If you want to do this:

Then follow these steps:

Shortcuts ▾ Notes ▾ Hints

—continued

    The manual flow icon

    The semi-autoflow icon

The autoflow icon

- PageMaker will take you back to your publication and you will have a new pointer—a *loaded text icon* (see left; read 3.81–3.88 for more info about autoflow, semi-autoflow, and manual flow).
- Position the loaded text icon where you want the type to begin.
- Click once to pour the text on the page.

- Be sure to read 3.84–3.86 about the important difference between manual and autoflow before you start to pour text.
- If the loaded text icon is positioned inside a column when you click, the text will flow to that column width.
- If the loaded text icon is *not* positioned inside a column when you click, the text will create a text block for itself that will be the width of your page margins.
- If you want to control the space that the text occupies as you place it, see 3.58.

3.52   Place text *as a new story* **without** retaining the format of the original document

- Follow the steps in 3.51 above, but this time make sure the checkbox for "Retain format" (3.46) has **no** check in it (if it does, click once on it to remove it).

- *Without* retaining the format, the text will flow in with the specifications of the style that has been chosen from the *style sheet* (Section 7 on Style Sheets). To see which style is chosen:
  - ☐ Click once on the pointer tool. From the Type menu, press "Style" (not "Type style") to get the submenu.
  - ☐ If the style selected is *"No style,"* then the placed text will flow in with the *default* type specs. Please read 3.20–3.21 and 3.34–3.36 for a more detailed explanation of default style sheets.

If you want to do this:	Then follow these steps:	Shortcuts ▾ Notes ▾ Hints
3.53 Replace an entire story	■ With the **pointer tool,** click once on the text block of the story you want to replace; **or** with the **text tool,** click once anywhere in the text to set the insertion point in the story. ■ From the File menu choose "Place...," *or* press Command D. ■ Locate the file you want to place; click once on the name of it to select it. ■ Click in the button "Replacing entire story." ■ Click OK, **or** double-click on the name of the file to be placed and it shall be done.	■ If the "Replace entire story" button is gray, it's indicating that a story has not been selected. Go back and make sure you did the first step. ■ If the story consists of more than one text block, you need to select only *one* block or set the insertion point into *one.* Either method will tell PageMaker to replace the *entire story,* even if it consists of many separate text blocks spanning several pages. ■ The text blocks that are being replaced will stay the same size, *except* the last one which will shrink if the new story is shorter, or show an arrow in the bottom loop if it's longer. (In 4.01, the last text block will grow deeper.)
3.54 *Insert* placed text into a story that is already on the page	■ With the **text tool,** click once in the story in the exact spot where you want the text to *begin* inserting. *See the note to the right.* ■ From the File menu choose "Place...," *or* press Command D. ■ Locate the file you wish to insert and click *once* on it. ■ Click on the button "Inserting text." ■ Click OK, *or* double-click on the name of the file to be inserted and it shall be done.	■ If the "Inserting text" button is gray, either (1) there is no insertion point flashing or text selected (3.137–3.138) on the page; go back and do the first step; **or** (2) the file you selected in the list box is not a text file; if you see the word "graphic" in the other buttons, you have selected a graphic file; **or** (3) if *all* the buttons are gray, the file you have selected to place is not place-able in PageMaker; e.g., you cannot place a folder. ■ The text will be *inserted* at the spot where the insertion point is flashing. If you are replacing text (3.55), just the portion that

If you want to do this:

3.55   *Replace a portion* of an existing story

Then follow these steps:

- With the **text tool,** press-and drag to select the text you wish to *replace* with another file. *See the notes to the right.*
- From the File menu choose "Place…," *or* press Command D.
- Locate the file you wish to replace the selected text with and click *once* on it.
- Click on the button "Replacing selected text."
- Click OK, *or* double-click on the name of the file to be inserted and it shall be done.

Shortcuts ▾ Notes ▾ Hints

is selected will be *replaced.* All the following text will just thread its way through the text block(s).

- If the insertion point or selected text is *inside* a paragraph, the new text will take on that paragraph's formatting, no matter how the new text was originally set.
- If the insertion point is *in its own* paragraph (meaning you hit a Return and it is flashing on its own line), or if you selected an entire paragraph to *replace,* you can choose to retain the format, read the tags, or let it come in with PageMaker's text defaults, just as when placing any story (page 112). The only difference is that, if you choose *not* to retain the format, the text will always default to "No style," *not* to the style sheet name you set as your style default (3.35).
- Inserting or replacing text this way is *not* Undo-able; that is, you cannot go to the Edit menu and choose "Undo edit." You can, of course, undo it yourself with the standard word processing functions, like cut, copy, delete, etc.

In the fields
of printing
and graphic design
it is generally agreed that
the poet in our midst is the type designer.

—Noel Martin

If you want to do this:	Then follow these steps:	Shortcuts ▾ Notes ▾ Hints

3.56 Place text and have PageMaker *read the tags*	■ If you are going to *insert* or *replace* text, then either set the insertion point where you want the text inserted, or select the text you want to replace. If you are going to place it as a *new story,* click once on the text tool or the pointer tool to make sure there is no insertion point lying around anywhere.
	■ From the File menu choose "Place...," *or* press Command D.
	■ In the list box (3.43), click once on the text file name you wish to place (you may need to switch drives [3.41] or open folders [3.45] to locate the file you want.
	■ Choose your option (3.51–3.55) to place the text as a new story, as inserted text, replacing a story, or replacing selected text.
	■ If the checkbox for "Retain format" is checked, "Read tags" will override it, so it doesn't matter if you switch it off or not.
	■ Of course "Convert quotes" (3.47) should be checked if real quotes or dashes were not used in the original.
	■ **Put a check in "Read tags"** (3.48).
	■ Click OK, *or* double-click on the name of the file to be placed; PageMaker will read the tags, eliminate them, and place the text with the formatting you previously specified in your style sheet. Wow.
		■ Boy, this is just the greatest thing since hinted PostScript. Imagine, you just buzz along in your word processor, not formatting anything, just typing in a few tags. Drop it into PageMaker and bingo—all heads are fomatted, body copy is set, charts are tabbed and indented, captions are small and italic, etc. etc. etc.
		■ Be sure to read Section 7 on Style Sheets, especially Scenarios #8 and #9 (7.69–7.71) to get a good grip on how to take advantage of this. You will find a very brief explanation in 3.36–3.39.
		■ You can ask PageMaker to read the tags when you place a file as a new story, as well as when you insert or replace text. But:
		  □ When you insert or replace text *into an existing paragraph* though, the new text will become part of the existing style— it *will not* follow the tag specifications.
		  □ If you replace *an entire paragraph,* the new text *will* follow the tag specifications.
		  □ If you insert text *while the insertion point is flashing on its own line* (in its own paragraph), the new text *will* follow the tag specifications.

If you want to do this:

3.57 Convert typewriter quotes (")
to real quotes (" ")

Then follow these steps:

■ You really must get in the habit of typing
these in automatically (see 3.237–3.241).
But if you didn't do it in the document
you want to place, simply click the
"Convert quotes" button when you
"Place...." This will convert all ugly (")
marks to beautiful open and closed
quotation marks (" and "). It will also
convert this mark (') to a real apostrophe (') or to open and closed single
quotation marks (' and '). A pair of
double hyphens (--) will be converted
to an em dash (—).

Shortcuts ▾ Notes ▾ Hints

■ This option will only convert the quotation marks from a document that is
being *placed* into PageMaker. If you typed
the story into the Story Editor, you can
"Find and Change" the marks (8.74).
■ If you think it is too much trouble to
"Find and Change" the marks, you can
export the story (15.36) and place it back
in, converting quotes along the way!
■ This little chart shows what the typewriter marks will transform into. Notice
PageMaker is smart enough to leave real
inch and foot marks after numbers:

"Scarlett"	"Scarlett"
'Scarlett'	'Scarlett'
Scarlett's	Scarlett's
--Scarlett	—Scarlett
3'4"	3'4"

■ This is not a foolproof feature, so it is a
good idea to double-check your marks.
See 3.240 for the key commands for typing
these, as well as other special characters.

If you want to do this:

Then follow these steps:

Shortcuts ▾ Notes ▾ Hints

3.58 Place text into a *bounding box* to hold it or to override column guides (**drag-place**)

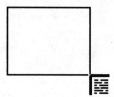

The bounding box created by drag-placing.

When you drag-place, the text stays just inside the bounding box; it doesn't expand. Extra text is

The text that has been drag-placed.

- Follow the steps in 3.51 to get a loaded text icon.
- When the loaded text icon appears, *don't click to place the text*—instead, **press-and-drag.** You will see a bounding box follow the loaded text icon as you drag it across the screen. When you let go, the text will be contained inside that space, even if autoflow is on.

- Great trick—be sure to get this one down! It's very handy for lots of things, such as:
  □ Let's say you have three columns on your page. You want the line length of this new story to be two columns wide—just *drag-place* the text across the two columns. Make the bounding box the size you want the text to fill.
  □ Let's say you are creating a newsletter and you want to have all the stories at hand to puzzle them together. *Drag-place* them all, one at a time, onto the pasteboard, creating a bounding box for each of them that is just big enough to see the first paragraph or so. Then, as you design the pages of the newsletter, you can just pull them in from the pasteboard. Even though you see just a paragraph, the text block holds the entire story.
- Also see 3.25 for using the I-beam to create a bounding box you can type into.

Placing PageMaker files into PageMaker

3.59 PageMaker does not allow you to open more than one publication at a time, which makes it very difficult when you want to take one great page from one PageMaker file and put it into another PageMaker publication. PageMaker 4.0 solves this dilemma with the Story Importer, which operates from the "Place..." command in the File menu. You can place any story from any other PageMaker 4 publication. If you want to place stories from a PageMaker 3 file, you will first need to convert it into a PageMaker 4 file (see 15.38).

3.60 You can place *all* the stories from another publication, or you can choose just the ones you want. Whichever you choose, they will import as a single story with carriage returns between each original story.

3.61 Often a publication is full of tiny text block stories, such as those containing page numbers, headers, footers, callouts, or captions. The Story Importer allows you the option of filtering out these small ones.

3.62 It is also possible to *view* any story from any other PageMaker publication, copy the text to the Clipboard, and then paste it into PageMaker or any other application. The on-line documentation does not recommend pasting directly into PageMaker this way because of limitations of this version of the Story Importer, but I haven't had any problem with it yet.

3.63 The Story Importer is limited in its ability to import indices: cross-reference index entries and alternate sort strings cannot be imported, and the range of the index entries is always converted to "Current page" (see Section 13 for info on Indexing).

3.64 You cannot import from the publication that is currently open. You cannot import inline graphics (9.91). The text you *do* import always comes in with pair kerning (4.173–4.175). Fonts used in the imported stories that are not in the System are turned into Chicago (you can use the Story Editor to replace the Chicago font with whatever else you have and want; 8.76).

3.65 The Story Importer has a good on-line Help file. There is no documentation in the current manual. See 3.72 for Help.

3.66 **Important note:** To use this feature, you need to have installed the Story Importer Filter when you originally installed PageMaker 4.0. If not, you will need to go back and install it (see 15.25).

3.67 If you don't know whether the Story Importer Filter is installed or not, you can find out right now:

- Hold down the Command key.
- From the Apple menu, choose "About PageMaker®..." to see the list of installed import and export filters.

OR you can also check this way:
- From the File menu choose "Place...."
- In the list box (3.43), see if you can locate the name of another Page-Maker file.
- If the name of the file shows up, then you have the Filter installed.
- Click Cancel.

The "Story Importer" dialog box

(from the File menu, choose "Place…"; double-click the name of another PageMaker publication; see 3.66)

3.68 *Click "Select all" to select all the stories in the list box to place (see 3.76).*

3.69 *Press Return or Enter to shortcut OK.*

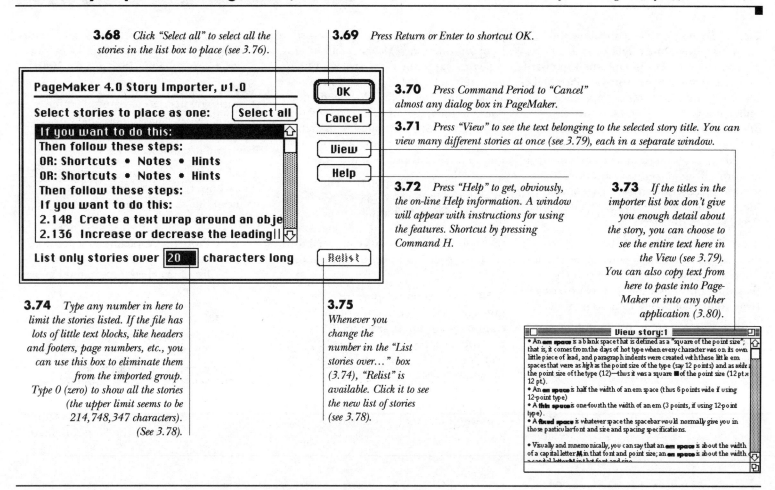

PageMaker 4.0 Story Importer, v1.0

Select stories to place as one: Select all

- If you want to do this:
- Then follow these steps:
- OR: Shortcuts • Notes • Hints
- OR: Shortcuts • Notes • Hints
- Then follow these steps:
- If you want to do this:
- 2.148 Create a text wrap around an obje
- 2.136 Increase or decrease the leading

List only stories over **20** characters long

OK

Cancel

View

Help

Relist

3.70 *Press Command Period to "Cancel" almost any dialog box in PageMaker.*

3.71 *Press "View" to see the text belonging to the selected story title. You can view many different stories at once (see 3.79), each in a separate window.*

3.72 *Press "Help" to get, obviously, the on-line Help information. A window will appear with instructions for using the features. Shortcut by pressing Command H.*

3.73 *If the titles in the importer list box don't give you enough detail about the story, you can choose to see the entire text here in the View (see 3.79). You can also copy text from here to paste into Page-Maker or into any other application (3.80).*

3.74 *Type any number in here to limit the stories listed. If the file has lots of little text blocks, like headers and footers, page numbers, etc., you can use this box to eliminate them from the imported group. Type 0 (zero) to show all the stories (the upper limit seems to be 214,748,347 characters). (See 3.78).*

3.75 *Whenever you change the number in the "List stories over…" box (3.74), "Relist" is available. Click it to see the new list of stories (see 3.78).*

View story:1

• An **em space** is a blank space that is defined as a "square of the point size"; that is, it comes from the days of hot type when every character was on its own little piece of lead, and paragraph indents were created with these little em spaces that were as *high* as the point size of the type (say 12 points) and as *wide* the point size of the type (12)—thus it was a square ■ of the point size (12 pt x 12 pt).
• An **en space** is half the width of an em space (thus 6 points wide if using 12-point type).
• A **thin space** is one-fourth the width of an em (3 points, if using 12-point type).
• A **fixed space** is whatever space the spacebar would normally give you in those particular font and size and spacing specifications.

• Visually and mnemonically, you can say that an **em space** is about the width of a capital letter M in that font and point size; an **en space** is about the width

If you want to do this:	**Then follow these steps:**	**Shortcuts ▾ Notes ▾ Hints**
3.76 Place (import) an *entire* PageMaker file	▪ If you are going to *insert* the file into existing text (3.54), *replace a portion* of existing text (3.55), *replace an entire story* (3.53), or place it *as a new story* (3.51–3.52), see the respective task for specifics on where the insertion point should be or how the text should be selected. ▪ From the File menu choose "Place...." ▪ Locate the name of the PageMaker file you wish to place (you cannot place any files from the currently open publication). ▪ In the list box (3.43), click once on the name of the file. ▪ Choose your options: whether you want to *retain the format* (3.33), *convert quotes* (3.57), or *read tags* (3.36–3.39; 3.56). ▪ Choose whether you are inserting text, replacing text, or placing a new story, depending on what you did in the first step. ▪ Click OK, **or** double-click on the file name. ▪ You should see the Story Importer dialog box, as shown on page 122. Click once in the "Select all" button (see 3.78). ▪ Click OK, **or** press Return or Enter. ▪ Depending on whether you are placing a new story or inserting or replacing text, you will either get a loaded text icon to place (3.82–3.87) or the text will automatically insert or replace.	▪ You can only import other PageMaker 4 files. To import a PageMaker 3 publication, you must first convert it to a PageMaker 4 file; see 15.38. ▪ You can treat an imported PageMaker file just as you do any other file you place; i.e., you can insert text, replace text, retain the format, read tags, etc., as detailed in the subsection on "Placing text into PageMaker" (3.27–3.58). ▪ All the original stories will be imported as one story with carriage returns between each one. ▪ A shortcut for the "Select all" button is Command A. ▪ A shortcut to "Cancel" is Command Period. Actually, this great shortcut works on every "Cancel" button in PageMaker (except in the Indents/tabs ruler!).

123

If you want to do this:	**Then follow these steps:**	**Shortcuts ▾ Notes ▾ Hints**
3.77 Place *selected* stories from another PageMaker 4 file	■ Follow the steps in 3.76 until you see the Story Importer dialog box. ■ Select the story you want to place by clicking *once* on it. If you want to select more than one story, hold the Shift key down and click once on each story. You can also press-and-drag with the Shift key down to select sequential stories. ■ If you select a story, then change your mind, you can deselect just that one story by holding the Shift key down and clicking once more on it. ■ When they are all selected, click OK, *or* hit the Return or Enter key. ■ Depending on whether you are placing a new story or inserting or replacing text, you will either get a loaded text icon for placing (3.82–3.87), or the text will insert or replace as you specified in the first step.	■ You can only import other PageMaker 4 files. To import a PageMaker 3 publication, you must first convert it to a PageMaker 4 file; see 15.38. ■ If you are going to import only one story, you can quickly shortcut by double-clicking on the story name. ■ If you change your mind and want *all* the stories, click on the "Select all" button *or* press Command A.
3.78 Limit the display of story titles in the list box to just those stories that are greater than a certain number of characters	■ Follow the steps in 3.76 or 3.77 until you see the Story Importer dialog box. ■ In the "List only stories over ___ characters long" box (3.74), type in a number between zero and 200 million. ■ The "Relist" button (3.75) will now be active; click on it, *or* press Return or Enter. ■ Only those stories with more than that number of characters will display.	■ This feature enables you to eliminate all those tiny little stories that just contain page numbers or captions or callouts, etc. ■ The list shows only the first few words of the story. If you need more, you can View any number of them (3.79). ■ Any story not displayed in the list will not be imported, even if "Select all" is chosen.

If you want to do this:	Then follow these steps:	Shortcuts · Notes · Hints
3.79 View any story	• Follow the steps in 3.76 or 3.77 until you see the Story Importer dialog box. • Click on any number of stories to select them. • Click the button "View," *or* press Command V; you will see a view window for each selected story. • If you have more than one view window on your screen, they will be in layers. Click on any layer to bring it to the front. • Click in the close box (upper left, in the title bar) of each view window to close it, **or** press Command W.	• The View displays the stories using the original font (if the font is installed in the Macintosh System), type size, type style, and carriage returns. Other attributes such as alignment, indents, leading, set width, etc., are not shown. • This View feature is very handy if the title in the list box is not enough for you to identify the story, or if you just want to see more of it. • You can copy text from the View to paste into any other application (3.80).
3.80 Copy text from the view window	• Follow the steps in 3.79 to open a view window. • Press-and-drag to select the text you want to copy. You can press Command A to select the entire story. • You can't access the menu while in the import story view, so you must use the keyboard command to copy the text: Command C. • Close the View by clicking in the close box of the window, *or* press Command W.	• When you select text, you can also Shift-drag (hold the Shift key down while you press-and-drag) to add on to or delete from the end of a selection. You can also click the insertion point at one spot, hold down the Shift key, and click the insertion point at another spot to select all the text between the two clicks. • The copied text can be pasted into PageMaker or into any other application, as long as it stays on the Clipboard (1.184–1.197). It typically will not hold its original formatting.

Text flow

3.81 In PageMaker you have several options of how you can physically put, or **flow,** the text on the page:

> **manual flow;**
> **semi-autoflow,** and
> **autoflow.**

3.82 When you choose "Place..." from the File menu to place a new story in your publication, the cursor shows a **loaded text icon.** When you click once with this icon anywhere in your publication, the text *flows* onto the page. (Even though your icon is loaded, you can still use the menu, the scroll bars, the rulers, and turn the pages.)

3.83 The three different icons:

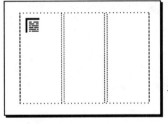 The manual flow icon

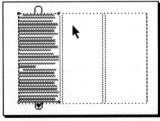 The semi-autoflow icon

The autoflow icon

3.84 If you use **manual flow,** when you click the mouse the text will flow onto the page until it runs out or hits the bottom margin or a graphic. Then it stops. If there is more text to be placed, a solid, down-pointing arrow will appear in the bottom windowshade loop of the text block (3.102). You must *manually reload the text icon* (by clicking once, lightly, on the arrow) in order to place the rest of the story (3.89).

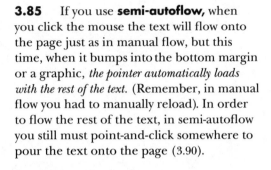

The manual flow icon loaded with text.

After clicking with manual flow, the arrow symbol in the bottom windowshade loop holds any extra text.

3.85 If you use **semi-autoflow,** when you click the mouse the text will flow onto the page just as in manual flow, but this time, when it bumps into the bottom margin or a graphic, *the pointer automatically loads with the rest of the text.* (Remember, in manual flow you had to manually reload). In order to flow the rest of the text, in semi-autoflow you still must point-and-click somewhere to pour the text onto the page (3.90).

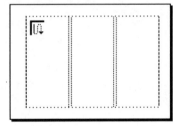

The semi-autoflow icon loaded with text.

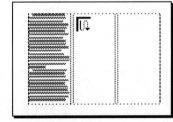

After clicking with semi-autoflow, the icon automatically loads extra text, ready for placing.

Text flow   *—continued*

3.86   If you use **autoflow,** when you click the mouse the text will flow onto the page (3.91); when it hits the bottom margin *the text will automatically begin flowing again at the top of the text column.* If you run out of pages, PageMaker will create more pages for you and continue placing the text. If there are graphics in the way, autoflow will jump over or around them as you have specified in text wrapping (Section 11).

3.87   Autoflow is particularly handy in combination with *reading tags* (3.36–3.39; 7.69–7.71): in your word processor, type your document with tags; set up your PageMaker publication with pages and margins and wrapped graphics; place the document with autoflow—as it pours into the publication, the text formats itself into heads and subheads and body text and pull quotes and wraps itself around graphics just as you previously specified. Tighten up the details and it's done! Magic.

3.88   You'll find yourself using different methods of flow as you work, depending on what you are doing at any particular moment. PageMaker thoughtfully provides keyboard shortcuts so you can switch instantly from one method to another at any time, no matter what the default happens to be (3.92).

The autoflow icon loaded with text.

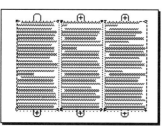

After clicking with autoflow, extra text is poured onto the page in a never-ending stream. Press Command Period to stop the flow.

If you want to do this:

3.89 Place text from a file, **or** place the rest of an existing text block, **using manual flow**

 manual flow icon

*The arrow in the windowshade loop indicates there is more text to that story and that it is **not** threaded into any other text block (3.100–3.103).*

*The + in the windowshade loop indicates there is more text to that story and that it **is** threaded into another text block (3.100–3.103).*

Then follow these steps:

- In the Options menu, make sure "Autoflow" has no checkmark next to it; if it does, choose it once more to take the checkmark off.
- Follow the steps in 3.51. In your publication, the cursor will become a loaded text icon for placing (see left).
- On the page, click once where you want the text to begin; it will pour itself in.
- If the text bumps into something before it is all placed, such as the bottom margin or a graphic, it will stop and you will see an arrow in a little windowshade loop at the bottom of the text block (see 3.95– 3.106 if you need more info on text blocks).
- To pick up the rest of the text manually, position the tip of the pointer on the arrow in the bottom windowshade loop; click *once* quickly and lightly. You will see the loaded text icon again.
- Repeat the previous three steps to place the rest of the text.

Shortcuts ▾ Notes ▾ Hints

- Of course, you can pick up text from any existing text block that shows an arrow or a plus sign in its bottom windowshade loop (with the **pointer tool,** click once on the text itself to see its windowshades— see 3.95–3.106 for more info on text blocks). Picking up extra text this way will give you the same loaded text icon for manual placement.
- An empty loop at the bottom of the windowshade indicates there is no more text to be placed—it's all there.
- Be sure to read the subsection on "Placing text into PageMaker" (3.27– 3.58) to understand how the text will be formatted when it pours in.
- Be sure to read 3.92 for info on how to override autoflow or manual flow whenever you feel like it, no matter what it says in the menu or which icon you see.

If you want to do this:	Then follow these steps:	Shortcuts ▾ Notes ▾ Hints

3.90 Use semi-auto text flow

 semi-autoflow icon

- Follow the steps in 3.51 to get the loaded text icon for placing, then:
- No matter whether you have a manual text icon or an autoflow text icon, **hold down the Shift key;** the cursor will change to a dotted snake with an arrow head.
- Click once to pour the text on the page; if the text hits the bottom margin or a graphic before the entire story is placed, it will stop and *automatically reload* the flow icon for further placement.
- Just click at the next point where you want to place more of the text, and keep repeating that sequence until the entire story is placed.

- Even if Autoflow is checked in the Options menu, pressing the Shift key will override it and create semi-autoflow.
- You can let go of the Shift key at any time to return it to manual flow or autoflow—whichever it was to begin with.

3.91 Use autoflow

 autoflow icon

- From the Options menu, check to see if "Autoflow" has a checkmark by it; if not, choose "Autoflow" to select it.
- Follow the steps in 3.51 to get the loaded text icon for placing, *but don't click yet.*
- In your publication, the cursor will show the *autoflow icon;* it looks like a snake with an arrow head (see left).
- Click where you want the text to begin. It will pour onto the page, filling column after column, turning pages itself, and even creating more pages if there aren't enough. **To stop, press Command Period.**

- **To stop autoflow, press Command Period.**
- Autoflow works whether you are placing text from the "Place..." dialog box or picking up extra text at the end of a text block (3.89).
- Autoflow will flow between the top and bottom margins and the columns. If you are placing graphic elements, such as rules (lines), be sure to either text wrap them (Section 11) or place them outside the actual margin guidelines; otherwise the text will flow right over them.

If you want to do this:	**Then follow these steps:**	**Shortcuts ▾ Notes ▾ Hints**

3.92 Override autoflow or manual flow	▪ To temporarily place text **manually** when Autoflow is *on*, hold down the Command key.
	▪ To temporarily **autoflow** text when Autoflow is *off*, hold down the Command key.
	▪ To temporarily place text **semi-automatically** when *either* manual flow *or* Autoflow is on, hold down the Shift key.
		▪ So the gist is this:
		  ▫ You will get the opposite of either manual flow or autoflow by pressing the Command key.
		  ▫ You will always get semi-autoflow by pressing the Shift key.
		▪ Even while the cursor is showing a loaded text icon, you can go up to the Options menu and check Autoflow on or off.

3.93 Stop autoflow	▪ Press Command Period.	
3.94 Cancel the loaded text icon *without* placing the text	▪ With the loaded text icon, click on any tool in the Toolbox.	▪ Important trick!

Aldus Manutius

Ever wonder why roman type is called roman and italic type is called italic? Well, you can stop losing sleep over it.

Strange as it seems, in 15ᵗʰ century Italy, land of the Romans, very few publications were printed with Roman letters—almost all scholarly or religious works were set in *Greek*. There weren't any other sorts of books anyway, except scholarly or religious works. No romance novels or horror stories yet.

When the man Aldus Manutius entered the publishing business with his company called the Dolphin Press, the printing industry was less than fifty years old. But there were already over a thousand presses operating across Europe, and literally millions of books had been printed. Aldus was proud and protective of his Greek fonts, but a bit sloppy and diffident about his Roman fonts. In fact, most of them were not very well designed, and he used them only for jobs sponsored by wealthy clients or academic friends. In 1496, though, Aldus published an essay for Pietro Bembo, an Italian scholar and friend. The Bembo typeface, with its lighter weight, more pronounced weight stress, and more delicate serifs, was an instant success. Claude Garamond picked it up in France and spread its influence throughout the rest of Europe. This "Aldine roman" affected type design for hundreds of years. *(You are reading the typeface Bembo right now.)*

Aldus himself produced well over 1200 different titles in his 25 years as a publisher. Over 90 percent of the books he produced were Greek classics. Aldus was a well-patronized scholar before he entered the printing and publishing trade, so the classics were close to his heart. His market for the books were the educated, the worldly, the wealthy. Aldus created small books, or *octavos,* intended for busy people, for nobility traveling across Europe on errands of state, for members of the "educational revolution" that were studying in the growing number of universities. The official writing style of the learned and professional scribes of southern Italy in the late 1400s was a relaxed, oblique, flourishy script called *cancellaresca*. To make his books more appealing to the higher-class market, Aldus took this exclusive writing style and developed a typeface out of it. It was a hit.

Aldus had his new type style copyrighted. He was trying to protect not just the one font—he wanted a monopoly on the cursive sort of style. He got it; he even got a papal decree to protect his rights. But as we all know, that doesn't mean no one will steal it anyway. People did. At least the other Italians called the style "Aldino"; the rest of Europe called it "italic," since it came from Italy. The first italic Aldus ever cut (well, actually, Francesco Griffo cut it) was produced in 1501 in Venice. Does the name Venice ring a bell?

These innovations of Aldus Manutius place him in history as perhaps the most important printer of the Renaissance, next to Gutenberg himself. Popularizing the roman typeface, albeit inadvertently, had a profound influence on typeface development for generations. Prior to Aldus's beautiful octavos, the only small, portable books were prayer books; all other works were massive volumes that sat on lecterns, designed for oral reading. With the development of his italic type, more text could be set on a page, thus saving paper and space and making books more affordable. Education became more accessible, and the world changed. Again.

—*rw*

Text blocks

3.95 PageMaker is an "object-oriented" program, which means that every object on the screen is its own little entity and is on its own layer (see 1.151–1.157 about layers). Even text is on a layer.

3.96 Text groups itself into **text blocks.** Every single piece of text, even if it is just one character, or reverse text, or even just blank space in the midst of a story, is in a text block, and each text block is on a separate layer.

3.97 You can see the outer dimensions of the block by clicking once on the text with the **pointer tool.** This shows you the **handles.** There is a handle in each of the four corners; by pressing-and-dragging on one of these handles, you can manipulate the text blocks in various ways—lengthen, shorten, widen, narrow, separate, etc.

3.98

This text is showing all its handles. Notice one in each of the four corners? They show up when you click on the text with the **pointer tool.** This text block is now **selected.**

Corner handle

3.99 At the top and bottom of each text block is a **windowshade loop.** These text boundary markers are called windowshades because they roll up and down just like windowshades. The top and bottom loops give you visual clues as to the text block's connection to other text blocks.

3.100 The **top windowshade loop** will either be empty or will have a plus sign (+) in it.

If the top loop is empty, it indicates that the *story* (3.106) *begins* with that text block.

If the top loop has a plus sign in it, it indicates that this text block is *threaded* (3.105) to a previous text block that contains more text from the same *story* (3.106).

3.101 If the text block contains the complete *story,* **or** if it contains the last section of a *story* (3.106), the **bottom windowshade loop** will be empty.

3.102 If there is more text than will fit into the current size of the text block, the **bottom windowshade loop** will show either a down-pointing arrow (▼) or a plus sign (+).

The down-pointing arrow indicates that there is more text in the *story* (3.106), but it is not placed into any text block.

The plus sign indicates that there is more text in the *story* (3.106), and it is contained in another text block that is *threaded* (3.103) to this one.

You can click once, lightly, on that ▼ or + symbol to pick up the rest of the text. Then if you click the loaded icon (3.82–3.83), the rest of the text will pour onto the page (3.89).

Text blocks *—continued*

3.103 When text blocks are **threaded,** as mentioned in 3.100 and 3.102, the text is *connected* through them all, as if a piece of thread runs through every character. As type is edited, deleted, added, or changed in any way in any one text block, the rest of the connected blocks adjust their text accordingly. This will happen whether the threaded text blocks are on the same page or on various pages in the publication.

3.104

The plus sign in the windowshade loop above indicates that this text block is not the beginning of the story, but that it is threaded to a *previous* text block. The plus in the loop below indicates that it is also threaded to a *following* text block. Notice the bottom loop in the text block in 3.98—it is empty, meaning "that's the end."

3.105 As the text blocks thread, they will not change size, so you needn't worry about your layout being interrupted when you edit —*except:* if changes are made that *decrease* the amount of text, the last text block will decrease in size or disappear, as necessary. If the amount of text *increases,* the last text block will not change size, but will show an arrow in its bottom windowshade handle, indicating there is more text to be placed (*if* you happen to look at the loops).

In PageMaker version 4.01, the last text block will expand to accommodate the next text, unless you have specifically rolled it up.

3.106 It is important to understand the difference between a **text block** and a **story.** The term *story* is referring to the entire document that was placed or typed into PageMaker. Let's say, for instance, that in your word processor or the Story Editor you type seven separate newsletter articles. You place them into a PageMaker publication one at a time so you can manipulate them easily. Each one of these articles becomes a PageMaker *story.*

You can keep a story in *one text block,* or you may choose to break the story up into *several text blocks.* If there is more than one block, the story is *threaded,* or connected, through them all, even if they are on completely different pages.

A story, then, starts with a text block that has an empty *top* windowshade loop, and ends with the last threaded text block that has an empty *bottom* windowshade loop.

(Excuse me for throwing this drop-shadowed box in here, but I was experimenting. That box is made of two PageMaker boxes pasted inline, 1 point leading, "Keep with next 3 lines" applied. I adjusted the baseline to fit the text inside. Now if I edit text, or roll up or move the text block, that paragraph will always stay inside that box. I learned how to attach one box to text from Steve and Ole in Real World PageMaker, *then spent some time experimenting to get the drop shadow. Zero-point leading does not work.)*

If you want to do this:	**Then follow these steps:**	**Shortcuts ▾ Notes ▾ Hints**

3.107 Select a text block or several text blocks

> Letters and characters are communication symbols on one hand, and attractive objects that stimulate sensitivity, on the other.
> —*Takenobu Igarashi*

A selected text block shows handles and windowshade loops.

- Choose an appropriate page view (from the Page menu) that will allow you to see the entire text block, or at least the top or bottom portion you need.
- With the **pointer tool,** click once on the text whose block you wish to select. You should see handles on all four corners.
- If you want to select **several** text blocks, hold the Shift key down while you click. To **de**select a block from the group, Shift-click it again.

- If you don't see handles, check to make sure the top or bottom edges of the text block are visible in that view.
- If you still don't see handles on the text of your choice, reduce the page view (Command W); you will see handles *somewhere*—perhaps there is another layer on top of your text that now has handles. If so, move or delete it (3.108; 3.112).
- If the layering concept is not quite clear to you yet, or if you are unfamiliar with selecting objects, please see 1.143–1.157.

3.108 Move a text block

> Letters and characters are communication symbols on one hand, and attractive objects that stimulate sensitivity, on the other.
> —*Takenobu Igarashi*

You'll see the four-headed arrow when you move a text block.

- With the **pointer tool,** click once anywhere on the text to select the block (see 3.107 if you have trouble selecting).
- With the **pointer tool,** point anywhere in the text; press-and-drag to pick up the text block and move it. When you let go of the mouse button, the text will be in that new position.
- If you want to restrain the movement of the text block to straight across or straight down, hold the Shift key down while moving; whichever direction you move first will be the one you are limited to. You can let up on the Shift key to switch direction without having to let up on the mouse.

- To move several text blocks at once, select several (Shift-click; see 3.107).
- Use a **fast move** (1.159) to move the entire text block quickly across the screen as an outline (press-and-drag with a *quick* start).
- Use a **slow move** (1.160) when you need to see the actual text in order to align it, as when aligning baselines or images (press, *hold a few seconds* until you see the four-headed arrow, then drag).

If you want to do this:	**Then follow these steps:**	**Shortcuts ▾ Notes ▾ Hints**
3.109 Widen a text block, or make it narrower *(lengthen or shorten the lines of text)*	■ With the **pointer tool,** click once on any part of the text block to select it (see 3.107 if you have trouble selecting). ■ With the **pointer tool,** position the very tip of the pointer on one of the four corner handles. ■ *Press* on the handle—you should see the diagonal, double-headed arrow (see left). ■ Press-and-drag either left or right to lengthen or shorten the line.	■ If you hold the Shift key down while dragging, you won't reposition the text block itself. ■ As you change the line length, the text will word wrap to fit the new length. And the symbol in the bottom windowshade loop may change (3.99–3.102).

Letters and characters are communication symbols on one hand, and attractive objects that stimulate sensitivity, on the other.
—*Takenobu Igarashi*

3.110 Shorten a text block	■ With the **pointer tool,** click once on any part of the text block to select it (see 3.107 if you have trouble selecting). ■ Position the very tip of the **pointer tool** in the middle of one of the windowshade loops—*do not click!* ■ *Press* the mouse button (you should see a double-headed, vertical arrow), and *drag* upward—the windowshade will roll up and stop when you let go. ■ If you accidentally click instead of press, you may get the *loaded text icon* (3.82–3.83). If so, click once on the pointer tool in the Toolbox and try again. If you get a dialog box that yells at you because there is no more text to place, it means you *clicked* instead of pressed. Just click Continue and try again.	■ If you drag the *top* loop downward, the bottom shade anchors to the page. Text will thread out of the *bottom* into a connecting text block, or into the arrow in the bottom loop. Dragging from the top *does not* send the first few lines back into a preceding text block! ■ If you drag from the *bottom* loop upward, the *top* shade anchors to the page. Any text that gets rolled up will thread into the connecting text block, if there is one, or else into the arrow in the bottom loop. ■ If the bottom loop was originally empty, it will now have an arrow symbol, indicating there is more to that *story* (3.106). ■ If the bottom loop already had a plus sign in it when you started, it will still have a plus sign when you finish.

Letters and characters are communication symbols on one hand, and attractive objects that

135

If you want to do this:	Then follow these steps:	Shortcuts ▾ Notes ▾ Hints

3.111 Lengthen a text block

Letters and characters are
communication symbols on one
hand, and attractive objects that

- With the **pointer tool,** click once on any part of the text block to select it (see 3.107 if you have trouble selecting).
- If both top and bottom windowshade loops are both empty, *you cannot lengthen the text block*—there is no more to it.
- If there is a symbol in either loop, position the very tip of the **pointer tool** in the middle of one of the loops that has a symbol—*do not click!* (If you accidentally click instead of press, you may get a *loaded text icon* [3.82–3.83]; click once on the pointer tool in the Toolbox and try again.)
- *Press* the mouse button down, and *drag* it outward—the windowshade will roll out and stop when you let go.

- If you pull up on the *top* loop, the bottom shade will anchor to the page and text will be added at the *bottom* of the text block. If you pull down on the *bottom* loop, the top shade will anchor to the page and text will be added at the *bottom* of the text block. If you want to add text at the *top*, you must shorten the *previous*, linked text block.
- No matter how far you pull the last text block handle down, it will snap back up to the last character in the story—you cannot pull it down farther. If you want more open space at the end of the text block, you can hit a few Returns after the last visible character; the Mac sees Returns as solid characters.

3.112 Delete a text block

- With the **pointer tool,** click once on any part of the text block to select it (see 3.107 if you have trouble selecting).
- When you see handles, hit the Backspace/ Delete key (*or,* of course, you could also choose "Clear" from the Edit menu). It's really gone now.

- If you change your mind, you can **Undo** the deletion if you do so *immediately:* from the Edit menu choose "Undo delete," *or* press Command Z.

If you want to do this:	Then follow these steps:	Shortcuts • Notes • Hints
3.113 Delete several text blocks	▪ With the **pointer tool,** click once on any part of the text block to select it (see 3.107 if you have trouble selecting). ▪ Hold the Shift key down and click on other blocks of text; each one you click on will be added to your selection. ▪ When you see all the handles, hit the Backspace/Delete key.	▪ If you want to *deselect* a text block, simply click on it again while holding down the Shift key. ▪ If you change your mind after you delete the text blocks, you can **Undo** the deletion if you do so *immediately:* from the Edit menu choose "Undo delete," *or* press Command Z.
3.114 Delete all the text blocks on the page *(this will also delete everything else on the screen, including any objects on the pasteboard, unless you Shift-click as noted under Shortcuts)*	▪ Click on the **pointer tool** in the Toolbox. ▪ From the Edit menu choose "Select all," *or* press Command A; everything on the screen will have handles (except master page items; 1.122–1.127). ▪ Press the Backspace/Delete key.	▪ If there are some objects you *don't* want to delete, hold down the Shift key and click on them to *deselect* those items before you hit Backspace/Delete. ▪ If you change your mind after you delete, you can **Undo** the deletion if you do so *immediately:* from the Edit menu choose "Undo delete," *or* press Command Z.

If you want to do this:

Then follow these steps:

Shortcuts ▾ Notes ▾ Hints

3.115 Divide a text block into two or more parts, keeping the separate text blocks threaded together

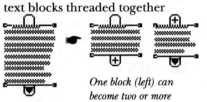

One block (left) can become two or more (above)

- With the **pointer tool,** click once on any part of the text block to select it (see 3.107 if you have trouble selecting).
- If this text block has a plus sign or an arrow in its bottom loop, indicating there is more text to the story, read **part a.**
- If the bottom loop is empty, indicating it is the end of the story, read **part b.**

---

a) If the text block has a symbol in the bottom windowshade loop

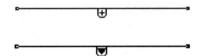

- With the **pointer tool,** click once on the symbol in the bottom windowshade loop; this will give you a loaded text icon (3.82–3.87).
- Wherever you click with that loaded icon, the text will pour itself in, beginning at that point; you will see a + sign in the loop at the *top* of the second text block, indicating the new block is threaded to a preceding one.
- If there is still a symbol in the bottom loop, click once on it to repeat the process. When the bottom windowshade loop is empty, there is no more text to place.

- Remember, the plus sign (+) indicates that the text block is *threaded* to another. If you pick up the text this way and create a new block, the new block will pull text from the *following* connected blocks.
- With a loaded text icon, you can *drag-place* to place the text (press-and-drag to create a bounding box; when you let go, the text will fill that space; 3.58).
- You could, of course, press-and-drag the bottom loop upward to shorten the existing text block before you separate it (3.110).
- As you place text blocks from one story across many (not even sequential) pages, PageMaker threads them all nicely together for you.

If you want to do this:	**Then follow these steps:**	**Shortcuts ▾ Notes ▾ Hints**
b) If the text block has an empty bottom windowshade loop 	■ With the **pointer tool** point to the empty loop, but *don't click yet*. ■ *Press* (don't click) on the loop and *drag* upward to the point where you want the text block to end; when you let go, there will be an arrow in the loop. ■ Now you can click once with the **pointer tool** directly on the arrow to pick up the extra text and place it somewhere else— just as in **part a** directly preceding this.	■ The purpose of this procedure is to shorten the text block so there will be a symbol in the loop, enabling you to pick up the text to start a separate block.
3.116 Remove one or more of several threaded text blocks in a story *without deleting the text in them* 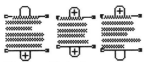 *Three text blocks from one story . . .* 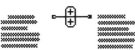 *roll one up and click . . .*  *the block disappears; the text threads on.*	■ With the **pointer tool,** click once on any part of one text block to select it (see 3.107 if you have trouble selecting). ■ Point to the bottom windowshade loop, no matter what symbol it has. ■ Press-and-drag upward until the top and bottom windowshade loops meet, like so:  ■ When they look like this (your loops may have different symbols in them), **click** once anywhere; the handles/loops will disappear and the text that was in that block will thread itself into the other text blocks. **Do not hit the Backspace/ Delete key!**	■ Using this technique, the text from the removed block will just move into the *following* text blocks, if there are any. The following text blocks will *not* get any bigger; only the last one with the empty loop will now show an arrow. You'll need to pull that down or place it somewhere. (In 4.01, the last text block will expand.) ■ Use this technique if you just want to *remove* a text block, but don't want to *delete* the text that was in it. ■ If you *delete* a text block that is threaded to another, or between two threaded ones, then that text is gone *permanently*. The other text blocks are still threaded together and will continue to thread the text, but whatever was in that deleted text block will be *missing*. It'll read funny.

If you want to do this:

Then follow these steps:

Shortcuts ▾ Notes ▾ Hints

3.117 Put separate, threaded text blocks
back into one text block

- If there is room in the column for the
entire story, follow **part a;**
OR if you want to put just one text block
back into another, like say the fourth text
block back into the third, follow **part a;**
OR if there is not room in the column
or even on the page for the entire story,
then read **part b.**

a) Reunite separate blocks back
into one, *if* there is room in one
column

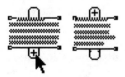

*Press in the previous text block's loop
and drag downward . . .*

to join the text blocks back into one.

- With the **pointer tool,** point to the + sign
in the bottom loop of the text block
preceding the one you want to *add* to it;
that is, if you want to add the fourth one
into the third, then point to the third. If
you want to combine *all the text blocks* into
the first one, then point to the first.
- Simply *press* and *drag* the bottom windowshade loop down as far as possible; it will
snap up to its end and show the empty
loop, indicating there is no more text.
Any threaded text blocks following will
disappear and their text will thread into
this one.
- If you still don't see an empty loop, you
need to press-and-drag down further.

- Use this technique anytime you want to
combine separate, but threaded, blocks
from one story, whether you want to
combine them all into one large block,
or just join a couple of the multitude
together.

If you want to do this:	Then follow these steps:	Shortcuts ▾ Notes ▾ Hints
b) Reunite several blocks back into one, if there is *not* room in one column for the entire story	▪ Follow the steps in 3.116 to remove text blocks, *without deleting any text,* starting at the last text block in the story. ▪ Even if the entire story cannot fit into one text block on one page, at least now it is all stored in that arrow symbol at the bottom of the first text block.	▪ Remember, the last text block in the story has an *empty* bottom windowshade loop. (See 3.106 for important clarification on the difference between a text block and a story.)
OR Place all the text *except the first block* on the pasteboard	▪ Click once in the symbol in the loop at the end of the *first* block to pick up all the following text (it won't disappear yet). ▪ If there is room on the pasteboard for the entire story, then click the loaded text icon (not *autoflow*) somewhere on the pasteboard to flow the rest of the story, or *drag-place* to create a bounding box (3.58) large enough to hold the text.	▪ Any text blocks that may have held parts of the story will now be gone, no matter how many pages they were spread across, and the entire story will be on the pasteboard.
OR Delete the entire story and re-place it into one block	▪ Choose the **text tool;** click once inside any text block belonging to the story. ▪ From the Edit menu choose "Select all," *or* press Command A; all the text will be highlighted. ▪ Press Command X; every text block of that story will be gone. You have just **cut** the entire story (3.118). ▪ With the text tool, set the insertion point where there is room for the entire story; press Command V to paste.	▪ You can, of course, just delete the entire story and start from scratch to place the file again, from "Place…" in the File menu (3.51).

If you want to do this:	**Then follow these steps:**	**Shortcuts ▾ Notes ▾ Hints**
3.118 Cut a text block	▪ With the **pointer tool,** click once on any part of the text block to select it (see 3.107 if you have trouble selecting). ▪ When you see the handles, from the Edit menu choose "Cut," *or* press Command X.	▪ Remember, anything on the Mac that is **cut** is *removed* from the document and placed on the Clipboard, ready for pasting. Keep in mind that the Clipboard can hold only one object at a time (1.184–1.187).
3.119 Copy a text block	▪ With the **pointer tool,** click once on any part of the text block to select it (see 3.107 if you have trouble selecting). ▪ When you see the handles, from the Edit menu choose "Copy," *or* press Command C.	▪ Remember, anything on the Mac that is **copied** is left in the document and a *copy* of it is placed on the Clipboard, ready for pasting. Keep in mind that the Clipboard can hold only one object at a time (1.184–1.187).
3.120 Delete a text block	▪ See 3.112 through 3.114 for deleting text blocks.	▪ Anything **deleted** is just plain gone—it is *not* placed on the Clipboard (1.184–1.190).
3.121 Paste a text block	▪ If you want to paste in a text block as a separate block, not threaded to any others, follow **part a;** ▪ **OR** if you want to *insert* the contents of the text block into another text block, follow **part b;** ▪ **OR** if you want to *replace* a portion of the text in another text block, follow **part c.** *—continued*	▪ When you paste text *as a separate block, it is no longer threaded to any other text block.* ▪ When you paste or insert a text block *into another text block,* the new text takes on the formatting and style of the *paragraph* it is inserted into, although the font specifications will remain intact. ▪ If you insert text *into its own paragraph,* though, by pressing Return *before* you insert, all of the original specifications of the text will remain intact (except line length).

If you want to do this:	Then follow these steps:	Shortcuts ▾ Notes ▾ Hints
a) Paste a text block as its own separate text block	▪ With the **pointer tool,** cut or copy the text block to the Clipboard (see 3.118–3.119). ▪ To paste it on the page as a separate text block, make sure you have the **pointer tool.** ▪ From the Edit menu choose "Paste," *or* press Command V; the text block will appear slightly offset from the original position, and you will have to move it to where you want it (press-and-drag with the pointer tool; 3.108).	This block will not be threaded to any other. It will retain all the formatting, including the line length, of the block it was originally copied or cut from. ▪ If the original text block is not visible on the screen, the new text block will paste into the middle of the window. ▪ Press Command Option V to *power paste* (1.194) the text block into exactly the position it was cut or copied from.
b) Paste a text block, inserted into existing text	▪ With the **pointer tool,** cut or copy the text block to the Clipboard (see 3.118–3.119). ▪ Choose the **text tool** from the Toolbox. ▪ Position the I-beam where you want the text to be inserted; click once to set the flashing insertion point. ▪ From the Edit menu choose "Paste," *or* press Command V.	*Inserted (pasted) text* will take on the formatting of the paragraph it is inserted into; some font specifications will stay the same, though. ▪ If the text to be pasted has formatting you wish to keep, hit a Return *after* setting the insertion point, but *before* pasting. Since this begins a new paragraph, the inserted text will keep its own formatting, *except* for line length.
c) Replace other text	▪ With the **pointer tool,** cut or copy the text block to the Clipboard (see 3.118–3.119). ▪ Choose the **text tool** from the Toolbox. ▪ Press-and-drag to select the text you want to replace (3.131). ▪ From the Edit menu choose "Paste," *or* press Command V.	▪ The text that is selected (highlighted) when you choose to paste will be entirely *replaced* with the new text. No other text in the block will be affected, except to adjust the space.

If you want to do this:	**Then follow these steps:**	**Shortcuts ▾ Notes ▾ Hints**
3.122 Separate a text block into two or more parts, making them separate, *unthreaded* stories	■ If the text blocks you want to unthread are already in two or more separate but threaded blocks, then follow **part a;** ■ **OR** if the text *can* be easily broken into separate text blocks first, do that—separate out what you want to unthread (3.115) and follow **part a;** ■ **OR** if the text you want to separate from a block is in the *body* of the text, such as a headline above body copy, follow **part b.**	■ **Part a** can help, for instance, when someone gives you one word processing document that contains four different newsletter articles; you really need four separate ones for easier placement and manipulation in PageMaker. Place the entire file, then separate it into smaller stories. (As a precaution, it also would be wise to export each one separately; 15.36.) ■ **Part b** is particularly helpful when you find you need to copy a portion of text as a separate story, such as a pull quote; or when you need to cut the headline so it can *span* two columns, while the story is *separated* into two columns.
a) Separate threaded text blocks *(unthread them)*	■ With the **pointer tool,** click once on the text block you wish to separate and unthread (see 3.107 if you have trouble). ■ When you see the handles of the text block, from the Edit menu choose "Cut," *or* press Command X; the block will disappear. ■ From the Edit menu, choose "Paste," *or* press Command V; the new text block will paste in slightly offset from where it originally was and will no longer be threaded to any other block (press-and-drag the new text block to move it; 3.108).	■ You could accomplish the same objective with the "Copy" command, realizing that the *original* text block would still be connected and threaded; the new, pasted text block would not be. ■ To paste the text block into exactly the same position it was cut or copied from, press Command Option V (that's a *power-paste;* see 1.194).

If you want to do this:

b) Separate a portion of the text from the body of the text block

Then follow these steps:

- With the **text tool,** press-and-drag over the text you wish to cut or copy so you can make a separate text block out of it; you should see light text on a dark background (it's highlighted, or selected; 3.131).
- If you want to *remove* it from the text block, from the Edit menu choose "Cut"; **or** if you want to leave it in the original text and make a *copy* of it for a new text block, from the Edit menu choose "Copy."
- With the **text tool**, click once to set the insertion point where you want the new text to appear (read the column to the right and decide which pasting method is best at the moment).
- From the Edit menu choose "Paste," *or* press Command V.

Shortcuts ▾ Notes ▾ Hints

- If you place the insertion point *in an existing text block,* the new text will become part of that text block and will pick up its formatting.
- If you press-and-drag the I-beam *to create a bounding box* (1.206–1.207), the text will flow into that space and that will be a new text block (great for spanning columns).
- If you place the insertion point *within a column,* the new text block will be the width of the column.
- If you place the insertion point *anywhere outside of any existing text block or outside of a column,* the new text block will be the width of your page margins (unless the insertion point is on the pasteboard to the left of the page, since the text block will stop when it bumps into the page).
- If there is *no insertion point flashing,* **or** *if the pointer tool is chosen,* the text will paste in as a block at the top of the screen and will be the width of the page margins.

Selecting and formatting text

3.123 PageMaker allows you incredible control over the text on a page. This subsection covers all the facets of formatting the text characters: type font, type size, type style, case, super- and subscript, set width, as well as rotated text and special characters.

3.124 You can also adjust the space between the lines (leading), the space between the paragraphs, between the letters, between the words. You can kern text and track text. You can define a hyphenation spacing zone. These spacing concepts are a little more complex and need more explanation, so you will find them in their own section, Section 4 on Spacing.

3.125 All of these text manipulations are done with the **text tool.** It is the exception to the rule of using the pointer to change things. But there is no exception to the rule: **select first, then manipulate.** The first part of this section deals with all the different ways to select the text before specifying and formatting.

3.126 When you select the **text tool,** you get the **I-beam** (pronounced eye-beam), as shown below. The I-beam is the visual clue indicating that you are now in the typing, or *text,* mode. It is simply a cursor, just like the pointer.

3.127 *Text tool cursor: the I-beam* ⎯⎯ ⌶
*(the little crossbar indicates
the baseline [1.156] of the text)*

3.128 And just like the pointer, the I-beam will accomplish nothing until you click the mouse. Click while you have the I-beam and you get the flashing **insertion point:** |

(Be sure to read 3.15–3.23 for a thorough explanation of the insertion point and how it decides what text specifications to type with.)

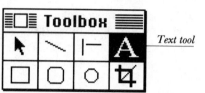

Text tool

Selecting text: character formatting *vs.* paragraph formatting

3.129 As noted in 3.125, text must be selected before it can be manipulated. There are two basic ways to select text in PageMaker, depending on whether you are going to change the formatting of the *characters,* or of the *paragraph.*

3.130 Character formatting applies *only* to those characters (including blank spaces) that are *selected.*

3.131 You can highlight, or *select* text by pressing-and-dragging the text tool over it, which makes it appear light on a dark background.

> If your text is not light-on-dark like this, try again. You must use the text tool.

3.132 You can add to or delete from a selection, but you cannot select two *unconnected* pieces of text, such as the first paragraph *and* the third paragraph. We all try to do it, thinking that of course there must be some way, but there isn't.

3.133 Text must be highlighted in order to format *characters* for any of the following:

Font	Leading*
Type size	Type style
Case	Position
Set width	Track
Color	To cut
To copy	To replace text

*Leading sometimes does and sometimes doesn't affect other characters; be sure to read about leading in Section 4.

3.134 Paragraph formatting applies to entire paragraphs, *whether you select the entire paragraph or not.* For this reason, you don't have to actually highlight the text you want to change—you can just set the insertion point within the paragraph. Of course, if you are changing more than one paragraph, you will need to select at least part of *all* the paragraphs you wish to affect.

3.135 The following are paragraph specific:

Alignment	Style sheets
Indents	Tabs
Hyphenation	Auto pair kerning
Leading method	Auto leading percent
Letter spacing	Word spacing
"Keep with" controls	Grid alignment

Paragraph rules above and below

Paragraph spacing before and after

Dictionary for spell-checking and hyphenation

3.136 Remember, the Mac sees every time you hit a Return key as a command to set up a new paragraph. See 3.230–3.236 for more info on this and on the terrific line-break feature.

If you want to do this:	Then follow these steps:	Shortcuts ▾ Notes ▾ Hints
3.137 Select text using the mouse (*To **deselect text**, click anywhere, even in a highlighted area*)	■ To select any text at any time, you must use the **text tool.**	■ See 3.107 for selecting *text blocks*, which is what you would need to do in order to move a block of text or to lengthen lines. ■ Check out the chart on page 733 that defines all the keyboard shortcuts. They come in very handy. ■ See 3.138 and 1.222–1.226 for greater detail on selecting text using the numeric keypad.
a) Select one character	■ With the **text tool,** position the I-beam to one side of the character to be selected. ■ Press-and-drag over the character.	■ **OR** click to set the insertion point, hold the Shift key down, and press the arrow key in that direction.
b) Select one word	■ With the **text tool,** position the I-beam in the middle of the word. ■ Double-click. ■ **OR** if your hands are on the keys anyway and the insertion point is at the end of a word, press Option Shift LeftArrow (use the RightArrow if the insertion point is at the beginning of a word; this will also select the space after the word).	■ This first technique also selects the blank space *after* a word. If you don't want that blank space selected or affected, use the press-and-drag method in **a)** above. ■ You see, Option plus the Left or Right-Arrow key moves the insertion point one word; whenever you add the Shift key to an insertion point movement, it *selects* text. That's true in many Mac programs.
c) Select one line	■ With the **text tool,** position the I-beam at the beginning of the line. ■ Press-and-drag to the end of the line. ■ If the line is a blank space, double-click.	■ **OR** hold down the Shift key and press the number 1 on the numeric keypad, **or** number 7 if the insertion point is at the *end* of the line. (If it types a *number* 1 or 7, press the Clear key and try again.)

If you want to do this:	Then follow these steps:	Shortcuts ▾ Notes ▾ Hints
d) Select one sentence	▪ With the **text tool,** position the I-beam at the *end* of the sentence; click once to set the insertion point. ▪ Press Command Shift 7 (on the key*pad*). ▪ If the insertion point is at the *beginning* of the sentence, press Command Shift 1 (number 1 on the numeric key*pad*).	▪ This technique selects a sentence. If the insertion point is in the middle of the sentence, the selection will extend to the other end from that point, depending on whether you press 1 or 7. (If you type an actual number, press the Clear key and try again; 3.138, 1.222–1.226.)
e) Select one paragraph	▪ With the **text tool,** position the I-beam anywhere in the paragraph. ▪ Triple-click.	▪ To add other adjoining paragraphs to that selection, press Command Shift and the Up or DownArrow. ▪ **OR** you can simply hold the Shift key down and click in any other paragraph on the screen in that *story* (3.106), even if it's in another text block—that one and all the paragraphs between will be selected.
f) Select a range of text *(in one story)*	▪ With the **text tool,** position the I-beam at the beginning point of the range of text to select; click once to set the insertion point. ▪ If necessary, scroll or change the page view to find the other end of the range of text; position the I-beam there—*don't click yet!* ▪ Hold down the Shift key and *now* click at this other end; everything between the two clicks will be selected, even if they are in separate text blocks (but the text blocks must be part of the same *story,* 3.106).	▪ This technique only works on one page or on a two-page spread—you cannot turn the page to get to the other end of the range of text. ▪ See **h)** for adding on to or deleting from this selection.

If you want to do this:	Then follow these steps:	Shortcuts ▾ Notes ▾ Hints
g) Select an entire story	▪ With the **text tool,** click anywhere in any text block belonging to the story. ▪ From the Edit menu choose "Select all," *or* press Command A.	▪ This technique will select all the text in the *entire story* (3.106), whether you can see it or not, even if it spans several pages and is made up of many text blocks, or even if it is not all placed yet.
h) Extend or shorten the selection	▪ After the text has been selected and you decide you need to adjust it, hold down the Shift key. ▪ Click once at the point at which you want the selected text shortened or extended, **or** press-and-drag from the *end* of the selection. (A funny thing—you can only adjust the selection from the *end* of where you pressed-and-dragged. That is, if you start pressing at the *beginning* of the paragraph, you can adjust the selection from its *end.* If you pressed at the *end* of the paragraph and selected by dragging upward, you can adjust the text from the selection area at the *beginning* of the paragraph.) ▪ You can use this trick in combination with the Command key and the numeric keypad to add characters, sentences, paragraphs, lines, etc., to your selection (1.222–1.226; 3.138).	▪ You can also press the Shift key down and *click* beyond or within the end of the selection; everything up to the click will be included in or excluded from the selection. ▪ You know those times when you press-and-drag over text to select it, and sometimes you miss the last character or maybe you go a word too far? You don't need to start over again—just use this Shift-key trick!

If you want to do this:	**Then follow these steps:**	**Shortcuts ▪ Notes ▪ Hints**
3.138 Use the keyboard to move the insertion point and to select text	▪ With the **text tool,** click to set the insertion point within the text. ▪ Hold the Shift key down while using any of these keyboard commands to select the text along the way.	▪ ***All numbers are numeric keypad numbers—not the numbers along the top of the keyboard!*** ▪ If you use the numeric keypad and it types a number, press the Clear key to switch it to arrow key mode. ▪ Another funny thing—all the numbers on the keypad move the insertion point, except the 5. 5 types a 5. ▪ Do you notice the pattern of these key commands? They follow the up-down-left-right placement on the keypad; using the Command key extends their movement. ▪ Also see 1.222–1.226 for more info on the numeric keypad.
a) One character to the left	Left arrow, *or* 4 on the keypad.	
b) One word to the left	Option LeftArrow, *or* Command 4 on the keypad.	
c) One character to the right	RightArrow, *or* 6 on the keypad.	
d) One word to the right	Option RightArrow, *or* Command 6 on the keypad.	
e) To the beginning of the line	7 on the keypad.	
f) To the end of the line	1 on the keypad.	
g) To the beginning of the sentence	Command 7 on the keypad.	
h) To the end of the sentence	Command 1 on the keypad.	
i) One line up	UpArrow, *or* 8 on the keypad.	
j) One line down	DownArrow, *or* 2 on the keypad.	
k) One paragraph up	Command UpArrow, *or* Command 8 on the keypad.	
l) One paragraph down	Command DownArrow, *or* Command 2 on the keypad.	
m) Up a screen	9 on the keypad.	
n) Down a screen	3 on the keypad.	
o) To the top of the story	Command 9 on the keypad.	▪ If the top or the bottom of the story is not on that page, you will get beeped.
p) To the bottom of the story	Command 3 on the keypad.	

3.139 The "Type specs..." dialog box *(from the Type menu, choose "Type specs..." or press Command T)*

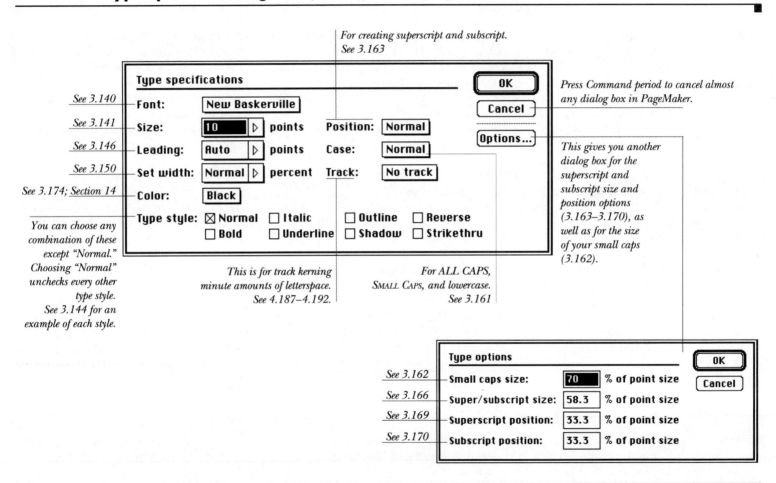

*For creating superscript and subscript.
See 3.163*

*Press Command period to cancel almost
any dialog box in PageMaker.*

See 3.140 — **Font:** New Baskerville

See 3.141 — **Size:** 10 ▷ points   **Position:** Normal

See 3.146 — **Leading:** Auto ▷ points   **Case:** Normal

See 3.150 — **Set width:** Normal ▷ percent   **Track:** No track

See 3.174; Section 14 — **Color:** Black

Type style: ☒ Normal ☐ Italic ☐ Outline ☐ Reverse
☐ Bold ☐ Underline ☐ Shadow ☐ Strikethru

OK   Cancel   Options...

*This gives you another
dialog box for the
superscript and
subscript size and
position options
(3.163–3.170), as
well as for the size
of your small caps
(3.162).*

*You can choose any
combination of these
except "Normal."
Choosing "Normal"
unchecks every other
type style.
See 3.144 for an
example of each style.*

*This is for track kerning
minute amounts of letterspace.
See 4.187–4.192.*

*For ALL CAPS,
Small Caps, and lowercase.
See 3.161*

Type options

See 3.162 — **Small caps size:** 70 % of point size

See 3.166 — **Super/subscript size:** 58.3 % of point size

See 3.169 — **Superscript position:** 33.3 % of point size

See 3.170 — **Subscript position:** 33.3 % of point size

OK   Cancel

If you want to do this:	Then follow these steps:	Shortcuts ▾ Notes ▾ Hints
3.140 Change the font	With the **text tool,** select the text you want to change (3.137–3.138). From the Type menu, slide down to "Font," then slide out to the side and choose the font you want. **Or** from the Type menu, slide down to "Type specs...." Press on the Font submenu and choose the font. Click OK.	▪ If you are going to be making several specification changes at once, such as font and size and style and case, see 3.151. ▪ If you are printing to a PostScript printer, such as an Apple LaserWriter, don't choose a font with a city name. City-named fonts are bitmapped. Their resolution is designed for the lower resolution of the screen and for printers like the Image-Writer; a PostScript printer doesn't know what to do with them. And an imagesetter really freaks out. See 18.5–18.10; 18.29–18.35.
3.141 Change the type size	▪ With the **text tool,** select the text you want to change (3.137–3.138). ▪ From the Type menu, slide down to "Size," then slide out to the side and choose the size you want. ▪ If you want a size other than the ones listed, choose "Other..." from that same pop-out menu. ☐ Type in a new point size, from 4 to 650. You can enter .1 increments. ☐ Click OK. ▪ **Or** from the Type menu, slide down to "Type specs...." Press on the Size submenu and choose a size, or enter a value from 4 to 650, in .1 increments. Click OK.	▪ There are 72 points per inch. Logically, then, the larger the point size, the larger the type. The Mac screen has a resolution of 72 dots per inch; each dot is one point, so we can see type fairly true to size. ▪ The type sizes that are in the *outline* style in the menu are the sizes that are *installed* in your system (they can be different for each font). If you don't have ATM, these specific sizes will look best on your screen, although a PostScript printer (such as the Apple LaserWriter) will print clean type no matter what it looks like on your screen (as long as it is not city-named). See 18.5–18.10 and 18.29–18.41 for info on printers and fonts.

153

If you want to do this:

3.142 Change the type size from the keyboard

You
can do
a good ad
without
good
typography,
but you
can't do
a great ad
without
good
typography.

—Herb Lubalin

Then follow these steps:

- With the **text tool,** select the text you want to change (3.137–3.138).
- **To make the type larger** one point at a time, hold down the Command, Shift, and Option keys all at once; each time you press the > key (above the period), the type will enlarge one point.
- **To make the type smaller** one point at a time, hold down the Command, Shift, and Option keys all at once; each time you press the < key (above the comma), the type will reduce one point.
- **To make the type larger or smaller in standard increments** (PageMaker calls them "graphic art" sizes, the ones you see listed in the size submenu), hold down just the Command and Shift keys while pressing the < or > key. This will change the type to the sizes listed in the Size submenu instead of point by point (e.g., from 14 to 18 to 24 to 30 to 36, etc.).

Shortcuts ▾ Notes ▾ Hints

- What a great shortcut—watch the size of the type change right in front of your very eyes!
- You can't change tenth-point increments (.1) this way, though. For instance, if the type you have selected is 14.7 point, using the key commands will take it down/up to the next *whole* size and continue from there in whole sizes.
- It's easy to remember which keys enlarge or reduce if you think of the < and > characters as the "less than" and "greater than" symbols, respectively.

- 9
10
11
12
14

  The "graphic art" sizes

If you want to do this:	Then follow these steps:	Shortcuts • Notes • Hints
3.143 Change the type style of selected text *(not to be confused with Style as in Style Sheets!)*	■ With the **text tool,** select the text you want to change (3.137–3.138). ■ From the Type menu, slide down to "Type style," then slide out to the side and choose the style you want (see the examples below); **Or** press Command T to get the "Type specs" dialog box to choose from.	■ If you are using *downloadable* (18.36–18.41) fonts, often you cannot change the type style from the Type menu; you need to go into the Font list and choose, for example, the actual italic or bold *font* (3.140). ■ Learn the simple keyboard commands for this process, as shown in the menu and directly below.
3.144 Change the type style of text from the keyboard *before* you type it *(what I call 'loading the insertion point')*	■ Say you are typing and the next word you want to type is to be in Italic, then the rest of the following text will be Normal again. Do this: ■ Type *up to* the word to be italicized. ■ Press Command Shift I (which is the keyboard combination for the Italic style). ■ Type the word—it will be Italic. ■ Press Command Shift I again; this will take the Italic style *off* and the rest of the text will type Normal. ■ Of course this works with changing to any style, including super- and subscript, all caps and small caps, as well as changing point sizes and even alignments. See the chart on page 733 for a list of all the keyboard shortcuts.	■ If you are typing directly into PageMaker, you don't want to have to pick up the mouse everytime you want to turn a word into italic, right? Then follow this simple method to speed your typing. ■ Normal Command Shift Spacebar **Bold** Command Shift B *Italic* Command Shift I Underline Command Shift U ~~Strikethru~~ Command Shift / Outline Command Shift D Shadow Command Shift W Superscript[hi] Command Shift + (**plus** on the key*board,* not the key*pad!*) Subscript[low] Command Shift - (**minus** on the key*pad,* or on the key*board;* actually it's the hyphen) ALL CAPS Command Shift K SMALL CAPS Command Shift H

If you want to do this:	Then follow these steps:	Shortcuts ▾ Notes ▾ Hints
3.145 Change text back to Normal	■ With the **text tool,** select the text to be changed (3.137–3.138). ■ From the Type menu, slide down to "Type style" and out to the submenu; choose "Normal"; **OR** after selecting the type, press Command Shift Spacebar.	■ Pressing Command Shift Spacebar is the quickest way to return your type back to the original font, even if you had it outlined-shadowed-bold-italic (yuck)— just hit these three keys and you're back to Normal. ■ This does not affect the style changes you don't see in the pop-out menu: super- and subscript (see 3.163 to change), or small caps, all caps, and lowercase (see 3.161).
3.146 Change the leading	■ With the **text tool,** select the line(s) that have leading you wish to change (see 3.137–3.138 re: selecting). If you want to *decrease* the leading, make sure you select the *entire line* (see 4.27–4.31). ■ From the Type menu slide down to "Leading" and out to the side submenu; choose the leading value. ■ If the only leading value in the submenu is "Auto" (meaning there is more than one value within the selected text), **or** if you want a leading value other than one listed, choose "Other...." ■ In the "Leading" box, type in the number of points for line space; click OK; **Or** you can use the "Type specs" dialog box (Command T) to select a standard value or enter your own value.	■ Leading can be specified in whole or tenth-point increments (.1), from 0 to 1300 points (don't ever type a comma in the number!). Leading can be larger or smaller than the point size of the type, depending on your objective. ■ Leading is a concept that needs to be fully understood in order to take advantage of the capabilities PageMaker gives you for adjusting it. Please read Section 4 on Spacing, especially the Leading section (4.12–4.51). This segment here is just a very brief synopsis.

If you want to do this:

Then follow these steps:

Shortcuts ▾ Notes ▾ Hints

3.147 Create reverse text

Boldness has genius, power, and magic in it.
—Goethe

- With the text tool, select the text you want to reverse (3.137–3.138 re: selecting text).
- From the Type menu slide down to "Type style," then to the pop-out menu on the side and choose "Reverse."

- Reverse text is white, which means if it is not on a dark background, it is invisible and can easily get lost. See 3.148 for finding it again. See 3.149 to prevent it from getting lost in the first place.
- Unfortunately (or maybe fortunately?) there is no keyboard command to reverse text.

3.148 Finding lost reverse text

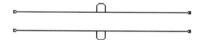

An empty text block like this can indicate reverse text. (It can also indicate a text block where the text was removed, but not the extra Returns, so PageMaker still thinks there is something in it. These'll drive you nuts.)

- View the area on the screen where you think the reverse text may have disappeared, **or** from the Page menu choose "Fit in window."
- Choose the **pointer tool.**
- From the Edit menu choose "Select all," *or* press Command A.
- You will see handles on every object on every layer (1.151–1.157; 1.175). Look for any handles that are holding an empty text block or that are under another layer—that will be your reverse text.
- Click once on the pointer tool to release all the handles; click in the area where you saw the empty block. Keep clicking until you find it.
- If the reverse text is under another layer, hold down the Command key and click on the layer above it. Click again, and just keep clicking until you get the handles of your object. Then press Command F to bring it to the front (1.177).

- Reverse text may just get lost on a white page, or it may be under another layer. If you don't quite get the layering concept, I strongly suggest you read that subsection in Section 1, 1.144–1.157.

If you want to do this:	**Then follow these steps:**	**Shortcuts • Notes • Hints**

3.149 Prevent reverse text from getting lost

Reverse Headline•

Text to be reversed.

Reversed text on the page, with the bullet marking the spot.

Reverse Headline

Reversed text on a black background, with the bullet disappearing.

- At the end of the text to be reversed, type an extra character, like a bullet (Option 8 will give you this bullet: •).
- With the text tool, select the text to reverse it, but don't select the bullet; the bullet will stay black and you will always know where your reverse text is.
- If you are planning to center that text, the bullet will throw off the centered alignment. In that case, simply type the same character at the beginning and the end of the line.

- Of course, this will only work well if you are placing the text on a black background; if the background is only a dark gray or other color, the bullet will show.

3.150 Expand or condense the type *(Change the set width)*

Expand the limits.

Text expanded 140%

Condense the prose.

Text condensed to 70%

- With the **text tool,** select the text you want to expand or condense (3.137–3.138 re: selecting text).
- From the Type menu, slide down to "Set width" and out to the pop-out menu to choose a percentage.
- Use the "Other..." option to type in any percentage you may want, from 5 to 250 percent, in tenth-point increments (.1).
- To remove the set width from text, select the text and choose "Normal" from the Set Width submenu (press Command Shift X).

- You can also set the width in the "Type specs" dialog box (press Command T to get it; 3.139).
- The set width of your type will affect the chosen letter and word spacing as well.
- This is great for those times when you need special effects for logos or headlines. It also works well when you have an unwanted hyphenated word—you can condense the type 98 or 99 percent, just enough to bring the hyphenated end back up onto the line.

If you want to do this:	**Then follow these steps:**	**Shortcuts ▼ Notes ▼ Hints**
3.151 Make several type specification changes at once	▪ Select the text with the **text tool** (3.137–3.138). ▪ From the Type menu, choose "Type specs..." ("specs" is for "specifications"), *or* press Command T. ▪ In this dialog box (as shown on page 152) you can specify all those items at once.	▪ If you are making only one or two changes to the text, such as a font or type style change, it is faster to use the single submenus directly from the Type menu. But if you want to make several changes without constantly running up to the Type menu, use "Type specs...." Case and Position cannot be found on the menu anyway.

3.152 Change the alignment	▪ With the **text tool,** select the text you want to change (3.137–3.138).
	    If you are changing just one paragraph, you only need to click once to set the insertion point within the paragraph (remember, PageMaker sees a paragraph every time you press the Return key, so a headline is considered a paragraph).
	 ▪ From the Type menu, slide down to "Alignment," then over to the submenu and choose your alignment.
		▪ Notice how easy the keyboard shortcuts are to remember:
		    Align left ....Command Shift **L**
		    Align right ......Command Shift **R**
		    Align center ....Command Shift **C**
		    Justify ....Command Shift **J**
		    Force justify ....Command Shift **F**
		 ▪ Just as in 3.144, you can choose an alignment either from the menu or from the keyboard *before* you type. Make sure the insertion point is flashing.
		 ▪ Be sure to read the following pages for practical information on alignment and its ramifications.

3.153 Alignment

How you choose to align your text plays a vital part in the look and the *readability* of your work (it is not the only factor—font, line length, typeface, style, size, line spacing, and case also contribute).

The term *readability* particularly refers to large amounts of text, as in a newsletter, brochure, magazine, etc. Extensive studies have shown what makes type easy and pleasant to read, and thus what encourages people to read what is written. Type that is not so readable can lose a significant part of its audience.

Sometimes, in short text, as in an advertisement or a package design, you can get away with using a particular design feature that detracts from the readability, but that does add to the attractiveness of the piece (such as extreme letterspacing, or all caps with a justified alignment), if you feel the *look* of the piece is more important than the loss of readability. You just need to be aware of the choice you are making and be able to qualify it.

Alignment in PageMaker is very interconnected with the word spacing, letter spacing, and hyphenation controls, particularly when working with justified text. I know you don't have time, but it would seriously behoove you to read through and understand Section 4.

3.154 Align left

> There is no single voice capable of expressing every idea; romance is still necessary, ornament is necessary, and simplification is not better than complexity.
>
> — Milton Glaser

Text aligned on the left is the most readable, as far as alignment is concerned. It is able to use the "Desired" word spacing and letter spacing (4.104–4.160) that the designer built into the font. With the alignment on the left, as you read, your eye can quickly find the beginning of the next sentence. And in this alignment, you can most easily make corrections and adjust lines when necessary, often without affecting the rest of the text at all.

When you align text left, the ideal is to keep the right, "ragged" side as smooth as possible. Often that means forcing line breaks in order to fill in holes or to prevent long strings from hanging beyond the rest of the lines. For instance, in this paragraph, the word "as" in the second line should be bumped down to the next line so it doesn't hang over like it is. To do that I would put my insertion point directly in front of the "a" and press Shift-Return (3.230–3.236).

3.155 Align right

> There is no single voice capable of expressing every idea; romance is still necessary, ornament is necessary, and simplification is not better than complexity.
>
> — Milton Glaser

Text aligned on the right creates a definite *look*. The letter and word spacing can still retain the "Desired" amount (4.104–4.160), and corrections can still be made fairly easily without affecting the rest of the text. The biggest drop in readability comes from the fact that the left edge, where our eye returns to find the next line to read, is not consistent. In short amounts of text, this isn't a great problem.

If you are using this alignment for the *look* it creates, then you might as well emphasize the look. Don't be a wimp. Rather than try to keep the left, ragged edge as smooth as possible, exaggerate it. There's no excuse to have hyphenated words here; bumping "necessary" down will eliminate a hyphen, as well as make the alignment more interesting. To bump "necessary," press Shift-Return (3.230–3.236) directly in front of it.

3.156 **Align center** ■

> There is no single voice capable of expressing every idea; romance is still necessary, ornament is necessary, and simplification is not better than complexity.
>
> — Milton Glaser

A centered alignment also gives a *look* to text, a more formal, serious sort of look. As with left- and right-aligned, it doesn't affect the letter and word spacing. But, as with right-aligned, if you're going to do it, then do it. Don't let the lines look ambiguous, as if it can't decide if it's justified or centered. A centered alignment gives you a perfect opportunity to group the lines into logical thoughts, rather than letting them fall where they want. Also, varying the line lengths makes it much more visually interesting. And there is never any excuse for hyphenated words. Break the lines with Shift-Returns (3.230–3.236).

> There is no single voice capable of expressing every idea; romance is still necessary, ornament is necessary, and simplification is not better than complexity.
>
> Milton Glaser

3.157 **Justify** ■

> There is no single voice capable of expressing every idea; romance is still necessary, ornament is necessary, and simplification is not better than complexity.
>
> — Milton Glaser

When you justify text, PageMaker forces the lines to extend to a certain length by adding or deleting space between the words and letters. You can specify the minimum and maximum amount you will allow the spacing to adjust, but if PageMaker can't do it the way you want, she does it the way she wants. (If you check "Loose/tight lines" in the Preferences menu, a colored or gray bar will indicate the lines where PageMaker refused to listen to you; 1.217.)

The biggest problem with justified text is the uneven word spacing; some lines have extra spacing, some less, and this visual irregularity interrupts the maximum readability. The shorter the line length, the worse the problem. It is also more difficult to correct dumb hyphenations and widows, as in the example.

Justify text *only* when the line length is long enough to be able to adjust the spacing equitably.

1.158 **Force justify** ■

> There is no single voice capable of expressing every idea; romance is still necessary, ornament is necessary, and simplification is not better than com-
> p   l   e   x   i   t   y   .
>
> — Milton   Glaser

Now this really looks stupid. The worst possible kind of widow (the end of a hyphenated word as the last line of a paragraph) really looks ridiculous when it is force justified. So do those last two words stretched across the line.

In regular justification, the last line of a paragraph retains its regular word and letter spacing. Occasionally the last line may be long enough that you would like it to justify to match the rest, in which case you could safely use force justification. Usually it isn't.

Force justification is a design technique created not so much for paragraphs as for headlines or a short body of letterspaced text. The example below was typed with an Option Spacebar between words, then force justified. See 3.159 for more details.

The Mac is not a typewriter

w r i t t e n   b y   R o b i n   W i l l i a m s

If you want to do this:

3.159 Force justify display text with wide letterspacing

ZOUNDS!

I   was   never

so   bethump'd

with   words

William   Shakespeare
King John   Act II

I typed this text normally and then force justified it. (The rules, or lines, are part of the paragraph; Section 6.)

ZOUNDS!

I was never

so bethump'd

with words.

William Shakespeare
King John ❧ Act II

I typed this text using the Option Spacebar between words, and then force justified it. (The rules, or lines, are part of the paragraph; Section 6.)

Then follow these steps:

- The trick to stretching text across a line is to make PageMaker think it is one word, which you can do by putting a *hard space,* also called a *non-breaking space,* between the words (4.207–4.218).
- Type each line of text, pressing Option Spacebar (which is a *hard space*) between each word instead of just the Spacebar.
- At the end of each line, where you really want the line to break after it is letterspaced, hit a Return or a Shift-Return (3.230).
- When you are done, select all the lines with the **text tool.**
- From the Type menu slide down to "Alignment" to get the pop-out menu, and choose "Force justify," **or** press Command Shift F.

- **An alternative sequence** is to create a bounding box (3.25) the width you want the text to occupy. With the insertion point flashing, press Command Shift F to force justify what you are about to type. Type, using Option Spacebar between words. This way you can see and decide exactly where lines should break as you type, rather than having to anticipate. *You do need to break the lines yourself,* as the text can't word wrap if it is one huge word.

Shortcuts ▾ Notes ▾ Hints

- Force justify forces *every* line to extend the maximum width of the line length. This differs from regular justification, which doesn't affect any line that has a Return character in it.
- The first thing justifying text affects is the space between words: it adds or removes minute amounts of space. Then, if that isn't enough, it adds or removes space between characters. So, in forcing the justification, if you can make PageMaker think there is just one word on that line, it will letterspace that line nearly perfect. This is much easier than trying to use the Spacing command.
- If you have already typed the text with Spacebars, or if you can't deal with typing the Option Spacebars, you can use the Story Editor to find and change all the Spacebars to Option Spacebars (8.78). Just make sure you type Returns where you want lines to break, or the entire text will come out as one word and will confuse PageMaker because she can't find that word in her dictionary in order to hyphenate it, in which case it may look something like this:

ZOUNDSIwasneverbethump'dwithwordsWilliamShakespeareKingJohnActII

If you want to do this:

3.160 Set indents or tabs

Then follow these steps:

- With the **text tool,** select the text you want to indent or tab (see 3.137–3.138 re: selecting text). If you just want to adjust a single paragraph, you only need to click the insertion point into the paragraph.
- From the Type menu choose "Indents/ tabs..." or press Command I.
- The margin edge of the tab ruler aligns with the margin edge of your text block, *if there is space in the window* (otherwise it just plops in the middle of the screen and you have to drag it into position).
- **To set a tab,** click in the ruler at the point where you want the tab to be. Then click on one of the tab alignment icons in the upper left of the ruler. If you want Leaders, choose one while the tab is selected.
- **To set the left or right indent,** press on the bottom half of the large black triangle at either end of the ruler. Press-and-drag on a marker to move it to where you want the text indented.
- **To set a first-line indent,** press on the top half of the left large triangle and move it where you want your first line to indent. The first line after every Return will align with that top marker, and the rest of the text will wrap back to the bottom half of the marker.

Shortcuts ▼ Notes ▼ Hints

- Indents and tabs are so important and so often misunderstood that they rate a separate section of their own. If this brief synopsis isn't enough for you, please read Section 5, where you will find in-depth explanations of indents and tabs, leaders, the ruler, how and when to use indents and tabs, and much more. Wow.

- You may need to scroll to the right to see the right indent marker.
- The left indent *marker* is made up of two separate triangles; to move the left *indent,* press on the lower one (the top one is the *first-line indent*).

If you want to do this:	**Then follow these steps:**	**Shortcuts ▾ Notes ▾ Hints**

3.161 Change the case
(as in uppercase or lowercase)
 	
Case: ✓Normal
      All caps
      Small caps
	■ With the **text tool,** select the text you want to change (3.137–3.138).
	■ From the Type menu choose "Type specs...," *or* press Command T.
	■ Press on the box next to the label "Case"; you will see a little menu drop down; then:
		■ Unfortunately, there is no way to turn text that was typed in UPPERCASE into lowercase with just the push of a key—it must simply be retyped. If the text was *originally* typed lowercase and then *transformed* into uppercase with the command, then you can change it back to lowercase with the command.

a) into UPPERCASE (all caps)	■ To turn *regular lowercase text* or SMALL CAPS into UPPERCASE, choose "All caps."	■ To change any text into all caps, select the text and then press Command Shift K; to turn it back into lowercase, press the key sequence again.
b) into SMALL CAPS *(where typed capitals remain normal-sized capitals, but lowercase letters become small-sized capitals)*	■ To turn *regular lowercase text* into SMALL CAPS, choose "Small caps." ■ To turn UPPERCASE into SMALL CAPS, retype it, *using lowercase letters.* Then follow the step directly above.	■ See 3.162 to change the size of the SMALL CAPS. The default is 70% of the point size. ■ Keyboard shortcut is Command Shift H. ■ You cannot change type set in all caps into small caps because "Small caps" only changes the lowercase letters.
c) into lowercase	■ To turn SMALL CAPS text into lowercase, choose "Normal." ■ To turn UPPERCASE into lowercase, retype it (unless you originally typed it lowercase and transformed it into uppercase; then you can choose "Normal").	■ The keyboard shortcut to turn SMALL CAPS into lowercase: Command Shift H. ■ If you originally typed the text in lowercase and transformed it into uppercase with the command, you can use the keyboard shortcut to turn it back into lowercase: Command Shift K.

If you want to do this:	**Then follow these steps:**	**Shortcuts ▾ Notes ▾ Hints**
3.162 Change the size of the SMALL CAPS Small caps size: **70** % of point size NOW IS THE TIME *(70%)* NOW IS THE TIME *(180%)* N. I T. T. *(10%)*	▪ With the **text tool,** select the text (3.137–3.138). ▪ From the Type menu choose "Type specs...," *or* press Command T. ▪ If the box next to Case does not say "Small caps," then press on it to pop out the menu and choose "Small caps." ▪ Press on the button "Options...." ▪ In the box next to "Small caps size," type in a number from 1 to 200; you can use tenth-point increments (.1).	▪ The keyboard shortcut for creating small caps is Command Shift H. Of course, you must first select the text with the text tool. ▪ Standard default is 70% of the point size. If you click on the pointer tool before you change that percentage, you can reset the default (3.166; 3.247). ▪ Press Option Return to close both dialog boxes with one motion.

3.163 Change the position
(Normal or ^{superscript} or $_{subscript}$)
 	
4th of July   *Superscript (th)*
 	
H$_2$O   *Subscript (2)*
	▪ With the **text tool,** select the text you want to change (3.137–3.138).
	  ▪ From the Type menu choose "Type specs...," *or* press Command T.
	  ▪ Press on the box next to the label "Position"; a little menu will pop-up; choose the position you want.
	▪ **OR** use the keyboard shortcuts:
	Superscript: Command Shift +
	(That's the plus sign from the key*board,* above the =; it doesn't work to use the key*pad* plus sign)
	Subscript: Command Shift -
	(That's the hyphen, from the key*board;* you can use the numeric key*pad* minus sign if you're in "arrow key mode" (1.223)—if you get a minus sign, press Clear; try again.)
		▪ See 3.164–3.170.
		▪ **Normal** position sets letters on the *baseline,* (3.168) which is the invisible line the type normally sits on.
		▪ **Superscript** sizes text to $\frac{7}{12}$ of the point size (which is 58.3 percent); that is, if the type is 12 points, the superscript size will be 7 points. Then it figures $\frac{1}{3}$ of the point size of the normal text (33 percent) and puts the superscript baseline just that high *above* the normal baseline. Example: 3rd becomes 3rd.
		▪ **Subscript** does the same as superscript, but places the baseline of the subscript character $\frac{1}{3}$ *below* the normal baseline. Example: H2O becomes H$_2$O.

Change the size and placement of superscript and subscript

3.164 To find this dialog box, from the Type menu choose "Type specs...," then click on the "Options..." button.

3.165 As with any character formatting, you must first *select* the text (use the text tool) that is to be super- or subscripted. If you change these settings while no text is selected and while no insertion point is flashing, you will set the defaults for the publication (3.247).

3.166 The **"Super/subscript size"** box defines the actual size of the character. You can enter values from 1% to 200% in tenth-point (.1) increments.

The default percent, 58.3, is $\frac{7}{12}$ of the point size of the type; that is, if the type is 12 points, the super/subscript character will be 7 points. If you change this number to 50%, then in a 12-point font your super/subscript character will be 6 points; in a 30-point font, the scripted character will be 15 points.

3.167 *Do you see a hidden possibility in this sizing option? You can set type up to 1300 points, simply by turning selected text into a superscript at 200%. Set the "position" to 0 (zero). See 19.20.*

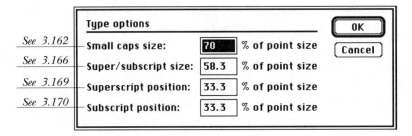

See *3.162*
See *3.166*
See *3.169*
See *3.170*

3.168 *The line below "Thomas Hardy" defines the invisible baseline from which super- and subscript characters position themselves above (1) and below (2): The normal text itself is positioned with ⅔ of the character body above the baseline, and ⅓ below.*

Thomas[1] Hardy[2]

3.169 The **"Superscript position"** box defines where the character will be placed in relation to the baseline of the normal text. The default is 33 percent, which places the baseline of the script character one-third of the way *above* the normal baseline, as shown in 3.168. You can enter any percentage value from 0 to 500 in tenth-point (.1) increments.

3.170 The **"Subscript position"** box defines where the character will be placed in relation to the baseline of the normal text. The default is 33 percent, which places the baseline of the script character one-third of the way *below* the normal baseline, as shown in 3.168. You can enter any percentage value from 0 to 500 in tenth-point (.1) increments.

If you want to do this:

Then follow these steps:

Shortcuts • Notes • Hints

3.171a Set a default for creating beautiful fractions easily

⅞   ¹⁵⁄₁₆   9¾

Super/subscript size:	70	% of point size
Superscript position:	33.3	% of point size
Subscript position:	0	% of point size

- Read the column to the right. ➡
- Choose the **pointer tool.**
- Press Command T to get the "Type specs..." dialog box; then click once on the "Options..." button.
- Change the number in the "Super/subscript size" box to 70.
- Change the number in the last box ("Subscript position") to 0 (zero).
- Press Option Return to close both dialog boxes. You have just set a *publication default* (3.247).

3.171b Type a fraction without having to select characters and open dialog boxes

- Set the defaults in the super- and subscript dialog box as shown above. Then you can use the following keyboard shortcuts:
  - ☐ Just before typing the 3, press Command Shift +; type the 3; press Command Shift + again.
  - ☐ To type the fraction bar, press Shift Option 1 (that's the number one).
  - ☐ Press Command Shift - (that's the hyphen); type the 8; press Command Shift - again to continue typing in the Normal style.

- **This technique sets a publication default** in the "Type options" dialog box, since creating fractions is probably the most useful way to take advantage of superscripts and subscripts. Setting the default means that whenever you start typing *a new text block*, you will have the new default specifications. As soon as you set your insertion point into a prevoiusly-created text block, the specifications from the character to the left of the insertion point take over.
- **If you don't want to set the default,** then just follow the steps to type the fraction. Then select the three characters in the fraction, get the "Type options" dialog box, and type the same numbers (70 and 0) in the same boxes as explained in the directions.
- **If you want to set these defaults for the entire PageMaker application,** simply follow the first five steps *while no publication is open*—you should see just the PageMaker menu, but no open window.
- You may want to change the size of the super/subscript from the 70 suggested here, depending on the size of your type and how it looks. You may also need to kern (4.165–4.186) to get the spacing correct.

If you want to do this:	**Then follow these steps:**	**Shortcuts ▾ Notes ▾ Hints**

3.172 Create interesting bullets

16-point Dingbats

◆ No ⁂ Boring ▾ Bullets ◆

16-point text used with
16-point Dingbats as bullets

- Type the character you want to use as a bullet, such as a Zapf Dingbat.
- Select the Dingbat with the **text tool.**
- From the Type menu choose "Type specs...," *or* press Command T.
- In the box next to "Position," press to get the submenu; choose "Superscript."
- Click once on the "Options..." button.
- In the "Super/subscript size" box, type 40.
- In the "Superscript position" box type 15.
- Press Option Return to close both dialog boxes.

- The standard "bullet" is the round dot you see before each paragraph in this column, produced by pressing Option 8 in any font.
- If you simply try to reduce the size of dingbats to use them as bullets, they appear too low in relation to the other characters.
- You can play around with the size and position in the "Type options" dialog box to get exactly what you want. The numbers noted here are just suggestions.

3.173 Make a line longer or shorter
(also see 3.109)

- With the **pointer tool,** click once on the text; you should see handles of the text block (see 3.98).
- Position the very *tip* of the pointer tool on one of the corner handles.
- Press-and-drag on the handle; this will stretch the width of the text block, making the line longer or shorter as you drag. All the text in the entire text block will wrap to the new line length.

- This is actually a function of the **text block.** If you don't understand the concept of text blocks very well, it would be a good idea to read all about them before you go too much further (3.95–3.122).
- If this technique does not change your line width, check the indents (Command I) to see if the black triangle on the right is aligned with the dotted line or not (5.44–5.46). If not, press-and-drag the right triangle all the way to the right until it won't go any further (which will be at the dotted line in the indent ruler).

If you want to do this:

3.174 Make the text or rules gray

What type shall I use?
The gods refuse to answer.
They refuse because they do not know.

W.A. Dwiggins

The lighter text is 65 percent black.

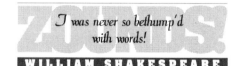

The light background text is 25 percent black; the 12-point rule is 77 percent black.

Then follow these steps:

If you haven't done so already, you need to create a Color style. Then you can apply the color to the text, rule, or border:

- From the Element menu, choose "Define colors...."
- Click "New...."
- Type in a name for this new color, a name that will give you a clue as to what it is, such as "Light Gray," or the percent value of the tint you are creating (e.g., 65%).
- Click in the radio button next to "CMYK."
- Use the scroll bars to set the values of Cyan, Magenta, and Yellow to 0 (zero), or you could just type a 0 (zero) in each.
- In Black, either enter a value (like 65) or use the scroll bars to get a low value. See the examples on the right.
- Press Option Return to close both boxes.
- From the Windows menu, choose "Color palette," or press Command K.
- With the **text tool,** select the text you want to shade gray; **or** with the **pointer tool,** select any number of rules (lines) or borders to shade gray.
- Click once in the color style name that you want to apply to the text or line. Unless you have a color or grayscale monitor, the items won't look any different on the screen, but they will print gray.

Shortcuts ▾ Notes ▾ Hints

- If you have already created the Color style, then you only need to **select** the text or rule, get the Color palette from the Windows menu, and choose the color. For text, you can also use the "Type specs" dialog box (press Command T).

- This technique is particularly useful for those of us who deal mostly in one color (black). If you have a color monitor or want to use spot color or any other kind of color, read Section 14 on Color.

- Examples of shades:

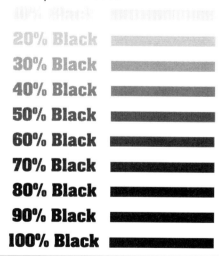

If you want to do this:	Then follow these steps:	Shortcuts ▾ Notes ▾ Hints
3.175 Delete text	■ With the **text tool,** select the text you want deleted (see 3.137–3.138 re: selecting). ■ From the Edit menu, choose "Clear," *or* press the Backspace/Delete key.	■ **Delete** or **Clear** does *not* put the deleted text on the Clipboard—it is just gone. ■ If you instantly decide you made a mistake, **UNDO** from the Edit menu. ■ Shortcut to Undo: Command Z. Note: you can only undo *the very last thing you did* (1.198). If you need more serious undoing, see the info on Reverting, 16.2–16.3 and 16.26–16.27.
3.176 Cut text	■ With the **text tool,** select the text you want to cut (see 3.137–3.138 re: selecting). ■ From the Edit menu, choose "Cut," *or* press Command X (easy to remember, since X is like X-ing it out).	■ **Cutting** removes the text from the publication and places it on the Clipboard (1.184–1.190), ready for pasting (3.178). ■ If you instantly decide you made a mistake, **UNDO** from the Edit menu. ■ Shortcut to Undo: Command Z. Note: you can only Undo *the very last thing you did* (1.198).
3.177 Copy text	■ With the **text tool,** select the text you want to copy (see 3.137–3.138 re: selecting). ■ From the Edit menu, choose "Copy," *or* press Command C (easy to remember— C for Copy).	■ **Copying** *leaves* the text in the publication and places a *copy* of it on the Clipboard (1.184–1.190), ready for pasting (3.178).

> **For more info on cutting,
> copying, and pasting, see 1.184–1.195
> and 3.118–3.121.**

If you want to do this:	**Then follow these steps:**	**Shortcuts • Notes • Hints**
3.178 Paste text	▪ With the **text tool,** cut or copy the text you want to paste (3.176–3.177); this will place it on the Clipboard. ▪ If you want to paste the text on the page **in its own text block,** follow **part a; OR** if you want to **insert the text** into a story currently on the page, follow **step b.**	▪ For more info on cutting, copying, and pasting, see 1.184–1.195.
a) Into its own text block	▪ With the **text tool, either** click the insertion point anywhere *outside* of another text block; **Or** create a bounding box for the text to flow into (press-and-drag with the text tool; when you paste the text, it will create a text block the width of the invisible box you just created; see 3.25). ▪ Either method will give you a flashing insertion point; from the Edit menu choose "Paste," *or* press Command V. The text will paste in, beginning at the flashing insertion point. The entire story will be contained in the text block.	▪ If the insertion point is inside a column, the text block will be the width of the column (1.75–1.81). ▪ If you create a bounding box (3.25), the text will be the width of the invisible box, but the depth will expand to fit the text. ▪ If the insertion point is neither in a column nor part of a bounding box, the text block will be the width of the page margins (1.75). It just knows how wide your margins are.
b) Into a current story	▪ With the **text tool,** click once to set an insertion point in the story at the spot where you want the text to begin. ▪ From the Edit menu, choose "Paste," *or* press Command V.	▪ Text pasted into a paragraph will take on the formatting of that paragraph—tabs, indents, margins, etc. ▪ Text pasted in as its own paragraph (by hitting Return before pasting) will retain its original formatting.

If you want to do this:

3.179 Replace existing text with the text that you cut or copied onto the Clipboard

Then follow these steps:

- With the **text tool,** select the text you want to replace by pressing-and-dragging over it (see 3.137–3.138 re: selecting). *Just the text you select will be replaced.*
- From the Edit menu, choose "Paste," *or* press Command V; the pasted text will completely *replace* whatever was selected.

Shortcuts ▾ Notes ▾ Hints

- If you want to replace text with a word processing file, see 3.55.
- Replacing text works exactly the same if the text you want to use is from the Scrapbook (see 1.201 and 1.204 for info on working with the Scrapbook).

Rotate Text

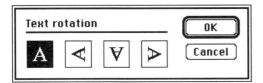

3.180 *The "Text rotation" dialog box, from the Element menu, shows the four increments you can choose for rotating text. The first one is the way we usually read text.*

3.181 *Examples of each of the four 90° increments. I must warn you: rotated text is not always WYSIWYG (what you see is what you get). It works best with resident fonts (18.38), and it works best if you have not extended or condensed the text.*

3.182 At last PageMaker has a text rotation command, albeit a very limited one. Like now you have a big choice between turning your text sideways or upside down, as shown in the example in 3.181.

3.183 Well, I shouldn't make fun of its limited capacity. At least now we can put photo captions running up the sides of photos, and we can position the return address of a mailing brochure directly on the PageMaker page. I assume this feature will develop over time.

3.184 Even though rotated text looks like a graphic, you cannot resize it, apply a text wrap to it, crop it, or make it an inline graphic. You can resize the *text block;* that is, you can lengthen or shorten the *line length* (3.190), but this will not condense, expand, or change the size of the *letters.*

When selected, this text looks like a graphic because of its handles. It isn't.

3.185 Other important things to know about rotating text:

- You cannot rotate text if more than one text block is selected.
- You cannot rotate text that contains an inline graphic (9.91).
- You cannot rotate a text block that is threaded to any other text block, or that has any text yet to be placed (that is, if there is any symbol in the bottom windowshade handle; 3.100–3.102).
- You cannot rotate text if its story is open in the Story Editor (8.6–8.8).
- If you condense or expand type (3.150) before rotating it, be sure to use the Aldus driver when printing, not the Apple driver (18.24–18.25).
- Most non-PostScript printers cannot print rotated text. If the "Text rotation" command in the menu is gray after you select a single, unconnected text block with no inline graphics present, then your designated printer (18.74) can't do it.

If you want to do this:	Then follow these steps:	Shortcuts ▾ Notes ▾ Hints
3.186 Rotate text	■ With the **pointer tool,** click once on the text block you want to rotate. ■ From the Element menu, choose "Text Rotation…"; if that item is gray, see 3.185 for possible reasons why. ■ Click once on the "A" that shows the angle at which you want to rotate your text; then click OK or press Return.	■ This is one dialog box where you can't double-click the item (like the "A") to shortcut the OK button.
3.187 Unrotate text **A** *This is the normal icon.*	■ With the **pointer tool,** click once on the rotated text you want to return to normal. ■ From the Element menu, choose "Text Rotation…." ■ Click once on the upright "A"; then click OK or press Return.	
3.188 Edit rotated text	■ Unrotate the text (3.187) and edit it with the **text tool** as usual, then rotate it back again. **OR** with the **pointer tool,** triple-click on the rotated text to bring up the Story Editor (Section 8). □ In the Story Editor window, edit the text as usual, then close the Story Editor window (Command W). After closing the window, you will see the changes on the page.	■ If you unrotate the text before editing, you can see your on-screen changes instantly. If you need to kern (4.165–4.186), set a new width (3.150), or use some other special technique, you *must* make those changes as unrotated text rather than in the Story Editor. ■ If you are just making "typo" sorts of changes, it may be faster to do it in the Story Editor. While there, though, you will see the text only as Geneva 12 point (or whatever you set your "Story view" text to; 1.210; 1.220).

If you want to do this:

3.189 Wrap rotated text around a graphic

Then follow these steps:

- Text wrap a graphic as usual (Section 11).
- With the **pointer tool,** press-and-drag the rotated text to position it near the text-wrapped object.

Shortcuts ▾ Notes ▾ Hints

- Rotated text will wrap around objects just as any other text will, although it will always "wrap all sides" even if one of the other text-wrapping options is chosen ("column break" or "jump-over"; 11.13–11.14). Lines will break as necessary and the *depth* of the rotated text block will expand as necessary.

W hen I get a little
money I buy books;
and if any is left,
I buy food and clothes.
—*Desiderius Erasmus*

Text before rotation

When I get a little money I buy books; and if any is left, I buy food and clothes. —*Desiderius Erasmus*

Text after rotation

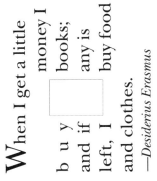

Rotated text that is wrapping on all sides, even though the object has a "jump-over" flow option (11.14) applied.

3.190 Resize a rotated text block

- With the **pointer tool,** click once on the rotated text.
- Press-and-drag on any handle you see, depending on which direction you want to resize the block. *This does not resize the text itself, just the rotated text block.*

- This is just like resizing any text *block;* the text will word wrap to fill the new size. Do you want to resize the text itself? See 3.188 re: editing. Do you want to stretch the rotated text, like a graphic? You can't. You can only unrotate it and set a new width (3.150).

Paragraphs

The "Paragraph..." dialog box holds a plethora of possibilities. Most attributes are discussed here; some are discussed more appropriately in Section 4 on Spacing.

3.191 All paragraph attributes apply to an entire paragraph. **Remember, the Mac sees a new paragraph every time you hit the Return or Enter key!** See 3.230–3.236 for intimate details on the paragraph concept and the *line-break* feature that provides the perfect option when you need a new *line*, but not a new *paragraph*.

3.192 Paragraph attributes apply to entire paragraphs. When you want to apply formatting, you only need to set the insertion point anywhere in the paragraph (click once with the text tool) to select it.

3.193 To select more than one paragraph, you must press-and-drag over each one, but you don't need to select *entire* paragraphs—even selecting just one character of each will do. As in any other program on the Mac, it is not possible to select two paragraphs that are not next to each other; e.g., you can't select the first and the third paragraphs, nor can you select the first paragraphs of two separate stories (3.106), even though they may be physically next to each other on the page.

The "Paragraph..." dialog box:

3.194 **"Indents"** is connected to the Indents/Tabs ruler. Use it for indenting left and right margins, as well as for indenting (or "outdenting") the first line of each paragraph. See 3.203–3.208.

3.195 Use **"Paragraph space"** for adding extra space between paragraphs or after heads and subheads, rather than using extra carriage returns. This extremely important and useful concept is covered in 4.63–4.87.

3.196 Use **"Alignment"** to determine whether text aligns on the left, the right, or both sides; is centered, or force justified. See 3.153–3.158 for examples and information on the uses of the different alignments, and 3.209 for using this dialog box to control it.

3.197 Use **"Dictionary"** to choose one of the many foreign language or specialized dictionaries for hyphenation and spell-checking. You can use more than one dictionary (up to ten) per publication, but additional dictionaries do slow down the composition and the spell-checker. (Spell-checking info is in 8.87–8.98; 8.106–8.126. Dictionary info is in 8.99–8.105. Hyphenation info is in 4.219–4.245.)

3.198 Use **"Options"** to control where columns and paragraphs break. Use it also to avoid widows and orphans (lines of a paragraph that straggle alone at the top or bottom of columns). See 3.211–3.229.

3.199 Use **"Rules..."** to place rules (or "lines," as they are called in the Element menu), at the top or bottom of a paragraph. This is a terrific feature. It takes a bit of time to learn to use properly, but I guarantee it's worth every minute of the effort. Section 6 is entirely devoted to paragraph Rules.

3.200 Use **"Spacing..."** to fine tune the space between letters, between words, and between lines (leading). This entire dialog box and its concepts are discussed in Section 4 on Spacing. You really should read it.

3.202 The "Paragraph specifications..." dialog box

"Paragraph space" Before and After is discussed in Section 4 on Spacing. See 3.195; 4.63–4.87.

Paragraph specifications

OK

See 3.194 — Indents:

Paragraph space:

Press Command Period to shortcut.

See 3.203 — Left `0` inches

Before `0` inches

Cancel

One of PageMaker's greatest features! See Section 6.

See 3.205; 3.207 — First `0` inches

After `0` inches

Rules...

See 3.204 — Right `0` inches

Spacing...

See 3.120. This dialog box is discussed in detail in Section 4 on Spacing.

See 3.209 — Alignment: `Right`

Dictionary: `US English`

See 3.197–3.210

See 3.211–3.215 — Options:

See 3.216 — ☐ Keep lines together ☐ Keep with next `0` lines

See 3.219

See 3.217 — ☐ Column break before ☐ Widow control `0` lines

See 3.222–3.229

See 3.218 — ☐ Page break before ☐ Orphan control `0` lines

See 3.222–3.229

☐ Include in table of contents

This automatically adds the paragraph to the Table of Contents list. See 3.220, as well as Section 13 on Book Publications; 13.28–13.32.

If you want to do this:	**Then follow these steps:**	**Shortcuts ▾ Notes ▾ Hints**

3.203 Indent a paragraph on the left
(To use the Indents/tabs ruler, also see 5.50; 5.71)

This paragraph has no indents. The text word wraps from one edge of the text block to the other.
    Now this paragraph has a **left indent** of .25—it is indented .25 inch from the left edge of the text block.

- With the **text tool,** select the paragraph(s) you want to indent (see 3.192–3.193 re: selecting paragraphs).
- From the Type menu, choose "Paragraph…" or press Command M.
- In the "Left" indent box, type a measurement for the indent. If "First" and "Right" are at 0, it will look similar to the example shown on the left, often called a "nested indent."

- **Indents** refer to how far the text is indented *from the edges of the text block*. They have nothing to do with column guides or margins or anything else—only text block edges as defined by the handles. See 5.49–5.53 for examples.
- These indents are all explained at great length in Section 5 on Indents and Tabs. There you will see examples of each indent, a Scenario using indents, and explanations on how to use them in combination with tabs to format your work most easily.
- The indent spacings you set here will be reflected in the Indents/Tabs ruler, and, conversely, any indents you set in the Indent/Tabs ruler will show up here.

3.204 Indent a paragraph on the right
To use the Indents/tabs ruler, also see 5.49; 5.72)

This paragraph has no indents. The text word wraps from one edge of the text block to the other.
Now this paragraph has a **right indent** of .5—it is indented .5 inch from the right edge of the text block.

- With the **text tool,** select the paragraph(s) you want to indent (see 3.192–3.193 re: selecting paragraphs).
- From the Type menu, choose "Paragraph…" or press Command M.
- In the "Right" indent box, type a measurement for the indent. If "Left" and "First" are at 0, it will look similar to the example shown on the left.

- An advantage to setting your indents in the Paragraph specs box, rather than in the Indents/Tabs ruler, is that you can enter a specific measurement, and even override the current measurement system being used (1.221). For instance, it is only here that you can get a *one-em indent* for paragraphs (3.207; which is what you really should be using if you're indenting first lines).
- Often, though, it is easier to use the Indents/Tabs ruler because you can actually see the physical width of indents.

If you want to do this:	**Then follow these steps:**	**Shortcuts ▾ Notes ▾ Hints**

3.205 Indent the first line of every paragraph
(To use the Indents/tabs ruler, also see 5.47; 5.51; 5.68)
 	
I put a .25-inch **first-line indent** in these paragraphs. The text word wraps between the left and right indents, which are at zero.
   Every time I hit a Return, the first line of the next paragraph automatically indents a quarter-inch.
   This is a terrific function. Use it.
	▪ With the **text tool,** select the paragraph(s) you want to indent (see 3.192–3.193 re: selecting paragraphs).
	▪ From the Type menu, choose "Paragraph..." or press Command M.
	▪ In the "First" indent box, type in a measurement. *This measurement will be added onto the "Left" indent,* since the first-line indent will indent itself *from the left indent, not from the edge of the text block* (e.g., if "Left" is .25 and "First" is .25, the indent will be actually .5 inch from the edge of the text block).
		▪ The "Left" and "Right" indents reference themselves from the left and right edges of the text block (5.46–5.53). "First," though, references itself from the "Left" indent. So then, the first-line indent can be to the left (a negative number) or to the right (a positive number) *of the left indent.* A negative number creates a hanging indent (as in 3.206), while a number larger than the left indent value creates a typical indent, as shown here in the first column.

3.206 Create a hanging indent *(To use the Indents/tabs ruler, also see 5.52; 5.69)* I put a .25-inch "Left" indent in these paragraphs so the text will word wrap at the right margin, then indent .25 inch on the left. I put a –.25-inch (that's a minus, or hyphen) indent in "First" so the first line will begin .25 inch to the *left* of the left indent. Remember that the first-line indent references itself from the *left indent,* *not* from the left edge of the text block.	▪ With the **text tool,** select the paragraph(s) you want to indent (see 3.192–3.193 re: selecting paragraphs). ▪ From the Type menu, choose "Paragraph..." or press Command M. ▪ Set a left indent by typing a number in "Left." That is where the text will align as it word wraps. ▪ In the "First" box, type in a *negative* number. That negative number can be no larger than the positive number in "Left" (that is, if the left indent is .25-inch, the first-line indent can be no more [less?] than –.25-inch).	▪ As noted in 3.205 above, a first-line indent to the *left* of the "Left" indent must be a *negative* number, since the first-line indent relates directly to the Left *indent,* not the left *margin* ("margin" as indicated by the edge of the text block).

If you want to do this:	**Then follow these steps:**	**Shortcuts ▾ Notes ▾ Hints**
3.207 Set a one-em indent for first lines	▪ *Before* you select the paragraph(s), know the point size of your text (to find out, with the **text tool,** double-click on a word, then from the Type menu check the "Size" pop-out menu). ▪ With the **text tool,** select the paragraph(s) you want to indent (see 3.192–3.193 re: selecting paragraphs). ▪ From the Type menu, choose "Paragraph..." or press Command M. ▪ In the "First" box, type a **0** (zero), then a **p**, then the point size of your type (e.g., **0p10**). There are variations of this, but this technique will work no matter what measurement system you are using and no matter what size your type is. If you change the size of your type, though, you will have to adjust this indent.	▪ Traditional typographic aesthetics long ago determined that a *one-em indent* is the most visually pleasing. An *em* is a typographic measure. When type was set with little pieces of metal, a typesetter would insert a little blank square of metal at the beginning of each paragraph. That little square was an *em* (also called a *mutton*). It is *approximately* the size of a capital letter M; it is *precisely* the size of the point size of the type. That is, if your type is 12 points, an em is 12 points wide. If your type is 36 points, an em is 36 points wide. Paragraphs that are indented more than an em space generally look awkward and clunky. Yes, an em space is much less than the five spaces or the half-inch we were taught to indent on a typewriter.
3.208 Set up paragraph indents *before* typing the paragraphs	▪ With the **text tool,** click to set the insertion point flashing anywhere except in another paragraph. ▪ From the Type menu, choose "Paragraph..." or press Command M. ▪ Type in the values for the First, Left, and Right indents; click OK. As long as you do not click the mouse anywhere else before typing, the insertion point is loaded with these specs, and they will be applied.	▪ If an insertion point is *not* flashing and if there is no text selected, then any specifications you set in the "Paragraph" dialog box will become the publication defaults (3.242–3.247).

If you want to do this: ■	Then follow these steps: ■	Shortcuts ▾ Notes ▾ Hints ■
3.209 Change the alignment of a paragraph	■ With the **text tool,** select the paragraph(s) you want to align (see 3.192–3.193 re: selecting paragraphs). ■ From the Type menu, choose "Paragraph...," *or* press Command M. ■ Press in the box next to "Alignment" to see the pop-up menu; choose the alignment.	■ I strongly suggest you read 3.153–3.158 for examples of each alignment and how each one affects readability. ■ As in 3.208, you can also load this function into the insertion point before you begin typing.
3.210 Change the dictionary, or add another one to check from Dictionary: ✓US English Deutsch Français Español Italiano UK English Svenska Dansk Norsk Nederlands Português Brazileiro	■ With the **text tool,** select the paragraph(s) you want to align (see 3.192–3.193 re: selecting paragraphs). ■ At any time, from the Type menu choose "Paragraph...," *or* press Command M. ■ Press in the box next to "Dictionary" to see the pop-up menu; choose the language.	■ Dictionaries are paragraph-specific; that is, the dictionary you choose applies only to the paragraphs you selected before you went to the dialog box. ■ The dictionary you choose here will be the one used in spell-checking that paragraph in the Story Editor (8.87–8.126). It is also used for guiding PageMaker in hyphenation (4.219–4.245). ■ You can use up to ten dictionaries per publication, although the more you use, the slower everything will become. ■ If the names of the dictionaries are gray, you do not have them installed. Only the US English dictionary comes with Page-Maker; if you want others, you must buy them separately. In addition to foreign language dictionaries, you can also get specialized dictionaries, such as medical or legal. ■ See 8.99–8.105 for more info.

The Paragraph dialog box "Options"

Options:

☐ Keep lines together ☐ Keep with next [0] lines
☐ Column break before ☐ Widow control [0] lines
☐ Page break before   ☐ Orphan control [0] lines
☐ Include in table of contents

3.211 The "Options" section of the Paragraph dialog box is something many people ignore because what it will achieve is not instantly clear, and if it is not instantly clear most of us don't have time to figure it out so we ignore it. So here are three pages of instant clarification. It's really quite simple.

3.212 These controls are often nicknamed "keeps," even though they are not all "keep" commands. All "keeps" are *paragraph specific;* that is, they will apply to the entire paragraph that is selected.

3.213 You set these paragraph controls and PageMaker tries to do what you say. But sometimes she can't. In the "Preferences" dialog box (1.210; 1.218) from the Edit menu, under "Show layout problems:" you can check "Keeps violations." Any line(s) where PageMaker has had to ignore your specs, you will see a gray bar (a yellow bar on a color monitor). That's just an indication to you that she had to think for herself, and it is your choice to leave it the way it is or to fix it manually. (The colored bar will not print.)

3.214 If your text starts to act funny, like jumps around on the page, or rolls itself up and refuses to budge, or appears and disappears as you type, there may be some paragraph option applied. To discover any applied options, don't select *all* of the paragraphs involved—select the suspects one at a time, then press Command M to get the dialog box. If you select more than one paragraph and they have different settings applied, PageMaker gets confused and will tell you that no options are applied at all.

What? You can't check the paragraph because the text block won't unroll? See 20.10.

3.215 If, however, you want to remove *all* paragraph keeps controls from selected paragraphs or the entire story, do this:

■ Press-and-drag to select the paragraphs you want to affect; **or** select the entire story: click once anywhere in the story with the **text tool;** then press Command A.
■ Press Command M to get the Paragraph dialog box.
■ Click in any "Options" checkbox to turn it on, then click in it again to turn it off (there should be no "X").
■ Click OK.

3.216 Keep lines together: When this option is checked, PageMaker will not break the lines of the selected paragraph into different columns, from page to page, or over text-wrapped graphics. This is an appropriate control for paragraphs of body text, but isn't really applicable to one-line paragraphs, such as headings (3.219).

"Options" —*continued*

3.217 Column break before: When you autoflow text, any paragraph with this option checked will jump to the next column, even if the next column is on the next page (and it will keep turning pages until it finds a blank column). If you are using manual or semi-autoflow, it will stop as usual and wait for you to place the rest of the text. If you apply this option to text you have already placed, paragraphs may disappear suddenly as they instantly go to find the top of a column.

It would not be a good idea to apply "Column break before" to the body text under a head, as it will leave the head stranded at the end of the previous column. It would make much more sense to apply it to the head itself. And it would be silly to bother applying this control to the first paragraph in a story.

3.218 Page break before: When you autoflow text, any paragraph you have applied this option to will jump to the next page, even if there is no next page (autoflow will create one). If you are using manual or semi-autoflow, the text will stop as usual and wait for you to place the rest. Even if you want to, PageMaker will not *allow* you to place a paragraph with this attribute on the same page as the paragraph before. If you try, it will just roll itself up and obstinately refuse to unroll until you move it to another page or to the pasteboard.

3.219 Keep with next ___ lines: This option enables you to keep the selected paragraph connected to the next 1, 2, or 3 lines of the following paragraph, which is great for making sure you don't have a headline stuck all by itself at the bottom of a column—at least it will have 1, 2, or 3 lines with it. If the 1, 2, or 3 lines won't fit at the end of the column with the head, the head will pop over to the next column to stay with its lines. If you want the head attached to the entire next paragraph, not just to a few lines, then also apply the "Keep lines together" (3.216) option to the paragraph *following* the head.

3.220 Include in table of contents: When you apply this to a selected paragraph, that entire paragraph will automatically be included when you create the publication's table of contents (see Section 13 on Book Publications; 13.28–13.32). If you have chapter heads, or perhaps subheads that you will be using to annotate the Contents page with, just add this to your head and subhead style sheets (Section 7).

3.221 Some of these controls are quite handy to add to your style sheets (Section 7). Look them over carefully; they can save quite a bit of time and trouble, like "Include in table of contents" for a style denoting chapter heads, or "Keep with next __ lines" for a subhead style.

"Options" and widows and orphans

3.222 There seems to be great puzzlement over the precise definition of a **widow** and of an **orphan.** Here is the low-down:

3.223 A **widow** is a very short last line of a paragraph, one that contains fewer than seven characters. The worst kind of widow is the last part of a hyphenated word, even if it is longer than seven characters. It's obnoxious.

Unfortunately, you see it all the time.

3.224 An **orphan** is the last line of a paragraph that is all by itself at the top of the next column, separated from the preceeding lines

of its paragraph.

Unfortunately, you see that all the time, too.

3.225 The widow and orphan controls in the "Paragraph specifications" dialog box are designed to control these bereft creatures.

3.226 Orphan control ___ lines: This works great. Type in a 1, a 2, or a 3. If you enter a 1, you are telling PageMaker never to let this paragraph leave one line alone at the top of a column (of a text block, actually)—you'll have at least two lines at the top. If you enter a 2, you'll have at least three lines; and if you enter a 3, you'll have at least four lines.

3.227 Widow control ___ lines: This does *not* mean that PageMaker will prevent leaving fewer than seven characters or a hyphenated word as the last line of a paragraph. Unfortunately, PageMaker has a bit of a mistaken notion of widows. She defines it as a small number of lines left at the bottom of a column, while the rest of the paragraph continues in the next text block.

3.228 You can type 1, 2, or 3 in the widow control box. If you type 1, PageMaker will not leave one lonely line from that paragraph at the bottom of the text block; the line will jump over to its mates in the following text block. If you type 2, PageMaker will not leave two lines; the two lines will jump over to the following text block. And I bet you can guess what will happen if you type 3.

There is no way in PageMaker to get rid of a real widow.

3.229 Now, it may or may not be obvious that if you "Keep lines together," exercising "Widow and/or Orphan control" in addition becomes redundant. If you do check them both, the entire paragraph will generally put itself at the top of the next text block.

Line breaks

3.230 The **line break** feature is a very small, yet very significant, addition to PageMaker. When you press Shift-Return, you cause the line of text to end, or *break,* but it does not start a new paragraph. Until you need it, this may not seem like much.

3.231 In almost every Macintosh program, every time you hit the Return key you are creating a new paragraph. A Return key makes what is called a "hard Return," meaning that when you edit the text, the line will always break at that point. This is opposed to a "soft Return," which is when the text automatically word-wraps at the margin edge. You can see the visual representation of each sort of Return character in the Story Editor (Section 8):

Soft·returns·show·no·visible·characters;· they·just·bump·into·the·edge·and·move·on.¶

A·hard·return·is·represented·by·the· paragraph·symbol,·as·it·shows·the·end·of· one·paragraph.¶

A·line·break,·which·creates·a·new·line· but·does·not·end·the·paragraph,·is· represented·by·a·right-pointing·arrow.↵

3.232 That hard Return character (¶) holds all the paragraph formatting. Whenever you hit a Return, that little Return character goes marching forward, bringing with it all the paragraph formatting to apply to the next paragraph. Paragraph formatting includes.

- Styles from the style sheet (Section 7), including whether to apply a "Next style" (7.27–7.31);
- Extra paragraph space before and/or after (4.63–4.87);
- First-line indent (5.47; 3.205–3.207);
- Paragraph rules (Section 6);
- Tabs and indents (Section 5);
- Hyphenation controls (4.219–4.237);
- Letter and word spacing specs (4.10);
- Alignment (3.153–3.158);
- Paragraph "Keeps" options (3.211–3.221).

3.233 This is where the **line break** comes in. By pressing Shift-Return, you can get a new line, *but you don't create a new paragraph* and all those things that come along with a new paragraph. In essence, if you press a Shift-Return you will get a new line that will **not**

- Apply a "Next style";
- Add any extra paragraph space before or after;
- Create a new first-line indent;
- Create any paragraph rules.

3.234 But the new line **will** keep the tabs and indents, the hyphenation controls, the letter and word spacing, the alignment, and the "Keeps" options—thus making it *appear* to be the same paragraph. And actually, PageMaker also sees it as the same paragraph (see 3.236).

3.235 A line break will not word wrap, though, so if you edit text that has line breaks, the sentences will retain the line endings.

- See the Scenario on the next page for instances of when to use the line break.

185

3.236　Scenario #4: Using the line break feature

Let's say you are typing a nice letter. You are very efficient: you choose your font and type specifications before you even begin to type. You put an extra 5 points of space between paragraphs. Now when you type the return address, every time you hit the Return key your lines are separated by those extra 5 points. Like this:

Ms. Scarlett Florence Williams

Toad Hall Annex

Santa Rosa, California 95404

But that's not what you want. So you retype it, this time using a Shift-Return at the end of each line instead of a Return. Now it looks like this:

Ms. Scarlett Florence Williams
Toad Hall Annex
Santa Rosa, California 95404

This also retains these three lines as one single paragraph! If you triple click with the text tool, all three lines will be selected.

Of course, you could just *replace* the Returns in your first address with Shift-Returns. Either backspace over the Returns and replace them with Shift-Returns, or use "Change" in the Story Editor (8.78).

Sometimes you may find a word that is hyphenated in a stupid place, as in the following paragraph:

For my part, I travel not to go an-ywhere, but to go. I travel for travel's sake. The great affair is to move.

Robert Louis Stevenson

So put your insertion point directly before the **a** in **an-** and press Shift-Return. The Shift-Return will just break the line without giving you the first-line indent. It also keeps the sentences as one entire paragraph.

For my part, I travel not to go anywhere, but to go. I travel for travel's sake. The great affair is to move.

Robert Louis Stevenson

Just to let you know, you could also type a discretionary hyphen (Command Hyphen) in front of the **a** *to prevent the word from hyphenating (4.224; 4.241).*

The Shift-Return line breaks can make it much easier to reformat columns of tabular material. At the end of each line, press Shift-Return instead of Return. This will retain all those separate lines as one paragraph. You can reformat all the rows of columns as easily as you reformat a single paragraph.

One➔　Two➔　Three◄┘
Einz.➔ Zwie➔　Drei◄┘
Un➔　Deux➔　Trois◄┘
Uno➔　Dos➔　Tres¶

Notice the right-pointing arrows (➔), indicating tabs. Notice the left-pointing arrows (◄┘), indicating Shift-Returns. Notice the paragraph symbol (¶), indicating the *end* of the one paragraph.

Special characters

3.237 Take advantage of the special characters the Macintosh keyboard provides to make your work look more professional.

3.238 In all of these keyboard sequences, **hold down** the Command key and/or Shift key and/or Option key while you press the other character.

3.239 The ellipsis (...) is a handy character, as it combines the three dots into one character and thus won't break at the end of a sentence (leaving you with one period at the end of one line and the other two on the line below). Professionally, though, typesetters still prefer a nicely-spaced ellipsis. You can create a nicely-spaced ellipsis that won't break by putting a non-breaking thin space (Command Shift T; see 4.215) between each period . . .

- Don't forget about the handy chart in Appendix E, located at the back of the book. It lists every special character currently available and how to type it.
- Also see Key Caps, 1.227–1.231. And be sure to read *The Mac is not a typewriter.*

3.240 To type a special character:

		Press these keys:
opening double quotation mark	"	Option [
closing double quotation mark	"	Option Shift [
opening single quotation mark	'	Option]
closing single quote mark; apostrophe	'	Option Shift]
en dash	–	Option hyphen
em dash	—	Option Shift hyphen
ellipsis	…	Option ;
bullet	•	Option 8
tiny bullet (a raised period)	·	Option Shift 9
copyright symbol	©	Option g
trademark symbol	™	Option 2
registered trademark symbol	®	Option r
degree symbol	°	Option Shift 8
cents symbol	¢	Option 4 *(the $, logically)*
fraction bar	/	Option Shift 1
ligature of f and i	fi	Option Shift 5
ligature of f and l	fl	Option Shift 6
inverted exclamation point	¡	Option 1 *(one, or !)*
inverted question mark	¿	Option Shift ?
monetary pound sign	£	Option 3 *(the #, or pound, sign)*
cedilla, lowercase	ç	Option c
cedilla, uppercase	Ç	Option Shift C

If you want to do this:

3.241   Accent marks

Then follow these steps:

- Find the key combination that will create the accent mark—either check the list below, the chart in Appendix F, or look in Key Caps (1.227–1.231).
- Type the word *up to* the letter that goes under the accent mark.
- Type the key combination that will produce the accent mark—*you did it right if nothing shows up on the page!* If you see the accent mark at this point, delete the word and start over.
- Now type the letter that is to be under the accent mark—*they will show up together;* type the rest of the word as usual.
  □ Example: to type **résumé:**
  - Type **r** .
  - Press **Option e.**
  - Type **e** .
  - Type the rest of the word (**sum**), and repeat the accent mark over the last letter **e**; you should see **résumé.**

  ´   Option e
  `   Option ~ (upper left or next to the spacebar)
  ¨   Option u
  ~   Option n
  ^   Option i

Shortcuts ▾ Notes ▾ Hints

- Now you have no excuse, as you did on a typewriter, not to take advantage of accent marks. If a word is supposed to have one, then use it.

Type specification defaults

3.242 When you type directly into PageMaker (but not into some text already on the page), the font specifications that show up are the ones that have been set as the **defaults;** that is, *there has to be* some sort of specifications, and if *you* don't *choose* what they are to be, you get the defaults.

3.243 In addition to the font itself, you can set the text to default to a different alignment, reverse type (be careful!), specific tabs and indents, autoflow or not, extra paragraph spacing, dictionary choices, "keeps" options, etc.—anything to do with the text can be set as a default, so every time you type you get those particular specifications.

3.244 See 1.6–1.16 for a list of the specifications that can be set as defaults, and for more detailed info. Basically, anything you see that is not gray when the pointer tool is selected can be set as a default.

3.245 Don't forget—text wrapping can also be set as a default (11.43); everything you draw, place, or paste in PageMaker as a graphic will then come in with a boundary around it. This can be very frustrating.

Life
is
uncertain.
Eat
dessert
first.
Christian
Nelson

If you want to do this:	**Then follow these steps:**	**Shortcuts ▾ Notes ▾ Hints**
3.246 Set the default type specifications for the entire PageMaker application	• Open PageMaker from the icon on the Desktop; **or** if PageMaker is already open, close any publication that may be on the screen. You should be looking at a *blank* screen with the PageMaker menu bar. • With the **pointer tool** that is available, from the Type menu choose the font, size, leading, and style of your choice (or choose "Type specs..." and make your choices there). (See 3.123–3.170 for info on setting specifications.)	• Any text specifications you choose while in PageMaker, *but with no publication open* (just the blank PageMaker screen), will be the new *application* defaults. Every publication you open from then on will *default to,* or automatically set you up with those specifications. • New application defaults do not affect any previously-created documents.
3.247 Set the default type specifications for the publication you are in	• At any point while the publication is open, choose the **pointer tool.** • From the Type menu choose the font, size, leading, and style of your choice (or choose "Type specs..." and make your choices there). (See 3.123–3.170 for info on setting specifications.)	• Any text specifications you choose with the **pointer tool** (with nothing whatsoever selected) *while a publication is open* will be the *publication* defaults. Just while you are in that publication, those are the specifications to which it will automatically revert. • Publication defaults do not affect any other document, whether previously created or yet to be created.

Containing better Instructions
than any which have yet appeared
on the Proper Handling
of those intimidating and mysterious
Spacing dialog boxes

4 ▾ TEXT SPACING

4.1   Minimums and maximums:

Item	Minimum	Maximum
Leading	0 pt.	1300 pt.
(tenth-point increments; .1)		
Autoleading	0%	200%
Para. space	0 pt.	1300 pt.
(tenth-point increments; .1)		
Word space	0%	500%
(1% increments)		
Letter space	-200%	+200%
(1% increments)		
Kerning	$\frac{1}{25}$th units	$\frac{1}{100}$th units
(.04 of an em)		(.01 of an em)
Set width	5%	250%
(.1% increments)		
Hyphenation zone	0	12 picas (2 inches)
(.1 increments)		
Number of consec. hyphens	1	255 or "No limit"
Word added to user dictionary	1	31 characters

4.2   PageMaker allows you to control practically *everything*. Now, you don't *have* to be in control—the default (automatic) settings for spacing are quite good for the average advertisement, flyer, or invitation. In fact, you could live a long time, never read this chapter, and never notice the lack of it in your life. If learning PageMaker itself is overwhelming you, *don't* read this yet. You'll get along fine for a long while. But when you're ready to really tap into the fine tuning, come back and study this section.

4.3   You'll know it's time to take control of spacing when you find yourself thinking, "Hmm . . . that's really too much space between those paragraphs," or "I wish I could tighten up that headline," or "I sure would like to set this copy with lots of white space between the letters and the lines." Understanding and using the spacing controls not only will make you a happier, more powerful person, but also will give your work a more professional appearance.

4.4   Even though I present each aspect of spacing in its own little subsection here, all aspects interweave. The leading affects the paragraph spacing, the letter spacing affects the word spacing, the kerning affects the tracking, the tracking affects the letter spacing, and on and on. It's a lot to grasp. Take it one space at a time.

4.5 What's the difference?

Leading is the space between every line of type, usually measured in points.

Paragraph spacing is the extra space that you can add between paragraphs, instead of a full line space.

Word spacing is the amount of space between words. **Letter spacing** is the amount of space between letters. Both are measured relative to the ideal spacing built into the characters by the font designer. Both apply to entire paragaraphs, and are typically used over a range of text, often for special effects

Auto kerning is an automatic adjustment to the letterspacing over a range of text, based on built-in font specifications. **Manual kerning** is the fine-tuning adjustment you apply between two characters, typically in display type (large type), to obtain visually-consistent letterspacing.

Tracking is an adjustment that automatically increases *or* decreases the letter and word space, based on the built-in kerning pairs and depending on the point size of the type. Tracking applies only to the selected characters.

Set width condenses or expands the type. It is not a spacing function, although it does affect the other spacing attributes.

Points and picas

4.6   Type size, leading, and paragraph space are measured in points. In case you are not clear on what **points** and **picas** are, here is the low-down:

A **pica** is the unit of measure used in typesetting, instead of inches. There are **6 picas per inch.**

Each pica is divided into **12 points.** Thus 72 points equal 1 inch.*

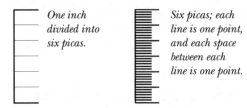

One inch divided into six picas.

Six picas; each line is one point, and each space between each line is one point.

4.7   Once you get beyond the basics in PageMaker, you will usually find it easier to set your measurement system to picas (4.9). If you still want to cling to inches, it's possible to leave your measurement system in inches, but set your vertical ruler in points and picas (or go all the way and customize the vertical ruler; 1.213).

** For those of you versed in traditional typography, 72 points do equal **exactly** one inch, not .996/inch, because the Macintosh screen is 72 dots per inch.*

Measurement system

Preferences

Layout view:

Measurement system: [**Picas**]

Vertical ruler: [**Picas**]

4.8   In all the dialog boxes that deal with spacing attributes, it is easier to work with points and picas, since that is what most of the spacing functions are based on.

4.9   To change your measurement system to picas, from the Edit menu, choose "Preferences...."

Next to "Measurement system," press on the submenu and choose "Picas." (This will affect all dialog boxes that have measurements in them, as well as the page rulers and the indents and tabs ruler.)

Next to "Vertical ruler," press on the submenu and choose "Picas." (This will affect just the vertical page ruler; see 1.212).

Click OK.

4.10 "Spacing attributes" dialog box *(from the Type menu, choose "Paragraph..."; click on the "Spacing..." button)*

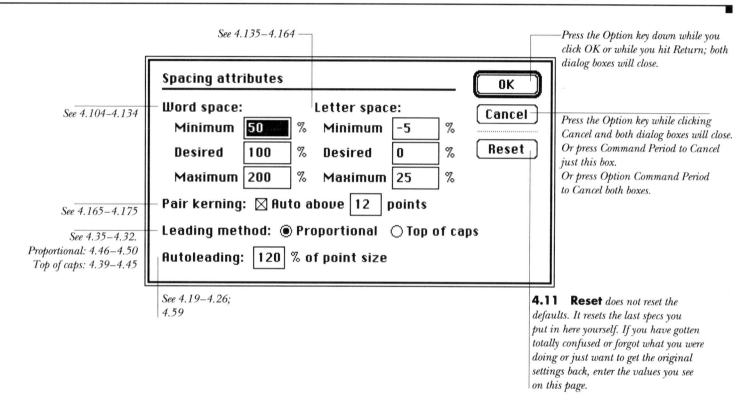

See 4.135–4.164

See 4.104–4.134

See 4.165–4.175

See 4.35–4.32.
Proportional: 4.46–4.50
Top of caps: 4.39–4.45

See 4.19–4.26;
4.59

Spacing attributes

Word space:
Minimum [50] %
Desired [100] %
Maximum [200] %

Letter space:
Minimum [-5] %
Desired [0] %
Maximum [25] %

Pair kerning: ☒ **Auto above** [12] **points**

Leading method: ◉ **Proportional**   ○ **Top of caps**

Autoleading: [120] **% of point size**

[OK]
[Cancel]
[Reset]

Press the Option key down while you click OK or while you hit Return; both dialog boxes will close.

Press the Option key while clicking Cancel and both dialog boxes will close. Or press Command Period to Cancel just this box. Or press Option Command Period to Cancel both boxes.

4.11   **Reset** *does not reset the defaults. It resets the last specs you put in here yourself. If you have gotten totally confused or forgot what you were doing or just want to get the original settings back, enter the values you see on this page.*

Leading

(pronounced 'ledding')

4.12   It is very important to understand the concept of **leading**—what it is, what it is doing, and how it is figured, in order to understand how to manipulate it aesthetically and sensibly and without going insane. It is easier to understand the *concept* if you understand its *physical origin*.

4.13   The term **leading** is a holdover from the days when all type was cast in metal. Literally, every single letter, space, and punctuation mark was on a separate piece of metal (guess what kind of metal they used). And they had to make a complete set of metal characters for each point size of type. The typesetter lined up all these tiny lead letters and spaces in little rows. Then, between each row of type, he inserted a thin strip of **lead** to separate them. Leading, therefore, is a term referring to the space between the lines of type.

4.14   Type has been measured in points (4.6) for a long time. Leading (the strip of lead), is also measured in points. If the typesetter wanted an extra 4 points of space between the lines of type, he inserted a thin strip of lead that was 4 points thick. That's easy enough, right? Now here's where you have to start paying attention, because it directly relates to what you have to work with in PageMaker's menu.

4.15   The typesetter would get out the case of 12-point letters to set a small booklet. He set the lines of 12-point type, and between the lines he put thin strips of lead that were 2 points thick. Now, you would think that he would call that a 2-point leading, right? Wrong.

4.16   **The size of the leading is added onto the point size of the type, and we call the leading (in this example) 14 point.** That's why you don't see 2 or 3 or 4 points of leading listed in the leading submenu in PageMaker. *What you see are the leading values that have been added together with the point size of the type you are working with.*

4.17   If you have 18-point type with an extra 4 points of space between the lines, you have a leading of 22 (written 18/22; spoken 18 on 22). If you have 30-point type with no extra space between the lines, you have a leading of 0, which we call *set solid* (30/30).

4.18   Today we can go even further with leading than the metal typesetters were able to—we can have *negative* leading. We can have 30-point type with a leading of 26 (30/26), which is −4, right? (Which is why, at this point in time, *leading* should really be called *linespace*.)

Auto leading

4.19 As with most things in life, leading has a standard from which we can deviate. **The standard value for leading is 20 percent of the point size of the type.** For instance, if you are using 10-point type, the standard leading value you would use is 12 point (20 percent of 10, added to the 10, equals 12).

4.20 PageMaker's standard value for automatic leading is 120 percent (which gives the same results as *adding* 20 percent). So when you see a leading value of **Auto** in any dialog box or menu, that Auto means 120 percent of the point size of your type, rounded off to the nearest tenth (.1).

4.21 An easy way to figure out the Auto leading is to pull down your calculator from the Apple menu and multiply the point size of the type by 1.2. The result is the leading value PageMaker has applied to your text. (I do wish she would just tell me the number, instead of making me figure it.)

4.22 *The 120 percent default autoleading value can be changed to suit your need for more or less auto-linespace (4.59). It is paragraph specific, meaning it will only apply to the paragraphs you select.*

Auto leading applied

4.23 Whenever the leading applied in a paragraph is Auto, *the space between the lines will adapt to any larger point sizes introduced into a line.* The characters with the largest amount of Auto leading take over the whole line. For instance, if the paragraph is 9-point type with Auto leading, and you insert an 18-point capital at the beginning of the paragraph, the leading on that entire first line will increase to the Auto specifications for 18 point. It will look like this:

I n the time of your life, live . . . so that in that wondrous time you shall not add to the misery and sorrow of the world, but smile to the infinite delight and mystery of it.

—*William Saroyan*

4.24 Does that awkward line space look familiar? With Auto leading applied, Page-Maker will take the Auto leading of the largest character on the line and apply it to the entire line.

Fixed leading

4.25 The solution to what you see in 4.23 is to use **proportional** (see 4.46–4.51) and **fixed leading.** Fixed leading is any leading amount that you *choose,* either from the Leading submenu or by typing in a value in a dialog box, *as long as it is not the word "Auto."* Even if you type in the exact amount that Page-Maker is already using for Auto, the fixed amount you enter does not adapt. It stays fixed.

4.26 Using the same example as in 4.23, I selected the entire paragraph (shown below) and changed the leading to 10.8, which is the exact amount PageMaker was automatically applying through "Auto" for the 9-point type (9 x 1.2). But by typing in the value, I *fixed* the leading amount. Then, when I changed the first letter to 18 point, it stayed fixed (see below). It doesn't matter whether you fix the leading *before* or *after* you change the type size.

I n the time of your life, live . . . so that in that wondrous time you shall not add to the misery and sorrow of the world, but smile to the infinite delight and mystery of it.

—*William Saroyan*

p.s. Not even fixed leading will help text using the "Top of caps" leading method (4.35–4.45).

Selecting text to change the leading

4.27 There is one important trick to remember when selecting the text whose leading you want to change: *you must select the entire line,* not just the characters that are visible. It is entirely possible (and happens all the time) that any leftover blank spaces have a different leading value or a larger point size. It is not so much a problem when you are *increasing* the leading, as PageMaker will apply the larger value. But if you try to *decrease* the leading, you will run into problems.

4.28 Here is an example. I wanted to decrease the linespace in this two-line headline, set at 12 point with Auto leading.

Never take anything too seriously.

At first, not knowing better, I selected the *characters* in the first line, ignoring the spaces at the end. ────────────

Never take anything too seriously.

When I changed the leading to 6 point (yes, that is radical leading), nothing happened! That's because those blank spaces after the word *anything* are also 12 point with Auto leading, just like the visible characters. Since PageMaker applies the largest leading value *to the entire line,* that larger Auto leading holds the linespace intact.

4.29 So I got more intelligent. This time I selected the entire line of text, all the way to the right margin. (The easiest way to select the entire line is to position the insertion point just before the first character in the line, and then drag *straight down* just a bit. Really. Try it. ────────────

Never take anything too seriously.

This time when I changed the leading of the first line to 6 point, it closed up the line space.

Never take anything too seriously.

4.30 When you want to change the leading of an entire *paragraph,* it's safest to triple-click on it (with the text tool), rather than press-and-drag. That way you are guaranteed that everything will be selected.

4.31 A quick way to select more paragraphs in addition to the first one is to hold down the Command and the Shift keys and press the Up or DownArrow.

Slugs

4.32   Leading values determine the size of the **slug** of type. When you press-and-drag over a line of type, what you see highlighted is the slug.

This slug shows 10-point type with Auto leading:

Dancing is a celebration of Life.

This slug shows 10-point type with a leading value of 20:

Dancing is a celebration of Life.

(Both of these slug examples are using the proportional leading method.)

4.33   If you find this fascinating and really want to read more about slugs, check out 6.14–6.18.

The leading submenu

4.34   This is just a tiny little tip regarding the "Leading" submenu in the Type menu. Since the leading depends on the size of the type, you first need to know what size the type is in order to manipulate the leading. Well, Aldus added this thoughtful little touch:

When you choose the "Leading" submenu, you are usually* offered a list of possible leading values, depending on the point size of the text that is selected. One of those numbers is in bold type—that number indicates the point size of the selected text. Isn't that nice?

Leading ▶	Other…
	✓Auto ⇧⌘A
	9
	9.5
	10
	10.5
	11
	11.5
	12
	15
	20
	30

* *If you only get the options for Other and Auto in this submenu, it is because the selected text has more than one leading value applied to it.*

Leading methods

4.35   PageMaker offers two ways to work with leading; one is inept and the other is a little better. If you have worked with traditional typesetting and the baseline-to-baseline method, you may find PageMaker's methods a little irritating at first. If you have never worked with traditional typesetting, as soon as you get comfortable with Page-Maker's version, Aldus will probably switch over to the baseline-to-baseline method and you'll have to figure it out all over again.

4.36   The inept method is called **Top of caps.** Earlier versions of PageMaker (before 3.0) used this method, and it is included in 4.0 mainly to be compatible with documents prepared in those earlier versions. Generally, you won't use "Top of caps" (see 4.44 for an instant clue why not). It does have *one* great use, though (4.45).

4.37   The other method is **Proportional.** This is much easier to deal with, and when you understand what it is doing and how to manipulate it, you can actually predict the results accurately.

4.38   The following pages explain the two methods in great detail. You can switch from one method to the other per paragraph. See 4.55; 4.56.

"Top of caps" leading and examples

4.39 **Top of caps** leading is a holdover from earlier versions of PageMaker. In this method, the slug (4.32–4.33) extends down from the top of the tallest *ascender* on the line. Now, that needs some explanation.

4.40 An *ascender* is the part of a letter that extends above the height of the letter **x.** The letters h, f, and b each have an ascender. *Ascenders are sometimes taller than the capital letters of the same font,* as in the example in 4.43. (So I don't know why they call it "Top of *caps*," when really the slug begins at the top of the *ascender*.)

4.41 Even if there is no letter with an ascender on that line, the slug begins where the ascender would be if it *were* there. If you have more than one point size of type on a line, the slug will begin at the top of the tallest ascender that *would* be there from the largest point size of type. (Now, remember, blank spaces also have sizes; 4.27–4.28.)

4.42 Because the leading slug begins at the ascender height and drops down from there, it is difficult to make the space between lines consistent if there are varying point sizes in a line. In fact, it is so inept that you will very rarely want to use it (4.44).

4.43 Here are a few examples of slugs indicating the leading values, using the "Top of caps" method. Notice how the slug stays in place along the top of the ascenders, and only the space *below* the line adjusts. (When you see a number like 10/12, it's pronounced "ten on twelve." The first number indicates the point size of the type; the second number indicates the leading.)

10/Auto When in doubt, don't.

10/20 When in doubt, don't.

10/6 When in doubt, don't.

4.44 Here is an example of a paragraph using "Top of caps" leading method. The text is 10/12 (fixed leading; 4.25). In the fourth line is a bullet •. This bullet is 14 point. Even with fixed leading, that line has a slug reaching from the top of the ascender that *would* be there in that 14-point type. So it takes the 12 points of fixed leading and puts most of it above the type, with very little left for the linespace below. Then the line below moves its slug up to meet the one above. This is very difficult, and sometimes impossible, to correct.

4.45 Although you are able to control *proportional* leading (4.46–4.51) more accurately than "Top of caps," there is one particular instance where "Top of caps" will help you retain your sanity.

You may have run across the problem of trying to change the amount of space between two or three lines in a headline. Using the default *proportional* leading, when you change the leading with the intent to bring the second line up closer to the first, you find that the first line also moves up, away from the second. That can be very irritating (below, and 4.51).

But if you apply the "Top of caps" method to the paragraph, the first line stays right in place when you change the leading, and the second line will move up to meet it.

10/Auto **PERFECT** IS GOOD ENOUGH

10/6 *Top of caps leading; second line moved up.* **PERFECT** IS GOOD ENOUGH

10/6 *Proportional leading; first **and** second line moved up.* **PERFECT** IS GOOD ENOUGH

"Proportional" leading and examples

4.46 When you use the **proportional** leading method, PageMaker divides the leading value into thirds. She places ⅔ of that value *above* the baseline, and ⅓ *below* the baseline. Like so:

Isn't this the most beautiful Q you've ever seen?

baseline

4.47 The example above is 36-point type on 36-point leading. The slug (4.32) is exactly 36 points deep; 24 points of it (⅔) are *above* the baseline, and 12 points of it (⅓) are *below* the baseline.

If the leading for the same example were 30, then 20 points of it would be placed above the baseline and 10 points below. The characters, of course, sit directly on the baseline at all times.

4.48 This is very consistent. In proportional leading, the leading slug arranges itself around the baseline. The slug of the largest leading value will take over, and any smaller type will just sit on the larger type's baseline.

4.49 This does present one problem. When you change the leading of a line, it does not just change the space *below* the line; it changes the space *above*, as well. Which means if you adjust the leading between two lines of a headline, both lines may move out of position, up or down. It can be very frustrating.

4.50 The examples below show how proportional leading can affect the same two lines so differently, depending on where you apply it.

Every home should have a stage and a dance floor

4.51 *This control headline is set with 10 point type and Auto leading (10/Auto). In the following examples, notice how the different leading values affect the text, depending on whether you change the first line, the second line, or both lines (the lower guideline through the examples is where the original text block ended). The discrepancy is because proportional leading applies the leading value to* **both** *the space* **above** *the baseline, as well as* **below** *the baseline.*

Every home should have a stage and a dance floor

a) *First line:* 10/18
Second line: 10/Auto

Every home should have a stage and a dance floor

b) *First line:* 10/Auto
Second line: 10/18

Every home should have a stage and a dance floor

c) *First line:* 10/18
Second line: 10/18

Every home should have a stage and a dance floor

d) *First line:* 10/8
Second line: 10/Auto

Every home should have a stage and a dance floor

e) *First line:* 10/Auto
Second line: 10/8

Every home should have a stage and a dance floor

f) *First line:* 10/8
Second line: 10/8

If you want to do this:

Then follow these steps:

Shortcuts ▾ Notes ▾ Hints

4.52 Figure out the actual value of "Auto" leading in a line of text

- With the **text tool,** double-click on a word.
- You need to know the point size of the type. From the Type menu, choose "Size" and see where the checkmark is. If the checkmark is next to "Other...," then slide over and see what it is; click Cancel.
- From the Apple menu, choose "Calculator." Multiply the point size of the type by 1.2. The answer, rounded off to the tenth point (.1), is the actual leading value.
- Put the calculator away by clicking in its close box (upper left).

- I sure wish PageMaker would just tell me a number instead of using the mysterious "Auto."
- If there is no checkmark next to any number, and the "Other..." box is blank, there is more than one point size in the text you have selected.

4.53 Figure out the current leading value of the selected text

- With the **text tool,** select the text you want to check.
- From the Type menu, choose "Leading."
  - ☐ If there is a number checked, that is the current leading value.
  - ☐ If "Other..." is checked, choose it to see the value; click Cancel.
  - ☐ If "Auto" is checked, follow the steps in 4.52 to find the value.
  - ☐ If the menu only shows "Other..." and "Auto," with no check next to either of them, *or* if it shows the complete list, but with nothing checked, there is more than one leading value in the selected text. You need to select a smaller portion of text to check.

- You can just click the insertion point in any text or blank space to check the leading at that spot. If you think there may be varying amounts of leading in the text, press-and-drag to select and confirm it.
- If the menu indicates that you have more than one leading value selected, select a smaller portion of text. If necessary, check separately to see what the other values are.
- If you type a value into the "Leading" edit box in "Type specs" or into "Other..." in the submenu at this point, you will change the leading of the *selected* text.

If you want to do this:	**Then follow these steps:**	**Shortcuts ▾ Notes ▾ Hints**
4.54 Increase or decrease the leading	■ With the **text tool,** select the entire line(s) you want to affect. ■ You must first know the *current* leading value. Follow the steps in 4.53. ■ From the Type menu, choose "Leading," then choose the number you want; **or** choose "Other..." and type in a leading value; click OK. **Or** choose "Type specs...," then press Tab (just a shortcut to the Leading edit box) and enter a leading value; click OK.	■ The higher the leading number, the greater the line space. You can apply leading from 0 to 1300 points, in tenth-point increments (.1). Don't type a comma in the number.
4.55 Use the *proportional* leading method (4.46–4.51) Leading method: ◉ Proportional ○ Top of caps	■ With the **text tool,** select the paragraph(s) you want to affect. ■ From the Type menu, choose "Paragraph specs...." ■ Click in the "Spacing..." button. ■ Click the "Proportional" button. ■ Click OK twice, *or* press Option Return.	■ "Proportional" leading is *paragraph-specific,* meaning that it will apply *to the entire paragraph* that has the insertion point in it, or to all paragraphs that have been highlighted (selected) with the text tool.
4.56 Use the *top of caps* leading method (4.39–4.45) Leading method: ○ Proportional ◉ Top of caps	■ With the **text tool,** select the paragraph(s) you want to affect. ■ From the Type menu, choose "Paragraph specs...." ■ Click in the "Spacing..." button. ■ Click the "Top of caps" button. ■ Click OK twice, *or* press Option Return.	■ "Top of caps" leading is *paragraph-specific,* just like "Proportional," as mentioned in the paragraph above. ■ The default method is *proportional.* Of course, if you like to create obstacles in your path just for the thrill of overcoming them, or if there is someone in your office you really don't like, set the application default to "Top of caps."

If you want to do this:	Then follow these steps:	Shortcuts ▾ Notes ▾ Hints
4.57 Adjust the leading of a paragraph so it is consistent	■ If you already know the leading value you want the entire paragraph to have, skip the next step. ■ If you want to match the inconsistent lines with the rest of the lines, then with the **text tool** double-click on a word that seems to hold the leading value you want. Follow the steps in 4.53 to discover its actual value. ■ Then, with the **text tool,** triple-click to select the entire paragraph. ■ From the Type menu, choose "Leading," then choose a number; **or** choose "Other..." and type in a value; click OK; **Or** from the Type menu, choose "Type specs...," then press Tab and type in the leading value for the entire paragraph; click OK.	■ This is a common procedure that you will need to follow whenever you increase the size of a character within a paragraph (see 4.23–4.26). ■ Pressing the Tab key in this step is only to select the Leading edit box. You could, of course, just double-click in the box.

If you want to do this:	Then follow these steps:	Shortcuts ▾ Notes ▾ Hints
4.58 Adjust the leading above the last line of a paragraph of body text	▪ Occasionally you will have a paragraph that seems to have more linespace above the last line than there is above the rest of the lines, yet the entire paragraph has the same leading value. ▪ With the **text tool,** set your insertion point directly after the last character in the paragraph. ▪ Hit a Return. This will bump the last line up to match the rest of the linespacing. ▪ If you have too much space between paragraphs now, hit the DownArrow key once, then press the Backspace/Delete key to remove the extra line you just inserted. **Or,** with the **text tool,** just double-click on the blank line and delete it.	▪ Make sure the paragraph is using the proportional leading method (4.55). ▪ Hitting the DownArrow key is meant to place the insertion point directly *in front of the first character* on the next line. Check to make sure that's where it is before you Backspace/Delete.
4.59 Change the Auto leading value **Autoleading: 120 % of point size**	▪ Read the notes to the right. ➡ ▪ From the Type menu, choose "Paragraph...," *or* press Command M. ▪ Click the "Spacing..." button. ▪ Double-click in the edit box next to "Autoleading." ▪ Enter a value between 0% and 200%, in 1% increments. ▪ Click OK.	▪ If the *insertion point* is flashing, you will set the auto leading for *that* paragraph. ▪ If there is any amount of *text selected,* you will set the auto leading for the *paragraphs* that contain the selected text. ▪ If you follow these steps when the *pointer tool* is selected, you will set a publication default (1.6–1.11). ▪ Include this spec in your style sheet (Section 7) for paragraphs that you always want with loose (extra) or tight (less) leading.

If you want to do this:	**Then follow these steps:**	**Shortcuts ▾ Notes ▾ Hints**

4.60 You want to change the leading, but it won't change

- If you are changing the leading of one line, make sure you select the *entire line,* including any white space at the end, before you change the leading value. You must highlight the line *clear to the end of the text block,* even if you have indents set (4.28–4.29).
- If you are changing the leading of a *paragraph,* make sure you select the *entire paragraph,* including any white space at the end, before you change the leading value. The most efficient method is to triple-click on the paragraph with the **text tool.**
- If you selected the text properly and it still doesn't change, check these: With the text selected, press Command M to get the Paragraph dialog box.
  - □ Any numbers in the "Before" or "After" edit box can affect your leading. Change them to zeros, if necessary.
  - □ Any "Options" applied don't really affect your leading, but they can make your type act very strange (3.214).
  - □ Click on the button "Rules...." Any rules applied to a paragraph affect the visible linespace.
  - □ While in the "Rules" dialog box, click on the button "Options...." A checkmark next to "Align to grid" will affect your leading. Deselect it, if necessary.

- Make sure your leading method is "Proportional" (4.55). Using "Top of caps" can really mess you up (4.44; 4.56).
- Sometimes the leading is really doing just what you told it, but you are *expecting* something else. Be sure to read 4.46–4.51 for examples of how proportional leading will affect the lines.

- If either the "Before" or "After" edit boxes in the Paragraph dialog box are *blank* (that is, they don't even have *zeros* in them), the paragraphs you have selected have *some* amount of space applied before or after, but the amounts differ in the different paragraphs. If you type a zero (or any other value) into either box, you will change the amount for all selected paragraphs.

If you want to do this:	**Then follow these steps:**	**Shortcuts ▾ Notes ▾ Hints**
4.61 Make the letters reappear after you decrease the leading H E L P — *The letters couldn't fit on the leading slug anymore.* H E L P — *Just redraw the screen*	▪ With the **pointer tool,** click once on the text block. ▪ From the Edit menu, choose "Bring to front," *or* press Command F. **Or** with any tool, select a new page view from the Page menu, or even select the same view. **Or** click in the zoom box with any tool you happen to have (the zoom box is the tiny little box way up in the upper right corner of the window: ⊡).	▪ Parts of the characters disappear because they are either out of the text block or hidden under the white space of the leading. No matter why, it is easy to make the character parts reappear. ▪ Actually, the letters will reappear whenever the screen is redrawn, as when the view is resized or scrolled across. These are just a couple of methods for redrawing the screen. ▪ Even if parts of the characters are missing on the screen, they will print.
4.62 Adjust the leading on an inline graphic so it doesn't make the linespace inconsistent	▪ With the **text tool,** click to set the insertion point on either side of the inline graphic. ▪ From the Type menu, choose "Paragraph...." ▪ Click on the button "Rules..."; then click on the button "Options...." ▪ Click on the checkbox "Align to grid." ▪ Next to "Grid size," type in the leading value of the text you are working with. ▪ Press Option Return to close all the boxes.	▪ Inline graphics are discussed in great detail in Section 9 on Graphics; the segment on this page is just meant for quick reference. ▪ For a full explanation of the purpose of "Align to grid" and what it is doing here, please see 4.89–4.101. ▪ Shortcut: typing in a value or selecting one from the submenu will automatically put a checkmark next to "Align to grid."

Paragraph spacing

(from the Type menu, choose "Paragraph...," or press Command M)

4.63 The **paragraph spacing** feature is terrific. On a typewriter, when we wanted extra space between paragraphs, we hit the carriage return twice. That was our only option. You may have noticed that now, with the professional-level type you are creating, those double spaces look a bit large and clunky. PageMaker provides you with the option of putting as much or as little space as you want between your paragraphs *automatically*, with just *one* press of the Return key.

4.64 The amount of space between paragraphs is determined in the "Paragraph specifications" dialog box ("Paragraph..." from the Type menu, or Command M). The only part of that confusing dialog box you need to be concerned with here is the "Paragraph space" section.

Paragraph specifications		OK
Indents:	Paragraph space:	Cancel
Left 0 picas	Before 0 picas	
First 0 picas	After 0p5 picas	Rules...
Right 0 picas		Spacing...
Alignment: Left	Dictionary: US English	
Options:		
☐ Keep lines together	☐ Keep with next 0 lines	
☐ Column break before	☐ Widow control 0 lines	
☐ Page break before	☐ Orphan control 0 lines	
☐ Include in table of contents		

4.65 Let's start with the paragraph space **After,** as it's easier to understand. For the text you are working on, decide how much extra space you want between the paragraphs. A general rule is to add about half a line's worth of extra space. For instance, if you are working with 12 point type, the Auto leading is 14.5 points (4.20). If you pressed a Return key twice, you would have a blank line of 14.4 points between the paragraphs. You want only half of that; you want a line space of about 6 or 7 points.

4.66 So *instead* of pressing the Return key twice, go to the "Paragraph space" dialog box and enter **0p6** (that's a zero, the letter p for picas, and the number of points you want; see 4.78) into the "After" edit box.

4.67 Every time you hit a Return, PageMaker thinks you just finished one paragraph and are about to start a new one. Once you have entered a number into the "After" box, you get those extra points of space *after* each paragraph.

4.68 The paragraph space **Before** is very similiar to "After," but *Before* inserts the extra points of space *above* the next line of type.

4.69 A classic case for applying extra space before is in a subhead. Typically a subhead follows several paragraphs of body copy, right? The body copy usually has extra space between its paragraphs. But after the last paragraph, you want even a little *more* space. You don't want to have to put extra space after that last paragraph every time you come to a subhead, do you? No. So you put extra space *before* the subhead. (See 4.76, as well as 4.83, Scenario 5).

4.70 Paragraph space before and after should be a natural part of your style sheets (Section 7). The example in 4.69 above would be a perfect situation in which to set up a style for body text with its extra space "After," and another style for the subhead with its extra space "Before."

4.71 A paragraph can certainly have space "After," in addition to any space "Before," which would be particularly appropriate for the subhead we were just talking about. It would *not* be appropriate for paragraphs of body text, though; see 4.72–4.76 for an important message.

An Important Note

4.72 *Paragraph space before, paragraph space after, and leading are cumulative.* That is, any values you enter into the "Before" and/or "After" edit boxes are added onto the literal leading value.

4.73 Let me explain. If your text is 12 point and you have 15-point leading, you actually (literally) have 3 extra points of space between the lines, right? (See 4.12–4.18). If you add an extra 5 points of space "After," the 5 points *are added onto the 3 points* that naturally come with the lines of text; you really have 8 points of space between the paragraphs (3 + 5).

4.74 So your paragraph has 3 literal points of leading and an extra 5 points of space "After." Then a subhead comes along that has an extra 4 points of space "Before." That space "Before" gets added onto all the other space—the 3 literal points of leading and the 5 extra points of paragraph space. So the subhead will actually have an extra *12 points* of visual space above it (3 + 5 + 4).

4.75 *Space before and after is literal.* That is, it does not get spread out through the slug as the leading does (4.32–4.33). It literally sits under or over the leading slug. You can count on it.

4.76 Paragraph space examples

This Headline is 18 point

The headline above is 18-point type with a leading of 18 points. It has no extra space "After."

These paragraphs of body copy are 11 point with 15-point leading (11/15). They have no extra space "After."

Subhead Number One

Subhead Number One is also 11/15, with no extra points of space "After."

This is just to show you a comparison.

This Headline is 18 point

The headline above is 18-point type with a leading of 18 points. It has a space "After" of 8 point. The dotted lines indicate the *extra* 8-point slug (4.32).

These paragraphs are 11 point with 15-point leading (11/15). They have a space "After" of 5 points. The dotted lines directly above indicate the *extra* 5-point slug.

Subhead Number One

Subhead Number One is also 11/15, with 5 points of space "After." But to separate it from the paragraphs above, it has an extra 4 points of space "Before." The dotted lines above the Subhead indicate the *combination* of the extra 5 points from the second paragraph, plus the extra 4 points "Before" from the Subhead.

Use points to override the measurement system

4.77   Since the basic unit of leading is points (4.6–4.7), the relationship between paragraph spacing and leading (linespace) seems clearer if you also use points for paragraph space. If you don't want to change your entire measurement system to picas (1.211; 4.82), you can override the existing measurement system by entering values in picas and points in the edit boxes.

4.78   If the value is less than one pica (less than 12 points), enter a **0** (zero), then the letter **p** (for picas), then the number of **points** (**0p5**). The **p** tells PageMaker not to use the current measuring system, but to use picas instead.

If the value is one pica or more, enter the **number,** then the letter **p** (**2p**). If there are points also, enter those after the **p** (**2p7** means 2 picas and 7 points).

4.79   The only problem with overriding is that when you return to the dialog box, you'll find that PageMaker has automatically translated those points and picas into the current measuring system (see 4.80–4.82). Then, if you want to change the space by a tenth point or several points, it is difficult to figure.

4.80   Overriding the measurement system looks like this. Notice it says "inches," but the value entered in the edit box is in picas and points.

Paragraph space:
Before [0] inches
After [0p5] inches

4.81   When you return to the dialog box, you'll find that PageMaker has turned the picas and points into the value of the current measurement system. That can make it difficult to work with.

Paragraph space:
Before [0] inches
After [0.069] inches

4.82   To see the actual value that you originally entered, go to the "Preferences" dialog box (from the Edit menu) and change the "Measurement system" to "Picas." When you go back to the "Paragraph space" dialog box, the value will have reverted to picas and points. *(This will change the entire measurement system to picas, including the horizontal ruler, the Indents/tabs ruler, and all dialog boxes. See 1.211.)*

Paragraph space:
Before [0] picas
After [0p5] picas

Mai: It would all be folly.
Mrs. Brown: Tell me, Mai, what's wrong with folly?

National Velvet

4.83   Scenario #5: Paragraph space "before" and "after"

Take note, in the example to the right, of the spaces *before* and *after* the subheads, as compared to the spaces *between* the paragraphs.

I set the **body copy paragraphs** with an extra 2 points of space **after** each (4.84). This means that every time I pressed the Return key, an extra 2 points of space was inserted *after* that last line. This 2-point space was *added onto* the current leading: the type size is 10-point with 12-point leading, so the space between the paragraphs is now 14 point.

I set the **subheads** with an extra 4 points of space **after,** because it usually looks best to have a slight bit more separation after a subhead than there is between paragraphs. Again, these points were *added onto* the leading of the subhead.

Now, to emphasize the connection of the subhead with the following text, I inserted a little bit of extra space **before** the subhead. The examples here have an extra 6 points. These 6 points are *added onto the leading of the line above it*—thus (read this carefully), the *leading* of the paragraph above, the *after* of the paragraph above, and the *before* of the subhead, are *all added together* to create that space above the subhead.

JOHN BASKERVILLE

A type design

In 1780 the 'transitional' typeface *Baskerville* was introduced to the world. Nobody liked it.

Baskerville is called a transitional typeface because its characteristics were crossing the threshold from the 'oldstyle' typefaces that were currently in use, to the 'modern' typefaces with their extreme contrasts of thick-and-thin strokes. But the public wasn't ready for this cold, dry look—they wanted the warmth of the oldstyles.

An inventor

John loved those thin strokes of his new font, made possible with the new technology of copperplate engraving. But the paper technology was not ready yet to accept those thin lines—when printed, paper was so absorbent that the lines mushed up and lost their fine quality.

So John had to invent a new paper process—*calendaring*—that is still used today to create a smoother finish for printing.

An entrepreneur

John was a wealthy man, making his money in the japanning trade of the 1700s—*japan* is a hard, durable, black varnish originating, of course, in Japan. At the age of forty, when he became a typefounder, John lost his fortune because nobody liked his typeface. They preferred Caslon.

A coincidence

Baskerville (the font) was lost to the world for the next 150 years. In 1923 The Monotype Corporation revived this lovely typeface, and it went on to become the most popular type in the world. The coincidence is that the country where Baskerville has been used most extensively is Japan, to whom John originally owed his fortune.

An aside

This book is set in ITC Baskerville, 10/12, from Adobe Systems Incorporated.

If you want to do this:	**Then follow these steps:**	**Shortcuts ▾ Notes ▾ Hints**

4.84 Add space *after* a paragraph

Paragraph space:

Before [0] picas

After [0p5] picas

- With the **text tool,** select the paragraph(s) to which you want to apply extra space (you can select just one paragraph simply by clicking the insertion point in it).
- From the Type menu, choose "Paragraph...," *or* press Command M.
- Enter the value for the amount of *extra* space you want in the "After" edit box. If your measurement system is in inches, you may find it easier to override the inches (4.77–4.78) or to change your measurement system to picas (4.9).

- Remember, a *paragraph* on the Mac is any line or group of lines that has a Return at the end of it (3.230–3.236). See 3.192–3.193 re: selecting paragraphs.

4.85 Add space *before* a paragraph

Paragraph space:

Before [0p3] picas

After [0] picas

- Follow the steps in 4.84 above. Enter the value for the amount of *extra* space you want in the "Before" edit box. Be sure to read 4.68–4.76 to understand what you are doing and what to expect.

- See 3.192–3.193 re: selecting paragraphs.

4.86 Break a line *without* adding a paragraph space

- Every time you press the Return key, Page-Maker thinks you want a new paragraph and so adds on any extra space before and/or after that you have specified. Sometimes you don't want that extra space. Instead of pressing a Return, press **Shift Return.** You will get a hard line break that will not add any extra space.

- See 3.230–3.236 for more info on the Shift Return line break.

If you want to do this:

4.87 Remove paragraph space

Then follow these steps:

- With the **text tool,** select any and all paragraphs from which you want to remove any extra space.
- From the Type menu, choose "Paragraph...," *or* press Command M.
- The "Before" and "After" edit boxes may be blank or they may have values in them. Either way, to remove space from either one, type a 0 (zero) into it.

    You don't need to change both the "Before" and "After" edit boxes. If one of the edit boxes is blank, you can leave it blank if you choose. **But:** *you **cannot** remove a value from an edit box and **then** leave it blank.* PageMaker will yell at you.

Shortcuts ▾ Notes ▾ Hints

- See 3.192–3.193 re: selecting paragraphs.
- If you remove the paragaraph space and there is still more space than you want, there may be something else going on. See 3.214.

Not only is typeset copy between 20 and 40 percent more readable and legible than typewritten copy, it saves space and is more likely to be read and remembered.   *~Allan Haley*

Align to grid   *(from the Type menu, choose "Paragraph..."; click on the "Rules" button; click on the "Options" button)*

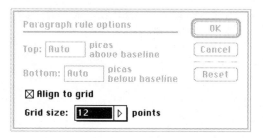

4.89   Some to-do has been made over what some people think is PageMaker 4.0's *vertical justification* feature. Well, this is it, but it isn't. Ideally, a vertical justification feature would take a body of text and align it vertically to fill a certain depth, just as horizontal justification aligns text to fill a certain width. PageMaker has always been capable of vertically aligning text by feathering in tiny increments of leading (well, always since 3.0). This "Align to grid" feature in 4.0 doesn't do quite the same thing, though.

4.90   Align to grid's principal claim to fame is that *you can force lines of text across columns to align on the same baseline.* Some people feel very strongly that every baseline (1.56) of every column should align on one common grid, as the baselines of this paragraph align with the baselines of the paragraph to the right. I believe there are other visual factors that are oftentimes more important. You can read this unbiased (ha!) report and make up your own mind.

4.91   With "Align to grid" on, PageMaker does not feather lines of text to fill a certain depth. No—she adds extra points of space after headlines, subheads, and between paragraphs. So then your body copy baselines are aligned, but you have another problem: the space between your paragraphs and headlines is inconsistent. Personally, I feel that is often a more flagrant visual inconsistency than baselines not aligning.

4.92   This is basically how "Align to grid" works: In your text, including any style sheets you may have created, you have set up a certain point size and leading for your body copy, and a different sort of size and leading for your headlines and subheads. You have incorporated a bit of extra space between your paragraphs, after your heads, and before your subheads (4.63–4.76). Well, with this extra space here and there, you find that your baselines across the columns do not match after a while, just like the columns on this page. The first part of this paragraph, as shown by the dotted lines above, aligns with the column to the left, because the type is the same size, with the same leading. But there are a few extra points of space after each paragraph, so now, at this point, the baselines of the two columns are no longer aligned.

Align to grid   —continued

4.93 With "Align to grid" turned on and your leading grid established, PageMaker will automatically insert extra space wherever it's needed to keep those baselines on the grid. The grid, according to this feature, is a set of invisible lines that you define using the leading value of your body copy. If your text is 12-point with 14-point leading, you would set your grid to 14 point.

4.94 On the previous page, I *could* select the text in the second column and align it to the grid so it would match the third column. PageMaker would insert extra points of space *between the paragraphs* until the baselines of the second paragraph matched the baselines directly across from it. But, personally, I don't want to do that because I don't want that much space between my paragraphs. If I did, I would have set them up that way. In this case, it is more important to me that I have half a line space between paragraphs, rather than have a large, clunky space.

4.95 "Align to grid" assumes you know how to work with a grid. A *grid* is an underlying structure, a framework, upon which to base your layout. Once a grid is established, all the elements of the job are aligned with it. The more complex the layout, the more essential a grid becomes. Grid theory is a very exciting and important part of graphic design. If you have studied grid theory, you will be able to take advantage of what the "Align to grid" feature has to offer without running into the problems it causes, or without having to use it at all.

4.96 You can set up your text to align with the grid at any point in the creation of your publication. You can apply it as a default, either for the publication or for the application (1.6–1.14). Or you can apply it to the appropriate styles in your style sheet. Or you can apply it as you go along. Or you can layout all the pages of your publication *without* using "Align to grid," and just apply it where it seems necessary (which is my preference).

The following pages also contain information relating to "Align to grid."

Notes

4.97   The "Align to grid" feature will "work" if:

- The body copy (the main text) all has the same leading.
- The text blocks all begin at a common point (they all hang from a "clothesline"), or at least they all "Snap to rulers," with the rulers having been customized to your leading increment (1.54–4.53; 4.99).
- You don't mind if PageMaker inserts extra linespace above the misaligned paragraph in order to stay on the grid.

4.98   "Align to grid" is paragraph-specific; that is, it is applied to the entire paragraph, no matter how few characters in that paragraph have been selected. In fact, it will apply to any paragraph that merely has the insertion point flashing in it. Since it is paragraph-specific, you can also include it in a style sheet.

With "Snap to rulers"

4.99   Using **Snap to rulers** is indispensable in conjunction with "Align to grid." Turn "Snap to rulers" on from the Options menu, then:

- In the "Preferences" dialog box (from the Edit menu), choose a "Custom" vertical ruler.
- Type in a point value that equals the point value of the leading of your body copy (4.53); click OK.

Now you will find as you move text blocks or graphics around on the page, they sort of hop from tick mark to tick mark on the rulers. In fact, you *cannot* place anything *between* tick marks. Since the markings on the vertical ruler are in the increments of your body text leading, it is not possible to place a text block anywhere but on one of the "grid" lines (also see 1.55).

With inline graphics

4.100   "Align to grid" is at its most practical when you are using *inline graphics*. An inline graphic is a graphic that you have placed as part of the text block. It can have leading and paragraph space applied to it, will conform to tabs and indents, and will move along with the text as you edit and format. The biggest problem with inline graphics is that they can throw off the leading. For instance, in this book, all the graphics you see in the first columns are inline (as in 4.84). The baseline of the first column is designed to align with the baseline of the second column. But when there is an inline graphic, it throws off that alignment.

4.101   So I select each inline graphic and align it to the grid (I check "Align to grid" and enter the leading value of the text). PageMaker then adds enough points to the space after the graphic (because now the graphic is a paragraph) to make the next line of text stay on the 12-point grid that aligns it with the adjacent column. The extra space is not a problem in this case, because the space below the inline graphic is so variable anyway.

See Section 9, 9.170–9.189 for more info on inline graphics.

If you want to do this:	Then follow these steps:	Shortcuts ▾ Notes ▾ Hints
4.102 Align text to a leading grid	■ First, make sure you know the point size of your leading (4.53). Then . . . ■ With the **text tool,** select the paragraphs you want to align to a grid. ■ From the Type menu, choose "Paragraph...." ■ Click on the "Rules..." button. ■ Click on the "Options..." button. ■ Click in the checkbox next to "Align to grid." ■ Type in the leading value of your body text in the "Grid size" edit box. ■ Press Option Return to *OK* all three dialog boxes (press Command Option Period to *Cancel* all three dialog boxes). ■ Customize your vertical ruler to the same leading value you set in "Align to grid" (4.99). ■ From the Options menu, make sure "Snap to rulers" is on (4.99). ■ With the **pointer tool,** press near the *top* of the text block and drag it into position. The text block will snap to the nearest ruler tick mark.	
4.103 Align graphics to a leading grid *(or to any other kind of grid)*	■ Customize your vertical ruler to the leading of your body text (4.99; 1.55). ■ From the Options menu, make sure "Snap to rulers" is on (4.99). ■ Now as you move and resize graphics, they will snap to the grid.	■ You don't have to set your grid with a *leading* value; you can customize the vertical ruler with any measurement, such as half-inches (36 points) or quarter-inches (18 points).

Word spacing

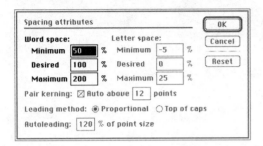

4.104 To get the "Spacing attributes" dialog box, choose "Paragraph..." from the Type menu, then click on the "Spacing..." button. In that overwhelming dialog box, only those three little boxes on the left deal with word spacing (see above). Ignore all the rest.

4.105 Word spacing applies to entire paragraphs, not just to selected text. Even if you have just a few of the characters selected, any changes entered here will affect the entire paragraph. This means you can use it in your style sheets.

4.106 The **Word spacing** segment of the "Spacing attributes" dialog box is concerned with the space *between the words*. When you hit the Spacebar, you create a space, right? That is a **word space.** A technical term for it is the *space band.*

4.107 When designers create fonts, they not only design the characters, but they also determine the ideal amount of space that should separate the letters and the words in that font and at each particular size.

4.108 The default value in the **Desired** edit box is 100%. That 100% indicates the ideal that the designer built into the font. If you leave that value as 100%, as text composes on the screen it keeps that

amount of space consistent between words, *as long as the text is not justified.*

4.109 If you change the Desired default to another value, such as 80%, the PageMaker will set the text using 80% of the ideal space between the words, *as long as the text is not justified.*

4.110 If your text *is not justified*, then it doesn't matter what values are in the Minimum and Maximum boxes; PageMaker will use the Desired value (unless you use an excessively large amount of space and the words can't fit on the line easily).

4.111 Any applied *word* spacing will *not* affect the *letter* space. Be careful, because too much or too little word space without appropriate letterspace can really make your text look dumb.

4.112 *This is an example of a font that needs to have its word spacing adjusted to make it more readable.*

"I believe that everyone should have a chance at an extravagant piece of folly."
  14-point type with default word spacing
  ~Mrs. Brown, National Velvet

"I believe that everyone should have a chance at an extravagant piece of folly."
  14-point type with 150% word spacing
  ~Mrs. Brown, National Velvet

Word spacing   —continued

4.113 When text is **justified** (aligned at both margins; 3.153–3.157), PageMaker increases or decreases space between the *words* in order to align the margins. In this process, often she can't use the 100% word space you desire.

4.114 The default value in the **Minimum** edit box is 50%. That 50% means that you won't mind if PageMaker has to squeeze the desired word space down to *half* of what the designer originally built into the space band.

4.115 The default value in the **Maximum** edit box is 200%. That 200% means that you won't mind if PageMaker has to increase the desired word space up to *twice the amount* of what the designer originally built into the space band.

4.116 You can change the values in either the Desired, the Minimum, or the Maximum edit boxes.

- You can set a Minimum of anywhere from 0 to 500 percent (1% increments).
- You can set a Maximum of anywhere from 0 to 500 percent (1% increments).
- The Desired spacing must be *equal to or between* the Minimum and the Maximum.

Word space:
Minimum 50 %
Desired 100 %
Maximum 200 %

4.117 PageMaker tries very hard to follow your word spacing specifications. But sometimes she just can't. PageMaker will let you know which lines disobey your rules *if* you have checked "Loose/tight lines" in the Preferences dialog box (from the Edit menu). Problem lines will have a gray bar (yellow, on a color monitor) behind them (4.122). The grey bar does not print; it is just a clue suggesting that perhaps you should take a closer look at that line. You may need to rewrite it, change the spacing, change the alignment, etc. But then again, it may be just fine for you.

4.118 Most of the time you can safely ignore the word spacing, as the Desired amount is generally adequate. Occasionally you may come across a font that looks a little too tight, or maybe it sets too loose. Then, of course, adjust it.

4.119 Rarely do you find that you can adjust the word spacing without adjusting the letter spacing as well. Extra word space with normal letter space usually looks like you don't know what you're doing. If you add extra letter space (4.142; 4.146), don't forget that letter spacing also affects the word spacing.

Examples of word spacing
All of the following examples use the font Futura Book (sans serif) or Goudy (serif), 12/Auto leading.

This column is **left aligned.**

4.120 Min: 50 Des: **100** Max: 200

Thou art thy mother's glass, and she in thee calls back the lovely April of her prime.

4.121 Min: 50 Des: **200** Max: 200

Thou art thy mother's glass, and she in thee calls back the lovely April of her prime.

4.122 Min: 50 Des: **500** Max: **500**

Thou art thy mother's glass, and she in thee calls back the lovely April of her prime. *(see 4.117)*

4.123 Min: **0** Des: **50** Max: 200

Thou art thy mother's glass, and she in thee calls back the lovely April of her prime.

This column is **justified, sans serif font.**

4.124 Min: 50 Des: **100** Max: 200

Thou art thy mother's glass, and she in thee calls back the lovely April of her prime.

4.125 Min: 50 Des: **200** Max: 200

Thou art thy mother's glass, and she in thee calls back the lovely April of her prime.

4.126 Min: 50 Des: **500** Max: **500**

Thou art thy mother's glass, and she in thee calls back the lovely April of her prime.

4.127 Min: **0** Des: **50** Max: 200

Thou art thy mother's glass, and she in thee calls back the lovely April of her prime.

This column is **justified, serif font.**

4.128 Min: 50 Des: **100** Max: 200

Thou art thy mother's glass, and she in thee calls back the lovely April of her prime.

4.129 Min: 50 Des: **200** Max: 200

Thou art thy mother's glass, and she in thee calls back the lovely April of her prime.

4.130 Min: 50 Des: **500** Max: **500**

Thou art thy mother's glass, and she in thee calls back the lovely April of her prime.

4.131 Min: **0** Des: **50** Max: 200

Thouartthymother'sglass,andsheinthee calls back the lovely April of her prime.

If you want to do this:	**Then follow these steps:**	**Shortcuts ▾ Notes ▾ Hints**
4.132 Increase the word space	▪ With the **text tool,** select the paragraph(s). ▪ From the Type menu, choose "Paragraph...," *or* press Command M. ▪ Click on the "Spacing..." button. ▪ Increase the value in the "Desired" edit box (e.g., 300% will increase the word space three times the normal amount). ▪ Increase the value in "Maximum" to at least as large as the value in "Desired." ▪ Click OK; click OK (or press Option Return to close both boxes).	▪ You can set Minimum or Maximum values anywhere from 0 to 500 percent, in increments of 1%. The Desired value must be *between,* or equal to, the Minimum and the Maximum. ▪ Be sure to read 4.104–4.119 to understand what you are doing.
4.133 Decrease the word space	▪ With the **text tool,** select the paragraph(s). ▪ From the Type menu, choose "Paragraph...," *or* press Command M. ▪ Click on the "Spacing..." button. ▪ Decrease the value in the "Desired" edit box (e.g., 25% will decrease the word space to one-fourth the normal spacing). ▪ Decrease the value in "Minimum" to at least as small as the value in "Desired." ▪ Click OK; click OK (or press Option Return).	▪ You can set Minimum or Maximum values anywhere from 0 to 500 percent, in increments of 1%. The Desired value must be *between,* or equal to, the Minimum and the Maximum. ▪ Be sure to read 4.104–4.119 to understand what you are doing.
4.134 Reset all the word space back to the original default **Word space:** Minimum `50` % Desired `100` % Maximum `200` %	▪ With the **text tool,** select the paragraph(s). ▪ From the Type menu, choose "Paragraph...," *or* press Command M. ▪ Click on the "Spacing..." button. ▪ Enter the values shown on the left. ▪ Click OK twice, or press Option Return.	▪ If the word spacing edit boxes are empty, it indicates that there is more than one value set for the selected paragraphs. What you enter will change *all* the selected paragraphs. ▪ See 4.11.

Letter spacing

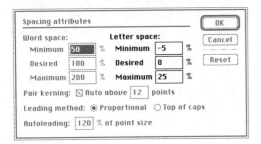

4.135 To get the "Spacing attributes" dialog box, choose "Paragraph..." from the Type menu, then click on the "Spacing..." button. In that overwhelming dialog box, only those three little boxes on the right deal with letter spacing (see above). Ignore all the rest.

4.136 Letter spacing applies to entire paragraphs; you cannot apply it to just a few words that are part of a larger paragraph. Using the letter spacing attributes is an easy way to get nicely "letterspaced" text, often so pretty. You can also include letter spacing attributes in your style sheets (Section 7), which is a great boon.

4.137 The **Letter spacing** segment of the "Spacing attributes" dialog box is concerned with the space *between the letters*. A technical term for it is the *pen advance*, a term for the amount of space you must move your pen before you begin the next letter.

4.138 When designers create fonts, they not only design the characters, but they also determine the ideal amount of space that the "pen" should advance before the *computer* creates the next letter; in other words, the designer decides how much space should surround each letter in a particular font and at a particular size.

4.139 The default value in the **Desired** edit box is 0%. That 0% indicates that *you do not want to deviate* from the ideal that the designer has built into the font. If you leave that value at 0%, then as text composes on the screen it keeps that consistent space between letters, *as long as the text is not justified.*

4.140 If you change the Desired default to another value, such as 20%, then Page-Maker will set the text using 20% *more* than the ideal space between the letters, *as long as the text is not justified.*

4.141 If your text *is not justified,* then it doesn't matter what values are in the Minimum and Maximum boxes; PageMaker will use the Desired value. Just remember: Desired must be *between* or equal to the Minimum and Maximum.

4.142 Letter space *does* affect the word space as well. It affects it because the space between words is just a Spacebar character. To us, it appears to be invisible. But to the Mac, it is a character. She doesn't know we can't see it. So as the letter space expands or condenses, the word space will expand or condense proportionally.

Letter spacing   —continued

4.143 When text is *justified* (aligned at both margins; 3.153–3.157), in order to align the margins, PageMaker first increases or decreases space between the *words,* according to the values set for word space (4.104–4.119). If it can't quite be done within the minimum and maximum word space settings, then she starts to work with the letter spacing settings.

4.144 The default value in the **Minimum** edit box is –5%. That –5% means that, when you choose to justify text, you won't mind if PageMaker has to squeeze up to 5% of the desired letter space *out* of what the designer originally built into the pen advance (4.137).

4.145 The default value in the **Maximum** edit box is 25%. That 25% means that, when you choose to justify text, you won't mind if PageMaker has to increase the desired letter space up to 25% *more* than what the designer originally built into the pen advance (4.137).

4.146 You can change the values in either the Desired, the Minimum, or the Maximum edit boxes.

- You can set a Minimum of anywhere from –200 to 200 percent (1% increments).
- You can set a Maximum of anywhere from –200 to 200 percent (1% increments).
- The Desired spacing must be *between,* or equal to, the Minimum and the Maximum.

Letter space:

Minimum	-5	%
Desired	0	%
Maximum	25	%

4.147 PageMaker tries very hard to follow your word and letter spacing specifications. But sometimes she just can't. PageMaker will let you know which lines disobey your rules *if* you have checked "Loose/tight lines" in the Preferences dialog box (from the Edit menu). Problem lines will have a gray bar (yellow, on a color monitor) behind them (4.122). The gray bar does not print; it is just a clue suggesting that perhaps you should take a closer look at that line and adjust it, if necessary (rewrite it, change the spacing, change the alignment, etc.; but then again, it may looks just fine to you the way it is).

4.148 Most of the time you can safely ignore the letter spacing, as the Desired amount is generally adequate. Occasionally you may come across a font that looks a little too tight, or maybe it sets too loose. Then, of course, adjust it.

Examples of letter spacing
All of the following examples use the font Futura Book (sans serif) or Goudy (serif), 12/Auto leading.

This column is **left aligned.**

4.149 Min: –5   Des: **0**   Max: 25

Thou art thy mother's glass, and she in thee calls back the lovely April of her prime.

4.150 Min: –5   Des: **25**   Max: 25

Thou art thy mother's glass, and she in thee calls back the lovely April of her prime.

4.151 Min: –5   Des: **75**   Max: **100**

Thou art thy mother's glass, and she in thee calls back the lovely April of her prime.

4.152 Min: **–25**   Des: **–25**   Max: 25

Thou art thy mother's glass, and she in thee calls back the lovely April of her prime.

This column is **justified, sans serif font.**

4.153 Min: –5   Des: **0**   Max: 25

Thou art thy mother's glass, and she in thee calls back the lovely April of her prime.

4.154 Min: –5   Des: **25**   Max: 25

Thou art thy mother's glass, and she in thee calls back the lovely April of her prime.

4.155 Min: –5   Des: **75**   Max: **100**

Thou art thy mother's glass, and she in thee calls back the lovely April of her prime.

4.152 Min: **–25**   Des: **–25**   Max: 25

Thou art thy mother's glass, and she in thee calls back the lovely April of her prime.

This column is **justified, serif font.**

4.157 Min: –5   Des: **0**   Max: 25

Thou art thy mother's glass, and she in thee calls back the lovely April of her prime.

4.158 Min: –5   Des: **25**   Max: 25

Thou art thy mother's glass, and she in thee calls back the lovely April of her prime.

4.159 Min: –5   Des: **75**   Max: **100**

Thou art thy mother's glass, and she in thee calls back the lovely April of her prime.

4.160 Min: **–25**   Des: **–25**   Max: 25

Thou art thy mother's glass, and she in thee calls back the lovely April of her prime.

If you want to do this:	Then follow these steps:	Shortcuts ▾ Notes ▾ Hints
4.161 Increase the letter space	■ With the **text tool,** select the paragraph(s). ■ From the Type menu, choose "Paragraph...," *or* press Command M. ■ Click on the "Spacing..." button. ■ Increase the value in the "Desired" edit box (e.g., 50% will increase the letter space half again as much as normal). ■ Increase the value in "Maximum" to at least as large as the value in "Desired." ■ Click OK; click OK (*or* press Option Return to close both boxes).	■ You can set Minimum or Maximum values anywhere from –200 to 200 percent, in increments of 1%. The Desired value must be *between,* or equal to, the Minimum and the Maximum. ■ Be sure to read 4.135–4.148 to understand what you are doing.
4.162 Decrease the letter space	■ With the **text tool,** select the paragraph(s). ■ From the Type menu, choose "Paragraph...," *or* press Command M. ■ Click on the "Spacing..." button. ■ Decrease the value in the "Desired" edit box (e.g., –25% will decrease the letter space by one-fourth the normal amount). ■ Decrease the value in "Minimum" to at least as small as the value in "Desired." ■ Click OK; click OK (*or* press Option Return).	■ You can set Minimum or Maximum values anywhere from –200 to 200 percent, in increments of 1%. The Desired value must be *between,* or equal to, the Minimum and the Maximum. ■ Be sure to read 4.135–4.148 to understand what you are doing.
4.163 Reset all the letter space values back to the original defaults **Letter space:** Minimum `-5` % Desired `0` % Maximum `25` %	■ With the **text tool,** select the paragraph(s). ■ From the Type menu, choose "Paragraph...," *or* press Command M. ■ Click on the "Spacing..." button. ■ Enter the values shown on the left. ■ Click OK twice, *or* press Option Return.	■ If the letter spacing edit boxes are empty, there is more than one value set for the selected paragraphs. What you enter will change all the selected paragraphs. ■ See 4.11.

223

If you want to do this:

4.164 Letterspace a headline

YOU CAN'T LET THE SEEDS
STOP YOU FROM ENJOYING
THE   WATERMELON

Then follow these steps:

- This really has nothing to do with the letter space segment of the "Spacing attributes" dialog box, but since you might look in this section for this information, here it is.
- Type the headline. Instead of just hitting the Spacebar between words, press the Option key while you hit the Spacebar. This creates a hard, or *non-breaking* space (4.207–4.212). If the headline is more than one line, *do* hit a Return or a Shift Return (4.86) between lines.
- When you are done typing, select all the lines of the text (if you used Shift-Returns, you only need to have the insertion point somewhere in the text).
- From the Type menu, slide down to "Alignment," then out to the submenu and choose "Force justify"; **or** press Command Shift F.

Shortcuts ▾ Notes ▾ Hints

- Also see 1.158 and 3.159 for other examples of letterspaced heads, using this same technique.
- You can use the letter space controls in the "Spacing attributes" dialog box to create this same effect, but it's a matter of trial and error to make it justify at both margins. Using the technique detailed here, the letters will spread or tighten to whatever length you widen or narrow the text block.
- That dialog box needs an "Apply" button, like the "Image control" box has, so you can see your changes before you OK them for the publication. Write to Aldus and tell them.

etaoin shrdlu

By Herb Caen
OF THE SAN FRANCISCO CHRONICLE

It just occurred to me, with the usual thull dud, that "etaoin shrdlu" is dead. If you are under a certain age, this will mean nothing to you, more's the pity. If you are over that age, and are a printfreak besides, the mere mention of "etaoin shrdlu" may bring a tear to your peepers—the same tear that is drawn by the mere mention of such words as "running board," "25-cent martini" and, well, OK, "peepers." In the pioneer days of print journalism, the intriguing "etaoin shrdlu," pronounced roughly "Etwan Sherdlu," was the most famous and most frequent of all typographical errors. And needless to say, The Old Chronicle had more than its share.

Once upon a time, children, reporters wrote their stories on typewriters. The result, called "copy" or "jeez that's awful," depending, was edited by copy editors (drunk, grizzled) using pencils. The copy, ruined or vastly improved by editing, depending, went to the composing room, where it was set into type by Linotype machines. These machines made wonderful, delicate tinkling noises as the operators' skilled fingers flew over the keys. The machines' hot lead, in great pots, was transformed into columns of type. The type, beautiful to see and touch, was transferred in trays to a metal frame, where compositors arranged it into a page, the layout of which had been sketched by a makeup editor, grizzled, drunk.

Every now and then, a Linotype operator would make a mistake. He would then run his finger down the two left-hand columns of the lower-case keyboard, producing the matrices "etaoin shrdlu," which filled out one line. Or, these words would be used as a guide on a galley of type, under the slug, say of "Caen." The compositor, a fellow who could read type upside down and backwards but no other way, was supposed to remove the slug and the "etaoin shrdlu." But in many cases, after too many trips to Hanno's, the M&M, or Breen's, the compositor would forget. And a front-page story would read: "The Mayor, shocked at reports that he would be indicted for mopery, called in reporters and said etaoin shrdlu." Or "Bryant Townsend II, socialite sportsman, announced his engagement to Miss etaoin shrdlu." The Chronicle became so famous for these it was sometimes called The Daily Shrdlu.

(continued on page 637.)

Linotype keyboard

San Francisco Chronicle

cument
of War
ngress Told

tained in a 27-page document prepared for the Senate Foreign Relations and Armed Services Committees, now considering the troops-to-Europe issue.

The document was drafted by legal experts of the White House and the State, Defense and Justice Departments. It spelled out arguments to support the view that President Truman has constitutional power to send troops to Korea in United Nations action and to assign troops to the North Atlantic Treaty defense force.

Clay Pleads For Europe

Senate Urged To Understand 'Little Man'

By VANCE JOHNSON
Washington Correspondent, The Chronicle
WASHINGTON, Feb. 28— Public hearings on the troops-for-Europe issue ended today with a three-star general begging Senators to look to the "little man" of Europe for the answer to their misgivings.

The witness was Lieutenant General Lucius D. Clay, retired, former commander of American occupation forces in Germany, now a deputy director of the Office of Defense Mobilization.

Pleading with the Senate Foreign Relations and Armed Services Committees not "to value freedom and Allies on the basis of two divisions to one division, or 10 dollars against 1 dollar," the general expressed the opinion that if the Europeans are given a chance they will prove themselves.

Limits, ratios or strings to American aid, said Clay, not only will fail to produce vigorous European rearmament but well might defeat the whole program.

Marines Attack

Stiff Fight in Center Sector; Han Crossed

By the Associated Press
TOKYO, March 1 — U. Marines led a powerful atta today (Thursday) by All troops and planes along a mile front in Central Ko against the heart of Chin Red defenses.

Simultaneously, U. S. 3d Divis infantrymen on the Western fr crossed the Han river in easi boats and attacked a two-mile-l sand island southeast of Red-h Seoul.

Both actions met fierce ene resistance.

Primary purpose of the big c tral front assault: make the Chi either stand and fight or withd from the one sector best suited any enemy counteroffensive.

Purpose of the 3d Division ac was: get troops across the sout loop of the Han; establish a bri head; then move tanks across shallow northern loop of the r into flatland southeast of Seoul

ISLAND BATTLE
Third Division soldiers ran hard-fighting Reds near Sinc on the north side of the island Chamsil near the southern shor

The central front assault ga ground despite bitter opposition
U. S. 1st Marine Division tro spearheading the assault, qui captured 600-foot "Clover Leaf l a strategic height in the Hoeng area. A Marine spokesman said attack was progressing on sched

The drive by American, Br Commonwealth and South Ko troops was aimed at heavily mai Communist mountain positions n of the road hub of Hoengsong. Correspondent Stan Swinton ported from U. S. Eighth A headquarters.

WEST OF HOENGSONG
The 25-mile attack front exte generally westward from Hoeng
The new attack amounted

1950s' hot lead

Kerning

4.165 Kerning is the process of adjusting the space between characters. It is slightly different than the *letter spacing* you may have just read about (4.135–4.138), in that kerning is *character* formatting, directly applied *between individual letters,* rather than entire paragraphs. Kerning is a fine tuning control, rather than a general attribute.

4.166 You may have read, here and there throughout this book, about the hot metal process used for centuries (until the 1970s), where every character was created on a separate little piece of metal (lead). These letters were lined up in rows to ready them for printing. Obviously, if each character was on its own little piece of lead, it could only get just so close to the one next to it. If a metal typesetter wanted letters closer to each other, he had to take a knife and trim the tiny blocks of lead. He didn't do it very often. You can pick up an old newspaper or magazine and instantly tell that it's old, right? A large part of the look that dates it is the loose letter spacing. The trend for the past twenty years has been to set tighter and tighter letter spacing. To do that we **kern** the letters—we take out tiny units of space between them.

Watermelon

Watermelon

Watermelon

Watermelon

Watermelon

4.167 The example to the left shows how the letters would be spaced if they were each on a separate block of lead. Notice particularly the gaps between the **Wa** and around the **o.** Curved letters and letters with extra white space, such as **T, W, A** (as opposed to letters like **H, I,** and **E**), always need kerning.

4.168 This example shows 18 point type set with no kerning.

4.169 This shows the same type set with *auto pair kerning;* the computer kerned the characters automatically (4.173–4.175; 4.180).

4.170 This example shows the same type set with *auto pair kerning,* then refined with *manual kerning* (4.173–4.179).

Visually consistent

4.171 The term *kerning* originally meant *reducing* the space between characters, but it has now come to mean *increasing* the space beween characters, as well, or simply *adjusting* the space.

4.172 The end result should be *visually consistent letter spacing*. Whether that means you increase space between tight letters or decrease space between loose letters, the spacing must be consistent. The eye should not stumble over spacing inconsistencies.

Auto kerning pairs

4.173 Most fonts have *kerning pairs* built into them. That is, as designers create fonts, they build in tighter spacing around certain *pairs* of letters that are known to cause inconsistent gaps—such as Ta, To, Yo, we, and many others.

4.174 You can choose to have PageMaker automatically kern those pairs *(auto pair kerning)* as you type. Kerning slows down the text composition on the screen, plus it is really only applicable to larger sizes of type (above 12 or 14 point). So you can choose to have PageMaker kern only type above a certain point size, and you can choose to turn it off altogether (4.180; 4.181). You can apply it to a style sheet (great for headlines) and you can set it as a default for your entire publication (1.14). **Auto pair kerning applies to the entire paragraph.**

4.175 Not all fonts have kerning pairs built in, and some that do have poorly adjusted pairs. And while some fonts have 200 or 300 kerning pairs, others have over a thousand. But just because a font has an excessive amount of kerning pairs does not necessarily mean it's better. In fact, where there are thousands of pairs it takes an interminable length of time to compose the text.

Manual kerning

4.176 Kerning is a totally visual skill. The computer does the best it can with what it has to work with, but the end result, especially for display type (type over 14 point) depends entirely on your judgment. So PageMaker also gives you the option to **manually kern** typc (4.182–4.185). You can manually kern between two characters or over a selection of text.

4.177 The space is increased or decreased between letters in units of an *em*. An em is a space the width of the point size of the type. That is, if you are using 12-point type, an em space is 12 points wide. If you are using 36-point type, an em is 36 points wide. PageMaker divides the em into 25 or 100 *units*.

4.178 You can kern in $1/25^{th}$ units or you can kern in $1/100^{th}$ units of an em, depending on the key combination you use (4.182–4.183). Because the amount of space is so tiny, often you won't see the result on the screen, but you will when you print.

4.179 Yes, that means you must print the page to check your kerning. If it's not right, you kern again and check again. (One of the greatest reasons to invest in Adobe Type Manager is that it allows you to see the effects of your kerning on the screen.)

If you want to do this:	**Then follow these steps:**	**Shortcuts ▾ Notes ▾ Hints**

4.180 Turn auto kerning on or off

Pair kerning: ☒ Auto above 12 points

- If you want to turn auto kerning on or off for the entire publication, then follow these steps after you click once on the **pointer tool** (click once on the pointer tool, even if it is already selected).
  Or, if you want to turn auto kerning on or off for just one or more paragraphs, then select the paragraph(s) with the **text tool.**
- From the Type menu, choose "Paragraph...," *or* press Command M.
- Click once on the "Spacing..." button.
- Find "Pair kerning." If you *do* want PageMaker to automatically pair kern, make sure there is a checkmark in the box for "Auto above." If you *don't* want auto pair kerning, make sure there is *no* checkmark in the "Auto above" box.
- Hold the Option key down as you click OK to close both dialog boxes (*or* press Option Return).

- The auto kerning function is *paragraph specific;* that is, it applies to an entire paragraph, not to individual characters. Turning it on or off while certain characters are selected will turn it on or off for the entire paragraph that the selected characters are part of.

4.181 Determine the point size of type that will be auto kerned

Pair kerning: ☒ Auto above 12 points

- Follow the steps in 4.180 above. After you turn pair kerning *on,* enter the minimum point size of the type *above which* you want to auto kern.
- Hold the Option key down as you click OK to close both dialog boxes (*or* press Option Return).

If you want to do this:	**Then follow these steps:**	**Shortcuts ▾ Notes ▾ Hints**

4.182 Decrease the space between two characters

- With the **text tool,** click once to set the insertion point *between* the two characters you want to kern together.
- To decrease the space in **coarse** amounts ($\frac{1}{25}$th units of an em; 4.177–4.178): press Command Backspace/Delete; **or** press Command LeftArrow.
- To decrease the space in **fine** amounts ($\frac{1}{100}$th units of an em; 4.177–4.178): press Option Backspace/Delete; **or** press Command Shift LeftArrow.

- You cannot do any kind of kerning in the Story Editor, nor can you include manual kerning as part of a style sheet.
- Kerning is cumulative with auto pair kerning, with letter spacing applied using the "Spacing attributes" dialog box, and with tracking (see 4.187–4.193).

4.183 Increase the space between two characters

- With the **text tool,** click once to set the insertion point *between* the two characters you want to kern apart.
- To increase the space in **coarse** amounts ($\frac{1}{25}$th units of an em; 4.177–4.178): press Command Shift Backspace/Delete; **or** press Command RightArrow.
- To increase the space in **fine** amounts ($\frac{1}{100}$th units of an em; 4.177–4.178): press Option Shift Backspace/Delete; **or** press Command Shift RightArrow.

Using the arrow keys

Coarse amounts (.04)
  delete: Command LeftArrow
  add: Command RightArrow

Fine amounts (.01)
  delete: Command Shift LeftArrow
  add: Command Shift RightArrow

Using the Backspace/Delete key

Coarse amounts (.04)
  delete: Command Backspace/Delete
  add: Command Shift Backspace/Delete

Fine amounts (.01)
  delete: Option Backspace/Delete
  add: Option Shift Backspace/Delete

4.184 Decrease or increase the kern spacing over a range of text

- With the **text tool,** press-and-drag over the range of text to be kerned.
- Follow the steps as in kerning between two characters (4.182; 4.183).

If you want to do this:	**Then follow these steps:**	**Shortcuts ▾ Notes ▾ Hints**
4.185 Remove all kerning from selected text	■ With the **text tool,** press-and-drag to select the text from which you want to remove kerning. ■ Press Command Option K, **or** press Command Option Shift Delete.	■ Retyping the text would also remove any kerning that had been applied. ■ A little note: the quick reference quide that comes with PageMaker says you can press Option Clear or Option Shift Clear, but those commands delete your text as well as the kerning. I guess that's one way to get rid of it.
4.186 Kern text or remove kerning while in the Story Editor	■ You can't.	

The image above is one word, including the black box.
I superscripted uidnunc, *kerned it all the way into*
the Q, *created a paragraph rule behind the lowercase*
letters, then reversed the letters.

Tracking
(from the Type menu)

Track ▶	✓No track ⇧⌘Q
	Very loose
	Loose
	Normal
	Tight
	Very tight

4.187 Tracking (also known as track kerning; "Track" in the Type menu) at first seems very similar to *letter spacing* in that you are adjusting the space between the letters. There are several differences, though.

4.188 Letter spacing applies to entire paragraphs; tracking applies only to the selected characters. Letter spacing is an arbitrary, overall measurement; tracking is dependent on the point size of the type and on the kern pairs built into each font. Letter spacing can be adjusted in .1 percent increments from –200 percent to +200 percent; tracking only offers you five options. And perhaps the most significant difference: it takes time to figure out how to use letter spacing; tracking provides instant gratification.

4.189 Tracking can be included in your style sheet (Section 7). Tracking can also be applied in the Story Editor, although you won't see any change until you return to the page layout.

4.190 More history: Remember those little pieces of lead that type used to be printed from? Every single font and every single point size of type had its own set of characters. When a typecutter made a 9-point font set, he built into it the appropriate letter spacing for 9-point. When he made a 36 point set, he built into it the appropriate letter spacing for 36-point, *which was not the same, relatively, as that for 9-point.* The larger the type size, the *less* space we need between the characters, proportionally. If you take 9-point text and enlarge it on a camera to 36-point, you can clearly see the loose letter space that results (4.193).

Computerized typesetting, though, does not create a separate font for each size, with its attendant adjustments in letter spacing, as well as in stroke width and proportions. Computers use one size as a standard, and all other sizes are created from that size.

4.191 Macintosh programs that work with proportional text and spacing use a *linear calculation* to determine the amount of space between words. That is, they take a size, such as 12-point, and proclaim that as the standard. With 6-point, they use half the amount of letterspacing that 12 point used. With 36-point type, they use three times as much letterspacing than 12-point used. This creates too much space in large type, and too little space in small type.

4.192 For the best readability, large type needs less space, small type needs more space. Tracking addresses this problem. A "Normal" track *reduces* the amount of letter space in large sizes, and *adds* letter space to small sizes. It does slow the text composition, so it's best to use it for what it is intended, rather than applying it to all your text indiscriminately. If you want a slightly tighter or looser letterspacing over a *broad* range of text, use the "Letter space" function (4.135–4.163).

4.193 *The small text is 9-point. I turned it into a graphic and enlarged it to 36-point. Notice how loose the same letter spacing appears at the larger size.*

The world, dear Agnes, is a strange affair. *Molière*

The world, dear Agnes,

Examples of tracking

4.194

36-point type with "No track"
("Molière" is 24-point)

The world, dear Agnes, is a strange affair. *Molière*

36-point type with "Very loose" tracking

The world, dear Agnes, is a strange affair. *Molière*

36-point type with "Loose" tracking

The world, dear Agnes, is a strange affair. *Molière*

36-point type with "Normal" tracking

The world, dear Agnes, is a strange affair. *Molière*

Examples of tracking   —*continued*

36-point type with "Tight" tracking

The world, dear Agnes, is a strange affair. *Molière*

36-point type with "Very tight" tracking

The world, dear Agnes, is a strange affair. *Molière*

4.195

5 point; "No track"   The world, dear Agnes, is a strange affair. *Molière*

5 point; "Very loose" track   The world, dear Agnes, is a strange affair. *Molière*

5 point; "Loose" track   The world, dear Agnes, is a strange affair. *Molière*

5 point; "Normal" track   The world, dear Agnes, is a strange affair. *Molière*

5 point; "Tight" track   The world, dear Agnes, is a strange affair. *Molière*

5 point; "Very tight" track   The world, dear Agnes, is a strange affair. *Molière*

4.196

10 point; "No track"   The world, dear Agnes, is a strange affair. *Molière*

10 point; "Very loose" track   The world, dear Agnes, is a strange affair. *Molière*

10 point; "Loose" track   The world, dear Agnes, is a strange affair. *Molière*

10 point; "Normal" track   The world, dear Agnes, is a strange affair. *Molière*

10 point; "Tight" track   The world, dear Agnes, is a strange affair. *Molière*

10 point; "Very tight" track   The world, dear Agnes, is a strange affair. *Molière*

Notice how a "Normal" track on this small, 5-point size **increased** *the letter spacing. "Normal" track on the 36-point and the 10-point type* **decreased** *the letter spacing.*

If you want to do this:	Then follow these steps:	Shortcuts ▾ Notes ▾ Hints
4.197 Apply tracking to selected text	■ With the **text tool,** select the text. Tracking will only apply to the highlighted (selected) text. ■ If the insertion point is flashing when you choose a track, then you are loading the insertion point and everything you type from that point on will track, *until you click the insertion point somewhere else.* ■ From the Type menu, slide down to "Track," then out to the side to select the track value. See 4.194–4.196 for examples of the effects on different sizes of type.	
4.198 Change the tracking	■ Just repeat 4.197 to change the tracking.	
4.199 Remove any tracking	■ With the **text tool,** select the text from which you want to remove tracking. If you are not sure exactly which characters have a track applied, it's okay to select extra text. ■ If the insertion point is flashing when you remove tracking, there will be no tracking in any text you type from that point on, *until you click somewhere else.* ■ You can go up to the File menu, down to "Track," and choose "No track," *or* it is much easier to just press Command Shift Q. *(Q? How'd they come up with Q?)*	

Set width

4.204 Examples of set width

4.200 Set width is not really a spacing function, but it is included here because it interconnects with and affects the other spacing values.

4.201 The "Set width" command actually expands and condenses the type: you can expand characters up to 250 percent, and you can condense them down to 5 percent, in .1 percent increments. Set width can be included in your style sheet. It can also be applied while in the Story Editor (Section 8), although of course you won't see the results until you return to the page layout.

4.202 When a designer creates an expanded or condensed font, she redraws the original characters that are in the Roman (straight) version, creating subtle differences in the strokes, the stress, the line weights, the thick/thin contrasts, the connections, etc. When the *computer* creates an expanded or condensed font, it just squishes or stretches the existing font.

4.203 Set width is *character specific;* that is, it applies to just the characters that are selected with the text tool, not to the entire paragraph.

"Open Sesame—I want to get out!" ~Stanislaw J. Lee	20%
"Open Sesame—I want to get out!" ~Stanislaw J. Lee	50%
"Open Sesame—I want to get out!" ~Stanislaw J. Lee	70%
"Open Sesame—I want to get out!" ~Stanislaw J. Lee	80%
"Open Sesame—I want to get out!" ~Stanislaw J. Lee	90%
"Open Sesame—I want to get out!" ~Stanislaw J. Lee	Normal
"Open Sesame—I want to get out!" ~Stanislaw J. Lee	110%
"Open Sesame—I want to get out!" ~Stanislaw J. Lee	120%
"Open Sesame—I want to get out!" ~Stanislaw J. Lee	130%
"Open Sesame—I want to get out!"	175%
"Open Sesame—I want to get out!" ~Stanislaw J. Lee	250%

If you want to do this:	**Then follow these steps:**	**Shortcuts ▾ Notes ▾ Hints**
4.205 Apply a set width to selected text, or change the set width of selected text	■ With the **text tool,** select the text. A set width will only apply to the highlighted (selected) text. ■ If the insertion point is flashing when you choose a width, then you are loading the insertion point and everything you type from that point on will condense or expand, *until you click the insertion point somewhere else.* ■ From the Type menu, slide down to "Set width," then out to the side to select the value. If you want a value other than those shown, choose "Other..." and type in a value of your choice from 5% to 250%, in .1 increments. See 4.204 for examples of the different effects.	■ You can also apply a set width to selected text through the "Type specifications" dialog box: choose "Type specs..." from the Type menu, or press Command T.
4.206 Remove any set width	■ With the **text tool,** select the text you want to remove a set width from. If you are not sure exactly which characters have a width applied, it's okay to select extra text. ■ If the insertion point is flashing, you will just be applying the normal width to any text typed from that point on, *until you click somewhere else.* ■ You can go up to the Type menu, down to "Set width," and choose "Normal," *or* it is much easier to just press Command Shift X.	■ You can also apply a set width to selected text through the "Type specifications" dialog box: choose "Type specs..." from the Type menu, or press Command T. ■ If you accidentally pressed Command X and your text disappeared, Undo immediately (from the File menu). If you are too late to Undo, do a mini-Revert: hold the Shift key down while you choose "Revert" from the File menu. Click OK. Your publication will revert to the way it was just before you removed the text.

Hard spaces (non-breaking)

4.207 PageMaker provides more than one way to get a blank space. Again, we go back to our historical roots. When printers were creating a page of type with those tiny little pieces of lead, they would use tiny little *blank* pieces to separate words and sentences, as well as to indent and to hang punctuation (19.16). These blank pieces came in several standard sizes, among them, **ems, ens,** and **thins.**

4.208 When the printer was setting a page, he would insert one **em** quad as a paragraph indent. An em quad was a little square of lead; it was as *tall* and as *wide* as the point size of the type (thus it was a *square* of the point size). On that 12-point page, then, the indent would be 12 points, the width of a 12-point em. If the type was 8 point, the em space would be 8 point. He could put several ems together to create a larger space.

4.209 An **en space** was the same as an em, but half the *width*. Thus a 12-point en was 12 points tall (as tall as the type), but only 6 points wide. And a **thin space** was one-quarter the width of an em. Thus a 12-point thin was 3 points wide.

4.210 Phototype and electronic type carried over the ems and ens and thins. We also have a *fixed space,* or *hard space;* that is, a non-breaking space the width of a normal space between the words, just like the Spacebar. "Set width" (4.200–4.207) affects the size of these special spaces; they will expand or contract at the same proportion you set the text.

4.211 Ems, ens, thins, and fixed spaces are all **non-breaking.** That is, even though they are blank, they are as solid as a character. If they are used between words, the words will not *break;* for instance, if you put a fixed space between *Ms.* and *Wollstonecraft,* the two words will never split at the end of a line.

4.212 When would you use ems and ens and thins? One very important use is for hanging punctuation (19.16). Or use them whenever you want a quick, dependable amount of space and don't necessarily want to set a tab. A thin can be used before leaders in tabs to customize the leaders (5.64; 5.65). A fixed space can be used between words to letterspace a headline (1.158; 3.159; 4.164) or to prevent an awkward line break (4.211). These spaces can be formatted with any text formatting you would use for regular characters, so you can select a space and make it smaller, for instance, if you need a tiny space less than the thin in your current point size.

An em was also called a "mutton," to distinguish it from an en, which was also called a "nut."

If you want to do this:	Then follow these steps:	Shortcuts ▾ Notes ▾ Hints
4.213 Create an em space	■ With the **text tool,** select the space you want to replace, **or** set the insertion point at the spot you want it to appear. ■ Press Command Shift M.	■ Hey! Is that an **M** for **em** space?
4.214 Create an en space	■ See the first step, above. ■ Press Command Shift N.	■ An **N** for **en** space!
4.215 Create a thin space	■ See the first step in 4.213. ■ Press Command Shift T.	■ A **T** for **thin** space!
4.216 Create a fixed space	■ See the first step in 4.213. ■ Press Option Spacebar.	■ See 4.211.
4.217 Create a non-breaking hyphen	■ See the first step in 4.213. ■ Press Command Option Hyphen.	■ This hyphen will not allow the word to break at the hyphen at the end of a line.
4.218 Create a non-breaking slash	■ See the first step in 4.213. ■ Press Command Option /.	■ This slash will not allow the word to break at the slash at the end of a line.

Hyphenation

(From the Type menu, choose "Hyphenation...")

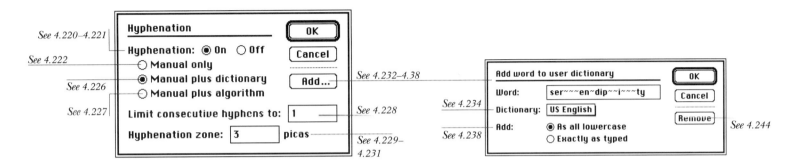

See 4.220–4.221
See 4.222
See 4.226
See 4.227
See 4.232–4.38
See 4.234
See 4.228
See 4.229– 4.231
See 4.238
See 4.244

4.219 PageMaker offers you the options to control whether there is any hyphenation allowed in the selected paragraph(s), where words will be hyphenated, how many line breaks can hyphenate in a row, and how close to the right margin a word has to get in order to be allowed to hyphenate. You can also add words to the user dictionary so she'll know where to hyphenate them. These hyphenation controls are paragraph specific (they affect just the paragraph that is selected), so they can be built into your style sheet, as well. You can set the controls as application or publication defaults, or you can just change the settings per paragraph in your text, before or after you create it.

4.220 Hyphenation off tells PageMaker not to hyphenate anything at all. In fact, you can't even *manually* hyphenate words (unless you insert a real hyphen; 4.222). Although, words that are just born with a hyphen in them will still break at the end of a line, at the hyphen (such as tongue-tied).

4.221 If you turn hyphenation **on,** you have these three choices, as you can see in the dialog box: *Manual only, Manual plus dictionary,* and *Manual plus algorithm.* These options determine how PageMaker makes decision about where to hyphenate words. They are explained on the following pages.

Manual only

4.222 Manual only means that Page-Maker will not automatically hyphenate words for you. You have to do it yourself. *That does not mean that you insert hyphens in words you want to hyphenate!* Oh no. If you type a regular hyphen to break a word at the end of the line, that hyphen will stay there when the text is edited. I'm sure you've seen this before:

> I declare! Sometimes it seems to me that every time a new piece of machin- ery comes in at the door, some of our wits fly out at the window.
> *(Aunt Abigail in* Understood Betsy*)*
> *Dorothy Canfield Fisher*

4.223 Somebody entered a hyphen to break the word at the end of the line. Then when the text was edited, or the line length changed, or the point size increased, or any number of things that made the text reflow, the hyphen stayed there. See 4.224 for a solution.

Discretionary hyphens

4.224 To prevent the problem illustrated in 4.222, you must enter a **discretionary hyphen:** press Command Hyphen. A discretionary hyphen is invisible until you need it. If the word has room to break at the end of a line, it will break and PageMaker will insert a visible hyphen. If the text reflows so that the word is no longer at the end of a line, the hyphen becomes invisible. It will wait there in the word until you need it again.

4.225 So with **Manual only** turned on, any words you want hyphenated you must hyphenate yourself with *discretionary hyphens* (see 4.239–4.241).

If you insert a discretionary hyphen and it doesn't hyphenate the word, it is because your hyphenation zone is too wide. See 4.229–4.231; 4.242.

PageMaker version 4.01 has a new diction-ary choice of "None." If you have applied the dictionary choice "None" through the "Paragraph specifications" dialog box (8.126), then the only option available to you in "Hyphenation" is "Manual." If you want either of the other methods of hyphen-ation, you must apply a different dictionary to the paragraph (8.126).

Manual plus dictionary

4.226 The second option, **Manual plus dictionary,** in addition to allowing Page-Maker to hyphenate at discretionary hyphens, also permits her to look words up in the dictionary and check the ranking of hyphenation breaks (4.236–4.237). If a word has a first, a second, and a third preference for hyphenating, PageMaker will try to hyhenate according to that order. If you have more than one dictionary installed, she will look in the dictionary that you have specified for that paragraph in the "Paragraph specifications" dialog box, plus its accompanying user dictionary (4.232).

Manual plus algorithm*

4.227 The option **Manual plus algorithm** allows PageMaker to hyphenate any word containing a discretionary hyphen (4.224), *plus* any word she finds in the dictionary, *plus* any word that is not in the dictionary, but which she can figure out how to hyphenate by using a dictionary algorithm.* This option gives PageMaker full range, which you may need to watch out for (such as two-character hyphenations, like words broken at -ed or -ly endings, or hyphenating jus-tif-i-ca-to-ry as if it was the same as jus-ti-fi-cate). At this point, the text layout itself and the hyphenation zone (4.229) will influence the hyphenation most seriously.

*Algorithm: a set of rules for solving a problem. Remember those rules we learned in the third grade about where to hyphenate words? PageMaker uses the same rules.

Limit consecutive hyphens

4.228 The option **Limit consecutive hyphens to** is a very important control. It allows you to control the number of consecutive hyphens per paragraph, anywhere from 1 hyphen to 255, or, for some strange reason, you can type in "No limit." Really, you never want to have more than one hyphen in a row. It looks very tacky to have stacks of hyphens (ladders), and it is not difficult to avoid them. Sometimes it takes a little copy editing, sometimes a little tracking (4.187–4.199), sometimes a little adjusting of the line length. But it must be done. You don't want to look tacky. Limit your consecutive hyphens to 1.

Hyphenation zone

4.229 In the **Hyphenation zone** you determine how far away from the end of the line a word has to be in order to hyphenate. For instance, if you enter 3 picas (.5 inch) as your hyphenation zone, nothing will be hyphenated *within that last half inch of the line.* You automatically weed out those two- and three-letter word breaks. If you enter .25 inch (or any equivalent, such as 1p6, which is 1 pica and 6 points), the beginning of a word can get to within a quarter-inch from the end of the line and still hyphenate. Obviously, that means shorter portions of the word can be left on the line above. You can enter any value from 0 to 12 picas (2 inches), in .1 increments.

4.230 *The smaller the hyphenation zone, the more PageMaker will hyphenate.* With greater ability to hyphenate, justified text can have more consistent word spacing, and unjustified text can have a smoother right margin. But there will be too many hyphenated words.

4.231 *The larger the hyphenation zone, the less PageMaker will hyphenate.* With less hyphenation, justified text will have more inconsistent word spacing. Unjustified text will have a more ragged margin.

Adding words to the user dictionary *(from the Type menu, choose "Hyphenation…," click on the "Add…" button)*

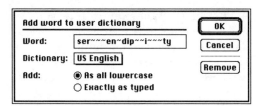

4.232 PageMaker allows you to add words to the *user dictionary* (also see 8.99–8.105), not to the main, Houghton-Mifflin dictionary. The *main* dictionary has 100,000 words; the *user* dictionary is where you can add words that are not in the main dictionary, but that you use regularly, such as jargon, technical terms, proper names, etc. PageMaker looks through both the main and the user dictionaries for hyphenating and spell-checking, so by adding your words to the user dictionary, PageMaker will be able to hyphenate them. Also, if a word is in neither dictionary, it is considered misspelled, so having the words in the user dictionary will prevent their being flagged as wrong.

4.233 This dialog box is exactly like the one in the spell-checker in the Story Editor; they operate the same way, and they accomplish the same thing (8.120–8.124).

4.234 If you have more than one *language* dictionary, each language has its own, separate user dictionary. You can choose the user dictionary in which to add the word by pressing on the submenu next to "Dictionary" (page 239). If you have the Legal or the Medical dictionary, they both share the same user dictionary as the US English one.

4.235 The main purpose of this little dialog box is to define where you want a word to be hyphenated as you add it to the user dictionary. You can also change the hyphenation points in words that are in the main dictionary (actually, you are really *adding* them to the user dictionary, but since PageMaker checks the user dictionary first, what she finds there will take precedence over what is in the main dictionary).

4.236 Type in the word you want to add. The tilde is the symbol used for **ranking** the hyphenation points: ~ . It is found on the upper left of some keyboards, or next to the Spacebar on the MacPlus keyboards; use it with the Shift key. (See the example in the dialog box, upper left.)

4.237 To rank the hyphenation points:
- Enter **one tilde** at the point in the word where it is most desirable to hyphenate.
- Enter **two tildes** at permissible hyphenation points.
- Enter **three tildes** where you want PageMaker to hyphenation the word only if it's absolutely necessary.
- **Remove all tildes** if you never want the word to hyphenate.

4.238 If you click **As all lowercase,** then no matter where you use capital letters as you type the word into the edit box, the word will be entered into the user dictionary as lowercase. PageMaker will spell-check and hyphenate any occurrence of that word, whether it contains capital letters or not.

If you choose **Exactly as typed,** then the word in the edit box will be entered into the user dictionary, *case-specific.* That is, Page-Maker will spell-check and hyphenate only the occurrences of that word that include the same capitalized and lowercase letters.

If you want to do this:	Then follow these steps:	Shortcuts · Notes · Hints
4.239 Enter a discretionary hyphen	■ First make sure the hyphenation feature is turned on: with the **text tool,** select the paragraph(s) containing the word(s) you want to hyphenate; press Command H; click in the "On" checkbox button if it isn't already checked; click OK. ■ With the **text tool,** click in the word at the exact spot you want to enter the discretionary hyphen. ■ Press Command Hyphen.	■ The hyphenation feature defaults to "On," with "Manual plus dictionary" selected. If you haven't changed it, it is probably still set. ■ If entering a discretionary hyphen still doesn't hyphenate the word, you need to widen the hyphenation zone; see 4.225; 4.242.
4.240 Remove a discretionary hyphen	■ With the **text tool,** click in the word, directly to the *right* of the discretionary hyphen. Even if you can't *see* the discretionary hyphen, you can do this—just click to the right of where it would be if you *could* see it. ■ Press the Backspace/Delete key.	
4.241 Prevent a word from hyphenating	■ Follow the steps in 4.239 to enter a discretionary hyphen, but place it *in front of the word.* That particular occurrence of that word will never hyphenate.	■ Also see 4.243 to add a word to the user dictionary so it *never* hyphenates.

If you want to do this:	Then follow these steps:	Shortcuts ▾ Notes ▾ Hints
4.242 Change the hyphenation zone	■ Select the paragraph(s) you want to affect. ■ From the Type menu, choose "Hyphenation...," *or* press Command H. ■ In the "Hyphenation zone" edit box, change the value. The larger the value, the less PageMaker will hyphenate; the lower the value, the more hyphenation will occur. Please see 4.229–4.231. • Click OK.	■ For instance, if the hyphenation zone is .5 inch and you want more words to hyphenate, change .5 inch to .25 inch. ■ Remember, anything you change in the "Hyphenation" dialog box is paragraph-specific; it applies only to the paragraphs that are selected when you choose the dialog box.
4.243 Add a word to the user dictionary, setting and ranking the hyphenation points	■ From the Type menu, choose "Hyphenation...," *or* press Command H. ■ Click the "Add..." button. ■ In the "Word" edit box, type the word you want to add to the dictionary. ■ Insert tildes (~; 4.236) where you want the word to hyphenate: 　□ **One tilde:** preferred hyphenation. 　□ **Two tildes:** less preferable, but acceptable. 　□ **Three tildes:** least acceptable; hyphenate at this point only if necessary. 　□ **No tildes:** never hyphenate this word. ■ Make sure the proper dictionary is selected, if you have more than one (4.234). ■ Select "As all lowercase" or "Exactly as typed"; see 4.238. ■ Click OK twice, *or* press Option Return.	■ Personally, I don't even bother entering tildes at the least acceptable point. Except for very lengthy words, I generally put one tilde at the only point where I would accept a hyphenation and don't even let PageMaker have any other options. ■ You can enter a maximum of 31 characters as a word.

If you want to do this:

4.244 Remove a word from the user dictionary

If the word is not in the user dictionary, you will get this dialog box when you try to remove it:

Couldn't delete word from dictionary.
Word not found in user dictionary.

Continue   7529:28683

Then follow these steps:

- From the Type menu, choose "Hyphenation...," **or** press Command H.
- Click the "Add..." button (yes, the Add button).
- In the "Word" edit box, type the word you want to remove from the dictionary.
- Choose the dictionary you want to remove it from.
- Click the "Remove" button. Click the OK button of the next dialog box.
- You can only remove words from the *user dictionary*. This means that if you or someone else did not input the word into the user dictionary, it cannot be removed from there. It is not possible to remove words from the main dictionary.

Shortcuts ▾ Notes ▾ Hints

- If you get told "Word not found in user dictionary" and you know you entered it earlier, you may have misspelled it, either when you entered it or just now when you tried to remove it. Remember, even blank spaces are characters, so if you hit the Spacebar after the word when you entered it, you have to type it with a Spacebar if you want to remove it.

  Also, each separate dictionary has its own user dictionary (except for Legal, Medical and US English, which all share one). If you are switching dictionaries around on different paragraphs, you may have entered the word originally into another user dictionary.

If you want to do this:

Then follow these steps:

Shortcuts ▾ Notes ▾ Hints

4.245 Change the hyphenation points of a word that is already in the dictionary

- If the word you want to add is typed on the screen, select it. Don't select any extra spaces at the end of the word, or any punctuation—just the word itself. It will be in the "Add word to user dictionary" dialog box when you get there (press Command H, then click "Add..."). Change the tildes as in 4.243. Click OK, and the new hyphenation points will take precedence over the original ones.

- If the word you want to change is not on the screen, you can add the word with the new hyphenation points to the user dictionary (4.243) as usual. Since Page-Maker checks the user dictionary first, the new version will take precedence over the original points.

- If you get a message telling you the word is already in the user dictionary, then first *remove* the word (4.244). You don't have to click the last OK button; just click the "Add..." button again and add the word with its new hyphenation.

- A great exercise would be to change the hyphenation of the word "dictionary." The Houghton-Mifflin main dictionary within PageMaker hyphenates it wrong (see 8.103). You should also change "dictionaries."

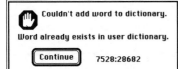

Couldn't add word to dictionary.

Word already exists in user dictionary.

Continue   7528:28682

5.1 Minimums and maximums:

Item	Minimum	Maximum
Tabs	0	40 per parag.*
	Can be as close as ¹⁄₃₂"	
Indents	The left and right indents cannot get closer than ¹¹⁄₃₂" to each other	

The tab limitation of 40 per paragraph is literally 40 per paragraph, not 40 per story or text block.

Note: *Indents and tabs can be very frustrating if you don't understand their logic. Once you understand it, you will find they are extremely consistent and dependable. You must keep in mind that tabs do exactly what you tell them. The problem is, we often don't know what we're telling them. If you find yourself screaming and yelling at tabs and indents, remember they are doing what you told them. It is your responsibility to* understand *what you are telling them.*

5.2 Indents and tabs are extremely important when working with *proportional type,* such as the type created on a Macintosh. On a typewriter, the text is *monospaced;* that is, each character takes up the same amount of space—the letter **i** takes up as much space as the letter **m.** When type is *proportional,* the letter **i** takes up about *one-fifth* the space of the letter **m.**

With monospaced typewriter type, you know that pressing the spacebar five times at one place will create exactly the same amount of space as pressing the spacebar five times somewhere else on the page. When working with proportional type, though (which means any font on the Mac except Courier and Monaco), using the spacebar is not accurate.

1. I inserted two spaces here after the period, and then spaced in this line.
2. Often it may look aligned on the screen.
3. But when it is printed, the misalignments are sadly obvious.

However, using tabs:

1. This is the first paragraph.
2. It will look aligned on the screen.
3. And when it is tabbed, you can rest assured it will really align when printed.

5.3 *Never* use the spacebar to align text. *Always* tab.

If you find you have trouble with indents and tabs, review the following principles:

5.4 ■ You must have the **text tool** chosen in order to set indents or tabs, and you must select the text *before* you try to create indents or tabs.

5.5 ■ Indents and tabs affect **only:**
   □ the flashing insertion point; **or**
   □ the paragraph in which the insertion point is flashing; **or**
   □ all *paragraphs* in which at least one character has been selected with the text tool.

   A new paragraph is created every time you press the Return key—a return address of three lines is actually three paragraphs (see 5.10).

5.6 ■ If any *portion* of any number of paragraphs is selected with the text tool, then the indent/tab formatting will affect *all* those paragraphs.

5.7 ■ Remember, no matter how many tabs you set in the ruler, in your text you must press the Tab *key* to move the insertion point over to the set tab before you begin to type!

5.8 ■ If the insertion point is flashing and it is not imbedded in any paragraph *but is sitting alone on its own line (and thus is its own paragraph),* then all the tab/indent formatting *will be put into that insertion point*—anything typed after that point will follow those specifications.

☞ *But,* let's say you format the insertion point, then move the mouse and *click* the insertion point down somewhere else, whether in another text block, the same paragraph, or even just a few characters over—*the second insertion point will not hold the formatting you just put into the first one* (5.9).

5.9 ■ Don't forget—standard Macintosh convention is that the insertion point *picks up the formatting of the character to its left.** That is, whatever font, style, size, leading, tabs, indents, paragraph spacing, etc., is in the character to the left of the flashing insertion point, even if that character is a blank space, that formatting will follow the insertion point as you create new characters.

So once you have your tabs and indents set up, as long as you press Returns you will carry on that formatting. Again, if you set your insertion point down somewhere else, you will lose it all—it will pick up its left neighbor's formatting.

* *If the insertion point is the first thing in a text block, it will pick up the formatting from the first character. If the insertion point begins a new text block, it will pick up the formatting from the defaults (1.6–1.9).*

Also read 5.14–5.21

Tabs and the line-break command

5.10   Tab formatting is *paragraph-specific;* that is, it applies to the *entire paragraph,* no matter what portion of it is selected. At the same time, it applies *only* to the paragraph that is selected. Of course, on a Mac every time you press a Return you create a new paragraph. Thus, changing a tab for a column of text means you must select every line of the entire column.

5.11   However, PageMaker offers a way to create separate lines of text, but keep them contained as a single paragraph. If you *do* need a new line of text, but you don't want to start a new *paragraph,* then use the **line-break** command: press **Shift-Return** instead of a regular Return. Doing this will create a hard line-break, but it will retain the line as part of the paragraph. See 3.230–3.236 for more info on this great little feature.

5.12

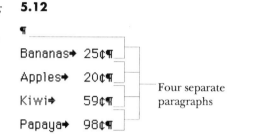

Four separate paragraphs

In the list of fruit (with tabs indicated by right arrows), I ended each line with a Return key, indicated by the ¶ marker. From the bottom of one marker to the bottom of the next is one paragraph.

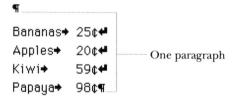

One paragraph

In the same list, I used a Shift-Return at the end of each line, indicated by the left-pointing arrows. This creates a line break, as you can see, but retains the text as one paragraph, between the two ¶ markers. Now I can format the entire unit as one paragraph.

5.13 Examples of tab alignments

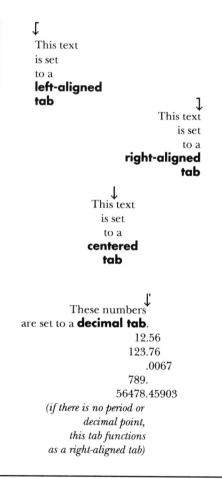

This text is set to a **left-aligned tab**

This text is set to a **right-aligned tab**

This text is set to a **centered tab**

These numbers are set to a **decimal tab**.
12.56
123.76
.0067
789.
56478.45903
(if there is no period or decimal point, this tab functions as a right-aligned tab)

How the tabs work:

Be sure to read the following pages for a thorough explanation of the ruler. See 5.13 for examples of the tab alignments.

5.14 When setting tabs in the Indents/tabs ruler, you must, in this order:
- **First** select the text you want to affect (5.5).
- **Then** get the Indents/tabs ruler (from the Type menu).
- **Click** in the ruler to set the tab.
- **Choose** a tab alignment (5.35).
- **Always** check to make sure the tail of the tab indicates the tab setting you want (5.13).
- Click OK.

5.15 PageMaker's **internal pre-set tabs** are set every half inch, indicated by tiny triangles (5.22a), so even if you haven't set any tabs yourself, hitting the Tab key will move the insertion point a half inch each time. As soon as you set one of your own tabs, all the internal pre-set tabs to the *left* of that one are eliminated; there are still internal pre-set tabs to the *right* of any you set yourself (5.22b/c).

5.16 Now, the following concept can be confusing, but it is a key to understanding tabs. Read it slowly and carefully:

Tabs are seen by the Mac as characters, the same as any other characters; they just have a different visual representation on the screen—to us they are invisible. When you press the Tab key one or more times before typing a word, that word hangs on to those Tabs, as shown in the word Hello below. Tab keys are indicated by the right arrows.

a) *In the Story Editor, you can see the visual representation of the Tab keys as little arrows (5.20). These three tabs will stay with* Hello *until you physically delete them.*

If no new tabs have been set in the indents/tabs ruler, then Hello will align with the third pre-set tab.

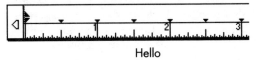

Hello

b) *The third pre-set tab is at 1.5 inches*

5.17 The tabs in a line are *cumulative;* for example, in the figure below: Mary will go to the first tab, Denny will go to the second tab, and Janyce will go to the third tab, wherever those tabs may be found.

More on tabs

5.18 Has something like this ever happened to your text?

- In your text, you hit the Tab key three times and arrived at the 1.5" default tab; you typed the word "Hello" (as in 5.16a).
- Then you went to the indents/tabs ruler, set a tab at 1.5", and clicked OK.
- Your tabbed info jumped over to 2.5", not 1.5"!
- That's because you had put *three* tabs into the word "Hello"; Hello said to itself "I'm going to the third tab—no matter where I find it, even if it's on the next line, I'm going to the third tab."
- Setting a tab at 1.5" deleted all the default tabs to its left, causing the tab at 1.5 to become the *first* tab.
- But remember, the default at 2" is still there, which is now the *second* tab. The default at 2.5" is also still there, which is now the *third* tab. Since the word "Hello" was told to go to the *third* tab, it goes to 2.5".

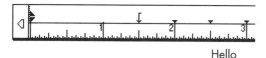

The defaults to the left of 1.5" disappear, making the 1.5" tab the first one.

5.19 To delete those extra tab characters, in the text simply backspace from the H in Hello—*tabbed spaces are deleted just as if they were characters*, whether you can see the arrows or not, and whether you are in the Story Editor or on the publication page.

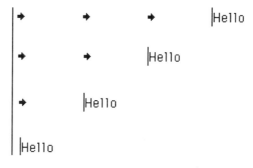

Set the insertion point to the left of the H; backspace once for each tab you want to delete.

5.20 In the Story Editor (Section 8) you can choose to see the tabs as visible characters, as in 5.19 (while in the Story Editor, from the Options menu choose "Display ¶"). This can help impress upon you that every time you hit the Tab key, you are creating a character that will stay there until you remove it. And as long as a Tab character is there, it will always try to find its spot on the ruler. You can also use the Story Editor to find and remove unwanted tabs (8.78).

5.21 The moral of the story: don't press the Tab key more than once per word/column until you get your tabs set up and know where you are going. You can always go back and adjust either the Tab characters or the tab settings if you decide later that they need to be moved.

The Indents/tabs ruler from the Type menu: Defaults and other important miscellaneous info

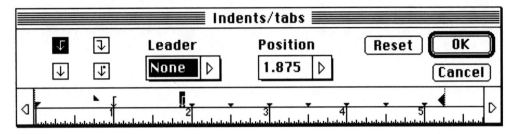

5.22 There are three kinds of **default tabs** that can be set in this ruler:

a) PageMaker's **internal pre-set default tabs,** set every half inch, indicated by the tiny triangles, as seen above. Clicking "Reset" eliminates all other tabs and restores these.

b) **Application default tabs,** indicated by regular tab markers (5.40). Set these defaults when there is no publication open (5.76). These will override the pre-set tabs and will apply to every new publication you create.

c) **Publication default tabs,** also indicated by regular tab markers. Set these defaults when a publication is open and the pointer tool is selected (5.75). These will override the application defaults, but will only apply to *new* text created in the current publication.

d) **Paragraph-specific tabs** are set while text is selected with the text tool (5.55). They are **not defaults,** and apply only to the selected paragraphs, overriding all other defaults.

Miscellaneous info:

5.23   The ruler always appears directly above the spot where the insertion point is flashing, with the zero point (5.37) aligned at the left edge of the text block. If the left edge is not visible or if there isn't enough space, the ruler places itself in the center of the screen.

It's not a bad idea to position the text you want to tab and indent so it is visible in the lower left part of the screen; this will enable you to see the entire ruler when it appears.

5.24   The ruler is actually a window; you can press-and-drag in its title bar (the top portion with the lines in it; 5.34) to move it around. If it isn't already, place the ruler so the zero point is sitting directly on top of the left margin of your text block, as shown in the examples 5.49 through 5.52. Use the ruler scroll bars also (5.36a/b), to help position the zero point.

5.25   The spacing and breakdown of the ruler markings changes with your page view, as the ruler adjusts itself according to the view at the moment; e.g., if you are viewing your page at 200%, the ruler will also show a 200% view. Thus, if you want to precisely place tabs and indents, get the ruler while in a larger view.

5.26   The measurement system of the ruler is determined by the measurement system used in the rest of the publication; i.e., if your page ruler is in inches, your tabs ruler will be in inches; if your page ruler is in picas, your tabs ruler will be in picas, etc. You can change this with the Preferences command (1.210–1.213).

Using the ruler

5.27 The Indents/tabs ruler has absolutely nothing to do with the horizontal ruler on the screen. In the Indents/tabs ruler you will see *dotted lines* (5.45). These dotted lines indicate *the outer edges of your text block*—the edges where the handles appear. If you don't see them on either end, press the little *scroll arrows* (5.36) to move the ruler back and forth.

5.28 The large right triangle, which is the *right indent* (5.44), is where all the text will align, within the handles.

5.29 The left triangle is made of two separate triangles: the top half is the *first-line indent* (5.39); the bottom half is the *left indent* (5.38). You can drag the top half back and forth by itself, but the bottom half always drags along the top half with it.

5.30 To move the bottom half of the left indent independently, hold the Shift key down, then drag.

5.31 Changes in your text will not be made until the OK button is clicked. Changes are not Undo-able (meaning you cannot use the *menu* to Undo changes)— you just have to go back and fix them.

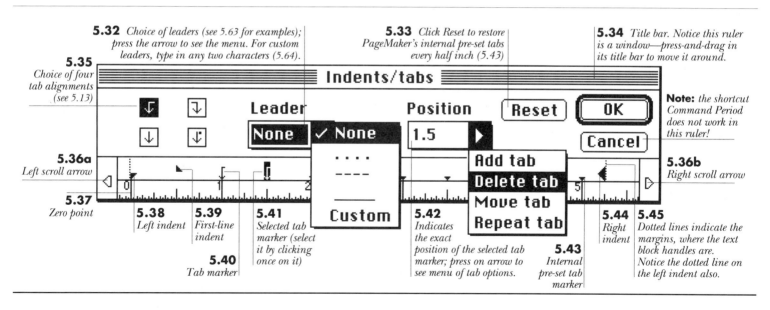

5.32 *Choice of leaders (see 5.63 for examples); press the arrow to see the menu. For custom leaders, type in any two characters (5.64).*

5.33 *Click Reset to restore PageMaker's internal pre-set tabs every half inch (5.43)*

5.34 *Title bar. Notice this ruler is a window—press-and-drag in its title bar to move it around.*

5.35 *Choice of four tab alignments (see 5.13)*

Note: *the shortcut Command Period does not work in this ruler!*

5.36a *Left scroll arrow*

5.36b *Right scroll arrow*

5.37 *Zero point*

5.38 *Left indent*

5.39 *First-line indent*

5.40 *Tab marker*

5.41 *Selected tab marker (select it by clicking once on it)*

5.42 *Indicates the exact position of the selected tab marker; press on arrow to see menu of tab options.*

5.43 *Internal pre-set tab marker*

5.44 *Right indent*

5.45 *Dotted lines indicate the margins, where the text block handles are. Notice the dotted line on the left indent also.*

Indents/tabs

Leader Position Reset OK

None ✓ None 1.5 ▶ Cancel

· · · ·
－ － － －
Custom

Add tab
Delete tab
Move tab
Repeat tab

Indents

5.46   You can **Indent** from the left or right *margin*. The margin, in this function, is not referring to any *page* or *column* margin, but to the margins of the *text block* as defined by its handles (for resizing the text block, see 3.97; 3.109–3.111). The margins show up in the indents/tabs ruler as dotted lines at either end, the left always being at zero. Neither indents nor tabs can be placed beyond either margin.

5.47   The **first-line indent** is only activated *on the first line after the Return key is pressed*. This is great for automatically indenting all paragraphs in body copy: you can either set up the indent before you begin typing so every paragraph will automatically indent, or select all the text afterward and set the indent. All first lines will be affected. (You can always re-adjust it at any time.)

5.48   Typical typewriter procedure was to use a tab for paragraph indents. The advantage of using the first-line indent instead of a tab is that you don't need to press the Tab key to activate it; it just happens on a Return. Also, you can more easily eliminate it from, or add it to, blocks of text, as it isn't dependent on your having pressed the Tab key.

Examples of indents

On the far right is a **solid dark triangle**—that is the **right indent.** If you move that triangle to the left, all the selected text will move in that far from the right margin edge.

5.49   *Right indent*

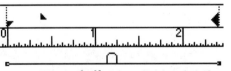

The **top half** of the split triangle is the **first-line indent.** If you move this top half to the right, the *first line* of each paragraph of the selected text will move in that far from the left margin edge.

5.51   *First-line indent*

On the far left is a **split dark triangle**—that is the **left indent.** If you press on the bottom half and move *both* the top and the bottom parts of the left triangle, the entire paragraph will *indent* to that point. Remember, the *margin* is still at the boundary defined by the text block handles, indicated on the ruler by the dotted line at either end.

5.50   *Left indent*

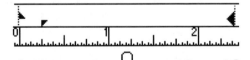

The **bottom half** of the triangle is the **left indent.** If you press the Shift key and move just the bottom half to the right, all lines of the selected text *except* the first line of each paragraph will move in that far from the left edge, or margin, where the text block handles are located.

5.52   *Hanging indent*

5.53

Scenario #6: Indents & tabs together—creating numbered paragraphs

a)

b)

1. A numbered paragraph needs the *first-line indent* set at the margin, and the *left indent* set far enough to the right to allow for the numbering, as shown above, **a).**

2. Notice in this arrangement there is also a *tab* set directly on top of the left indent. This is to get the first word of the text over to the indent.

3. When typing the text, type the number and then the period.

4. Next press Tab to get to the left indent (the bottom triangle), which is where all the type is going to align.

5. As you type, the text will *word wrap at the right indent, and align at the left indent,* just as you see here.

8. If the numbers are going to go beyond one digit, as in the number 10, then you must use *another* tab in order to keep the numbers aligned and to prevent this look:
   8. Aligned.
   9. Aligned.
   10. Not aligned. Oops.

9. So, even before typing the first number, set the ruler in this manner, shown in **b):**
   - Set the first-line indent (top triangle) all the way to the left margin.
   - Set the left indent (bottom triangle) to where text will align (allow room for increasing numbers).
   - Set a decimal tab *between* the two indents (allow more room on the left side of the tab for numbers to grow larger). If you're not using a decimal or a period, you can set a right-aligned tab to produce the same effect.
   - Set a left-aligned tab directly on top of the left indent (bottom triangle).

10. When typing the text, follow these steps:
    - Between numbered paragraphs, hit Return.
    - Press Tab; this will take you to the decimal tab; type the number and the period.

- Press Tab again; this will take you to the tab on the left indent; begin typing.
- As your text word wraps, it will come back to the left indent (the bottom half of the triangle) and align there, making your text look like these last three numbered paragraphs (without the bullets).

11. Remember, **never** use the space bar to align text or numbers—**always** use a tab, even if you're aligning only one or two spaces.

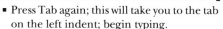

5.54 Scenario #7: Example of nested indents

Nested indents is a term used for indents within indents, such as in this column. Oftentimes this necessitates changing the ruler formatting several times in one document.

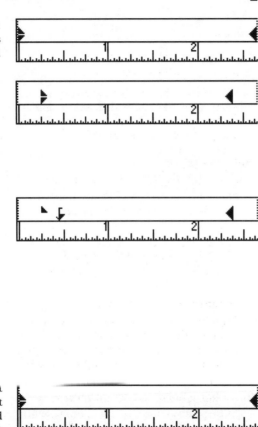

> To nest *this* paragraph, I pressed the Return key after the word *document,* then set a new ruler. In the new ruler, I moved *both* the left and right indents inward from the margins. Since the Return key had created a new paragraph, the indents/tabs ruler only affected the text *following* the insertion point.
>
> - Now, on *these* bulleted paragraphs I used a combination of the tabs and indents.
> - I placed the first-line indent marker where you see the bullet.
> - I placed the left indent marker where I wanted the text to align.
> - I put a tab directly on top of the left indent marker, so I could tab the first line to the spot where I wanted the rest of the text to align.
> - I left the right indent marker right where it was.

Now, in this paragraph I set the indents back out to the margins, returning to the format of the first paragraph. You may have also noticed I deleted the extra space between those paragraphs (4.87) in the bulleted section to further emphasize their grouping.

If you want to do this:

Then follow these steps:

Shortcuts ▾ Notes ▾ Hints

Tabs

5.55 Set a new tab,
or add a tab

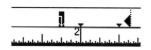

Tab marker, selected, in the ruler

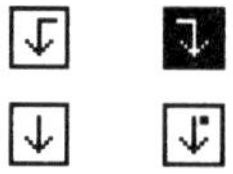

*Choice of tab alignments (see 5.13
for examples of each alignment)*

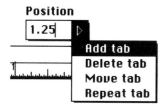

- With the **text tool,** click to set an
insertion point;
or select *all* the paragraphs in which
a tab is to be set.
- From the Type menu, choose "Indents/
tabs…" *or* press Command I.

Either Manually:
- In the Indents/tabs ruler, click at the
point on the ruler markings where you
want to set the tab; a tab marker as shown
at left should appear.
- In the upper left of the ruler, click on the
tab icon (as shown at left) symbolizing the
alignment you want (5.13); click OK.

Or using the Position box:
- Type in the exact measurement for where
you want the tab to appear;
- Press on the arrow in the box;
- Slide down and choose "Add tab."
- In the upper left, click on the tab icon
symbolizing the alignment you want
(5.13); click OK.

- Remember, the Indents/tabs function
only applies to the **paragraph** that has
the insertion point in it, or the paragraphs you have selected. Mac sees a
new paragraph *every* time you press the
Return key, so if you have a column
of information, each *line* is a separate
paragraph—unless you have used the
Shift-Return line break (5.11).
- Check to make sure the tail of the tab
is indicative of the type of tab you want
(see 5.13). If it isn't, **change** that tab
by selecting a new icon (5.59). You can
always click OK in the ruler and go check
out your text, then come back and change
the tab if you don't like it. Don't you
think this ruler should have an "Apply"
button? Write to Aldus and tell them.

257

If you want to do this:	Then follow these steps:	Shortcuts ▾ Notes ▾ Hints

5.56 Set a tab directly on top of an indent marker

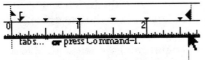

Click here in the tick marks, and the tab will pop up to the top of the ruler.

- Follow the same procedure as 5.55, but this time click in the ruler markings on the *bottom* half of the ruler, directly under the indent marker—the tab will slide right up the tick mark and land directly on top of the indent marker. Sometimes if the right indent marker is directly on the right margin, you must set the tab in just a fraction of an inch.

- If the two halves of the left indent are separated, you cannot place a tab on the left-most one; and it doesn't make sense to place anything except a right-aligned tab on the right indent.
- If you still have trouble setting a tab directly on top of an indent marker, set a tab anywhere else and just drag it over on top of the indent.

5.57 Delete a tab

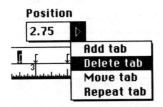

- With the **text tool,** click to set an insertion point in the paragraph; **or** select *all* the paragraphs from which you want to delete the tab(s).
- From the Type menu, choose "Indents/tabs…" **or** press Command I.

Either Manually:
- *Press* on the tab you wish to delete and drag it *down* off the ruler; when you let go of it, the tab will disappear.

Or use the Position box:
- Click once on the tab;
- Press on the Position box arrow; choose "Delete tab."
- **Or** in the Position box, type in the ruler measurement of the tab you want to delete;
  □ Press on the arrow; choose "Delete tab."

- **Note:** You cannot delete the internal pre-set tabs—those tiny triangles (5.22a).
- Deleting a right-most tab that *you* have set causes all pre-set tabs to reappear that were originally between the deleted tab and the next tab to the left.
- Now, you must understand that this only deletes *the tab marker in the ruler*—it does *not* delete the tab character you typed into your text! Even though you delete a marker, the text is still going to look for another tab marker to jump to. To delete the tab character itself from your text, backspace it, just as if it were a visible character (5.19).

If you want to do this:

Then follow these steps:

Shortcuts ▾ Notes ▾ Hints

5.58 Move a tab

- With the **text tool,** click to set an insertion point in the paragraph; **or** select *all* the paragraphs in which you want to move the tab.
- From the Type menu, choose "Indents/tabs…," *or* press Command I.

Either Manually:

- Simply *press* on the tab you wish to reposition and drag it to its new location; you can drag any tab marker right across any others without bothering them.

Or use the Position box:

- Click once on the tab to select it;
- Type the new ruler measurement into the Position box;
- Press on the Position box arrow; choose "Move tab."

- You can't move the internal pre-set tabs (the tiny little triangles).
- You *can* set new *application* defaults (5.22b) or override the pre-set tabs with *publication* defaults (5.22c).

- Remember, pre-set tabs will appear and disappear as the right-most tab is moved.

- Specifying a measurement in the Position box is great for getting precise placement, even in a small view.

Position

Add tab
Delete tab
Move tab
Repeat tab

5.59 Change a tab from one alignment to another

- With the **text tool,** click to set an insertion point in the paragraph; **or** select *all* the paragraphs in which you want to change the tab.
- From the Type menu, choose "Indents/tabs…," *or* press Command I.
- Click once on the tab *marker* you wish to change.
- In the upper left of the ruler, click on the new tab alignment (5.13) you wish to change to; click OK.

- This particular step cannot be done from the Position box—*you must select the tab itself* by clicking once on it; that is, typing a tab's ruler measurement in the Position box and then clicking on a new tab alignment will *not* change the tab specified in the Position box.

If you want to do this:	Then follow these steps:	Shortcuts ▾ Notes ▾ Hints

5.60 Repeat a tab

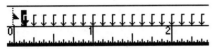

a) Notice the tabs are repeating the space between the selected tab and the zero point.

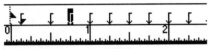

b) Notice the tabs repeat the space between the selected tab and the tab to its left.

- With the **text tool,** select *all* the paragraphs in which you want tabs; **or** just set an insertion point at the point where you want new text to begin.
- From the Type menu, choose "Indents/tabs…," *or* press Command I.
- Either set a tab (5.55) or select an existing tab by clicking once on it;
- Press on the arrow in the Position box;
- Choose "Repeat tab."
- Read the next column ☞

- Ever try to set a tab every 3/16"? Well, this procedure sets up a series of tabs that will repeat an equidistant measure across the ruler. That distance is determined by either the space between the zero point and the first tab *(figure a)*, or between the tab selected and the tab to its left *(figure b)*.
- If there are currently tabs to the right of the tab selected to repeat, they will be *replaced* by the repeated tabs.
- If you change your mind and you want the ruler you had originally set, you must *Cancel;* choosing *Reset* will *not* reset your original ruler! (5.61)

5.61 Reset the tabs

[**Reset**]

- With the **text tool,** select *all* the paragraphs in which you want tabs reset; **or** just set the insertion point in the one paragraph you want to affect.
- From the Type menu, choose "Indents/tabs…," *or* press Command I.
- Click the "Reset" button; click OK.

- Resetting the tabs deletes all *publication and application* tabs (5.22b/c) and restores all the *internal pre-set* tabs (the tiny triangles; 5.22a); it does not affect the indents.
- Resetting *when no text is selected* will reset the default tabs back to the *internal pre-set* tabs (5.22a).

5.62 Clear all tabs

- With the **text tool**, select *all* the paragraphs in which you want to clear all tabs.
- From the Type menu, choose "Indents/tabs…," *or* press Command I.
- Click the Reset button.

- Clearing all the tabs *does not mean you have no tabs;* you can't get rid of the internal pre-set tabs. You can't even set a default of zero tabs—there must be at least one.

If you want to do this:

5.63 Set a tab with leaders

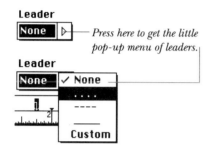

Press here to get the little pop-up menu of leaders.

Example of dot leaders 1

Example of dash leaders——————2

Example of line leaders _____3

Example of custom leaders • • • • • • 4
This custom example is a bullet and an en-space combination

The line leaders are great for quick forms; just hit a Return at the end of each line, instead of a number. Move the tab to make the lines longer or shorter. Change the leading or paragraph space to change the space between the lines.

Then follow these steps:

- With the **text tool,** select *all* the paragraphs in which you want tabs with leaders;
  or just set an insertion point at the point where you want new text to begin.
- From the Type menu, choose "Indents/tabs…" **or** press Command I.
- If you don't want the current tabs, click Reset;
  or at least delete any tabs to the left that you don't need.
- As usual, click in the ruler to set a new tab; **or** type a ruler measurement in the Position box; press on the arrow and choose "Add tab."
- Click on a tab alignment icon (5.35) to choose the alignment; typically, with leaders you want a **right-aligned** tab ⬇.
- Press on the arrow next to the Leaders box; choose the leader of your choice (for custom leaders, see 5.64); click OK.
- On your publication page, type the text that precedes the leaders; press Tab—if you don't see the leaders yet, that's okay!
- Type the text that is to be on the other end of the leaders—the leaders will then appear, if they haven't already.

Shortcuts ▾ Notes ▾ Hints

- The font, size, and style of the text at the *end* of the leaders can be different than that at the *beginning* of them; the leaders themselves will always be in the same font, etc., as the last character they *follow* (see 5.65 for tips on circumventing that situation).
- The "Custom" choice allows you to create leaders from any single character on the keyboard, or any combination of two characters, including a space (5.64; 5.65).
- If you want leaders with nothing at the end and the leaders won't show up until you type something, then insert whichever of these characters works for your project:

Spacebar ....
  (just the Spacebar)
Fixed space ....
  (Option–Spacebar)
Thin space ....
  (Command Shift t)
En space ....
  (Command Shift n)
Em space ....
  (Command Shift m)
Return ....
  (Return)
Line break ....
  (Shift-Return)

If you want to do this:

Then follow these steps:

Shortcuts ▾ Notes ▾ Hints

5.64   Create your own custom leaders

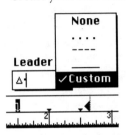

- With the **text tool,** select *all* the paragraphs in which you want to have custom leaders;
or set the insertion point at the point where you want to begin using leaders.
- From the Type menu, choose "Indents/ tabs…" **or** press Command I.
- If you don't want the current tabs, click Reset; **or** at least delete any tabs to the left that you don't need.
- Either set a new tab or click once on the one you want to add custom leaders to (usually a right-aligned tab).
- While the tab marker is selected, in the Leaders box press on the arrow; choose "Custom."
- Type any two characters of your choice, including any of the non-breaking spaces or alternate characters (3.240, or see Appendix E); click OK.
- On the publication page, type the text; press Tab—*you will probably not see the leaders!* Type the text at the end of the leaders—the leaders will then appear (if they haven't already). Also see 5.65.

- The font, size, and style of the text at the *end* of the leaders can be different than that at the *beginning* of them; the leaders themselves will always be in the same font, etc., *as the last character they follow.* If this is a problem, see 5.65 for solutions.

- Even though the alternate character may appear as just an empty square or some other strange symbol in the entry box in the ruler, it will turn into the corresponding character in the font of your text.

What an easy way 🐇🐇🐇🐇🐇🐇🐇🐇🐇🐇🐇🐇🐇🐇🐇🐇🐇🐇🐇🐇🐇🐇🐇🐇🐇🐇 to get bunnies running backward across the page.
(see 5.65)

If you want to do this:

5.65 Create fancy custom leaders, where the font of the leaders is different than the font before or after the leaders

Examples:

Isn't this fancy? ◆◆◆◆◆Oh my yes!

Get practical •••••••••••••••••••••••••••••••OK

Leader

This is the character I entered to get the diamond leaders in the second example. Then in the line of text, I typed the thin space, selected it, and turned it into 6-point Zapf Dingbats. (Extra trick: to get the diamond so small, I subscripted it and changed the size to 50 percent. Unfortunately, you can't change the baseline of the leader this way. See 3.163–3.170 for super- and subscripts).

Then follow these steps:

- Create custom leaders as in 5.64. In the Leader box, type in the character you want to be your leader. Don't worry if it's an alternate character that appears as a blank box or some other strange symbol. (For instance, in the example to the left, the text font is Baskerville, but to get the little hand in the Zapf Dingbats font, I typed Shift 8, which looks amazingly like an asterisk.) Click OK.
- Type your info, press Tab, type the text at the end of the leader. Of course the leader at this point is still in the text font.
- Just after the last character *before* the Tab (in the first example, just after the question mark), insert a thin space (Command Shift T).
- Select that blank thin space and change the font of it (in these examples, to Zapf Dingbats). The leaders will pick up that font. You do have that little extra space, though. If you don't like it you can always select it and reduce the point size, thus reducing the point size of the leaders also. You can also kern between the last character and the thin space (4.182).

Shortcuts ▾ Notes ▾ Hints

- Use this trick also for those times when you need consistent leaders, but the preceding text is not always consistent; e.g., sometimes bold, sometimes light:

Tostadas **$1.95**
Enchiladas
　　with green sauce **$2.50**
　　with red sauce **$2.25**

Insert a consistent thin space (say, an 8-point light italic) after each item, before the leaders:

Tostadas **$1.95**
Enchiladas
　　with green sauce **$2.50**
　　with red sauce **$2.25**

- The easiest way to select that thin space you inserted, if your insertion point is still there just after it, is to hold down the Shift key and press the left arrow key.
- You may want to kern (4.182) between the last character and the inserted thin space.

263

If you want to do this:	Then follow these steps:	Shortcuts ▾ Notes ▾ Hints
5.66 Remove the leaders, not the tab	■ Select the paragraph(s) as noted in 5.64. ■ Click once on the tab that holds the leaders. ■ In the Leader box, press on the arrow; choose "None"; click OK.	
5.67 Set a tab with leaders that go right over the top of a text-wrapped object	■ Follow the steps for creating a tab with leaders (5.63; 5.64). ■ Just make sure that *both ends* of the tabbed line are *beyond the borders* of the text wrapping boundary.	■ The leaders can go in front of or in back of the text-wrapped object (select the text block with the *pointer tool*, and from the Element menu choose "Bring to front" or "Send to back"). ■ If the leaders don't all appear, you may need to redraw your screen—simply change page view sizes, click in the zoom box in the upper right corner of the window (⊟), **or** select the text block with the *pointer tool* and from the Element menu choose "Bring to Front."

L E T T E R S

are symbols

which turn matter

into spirit.

Alphonse de Lamartine

If you want to do this:	**Then follow these steps:**	**Shortcuts · Notes · Hints**

Indents

5.68   Set a first-line indent
(example and ruler: 5.51)

This paragraph has a first-line indent; that is, the first line indents to the right of the main body of text.

- With the **text tool,** click to set an insertion point in the paragraph;
  or select *all* the paragraphs in which you want to have a first-line indent;
  or set the insertion point at the point where you want text to begin.
- From the Type menu, choose "Indents/tabs…," *or* press Command I.
- Press on the **top** half of the large triangle on the far left of the indents/tabs ruler; press-and-drag it to the spot on that ruler where you want the first lines to indent; click OK.

- Remember, a *first line* is any line you type after pressing the Return key (5.47).
- As you hit Return, the next paragraph will pick up the same ruler formatting.
- You can also set your first-line indents from the Paragraph dialog box (3.203), **or** within your Style Sheets (Section 7).
- Typographic standards traditionally dictate a *one-em indent;* that is, an indent equivalent in width to the point size of your type—in 12-point type, the indent should be 12 points wide.
- You can set an indent in points in the Paragraph dialog box (from the Type menu; 3.203); override the current ruler measurement if necessary (1.221).

5.69   Set a hanging indent
(example and ruler: 5.52)

This paragraph has a hanging indent; that is, the first line is to the left of the main body of text.

- Select the text as in 5.68.
- From the Type menu, choose "Indents/tabs…," *or* press Command I.
- Hold the Shift kcy down and press on the **bottom** half of the large split triangle on the far left of the indents/tabs ruler; press-and-drag it to the spot on that ruler where you want the **body** of the paragraph to align; click OK.

- Remember, a *first line* is any line after pressing the Return key. The first line will align at the **top half** of the triangle; the rest of the text will word-wrap to align at the **bottom half** of the triangle.
- If the top half is at zero, the bottom half will not move to the left unless you hold down the Shift key while dragging.

If you want to do this:

5.70 Delete any first-line indent or hanging indent

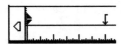

If both halves are at the zero marker, there will be no indents of any kind.

Then follow these steps:

- With the **text tool**, click to set an insertion point in the paragraph;
  or select *all* the paragraphs in which you want to have a first-line indent;
  or set the insertion point at the point where you want text to begin.
- From the Type menu, choose "Indents/tabs…," *or* press Command I.
- Press on the **top** half of the large split triangle; press-and-drag it to place it *directly on top of* the bottom half of the triangle.
- If necessary, press-and-drag on the **bottom** half of the black triangle to drag them *both* to wherever you want the text to align.

Shortcuts ▾ Notes ▾ Hints

- Take them both back to the zero point if you don't want to have any indent at all.

Experience is what you get—when you don't get what you want. Richard Thomas Cella

If you want to do this:

Then follow these steps:

Shortcuts • Notes • Hints

5.71 Indent from the left margin
(example and ruler: 5.50)

This first paragraph has no indent; that is, everything aligns with the left edge, or margin, *of the text block handles.*

   This second paragraph, however, is indented from the left margin of the same text block.

And this paragraph is reverted back to the specifications of the first one.

- With the **text tool**, set the insertion point in the paragraph;
  or select *all* the paragraphs you want to have indented;
  or set the insertion point at the point where you want text to begin.
- From the Type menu, choose "Indents/tabs…," *or* press Command I.
- If the top half of the left large triangle is not on top of the bottom half, then press-and-drag to place it on top.
- Press on the *bottom* half of the triangle (both halves will now move together); press-and-drag to the spot on the ruler where you want the text indented.

- Remember, the term "left *margin*" is *not* referring to the page margins or the column margins you set up, nor is it necessarily where the text is aligned in the text block—the left *margin* is where the left-side *handles* of the text block are. See the example in 5.50.

- Or hold the Shift key down and just drag the bottom half to meet under the top half.
- Take them both back to the zero marker if you don't want to have any indent at all.

5.72 Indent from the right margin
(example and ruler: 5.49)

This paragraph has no indent; that is, the text is justified with both edges, or margins, *of the text block handles.*

This second paragraph, however, is indented from the *right* margin of the same text block.

And this paragraph is reverted back to the specifications of the first one.

- Select the text the same as in 5.71 above.
- From the Type menu, choose "Indents/tabs…," *or* press Command I.
- If you don't see the large solid right triangle in the ruler, press on the right scroll arrow.
- When you find the large solid triangle, press-and-drag it to the spot on the ruler where you want the text indented.

- Remember, the term "right *margin*" is *not* referring to the page margins or the column margins you set up, nor is it necessarily where the text is aligned in the text block—the right *margin* is where the right-side *handles* of the text block are. See the example in 5.49.

If you want to do this:

5.73   Remove any indents

There
is
no
duty
we
so
much
underrate
as
the
duty
of
being
happy.

Robert Louis Stevenson

Then follow these steps:

- With the **text tool**, set the insertion point in the paragraph;
  or select *all* the paragraphs you want to remove indents from;
  or set the insertion point at the point where you want text to begin with no indents.
- From the Type menu, choose "Indents/tabs…," *or* press Command I.
- To remove the **right indent,** press-and-drag the large solid right triangle (if you don't see it, press on the right scroll arrow); drag the triangle all the way back to the dotted line on the right, which indicates the edge of your text block.
- To remove the **left indent,** press-and-drag both halves of the large left triangle back to the zero point. Hold down the Shift key to drag the bottom half, if necessary.

Shortcuts ▾ Notes ▾ Hints

- Remember, the term "*margin*" is *not* referring to the page margins or the column margins you set up, nor is it necessarily where the text is aligned in the text block—the *margins* of your text are defined by the *handles* of the text block. See the examples in 5.49 to 5.52.

If you want to do this:	Then follow these steps:	Shortcuts ▾ Notes ▾ Hints

Miscellaneous tab and indent info

5.74 Copy the entire tab/indent formatting to other *adjacent* paragraphs

- Select the text with the **text tool.** The trick here is to select the paragraph that has the formatting you want to apply to the others, *and* the paragraphs that you want to apply it to. You can drag up or down to select the separate, adjacent paragraphs, *but it is the ruler formatting in the paragraph* **at the top of the selection** *that will apply to all the other selected paragraphs.*
- From the Type menu choose "Indents/ tabs...," *or* press Command I.
- The ruler shows the format for the *topmost* paragraph you selected; just click OK and that formatting will be applied to the other selected paragraphs.

- Unfortunately, there is no way simply to copy the ruler formatting from one paragraph and apply it to other paragraphs that are not sequential. If you copy *text* from one format and paste it (using the text tool) into another, the pasted text takes on the formatting of the paragraph it is pasted *into.*
- You can, though, select some text that has the formatting you wish to copy, *create a style name,* and apply that *style* to other paragraphs (see Section 7 on Style Sheets).

5.75 Set the default tabs and indents for the current open publication

- While the publication is open, choose the **pointer tool,** even if it's already chosen.
- From the Type menu choose "Indents/ tabs...," *or* press Command I.
- Set any tabs and indents you like. PageMaker's *internal pre-set* tabs will still be the tiny triangles, and your publication defaults will look like regular tab markers. These defaults will apply only to this particular publication.

- Clicking "Reset" in the ruler will restore the tiny triangles—the *internal PageMaker pre-set tabs*—every half inch, *not the application defaults you may have set!*
- Set publication default tabs when you find you regularly need a particular set-up; for instance, rather than every half inch, you really need tabs every 1.25 inches.

If you want to do this:	Then follow these steps:	Shortcuts ▾ Notes ▾ Hints
5.76 Set the default tabs and indents for the entire application	▪ *While no publication is open,* from the Type menu choose "Indents/tabs...." ▪ Set any tabs and indents you like. You'll notice your application and default tabs look like regular tab markers, as opposed to the triangular, internal, PageMaker pre-set tabs every half inch.	▪ If a publication is open, close it. You need to be looking at PageMaker's empty desktop, with a blank screen—no window open—and the PageMaker menu along the top. ▪ If you click the "Reset" button in the ruler, you will reset all the tabs back to the *pre-set internal PageMaker tabs,* indicated by the tiny triangles every half inch. ▪ See 1.6–1.16 for more info on setting defaults in general.
5.77 Reset the tiny triangular pre-set tabs	▪ You can't.	
5.78 Replace spaces with tabs throughout an entire story, where someone spaced more than twice, or remove tabs that someone entered in the wrong places	▪ Use the Story Editor (Section 8). Task 8.78 specifically walks you through finding and changing invisible characters, like tabs.	
5.79 Deselect a tab in the Indents/tabs ruler	▪ Click once in the white space above the measuring part of the ruler, like next to the word "Leader" or under "Reset."	

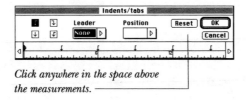

Click anywhere in the space above the measurements.

Containing matter of such Import
as will Astound and Delight
the User.

6 ▾ Paragraph Rules

6.0 Minimums and maximums:

Item	Minimum	Maximum
Length	-22.75 inches (indented or extended beyond the text or the text block)	+22.75 inches
Above or below the baseline	0 inches	22.75 inches

Marry, sir,

she's the kitchen wench

and all grease.

I know not what use to put her to,

but to make a lamp of her

and run from her

by her own light!

Dromio
The Comedy of Errors
William Shakespeare

6.1 This section deals with the incredible paragraph rules. No, these are not rules like "Every paragraph must contain a beginning thought, a developed idea, and a conclusion." "Rules," in design jargon, means "Lines." In PageMaker, in the Element menu they are called Lines, and in the Paragraph dialog box they are called Rules. Hmmm . . .

6.2 Anyway, this Rules feature is one of the greatest little inventions. Absolutely terrific. Now you can put rules under and over text, and as you edit the text, enlarge or reduce the type size, change the font, or move the text block, the rules come right along with it. Getting the rules placed in exactly the right position can take a little figuring and trial-and-error, but it is definitely very well worth the time spent.

6.3 In this book, every line you see embedded within text is actually a rule applied to the paragraph. Take a look at the little chart on page 119 or the quote on page 264. Or, hey, take a look at the far left column on this page. One amazing thing about these rules is that *they can extend beyond the borders of the text block!* I had a hard time believing they could be that wonderful. In this book, created entirely in PageMaker (really—I never touched Word), each column is a separate text block, threaded through all the pages of one section. But there are those hairline rules between each task that span all three columns. At first I was drawing them in. Then, of course, when I edited text I had to move them all. Now I have a style in my style sheet (see Style Sheets, Section 7) called "Hairline" that consists of a paragraph rule that starts in the left column and extends across the page; I just click the style name and it appears. I rearrange the text and it follows along. I'm so happy now.

6.4 The "Paragraph rules" dialog box *(from the Type menu, choose "Paragraph…"; click on the "Rules…" button)*

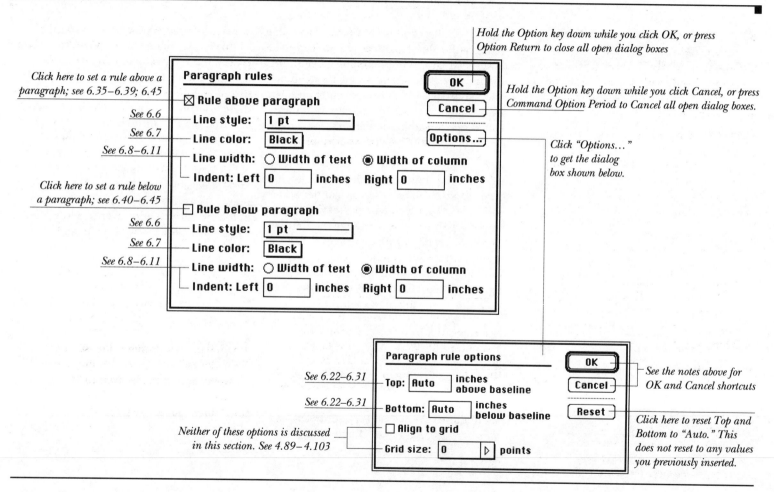

Hold the Option key down while you click OK, or press Option Return to close all open dialog boxes

Click here to set a rule above a paragraph; see 6.35–6.39; 6.45

Paragraph rules

☒ **Rule above paragraph**

See 6.6 — Line style: `1 pt ———`

See 6.7 — Line color: `Black`

See 6.8–6.11 — Line width: ○ **Width of text** ● **Width of column**

Indent: Left `0` inches Right `0` inches

Click here to set a rule below a paragraph; see 6.40–6.45

☐ **Rule below paragraph**

See 6.6 — Line style: `1 pt ———`

See 6.7 — Line color: `Black`

See 6.8–6.11 — Line width: ○ **Width of text** ● **Width of column**

Indent: Left `0` inches Right `0` inches

`OK`

`Cancel`

`Options…`

Hold the Option key down while you click Cancel, or press Command Option Period to Cancel all open dialog boxes.

Click "Options…" to get the dialog box shown below.

Paragraph rule options

See 6.22–6.31 — Top: `Auto` inches above baseline

See 6.22–6.31 — Bottom: `Auto` inches below baseline

Neither of these options is discussed in this section. See 4.89–4.103

☐ **Align to grid**

Grid size: `0` ▷ points

`OK`

`Cancel`

`Reset`

See the notes above for OK and Cancel shortcuts

Click here to reset Top and Bottom to "Auto." This does not reset to any values you previously inserted.

The "Paragraph rules" dialog box —*continued*

6.5   The "Paragraph rules" dialog box is where you define the look and length of the line (rule). The choices "Rule above paragraph" and "Rule below paragraph" look exactly the same, but can have different specs in them.

6.6   **Line style** is simply the same pop-up menu you are accustomed to using from the Element menu. See 6.32–6.33 for examples and point sizes of the patterned lines.

6.7   **Line color** is the same menu that appears in the "Color palette" (from the Windows menu), which holds all the default colors plus the ones you defined (14.91). See 6.49 for specifics on how to make your rules in colors or in shades of gray.

6.8   **Line width** offers you two choices. If you choose to extend the line the width of the *text,* then the rule will lengthen or shorten as you edit the words. If you choose to extend the line the width of the *column,* the line will lengthen or shorten as you change the width of the *text block* (which really has nothing to do with the *column*).

6.9   **Indent** allows you to indent the width of the line a certain distance from the beginning and end of the words (if you have "Width of text" chosen), or from the edges of the text block (if you have "Width of column" chosen). You can enter positive or negative values in the Left and Right boxes. **You can specify any value up to ±22.75 inches** (which is really a bit excessive because you can't have a page that large anyway).

6.10   If you have chosen **Width of column,** the value **0 (zero)** in the indents boxes will extend the line exactly the width of the **text block.**

YOUR ATTITUDE IS YOUR LIFE.

If you type in a **positive** value, such as .5, the rules will *indent* that amount from the left and right edges of the text block.

YOUR ATTITUDE IS YOUR LIFE.

If you type a **negative** value, such as -.5, the rules will *extend* that far beyond the text block! *You may not see it on the screen,* but it will print.

YOUR ATTITUDE IS YOUR LIFE.

6.11   If you have chosen **"Width of text,"** the value **0 (zero)** in the indents boxes will extend the line exactly the width of the words it is directly above or below. "Text," or words, includes any tabs or spaces!

YOUR ATTITUDE IS YOUR LIFE.

If you type in a **positive** value, such as .5, the rules will *indent* that amount from the beginning and end of the words.

YOUR ATTITUDE IS YOUR LIFE.

If you type a **negative** value, such as -.5, the rules will *extend* that amount from the from the beginning and end of the words. Notice this can also extend beyond the boundaries of the text block!

YOUR ATTITUDE IS YOUR LIFE.

273

6.12 **Notes about paragraph rules**

❖ Rules can be applied to style sheet definitions (Section 7).

❖ Rules can have a color applied to them (6.49).

❖ You cannot select paragraph rules with the pointer tool.

❖ You cannot edit rules (change anything about them) except through the Paragraph dialog box from the Type menu, or, if the rule is part of a style you created, the Paragraph dialog box found in "Define styles...."

❖ Paragraph rules will text wrap just like text (Section 10).

❖ The extra space for positioning the rule is added onto any space "before" or space "after" (4.63–4.75).

❖ The rules are actually *behind* the text, so you can put reverse text over black or colored rules and create other fancy effects.

The text to the left has the following specs:

Column width: 15.75 *picas (2.625 inches)*
Body text: Baskerville 10/auto (12)
Bullet: *Zapf Dingbats, Shift E; 10/auto (12); reverse; superscripted at 100% size, 25% position*
Indents:

	Left	*3p5*
	First	*-3p5*
	Right	*0p7*

Space after: 0
Rule above: 12 point
  Color: black
  Width of column
  Indent left: 2p
  Indent right: 13p
Rule below: Hairline
  Color: black
  Width of column
  Indent left: 2p
  Indent right: 0
Top of rule: 1p above
Bottom of rule: 0p6 below

p.s. For some reason if I pressed a tab after the Zapf Dingbat, the Dingbat would not show up. In fact, if I inserted a tab anywhere in the paragraph, the Dingbat would not come forward. I had to remove the tab and put in hard spaces. Tabs often present a problem in connection with paragraph rules.

6.13 **Points and picas**

To work efficiently with paragraph rules, it helps to understand points and picas.

In typesetting, inches are not used at all. Instead, the measuring system is **picas.**

There are **six picas in one inch;** one pica equals .167 of an inch (have you seen that number before?). Picas are generally used to measure width (as of columns or line lengths), or depth (as in columns, text blocks, or ad space). Anytime you would typically use inches, you can use picas.

Each pica is divided into 12 points.
Type size is measured in points; linespace (leading) is measured in points. There are, of course, 72 points in one inch.

Typing a value like **3p6** means you want 3 picas and 6 points. If you want less than one pica's worth, you must type the 0 (zero) before the p: **0p7** means 7 points.

One inch divided into 6 picas.

One inch divided into 72 points. Each line and each space between the lines is 1 point.

How paragraph rules work

6.14 Paragraph rules are actually attached to the paragraph. The rules are paragraph-specific, meaning they apply to the entire paragraph, even if only a portion of it is selected. To understand exactly where they attach, you need to understand *slugs*.

6.15 When you press and drag with the text tool over a line of type to select it, the black area you see is the line *slug*, a term held over from metal type.

This is not a banana slug.

6.16 The example directly above is 10-point type with auto leading (auto leading would be 12 points; 4.20–4.21). If you add more leading, the line slug will enlarge, because the slug in PageMaker is actually the size of the line of *leading*, not the size of the type. The slug below shows 10-point type with 20-point leading.

Visit the Guerneville Slug Fest.

6.17 Now, a *paragraph* slug (triple click with the text tool) also shows any "space after" you have set, as well as any "space before" from the following paragraph (4.63–4.75), as shown below.

Every year in Sonoma County we celebrate slugs at the Slug Fest: slug races, beauty contests, and prizes for the best slug recipes. You've just got to try Banana Slug Bread with walnuts, or Black Slugs Sautéed with garlic and our world-class wines. Yum.

6.18 Paragraph rules are automatically placed at the top and bottom of the *line* slugs, though, not the *paragraph* slugs. Here are the three previous examples with the default "Auto" rule specifications above and below.

This is not a banana slug.

Visit the Guerneville Slug Fest.

Every year in Sonoma County we celebrate slugs at the Slug Fest: slug races, beauty contests, and prizes for the best slug recipes. You've just got to try Banana Slug Bread with walnuts, or Black Slugs Sautéed with garlic and our world-class wines. Yum.

6.19 Obviously, the default specs are not usually what you will want. So we need to discuss the *baseline* of text lines, because you position the rules up or down from the baseline. The baseline is simply the invisible line that the letters sit on:

Slugs for Supper!   *baseline*

6.20 **No matter what the leading or the type size, the baseline stays the same.** With proportional leading (4.46–4.48), PageMaker takes the point size of the leading and divides it into thirds. Approximately two-thirds of it is positioned above the baseline, and one-third is positioned below the baseline. *That defines the slugs you see in 6.15–16.16, which in turn determines where the rules are automatically placed.* The **type size** is also divided the same way—two-thirds above and one third below. For instance, with 24-point type, PageMaker puts 16 points above the baseline and 8 points below.

6.21 So, if you want the rules placed somewhere other than where those "Auto" defaults place them, you need to insert a measurement in the "Paragraph rule options" dialog box (6.23–6.31).

The "Paragraph rule options" dialog box *(from the Type menu, choose "Paragraph…"; click "Rules…"; click "Options…")*

```
Paragraph rule options                    ┌──────────┐
                                          │    OK    │
Top:  [Auto]   picas                      └──────────┘
               above baseline             ┌──────────┐
                                          │  Cancel  │
Bottom: [Auto] picas                      └──────────┘
               below baseline             ┌──────────┐
☐ Align to grid                           │  Reset   │
                                          └──────────┘
Grid size: [0      ▷]  points
```

6.22   Read page 275.

6.23   "Top" affects the rules above, and "Bottom" affects the rules below (the ones you specified in the "Paragraph rules" dialog box). If you chose no rules, these values do nothing.

6.24   It is generally easier to work with the "Paragraph rule options" if you have your measuring system set to picas. To do that, from the Edit menu choose "Preferences…." Press on the box next to "Measuring systems" to get the pop-up menu, then choose "Picas." Click OK. (For more info on the "Preferences" dialog box, see 1.210–1.213.) No matter what your measuring system is, though, if you use the **0p_** sorts of values that I'll be mentioning here, (**zero, p** for picas, then a **point** value), they will override whatever system is currently in effect (1.221).

6.25   The values you enter in the "Top" or "Bottom" boxes determine how far above and below the baseline the rule will be placed. You have seen where "Auto" places the rules (6.18). **"Auto" places the rules on the slug boundaries, but any** *values you type in* **are literal. Note:** If you enter any value in "Top" or "Bottom" besides "Auto," then the placement of your rules will not be affected if you later decide to change the leading (see 6.31).

6.26   The values are literal; that is, if you specify 2p in the "Top" box, the rule will begin literally two picas above the baseline. That is, the *top* of the rule will begin 2 picas above the baseline, and the thickness of it will *hang down* from there (6.30).

6.27   If you specify 1p in the "Bottom" box, the rule will begin literally one pica below the last baseline: the *bottom* of the rule will begin one pica below the baseline, and the thickness of it will *build up* from there (6.30).

6.28   So you must take into consideration the size of the type. Since two-thirds of the point size of the type is above the baseline, and one-third is below the baseline (6.20), add up those figures plus the point size of the rule (6.33) to determine the exact distance above or below. You'll probably still have to experiment.

Maximize
Your Options

2 picas

1 pica

6.29   *These hairline rules are set at 2 picas above and 1 pica below the baselines (type is 24/23). You can see that these measurements are literal.*

Maximize
Your Options

2 picas

1 pica

6.30   *The paragraph now has 4-point rules. Notice the top rule hangs* **down** *from the top of the 2 picas, and the bottom rule* **builds up** *from the bottom of the 1 pica specification.*

Maximize
Your Options

2 picas

extra leading

1 pica

6.31   *Notice that changing the leading does not affect the relative positions of the rules. Neither will changing the font size. That's usually good.*

6.32 Line styles and point sizes

6.34 Wow

6.32 Line styles are shown at their actual size in the menu, except None, Hairline, and .5 point because of the resolution of most screens. See 2.19–2.21 for examples of actual printed lines, which may look slightly different than what you see on your screen.

6.33 Below are the literal point sizes of the patterned rules, so you can figure out how far to place them above and below.

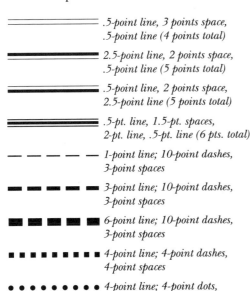

.5-point line, 3 points space, .5-point line (4 points total)

2.5-point line, 2 points space, .5-point line (5 points total)

.5-point line, 2 points space, 2.5-point line (5 points total)

.5-pt. line, 1.5-pt. spaces, 2-pt. line, .5-pt. line (6 pts. total)

1-point line; 10-point dashes, 3-point spaces

3-point line; 10-point dashes, 3-point spaces

6-point line; 10-point dashes, 3-point spaces

4-point line; 4-point dashes, 4-point spaces

4-point line; 4-point dots, 4-point spaces

To the right is an example of how using paragraph rules with style sheets (Section 7), saved countless hours. I created a 12-page program for the Tap Dance Studio, listing 32 dances. I created three styles in my style sheet: one for the song title with the reverse text on the black rules; one for the choreography by-line, which placed the hairline rule above; and one for the list of dancers. *Combined with the feature "Next style"* (7.27–7.31), I was able to type the song title, hit a Return, type the choreography line, hit a Return, type the list of dancers, hit Shift-Returns (3.230–3.236) until the last name, then hit a Return and start over with the next song title. As I typed, *all* the formatting, including the rules and the reverse text, just appeared. As I edited, all the rules adjusted automatically. I could roll up the text block and pour it somewhere else, and all the rules came right along. Awesome.

Opus One

choreographed by Vicki Suemnicht

Betsy Waliszewski, Harrah Argentine, Ronni Madrid, Anne Marie Ginella, Jimmy Thomas, Mary Grady, John B. Rose

Anything Goes

choreographed by Nina Raggio

Marjori Cerletti, Barbara Sikora, Robin Williams, David Peters, Gary B. Jones, Janyce Bodeson, Shannon Mills, Ryan Williams, Mary Boston, Beverly Scherf

If you want to do this:

6.35 Set a paragraph rule **above** that is the width of the column or of the text

• • • • • • • • • •

This paragraph rule
is the width of the text.

• •

We
• • • • • • • • •
haven't the money,
• • • • • • • • •
so we've got to think.

Lord Rutherford

Paragraph rule: column width

Font size: 10 point/Auto

Extra paragraph space after: 0p2.5

Rule position: 1p1.5 above

Text indent: left 2p

Then follow these steps:

- With the **text tool,** select the paragraph(s).
- From the Type menu, choose "Paragraph...," **or** press Command M.
- Click on the "Rules..." button.
- Under "Rule above paragraph," press on the "Line style" pop-up menu and choose a line width or pattern (this will automatically put a check in the "Rule above paragraph" box).
- ★ Click in either the "Width of text" or "Width of column" box.
- Click on the "Options..." button.
- Next to "Top," type in the number of picas and points that measure how far above the baseline you want to position the rule. Allow for two-thirds of the point size of the type, plus the point size of the rule (6.33), plus a few points for space. You can use the **0p__** format, no matter what measuring system is currently in use (6.24; 1.221).
- Click all the OK buttons; or hold the Option key down while you click one OK button; or press Option Return once.
- Check it out. You may need to return to the paragraph rules dialog boxes to adjust the precise placement of the rules.
- Paragraphs with rules *above* often need to have a few points of paragraph space added *after* (4.63–4.75).

Shortcuts ▾ Notes ▾ Hints

- You have to be careful about pressing on the "Line style" submenu in the dialog box. You may *think* you are just checking things out, but pressing on this submenu automatically puts a rule above the selected paragraph for you, whether you notice or not. That's another reason to always *Cancel* out of boxes you were just nosing around in, rather than click OK.
- A problem with overriding the current measuring system rather than changing it to picas (6.24), is that PageMaker converts your overriding measure into the current measure. For instance, say you are using inches for the measurement system and you type in 0p4 because you want a rule 4 points below the baseline. You click OK to go check it out. The next day you decide you want more space, so you go back to the dialog box. Now the dialog box says 0.056 inches and you haven't the foggiest idea how many points you inserted originally. Just change the whole measurement system to picas.

If you want to do this:	Then follow these steps:	Shortcuts ▾ Notes ▾ Hints

6.36 Set a paragraph rule **above,** *indenting* from the width of the column

---

This paragraph rule is the width of the column, indented 3p from the left and 3p from the right. The text is 9 point, with 3p of paragraph space after. The rule is 1p5 above the baseline.

With a paragraph rule above, every time you hit the Return key, the paragraph will start with that rule.

This group of paragraphs may look like they have a rule above and also a rule below, but they are fooling you.

- Follow the steps in 6.35 until you get to the star (★).
- Click in the "Width of column" button.
- In the left and/or right indent boxes, type a **positive** number. If you type a number in both boxes, make sure they don't add up to more than the width of the text block.
- Go back to 6.35 and continue on with the steps to position the rule above.

- Though PageMaker calls this the "Width of column," it is actually the width of the *text block.* The rule doesn't give a darn what your *column* measurements are.
- As you widen or narrow your text block, this rule will adapt to the new width. Just what we've been waiting for.
- The "Width of column" ignores any tabs or indents set for the text.
- The example to the left looks like it has a rule *below* the last paragraph. Actually, it is just the rule *above* from the next paragraph (but the next paragraph has no text, obviously).

6.37 Set a paragraph rule **above,** *extending* beyond the width of the column

---

This paragraph rule is the width of the column. It is extended –1p5 from the left and –1p5 from the right. The text is 9 point and the rule is placed 1p5 above the baseline. The dotted lines on either side indicate the text block edges.

- Follow the steps in 6.35 until you get to the star (★).
- Click in the "Width of column" button.
- In the left and/or right indent boxes, type a **negative** number. You can enter up to –22.75 inches on either side, but of course your page isn't that big.
- Go back to 6.35 and continue on with the steps to position the rule above.

- If your rules extend beyond the text block, you may not see them on the screen. In fact, you probably won't. If you redraw the screen, they usually show up (change the page view; click in the zoom box; click on the text block with the pointer tool and press Command F). The rules seem to be very trustworthy, though, and will show up on your page when you print.

279

If you want to do this:

Then follow these steps:

Shortcuts ▾ Notes ▾ Hints

6.38 Set a paragraph rule **above,** *indenting* from the width of the text

• • • • • • • •

You can't let the seeds

• • • • • •

stop you from enjoying

• • •

the watermelon.

• •

- Follow the steps in 6.35 until you get to the star (★).
- Click in the "Width of text" button.
- In the left and/or right indent boxes, type a **positive** number. If you type a number in both boxes, make sure they don't add up to more than the width of the first line of text in each paragraph.
- Go back to 6.35 and continue on with the steps to position the rule above.

- When it is the width of text, the rule reads *every* character, including spaces, hard spaces, and tabs. This can be to your advantage or no. In the example, the indent was 2p on both sides. There are dots after the last line because I hit a Return, then typed em spaces (Command Shift M). I also inserted an em space on either side of the first line to make PageMaker think there was more text, thus making more dots.

6.39 Set a paragraph rule **above,** *extending beyond* the width of the text

━ ━ ━ ━ ━ ━ ━ ━

Tahiti people say:

━ ━ ━ ━ ━ ━

You eat Life,

━ ━ ━ ━

or

━ ━ ━ ━ ━ ━

Life eats You.

━ ━ ━ ━ ━ ━ ━

Mutiny on the Bounty

- Follow the steps in 6.35 until you get to the star (★).
- Click in the "Width of text" button.
- In the left and/or right indent boxes, type a **negative** number. You can extend the line -22.75 inches on either side. Supposedly. How could we ever check?
- Go back to 6.35 and continue on with the steps to position the rule above.

- If extending the rule beyond the text also extends it beyond the text block, the full length of the rule may not show up on your screen. It will print, though. You can usually see most of the rule if you redraw the screen: click in the zoom box, located in the upper right corner of your screen (回); *or* change the page view, or select the same view you are looking at already; *or* just redraw the text block by clicking on it with the pointer tool and pressing Command F.

If you want to do this:

6.40 Set a paragraph rule **below** that is the width of the column or of the text

When a rule below is the **width of the text,** it will be as long as the last line in the paragraph.

When a rule below is the **width of the column,** it stretches the width of the text block, no matter what the text does.

So you can have the same paragraph rule specs, but adjust the tabs and indents to suit your fancy.

This gives you a great deal of flexibility. You'll start trying to dream up work to do just so you can play with paragraph rules.

On all paragraph rules above and below, you may want to add a few points of paragraph space before or after (see 4.63–4.75).

This is 9-point type, with an extra 6.5 points of paragraph space added before (see 4.85). The rules are .5 point, positioned 0p7.5 below.

Then follow these steps:

- With the **text tool,** select the paragraph(s).
- From the Type menu, choose "Paragraph...," *or* press Command M.
- Click on the "Rules..." button.
- Under "Rule below paragraph," press on the "Line style" pop-up menu and choose a line width or pattern (this will automatically put a check in the "Rule below paragraph" box).
- ★ Click in either the "Width of text" or "Width of column" box.
- Click on the "Options..." button.
- Next to "Bottom," type in the number of picas and points that measure how far below the baseline you want to position the rule. Allow for one-third of the point size of the type, plus the point size of the rule (6.33), plus a few points for space. You can use the **0p__** format, no matter what measuring system you're currently using (6.24; 1.221).
- Click all the OK buttons; or hold the Option key down while you click one OK button; or press Option Return once.
- Check it out. You may need to return to the paragraph rules dialog boxes to adjust the precise placement of the rules.
- Paragraphs with rules positioned *below* often need to have a few points of paragraph space added before (4.63–4.75).

Shortcuts ▾ Notes ▾ Hints

- In the second example, do you wonder how there can be a rule *above* the first paragraph in the example, if it is supposed to contain only a rule *below?* Actually, that line is just a paragraph with no text. Hitting the Return key makes PageMaker think there is a paragraph, so she throws in a rule.

If you want to do this:	**Then follow these steps:**	**Shortcuts ▾ Notes ▾ Hints**

6.41 Set a paragraph rule **below,** *indenting* from the width of the column

Question 1 _____

Question 2 _____

Question 3 _____

- Follow the steps in 6.40 until you get to the star (★).
- Click in the "Width of column" button.
- In the left and/or right indent boxes, type a **positive** number. If you type a number in both boxes, make sure they don't add up to more than the width of the text block.
- Go back to 6.40 and continue on with the steps to position the rule below.

- The example is 9-point Futura Book on 20-point leading. The rule is a hairline indented 4 picas from the left, positioned 1.5 points below the baseline.

6.42 Set a paragraph rule **below,** *extending beyond* the width of the column

- Follow the steps in 6.40 until you get to the star (★).
- Click in the "Width of column" button.
- In the left and/or right indent boxes, type a **negative** number. You can input a number up to (down to?) –22.75 inches.
- Go back to 6.40 and continue on with the steps to position the rule below.

- Rules extending beyond the width of the text block may not show up on the screen. Don't worry, though, they print.
- The specs for this example are the same as for the one above (6.41), except that it now has a –17p right indent, taking the rules 17 picas past the right margin, which is out of their 16-pica text block and over to span the second column.

Question 1 _____

Question 2 _____

Question 3 _____

If you want to do this:	**Then follow these steps:**	**Shortcuts ▾ Notes ▾ Hints**
6.43 Set a paragraph rule **below,** *indenting* from the width of the text A <u>Points:</u> B <u>Picas:</u> C <u>Ems:</u> D <u>Ens:</u> E <u>Thins:</u>	▪ Follow the steps in 6.40 until you get to the star (★). ▪ Click in the "Width of text" button. ▪ In the left and/or right indent boxes, type a **positive** number. If you type a number in both boxes, make sure they don't add up to more than the width of the last line of text in each paragraph. ▪ Go back to 6.40 and continue on with the steps to position the rule below the baseline.	▪ The specs for the example: 9-point Futura Book, auto leading; an extra 9 points of space between paragraphs (4.84); a 2-point rule, indented 3 picas from the left; positioned 5.5 points below the baseline. Notice that this position (5.5 points below the baseline) works here because the text has no *descenders* (those parts of the letters that hang below the baseline, as in p, q, y, g, etc.). If there were descenders, I would have had to allow more space for them.
6.44 Set a paragraph rule **below,** *extending beyond* the width of the text A Points: B Picas: C Ems: D Ens: E Thins:	▪ Follow the steps in 6.40 until you get to the star (★). ▪ Click in the "Width of text" button. ▪ In the left and/or right indent boxes, type a **negative** number. You can input a value down to −22.75 inches. ▪ Go back to 6.40 and continue on with the steps to position the rule below the baseline.	▪ The specs for the example are the same as those above (6.43), *except* that the left indent is extended -1p6 beyond the text, which takes it beyond the text block itself. The right rule indent is still set at zero, but the text is now aligned at a right tab (Section 5 on Indents and Tabs, 5.55).

This dotted line indicates the edge of the text block.

If you want to do this:

6.45 Set paragraph rules **above and below**

The Three Rules of Life

Rule 1: Your attitude is your life.

Rule 2: Maximize your options.

Rule 3: Never take anything too seriously.

■ **Rousseau**   Myself alone . . . I am not made like anyone of those who exist. If I am not better, at least I am different.

■ **Voltaire**   Everything must end; meanwhile, we must amuse ourselves.

■ **Kazantzakis**   I'm laughing at the thought of you laughing, and that's how laughing never stops in this world.

Those little black boxes are actually 8-point paragraph rules. They are indented from the right, so they appear to be little boxes. They automatically show up when I hit the Return key.

Then follow these steps:

- With the **text tool,** select the paragraph(s).
- From the Type menu, choose "Paragraph...," *or* press Command M.
- Click on the "Rules..." button.
- Choose line widths or patterns from both "Line style" pop-up menus (this will automatically put checks in the "Rule above/below paragraph" boxes).
- Click in either the "Width of text" or "Width of column" buttons.
- Enter values for indenting or extending the rules (6.36–6.39; 6.41–6.44).
- Click on the "Options..." button.
- Next to "Top," type in the number of picas and points you want the rule to be positioned *above* the text. Allow for two-thirds of the point size of the type, plus the point size of the rule (6.33), plus a few points for space.
- Next to "Bottom," type in the number of picas and points you want the rule to be positioned *below* the text. Allow for one-third of the point size of the type, plus the point size of the rule (6.33), plus a few points for space.
- Click all the OK buttons; or hold the Option key down while you click one OK button; or press Option Return once.

Shortcuts ▾ Notes ▾ Hints

- You may need to fuss around with extra paragraph space (4.63–4.75) and/or leading values (4.12–4.64) to get the precise amount of white space above and below the rules.

- The specs for the first example: Futura Book and Bold, 8-point type; 20-point leading; 15.75 pica column. Extra paragraph space of 0p4. Rule above is 4 point; width of column; indented from the right 13p3; positioned 1p2 above the baseline. The rule below is a hairline; width of column; no indents; positioned 0p8 below the baseline. I removed the rule above from the first paragaraph.

- The specs for the second example: Futura Book and Bold, 8-point type; auto leading; 15.75 pica column. Extra paragraph space of 0p6.5. There is an 8-point rule above; width of the column; indented 15p3 from the right; positioned 0p7 above the baseline. The rule below is .5 point; width of column; indented from the left 7p; positioned 0p8 below the baseline. There is also a left paragraph indent of 7 picas, and a first-line indent of -5p9.

If you want to do this:

6.46 Create reverse text in a rule

Herb Lubalin said:

It stinks.

Christophero Sly: Come, madame wife, sit by my side and let the world slip; we shall never be younger.

Taming of the Shrew

Child	Birthdate
Ryan	12/2/77
Jimmy	4/19/82
Scarlett	5/01/86

Then follow these steps:

- Follow the steps in 6.35, 6.40, or 6.45 to position paragraph rules above and/or below.
- The largest rule you can choose is 12 point, but if you strategically place a rule above *and* a rule below, both 12 point, you can actually get a bar 24 points deep to reverse text out of (as in the first example).
- Keep in mind: the rule above *hangs down* from the value you type into "Top," and the rule below *grows up* from the value you type in "Bottom" (6.26–6.27).

   You can type a value as low as 0 (zero) into "Top," which means the rule will start at the baseline and hang down from there; essentially it is hanging down over the next line of type, even though it is a rule "above."

   In "Bottom" you can type a value that is less than the point size of the rule (down to zero, in fact), thereby making the rule grow up and over the baseline, into the text above.
- So then, if a black rule is positioned over text, obviously you must select the text and reverse it (from the Type menu, choose the submenu "Type style," then choose Reverse).
- You'll find that the reverse text will constantly disappear. Just click on it with the **pointer tool** and press Command F to bring it forward.

Shortcuts ▾ Notes ▾ Hints

- See page 208 for specs of the examples.
- The rules are actually on a separate layer, *behind* the text (see 1.151–1.157 re: layers). But they would rather be in front and so pop forward every time you edit the text or change the specs. The text will become visible whenever you redraw the screen: click in the zoom box, located in the upper right corner of your screen (⊡); *or* change the page view, or select the same view you are looking at already; *or* just redraw the text block by clicking on it with the pointer tool and pressing Command F. Yes, it's irritating. Even if you don't *see* the reverse text, it will print (unless it has gone into hiding because of the tabs...)
- Tabs often create a problem with reverse text, typically just with the text *in front* of the tab. Not always, but often. If your text won't come forward, take out any tabs and replace them with hard spaces (6.207–4.216). If your text isn't visible because of a tab, *it won't print!*

285

If you want to do this:

Then follow these steps:

Shortcuts ▾ Notes ▾ Hints

6.47 Remove *or*
Change the rule and/or
the position

- To **remove** rules, select the text with the **text tool,** go back to the paragraph dialog box, and uncheck the Rule checkboxes.
- Now, you already know that to **change** something, you select it and go back to the paragraph dialog boxes, input new information, and click all the OK buttons.

  But you may be reading this because you already tried that and it didn't work.
- ☞If you select *one paragraph,* you can go into the dialog boxes and change the specs.
- ☞If you select more than one paragraph *that all have the exact same specs,* you can go into the dialog boxes and change the specs.
- ☞If you select more than one paragraph *and the paragraphs have different rule specifications,* PageMaker will ignore any changes you make in the "Paragraph rules" and the "Paragraph rule options" dialog boxes. You can *remove* all the rules, but you can't put them back consistently.
- Here are your options, if you want to change several paragraphs to make them consistent:
  - ☐ Change the inconsistent one(s) to match the others' current specs; select them all and make overall changes.
  - ☐ Create a style sheet and apply it to the concerned paragraphs.
  - ☐ Delete all the paragraphs and start over.

- I can't figure out if this limitation is a wonderful protective device or an irritating bug.

  On the one hand, it is not always easy to tell whether a rule is a "rule below" from the paragraph above, or a "rule above" from the paragraph below. Thus, it is not always clear whether the paragraphs you select have the same specs or not. This limitation prevents you from accidentally changing a paragraph you didn't mean to.

  On the other hand, this limitation means you cannot consciously select an entire group of paragraphs with different specs and change the rules to make them all consistent. You can't even pull the old Indents & Tabs trick (5.74).

  I mean, this is serious. *You cannot even select all the varying paragraphs, take all the rules out, and start over.* The dialog boxes delude you into thinking you can, until you click OK and see that they really didn't listen to you at all.

  Now what do *you* think? Is this a bug or a blessing?

If you want to do this:

Then follow these steps:

Shortcuts ▾ Notes ▾ Hints

6.48   Create a reverse rule

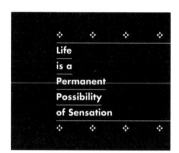

Robert Louis Stevenson

- Ah—so you noticed that the line width submenu is missing the "Reverse" option! But that's easy to take care of.
- Select the paragraphs and position the rules as in 6.35, 6.40, or 6.45. Before you click the final OK, press on the submenu next to "Color" and choose "Paper."
- Of course, the paper-colored rule must be over a dark background in order to be visible. The dark background can be an object you draw with the PageMaker tools or any graphic you import. Or you can overlap the white rule on a dark rule, as in the example to the left.

- Specs for the example: Futura Bold 7 pt.; 11.5 leading; paragraph indent of 3 picas. Rule above: 12 point; width of column; right indent of 7.5p; positioned 0p8 above baseline. Rule below: .5; width of text; left indent of 3p; positioned 0p4 below baseline. I extended the first and last paragraph rules by inserting em spaces (Command Shift M), since the rules follow the width of the text. I removed the rule below the last paragraph.
- Just a note: I never could see all the text on the screen; most of the time just the white lines and the Dingbats would appear, and those only occasionally. But it printed. I'm assuming future updates will fix that.

6.49   Change the rule to a color
or to a shade of gray

they: used with an indefinite singular antecedent in place of the definite masculine "he" or the definite feminine "she."

The Random House College Dictionary

- Select the paragraphs and position the rules as in 6.35, 6.40, or 6.45.
- In the "Paragraph rules" dialog box, press on the submenu next to "Color." This menu holds all the default colors, as well as any colors you defined in the "Define colors..." dialog box (15.49). Choosing one will change the color of the rule for that paragraph.
- On a monochrome screen, even a gray rule may appear as solid black, but it will print in the tint percentage.
  (Avoid using tabs after the word(s) that overprint a gray rule; 6.46).

- It's very easy to make a gray rule. Details are in Chapter 14, but here is a brief synopsis:
  - □ From the Element menu, choose "Define colors...."
  - □ Click "New." Type a name for your color (you can use numbers, like 15%). Click the CMYK button. Put zeros in the first three boxes (Cyan, Magenta, Yellow). Type a value in the Black box (like 15 for a 15% tint of Black). Click OK. Now this color will show up in the "Paragraph rules" dialog box.

6.50   Specs for the examples on page 285

Herb Lubalin said:

It stinks.

- In these two lines (each a paragraph), there is no extra paragraph space before or after, and no extra leading. It's the 12-point rule below that extends the line slug (6.18) to create that nice white space, since the line uses auto leading.

"Herb Lubalin said:"

- Futura Bold, 14-point type with auto leading.
  Rule above: 12-point; width of text; left and right indents –0p3; positioned 1p5 above the baseline.
  Rule below: 12-point, width of text; left and right indents –0p3; positioned 0p7 below the baseline (notice the positions above and below add up to 24 points).

"It stinks."

- Futura Book, 9/auto.
  Rule above: hairline; width of column; positioned 1p6 above the baseline, which just tucks under the thick rule above it.

Christophero Sly: Come, madame wife, sit by my side and let the world slip; we shall never be younger.

Taming of the Shrew

- Futura Book; 9 point type with 13-point leading; "Christophero Sly:" is 8-point Bold.
  Rule above: 12 point; width of column; indented from the right 9 picas; positioned 0p8.5 above the baseline. Notice it is a 12-point rule positioned only 8.5 points above the baseline, which means a few points will hang down below the baseline, covering the descenders.
- There is a paragraph left indent of 0p7.

Child	Birthdate
Ryan	12/2/77
Jimmy	4/19/82
Scarlett	5/01/86

- Except for the first line, the specs are Futura Book, 9-point type on 13-point leading. There is no extra paragraph space before or after. There is a left paragraph indent of 0p7.
  Rule above: 12 point; width of column; right indent of 10p; positioned 0p9 above the baseline.
  Rule below: .5 point; width of column; no indents; positioned 1p1.5 below the baseline.
- **First line:** (Child...Birthdate) The first line has the same specs, except that the font is 8 point Futura Bold, and the rule above has no right indent. I couldn't insert a tab to align "Birthdate," because it made "Child" disappear on the screen; it wouldn't even print. I had to insert em spaces (4.208) to move "Birthdate" over.

A Chapter very full of learning,
nicely adapted to the present taste and times,
and calculated for the
Instruction and Improvement of the User.

7.1 Style sheets have got to be the most wonderful invention since the Mac and the LaserWriter—it's hard to imagine how we ever lived without them. Even on a one-page document, style sheets can save hours of time and frustration. It doesn't take long to learn how to use them, and the time spent is one of the best investments you could make for yourself. If you are not using style sheets, you are not tapping into the true power of PageMaker.

7.2 What style sheets allow you to do is label, or *tag*, paragraphs with a *style name*, or *definition*. That name, or definition, tells a paragraph exactly what form to take. You can apply any text formatting (7.32). Once a style definition has been set up, you simply click in a paragraph and choose the style name (from the Style palette, or from the "Style" submenu in the Type menu), and all the formatting will be applied to that paragraph. At any time later you can change the specifications in that style *definition* and all paragraphs that have had that particular tag, or name, applied also change instantly. (See the Scenarios, 7.69–7.71).

7.3 Even though a paragraph has a style definition attached to it, you can certainly customize any paragraph; you can italicize words, add tabs, create indents, specify paragraph rules, change the track, etc. These are *overrides* (7.34; 7.36–7.41).

7.4 You can even *tag* the text in your word processor (7.64) as you create it, labeling text with the style definitions. When you place the document into Page-Maker, all the appropriate formatting will automatically be applied!

7.5 Style sheets are saved along with each publication or template. So if you set up a style sheet in a template (Section 12), each new publication you create from that template will be perfectly consistent with the original. Or you can copy the style sheets (7.50) from one publication into another rather than recreate them all from scratch. Or copy and then edit them to suit. Oh, it is just amazing what you can do with style sheets.

7.6 **Be careful:** Don't get *style sheets* confused with *type styles* (they should have named them something else). *Type styles* are things like bold, italic, underline, etc.

Please note:

The procedures in this section assume you understand how to use the tabs and indents ruler, the type specification dialog box, the paragraph dialog box, and the color specifications. When a direction assumes something, I've added references to the specific paragraphs where you'll find the other information.

The "Define styles" dialog box   *(from the Type menu, choose "Define styles…," or press Command 3)*

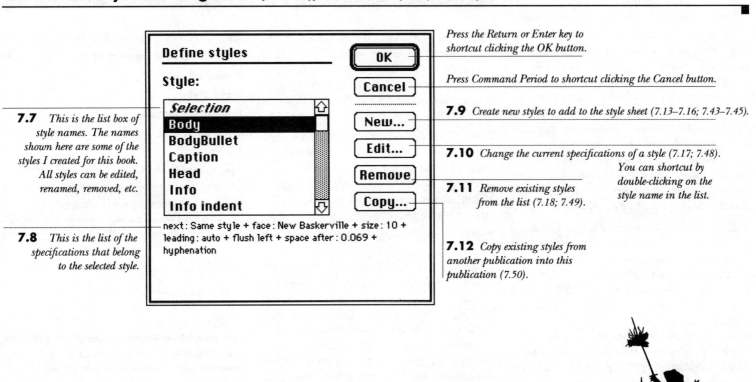

Define styles

Style:

Selection
Body
BodyBullet
Caption
Head
Info
Info indent

next : Same style + face : New Baskerville + size : 10 + leading : auto + flush left + space after : 0.069 + hyphenation

OK

Cancel

New…

Edit…

Remove

Copy…

Press the Return or Enter key to shortcut clicking the OK button.

Press Command Period to shortcut clicking the Cancel button.

7.7   *This is the list box of style names. The names shown here are some of the styles I created for this book. All styles can be edited, renamed, removed, etc.*

7.8   *This is the list of the specifications that belong to the selected style.*

7.9   *Create new styles to add to the style sheet (7.13–7.16; 7.43–7.45).*

7.10   *Change the current specifications of a style (7.17; 7.48). You can shortcut by double-clicking on the style name in the list.*

7.11   *Remove existing styles from the list (7.18; 7.49).*

7.12   *Copy existing styles from another publication into this publication (7.50).*

Make definite assertions. William Strunk, Jr.

New...

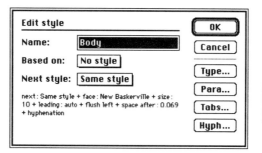

7.13 If you click the **New...** button, you will get this dialog box. You need to type in a name (it's a good idea to give it a descriptive name so you will have a clue as to what it will do).

7.14 The name that appears automatically in **Based on:** is the name that was highlighted in the list when you clicked "New...." See 7.20–7.26 on the importance of the name in that box.

7.15 The name selected for **Next style:** is the style *that PageMaker will switch to automatically* when you hit the Return key (7.27–7.31).

7.16 The buttons along the side (*Type...*, *Para...*, *Tabs...*, and *Hyph...*) will give you the standard dialog boxes that you already know and love (7.43–7.44).

Edit...

7.17 If you click the **Edit...** button, you will get this dialog box. It's exactly the same as the "New..." box, except that the name of the style-to-be-edited is already entered. Notice at the bottom you see the specifications that have been already defined for this style. Use this box to make any changes to an existing style (7.48).

7.18 If you click the **Remove...** button, you will not get a dialog box (7.49). You will not even get an alert box asking if you really want to remove the selected style. It's just gone. Instantly. If you decide that was *not* a smart thing to do, **click the Cancel button.**

Copy...

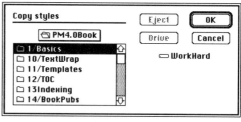

7.19 If you click the **Copy...** button, you will get this dialog box. It's just like any other "Open" dialog box you see on the Mac, and you navigate the same way. Double-click on any PageMaker file and you will copy any style sheets from that publication into the current one. If any styles you are copying have exactly the same name as *existing* styles in your current publication, PageMaker will ask if you want to copy over existing styles; if you click OK, the specifications of the publication you are copying *from* will *replace* your current specifications. All other copied styles will be *added* to your list; nothing will be removed.

Based on:

7.20   A style can be **based on** another style. This is a very important concept to grasp and to take advantage of, as it can either help you tremendously or foul you up royally.

7.21   The basic idea is that you can *base* a new style on an existing one. That means you don't need to go through and re-specify all the formatting for the new style—it will pick up all the formatting from the one it is *based on*. Then you can adapt the *new* one to make it different than the original. For instance, let's say you have a style for Headlines. You want your subheads to have all the same formatting as the headlines, except a smaller size. So you base your new style Subhead on the existing style Headline, and change only the *size* of the style Subheads.

7.22   This has another advantage besides making it faster to create the style. Let's say your font for Headlines is Times Bold. Your client now wants you to change it to Palatino Bold. So you go to your style sheet and change the Headline font. *All styles that are based on Headline will also change to Palatino Bold.* Your Subheads will change to Palatino Bold, *but they will stay the smaller size.*

7.23   Take a look at the specifications at the bottom of this "Edit style" dialog box.

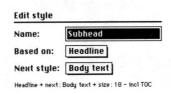

```
Edit style
Name:        Subhead
Based on:    Headline
Next style:  Body text
Headline + next: Body text + size: 18 – incl TOC
```

You see that it is based on "Headline," then the specs show a plus sign and more formatting. Anything I change in "Headline" will also change in "Subhead," *but "Subhead" will retain all the formatting listed after the plus sign.*

You can also *remove* parts of the "Based on" style that you don't want to apply to the new style. For instance, anything tagged with the style Headline is to be included in the Table of Contents (a specification in the paragraph dialog box). In the new style Subhead, I *removed* "Include in Table of contents," as indicated in the example above by the notation "– incl TOC."

7.24   The power of this is that you can make global changes to a publication with only a few seconds of work. *It also means you can inadvertently change styles you didn't mean*

to if you based one style on another without understanding the purpose of "Based on."

7.25   If you *remove* a style from your style sheet, all paragraphs that had been previously tagged with that style *will revert to whatever the removed style had been based on.* Now, this does not mean they will turn into that style, though. *They will retain the formatting of the style that was removed,* but they will be *tagged* with the "based on" style name. If you click in one of those paragraphs and take a look at the style sheet palette (Command Y), you will see a plus sign after the style name, indicating that the paragraph has an override (7.33–7.34) in it. These paragraphs *will* respond to any changes you make in the style they are now tagged with, but they will keep their overrides.

7.26   If you remove a style, and you *do* want to revert all those paragraphs with the overrides back to the original formatting that is in the "based-on" style, see 7.49 and 7.58–7.60.

Next style:

7.27 This "Next style" feature is hot. You gotta get this one down. You can set up your style sheet and include in the specifications which style you want to appear *next,* when you hit the Return key. Let's say that in your work you see that every time you tag a paragraph with your Subhead style, the next style you work with is Body Text. If you set your style Subhead to include a "Next style" of Body Text (as you can see noted in the example in 7.23), then this will happen: You choose Subhead from your style sheet and type the subhead text; when you hit the Return key to go to the next line, *the text automatically turns into the style Body Text.* Body Text would most likely have a "Next style" of "Same style," since you will probably have several paragraphs of Body Text before you need to switch back (manually) to your Subhead style.

7.28 You can get very tricky with this. You can set your Subhead style to follow next with First Paragraph style, a paragraph formatting you have set up that does not include an indent (which is a standard typographic format). Then First Paragraph has a "Next style" of Body Text, which *does* have a one-em indent, as is typical of body copy. So: you type the Subhead, hit Return; then type the next text, which is now *automatically* First Paragraph, hit Return, and then type the rest of the text, which is now *automatically* Body Text.

7.29 In a parts list, a catalog, a program, a résumé, any publication where certain styles often follow other styles, you can set up your "Next styles" and just buzz along, watching the formatting appear before your very eyes. Take a look at 6.34 for one example of this feature, and see Scenario #8 (7.69). Oh, it's truly wonderful.

7.30 *"Next style" only goes into effect as you are typing.* That is, let's say you have several paragraphs already on the page. You create a style that has a "Next style" in its formatting. If you apply that style to the first of the paragraphs that have already been typed, the second existing paragraph *will not* become whatever is the "Next style." If you go back and edit a style and change its "Next style," that change *will not be reflected anywhere*—it will only appear as you type new text with that style.

7.31 If you don't want the "Next style" to be applied to the next line of text, then use a **line break** instead of a Return; that is, press Shift-Return (hold the Shift key down while you press Return; 3.230–3.236). This will break the line, but will *keep* the current paragraph formatting and style. For instance, you may want to force a line break in your subhead so it doesn't hyphenate. If you hit a Return, you will get the "Next Style." But if you hit Shift-Return, you will get a line break, and retain the Subhead style.

Formatting options

7.32   This is a list of the format options you can apply to each style name:

> Font
> Size
> Leading
> Set Width
> Position
> Case
> Track
> Type style
> Left indent
> Right indent
> First-line indent
> Alignment
> Paragraph space before
> Paragraph space after
> Word spacing
> Letter spacing
> Auto pair kerning
> Leading method
> Auto leading percent
> Paragraph keeps options
> Paragraph rules
> Tabs
> Hyphenation
> Color
> Next style
> Include in table of contents

The + and the * (overrides and imported styles)

7.33   A style applies to an entire *paragraph* (remember, you create a new paragraph every time you press the Return key). Whenever the insertion point is in a paragraph, the style belonging to that paragraph will be highlighted in the Style palette (if the palette is showing; Command Y) or in the menu ("Style" in the Type menu). You may see a plus sign (**+**, indicating an *override*), or an asterisk (*, indicating an *imported* style) after a style name.

7.34   Because styles apply to entire paragraphs, if you change the formatting of even one character (italicize a word or make it bold or change the font or add a tab, etc.), that paragraph no longer carries the pure style formatting—it has an **override** in it. It is that *override* that makes the plus sign (**+**) appear in the Style palette. (If the override is from local *character* formatting, such as bold or italic, the plus sign will only appear if the insertion point *is in the word itself* that is creating the override.) Overrides are fully discussed in 7.36–7.41.

7.35   If you place text into PageMaker that has been prepared in a word processing program, and that program also uses style sheets, the styles imbedded in the text will be added to your list as **imported** styles. They are indicated with the asterisk (*). *If an imported style name matches the name of one of your PageMaker styles, the formatting from PageMaker will take over.*

Microsoft Word automatically applies the style "Normal" to text, even if you think you have never used style sheets. This can create a problem; see 7.52. Also see 7.51 for more info on importing styles.

"What type shall I use? The gods refuse to answer.

Overrides

7.36 Styles apply to entire paragraphs, although it is possible to **override** them. In other words, even though the paragraph is set up as ITC Baskerville 10 point, for example, you can throw in an italicized word or perhaps another font altogether. These changes *(local formatting),* are called *overrides.* It is important to understand how the overrides work so they won't frustrate you. There are two kinds: **temporary** and **permanent**.

Temporary Overrides

7.37 If a paragraph contains a **temporary** override, when you *apply a new style* or when you *reapply the same style,* the temporary override (local formatting), *disappears* and the characters revert back to the standard for that style.

7.38 *Temporary* overrides are created using any type specifications *except type style,* (that is, bold, italic, outline, etc.), either from the menu or from any of the dialog boxes. Specifications such as paragraph spacing, leading, size, tabs and indents, alignments, font changes, etc., *and the type style Reverse,* will all disappear when the style belonging to the paragraph changes.

Permanent Overrides

7.39 A **permanent** override not only stays through the change, but adapts itself to its purpose—e.g., if you *underline* a word for emphasis and then change the style definition to underline, the underline override you made earlier becomes *not underlined* so it is still emphasized! Amazing. How does it know?

7.40 *Permanent* overrides are created when you use any of the *type styles* (except Reverse) from the Type menu **or** from the Type specs dialog box. *Case* options (caps or lowercase) and *position* options (superscript and subscript) are also permanent in that they will stay in place when the style definition is changed, although they don't adapt themselves by reversing as the *type styles* do.

7.41 When you change the style of a paragraph, you can choose to hang onto any override (7.57). You can also get rid of permanent overrides (7.59–7.60).

They refuse because they do not know." —*W.A. Dwiggins*

If you want to do this:	Then follow these steps:	Shortcuts ▾ Notes ▾ Hints
7.42a Show the Style palette	■ From the Windows menu choose "Style palette," *or* press Command Y.	■ It is very handy to have this on your screen—you can use this palette instead of going through the Type menu.
7.42b Hide the Style palette	■ From the Windows menu choose "Style palette," *or* press Command Y.	■ Since the palette is a window, you can also click in its little close box (upper left).

7.43 Create a new style from scratch **One method** *(also see 7.44)* *Be sure to read Scenario #8 and Scenario #9 (7.69–7.71)* Based on: No style ✓Body BodyBullet Caption Hairline Info Next style: Same style No style ✓Body BodyBullet Caption Hairline Info	■ From the Type menu choose "Define styles...," *or* press Command 3. ■ From the "Define styles" dialog box that appears, click "New" (7.9) to get to the "Edit style" dialog box for a new style (7.17). ■ Type in the name of your new style where it says "Name"; any name that describes the purpose of this new style will do. ■ "Based on": read 7.20–7.26 to clarify this option. Press on the box to get the sub-menu of other styles in your style sheet; choose the style you want to base this new style on. If you don't want it based on any style, then choose "No style." ■ "Next style": read 7.27–7.31 to clarify this option. Press on the box to get the submenu of other styles in your style sheet; choose the style you want to automatically appear next. If you don't want a different style to follow next, then choose "Same style."	■ Use this method when you have a defnite idea of what the specifications should be. You can always change things later. ■ The name should be something that will identify the style's purpose when you see it in a list. Don't make it too vague, such as "#1."

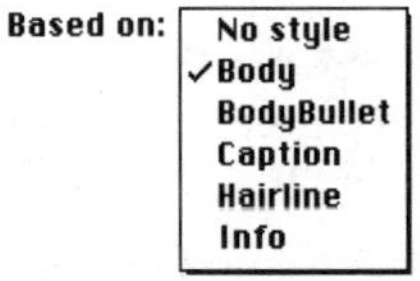

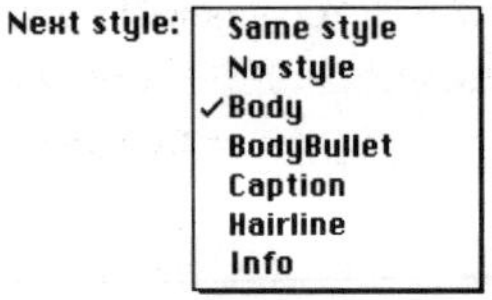

—continued

If you want to do this:	Then follow these steps:	Shortcuts ▾ Notes ▾ Hints
—continued	▪ Click the button "Type..." to get the type specifications dialog box; choose any of the specifications you see (3.139), including color or varying shades of gray for your text (3.174); click OK. You are still creating/editing.	
	▪ Click the button "Para..."; set any specifications you see (3.202; 4.63–4.87). Don't forget about those amazing paragraph rules (Section 6)—take advantage of using them in a style sheet! Click OK; you are still creating the style.	▪ If you set indents in the "Para" box, they will show up in the tab ruler.
	▪ If you want any tabs or indents, click the button "Tabs..." (5.55); you can set your indents here rather than in the "Para..." box. Click OK; you are still creating the new style.	▪ If you choose to set the indent in the tab ruler, the specs will also appear in the "Para..." box.
	▪ If you want control over the hyphenation that is different than the default controls, click the button "Hyph..." (4.219–4.231); click OK.	▪ If you are nested deep in these dialog boxes, you can hold the Option key and either press OK *or* hit Return (or Enter) and all the dialog boxes will close. **Or** you can press Command Option Return.
	▪ Click all the OKs to close the "Define styles..." dialog boxes and you've got it!	▪ To Cancel out of *all* the boxes, hold the Option key down while you click Cancel. **Or** press Command Option Period. Command Period will cancel just one box at a time.
	▪ This process just *defined* the style. Now you must go to your text and *apply* the styles, also called *tagging* the paragraphs (7.54).	

If you want to do this:	Then follow these steps:	Shortcuts ▾ Notes ▾ Hints

7.44 Create a new style from scratch
A second method *(also see 7.43)*

See Scenario #9 (7.70–7.71)

- With the text on the page, format a paragraph the way you want it—set the font, size, leading, tabs, spacing, rules, etc.
- With the **text tool,** click the I-beam within the formatted text.
- From the Type menu choose "Define styles...," *or* press Command 3.
- "Selection" should be highlighted in the list box; click on "New..." to get the "Edit style" dialog box (*or* just double-click on "Selection").
- Type in a name that will give you a clue as to the purpose of this new style.
- "Based on": read 7.20–7.26 to clarify this option. Since you are creating the style this way and not as in 7.45, you probably want it based on "No style."
- "Next style": read 7.27–7.31 to clarify this option. Press on the box to get the submenu of other styles in your style sheet; choose the style you want to appear next automatically. If you don't want a different style to follow next, then choose "Same style."
- Click all the OK buttons.

- With this method you are setting up all your specifications in the text itself, watching what you are doing. It is often easier to do it this way, where you can make instant changes to the appearance, than to do it from inside a dialog box. Then when it meets your standards, create the new style and it will hold all the formatting you set. Of course, you can always go back and edit changes later. That's the whole idea.
- When formatting the paragraph to create a style, *make sure you are using only* **one** *specification from each category.* That is, the paragraph cannot have some words bold and some italic; it cannot have two variations of leading or spacing, etc. You can override things later with local formatting (7.36–7.41; 7.56), if you choose.
- If you are nested deep in these dialog boxes, you can hold the Option key and press OK *or* hit Return (or Enter) and all the dialog boxes will close. **Or** you can press Command Option Return.
- To Cancel out of *all* the boxes, hold the Option key down while you click Cancel. **Or** press Command Option Period. Command Period will cancel just one box at a time.

If you want to do this:	Then follow these steps:	Shortcuts • Notes • Hints
7.45 Create a new style **based on** an existing style	**Either:** ■ With any tool, from the Type menu choose "Define styles...," *or* press Command 3. ■ In the list box, click once on the style name you want the new style to be *based on*. ■ Click "New" in the "Edit style" dialog box; make your format changes the same as with a new style (7.43). *See Notes* ☞ **Or:** ■ With the **text tool,** click in a paragraph that has the style on which you want to base your new one. ■ From the Type menu choose "Define styles...," *or* press Command 3. ■ Click "New" in the "Edit style" dialog box; make your format changes the same as with a new style (7.43). *See Notes above* ☞ **Or:** ■ With the **text tool,** click in a paragraph that has the style on which you want to base your new one. ■ If the Style palette is not showing, press Command Y. Hold the Command key down and click once on the style "No style." ■ This shortcuts to the "Edit style" dialog box; make your format changes the same as with a new style (7.43). *See Notes above* ☞	■ Each of these methods automatically puts the style name of the *selected* text in the "Based on" submenu for your new style. All the formatting from the "Based on" style automatically applies to this new style you are creating—you only need to *revise* it. ■ If one style is "Based on" another, when *the original style it is based on* is changed, this one changes too. Be sure to read 7.20–7.26 to understand this important concept. ■ This is the quickest and easiest method. You will not replace the style "No style," as it is part of the PageMaker program. (Actually, "No style" holds the type spec defaults for the publication; 1.6–1.9.)

If you want to do this:	Then follow these steps:	Shortcuts ▾ Notes ▾ Hints
7.46 Rename a style	■ If the Style palette is showing (press Command Y), hold down the Command key and click once on the name you wish to change; you will get the "Edit style" dialog box. Type the new name; click OK. ■ **OR** hold down the Command key; from the Type menu, slide down to near the bottom to get the Style submenu *(not "Type style")*. Choose the style name you wish to change; you will get the "Edit style" dialog box. Type the new name; click OK. ■ **OR** from the Type menu choose "Define styles...." Double-click on the name you wish to change (which is a shortcut to the "Edit style" dialog box). Type in the new name; click the OK buttons, **or** press Option Return.	
7.47 Replace an existing style	■ Follow the steps in 7.43 or 7.44 to create a new style. ■ Name it exactly the same as the one you want to replace; click OK. ■ You will get an alert box asking if you want to replace this one; click OK; then click OK again.	■ Sometimes it's easier to start from scratch and just *replace* an existing style, than to try to Edit the entire thing. Any paragraphs that were tagged with the original style name will turn into the new style with the same name. ■ Also see 7.53 about having one existing style transform, or merge, into another.

If you want to do this:	**Then follow these steps:**	**Shortcuts • Notes • Hints**
7.48 Edit an existing style *(Change its definition)*	■ With any tool, from the Type menu choose "Define styles...," *or* press Command 3. ■ In the list box, click once on the style name you want to edit; then click the "Edit..." button (**or** just double-click on the style name); you will see the "Edit style" dialog box. ■ Click on any of the buttons (Type, Para, Tabs, Color) to make any changes. ■ Click the OK buttons, *or* press Command Return to close one box at a time, *or* press Command Option Return to close all boxes.	■ A great shortcut to the "Edit style" dialog box: in the Style palette (Command Y), hold down the Command key and click once on the style name. ■ A point to remember: changing the specs for a style *will not automatically change any local formatting* (overrides; 7.33–7.35) that you previously made in a paragraph, whether the overrides were permanent or temporary. The changes will, of course, take effect in any new text created with this style, and in any existing paragraph that you *re-apply* this style to (click in the paragraph, click again on the style name).
7.49 Remove any style	■ From the Type menu, choose "Define styles...," *or* press Command 3. ■ Click once on the name of the style you want to remove. ■ Click the button "Remove." **Be careful**— this is inconsistent with our Macintosh expectations. Typically, if you are going to do something potentially disastrous you get an alert box asking if you really want to do this. Not here—it just gets instantly removed and is never seen again. *If you accidentally Remove something you really do want, click* **Cancel.** ■ If you want the style removed, click OK.	■ When you Remove a style, every paragraph that had that style attached to it *changes its tag* to the style the Removed one was *based on*. But *the text formatting will not change;* that is, existing text will not look any different, as PageMaker will consider the old formatting as overrides (7.33–7.41) to the new style. If the removed style was *not* based on anything, all paragraphs that were tagged with the Removed style will change to "No style," which means it really has no tag of any style at all. Be sure to read 7.20–7.26 about the "Based on" concept.

If you want to do this:	Then follow these steps:	Shortcuts ▾ Notes ▾ Hints

7.50 Copy styles from another PageMaker publication

- From the Type menu choose "Define styles...."
- In the dialog box, click the button "Copy." You see the same kind of dialog box you get with "Open" or "Save as..." and you navigate around in it the same way (opening folders, changing disks, etc.; see page 576).
- Find the publication that has the style sheet you want to copy; double-click on its name. If there are styles with the same name, PageMaker will ask if you want the new ones to copy over existing styles, giving you a chance to Cancel; click OK.

- Be sure to read 7.19 to understand exactly what copying styles does for you. Any changes will be implemented throughout the entire publication as soon as you click the OK button.
- If you change your mind before you click OK, click "Cancel"!
- It's a good idea to **Save** your publication right before you Copy styles, just in case you change your mind *after* you click OK. Copying styles *is not Undo-able*, but you *can* Revert to the last time you saved (16.26), or mini-Revert to the last update on the mini-Save (16.27).

7.51 Import styles from a word-processing program

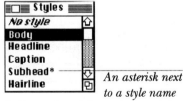

An asterisk next to a style name indicates that style was imported from another document. See the note in 7.52!

- When you *place* a word-processed document in PageMaker (3.32), any styles you applied to the original incoming document are *added* to PageMaker's style sheet. These **imported styles** are indicated in the Style palette with an asterisk (*).
- If you choose to "Retain format" when you place, the document places with the text formatted and tagged with the word processing style names. If you do *not* choose to "Retain format," the document places with PageMaker's default style (7.68); you will usually see a plus sign (**+**; 7.33–7.35) in the Style palette, in addition to the asterisk.

- If there are style names in that word processing style sheet that are not *used* in the document, they will not be imported.
- **If an imported style has exactly the same name as a PageMaker style, the formatting of the PageMaker style takes over.**
- Not all features of the imported style can be applied; basically, the features for which PageMaker does not have an equivalent will be lost, such as hidden text, bar tabs, headers and footers, etc.
- All other tabs, Returns, and first-line indents will carry over, whether "Retain format" is checked or not.

If you want to do this:

7.52 Fix a "Bad record index"
*(Thanks to Ole and Steve,
in* Real World PageMaker, *
for this great tip!)*

■ **Note:** A good preventive measure to protect yourself from a bad record index is to make sure you turn imported styles (7.51) into PageMaker styles as soon as they appear. Imported styles are indicated with an asterisk (*) next to the style name. To turn them into PageMaker styles, simply hold the Command key down and click once on the style name in the Style palette; when you see the Edit dialog box, click OK.

Remove any imported styles that you don't use, need, or want (7.49).

Then follow these steps:

■ Read the column to the right.
■ If you don't have the Style palette on your screen, press Command Y.
■ Check each style to see if it is confused. Start with the imported styles (the ones with an asterisk [*] next to their names): Hold down the Command key and click once on the style name; you will see the "Edit style" dialog box.
■ Click OK; if you *do not* get a "Bad record index" message, this style feels fine.
■ If you *do* get the message, hold down the Command key and click on the style *"No style."* Type the *exact* name (but not the * or the ◆) of the confused style you just found. Click OK and PageMaker will ask if you want to replace the original one; click OK.
■ After changing all the offending styles, use "Save as..." to compress and protect your publication (16.25).
■ Now go to the "Define styles..." dialog box (press Command 3) and *remove* those styles you just renamed (click on the style name, then click the Remove button).
■ Use "Save as..." again to compress and protect your publication (16.25).

Shortcuts ▾ Notes ▾ Hints

■ A bad record index is indicated by an alert box, often after you've been in your "Define styles" dialog box and made changes to styles; after you click OK, PageMaker tells you the changes couldn't be made. Or she may tell you that you "Cannot turn the page" when you try to define styles. If you start getting funny (yeah, very funny) messages, go through the procedure noted to the left.
■ A bad record index is most often the result of imported word-processing styles getting confused. Whenever you place a file into PageMaker that was created in Microsoft Word, you bring in the style "Normal," whether you used style sheets or not. If you *did* use style sheets in Word or another program, those styles are *also* imported when you place the file. If any of these styles have the same name, like "Normal," but not the exact same specifications, they try to come into PageMaker, but the existing imported styles do not really belong to PageMaker, so they are not replaced and PageMaker gets confused and freaks out. These alien styles sneak into your PageMaker document whether you have clicked "Retain format" in the Place dialog box or not. *They will not come in if you choose to "Read tags," whether there are actually tags to be read or not.*

If you want to do this:	Then follow these steps:	Shortcuts ▾ Notes ▾ Hints

7.53 Transform one existing style (Style A) into another existing style (Style B) (*Another valuable technique from Steve and Ole, of* Real World PageMaker*)*

Note: *You may find it easier to use the Story Editor to find all paragraphs tagged with a certain style, and change them all into another style (8.76). There may be a time when find-and-change will not work effectively, in which case you can always use this technique.*

To transform Style A into Style B:

- Click once on the **pointer tool,** *even if it is already selected.*
- If the Style palette is not showing, press Command Y. Click once on **Style B.**
- Press Command 3 to get the "Define styles" dialog box.
- Double-click on the style name "Selection." You will see the "Edit style" dialog box, but with a blank name, *based on* **Style B.**
- Type in the *exact* name of **Style A.** Click OK; when PageMaker asks if you want to replace the existing style, click OK again. *Don't close the "Define styles" box yet!*
- Double-click on **Style A;** you will see the "Edit style" dialog box. Type in the *exact* name of **Style B** (replacing Style A's name).
- Change "Based on" to "No style."
- Click OK; click OK again when Page-Maker asks if you want to replace the existing style of that name.
- Now you can click OK to close the "Define styles" dialog box. Everything that was previously tagged **Style A** is now tagged **Style B.** Not only are they tagged, but they have changed their formatting to **Style B.**
- Permanent overrides will be kept through this transformation, and temporary overrides will disappear (7.37–7.38).

- Use this technique when you want to take two separate, existing styles and eliminate one of them, *transforming* it into the other style. Perhaps you have two separate styles, like Subhead1 and Subhead2, and you want to turn them all into Subhead2. Or perhaps you want to turn all the stupid Normal text into Body Copy. If you follow the procedure outlined here, you will not only change the two style *names* into one, but you will transform all the *text* of the two separate styles into the one style.
- You may think: If I just *base* (7.20–7.26) Subhead1 on Subhead2, then I can *remove* Subhead1. All the paragraphs that were Subhead1 will then *become* Subhead2, since that's what they were *based on.* Well, that's true to a certain extent—all the paragraphs that were Subhead1 will be *tagged* with the style Subhead2, *but their actual formatting won't change.* They will still *look like* Subhead1 and the old formatting will be thought of as *overrides* (7.36–7.41).
- What you are actually doing here is making the two styles identical, except for their names. Then you are making their names identical as well, so they actually become one.

If you want to do this:	Then follow these steps:	Shortcuts ▾ Notes ▾ Hints
7.54 Apply a style to a paragraph	■ With the **text tool,** select the text: □ if you want to **select just one paragraph,** simply click the I-beam anywhere in it; □ if you want to **select more than one consecutive paragraph,** press-and-drag to select all of them; □ if you want to **select an entire story,** click with the I-beam anywhere in the text block, then press Command A to select all. ■ From the Type menu, slide down to Style (near the very bottom—*not* Type Style!); move out to the right and choose the Style of your fancy. **Or** press Command Y to show the Style palette; click on the style name to apply it to the selected paragraph(s).	■ Applying a style removes any other fonts and formatting that were in the text. Permanent overrides are preserved (7.39–7.41). ■ After you apply a style to a paragraph, that paragraph is now considered *tagged.*
7.55 Change a paragraph's style	■ Changing a paragraph's style is exactly the same as applying a new style (7.54). ■ If you want to change the *definition,* or specifications of the style, see 7.48.	■ Changing the style, though, may have an effect on any overrides (7.36–7.41) that may be in the paragraphs. To preserve the temporary overrides, see 7.57.
7.56 Override the style sheet *(change the formatting in any paragraph)*	■ If you want to change any specifications in the paragraph itself, just go ahead and do it—size, font, tabs, indents, etc. ■ Be sure to read about temporary and permanent overrides (7.36–7.41) to see how they will affect future changes in style names or in paragraph formatting.	■ A plus sign (+) next to the style name on the Style palette indicates the presence of an override (7.36–7.41). *That plus sign will only appear, though,* when the insertion point is in the actual word or section of text that is creating the override.

305

If you want to do this:	Then follow these steps:	Shortcuts ▾ Notes ▾ Hints
7.57 Preserve temporary overrides (7.37–7.38) when changing a paragraph's style	■ If you want to retain the temporary overrides in a paragraph, press the Shift key when changing the style.	■ Changing the *definition,* or specifications of a style ("Edit..." from the "Define styles" dialog box), *will not change any overrides, even if they are temporary (see 7.58).*
7.58 Eliminate all temporary overrides from tagged paragraphs	■ With the **text tool,** click once in the paragraph, **or** press-and-drag to select more than one paragraph, **or** click once in any paragraph and press Command A to select the entire story. ■ From the Type menu, pop out the submenu "Style" and choose the style for the selected text, *even if it is already checked.* **Or** show the Style palette (Command Y) and click once on the style name, *even if it is already highlighted.* The plus sign should disappear (unless there are also *permanent* overrides in that paragraph; 7.59).	■ The plus sign (**+**) in the Style palette indicates an override (7.33–7.41), whether temporary or permanent. ■ A temporary override is any formatting except type style (bold, italic, outline, etc., as well as case [caps vs. lowercase] and position [super- and subscript; 3.163–3.170]). Temporary overrides include reverse, size, leading, font, paragraph specs, tracking, set width, tabs and indents, etc.).
7.59 Eliminate permanent overrides from tagged paragraphs *(bold, italic, underline, strikethru, outline, and shadow)* *(See **7.60** to get rid of case and position overrides)*	■ Some permanent overrides are trickier to get rid of than others. To get rid of the easy ones—the type styles you see listed in the menu (bold, italic, underline, strikethru, outline, and shadow)—do this: ■ Select the text with the **text tool.** ■ From the Type menu, pop out the "Type style" submenu and choose "Normal," **or** just press Command Shift Spacebar.	■ These type style overrides are easy to get rid of. It is not Undo-able though; that is, after you eliminate the type styles this way you cannot go to the Edit menu and choose Undo to bring them back.

If you want to do this:

7.60 Eliminate really permanent overrides from tagged paragraphs (*case, as in uppercase or lowercase; and position, as in superscript or subscript*)

(See **7.59** *to get rid of type style overrides*)

Then follow these steps:

- These permanent overrides are trickier to get rid of than the simple type style formatting. You will have to change all the selected text into the same case or position, then change it back again.
- Save your publication before you do anything, just in case you blow it. Then if you do blow it, from the File menu you can choose "Revert" (16.26).
- Select the text by pressing-and-dragging over it, **or** click once in any paragraph and press Command A to select the entire story.
- Now, *you have to change the entire selection of text into the offending override.* That is, if you want to get rid of all the superscripts contained in the text, first *change all the text to superscript* (press Command Shift +; that's a plus, but don't use the plus sign from the numeric keypad). Then change it all back again (press the keyboard shortcut again).

    If you have some text *that you typed in lowercase and used the menu to transform into all caps,* you can turn everything back into lowercase: select it and turn it *all* into uppercase (Command Shift K), then back into lowercase (same keys). You can do the same for text in small caps (Command Shift H).

Shortcuts • Notes • Hints

- All caps, small caps, superscript, and subscript really hang in there; you need to go to extra lengths to get rid of them.
- Remember, you can only turn all caps into lowercase *if the text was originally typed in lowercase and then turned into all caps through the menu or the keyboard shortcut.* If you *typed* the text all caps, then the only way to transform it back into lowercase is to retype it. Really. With all the magic this machine can do, it's unbelievable how pitifully few programs can turn caps into lowercase.
- If you have just a few of these overrides, of course you can select just the specific pieces of text and change them one at a time. Use the technique explained here when you want to eliminate several instances of the override throughout the story. *The paragraphs you select do not have to be tagged with all the same style.*

If you want to do this:	**Then follow these steps:**	**Shortcuts ▾ Notes ▾ Hints**
7.61　Use the Story Editor to find and change local formatting (overrides; 7.33–7.41)	▪ If you are not familiar with using the Story Editor, first read Section 8; 8.76. ▪ For instance, if you want to get rid of all the italic overrides throughout the publication, leave the "Change" box empty, and just select the "Attributes" for the text you want to change. You can set it to change any italic it finds, in any font or a specific font, in any size or a specific size, etc. You can find and change bold text to normal, or all occurences of 12-point text to 10-point text. ▪ You can also change specific text to local formatting. Let's say you are writing about a book titled *The Mac is not a typewriter*. You can just speed type the initials "tm." Then go to the Story Editor, find any occurence of "tm," and change it into the full title in the italic font of your choice, thus overriding the style sheet with ease and elegance (8.75).	▪ In this book, style sheets were used for all text. In the first column, though, you can see that style has an override in every paragraph; the main text is 10-point Baskerville, but the number is 9-point Futura Bold. Also scattered throughout the text are various references, also in 9- point Futura Bold. Changing text into 9-point Futura Bold is a multi-step process: First I have to select the text, then go to the menu and change the font, reduce the point size, and make the style bold. But by using the Story Editor in combination with style sheets, I was able to save hours of time: 　　As I typed the text, I used the keyboard command to underline all the characters I knew would eventually be Futura Bold; that is, I typed along, then pressed Command Shift U *before* I typed the characters that were to change, then pressed Command Shift U again *after* I typed the characters, to turn the following text back to normal. When I finished the chapter, I opened the Story Editor and changed all the underlined text into 9 point Futura Bold in all stories. Wow. I'm impressed. Thank you Aldus.
7.62　Use local formatting (overrides; 7.33–7.41) intentionally, then use the Story Editor to find and change it	▪ Taking advantage of the Story Editor, you can *intentionally* insert overrides in your text, especially the ones using keyboard commands, as you can do those so quickly. Then you can use the Story Editor to change all those easy keyboard overrides into more complex formatting (see the column to the right).	

If you want to do this:

7.63 Apply styles to text in the Story Editor

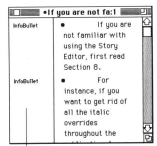

The sidebar in the Story Editor, displaying the style names.

Then follow these steps:

- Apply the style name to paragraphs while you are in the Story Editor just as you would while on the publication page:
- Click in the paragraph, or select a series of paragraphs.
- You can still use the Type menu, although using the Style palette is so much easier and quicker (Command Y to show the Style palette). Just click on the name in the style sheet list.
- While in the Story Editor, *you will not see any type changes.* They will not appear until you place or close the story. Yes, that can be frustrating. You will see the *type styles*, though, if your style specifications include any of those (bold, italic, underline, strike-thru, outline, and shadow; not Reverse).
- While in the Story Editor, if you choose "Display style names" from the Options menu, you will see the style names tagged to each paragraph; they will be in a list in the sidebar on the left. If there is no style attached to a paragraph, you will see a bullet (•) in the sidebar.

Shortcuts ▾ Notes ▾ Hints

- Be sure to read Section 8 on the Story Editor for all the details on this great adjunct to PageMaker.
- You can apply styles while in the Story Editor, and you can create them there as well. Of course, you can't see the results of what you're doing until you get back to the page layout.

If you want to do this:

7.64 **Create** a word-processing document so PageMaker can read the tags *Also read Scenario #9; 7.71*

(See 7.63 for word processing with style sheets in PageMaker's Story Editor)

Then follow these steps:

- In your word processing document, don't format anything—don't bother to change fonts or sizes or set paragraph spacing or indents. Just type the text with your favorite city-named font. Use Returns only when you want a paragraph break (3.230–3.236). Read Section 5 to understand tabs and indents; don't *format* with tabs, just *insert* them where you know you will need them later to work with them. Let the word processor do what it does best—process words.
- At the beginning of each paragraph that will have a new style attached, type in the style name that you want PageMaker to read, and enclose it between angle brackets, like so:

```
<Headline>William Strunk, Jr.
<Body text>If you don't know
how to pronounce a word, say
it loud.
```

- Not *every* paragraph needs a tag—just the first one in that style. Any paragraph following will pick up the same specifications as the one above it until a new tag is applied.
- It doesn't matter which letters are capitals.
- Leave no space or tab between the tag and the first word of the paragraph, unless you want it to appear in the final version.

Shortcuts ▾ Notes ▾ Hints

- Actually, this is the best way (from my point of view, which you are stuck with in this book) to prepare text for placement in PageMaker.
- **Either use style names you have already created in the PageMaker publication, or make up style names in the word processor; then when you get to PageMaker, create styles using those same names (of course, *before* you place this document).**
- With the tags in position, when you place this document PageMaker will *read the tags* (if you checked that Option in "Place..."; 7.65), *eliminate the tags* from the text, and *apply that style* to the paragraphs. Do you realize what this means? You can type, for instance, 66 pages in MacWrite II, tag the heads and subheads and indented tables and body text and captions and pull quotes without ever having to select text and use the menus, then drop it into PageMaker (where you have set up your style sheet), and all 66 pages will instantly have its final formatting. Amazing! Used with Autoflow (3.86–3.87) and text wrapping (Section 11), PageMaker will just pour text in and make new pages for you as she needs them.
- If your word processor can do it, set up a macro or a glossary entry to input the tags.

If you want to do this:	**Then follow these steps:**	**Shortcuts • Notes • Hints**
7.65 Place a word-processed document that has been tagged with style names	▪ In the PageMaker publication, set up your style sheet (7.43; 7.44), **or** copy it in from another publication (7.50); **OR** open a template that already has style sheets prepared. ▪ From the File menu choose "Place...." ▪ Navigate, if necessary, to find the tagged document you want to place (page 576). ▪ Click once on the name of the file you want to place. ▪ Uncheck "Retain format" by clicking once on it. ▪ Click on "Read tags" to check it. ▪ Double-click on the name of the file you want to place, or click OK. ▪ With the loaded text icon that is now on the screen, click to start pouring the text. (Read 3.27–3.58 for detailed info about placing text.)	▪ Make sure the names on the PageMaker style sheet *exactly* match the tags you used in the word processor! ▪ You can always go in and edit the styles after the document has been placed. ▪ If "Retain format" and "Read tags" are both checked, "Read tags" will take precedence on paragraphs that are tagged. Untagged paragraphs will retain the format in which they were originally word processed. ▪ See 7.64 for info on putting the tags in the word-processing document.

The good type designer knows that, for a new font to be successful, it has to be so good that only a few recognize its novelty.   —*Stanley Morison*

If you want to do this:

7.66 Export a story, tagging it with the style sheet names

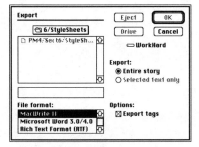

The "Export" dialog box; also see 15.36.

Then follow these steps:

- With the **pointer tool,** click once in any paragraph in the story. If you want to export just a selected portion of the story, then press-and-drag over that portion.
- From the File menu, choose "Export..."; you'll see the dialog shown at the left.
- Click the appropriate "Export" button, depending on whether you want to export the entire story, or just the portion you selected. If you didn't select a portion, the "Selected text only" button will not be available.
- Click the "Export tags" box under "Options."
- Choose the "File format," which is the word processing format or application you want the story to turn into.
- Type a name for the file. Make sure you are putting it in the right folder; navigate if necessary (see page 576).
- Click OK. There will be an icon or file name on your disk representing this file, and the document will contain all the tags in angle brackets; i.e., <Headline>.

Shortcuts ▾ Notes ▾ Hints

- The exported story will have tags, that is, angle brackets with the name of the paragraph style: <Body Copy>. You'll see them typed in front of each paragraph. This file can then be placed into any other PageMaker publication that carries the same style sheets with the exact same names. (The tags themselves are simply *text;* they do not indicate formatting that is applied. These tags *will not be added to the style sheet* of any PageMaker publication.)
- When you place one of these files, remember to click the "Read tags" button, or the text will come in with a tag still visible in front of each paragraph.
- The "File format" list displays the export filters you installed when you first loaded PageMaker onto your Mac. If you need another filter, you can copy just the filter icon onto your disk at any time. Put the filter in the "Aldus Filters" folder, which is in the "Aldus Folder," which is in the System Folder on your hard disk. I know, you don't remember making that folder. You didn't—PageMaker did when you installed it.

If you want to do this:	**Then follow these steps:**	**Shortcuts ▾ Notes ▾ Hints**
7.67 Set a particular style as the publication default when *typing* in PageMaker	▪ With the **pointer tool,** choose a style from the Style sheet submenu, either at the bottom of the Type menu, or from the Style palette, if it is showing (Command Y). ▪ Take advantage of this. For instance, if you are going to type several captions, default to your Caption style. When you are about to go through your publication and write pull quotes, default to the style you previously set up for pull quotes.	▪ Every time you click the insertion point *outside* of a text block and begin to type, PageMaker uses the text specifications from the style that has been set as the default. Typically the default is *"No style."* ▪ You can check to see what the current default is: click once on the pointer tool, then check the Style submenu. The font with the checkmark is the default font. ▪ The specs for *"No style"* are whatever you choose while the pointer tool is selected; see 3.20–3.21. You can change them at any time.
7.68 Set a particular style as the default when *placing* text from a word-processor into PageMaker	▪ With the **pointer tool,** choose a style from the Style sheet submenu at the bottom of the Type menu, *or* from the Style palette if it is showing (Command Y). See Scenario #9, 7.70.	▪ When you *place* text into PageMaker, if there is **no** check in the "Retain format" checkbox, the text will transform itself into the specifications of whichever style from the style sheet is the default. ▪ If the default style is *"No Style,"* then PageMaker uses the standard text defaults. You can set these standards simply by choosing the specifications with the **pointer tool** (more info on publication and application defaults: 1.6–1.11). ▪ Whenever you set a style as the default, the style "No style" picks up all those specifications (which essentially changes your "standard" text defaults).

Scenario #8: Using Style Sheets—the "create as you go" method

7.69 Scene One: OK. You're about to create a résumé. You have a blank, one-page publication open on the screen. Since there is not a significant amount of text involved in a résumé, you decide to just create it on screen. So you type in a head, hit a Return, and type some supporting information.

Before you go too much further, you start playing around with fonts, styles, spacing, leading, set widths, paragraph rules, etc. You format the head and finally are fairly happy with something. So you select the head text, press Command 3, double-click on *Selection*, name it Head, and click OK. While you're there, you remove all the default styles Page-Maker provided you with. You click OK again, and apply that new style to the selected head.

Well, you like that Head all right. So now you format the supporting text with a lighter weight font, less space after, no set width, etc. You go back to the "Define styles" dialog box and name this new one Support. While you are there, you also set the "Next style" for Head to be Support, so as you type a Return after each head, the formatting automatically transforms into the Support style.

As you create this résumé, you start to notice a pattern. You notice that after each Support line, the next two or three lines are always indented. So you name a new style, Indent, *based on* Support, and actually you set the *next style* as Support, also. And you edit the Support style so the *next style* is Indent.

Now you can type a Head. When you hit the Return key, the style automatically switches to Support and you type a supporting line of text. When you hit Return, the style automatically switches to Indent. You want to type two or three lines indented, but Indent's *next style* is specified as Support. Well, you don't want a Support paragraph yet, so instead of pressing Return, you press Shift-Return to get a line break but not a new paragraph. So with the Shift-Returns you type a few lines of Indent. Then you hit Return and it switches to Support.

Now the résumé is all keyed in. You want to make some refinements in the look of it, like you want the Heads to be a little larger and bolder. You want the paragraph rule to be a little closer to the text. So you edit the Head style and all the changes are made to the page. You decide you want a completely

different font for the Support and Indent text. So you edit Support—change the font. Because Indent was *based on* Support, the font in Indent *automatically* changes. Oh, life has never been so easy.

This beautiful résumé is so wildly successful that people are begging you to create a similar one for them. Fortunately, you saved this original document as a *template,* as well as a publication (12.14). Now when you open the *template,* the style sheet you so laboriously created is still there and you can whip out those résumés like cookies.

Scenario #9: Using Style Sheets—the "I know what I want" method

7.70 Scene Two: All right, so you know what you want. You're doing a six-page brochure and you've already decided in your loose comps what all the text formatting will be. You create six blank pages. You create a style sheet for Headlines, Subheads, Body Copy, Pull Quotes, and Captions.

Unfortunately, whoever input the text in the word processor didn't know how to add tags (7.64). So after you place each file you are going to have to select the paragraphs and apply the styles.

To make life a little easier, you set a new default style. Since most of your text is going to be Body Copy, you set Body Copy as the default (simply by clicking once on the pointer tool, then selecting Body Copy from the Style palette). Now when you *place* each story for the brochure, you make sure the "Retain format" box is *not* checked. When the text drops into PageMaker, the entire story will turn into Body Copy. At least that saves you the time required to select the body text and change it. Now you only need to select the heads, subheads, pull quotes, etc., and apply their styles.

7.71 Scene Three: Your office is working on an annual report, about thirty pages long. A typist is inputting the text and you will be doing the layout in Page-Maker. Since you are so smart, you have taught the typist how to input the tags.

You don't know exactly what the text formatting will eventually be, but you do know there will be Heads, Subheads, Body Copy, Tables, and ByLines. So in the rough copy that the typist will be keyboarding from, you mark the spots where he is to insert tags.

As the typist types, when he sees one of your callouts, he types the tag so: <Heads>. He types the text following the tag, with no space between the tag and the text. You've trained him not to put any *extra* carriage returns between paragraphs—you will specify extra paragraph space in the style sheet. You've trained him not to indent— you will specify indents in the style sheet. You've trained him not to input any extra tabs; he is to hit the Tab key *once* before each item in each column, *even if on the screen in the word processor it doesn't line up*— you will specify the tabs in the style sheet.

By the way, you've also given him the book *The Mac is not a typewriter* so he doesn't put two spaces after periods, or use two hyphens instead of a dash, and so he knows where to use an en dash, and whether a comma goes inside the quotation marks or not, etc. etc. etc. He's so grateful.

You see (and thank goodness you know this), if someone inputs extra carriage returns, tabs, indents, spaces, etc., you will have to go through the text when it gets to PageMaker and delete them all. It is possible to use the Story Editor to find and change those extra characters, even those invisible ones (8.78). But it's wise, as well as more efficient, to keyboard it in the most efficient manner to take advantage of the style sheets.

While your typist is keyboarding, you are busy preparing the thirty-page PageMaker publication in which to place the finished document. You're setting up your master pages with columns, guidelines, and auto-numbering; you're creating text wraps to control the text flow, and definitions for the style sheets. And you're thinking about what you are going to do with all the time you will save by using style sheets.

A discourse between the Poet and the Player: of no other use in this manual but to divert the reader.

A special blessing expressing praise of the new printing technology.

 LESSED BE HE WHO FORMS MAN WITH KNOWLEDGE

AND TEACHES HUMANS UNDERSTANDING,

WHO AMPLIFIED HIS GRACE WITH A GREAT INVENTION,

ONE THAT IS USEFUL FOR ALL INHABITANTS OF THE WORLD,

THERE IS NONE BESIDE IT AND NOTHING CAN EQUAL IT

IN ALL THE WISDOM AND CLEVERNESS

FROM THE DAY WHEN GOD CREATED MAN ON EARTH.

R. David Gans ✒ 1592 ✒ Prague
(the first Hebrew histographer)

8 ▾ STORY EDITOR

8.1 Minimums and maximums:

Item	Minimum	Maximum
Open story windows	1	10
Number of char. to change	0	32,767

Type
**is one of the
most eloquent
means of expression
in every epoch of style.
Next to architecture,
it gives the most
characteristic portrait
of a period
and the most
severe testimony
of a nation's
intellectual status.**

—*Peter Behrens*

8.2 The **Story Editor** is the word processor that is built into PageMaker. Yes, people have complained that it is clunky and inelegant. But personally, I think it's terrific. This entire book was done entirely within PageMaker—I never even looked at Word. (Actually, if I was going to use a separate word processor, I would have used MacWrite II anyway.)

8.3 The Story Editor allows you to create text much more quickly than it can appear on the layout page. What upsets some people is that the text formatting you see in the Story Editor is *not* what you see on the Layout page. But I say, "So what." Use the word processor to process words, not to format your text. Use it to find and change words. Use it to check your spelling.

8.4 Use it to find and change text attributes; for instance, use it to find all instances of Baskerville Italic and change them all to Franklin Gothic Bold. Or find all text that is tagged with a Subhead1 style and change them to the Subhead2 style. Oh, it is the most marvelous invention. Please see Scenarios #10 and #11 for other ways to take advantage of this great feature.

About the Story Editor

8.5 Move *a window by dragging in its title bar.* **Resize** *a window by dragging in its size box. This shows several windows open in the Story Editor. Notice in the background you can see the page layout window as well.*

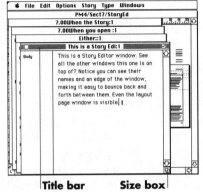

Title bar   Size box

8.6   When you open the Story Editor (8.30–8.31), you are looking at the **story view.** The actual PageMaker publication page is referred to as the **layout view.** I will also refer to it as the *page layout view* or the *publication page* to make it as clear as possible here.

8.7   What you see when you open the Story Editor is a **window** that operates just like any other window on the Mac. It has a title bar, a scroll bar, a zoom box, a size box, and a close box (if you are not familiar with these parts and how to operate them, you really should read *The Little Mac Book*). The Toolbox disappears, because you don't need it.

8.8   Each window holds only one story (if you are not clear on the difference between a *text block* and a *story*, please pop over to 3.106). You can get a window for each and every story in the entire publication, including every little pull-quote and caption, no matter how small. In addition, each is named with the first few characters in the first paragraph of the story. If there is more than one story that begins with the same characters, the title bar will number them (Hello:1; Hello:2; etc.).

8.9   You can have up to ten story windows open at a time, each holding a different story. As is typical with windows, they will layer over the top of each other. You can easily get to the different windows either by clicking on the visible part of the one you want (it will come forward), **or** by choosing it from the Windows menu. All open windows, including the publication itself, will be listed in the Windows menu (8.29).

Window tricks: To move a window all the way to the back, hold the Option key down and click in its title bar. To move a window without making it active (in front), hold the Command key down as you drag its title bar.

8.10   You cannot **print** the document directly from a story window; the story must be placed on a page (8.79). But, if you have an ImageWriter printer, you can print what is visible in the window or what is visible on the screen:

- To print the window, have it visible as the top layer. Press Command Shift 4.
- To print what is visible on the screen (which may be several different windows, depending on how you arrange them), press the Caps Lock down, then press Command Shift 4.

8.11   You can open story windows only when the publication itself is open. When you close the publication, all *unplaced* (8.81) story windows close also. Only *unplaced* stories will automatically open again when you re-open the publication. PageMaker

The Story Editor
—continued

considers any story as *unplaced* that has not yet been put on a publication page—it exists only in the Story Editor.

8.12　PageMaker will automatically save all *unplaced* stories (8.81) in their present state and they will re-open along with the publication.

8.13　The **font** (typeface) displayed in the Story Editor defaults to 12-point Geneva. This means that *everything* you type is in 12-point Geneva. Even if you select text and change its font to 36-point Garamond Ultra, it will appear as 12-point Geneva in the window. Neither will you see line breaks, columns, letter or word spacing, hyphenation, text color, rotation, or kerning. Just 12-point Geneva text. You *will* see any type *style* changes (bold, italic, etc., except reverse), and you will see some kind of blank space where a tab or indent has been set.

8.14　As you type, though, PageMaker keeps track of any changes, and when you close the story window, the text with all its attributes will flow onto the page. When you are in the Story Editor, you may notice, if it is visible, that the story on the layout page is gray when its window is open. And

when you are on the layout page, the story window, if it is open, will be gray.

8.15　You can change the font in which the Story Editor displays to any other font in your System (8.45). But you will find it easier to read a bitmapped font, as they are designed for the resolution of the screen. Almost all bitmapped fonts have city names (Geneva, Boston, New York, Chicago, etc.). Also, to make it easiest to read, choose a font size that is installed in your System. You can tell which sizes are installed by looking in the Size submenu: the numbers in outline form indicate installed sizes.

8.16　The Style palette and the Color palette are both available while you are in the Story Editor, and you can use them to apply styles to paragraphs and colors to text, but you won't see the effect. You *can* choose to see the *name* of the applied style in the sidebar next to the paragraph, though (from the Options menu, choose "Display style names").

8.17　This is a great little feature: if you choose "Display ¶" from the Story Editor Option menu, you can hide or show all those invisible characters, like Returns,

Tabs, Line-breaks, and Spaces. This is great for those times when you are trying to discover why your tabs are acting bizarrely, or where someone has used spaces instead of first-line indents. You can also find-and-change any misformatting (Scenario 11).

8.18　An inline graphic (9.91) in the Story Editor will appear as a little box (▓), just a placeholder. Index entries (Section 12) will appear as ◊. Automatic page-number markers (1.139a) will appear as #. The end of the story is indicated by a small, vertical bar (▮).

8.19　**Important note:** When you place a story into PageMaker that you created in an outside word processor, you know you can always throw away the version you have in PageMaker because the word-processed version is still on the disk and you can place it again. **But** if you create a story directly in the Story Editor and then place it on a page, **there is no other copy of it.** The Story Editor just gives you another view of what is on the page. If you eliminate the story on the layout page, you eliminate the story view of it also. If you want to keep an outside copy of the story, export it (8.38).

The Story Editor menu *(from the Edit menu, choose "Edit Story," or press Command E)*

8.20 When the Story Editor is open, you will see a slightly different menu bar:

⁂ File Edit Options Story Type Windows

8.21 Some of the Story Editor menu commands are the same or similar to the layout menu commands, but they don't really do the same thing, particularly "Place" and "Close story."

8.22 Place... in the *layout view* brings in a file from another program, and you get a loaded icon (3.82–3.83). "Place" in the *Story Editor* will also load the pointer, but with the *new* story that is in the current window, and you can place it as you would any outside file (3.27–3.77). If the window is *not* a new story, but a story that has been placed on the page previously, the File menu changes "Place" to "Replace" (8.24; 8.82).

8.23 Close from the *File* menu, in either story or layout view, will close the publication. "Close story" from the Story menu will close just the window that is on the top layer (the *active* window). If the story is a new one that hasn't been placed yet, you will get a dialog box asking if you want to place or discard it (8.78).

8.24 *"Close" from the File menu closes the* **publication,** *not just the story window. You cannot open a new story from here (8.30). Notice this File menu has "Replace" instead of "Place" (sometimes: 8.22; 8.82). You cannot change the "Page setup," nor can you "Print."*

8.25 *In the Story Editor, the Find, Change, and Spelling commands are black and available (in the layout view, they are always gray). While you're in the story view, the last command is "Edit layout," to return to the page layout. While you're in the layout view, this command is "Edit story."*

8.26 *Indexing and creating tables of contents can be done from the story view. You can also choose to see the style sheet names, as well as invisible characters (8.43).*

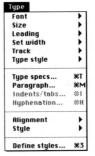

8.27 *From the Story menu you can open a new, blank story window (8.30), close an existing one (8.79), or import a word processing document (8.35) or another PageMaker file (8.37).*

8.28 *You can use almost any of the type specifications, just as in the layout view, except indents and tabs and the hyphenation controls. Remember, though, you won't see any of your specs in the story window (8.13).*

8.29 *The Windows menu lists all the open windows, including the page layout view window. If you leave the Story Editor by choosing the layout page, all those story windows just go* behind *the publication page; they are actually still open back there.*

You can also show and hide the palettes from this menu.

If you want to do this:	Then follow these steps:	Shortcuts ▾ Notes ▾ Hints

Opening windows; editing

8.30 From the publication page, open the Story Editor to a new, blank story window *(If you are already in the Story Editor, just choose "New story" from the Story menu)*	▪ **Either:** With the **text tool,** click once *outside of any existing text block;* **Or:** Click once on the **pointer tool,** even if you already have the pointer tool selected. ▪ **Then:** From the Edit menu, choose "Edit story," *or* press Command E. ▪ In the story view you will get a blank window that is named "Untitled:1."	▪ Every existing text block already has its own story window that will open if there is an insertion point anywhere in it, or if any of its text is selected, so the trick to begin a new, *blank* text block is to click the insertion point somewhere else, or make sure no text block has been selected with the pointer tool.
8.31 Open the Story Editor to view a particular story you want to edit: **a)** So that the insertion point is flashing before the first character of that text block, even if it is not the first text block in the story	There are several ways to do this, depending on exactly what you want to view in the story: **a)** With the **pointer tool,** triple-click on the text block. ▪ **Or,** with the **pointer tool,** click once on a text block to select it, then from the Edit menu choose "Edit story," *or* press Command E.	
b) So that the insertion point is flashing in the story window at the same spot it was flashing in the layout	**b)** With the **text tool,** click once at the particular spot you want to start editing. ▪ From the Edit menu, choose "Edit story," *or* press Command E.	▪ You can also select text (press-and-drag over it) and then press Command E. The selected text will still be highlighted when it appears in the Story Editor.
c) If you previously opened this window and it is now tucked behind the layout view	**c)** With any tool, from the Windows menu choose the name of the story (the "name" is the first few letters of the story); *or* if you can see the story window edge behind the layout, click once on it.	▪ Whichever window is *active,* or on the top layer, determines whether you are in story view or layout view (8.6). You can resize your publication window so you can see the story windows behind it (8.5).

321

If you want to do this:	**Then follow these steps:**	**Shortcuts ▾ Notes ▾ Hints**
8.32 While the Story Editor is active, bring to the front a story window that is already open, but is buried under other windows	■ From the Windows menu, choose the name of the story (the "name" is the first few characters in the text block); ■ **Or,** if it is already open you should be able to see its title bar (with the name in it); just click in the title bar.	■ To send a window behind all the others, hold the Option key and click its title bar. To move a window without making it come to the front, hold the Command key and press-and-drag in its title bar (actually, this trick works on any window on the Mac).
8.33 While the Story Editor is active, open a story that is still on the layout page	■ To open a story window for an existing text block, you must return to the page layout view. *This does not mean you must close the story view.* Just click once on the exposed portion of the publication page, **or** choose the publication name from the Windows menu. ■ Find the story you want to open, and then open it as usual (triple-click on it with the pointer tool, or click the insertion point in it and press Command E). You will return to the Story Editor, and all the other windows that were open will still be open.	■ It does seem a little awkward to have to go back to the layout view to get another story. If you are working with only one meg of RAM, you really should close all story windows (press Command W for each window) before you bring in another one.
8.34 Import a word-processing file from outside PageMaker into its own separate window *(see the dialog box in 8.35)*	■ From the Story menu, choose "Import...." ■ Notice it is the same dialog box as "Place..." in the layout view (3.40–3.50). You use it the same way here. Find the name of the document you wish to import, check your options at the bottom (8.35; 3.46–3.50), and double-click on the file name. You will get a new window with your imported story in it.	■ Importing into the Story Editor is just like "placing" into the publication (3.27–3.77), except that you don't get a loaded text icon—you get a story window.

If you want to do this:	Then follow these steps:	Shortcuts ▪ Notes ▪ Hints
8.35 Import a story, *inserting* the text into the current story, *replacing the entire story*, or *replacing a portion* of the current story 	▪ Open the story that you want to edit (8.31). ▪ If you want to **insert new text** into the existing text, click once to set the insertion point where you want the new text to begin; ● **or** if you want to **replace an entire story,** click once anywhere in the story; ● **or** if you want to **replace a portion of text,** select the portion you want to replace (press-and-drag, or see 8.39). ▪ From the Story menu, choose "Import...." ▪ In the dialog box, find the file to import and click once on its name. ▪ Under "Place," click in the button of your choice. If you left an insertion point flashing in your story window instead of selected text, there will be a button "Inserting text." ▪ Choose whether you want to "Retain format" (3.51–3.52), "Convert quotes" (3.57; always, really), or "Read tags" (3.56; 7.64–7.65). ▪ Click OK, or double-click on the file name.	▪ If you have trouble "navigating" to find other files, you may want to spend some time studying page 576. Or use Find File (1.232–1.233).
8.36 Import stories from another PageMaker publication	▪ This works exactly the same as it does in the layout view, so please see 3.59–3.80. The only difference is that the file you're importing drops into the story window as text, rather than as a loaded icon on the layout page.	▪ This is really a terrific trick. It allows you to get separate stories or the entire file belonging to another PageMaker publication and add it to this one.

If you want to do this:	Then follow these steps:	Shortcuts ▾ Notes ▾ Hints

8.37　Import a graphic into a story, either as a *new* inline graphic or to *replace an existing* inline graphic

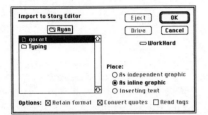

- Open the story window where you want to insert or replace a graphic (8.31).
- If you want to **insert an inline graphic,** then just click the insertion point at the spot you want it inserted;
  Or if you want to **replace an inline graphic,** then select the little icon (▓) representing the graphic you want to replace (double-click it, or press-and-drag over it).
- From the Story menu, choose "Import...."
- Find the graphic file you want to import. You will know the file is a graphic when you click once on it: the buttons "As inline graphic" or "Replacing entire graphic" will show up and be black. The story window cannot accept an independent graphic (9.90).
- Click once on the file name, then click OK; **or** double-click on the file name.
- In the Story Editor window, the graphic will appear as that little icon (▓). I know, you can't tell one from the other. But it works.
- If you are replacing one graphic with the other, remember that *the new one will assume the size and proportions of the one it is replacing,* which may or may not be what you want.

- The only kind of graphics you can have in the story window are *inline graphics.* Inline graphics are those that are imbedded within the text. They move along with the text as you edit, and are actually part of the text block. Inline graphics are too cool. Learn to take advantage of them (9.170–9.205).

- If the replaced graphic in the page layout view is not proportioned properly, you can do this: Get the **pointer tool.** Click once on the graphic. Hold the Shift key down. *Press* on any handle and count to three. It will snap back into the original proportions (not the original size) it was created in.

If you want to do this:

8.38 Export and link a story, either the *entire* story, or a *selected portion* of the story

(for complete info on linking, see Section 10 on Linking Text and Graphics)

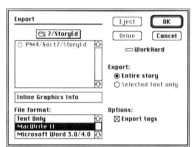

Then follow these steps:

- Open the story window you want to export.
- If you want to export the **entire story,** just click the insertion point anywhere; **or**
- If you want to export just a **portion of the story,** select just a portion (press-and-drag, or see 8.39).
- From the File menu, choose "Export...."
- If there is already a name in the edit box (directly above "File format:"), then this file is already linked to something. If you can see the same name in the list box, you will be asked if you want to replace the existing file.

  If you change the name, you create a second version of this same file, *but the story will still be linked to the first version.*

  If there is no name in the edit box, then type one in.
- Click the button to export the entire story or selected text only. Even if text is selected in the story, you can choose to export the entire story anyway.
- Choose the file format you want the exported document to be in (15.14–15.15).
- Click "Export tags" if you used them and want to keep them.
- Click OK. The link (10.2–10.11) is established automatically.

Shortcuts ▼ Notes ▼ Hints

- When you export a story you are putting it into a format that can be read by a word processor.
- The link is established automatically. See Section 10 for detailed information on linking text and graphics. The basic idea is that if you make any changes in the linked word processing or graphic document after you close PageMaker, the changes can be automatically updated. **But** if you make changes in the *PageMaker version* after establishing the link, and then choose to update the changes that were made in the *word-processing version,* you will lose all those changes you made in the *PageMaker version.*
- Each story must be exported as a separate document. You can't expect to name two or three files with the same name and have them funnel into one—they won't.
- Exporting from the Story Editor is exactly the same as exporting from the page layout view, actually. If you need more information, please see Section 10 on Linking and Section 15 on Exporting.

If you want to do this:

Then follow these steps:

Shortcuts ▾ Notes ▾ Hints

8.39   Select text in a story

Selecting text in a story window is similar to selecting text in the layout text blocks (3.129–3.138).
- You can, of course, press-and-drag to select text.
- You can use the arrow keys or the keypad keys in combination with the Shift key to select text in increments of characters, words, lines, sentences, paragraphs, screens, or the entire story (1.224; 1.226).
- Command A selects the entire story, whether it is all visible or not.
- If the style names are showing in the sidebar (from the Options menu, choose "Display style names; 8.41), you can use them to select paragraphs: Click once on the style sheet name (even if it is just the bullet indicating "No style") that appears in the sidebar. You can't press-and-drag down through those style names, not even with the Shift key, but you *can* Shift-click to add to the selection. That is, click once on a style name. If you want to add the next three paragraphs to the selection, hold down the Shift key and click on the style name three paragraphs below (or above).

- If you miss a few characters at the end when pressing-and-dragging to select, or if you went a few characters too far, hold the Shift key down and pick up the drag at the end to add to or delete from the selection. You can only do this from the *end* of the selection; that is, if you pressed-and-dragged upward, the *end* is on the up side. Try it!
- On the keypad, the 3 and the 9 work a little differently in the story view than they do on the publication page:
  - If you press 3 or 9, the screen moves, *but not the insertion point.*
  - Hold Shift and press 3 to select all the text *visible* in the window *above* the insertion point (the window may scroll up so you don't see the selected text; if so, press on the down scroll arrow). Hold Command Shift and press 3 to select all the text *below* the insertion point, whether it is visible or not.
  - Hold Shift and press 9 to select everything visible in the window, *plus* one window up. Hold Command Shift and press 9 to select from the insertion point *all* the way up to the beginning of the story.

If you want to do this:	**Then follow these steps:**	**Shortcuts ▾ Notes ▾ Hints**
8.40 Edit in a story window	▪ Edit in a story window just like you edit in a text block. The only difference is that you won't see any formatting changes except type style. ▪ You cannot use the keyboard to change the size of text. ▪ You can press Option Backspace/Delete to delete the character to the *right* of the insertion point. (That key combination in the page layout view, though, will *kern* in small increments; 4.182–4.184).	▪ Just remember the basic Mac rule (Rule #2): Select first, then operate. Select the text you want to edit, then use the menu or keyboard commands to change it. Also remember to set the insertion point down first before you being to type or delete.
8.41 Use style sheets in the Story Editor *This is the sidebar where the style names will appear.*	▪ **Create** style sheets just as you would in the layout view (Section 7). ▪ **Use** style sheets in the Story Editor just as you would in the layout view: Select the paragraph(s), then choose the style name from the Style palette or the "Style" submenu under Type. ▪ From the Windows menu, choose "Style palette" to show or to hide it.	▪ You won't see any effect of the style sheet while you are in the Story Editor. ▪ You can choose to see the style names in the sidebar: From the Options menu, choose "Display style names."
8.42 Edit rotated text	▪ On the layout page, triple-click on the rotated text with the **pointer tool.** ▪ Edit as usual. ▪ Close the window (from the Story menu, or press Command W).	▪ You cannot kern in the Story Editor, nor can you see the effects of word or letter spacing. If you need to make those kinds of adjustments, it is better to unrotate your text (3.187), do it visually on the layout page, and then rotate it back.

If you want to do this:	**Then follow these steps:**	**Shortcuts ▾ Notes ▾ Hints**

8.43 Display or hide invisible text characters

Spaces · (a raised period)

Return ¶

Line break ↵
   (*Shift-Return*)

Tab ➡

- To display the invisible characters while in a story window, from the Options menu, choose "Display ¶." A checkmark will appear next to it.
- To hide the invisible characters, from the Options menu, choose "Display ¶"; the checkmark will disappear.

- In the Story Editor, any kind of space is symbolized with the little raised period: normal spaces with the Spacebar; hard spaces (Option Spacebar); and em, en, and thin spaces (4.207–4.216).
- See 8.61 for a chart of the symbols to input into the Find box in order to find these characters.
- It is so nice to be able to see those characters. It makes it much easier to remove troubling tabs or Returns.

8.44 Move a story window without making it active (that is, without bringing it to the top layer)

- Hold down the Command key.
- Press-and-drag in the title bar of the window you want to move. You will be able to move it, but it won't come forward.

- This comes in handy quite often, actually. It saves you from having to wait for the windows to redraw as they switch layers, and helps prevent windows from getting lost. (Actually, this trick also works on any windows on the Mac.)

8.45 Change the font and/or size text that the Story Editor displays

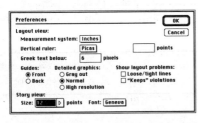

- In either the story view or the layout view (8.6), from the Edit menu, choose "Preferences…."
- Under "Story view," either type a size into the size box, **or** press on the little arrow to get the size submenu and choose a size.
- Next to "Font," press on the box to get the font submenu and choose a font.
- Click OK, *or* press Return or Enter. (To Cancel, press Command Period.)

- As noted in 8.15, city-named fonts are bit-mapped and easier to read on the screen (fonts such as Geneva, Boston, New York, Chicago, etc.). Personally, I prefer to use New York or Boston.
- 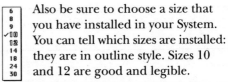 Also be sure to choose a size that you have installed in your System. You can tell which sizes are installed: they are in outline style. Sizes 10 and 12 are good and legible.

"Find"

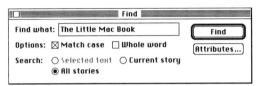

8.46 The **Find** window enables you to instantly find any occurrence of a word or any part of a word, or even of alternate or invisible characters, such as Returns and tabs and em spaces (8.57–8.62). Notice it is just a *window,* and so can be moved around on the screen. It can also get lost behind other windows, but if it does, just choose it again from the menu, or press Command 8.

8.47 Now, "Find" goes one step beyond just finding characters: You can find text **attributes.** For instance, you can search for occurrences of any 18-point type, or any italics, or any paragraphs that are tagged with a certain style from your style sheet, or any font, or any combination (8.59).

8.48 You can combine finding words with finding attributes (8.58). For instance, you can find just the word *rat* that is in 24-point Bodoni Bold, and the Story Editor will ignore any other *rat.*

8.49 If **Match case** is checked, the Story Editor will only find those words with capital letters that exactly match the capital letters you have typed here. Otherwise it is *case insensitive,* meaning it will ignore whether letters are capital or not, both in how you typed it in the "Find" box and in the words it finds.

8.50 If **Whole word** is *not* checked, the Story Editor will find any word that has that string of characters in it. For instance, looking for *rat* will also find you *brat* and *rather.* Now, the string includes any spaces you type, also. That means you have to be careful—if you ask to find *"rat "* with a space after it, you will find *brat* but not *rats.*

8.51 If **Whole word** *is* checked, the Story Editor will only find words that *exactly* match the words you have typed.

8.52 **Whole word** and **Match case** are checkboxes: You can select one or *both* of them.

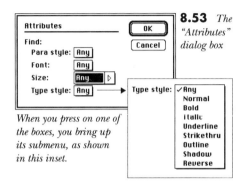

8.53 *The "Attributes" dialog box*

When you press on one of the boxes, you bring up its submenu, as shown in this inset.

8.54 You can choose to **search** for the characters or attributes in three ways: In **Selected text** (provided you had some text selected *before* you chose "Find"); in the **Current story;** or in **All stories** in the entire publication. The more text it has to search, though, the longer it will take.

8.55 As the Story Editor finds the characters, it displays their story window on the screen. The characters are highlighted, ready for you to deal with. When you click on the highlighted text to do something to it, the "Find" window will disappear behind the other windows. Just press Command 8 to bring it forward again.

8.56　Scenario #10: Using "Find..."

Let's say you have a 130-page publication. You need to edit the story about the walruses that have been beaching themselves in Bodega Bay. So when you open PageMaker, rather than try to find the page with that story on it, you simply press Command E. This brings up the Story Editor, with a blank window. You then press Command 8 to get the "Find" window. You type *walrus,* choose the button "All stories," and hit the Return key (which, you know, is a shortcut for the Find button, since the Find button has a dark border around it). Oops, PageMaker shows you a poem about *The Walrus and the Pussycat.* The "Find" button has now turned into the "Find next" button, so you just click again. *Now* the story about the walrus and Bodega Bay is on the screen and you can edit away.

So you have edited that story, but now you need to find the photo of Ms. Hassenpfeffer because you have a new TIFF file you want to replace it with. You can't "find" specific graphics, but you know the caption had her name in it. So in the "Find" window you type *hassen.* You only type part of the name because you're not sure if it's spelled right in the caption or if you even know how to spell it right anyway. The search finds and shows you the story window for the caption on the screen. You press Command E and PageMaker takes you right to the page that has that caption story on it. Neato.

You created a four-page newsletter and took it to your service bureau for output. They say you have the font New York somewhere in your file and you need to get rid of it. But you can't see it anywhere. Since you did place some MacWrite II files in the newsletter that someone else wrote, you think perhaps there may be some blank spaces or blank lines that are still formatted as New York.

So, in the "Find" window, you don't type anything. You leave it completely blank, with not even a spacebar. You click on the "Attributes..." button and choose the font New York from the submenu. Since Find cannot find just a font, you must also choose something like the type style "Normal," or a paragraph style. You click OK, click "All stories," and then click Find. Et voilà! All those darn little New York buggers will show up and you can choose to do whatever you want with them, like delete them or turn them into Times.

Also use the Story Editor to find all those paragraphs that are still tagged with that irritating style "Normal*" that got imported from Word (we're talking *style sheet Normal,* not *type style Normal*).

If you want to do this:	Then follow these steps:	Shortcuts ▾ Notes ▾ Hints

8.57 Find a word or words with no particular text attributes 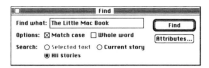 	■ You must be in the Story Editor to **Find.**
	  □ If you want to search only **Selected text,** then select that portion (8.39);
	  □ If you want to search the **Current story,** then make sure the story is in the *active* window (you should be able to see the horizontal lines in its title bar); click the "Current story" button;
	  □ If you want to search **All stories** in the publication, then it doesn't matter which window is active or if any text is selected; click the "All stories" button.
	■ From the Edit menu, choose "Find...," *or* press Command 8.
	■ Type the characters you want to find. Be careful not to type any superfluous spaces.
	■ If there is an underline under "Find what:," hold the Option key down and click once on the "Attributes..." button.
	■ Click "Match case" and/or "Whole word" if necessary (8.49–8.52).
	■ Click the "Find" button, *or* press Return.
	■ If you get the "Continue from beginning of story?" alert box, make your choice (*see the paragraph directly to the right* ☛).
	■ To put "Find" away, click in its close box *or* press Command W. Clicking on another window will simply *hide* "Find" behind a larger window.
		■ If "Find..." is not available in the menu, it means the "Change" window is open somewhere. If you don't see the "Change" window, then choose it from the Edit menu or press Command 9. Then close it with the close box, or press Command W —don't just click on another window to make it disappear.
		■ An underline under "Find what" indicates that there are some attributes applied to the characters to be found. This will limit your search. Using the Option-click, as mentioned, changes all the attributes back to "Any."
		■ Once you have found characters, in order to do anything to them you need to click in their window. This makes that window *active,* and may hide the "Find" window. To bring the "Find" window back, choose it again from the menu, or press Command 8.
		■ If you are searching just the current story, the search starts at the insertion point and goes to the end. There you will be asked if you want to "Continue from beginning of story?" in order to search back to where "Find" started from.

331

If you want to do this:

8.58 Find characters with special text attributes

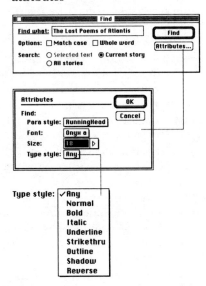

Then follow these steps:

- Follow the steps and read the info in 8.57.
- Before you click the "Find" button, click the "Attributes..." button. You will see the dialog box shown on the left.
- Each of the little boxes is a submenu that you can choose from.
  - □ **Para style** has all the style sheets that are in the current publication.
  - □ **Font** has all the fonts installed in your System.
  - □ **Size** has all the standard font sizes. Or you can type in any size you like, from 4 point to 650 point, in tenth-point (.1) increments (as usual).
  - □ **Type style** has the standards styles. This is the only submenu where you can choose more than one attribute. Choose the first one, then go back and choose others. A plus sign (✦) will appear next to the style name, indicating there is more than one style selected. To take away one of them, choose it again. To take away all of them, choose Normal or Any, depending on what you are looking for.
- Choose the other "Search" and "Options" buttons as in 8.57, and then click the "Find" button.

Shortcuts ▾ Notes ▾ Hints

- As soon as you choose any other attribute besides "Any," you'll see an underline beneath "Find what." It's a great little visual clue that tells you an attribute is selected, without having to check the dialog box.
- To return all the attributes back to "Any," hold down the Option key and click once on the "Attributes..." button. The underline beneath "Find what" will disappear.
- If you haven't done so yet, you may want to read Scenario #10 for some ideas about when this feature comes in handy.
- The edit box (where you type in the characters) will not reflect any of the attributes—it will always stay 12-point Chicago.

If you want to do this:	Then follow these steps:	Shortcuts ▾ Notes ▾ Hints

8.59 Find just attributes

- If you want to search for just text attributes, no matter what words they belong to, then **leave the edit box blank** and choose the attributes. *Make sure the edit box is really blank;* the flashing insertion point must be all the way to the left. Otherwise, if you have even a blank space in the edit box, the Story Editor will search for blank spaces with the necessary attributes.
- "Find" cannot find just a font. You need to give it more definition, such as a size or a style.
- Notice that if there are attributes selected, "Find what" is underlined.

- To return all the attributes back to "Any," hold down the Option key and click once on the "Attributes..." button.

8.60 Change all the attributes back to "Any"

Find what: [   ]

Change to: [   ]

The underline indicates that some attributes are applied.

Find what: [   ]

Change to: [   ]

No underline indicates that no attributes are applied.

- Hold down the Option key and click once on the "Attributes..." button. The underline beneath "Find what" will disappear.

If you want to do this:

8.61   Find invisible or special characters

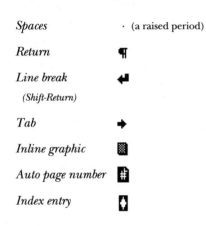

Spaces	· (a raised period)
Return	¶
Line break	↵
(Shift-Return)	
Tab	➡
Inline graphic	▨
Auto page number	⊞
Index entry	◘

Then follow these steps:

- See 8.57 and 8.58 for the general steps.
- To find some of the invisible and special characters, you need to type in a code (the ^ symbol, a caret, is Shift 6).
- To find a **Spacebar space,** type a space.
- To find a **non-breaking space,** type a non-breaking space (Option Spacebar)

or type:	^S *or* ^s
Non-breaking slash	^/
Non-breaking hyphen	^~
Em space	^M *or* ^m
En space	^>
Thin space	^<
Any kind of blank,	
white space	^W *or* ^w
En dash	^=
Em dash	^_ *(Shift Hyphen)*
Return	^P *or* ^p
Line break	^N *or* ^n
Tab	^T *or* ^t
Discretionary hyphen	^-
Caret	^^
Automatic page number	^# *or* ^3
Index entry	^;
Inline graphic	Control Q
	(in the edit box,
	it will look like
	the Command
	key symbol: ⌘)

Shortcuts ▾ Notes ▾ Hints

- Any special characters that are not in this list can be found by simply typing the standard keys for that character (see Appendices D and E for a complete list).
- Many special characters will appear as empty boxes (□) in the edit box because Chicago (which is the only font you will see in the edit box) doesn't have all those special characters. Don't worry—as long as you type in the correct key combination, PageMaker knows what you actually want and can find it.
- By the way, a funny thing happens if you type the keys for the fi and fl ligatures in version 4.0: the edit box will display the opposite ligature; that is, if you type fi (Shift Option 5), it appears as fl. Don't worry, though, the Story Editor will search for and replace with the correct ligature, even though it looks wrong in the edit box. Version 4.01 fixed this oversight.
- "Change" seems to have trouble with finding the caret (^). On my machine it will find any carets that appear *after* the insertion point, but if I ask it to go back and check from the beginning, it can't find any more, even though they are there. Odd.

If you want to do this:

8.62 To find a wildcard character

Then follow these steps:

- See 8.57 and 8.58 for steps on the general process of finding characters.
- In the edit box, type ^? (that's Shift 6 and a question mark) in place of the wildcard character. You can use attributes with it.

Shortcuts ▾ Notes ▾ Hints

- A wildcard character allows you to find words that may be misspelled, or ones that you just don't know quite how to spell. For instance, if you want to find *Allen,* but you are not sure if it is spelled *Allen* or *Allan,* you could search for *All^?n* and PageMaker would find either one.
- You can use any number of wildcard characters in a string of characters. Wildcard characters will indicate any character, including spaces, except Returns and Tabs.

I remember that T.M. Cleland, the famous American typographer, once showed me a very beautiful layout for a Cadillac booklet involving decorations in colour. He did not have the actual text to work with in drawing up his specimen pages, so he had set the lines in Latin. This was not only for the reason that you will all think of, if you have seen the old type foundries' famous Quousque tandem copy (i.e., that Latin has few descenders and thus gives a remarkably even line). No, he had told me that originally he had set up the dullest "wording" that he could find, and yet he discovered that the man to whom he submitted it would start reading and making comments on the text. I made some remark on the mentality of Boards of Directors, but Mr. Cleland said, "No, you're wrong; if the reader had not been practically forced to read—if he had not seen those words suddenly imbued with glamour and significance—then the layout would have been a failure. Setting it in Italian or Latin is only an easy way of saying, 'This is not the text as it will appear.'"

Beatrice Warde, *Printing Should Be Invisible,* 1927

335

"Change"

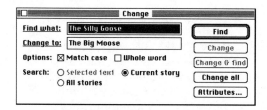

8.63   The **Change** window enables you to find instantly any occurrence of a word or any part of a word, or even of invisible or alternate characters, such as Returns and tabs and em spaces (8.74–8.76), and *change* them into any other characters.

8.64   "Change," like "Find," goes one step beyond just finding characters: it can find and change certain text **attributes** (formatting). For instance, you can search for occurrences of any 18-point bold type and change it into 12-point italic in another font (8.76).

8.65   You can combine finding words with finding attributes (8.75). For instance, you can find just the word *dog* that is in 24-point Bodoni Bold, and the Story Editor will ignore any other *dog*s.

8.66   If **Match case** is checked, the Story Editor will only find those words with capital letters that exactly match the capital letters you have typed here. Otherwise it is *case insensitive,* meaning it will ignore whether letters are capital or not, both in how you typed it and in the words it finds. But words will always **change** into the case you type in.

8.67   If **Whole word** is *not* checked, the Story Editor will find any word that has that string of characters in it. For instance, looking for *dog* will also find you *hotdog* and *dogfood.* If you change *dog* to *cat,* you will get *hotcat* and *catfood.* Now, that includes any spaces you type, also. That means you have to be careful—if you ask to find *"dog "* with a space, you will find *hotdog* but not *dogfood,* because *hotdog* will have a space after it. If you find *dog* and change it to *"cat "* (with a space), *dogfood* will become *cat food.*

8.68   If **Whole word** *is* checked, the Story Editor will only find words that *exactly* match the words you have typed and will *replace* them with exactly the words you have typed.

8.69   **Whole word** and **Match case** are checkboxes, which indicates that you can select one or *both* of them.

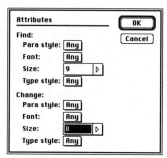

8.70   *The "Attributes" dialog box; the top half identifies attributes you want to find, and the bottom half identifies attributes to which you want to change the found words. Each little box is a submenu.*

8.71   You can choose to **search** for the characters three ways: in **Selected text** (provided you had some text selected *before* you chose "Change"); in the **Current story;** or in **All stories** in the entire publication. Of course, the more text the Story Editor has to search, the longer it will take.

8.72   Notice the "Change" box is just a *window;* you can move it around on the screen. It can also get lost behind other windows, but if it does, just choose it again from the menu, or press Command 9.

8.73 Scenario #11: Finding and changing text

This is the greatest thing. You have probably noticed that the text in this book is Baskerville, 10 point. But every paragraph has a number and many important words in 9-point Futura Bold. Well, when I originally started drafting this book in PageMaker 3.02, I had to press-and-drag over those words, go to the Type specs dialog box, and change the selected text to 9 point, Futura, and bold. What a pain in the you-know-what.

Well, this is what I do now: I just type away in my 10-point Baskerville paragraphs (which are all tagged with a style definition, of course; Section 7). When I come to a word that is to be 9-point Futura Bold, I press the keyboard shortcut to underline it *before* I type the word(s). Then I type the word(s). Then I press the keyboard shortcut again to take the underline off.

When I am finished with the entire section, I open the Story Editor. I tell it to go find all the underlined words and turn them into 9-point Futura Bold with no underline. Then I tell it to go find every occurrence of **fi** and **fl,** no matter what the attributes ("Any") and change them into the ligatures **fi** and **fl.** Oh my gosh. It's too wonderful.

Let's say you are working on a form. There are lots of little checkboxes: □ . You know the checkbox is just a Zapf Dingbat letter **n,** outlined. You can't just type an **n** wherever you are going to want the box to appear, because then every other letter **n** would also turn into a box. So you need to identify it somehow.

You could use the keyboard shortcut to outline it as you type. Or you could type a bullet (•, Option 8) instead. Or you could type **xx.** Use anything that will be a consistent flag, but that couldn't be mistaken for anything else in the publication. Then, when you are done with the form, you go into the Story Editor and change the flagged characters from one setting into an **n** in Zapf Dingbats, outline, and maybe a point size or two larger or smaller.

(Actually, in this particular case you *could* use just a letter **n.** All you need to do is make sure to check the boxes "Whole word" and "Match case." Because we never otherwise type a lowercase **n** all by itself, the ones you want would be the only ones found. Oh, there are a myriad of solutions.)

Or, let's imagine someone else has input the copy for the entire 16-page tabloid you are responsible for editing. They haven't read *The Mac is not a typewriter* yet, so the copy is full of typewriter mentality. The first thing you do is give them that book to read so you won't have to repeat this chore next month. Then you set to work with the Story Editor and find-and-change.

You find every *Period Space Space* with Any attributes, and change them all into *Period Space* (just type a period and hit the space bar twice for two, once for one) with Any attributes. You then find all the double hyphens and change them into em dashes (8.78). You find any text than has an underline and turn it into italic. You find all the fi and fl combinations and turn them into the fi and fl ligatures (8.78). You find every instance of where the typist typed five spaces for a paragraph indent, and you remove them (change them into nothingness by typing nothing in the "Change to" box). Later you will set a paragraph indent in your style sheet. You find all the foot marks (') that some people use as an apostrophe, and turn them all into true apostrophes ('), watching out, of course, for any numbers that really need the foot mark. You find . . .

If you want to do this:	Then follow these steps:	Shortcuts ▾ Notes ▾ Hints

Change

8.74 Change characters, regardless of their particular attributes

- You must be in the Story Editor (8.30–8.31) to **Change.**
  - ☐ If you want to search only **Selected text,** then select that portion of text (8.39); click the "Selected text" button.
  - ☐ If you want to search the **Current story,** then make sure the story is in the *active* window (you should be able to see the horizontal lines in its title bar; 8.7; 8.9); click the "Current story" button.
  - ☐ If you want to search **All stories** in the publication, then it doesn't matter which window is active or if any text is selected; click the "All stories" button.
- From the Edit menu, choose "Change...," *or* press Command 9.
- Type the characters you want to find. Be careful not to type any superfluous spaces.
- If there is an underline under "Find what:," hold the Option key down and click once on the "Attributes..." button.
- Click "Match case" and/or "Whole word" if necessary (8.49–8.52).
- If you want to change every occurrence of the characters, then click "Change all."

—continued

- If "Change..." is not available in the menu, it means the "Find" window is open somewhere. If you don't see the "Find" window, then choose it from the Edit menu or press Command 8. Then close it with the close box or press Command W— don't just click on another window to make it disappear.
- An underline under "Find what" indicates that there are some attributes applied to the characters to be found. This will limit your search. Using the Option-click, as mentioned, to change all the attributes back to "Any" (8.59).
- Once you change all the occurrences, you cannot undo those changes simply by choosing Undo from the menu. If you seriously need to undo, you can Revert; see 16.26–16.27.

If you want to do this:

—continued

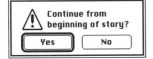

Then follow these steps:

- If you want to be selective about the characters you are changing, then click the **Find** button, *or* press Return or Enter.
- If you are being selective and have found the first occurrence of the characters, you then have a choice:
  - ☐ The "Find" button turns into a **Find next** button. This allows you to skip the change and go find the next one.
  - ☐ Click the **Change** button to change it and stay right there on that selected word. This allows you to pop into the story window if you like and work with the selected text. The "Find" button turns into a "Find next" button.
  - ☐ Click the **Change & find** button to change it and move on to the next one.
- If you are searching just the current story, the search starts at the insertion point and goes to the end. You may be asked if you want to "Continue from beginning of story?" in order to search back to where it started from.
- To put "Change" away, click in its close box *or* press Command W. Clicking on another window, including the publication window, will simply hide "Change" behind a larger window.

Shortcuts ▾ Notes ▾ Hints

- Remember, when you close the Story Editor by choosing "Edit layout" from the Edit menu, or by pressing Command E, you are simply *hiding* the story windows, including the Change window, behind the page layout view. If you want to close the Change window, or any story window, press Command W once for each window.

If you want to do this:

Then follow these steps:

Shortcuts ▾ Notes ▾ Hints

8.75 Find and change characters with text attributes

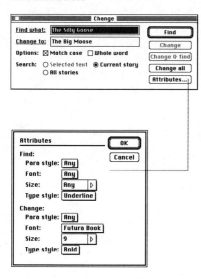

- Follow the steps in 8.74 to get the "Change" window.
- Input the characters you want to find, then input what you want to change them to.
- Select your choices for "Options" and "Search" (8.66–8.71).
- Click the button "Attributes...." In the Attributes dialog box (shown at left), press on the little boxes to pop up the submenus.
  - □ **Para style** has all the style sheets that are in the current publication.
  - □ **Font** has all the fonts in your System.
  - □ **Size** has all the standard font sizes. Or you can type in any size you like, from 4 point to 650 point, in tenth-point (.1) increments (as usual).
  - □ **Type style** has the standards styles. This is the only submenu where you can choose more than one attribute. Choose the first one, then go back and choose others. A plus sign (+) will appear next to the style name, indicating there is more than one style selected. To take away one of them, choose it again. To take away all of them, choose Normal or Any, depending on what you are looking for.
- Now go through your finding and changing as described in 8.74.

- The text in the edit box will always be 12-point Chicago, no matter what attributes you apply to it, so don't worry if it doesn't look like what you want.
- Unfortunately, you can't apply such attributes as set width or superscript specs, nor can you even search for them.
- If you have applied attributes to the characters you want to *find,* you will see an underline below "Find what."

  If you have applied attributes to the characters you want to *change into,* you will see an underline below "Change to."

  It's important to be aware of whether there are attributes applied or not because they can seriously affect the search. To remove all applied attributes (turn all the little boxes back to "Any"), hold the Option key down as you click once on the "Attributes..." button. You will see the underlines disappear.

If you want to do this:	Then follow these steps:	Shortcuts · Notes · Hints
8.76 Find and change just text attributes	■ Follow the steps in 8.74 to get the "Change" window. ■ If you want to search for just text attributes, no matter what words they belong to, then just **leave the edit boxes blank** and choose the attributes, *both* for finding and changing. *Make sure the edit boxes are really blank;* the flashing insertion point must be all the way to the left. If you have even a blank space in the edit boxes, the Story Editor will search for and/or change blank spaces with the necessary attributes. ■ **If you don't select any "Change" attributes (if they all remain as "Any"), then all characters with the "Find" attributes will be *eliminated!*** ■ If there are attributes selected, "Find what" and "Change to" *are underlined.*	■ To return all the attributes back to "Any," hold down the Option key and click once on the "Attributes..." button.
8.77 Find and **eliminate** characters and/or text attributes	■ Follow the steps in 8.74 to get the "Change" window. ■ The deal is this: if there is no text in the "Change to" edit box, and if there are no "Change" attributes selected, then any text or any attributes from the "Find what" edit box will just be *eliminated.*	■ If you are asking to find just attributes, *then any text with those attributes will be eliminated.* Although this can be scary, you can certainly use it to your advantage. ■ Watch those visual clues: if there is no underline below "Change to," then there are no attributes selected.

If you want to do this:

8.78 Find and change special characters

Spaces	· (a raised period)
Return	¶
Line break	◀┙
(Shift-Return)	
Tab	→
Inline graphic	▨
Auto page number	⌗
Index entry	◆

Then follow these steps:

- See 8.74 and 8.75 for the general steps.
- To find some of the invisible and special characters, you need to type in a code (the ^ symbol, a caret, is Shift 6).
- To find a **Spacebar space,** type a space.
- To find a **non-breaking space,** type a non-breaking space (Option Spacebar) **or** type: ^S *or* ^s

Non-breaking slash	^/
Non-breaking hyphen	^~
Em space	^M *or* ^m
En space	^>
Thin space	^<
Any kind of blank, white space	^W *or* ^w
En dash	^=
Em dash	^_ *(Shift Hyphen)*
Return	^P *or* ^p
Line break	^N *or* ^n
Tab	^T *or* ^t
Discretionary hyphen	^-
Caret	^^
Automatic page number	^# *or* ^3
Index entry	^;
Inline graphic	Control Q

(in the edit box, it will look like the Command key symbol: ⌘)

Shortcuts ▾ Notes ▾ Hints

- Any special characters that are not in this list can be found by simply typing the standard keys for that character (see Appendices D and E for a complete list of codes and special characters).
- The text in the edit box is always 12-point Chicago, no matter what attributes are applied. Many special characters will appear as empty boxes (□) in the edit box because Chicago doesn't have all those special characters. Don't worry—PageMaker knows what you actually want and can find it.
- By the way, a funny thing happens if you type the keys for the fi and fl ligatures in version 4.0: the edit box will display the opposite ligature; that is, if you type fi (Shift Option 5), it appears as fl. Don't worry, though, the Story Editor will search for and replace with the correct ligature, even though it looks wrong in the edit box. Version 4.01 fixed this oversight.

If you want to do this:	Then follow these steps:	Shortcuts ▾ Notes ▾ Hints

Closing windows; placing text

8.79 Place a *new* story
(Untitled or imported; 8.22)

- To place a new story, the new story must be the *active* window (in the front, with horizontal lines its title bar). There are four ways to place it; choose one:
  - ▢ From the File menu, choose "Place," (or press Command D); **or** from the Edit menu, choose "Edit layout" (or press Command E). Either way, you will get the standard loaded text icon (3.82–3.83). Click to flow the text onto the page.
  - ▢ **Or** you can just click in the close box (tiny box in the upper left of the window), **or** from the Story menu, choose "Close story" (or press Command W). Either way, you will get an alert box warning you that the story has not yet been placed. Click the "Place" button and you will get the standard loaded text icon. Flow the text onto the page, as usual (3.81–3.94).

- You can always tell if a story is *new* because the name in the title bar is "Untitled:1." If there is more than one new story, they will be called "Untitled:1," "Untitled:2," etc.
- If you do not place a story before you quit PageMaker, it will still be saved along with the publication (as long as you didn't "Discard" it!). Next time you open Page-Maker, that story will be the active window, right in front of your face, reminding you that it is still unplaced.
- If this new story is the only story window open, then placing it will close the Story Editor. Otherwise, if there are more windows open, the Story Editor will stay open and all the story windows will just hide behind the page layout window.
- Remember, you can turn or create pages with a loaded text icon if you need to place the story on another page.

> The story has not been placed.
> [Place]
> [Discard]
> [Cancel]

This alert box appears if the story has never been on the publication page before.

8.80 Discard a *new* story
(Untitled or imported)

- To discard a new story, click in its close box (the tiny box in the upper left of the window). You will get an alert box warning you that the story has not yet been placed. Click the "Discard" button. *This is not Undo-able—it is really gone.*

- **Note:** If you created the story in the Story Editor, then you have no other copy of it! If you discard this story, this story is destroyed. See 8.19.

If you want to do this:	Then follow these steps:	Shortcuts ▾ Notes ▾ Hints
8.81 Leave a new story (Untitled or imported) *without* placing or discarding it	■ Don't *close* the Untitled window; just click on the layout page of your publication, **or** from the Windows menu, choose the name of your publication. Either way, the Story Editor will actually stay open, and it and all the other windows will hide behind the publication page window.	■ If you do not place a story before you *quit* PageMaker, it will still be saved along with the publication. Next time you open PageMaker, that story will be the active window, right in front of your face, reminding you that it is still unplaced.
8.82 Replace an existing story	■ If you open a story window for a story that already exists on the layout page, then the Edit menu has the command "Replace" instead of "Place." There are three ways to replace the original with the edited version: ■ Choose "Replace" from the Edit menu; ■ **or** click in the story window close box; ■ **or** click on the publication layout page. ■ You will *not* get a loaded text icon; the text will just flow into the text block it came from, whether you can see it on the current page or not. See 8.84 for replacing the story, and at the same time, turning to the page it is laid out on.	■ If the story you are replacing is the last story window open, the Story Editor will close up. If there are other story windows open, replacing the story in this way will not close the Story Editor—all the open windows will just hide behind the publication window, taking up valuable memory.
8.83 Return to where you left off in the layout view	■ No matter which story you are editing, you can return to the exact page you left before you entered the Story Editor simply by clicking on the publication page window, or by choosing the publication name from the Windows menu.	

If you want to do this:	**Then follow these steps:**	**Shortcuts ▾ Notes ▾ Hints**
8.84 Return to the layout view in the exact spot in the story you are currently editing *(You can't do this with an "Untitled" or imported story.)*	▪ When you are finished editing in a story window, *don't* choose to "Replace" the story from the file menu, *don't* click on the publication page, and *don't* choose the publication name from the Windows menu. *Instead,* from the Edit menu, choose "Edit layout," *or* press Command E. ▪ The entire Story Editor will hide, the pages will turn, if necessary, and you will arrive at the page where your insertion point was flashing in the story window, and with any new changes applied.	
8.85 Save a new (Untitled, or imported) story *without* placing or discarding it	▪ To save the story without actually placing it on the page, do not hide the Story Editor (that means, do not choose "Edit layout" from the Edit menu, and do not press Command E). Instead, click on the publication layout page, or choose the name of the publication from the Windows menu. ▪ Now you can go ahead and close the publication or quit PageMaker. When you open PageMaker next time, any untitled or imported-but-not-yet-placed windows will appear in front of you.	

The spell checker

8.87 I do like PageMaker's spelling checker. It is simple, complete enough, and fairly clever. It takes about five minutes to figure out. You probably don't even need to read this.

8.88 Remember, a spell checker is always limited. It will check for obviously mis-spelled words, but it cannot tell you if you should be using *pair* where you have typed *pear*, or if you mean *effect* where you have typed *affect*. You still need someone with a spelling brain to proof the text.

8.89 Besides spelling, the spell checker will check for other errors, such as dupli-cate words (the the), or for words that should be capitalized.

8.90 If the potentially misspelled word is capitalized, all the suggestions for correct spelling replacements are also capitalized. (Deplorably, though, whenever the diction-ary has an apostrophe in its word, it uses the typewriter symbol ['] instead of a true apostrophe [']. I can't believe it.)

8.96 The spell checker is in a **window,** not a dialog box (pages 8.49). If you like, you can move the window around on the screen so it is out of the way. While it is open, you can still use the menus and desk accessories. If you click on another window to make it *active*, the spell checker may hide behind the active window. Just choose it again from the menu (or press Command L) to bring it forward.

8.97 When you installed PageMaker, you automatically installed the 100,000 word U.S. English dictionary. What? You don't see it? Didn't you look in the US English folder, which is in the Proximity folder, which is in the Aldus folder, which is in the System folder, which is on your hard disk? If you don't have a dictionary installed when you ask to check spelling, PageMaker will yell at you (8.119). See 8.102 for installing the dictionary.

8.98 You can buy other dictionaries from Aldus, such as Legal and Medical, as well as foreign languages. Be sure to read the following page regarding the installation of these dictionaries and how they operate. One **important note:** although you can have at least ten dictionaries installed, *you can only use one at a time.* The dictionaries are **paragraph-specific;** that is, you must choose one dictionary per paragraph, and you must choose it from the "Paragraph" dialog box (8.104). It is that particular, chosen dictionary that the spell checker will use for that paragraph, both for spell-checking and for hyphenation. Because dictionaries are paragraph-specific, you can include them in a style sheet (Section 7). If you want PageMaker to search more than one dictionary in a paragraph, see 8.125.

PageMaker 4.01 includes an option of not using any dictionary at all, called "None." PageMaker will not spell check or hyphen-ate paragraphs with "None" applied.

The user dictionary and other dictionaries (foreign, legal, and medical)

8.99 PageMaker uses a 100,000-word Houghton-Mifflin dictionary. That's a lot of words, but in most of our work, there are always words that are not in a standard dictionary, such as jargon, nicknames, proper names, etc. ("PageMaker" isn't even in the dictionary, and thus it can't be hyphenated). To prevent PageMaker from constantly reporting those words as misspelled, you can add them to a **user dictionary.** Whenever you use the hyphenation dialog box or the spell checker to add words, those words are added to the *user dictionary,* not to the main dictionary. When you remove words, they are removed from the *user dictionary.*

8.100 PageMaker checks both the English dictionary and the user dictionary whenever you spell-check in the Story Editor or whenever a word needs to be hyphenated.

8.101 It is possible to create more than one user dictionary, but you can only access one at a time (see 8.124 for a tip on switching user dictionaries). However, a specialized user dictionary may come in handy sometime for a particular project. You can copy any customized user dictionary into someone else's dictionary folder so they can use it also (8.123).

8.102 If you order **foreign dictionaries** from Aldus, you must *install* them, not just copy them into the Proximity folder, as the dictionaries are compressed files. Just click on the "Install" icon on your dictionary disk and it will walk you through the process. Each foreign dictionary is in its own folder. *Each foreign dictionary will have its own user dictionary.* As you spell-check or add words for hyphenation while using a foreign dictionary, the words will automatically be added to the user dictionary for that particular language.

8.103 If you order either the **Legal** or the **Medical** dictionary, you get both. You must *install* them, not just copy them into the folder, as the dictionaries are compressed files. Now, a funny thing happens when you install either of those dictionaries: If you install Legal, the English disappears. If you install Medical, the Legal disappears. If you re-install English, the Medical *and* the Legal disappear. Apparently you can have only one of these three dictionaries installed. The secret is this: The Legal dictionary *includes* the US English dictionary. The Medical dictionary *includes* the US English *and* the Legal

Dictionary: ✓None / Deutsch / Français / Italiano / Nederlands / **US English Medical** / Español / UK English / Svenska / Dansk / Norsk / Português / Brasileiro

8.104 *This shows the list of dictionaries Aldus has available. If you have Legal or Medical included, "US English" will appear as "US English…," indicating it is more than just the standard dictionary. (The option "None" is only available in version 4.01.)*

dictionaries. So by installing the Medical dictionary you have them all, although your dialog boxes will only list the Medical one.

8.105 Although you essentially have three dictionaries rolled into one, you will only have one user dictionary for the set.

I had to prove this to you—it just cracks me up. Look where the dictionary hyphenates the word "dictionary"! This would be good practice—go into the "Hyphenation" dialog box and change the hyphenation of that word so it doesn't look stupid (4.245).

The "Spelling" window *(from the Edit menu, while the Story Editor is open, choose "Spelling...")*

8.106a *Watch this* **message;** *it changes frequently to tell you what's going on.*

8.107 *The selected wrong spelling (8.107) will change into whatever is in this* **edit box.**

A smart man learns from his mistakes.

Spelling

Ready...

Change to:

Search: ○ Selected text ● Current story ○ All stories

Start
Replace
Add...

8.108 *Click here (or just press Return) to start the spell check (8.117).*

8.109 *Click this button to add words to the* **user dictionary** *(8.120)*

8.110 *Choose one of these to tell PageMaker where to check the spelling.*
Selected text *will be available only if you selected a portion of text before you brought up the Spelling window.*
Current story *means the window on the top layer—the window that was* active *when you chose "Spelling..." from the Edit menu.*
All stories *means every story in the entire publication, not just those windows that are open.*

The "Spelling" window —*continued*

8.111 *The* **Title bar;** *press-and-drag here to move the window around.*

8.106b *Now the* **message** *tells you there is a misspelled (unknown) word.*

8.114 *Click here to skip the word and move on. Ignored words will be remembered and ignored again until you close the publication.*

8.112 *The* **edit box** *shows a possible correct spelling. You can type into this box.*

```
Spelling
Unknown word : gide

Change to:  gide

            side
            wide
            give
            died

Search:  ○ Selected text   ● Current story   ○ All stories

            Ignore
            Replace
            Add...
```

8.115 *Click here to replace the unknown word with the word in the "Change to" edit box.*

8.116 *Notice this list is a scrolling box. PageMaker gives you a wider choice of possibilities, more than just other words with the same first letter.*

8.113 *If you click on a word in this* **suggestion list,** *it will appear in the "Change to" edit box, ready to replace the unknown word.*

If you **double-click** *on a word in the list, that word will replace the unknown word and the spell checker will automatically move on to find another misspelling.*

A wise person learns from others' mistakes.

349

If you want to do this:	**Then follow these steps:**	**Shortcuts ▾ Notes ▾ Hints**

8.117 Check spelling

Notice the messages in the upper left corner of each of these examples

a) *The spell checker, ready to start.*

b) *A misspelled word has been found. Notice that the "unknown" word is in the edit box.*

c) *An* improper *word has been found. Notice the most likely proper word is in the edit box.*

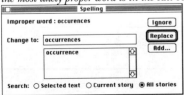

- If you want to check the *entire publication,* press Command E; **or** with the **pointer tool,** triple-click on any text block.
- **Or,** if you just want to check *one story,* either triple-click on that story with the **pointer tool; or,** with the **text tool** click once in the story and then press Command E.
- **Or,** if you want to check just *a selected portion of text,* either select the text on the page (press-and-drag over it with the text tool) and then press Command E; **or** open the story window first (click once in the story with the text tool, and press Command E) and then select the text.
- While a story editor window is on the screen, from the Edit menu choose "Spelling...," *or* press Command L. You will see the Spelling window (**a**).
- Click the "Search" button of your choice (8.110); then click the "Start" button, or press Return.
- If the spell checker finds a misspelled word, the window contents will change to look something like (**b** or **c**). Always check the little message in the top left corner (8.106a/b).
- If you want to skip this word, click the **Ignore** button (8.114).

—continued

- My father would have been so happy with a spell checker. He always complained: "How can anyone look up the correct spelling in the dictionary if he doesn't know how to spell it?" Now he would be able to type 'sikology' and the spell checker would suggest politely that perhaps he meant 'psychology.'

- Notice in **b** and **c** that the Return key default (the button with the dark border) is different, depending on whether the word in the edit box is unknown or improper. In the *improper* box, when you click "Replace," the "Ignore" button becomes a "Continue" button.

If you want to do this:

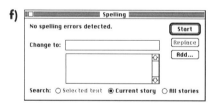

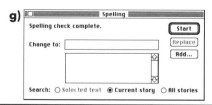

Then follow these steps:

- If you want to replace the unknown word with the word in the "Change to" edit box, then click "Replace." You can, of course, edit the word in the edit box first.
- If you want to replace the unknown word with a word from the list, click once on the list word, then click "Replace," **or** just double-click on the list word (8.113).
- If the spell checker finds two of the same words in a row, the second is selected as an unknown and the "Change to" box will be empty (**d**). Click "Replace," which will *remove* the duplicate word (you are actually replacing the duplicate word with the nothingness in the "Change to" edit box).
- Other messages may appear in the window, depending on what the checker finds (**e**).
- If there are no spelling errors, you will get a message in the spell-checking window informing you so (**f**).
- No matter where the insertion point is flashing, the spell checker will check the entire area you asked it to search (8.110). When it is finished, the message will tell you so (**g**).
- You can leave the spell-checking window off to the side somewhere (press-and-drag in its title bar), **or** click in its close box to put it away.

Shortcuts ▾ Notes ▾ Hints

- If you double-click on a word in the list, the unknown or misspelled word will be replaced and the spell checker will move on to find another word.

If you want to do this:	**Then follow these steps:**	**Shortcuts ▾ Notes ▾ Hints**

8.118 Check the spelling of just one word

- To check just one word, you need to select the word and have the spell checker go through its motions for the "Selected text." It may seem, at first, like a lot to go through, but if you use the keyboard commands, you can check a word in less than four seconds.
- **If you are in the layout view,** do this:
  - Double-click on the word.
  - Press Command E and L (one after the other). Click in the "Selected text" button, if it isn't already on, then hit Return.
  - Find the correct spelling in the suggestion list and double-click on it.
  - Press Command E again, **or** just click once on the layout page.
- **If you are in the story view,** do this:
  - Double-click on the word.
  - Press Command L (even if the window is visible; these keys will make it *active*). Click in the "Selected text" button, if it isn't already on, and hit Return.
  - Find the correct spelling in the suggestion list and double-click on it.
  - Click once on your story window to make it active again.

- If you previously clicked the "Selected text" button, the spell checker will stay in that mode. Then you can really speed along— just press Command E and L and hit Return, without even waiting for anything to appear. It will catch up to you.
- You don't need to worry about that extra space after the word that PageMaker selects when you double-click on a word. The spell checker knows to ignore it.
- Of course, if the correct word is not in the suggestion list, you may have to spend a few seconds typing the correction.

If you want to do this:

8.119 Find out why you get the "Cannot open dictionary for this paragraph" message

Then follow these steps:

■ This message will appear if PageMaker cannot find a dictionary with which to spell-check or hyphenate. When you originally installed PageMaker, the dictionary was automatically installed into the Aldus folder in the System folder. If you have the Medical/Legal dictionary set, installing the Medical dictionary will provide you with the US English, the Legal, and the Medical dictionaries. To install a new dictionary, just click on the "Install" icon that is on the same disk. It will walk you through the process.

Shortcuts ▼ Notes ▼ Hints

■ The dictionary icons looks like this when they are on the floppy disk:

AldEng00.VPX   AldEng.BPX

They look like this after they have been installed:

AldEng00.VPX   AldEng.BPX

If you want to do this:	Then follow these steps:	Shortcuts ▾ Notes ▾ Hints

8.120 Add words to the user dictionary 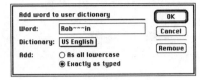	■ You need to be in the Story Editor, with the spell checker up (8.117).
	■ If the word you want to add is already in the spell checker's "Change to" box, then click the "Add" button.
	
	    Even if the "Change to" box is empty or contains a word you don't want to add to the user dictionary, click the "Add" button.
	■ You will see the dialog box shown on the left. Any word in the "Change to" box appears here with tildes (~) indicating hyphenation points. You can change the tildes: zero tildes prevents hyphenation; one tilde indicates the best hyphenation; two is okay; three is the least desirable.
	
	    If the "Change to" edit box was empty, the "Word" box here will be empty. Type the word and insert tildes as you prefer.
	■ Click "As all lowercase" if you want to enter the word as lowercase, no matter how you typed it. This allows the spell checker to find the same word with caps or lowercase.
	■ Click "Exactly as typed" if you want to enter the word with the capital letters as you specify.
	■ You can choose to which language dictionary you want to add these words, although the words are not added to the dictionary itself, but to the supplemental user dictionary (8.99–8.101).
		■ Depending on the keyboard, the tilde is found either in the upper left corner or next to the spacebar. Hold the Shift key down and press the tilde key.
		■ See 4.219–4.245 for more info on the hyphenation system in PageMaker.
		■ You cannot add words to the main Houghton-Mifflin 100,000 word dictionary. You *can* add words to the *user dictionary*. PageMaker automatically checks the user dictionary first *in addition* to any language dictionary whenever she checks spelling and hyphenation.
		■ In the user dictionary you can permanently set up all your technical terms, proper names, swear words, etc., so you don't have to keep clicking the "Ignore" button.
		■ Choosing a dictionary here does not tell PageMaker which dictionary to use to check spelling—that choice is made from the "Paragraph specs" dialog box (Command M; 8.126).

If you want to do this: ∎	**Then follow these steps:** ∎	**Shortcuts ▾ Notes ▾ Hints** ∎
8.121 Hyphenate a word you are adding to the user dictionary 	▪ When the word is in the "Add" edit box (8.120), you may see tildes (~) indicating the points where PageMaker will hyphenate the word. One tilde indicates the ideal point to hyphenate; three the least. You can add or delete them as you see fit. ▪ In this dialog box, if you never want the word to hyphenate, take out all the tildes.	▪ Depending on the keyboard, the tilde is found either in the upper left corner or next to the spacebar. Hold the Shift key down and press the tilde key. ▪ See 4.219–4.245 for more info on the hyphenation system in PageMaker.
8.122 Remove a word from the user dictionary  	▪ You need to be in the Story Editor, with the spell checker up (8.117). ▪ If the word you want to remove is already in the spell checker's "Change to" box, then click the "Add" button. Even if the "Change to" box is empty or contains a word you don't want to remove, click the "Add" button. The point is, you want to see the "Add to user dictionary" dialog box. ▪ If the word is not already in the edit box, then type it in. ▪ Click the "Remove" button. If it worked, you'll get a message "Word removed." If PageMaker could not find that exact word, you'll get a message "Word was not found in user dictionary." Maybe you mistyped it, or it may not be in the *user* dictionary.	▪ You are removing this word from the *user dictionary*, not from the main dictionary.

If you want to do this:

Then follow these steps:

Shortcuts ▾ Notes ▾ Hints

8.123 Make a new user dictionary
(or copy it to give to someone else)

AldEng.UDC

- You have to leave PageMaker and go back to the Finder (Desktop) to make a new user dictionary.
- In your System folder is a folder named Aldus. In the Aldus folder is a folder named Proximity. In the Proximity folder is a folder called US English. In the folder US English is a file named AldEng.UDC.
- Take that AldEng.UDC file and put it somewhere else. Perhaps you want to give it to a co-worker, or put it in another folder, or throw it in the trash.
- Go back to your PageMaker publication. As soon as you add a word to the user dictionary, a new file will be created, tucked away deep in that same folder.

- To put a copy of this file into another folder on the same disk, hold the Option key down as you drag the icon into the other folder.
- If you hate having to close all those windows on the Desktop again, hold down the Option key as you click them open. As you open each one, the one before it will close.
- These directions assume you are working with the US English dictionary. If you are working with any other language or specialty, of course, you need to go into its dictionary folder, which will also be found in the Proximity folder. Each language has its own user dictionary.

8.124 Switch user dictionaries

- If you have created more than one user dictionary (8.123), you can switch from one to the other simply by putting the one you want to use into the US English folder, which is inside... etc. etc. etc. (see above). It must be named AldEng.UDC (caps or lowercase doesn't matter; the *Eng* indicates it belongs with the English dictionary). You can only have one user dictionary in that folder at a time, though.

- These directions assume you are working with the US English dictionary. If you are working with any other language or specialty, you need to go into its dictionary folder, of course, which will also be found in the Proximity folder.

If you want to do this:

8.125 Check spelling, using more than one dictionary

Then follow these steps:

- This segment will only apply if you have any foreign dictionaries installed.
- While you are in the Story Editor, check the spelling as usual (8.117).
- Then *select* the paragraphs (8.39) that you want to check with another dictionary.
- While the paragraphs are selected, from the Type menu, choose "Paragraph...," *or* press Command M.
- Press on the "Dictionary" submenu and choose another dictionary. Click OK.
- Press Command L to bring back the spell checker.
- Check the selected text again.
- If you will be editing that text again, you may want to select the paragraphs and apply the original dictionary to them.

Shortcuts ▾ Notes ▾ Hints

- The spelling is checked using the dictionary that was applied to the paragraph through the "Paragraph" dialog box (from the Type menu). I know, you probably think you didn't apply one. But just like everything else, if you didn't change it yourself, a default was applied. If you only have one dictionary installed (typically US English), then that is your only choice.
- If you do have a foreign dictionary and are checking occasional foreign words, it works best to select just the foreign words in question and spell check just the selected text. Otherwise, the foreign dictionary will think every English word is a misspelling.

If you want to do this:	**Then follow these steps:**	**Shortcuts ▾ Notes ▾ Hints**
8.126 Change dictionaries in a paragraph	■ With the **text tool,** select the paragraph(s) in which you want to change the dictionary. ■ From the Type menu, choose "Paragraph…," *or* press Command M. ■ Press on the submenu next to "Dictionary" and choose another dictionary. ■ Click OK. PageMaker will now look through *this* dictionary when you choose to spell check in the Story Editor.	
8.127 Change the default dictionary	■ To change the **application default,** follow this procedure when there is no publication open; all you should see on the screen is the PageMaker menu. ■ To change the **publication default,** follow this procedure when a publication is open. Click once on the pointer tool (even if it is already chosen) before you follow this procedure. 　■ From the Type menu, choose "Paragraph…," *or* press Command M. 　■ Press on the "Dictionary" submenu and choose another dictionary. Click OK.	■ Changing the default dictionary does not change anything in any text that is already on the page. ■ PageMaker will check both spelling and hyphenation from the dictionary that is chosen in the "Paragraph specifications" dialog box.

9 ▾ GRAPHICS

9.1 Minimums and maximums:

Item	Minimum	Maximum
Graphic file size automatically stored in publication	0	256K (depending on your link options; Section 10)
Lines/inch	5	300
Screen angle	0°	90° *(actually, you can enter a value up to 360°, but since certain angles repeat others, only values up to 90° are practical)*

9.2 There are two general categories of graphics in PageMaker: 1) those you create within PageMaker with the drawing tools; and 2) those you create in other software programs and then bring into PageMaker. Section 2 covers the first category of graphics; this section covers the second.

9.3 There are two ways you can bring in graphics that were created outside Page-Maker. You can *paste* them in from the Clipboard (which includes those that come from the Scrapbook). Or you can *place* them from a graphic file. Files that are placed fall into one of two categories: scanned images; and images created in paint, draw, or illustration programs.

9.4 PageMaker can read any file saved as MacPaint (paint-type, or PNTG), TIFF, PICT, PICT 2, or EPS formats (all of which are explained in the following pages).

9.5 One of PageMaker's particularly exciting features is the ability to place graphics **inline;** that is, you can embed a graphic into a text block and it will move along as you edit text (9.170–9.205).

Paint-type graphics

9.6   A paint-type graphic is always **bitmapped.** Bitmapped means it is made out of the bits of dots (pixels) on the screen; 72 dots per inch (dpi), to be precise. The screen is made up of all those tiny dots, and a bitmapped image tells the screen which dots to turn on (black) and which dots to turn off (white). Here is an image that was created as a paint-type graphic:

Below is an enlarged view of the bottom left part of this image. It shows clearly how the image is made of a collection of pixels, either on or off.

9.7   Paint-type graphics are always black-and-white (meaning pixels are either on or off; you can *assign* color to the pixels). Paint-type are always 72 dots per inch, with a maximum size of 8 x 10 inches. Their white background is usually transparent. You can create a paint graphic in most any *paint* program (such as SuperPaint, MacPaint, and Desk-Paint, or in HyperCard's paint program; 9.77). The biggest problem with paint-type graphics is that when you enlarge them, the dots get bigger; when you reduce them, the dots smoosh together.

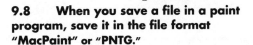

9.8   When you save a file in a paint program, save it in the file format "MacPaint" or "PNTG."

9.9   PageMaker can *read* any bit-mapped MacPaint graphic file, but once it is *placed* into PageMaker, it is no longer literally bit-mapped, in that you cannot edit it. The image still holds onto its pixel-by-pixel *look*, but the graphic itself actually becomes a TIFF ("Image"). If a paint image is *pasted* in from the Scrapbook, it becomes a PICT.

9.10   When you place a paint graphic, the cursor changes to a paintbrush, giving you a visual clue as to what type of graphic you are about to lay on your page:

9.11   When you resize a 72-dot-per-inch paint-type graphic, any patterns that may be in the graphic get scrunched or expanded, often creating a moiré pattern or a series of odd lines through the image. PageMaker provides a way to resize the graphic so the dots will match the resolution of the printer on which you will create the final output. It will still be a 72-dot-per-inch image, but it will be resized so the printer resolution can best accommodate it. PageMaker calls this "magic-resizing." See 9.103.

9.12   *A paint-type graphic resized normally.*

9.13   *A paint-type graphic resized using the "magic-resize" technique.*

PICT graphics

9.14 PICT graphics are not bitmapped; they are **object-oriented.** PICTs are created in draw-type (vector) programs, such as MacDraw or CricketDraw. *Paint* graphics are created by turning dots on and off; *PICT* graphics are created as entire *objects,* defined by a mathematical formula. When a PICT is resized, it is not the dots that get larger or smaller. Using the formula, the computer actually redraws the image in a different size, so the resolution stays exactly the same. It is the *object* that gets resized, not the dots.

9.15 Almost any paint-type graphic can also be saved as a PICT; *this does not mean that it turns the existing paint dots into a math formula for a clearer image!* It just means that now, instead of being read dot-by-dot, the entire bunch of dots has been grouped into one inseparable image. If the image was created with paint dots to begin with, the dots will get bigger as the image is resized. Paint-type graphics pasted from the Scrapbook are turned into PICTs (as shown directly below).

9.16 You cannot use image control (9.118–9.168) on a PICT, nor can you magic-resize it (9.23; 9.103).

9.17 There are two basic formats for PICT: PICT and PICT 2. Mac IIs and the SE30 can save in the PICT 2 format (if that's an option in the software you're using), which has more enhanced capabilities, including high-resolution color. PageMaker can read both (although I haven't been able to place even a tiny line-art PICT 2 without crashing).

9.18 PICTs are not as dependable as the other file types. The graphic on the right was created in the draw portion of SuperPaint and saved as a PICT and also as a MacPaint file. The MacPaint file has faithfully reproduced the original, with the only problem being the bitmapped type (which can be a major drawback). The PICT, on the other hand, has unpredictably changed a number of elements, including the font. Their inconstancy is even worse when printed to non-PostScript printers.

9.19 **As a general rule,** avoid saving files as PICTs unless that is your only choice. If you must save as a PICT, limit the image to *objects;* that is, don't try to include paint-type

9.20 *A paint-type file, created in the draw portion of SuperPaint and saved in the MacPaint format (the cat and rug are bitmapped)*

9.21 *This is the exact image as above, but saved as a PICT file.*

graphics in them, such as from MacPaint or the paint portion of SuperPaint. If you set type within the graphic, avoid *downloadable* fonts (18.33–18.37)—stick to the fonts that are installed in the printer's ROM (in the Apple LaserWriter, those are Helvetica, Times, Bookman, Avant Garde, Courier, Palatino, New Century Schoolbook, Zapf Chancery, Zapf Dingbats, Symbol, New Helvetica Narrow).

TIFF graphics

9.22 TIFF (tagged image file format) images are all bitmapped images, although they can be any size and resolution, and even grayscale or color. TIFFs come in three varieties:

- Black-and-white bitmaps (bi-level), usually created in a paint program and saved as a TIFF, or scanned in as line art (9.41).
- Palette-color TIFFs created in paint programs (16- or 256-color images).
- Grayscale or full-color TIFFS, created by scanning photographs or artwork (9.54).

9.23 Once a TIFF is placed in PageMaker, you can use image control on it (9.118–9.168). You can magic-resize bi-level TIFFs (9.11–9.13; 9.103). TIFF is the best format in which to save scanned images (9.36–9.47).

9.24 TIFFs can be quite large, so Page-Maker allows you to **compress** them (9.109). The printing quality is the same, and the compression can be sizable, so I recommend you get in the habit of regularly compressing the files as you place them. PageMaker also gives you a choice when the file is large, of whether or not to include the entire file within the publication (9.88).

9.25 A color TIFF image will display as a grayscale image on a monochrome monitor, and will print as a grayscale.

9.26 In the "Preferences" dialog box (from the Edit menu), you have a choice of viewing your detailed graphics on-screen as gray boxes ("Gray out"), as "Normal" low-res versions, or as "High resolution" (9.112–9.114). The High-res *vs.* Normal choices visibly affect TIFFs more than any other format. If you've selected "High resolution," you'll find that it takes a great deal of time to redraw high-res TIFFs as you are working on the page. However, you can set your preference to "Normal," enjoy a quick-drawing screen, but at any time still *temporarily* view the images in high resolution just until you redraw the screen again: simply hold down the Control key (yes, that's Control, not Command) as the screen redraws (as when you resize an image, text wrap, change views, etc.; 9.115).

9.27 *Black-and-white bitmapped TIFFs, scanned as line art.*

9.28 *Scanned photograph, saved as a grayscale TIFF.*

EPS graphics

9.29 EPS graphics (Encapsulated Post-Script; aka EPSF) are created with high-end drawing programs, such as Adobe Illustrator or Aldus Freehand. *PostScript* is a page description language that can be read by PostScript printers, such as the Apple LaserWriter or the Linotronic, and the output is smooth and clean and beautiful. Other printers use other languages, such as *QuickDraw* or *QuickScript,* and oftentimes can't interpret EPS files. Your printouts of EPS graphics from these printers will usually show just the low-resolution screen version, or they may ignore the image altogether.

9.30 It's possible to save a scanned image as an EPS, but the files are huge and you can't edit or image control them. And it's not recommended that you save any bit-mapped images as EPS, especially color bitmaps. On the plus side, some draw programs allow you to save as EPS, which is often more preferable than those undependable PICTs. You can also save a PageMaker page as an EPS file, which means you can then place it into any other PageMaker publication as a graphic image (9.117).

9.31 An EPS file is actually made up of two parts—the high-resolution PostScript code and the low-resolution screen version. The PostScript code is a text document that tells a Postscript printer how to print the high-res image on paper. The low-res version is what you see on the screen. A non-PostScript printer can generally output only the low-res screen version.

9.32 If you're a programmer, you can write your own code to create or to edit EPS files. If you're mortal like the rest of us, you can create an EPS image in a software package like Aldus Freehand or Adobe Illustrator (see 9.79 and 9.80 for tips on how to save those images so PageMaker can read them).

9.33 It is possible to place into PageMaker just the EPS code, rather than the screen version. This would happen if you inadvertently saved the graphic without following the advice in 9.79 or 9.80. Even though you may see only the code, the graphic itself will print. It is a little disconcerting, though.

9.34 *This is what an EPS file will look like on your screen if the screen version is not available.*

9.35 *Even if your screen shows just the code, as above, the graphic will print to a PostScript printer.*

```
TITLE  ToadHallLogo.ps
CREATOR: Freehand
CR DATE: 7/11/90 12
```

Toad Hall
on Montecito

An EPS file, created in Illustrator by Tuan Pham.
Based on the logo for The Tap Dance Studio.

Scanned images

9.36 Scanned images are images that have been created outside the computer and brought onto the screen through scanning hardware and software, rather than having been created in a graphics program and just placed or pasted onto the screen. The following recommendations are only for using with PageMaker; other programs may have different needs.

9.37 Scans come in three basic varieties: **line art, halftone,** and **grayscale** (sometimes called ConTone). Each variety can usually be saved as a TIFF (9.22–9.28), as an EPS (9.29–9.35), or as a PICT (9.14–9.21). **The preferred format is TIFF,** developed especially for scanning. Bitmapped EPS files are huge and ungainly, plus you cannot image-control them in PageMaker. PICTs are unreliable, and cannot be image-controlled.

9.38 When you're scanning, it's generally best to scan as close to the finished size as possible, perhaps just a little bigger. You can always resize it in PageMaker, but you'll get the best results and save disk space if you don't have to make a radical correction.

9.39 Also, crop the image as much as possible when you create the scan. You can,

of course, crop it in PageMaker (9.104), but PageMaker holds onto the entire image, even the part that has been cropped off.

Thus the file size remains just as hefty for a small portion of the graphic as it does for the entire image.

9.40

Scan as Line Art:	Advantages	Disadvantages
·Anything black-and-white, any image from a book or newspaper, pen-and-ink drawings, engravings, most clip art, most any logo.	·It's easy to create good quality images. ·Files are small. ·They print quickly. ·They resize well.	·Image has no gray values. ·It's sometimes difficult to hold both the fine lines plus the detail in the dark areas.
Scan as Halftone:	**Advantages**	**Disadvantages**
·Any image that has shades of gray or color, such as pencil or charcoal drawings, photographs. ·If you are printing to a non-PostScript printer, it is usually best to use a halftone scan.	·You can usually control the pattern. ·Files are small. ·They print quickly. ·Some scanning software corrects for laser printers, in which case it can be better than grayscale when printed on a laserwriter.	·Must be scaled integrally (magic-resized; 9.11–13). ·Difficult to edit. ·Prints the same at high-res or low-res. ·Cannot adjust contrast or brightness in PageMaker.
Scan as Grayscale:	**Advantages**	**Disadvantages**
·Any image that has shades of gray or color, such as pencil or charcoal drawings, photographs. ·If you are printing to a high-res PostScript printer, use a grayscale scan.	·Can edit and scale well. ·Can adjust contrast and brightness in PageMaker. ·Can scan at lower res. ·Extremely high quality available on high-res printer.	·Large files. ·Slower printing. ·White areas are opaque in PageMaker. ·Can require large amounts of memory.

Line art scans

9.41   Scan black-and-white images as **line art TIFFs,** at the highest resolution possible. A black-and-white image is one that has no shades of gray. Sometimes an area may appear gray, but it is really an illusion, with small black or white dots—when little black dots are in a white space, or vice versa, it *appears* gray. Anything that has previously been printed is black-and-white, actually. Any clip art you find in books, any photo in a newspaper, any logo that has been printed on a page—these are all black-and-white line art. (Keep in mind that if it has been printed before, it may be copyrighted! Check.)

9.42   When scanning a black-and-white image, it doesn't do any good to adjust the "Contrast," because there is only one form of contrast and it's already there: black vs. white.

You *can* adjust the "Brightness," though. It's always a trade-off. You can brighten the image as you scan it to get more detail in the dark areas, or to drop out dirt on the original. But fine lines in the light areas will fall apart. You can decrease the brightness to pick up fine details, but the dark areas will fill in. Below are examples.

9.43   Occasionally you may want to save a scanned black-and-white image as a gray-scale in order to pick up the fine details (9.53). Again, it's a trade-off, this time between sharp, visual clarity and the detail in the darker areas. When making your choice, you'll also want to remember that white areas in line art are transparent; white areas in grayscale images are opaque (as shown by the black line below).

9.44 *Scanned with -12% brightness. Lines are heavier and blacks more solid. Notice the tiny spots where it's picking up dust on the page.*

9.45 *Normal line art scan with no adjustments made. White areas are transparent.*

9.46 *Scanned with +12% brightness. Notice the added detail in the dark areas, but the fine lines are falling apart.*

9.47 *Scanned as a grayscale TIFF. There's more detail, but it is also halftoned. White areas are opaque.*

Halftones, grayscales . . .

9.48 With digital halftoning, things can get complex, what with the different resolutions and halftone/dithering options and gray levels and screen frequencies all affecting each other. **This segment is meant only as a guide.** There are entire books written on scanning, halftones, and the variables and variations. You will always need to experiment to get your image just right, but my hope is that this section will cut down on the time and frustration it takes.

9.49 Any image that is not strictly black and white, such as a pencil or charcoal drawing, a color image, or an actual photograph, must be turned into black and white so it can be printed. Neither the laser printer nor the printing press can print shades of gray with black ink (or black toner)—each only prints a black-and-white *illusion* of gray. This has been true since printing began, and it will be true for a while to come.

9.50 So in order to get a charcoal drawing or a photograph printed, you must turn those shades of gray into black dots. Tiny black dots on a white background look light gray; big black dots with less white area in the background look much darker—it's in this way that a printer is able to replicate

various shades of gray, using only black ink or toner on white paper. An image that has had its shades turned into dots is **halftoned** (giving it half the tone it started with), or **screened.**

9.51 A halftone can have a very fine *screen* or a very coarse *screen* (or anything in-between). The fineness of the screen is measured in **lines per inch.** A halftone with a 53-line screen would have 53 rows of dots per inch; a 133-line screen would have 133 rows of dots per inch. You can see from the examples below that the 53-line screen is much coarser.

9.52 No matter which of the following methods you choose to halftone your image (9.56), you need to know what line screen

105-line screen *53-line screen*

your commercial press will need in order to produce your job. Newspapers generally use a 75- or 85-line screen (look carefully at a newspaper photo and you can easily see the dots that create the image). Any printing press with the word *speedy, quick,* or *instant* in its name generally uses an 85- to 100-line screen (copy machines deal best with that frequency, also). Glossy magazines generally use 120- or 133-line screens. High-quality art books use 150- or 175-line screens (but if you're doing a high-quality art book you are probably not scanning the images in on the computer at this point in technology). Line screens over 110 should be printed onto film.

9.53 When you choose to scan an image (9.36–9.47) as a **halftone,** the scanner turns the gray tones into printer-readable black-and-white dots; each dot on the screen is either black or white. The scanned halftone is then called a "flat" or "bi-level" bitmap.

9.54 When you choose to scan an image as a **grayscale,** each dot on the screen holds more information than just whether it is black or white; it goes four to eight levels deep, and each dot can register a different depth, or gray value. Sort of like looking into a pond—where the water is deep, it

... and scanning

looks darker; where it is shallow, it looks lighter. The many levels of gray it contains are trying to approximate the *continuous gray tone,* the gradual blend of black to white, of which photographs are comprised. *In order to print a grayscale image, either on your laser printer or on a commercial press, you must still halftone the grayscale image (9.56–9.60).*

9.55 There is a complex connection between the printer resolution, the line screen, and the number of gray levels an image can have. Generally you will hear about 16-level and 256-level grayscale values. Some scanners let you choose the grayscale depth level, and some just give you the deepest possible and let you monkey with the levels that will eventually be visible as you change the line screen and the printer.

9.56 So, there are three ways to halftone an image you want to work with in PageMaker:

- You can halftone it when you scan it.
- You can scan the file as a *grayscale* and halftone it on the PageMaker publication page through the "Image control" (9.118–9.168).
- You can scan the file as a *grayscale* and let the PostScript printer halftone it as it gets printed (9.59).

9.57 As a rule of thumb, **it's best to scan the image as a grayscale** and then halftone it in PageMaker or on the printer. If you scan it as a halftone, the file will be nice and small, as it turns into just a black-and-white image. But you will always be stuck with the line screen you scanned it in with, and you won't be able to adjust the brightness or the contrast. You have more options using a grayscale.

9.58 You still must halftone a grayscale image before you can print it. One way to do this is through the "Image control" dialog box (9.118–9.123), which allows you to give your image the line screen and the angle you want, as well as to adjust the brightness and the contrast (9.147–9.159).

9.59 Or you can let a PostScript printer halftone it for you. The Apple LaserWriter will apply a 53-line screen (see 9.62) to any grayscale image it finds that doesn't have a screen already applied. A laser printer doesn't have high enough resolution to distinguish between 16 levels of gray and 256 levels of gray. If your final output will be to a laser printer, save the image as a 16-level TIFF (if your scanning software gives you a choice) to keep the file size to a minimum. It will look just as good as a 256-level image.

9.60 High-resolution imagesetters can take advantage of the information provided in a 256-level grayscale. They have a much higher default line screen; for instance, a Linotronic will automatically apply a default of a 150-line halftone screen. Most service bureaus reset the default to around 105 (see 9.52), as 150-line is too fine for most work. If you want a different line screen than the imagesetter's default, you can apply it through the "Image control" dialog box (9.132–9.143) to each grayscale image, one at a time. Or you can ask the service bureau to change the APD (18.11) so all the images will use the same line screen automatically.

9.61 By the way, the printer's default line screens (in laser printers, as well as in high-resolution imagesetters), apply to any and all screens in the publication—drawn boxes with fills, gray tints applied to text or lines, etc.

Halftone examples   *(Always magic-resize images that have been scanned as halftones! See 9.11–9.13; 9.103)*

Scanned as a halftone *(9.48–9.53)*

9.62 *Halftoned with a 53-line screen; Apple LaserWriter IINT. If you don't like the way a scanned halftone looks after you print it, you have to rescan it; you can't adjust it within PageMaker.*

9.63 *Halftoned with a 71-line screen; Apple LaserWriter IINT.*

9.64 *Halftoned with a 71-line screen; Linotronic (1270 dpi).*

Scanned as a grayscale, halftoned through Image Control *(9.118–9.123)*

9.65 *Grayscale; Apple LaserWriter IINT; 53-line screen applied. Notice it looks the same as when the Laser printer applies the screen itself (9.68).*

9.66 *Grayscale; HP DeskWriter; 53-line screen applied. Any screen you apply in Image Control will override the printer's default screen.*

9.67 *Grayscale; Linotronic (1270 dpi); 85-line screen applied. Any screen you apply in Image Control will override the printer's default screen.*

Scanned as a grayscale, halftoned through the printer *(9.59–9.61)*

9.68 *Grayscale; Apple LaserWriter IINT; 53-line screen default.*

9.69 *Grayscale; HP DeskWriter; 53-line screen default.*

9.70 *Grayscale; Linotronic (1270 dpi); 105-line screen default.*

yes, that's me in 1953.

Rules of thumb for grayscale scans

9.71 In general, don't halftone at the scanner; apply the halftone in the "Image control" dialog box (9.118–9.123), **or** let the printer halftone it (see 9.59 and 9.60).

9.72 When you scan an image as a grayscale, set the dpi (dots per inch) at no more than twice the line screen at which it will be printed. For instance, even though the LaserWriter has a resolution of 300 dpi, the default line screen for halftoning is **53 lines per inch.** So scan the image at around 106 dpi. Any extra image data that is more than twice the line screen is ignored, and just makes your file larger. To find out the default line screen of your printer, ask your service bureau or your printer's tech support.

Scanned at 210 dpi; printed with 105-line screen *Scanned at 300 dpi; printed with 105-line screen*

9.73 What a grayscale image looks like on the screen doesn't have much to do with what it will look like when printed. That's not very comforting, I know.

This is what the photo in 9.64 looked like on my screen at Actual Size.

9.74 If you will be printing to a high-resolution imagesetter, the output on the laser printer will not give you a very good representation of what to expect from the imagesetter. That's not very comforting, either. Below, the first photo was printed on an Apple LaserWriter IINT; the second photo, with the same image-control settings, was printed on a Linotronic 200.

LaserWriter

Linotronic

9.75 When a halftone is printed on a commercial press or on a copy machine, the tiny little black dots you see in the white

areas will drop out (disappear). The tiny little white dots you see in the black areas will clog up. So inevitably, every image that comes out of any imagesetter is going to develop more contrast when it's finally reproduced—the lights will be lighter and the darks will be darker. **It's important to adjust for this** by image-controlling the TIFF so it comes out of *your* printer rather gray and flat-looking. When you first start working with halftones, it's hard to make yourself create a flat-looking image; we want to see it sharp and crispy. Control yourself. The photo below, on the left, was gray and dull on the screen, as well as from the LaserWriter. The photo on the right was adjusted so it looked crispy on the screen, with dark blacks and light whites. But after going through the imagesetter and then the printing press, the crispy one has lost too much detail in both the dark and light areas; the grayer one on the left picked up contrast in the process. See 9.155 for a standard setting for producing a decent halftone.

The best way to save a graphic image for later placement into PageMaker

9.76 When you create a graphic in a graphic program, generally you have a choice of file formats in which to save the image. You make the choice as you "Save as…" and name the file. If you have already created and saved the graphic with a name, you can open it in its program and choose "Save as…" again, give it another name, and thus save a copy in another format. It's a good idea to include the type of file format in the name, so when you see the name in a list box you will know what you are looking at (e.g., Cats/macpaint, or Cats/tiff).

The following are the file formats in which to save graphics so PageMaker can read them:

9.77 Paint programs: Save as a **MacPaint** file. Even in SuperPaint, you must save it as a MacPaint file if you want PageMaker to read it. A paint program is any software package with the word *Paint* in it, such as MacPaint, SuperPaint, CricketPaint, etc. Paint programs are the ones where you can use brushes to wipe a pattern across the screen, and an eraser to remove things. They are bitmapped. Don't save paint images as PICTs (9.18).

9.78 Draw programs: Save as a **PICT** file. A draw program is any software package with the word *Draw* or *Draft* in it, such as MacDraw, MacDraft, CricketDraw, etc. Draw programs are *object-oriented*. If the images you create have handles on them, like PageMaker-drawn boxes, and you select items by clicking on them with a pointer tool, then it is a draw program. Save as a PICT if the image contains only object-oriented graphics or type (preferably ROM fonts; 9.19)—if you add any paint stuff to it, the PICT will be very undependable (9.18–9.21), and you may be better off saving it as a MacPaint file.

9.79 Adobe Illustrator: Illustrator files automatically save as **EPS** files. You have a choice of whether to include the screen version along with the PostScript code in the file (9.31–9.35). If you want to make sure you will be able to see the graphic itself on the PageMaker page, rather than just the structuring comments in a gray box, then make a selection in the "Include preview for"—select either "Black and White Macintosh" or "Color Macintosh," depending on the screen on which you will be viewing it. If you have placed other EPS files within this graphic, then also click the checkbox to "Include copy of placed EPS files for other applications."

9.80 Aldus Freehand: PageMaker cannot read a Freehand file. You must use the "Export…" command under the file menu. This gives you the "Export as Encapsulated PostScript" dialog box. Click in the "Macintosh" picture format button. Notice the edit box suggests you use **.eps** in the file name for easy identification. *If you update the original illustration,* the EPS version is *not* automatically updated along with it! You need to export the altered file again, save it with the same name as the EPS file, and click "Yes" when you are asked if you want to replace the existing file with the same name (very much like updating Table Editor files; 17.128).

9.81 DeskPaint: With most other graphic programs, it is always safe to save as a TIFF (preferably) or as a MacPaint file. A TIFF is usually preferable because you can get a higher resolution in the image; MacPaints are limited to 72 dots per inch. **TypeAlign:** save files in the EPS format.

"Include complete copy?" ∎

9.82 When placing a large graphic file, you may see this alert box:

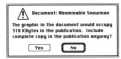

9.83 This information is connected to the Linking process in PageMaker, which is explained in great detail in Section 10. Potentially, the links allow PageMaker to update the files you placed in the publication with any changes you make in the original files. Pretty amazing.

9.84 The default link option is to "Store copy in publication." This means that Page-Maker will keep a copy of the graphic as part of the publication itself, as opposed to keeping only a low-resolution screen version in the publication. If only the low-res version is stored, PageMaker *links* it to the external, original file; when she needs complete information in order to display or print the publication, she follows the link to the original file.

9.85 However, if a graphic file is larger than 256K, PageMaker will ask if you really do want to store the whole thing in the publication, even if "Store copy in publication" is checked. If you choose "Yes," your publication size will increase by that amount. This can be significant if you have more than a couple of graphic images. The larger and more ungainly the publication size, the slower PageMaker operates.

9.86 You will also see this alert box when you update an existing publication file that is over 256K, or when the update will enlarge the file to more than 256K.

9.87 If you are not using large files, or if you don't care about updating changes in them, then you don't ever need to worry about this. All your graphics can be stored in the publication and everything will act just the same as it did before linking was invented.

9.88 *p.s.* All EPS (9.29–9.35) files and all text files are always stored in the publication anyway, whether you like it or not. They are still linked to their external originals and can be updated (see Section 10 on linking and updating revisions).

Independent *vs.* inline graphics ∎

9.89 Any kind of graphic in PageMaker can be placed or pasted on the page in one of two ways: either as an **independent** graphic or as an **inline** graphic.

9.90 An **independent** graphic is one that is not imbedded in any text block, but is just sitting on the page all by itself, just like you would expect it to. If you move the graphic, nothing else moves with it. If you do anything to any other element on the page (such as cut, delete, copy, or resize), the action doesn't affect an independent graphic.

9.91 An **inline** graphic is one that you place or paste directly into a text block, just as you would a text character. You can apply some text attributes to it, but you can still treat it as a graphic in other respects. As part of the text, it will move along just like a character as you edit. You can roll it up in a windowshade, or cut it along with the text block. See 9.170–9.205 for full details.

If you want to do this: Then follow these steps: Shortcuts ▾ Notes ▾ Hints

Independent graphics

9.92   Place a graphic

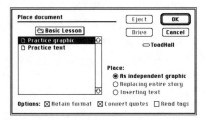

 A bitmapped, paint graphic (9.6)

An object-oriented draw graphic; PICT (9.14)

A bitmapped TIFF graphic (9.22)

An Encapsulated PostScript graphic; EPS (9.29)

A Scrapbook PICT graphic (9.96)

- Click once on the **pointer tool,** even if the pointer tool is already selected. This is to prevent accidentally placing the graphic inline.
- From the File menu, choose "Place...."
- Find the name of the graphic file in the list box; you may need to switch drives and folders to find it. You will know it is a graphic when you click once on it, because the top button under "Place" will become "As independent graphic."
- Click once on the name of the file, then click OK; **or** double-click on the name of the file.
- Depending on the file format of the graphic, you will get one of the cursors shown on the left (a loaded graphic icon). Simply click the loaded cursor on the page and the graphic will pour on; the top left corner of the graphic will be positioned wherever you click.
- If you immediately decide you don't want it at all, just hit the Backspace/Delete key.

- See 9.89–9.91 to understand the difference between independent graphics and inline graphics. Basically, an independent graphic is its own little entity on the page, separate from anything else. An inline graphic is actually part of the text block, and will reflow with any text editing.

If you want to do this:

Then follow these steps:

Shortcuts ▾ Notes ▾ Hints

9.93 Drag-place a graphic

- Select a file to place, just as in 9.92.
- Instead of clicking to put the graphic on the page, press-and-drag with the loaded graphic icon. You will see a bounding box. When you let go of the mouse button, the graphic will flow into the space you created.

- Unfortunately, you can't use the Shift key to restrain the bounding box to the proper proportions of the graphic. If you don't like the proportions, see 9.102.

9.94 Replace a graphic

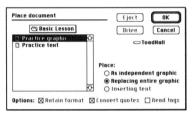

- On the publication page, select the graphic you want to replace (click once on it with the **pointer tool**).
- From the File menu, choose "Place...."
- Find the name of the file you want to place; click once on it.
- On the right, under "Place," you will have an option of "Replacing entire graphic." Click in that button.
- Click OK, *or* double-click on the file name.
- You won't get a loaded graph, icon this time; PageMaker will just go ahead and get rid of the graphic on the page that you selected earlier, and replace it with this one. *This new one will take on the size and shape of the one it is replacing.* Of course, this means the new one may have the wrong proportions; if it is out of proportion, see 9.102.

- The new graphic will replace the selected graphic, taking on the size and shape of the selected one. If you are replacing a file with the *same* file updated, the new one will drop in with the same cropping as the old one it is replacing.

If you want to do this:	Then follow these steps:	Shortcuts ▾ Notes ▾ Hints

9.95 **Paste** a graphic from the Scrapbook

- Choose the **pointer tool.**
- From the Apple menu, choose "Scrapbook."
- Find the image you want to paste. From the Edit menu, choose "Copy," *or* press Command C. Click in the close box.
- While on the publication page, from the Edit menu choose "Paste," *or* press Command V.

- Graphics from the Scrapbook will retain their format when they paste into Page-Maker, except for paint-type graphics, which become PICTs.

9.96 **Place** a graphic from the Scrapbook

The Scrapbook File is in the System Folder, as you can see in the list box above.

 This is the loaded graphic icon you will see when you place the Scrapbook. The number indicates the number of items loaded into the icon. Each time you click, this number will decrease.

- Click once on the **pointer tool.**
- Make sure the Scrapbook is *closed,* not just hiding behind the PageMaker window (click in the Scrapbook close box).
- From the File menu, choose "Place...."
- Navigate to the System folder (see 16.6–16.9 if you need help).
- Click once on "Scrapbook File."
- Under "Place," make sure the button "As independent graphic" is clicked on.
- Double-click on the "Scrapbook file."
- You will get a loaded graphic icon, as shown on the left. The number indicates the number of items in the Scrapbook.
- Each time you click the mouse, the next item in the Scrapbook will place on the page, starting with the first.
- When you don't want any more items, click the pointer tool in the Toolbox to absorb the extras.

- It's extremely important to make sure you click on that pointer tool to ensure that there is no insertion point lying around somewhere. You can inadvertently place an entire Scrapbook into an insertion point that may even be on another page altogether. You probably won't even know it because the text block can't figure out what to do with all those things that were in your Scrapbook, so it rolls itself up and you can't figure out where the heck the stuff went. So maybe you even try it again and then you're really in trouble 'cause you can't even unroll the text block to remove the stuff once you figure out where it landed. Do you wonder how I know about this dilemma? See 9.198 for a tip on how to deal with it.
- Any lines finer than 1 point will be converted into 1-point lines when placed.

If you want to do this:	**Then follow these steps:**	**Shortcuts ▾ Notes ▾ Hints**
9.97 Paste a graphic from the Clipboard	▪ In any program, you can put any graphic on the Clipboard: select it; cut or copy it as usual. See 9.99 and 1.191–1.192. ▪ Quit that program and open PageMaker. ▪ Just press Command V to paste the graphic right on the page. You have to remember not to cut or copy anything else before you paste into PageMaker.	▪ The Clipboard is part of the Macintosh System; it is not part of any particular program. So whatever you put into it in one application (say, SuperPaint), will stay right there while you go to another program (say, PageMaker). When you turn off the Mac, anything that was on the Clipboard will disappear.
9.98 Move a graphic ✛ *The four-headed arrow, indicating the graphic is in moving mode.*	▪ With the **pointer tool,** press-and-drag on the graphic. *Make sure you don't press on any handle.* You should see a four-headed arrow; if you see a two-headed arrow, you have grabbed a handle and will end up *stretching,* not *moving,* the graphic (9.101). ▪ If you press-and-drag *quickly,* you will see just a rectangular outline as you move the graphic. This is a **fast move** (1.159). ▪ If you press and *hold it,* waiting until you see the watch cursor, *then* the four-headed arrow, you will see the entire graphic as you move it. This is a **slow move** (1.160).	▪ If you see this symbol when you press: ⬍ it means the graphic is an *inline* graphic. You cannot move an inline graphic with the pointer tool in the same way you move an independent graphic; see 9.188–9.189 or 9.199. ▪ If you accidentally stretch the graphic, instantly press Command Z to undo the stretch.
9.99 Cut or copy a graphic	▪ First select the graphic with the **pointer tool.** Cut or copy it just as you cut or copy anything on the Mac: ▪ From the Edit menu, choose "Cut" (Command X) or "Copy" (Command C).	▪ See Section 1, Basics, for info on cutting, copying, pasting, and the Clipboard: 1.184–1.187 and 1.192–1.199.

If you want to do this:	Then follow these steps:	Shortcuts ▾ Notes ▾ Hints
9.100 Delete a graphic	▪ Delete a graphic as you delete anything on the Mac: click once on it with the **pointer tool,** then hit the Backspace/Delete key (*or* choose Clear from the Edit menu).	▪ When you cut or copy a graphic, it goes onto the Clipboard. When you Clear or Backspace/Delete it, it is really gone. You can Command Z to undo.

9.101 Resize a graphic

 Original graphic

 Stretched horizontally

 Stretched vertically

 Stretched proportionally with the Shift key

▪ With the **pointer tool,** click once on the graphic.
▪ With the very tip of the **pointer tool,** press-and-drag on a handle.
  ▪ Pressing on a side handle will resize the graphic horizontally.
  ▪ Pressing on a top or bottom handle will resize the graphic vertically.
  ▪ Pressing on a corner handle will resize the graphic in both directions.
▪ To resize the graphic **proportionally,** hold down the Shift key while stretching on any handle.

9.102 Resize a graphic back into its original proportions

▪ With the **pointer tool,** click once on the graphic.
▪ Position the very tip of the pointer on one of the handles.
▪ Hold the Shift key down and *press* on that corner handle to the count of three. The graphic will pop back into its original *proportions,* although not its original *size.*

If you want to do this:

9.103 "Magic-resize" a bi-level graphic

Press on the submenu next to "Printer" to choose the printer destination.

LaserWriter II NT.apd

This is what an APD file looks like on your disk.

A graphic resized normally.

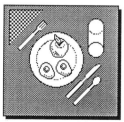

A graphic resized magically.

Then follow these steps:

- In order to magic-resize, you must have the APD (Aldus printer description; 18.11) for the printer on which you are going to produce your final output, even if you don't own the printer. For instance, if you are going to print to a Linotronic 300, its APD must be in your System folder. Only those printers whose APDs are installed will appear in the Print dialog box. If you don't see the printer you want listed there, you must install its APD in order to magic-resize a graphic to it (see 18.168).
- Back in PageMaker, from the File menu, choose "Print...."
- In the "Print to" dialog box, choose the name of the printer you will use for final output (see above left). Click "Cancel" (even though you Cancel, the dialog box will hang on to the printer destination).
- Follow the steps in 9.101 to resize a paint-type graphic, either vertically, horizontally, or both. *Before you press-and-drag, though, hold down the* **Command** *key.* The graphic will resize in jumps.
- To magic-resize *proportionally,* hold down both the Command *and* the Shift keys.

Shortcuts ▾ Notes ▾ Hints

- Magic-resizing only works on black-and-white bitmapped images (grayscale TIFFs don't need it); it does not work on PICTs, even if they hold a bitmapped image, and it doesn't need to work on EPS files.
- Magic-resizing is a technique to enhance the look of bitmapped graphics by matching the screen pattern of the graphic with the resolution of the printer. This means, though, that PageMaker must know the resolution of the printer on which you are going to print *the final output.* For instance, if you are doing proofs on a laser printer, but you are going to an imagesetter for the final output, you need to resize the graphics for the imagesetter. Yes, this does mean you have to switch printers back and forth in the Print dialog box, depending on whether you are printing or resizing. **Note:** magic-resizing defaults to 300 dots per inch if you use the Apple driver (18.20–18.28).
- Magic-resizing works on files that have been *placed.* You will know if it's working or not because when you magic-resize, the image jumps from size to size in big leaps. Thus your image size is more limited than when you are resizing normally. The higher the printer resolution, the more sizes you can adjust to.

If you want to do this:

9.104 Crop a graphic,
uncrop a graphic,
and pan a graphic

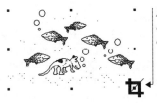

The cropping tool

*Position the
cropping tool
over a handle.*

*When you press on
a **handle** with the
cropping tool, you
will get an arrow
to resize with.*

*When you press on
the **image** with the
cropping tool, you will
get the grabber hand.
Press-and-drag to move
the image within the
frame.*

Then follow these steps:

- With the **cropping tool,** click once on the graphic. The handles you see will look like standard handles.
- Center the *inside* of the cropping tool directly over one of the handles (see left).
- Press-and-drag the handle in toward the center. This does not *resize* the image; it actually chops off, or *crops*, the part you drag over. Dragging the side handles will crop just horizontally or just vertically, the same as when you resize. Dragging a corner handle will crop in both directions at once.
- Cropping is not like using scissors; if you want to **uncrop the image,** simply drag back out. You can uncrop it even after you have resized it, or cut and pasted the image. Even though you can't see the entire image, it will always hang onto its whole self and you can pull it back out any time.
- After you have cropped it down to the necessary size, you can **pan the image.** This is too cool; you really must try it. After it's cropped, with the **cropping tool,** *press* on the center of the image. The tool will turn into the grabber hand and you can move the image around *within the frame.* Even after you cut and paste a cropped image, you can always go in and pan the pasted version again.

Shortcuts ▾ Notes ▾ Hints

- The cropping tool icon is derived from the L-shaped pieces of cardboard that designers and photographers have traditionally used for making decisions as to where an image should be *cropped,* or chopped off. We put the two Ls together, as shown in the cropping tool icon, and moved them in and out from each other to frame just the part of the image to keep. An image is rarely used full-frame, unless the photographer has a great design sense, or unless the photos have been very tightly directed by an art director. Even so, often it is necessary to crop out an awkward corner, or a bit off the top, or some fingers along the bottom that happened to get stuck in the photo. Or the original has three people in it and you want only one person's face. Or often you may find a little piece of something useless attached to some clip art you copy in from somewhere. These are all typical uses of the cropping tool.
- In general, though, avoid major cropping. Whenever possible, take the image into a graphic program and remove what you don't need. Even though you may see only a fraction of the original graphic, the entire image is still there, taking up lots of space, potentially causing printing problems.

If you want to do this:

Then follow these steps:

Shortcuts ▾ Notes ▾ Hints

9.105 Text-wrap a graphic

The text wrap dialog box. The standoff has been defined as .2 picas.

a) "Everybody wants to be someplace he ain't. As soon as he gets there he wants to go right back."
Henry Ford

A rectangular text wrap with a standoff of .2 picas

b) "Everybody wants to be someplace he ain't. As soon as he gets there he wants to go right back."
Henry Ford

A custom text wrap

- With the **pointer tool,** click on the graphic.
- From the Element menu, choose "Text wrap...."
- Under "Wrap option," click on the middle icon, as shown at left.
- Under "Text flow," the third icon will automatically select itself, as shown at left.
- Enter values in the "Standoff" boxes for the amount of space you want between the graphic boundary and the text wrap boundary (as seen in **a**). Click OK.
- If you want a custom wrap (**b**), then use the **pointer tool** to click on the dotted line around the graphic (the wrap boundary). Each click will create a new point. Press-and-drag to move the point. (See 11.30.)
- With each move, the text will reflow. To pause the reflow until you finish moving the points, hold down the Spacebar while you press-and-drag. When you let go of the Spacebar, the text will re-wrap.

- Text wrapping is explained in great detail in Section 11. This segment is just a brief synopsis of the process.
- You cannot text wrap inline graphics. You can text wrap any other graphic, whether you have placed it, pasted it from the Clipboard, or drawn it in PageMaker (including lines).

9.106 Remove text wrapping from a graphic

Wrap option:

Text flow:

- With the **pointer tool,** click once on the graphic.
- From the Element menu, choose "Text wrap...."
- Under "Wrap option," click on the first icon, as shown at left.
- Click OK.

- If everything you place or paste drops into PageMaker with a text wrap, there is a default set. To remove a text wrap default, click once on the pointer tool *instead* of on the graphic (click on the pointer even if it's already selected). Then follow the rest of the steps. See 11.44.

379

If you want to do this:

Then follow these steps:

Shortcuts ▾ Notes ▾ Hints

9.107　Turn text into a graphic

a) *Type the text into its own text block*

Item 1 out of 2

b) Before *you paste into the Scrap-book, check the bottom left to make sure you are viewing the first item.*

c) *Click on this name to get back to the hard disk.*

d) *The icon indicates the number of items the Scrapbook holds.*

e) *Notice the text now has graphic handles.*

f) *Stretch it just like a graphic. Cuz it is one.*

- With the **text tool,** type the letter(s) you want to use as a graphic; type them in their own separate text block (**a**). It's easiest, although not imperative, if you make the text as close to the finished size as you can. Make any style changes (bold, italic, etc.).
- With the **pointer tool,** click once on the text block.
- Copy the graphic (press Command C).
- From the File menu, open the Scrapbook. *Make sure you are viewing the first item* (**b**).
- Paste the graphic (press Command V).
- **Close** the Scrapbook (click in its close box).
- Make sure the **pointer tool** is still selected. From the File menu, choose "Place...."
- Navigate to your System folder (click on the name of your hard disk until you see the list of files that are on your disk [**c**]; double-click on "System folder").
- Double-click on "Scrapbook file."
- You should now have the loaded "place" icon for the Scrapbook (shown at left, **d**). Click once on the page to place your item. Then click on the pointer tool to let it absorb the rest of the Scrapbook images.
- Now your text is a graphic, complete with graphic handles, as shown at left, **e.** You can stretch and maneuver it just like any graphic. Wow.

- This is the perfect trick to use when you want to text wrap an initial cap: first turn the letter into a graphic, then apply the text wrap (9.105; Section 11). Notice that this technique involves the place-the-Scrapbook maneuver (9.96).
- When you turn a PostScript letter into a graphic this way, it becomes a PICT. When printed, it will retain the same smooth edges it would have had as a plain ol' letter, no matter how you may resize it.
- Some third-party Scrapbooks, such as SmartScrap, make this process much easier. In SmartScrap, if you copy the entire text image out of the Scrapbook, it will paste into PageMaker as editable text. But if you use the selection tool and *select* the text before you copy, it will paste into PageMaker as a graphic.

If you want to do this:

9.108 Group several objects into one graphic

This group is made up of many separate objects with lots of different handles.

Now the group is one object, with one set of handles.

Resize it. *Crop it.*

Stretch it.

Then follow these steps:

- With the **pointer tool,** hold the Shift key down and click once on each object that you want to group. You may also need to use the Command key to get to objects under other layers (1.176). **Or** you could use the Shift-click or marquee methods to select the objects (1.168–1.169).
- Once they are all selected, copy them to the Scrapbook. Follow the rest of the steps in 9.96 for *placing* the Scrapbook file.
- Once the Scrapbook item has been *placed,* not pasted, that group of objects is one graphic with one set of handles. You can resize it, crop it, move it as one image.
- To edit the image, *paste* it in from the Scrapbook, make the changes, put it back in the Scrapbook, and *place* it again.

Shortcuts ▾ Notes ▾ Hints

- When the item is placed from the Scrapbook, it is in PICT format. PICT often has trouble keeping line weights consistent; notice in the example on the left that the grouped object, after it was placed, grew an extra line around part of it. Often opaque boxes will become transparent, a habit that is also very irritating.
- If you have a lot of grouped images that you want to back up, you can make a copy of the Scrapbook File and save the copy in another folder. The easiest way to make a copy is to hold down the Option key while you drag the Scrapbook file from the System folder into the other folder (perhaps into the folder that also holds the publication). Add a descriptive word to the name of the Scrapbook File to identify it (e.g., Scrapbook File/frogs). Keep in mind that the Scrapbook will automatically use the file that is in the System folder, so if you want to open the *copy* you made, you will need to *switch* the two. In the System folder, you must name the Scrapbook File *exactly* "Scrapbook File," or the Mac can't find it. If there is no Scrapbook File in the System folder when you open Scrapbook from the Apple menu, Mac will create a new, empty one for you.

If you want to do this:	Then follow these steps:	Shortcuts ▾ Notes ▾ Hints

9.109 Compress a TIFF file to save space on the disk

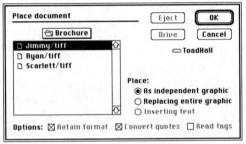

The list shows three uncompressed TIFFs.

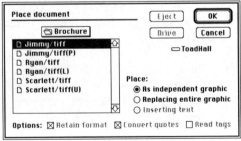

The list now shows compressed copies of the original TIFFs.

- Click once on the **pointer tool,** even if the pointer tool is already chosen.
- From the File menu, choose "Place...."
- Locate the TIFF file you want to compress and click once on it.
  - □ To create a **moderately-compressed** copy, hold down the Command and Option keys. Click on the OK button (or hit Return), *and keep holding those two keys down to the count of five.*
  - □ For **maximum** compression, hold down the Command, Option, and Shift keys. Click on the OK button (or hit Return), *and keep holding those three keys down to the count of five.*
- You will get the typical TIFF loaded icon with which to place the graphic. Click as usual to put it on the page.
- Now there is a new file on your disk. If you go back to the File menu and choose "Place...," you will see it listed. PageMaker has added an initial after the file name to indicate what you did to it (see the chart on the right).

- This procedure does not compress the *original* TIFF; it creates a compressed *copy.* In order to take advantage of the extra disk space the compression creates, you need to remove the original TIFF from the disk (to a back-up disk, right?). PageMaker will automatically link (Section 10) the publication version to the compressed copy.
- The amount a file can be compressed depends on the complexity and size of the original. I've seen a TIFF reduce from as much as 1267K to 206K.
- You can always decompress any compressed TIFF (9.111). Most other programs cannot read a TIFF that was reduced in PageMaker.
- You can also compress paint files. When you next place that compressed paint file, you'll notice it has turned into a TIFF.

P	=	Moderate compression of black-and-white or palette-color TIFFs
LD	=	Moderate compression of grayscale or color TIFFs
L	=	Maximum compression of black-and-white or palette-color TIFFs
LD2	=	Maximum compression of grayscale or color TIFFs
U	=	Decompressed TIFF of any sort

If you want to do this:	Then follow these steps:	Shortcuts ▾ Notes ▾ Hints
9.110 Replace a TIFF file on the page with a compressed TIFF file	▪ Follow the steps in 9.109 to compress a TIFF, but with these exceptions: ▫ Before you go to the File menu, with the **pointer tool,** click on the graphic you want to replace. ▫ In the "Place…" dialog box, after you click on the file name, click in the button "Replacing entire graphic."	▪ This trick will eliminate the current graphic image from the page (whether it is a TIFF or not) and replace it with the compressed version as you create it from the "Place" dialog box. If you are replacing the current graphic with the same file compressed, it will drop in with the exact size, cropping, and image control settings.
9.111 Decompress a TIFF file	▪ Click once on the **pointer tool,** even if the pointer tool is already chosen. ▪ From the File menu, choose "Place…." ▪ Locate the compressed TIFF file you want to decompress and click once on it. You will know the file is compressed by the letter in parentheses after its name; see 9.109. ▪ Hold down the Command key and click OK. *Keep holding the Command key down to the count of five.* ▪ You will get the typical TIFF loaded icon to place the image. Click on the page. **If you don't want to place it, click on the pointer tool.** The decompressed copy will stay on your disk, even if you don't actually place the file on the page.	▪ This decompressing technique does not decompress the compressed file—it creates an *additional* copy that is decompressed. If you return to the "Place…" dialog box you will see the previously-compressed file listed, this time with a (U) after its name, in addition to the original compression code (P, L, or LD2; see 9.109). When you look on your disk, you may not find the (U) version, but you will see a new icon labeled PMF000. That PMF000, *in this case,* is the decompressed TIFF file. If you close the folder and reopen it, that file will rename itself with the appropriate abbreviations in parentheses.

If you want to do this:	Then follow these steps:	Shortcuts ▾ Notes ▾ Hints
9.112 Display all graphics as gray boxes for fastest screen display 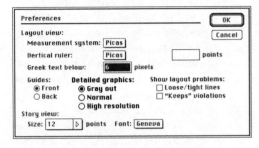	■ From the Edit menu, choose "Preferences...." ■ Under "Detailed graphics," click in the "Gray out" button. ■ Click OK.	■ If your graphics are merely placeholders, or if you are in a major rush, turn this option on. It will change the graphic: becomes: ■ When you print the publication with this option turned on, Page-Maker will still print the real graphics; this preference is just for quick screen display.
9.113 Display all graphics as low-resolution screen images Detailed graphics: ○ Gray out ◉ Normal ○ High resolution	■ This option is actually the default, so you won't need to reset it, unless someone has gone in and changed it. If so: ■ From the Edit menu, choose "Preferences...." ■ Under "Detailed graphics," click in the "Normal" button. ■ Click OK.	■ This option places TIFF images as low-resolution screen versions. PICTs that are over 64K will be displayed as monochrome TIFF images. You can temporarily view the graphic at high-res at any time; see 9.115.
9.114 Display all graphics at high-resolution Detailed graphics: ○ Gray out ○ Normal ◉ High resolution	■ From the Edit menu, choose "Preferences...." ■ Under "Detailed graphics," click in the "High resolution" button. ■ Click OK.	■ This will make all graphics display at their highest resolution, which can significantly slow down your work on the screen. It's best to leave this option at "Normal," and display the high-res version only when it's necessary. See 9.115 for displaying high-res images one at a time temporarily.

If you want to do this:	**Then follow these steps:**	**Shortcuts ▾ Notes ▾ Hints**
9.115 Display a single graphic at high-resolution	■ This technique won't work if the "Detailed graphics" option in the "Preferences" dialog box is set to "Gray out." ■ To display a high-res version of a graphic, hold down the **Control** key as you place the graphic, or as the screen redraws. (The screen redraws anytime you change views, use the scroll bars, resize an image, click in the zoom box, etc. You can hold down the Command and Shift keys as if you were going to resize an image, hold down the Command key also, and press on a corner handle to re-display in high-res.)	■ Actually, this will display any and all of the high-res graphics that happen to be on the screen, not just one single image. ■ Notice this technique uses the **Control** key, not the Command key. That means if you have a keyboard that does not have a Control key, like the Mac Plus keyboard, you can't do this.
9.116 Apply color to a graphic	■ With the **pointer tool,** click once on the graphic(s). ■ If the Color palette is not showing, press Command K (or choose it from the Windows menu). ■ Select the color to apply to the graphic(s).	■ See Section 14 for details on using color in your publication. This segment is just a brief synopsis. ■ Black-and-white TIFFs and paint-type graphics will display the colors you apply. PICT, EPS, and color TIFF graphics can have color applied to them, but they will not display their assigned colors. ■ You cannot apply color to objects through the "Define colors..." dialog box. That box is just for *creating* colors.

If you want to do this:

9.117   Create an EPS file
of a PageMaker page

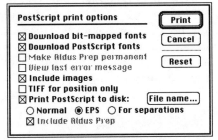

This is the dialog box for printing to disk.

*This is an EPS graphic of a 4 x 6 page
in another PageMaker publication.*

Then follow these steps:

- You need to be in the publication that
has the page you want to make into a file.
You don't have to be viewing that page,
though; just know its page number.
- From the File menu, choose "Print...,"
or press Command P.
- In the Print dialog box, enter the page
number (of the page you want the EPS file
of) in the "From ___ to ___" edit boxes. You
can only do one page at a time, so both edit
boxes must have the same number.
- The "Scaling" must be 100%.
- Click on the "PostScript..." button.
- In the "PostScript print options" dialog
box, click on the "Print PostScript to disk"
button. Leave the other defaults as they
are. Directly below, click on the "EPS"
button.
- Click in the "File name..." button and
name the file. It's a good idea to type **.eps**
on the end of the name for identification.
Click OK.
- Click the "Print" button.
- You will see messages across the screen
similar to a regular printing session.
When the process is done, you can go
to the "Place" dialog box (from the File
menu) and see the new file listed. It will
place just like any other graphic.

Shortcuts ▾ Notes ▾ Hints

- This procedure allows you to create a
graphic image of any *one* PageMaker
page (one at a time, that is; of course
you can make separate files of as many
pages as you like). You can then place the
image in any PageMaker publication. As
an EPS file, you can resize it, stretch it,
crop it, etc., just like any other graphic.
- *The graphic will be as large as the page
it was created on.* If you want a smaller-
sized graphic, change the page size in the
"Page setup" dialog box (from the File
menu) to as small as you can get away with.

Nelson Hawks

"In the 1600s, type foundries grew out of the printing trade. There was no order to the new foundries' product offerings and nothing matched from one foundry to another. If printers limited themselves to one foundry's products, the situation was usually under control; but as soon as another foundry's type was introduced, havoc resulted. No type from any two foundries aligned the same, was the same size, or was even consistent in height; nothing matched. The same faces from different foundries simply could not be used together, and careful attention had to be paid not to mix various foundries' faces when storing type. Even spacing material did not match, which meant that printers had to purchase multiple sets of everything." *

Does that scenario sound familiar? Read it again, substituting "1980s" for "1600s," "vendor" for "foundry," and "Mac user" for "printer."

In the 1400s when a print shop had a job to do, they made their own type for that job. Every print shop made their own type. It wasn't until the early 1600s that Claude Garamond had the idea to create type and sell it to others—the very first type foundry. But as other type foundries developed, type was made in all sorts of ways, as there were no established standards. By the 1800s there were thousands and thousands of print shops all over the world, each with thousands of pounds of metal type that couldn't be consolidated in any way. Oftentimes even the same typeface from the same foundry ordered on two different days didn't match each other. One printer complained in the late 1880s that "there are no two foundries . . . whose body types, either in depth, or in width, are cast by the same standard."

In 1877, Nelson Hawks was a junior partner in Marder, Luse and Company, a large type foundry in Chicago. Nelson was sent to San Francisco to establish a branch office. He was directly confronted with the inventory problems of metal type. So, being a very simple and practical man, he created a solution. Nelson came up with a workable standard, the one we now know and love: points and picas. All he had to do was convince all the printers in the country to adopt the new system.

Mr. Hawks presented the idea to his boss, Mr. Marder. Mr. Marder saw that the time was ripe for this sort of change, and since all their type had been melted in the Great Chicago Fire anyway, he wanted to go into production immediately, patent the system, and establish a monopoly. Marder told Nelson to keep this a great secret.

But Nelson was enthusiastic and altruistic and he thought everyone should know about this new system because it would make everyone's life easier. So when Mr. Marder went back to Chicago, Nelson stayed in California (Alameda, actually) and vigorously promoted this new idea all over the west coast. Of course this irritated his cantankerous partners in Chicago, so Nelson just up and quit. Sold out his interest in 1882 for $12,000. Then he got to do what he really wanted to do: evangelize the point system. He traveled all over America, meeting with the owners of the largest foundries, taking out ads in trade journals, writing letters to every type foundry in the United States. He didn't do it for money—he did it because it was the right thing to do.

Nelson's system did become the standard in America and in Britain, and he was fortunate enough to live to see the day (in fact, he lived to be 89). At the age of 80, Nelson remarked, "The only benefit I have derived from it lies in the satisfaction of having been successful in giving the printing craft something useful and lasting."
Thank you, Nelson.

This passage is from Allan Haley's article in U&lc, May, 1985. Many thanks to Mr. Haley and his historical research for the basis of this article.

Image control
(with the pointer tool, click on a TIFF or paint-type image; from the Element menu, choose "Image control...")

9.118 Image control is a dialog box that allows you to control several aspects of bitmapped graphics (which in PageMaker are the TIFF images). You can use it to change the screen pattern (dots vs. lines), adjust the contrast of the darks and lights, alter the lightness or darkness of the entire image, and change the dot-screen angle and lines-per-inch frequency.

9.119 Image control only works on one image at a time. It doesn't work at all on PICTs, color TIFFs, or graphics pasted from the Scrapbook (PageMaker turns them into PICTs). If you really need to apply image control to a PICT, you can copy the item into a paint program, save it as a TIFF or as a MacPaint file, and then *place* it back into PageMaker (9.168).

9.120 The "Link info" dialog box from the Element menu can tell you the format of the *selected* graphic, next to the label "Kind." If the image is a TIFF, "Kind" will call it "Image" (for Tagged Image File Format). Or you can just pull down the Element menu and see if the "Image control..." command is black; if it is, the *selected* image is a TIFF.

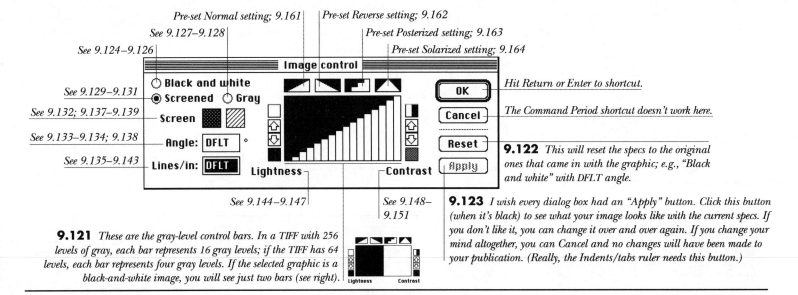

Pre-set Normal setting; 9.161
Pre-set Reverse setting; 9.162
See 9.127–9.128
Pre-set Posterized setting; 9.163
See 9.124–9.126
Pre-set Solarized setting; 9.164

See 9.129–9.131
See 9.132; 9.137–9.139
See 9.133–9.134; 9.138
See 9.135–9.143

Hit Return or Enter to shortcut.

The Command Period shortcut doesn't work here.

9.122 *This will reset the specs to the original ones that came in with the graphic; e.g., "Black and white" with DFLT angle.*

See 9.144–9.147
See 9.148–9.151

9.123 *I wish every dialog box had an "Apply" button. Click this button (when it's black) to see what your image looks like with the current specs. If you don't like it, you can change it over and over again. If you change your mind altogether, you can Cancel and no changes will have been made to your publication. (Really, the Indents/tabs ruler needs this button.)*

9.121 *These are the gray-level control bars. In a TIFF with 256 levels of gray, each bar represents 16 gray levels; if the TIFF has 64 levels, each bar represents four gray levels. If the selected graphic is a black-and-white image, you will see just two bars (see right).*

Image control:
Black and white

9.124 The **Black and white** button is automatically chosen if the selected graphic is a bilevel bitmap (9.6), meaning it is strictly black and white with no gray levels.

9.125 If the image is already "Screened" or "Gray," clicking on the "Black and white" button will convert it to a bilevel image.

"Gray"   *"Black and white"*

9.126 If an image is black and white, your only option in "Image control" is to reverse it; that is, what is black will be white and what is white will be black (9.162).

Image control:
Gray

9.127 The **Gray** button will only be chosen if the selected graphic is a grayscale TIFF *and* you have a grayscale monitor that has the gray levels turned on (from the Control Panel). Without a grayscale monitor, the "Gray" button will be dim, and the "Screened" button will be selected. You can still adjust the gray levels (9.129–9.131; 9.151), you just won't see the effect so clearly on the screen. (Grayscale TIFFs sure do look pretty on a grayscale monitor.)

9.128 With the gray-level control bars (9.121; 9.144–9.151) you can control the lightness and the darkness of the pixels. See 9.152–9.159 for examples.

Image control:
Screened

9.129 The **Screened** button is automatically chosen if you have selected a grayscale TIFF image but you don't have a grayscale monitor. If you leave the "Screen," "Angle," and "Lines/in" options as they are, the grayscale image will reproduce the same as if you had the option of the "Gray" button.

9.130 If the selected object is a black-and-white TIFF, you can click the "Screened" button to apply a halftone to it. This can occasionally bring out some extra detail in the image (9.165), but it comes in most handy when you want to lighten the image. You can lighten it just a touch so the image is not so harsh, or you can lighten it quite a bit so the image becomes just a shadow on the page (9.166).

9.131 If the selected object is a grayscale TIFF, you can use the "Screened" button to apply a halftone to *override* the default settings of the designated printer. For instance, the LaserWriter defaults to a dot pattern, 45° angle, and 53 lines/inch. For a special effect, you might want to apply a line pattern (9.138) with 30 lines/inch; it will replace the LaserWriter's defaults for that particular image.

Image control:
Screen (or pattern)

Screen

Standard dot pattern | Line pattern

9.132 If you applied a halftone screen as you scanned your image, you probably had options as to what sort of pattern to use. If you scanned the image as a grayscale TIFF (which is preferable), PageMaker also gives you options: the standard dot pattern or a line pattern. (They are usually called dot "screens" and line "screens," but many other things are also called screens; to keep the confusion down at the moment, I will refer to them as patterns.) As you click on either of the patterns, it is instantly applied to the image.

Image control:
Angle

Angle: 90 °

9.133 **Angle** refers to the direction in which the dots or lines are lined up. The standard default for black-and-white halftones is 45°. You will rarely need to change it, unless you are doing special effects, or you are fine-tuning patterns on different colors that will be overlaying each other.

9.134 You can specify any angle from 0° through 360°. When the value in this box is **DFLT,** the angle will adjust to whatever the default is for the printer that is printing the publication. Your service bureau can change its imagesetter's default, if necessary.

Image control:
Lines/in

Lines/in: 53

9.135 **Lines/in** refers to the *line frequency,* or how many rows of dots or lines there are in one **inch.** The higher the number, the finer the dot. The finer the dot, the more difficult to print.

9.136 A PostScript printer will automatically apply a default line/inch value as it goes through the printer. The LaserWriter uses 53 lines per inch; a Linotronic uses 150 lines per inch, *generally* (9.142). **Any number you enter in this box will override the printer's default.**

9.137 *The image below is 105 lines per inch, using the standard dot pattern at the standard 45° angle.*

9.138 *The image below is 45 lines per inch, using a line pattern at a 90° angle.*

9.139 *The image below is 53 lines per inch, using a line pattern at a 0° angle.*

Image control:
Lines/in   —continued ▪

9.140 You can enter a line frequency of from 5 through 300 lines per inch. You must keep in mind, however, the printing method you'll be using for final reproduction.

9.141 If you will be using a copy machine to reproduce the work, use a line frequency of not more than 60 to 80. You can go towards the higher end (70 to 80) if the paper from the laser printer and the copy machine are both smooth (not plain ol' copy paper), or if you are printing to a high-resolution imagesetter.

9.142 If you are printing to a high-res imagesetter and a commercial press will be making reproductions, *ask the presspeople* what line screen (frequency) they will prefer for the press. You can either enter that number here in the "Lines/in" edit box, **or** tell your service bureau to print all the screens in your publication at that frequency (18.00–18.00).

9.143 When the value in the edit box is **DFLT,** the frequency will adjust to whatever the default is for the printer that is printing the publication.

Image control:
Lightness ▪

9.144 The **Lightness** control bar adjusts the brightness of the **dark pixels** (dots).

9.145 If your image is **Black-and-white,** you can only adjust this to all or nothing—either your image is black-and-white or it is white-and-black. Click towards the top of the large black bar to switch settings, or click in the pre-set Reverse button (9.162).

9.146 Even though your image is black-and-white, you can click in the "Screened" button and adjust the *lightness.* You still cannot adjust the *contrast,* even though you can move the bar up or down.

9.147 If the **Screened** or **Gray** buttons are selected, you can adjust the varying levels of gray. You can use the little scroll arrow to move the bars, but you will have more control over the individual bars if you just press-and-drag on them. You can start from one bar and just sweep across—the bars will follow the pointer. See the following pages for examples of lightness and contrast settings and how they affect an image.

Image control:
Contrast ▪

9.148 The **Contrast** control bar adjusts the brightness of the **light pixels** (dots).

9.149 If your image is **Black-and-white,** you can only adjust this to all or nothing—either your image is black-and-white or it is white-and-black. Click towards the top of the black chunk to switch settings, or click in the Reverse pre-set button (9.162).

9.150 Even if you halftone your black-and-white image by clicking in the "Screened" button, you can't adjust the contrast because there is no contrast to adjust. Either a pixel is black or it is white; you cannot adjust the levels in-between to make black less of a contrast to white.

9.151 If the **Screened** or **Gray** buttons are selected, you can adjust the varying levels of gray. You can use the little scroll arrow to move the bars, but you will have more control over the individual bars if you just press-and-drag on them. You can start from one bar and just sweep across—the bars will follow the pointer. See the following pages for examples of lightness and contrast settings and how they affect an image.

Image control lightness and contrast settings

9.152 The following are some examples of what to expect with different lightness and contrast settings. These are all printed on a Linotronic (1270 dpi) at a default angle and line frequency (105), unless otherwise noted. Remember, avoid the tendency to make the image appear sharp and crisp on the screen (9.75). In your laser printer proof, you want to be able to see a few white dots in the black areas, and a few black dots in the white areas, realizing that those few tiny dots will probably disappear when it gets reproduced, and the general contrast will be sharpened even more when it goes through the printing press or the copy machine.

9.153 It takes a good deal of experimentation and experience to get these controls adjusted so you know what to expect. And even then, often it's a surprise. And you're never quite satisfied. Well, that's what we get for being on the cutting edge. I'm sure Gutenberg felt the same way, trying to get the ink just right for the impressions on varying types of paper.

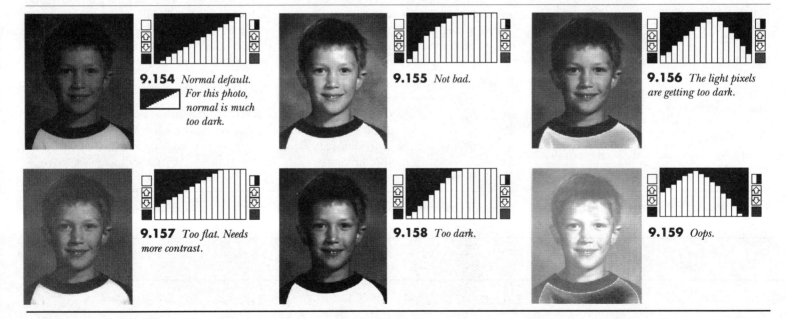

9.154 *Normal default. For this photo, normal is much too dark.*

9.155 *Not bad.*

9.156 *The light pixels are getting too dark.*

9.157 *Too flat. Needs more contrast.*

9.158 *Too dark.*

9.159 *Oops.*

Pre-set settings

9.160 For any of these pre-set settings, simply click in the little icon in the "Image control" diaog box. Then you can adjust individual bars, if necessary. These were all printed on a Linotronic, 1270 dpi, with a 105-line screen (frequency) with the default angle.

Normal

9.161 *This is a Normal setting for comparison. This is Serena Pickering Catt, my great-great-great-grandmother. My alter ego. They say I'm her spittin' image.*

Reverse

9.162 *This is a pre-set Reverse setting. All the white pixels are now black, and all the black pixels are now white. This is probably a fair representation of what Serena looks like at the moment.*

Posterized

9.163 *This is a pre-set Posterized setting. Serena would probably like this view of herself— strong, sharp, no nonsense.*

Solarized

9.164 *This is a pre-set Solarized setting. A little too psychedelic for Serena.*

If you want to do this:	Then follow these steps:	Shortcuts ▾ Notes ▾ Hints

Image control

9.165 Adjust the appearance of a TIFF image

- With the **pointer tool,** click once on *one* graphic.
- From the Element menu, choose "Image control...." If the command is gray, either you have selected more than one graphic, or the image you selected is not a bitmapped (TIFF) image. If it's not a TIFF, you can't image control it; see 9.168 for turning another sort of graphic format into a controllable TIFF graphic.
- In the "Image control" dialog box, adjust everything to your liking. Segments 9.118–9.164 explain, and give examples for, all those mysterious controls.
- Regularly click the "Apply" button to see how you are affecting the image. When you like it, or at least when you are through controlling, click OK.

A good laugh is a mighty good thing, and rather too scarce a good thing; the more's the pity. So, if any one man, in his own proper person, afford stuff for a good joke to anybody, let him not be backward, but let him cheerfully allow himself to spend and to be spent in that way, and the man that has anything bountifully laughable about him, be sure there is more in that man than you perhaps think for.

—Herman Melville
Moby Dick

If you want to do this:

Then follow these steps:

Shortcuts ▾ Notes ▾ Hints

9.166 Lighten a TIFF or paint-type image to a shadow so you can print text right over the top of it

The setting below produced the shadow on the left.

Black-and-white TIFF

The setting below produced the shadow on the left.

Grayscale TIFF

- Select the graphic and open the "Image control" dialog box, as noted in 9.165.
- If the image is **black-and-white,** click the button "Screened."
  □ Choose whether you want the dot screen or the line screen (9.132–9.139).
  □ Drag the first control bar, the "Lightness" bar, upward. You can use the little scroll arrows, but you'll have more control if you just press-and-drag the bar itself (9.121).
  □ Press the "Apply" button to see the effect. When it's appropriate, click OK.
- If the image is a **grayscale,** the button "Gray" should already be selected.
  □ Position the pointer tool in the first of the bars, on the far left. Press the mouse button, and sweep across the bars to get the same general pattern you see on the left. You can also adjust each bar individually.
  □ Experiment with the bars, clicking "Apply" regularly to check it out. When you like it, click OK.
- You can return to "Image control" at any time (when the image is selected, of course) and re-adjust the settings.

If you want to do this:	Then follow these steps:	Shortcuts ▾ Notes ▾ Hints
9.167 Return a TIFF image to its original specifications	■ With the **pointer tool,** click on the graphic. ■ From the Element menu, choose "Image control…." ■ Click the "Reset" button. Click OK.	■ This Reset button will return the graphic to the specs it came into PageMaker with.

9.168 Turn a PICT or EPS graphic into a TIFF so you can image-control it

EPS graphic

EPS turned TIFF

PICT graphic

PICT turned TIFF

■ Simply click once on the graphic with the **pointer tool.**
■ Copy it (Command C).
■ Paste it into a paint program. DeskPaint™ is a great little desk accessory for this, if you have enough memory to use it in combination with PageMaker. Save the graphic as a TIFF or as a MacPaint file.
■ Back in PageMaker, *place* the graphic as you would any other (9.92). It is now a TIFF.

■ If your original image for the PICT was bitmapped (which it really shouldn't be), this procedure will be acceptable. If the original was a nice, smooth draw-type or EPS image, you may be disappointed in the results, because converting the graphic to a TIFF converts it to a bitmap, as you can see in the examples to the left. This may be all right in some cases, especially if you are going to screen it way back to a dim shadow, or if it was bitmapped in the first place.

If you want to do this:

9.169 Lighten a PICT to a shadow

Edit color		OK
Name: 20%		Cancel
Model: ○ RGB ○ HLS ● CMYK		PANTONE®...
Cyan:	0 %	
Magenta:	0 %	
Yellow:	0 %	
Black:	20 %	

The "Edit color" dialog box, useful for specifying tints.

Then follow these steps:

- You can't use image control on a PICT, but you *can* apply a black tint screen. If you have black tint screens already in your Color palette, just select the image and then select the tint. If you need to make a tint to apply, follow these steps:
- From the Element menu, choose "Define colors...."
- Click "New...."
- Click the "CMYK" button.
- Type in a name that will give you a clue as to what tint this is, such as "20%."
- Hit the Tab key. Type 0 (zero).
- Hit the Tab key. Type 0 (zero).
- Hit the Tab key. Type 0 (zero).
- Hit the Tab key. Type 20 (or any number that gives the tint value you want; the example is 20%). Your dialog box should look like the one on the left.
- Press Option Return (to close both boxes).
- From the Windows menu, choose "Color palette," *or* press Command K.
- With the **pointer tool,** click once on the PICT you want to lighten.
- In the Color palette, click on the name of the tint you just made.
- On a monochrome screen, the image will look solid black, but on a PostScript printer it will print in the tint (see left).

Shortcuts ▾ Notes ▾ Hints

- This doesn't really come under the topic of "Image control," but I thought you might get frustrated trying to screen back (lighten) an image other than a TIFF, so I included it here. You'll find more detailed info on tints in Section 14 on Color.

Inline graphics

9.170 Inline graphics are one of the very greatest features of PageMaker 4.0. Any graphic that can be placed or pasted independently, or that can be drawn in PageMaker, can also be placed or pasted *inline;* that is, imbedded as part of the text. When it is inline, a graphic will move along with the text as it is edited. And then it can also be cut, copied, and pasted along with the text it rides with.

9.171 An inline graphic can take on some text attributes, but can also be manipulated as a graphic. To apply text attributes, select the inline graphic with the text tool; to apply graphic attributes, select the inline graphic with the pointer tool. (Selecting an inline graphic with the pointer tool selects *just* the graphic, not the text block; to select the text block, click in the text area or Command-click on the graphic until you see handles on the text block.)

9.172 Since an inline graphic is part of the text, you can include it in tracking, kerning, leading, leading method, word and letter spacing, and color. It will align with tabs, will move over with the spacebar or any hard spaces (4.207–4.218), and will respond to Returns and indents. It will

listen to paragraph-level formatting, such as space before and after, keeps controls, and alignment. (Are you thinking that you can imbed a graphic into a text block and then rotate the text block, thus getting a rotated graphic? You can't.)

9.173 You cannot apply a point size to inline graphics, nor a font, nor a style, such as bold or italic. You cannot use super- or subscript options to reposition the graphic. You cannot rotate a text block containing an inline graphic.

9.174 As a graphic, you can crop it; resize it; cut, copy, and paste it; adjust the resolution; apply color; and modify it with image control (if it's a TIFF). If the graphic is a PageMaker-drawn object, you can change its line widths and corners.

9.175 You *cannot* apply a text wrap. The "Bring to front" and "Send to back" commands don't work on inline graphics, either, except as part of the entire text block.

9.176 An inline graphic has a *boundary* around it, just like any other graphic, indicated by its handles. This boundary is sometimes wrapped directly around the image itself, but oftentimes is much larger than the

graphic. This can create problems, because the boundary is what determines the space between the graphic and the text, the tab, the indent, etc. The simple solution is to crop the excess away from the graphic (9.104). You can do this before or after you place the graphic inline.

The text cannot get closer to the actual image than the boundary (indicated by the eight handles).

After cropping the boundary away, you have more options for spacing the graphic.

9.177 An inline graphic also has its own *baseline,* which is two-thirds of the distance from the top of the graphic boundary (assuming you are using the Proportional leading method; 4.46–4.51), just as text has its baseline two-thirds of the distance down from the top of its leading slug (4.47). You can actually adjust the baseline of the graphic by moving the graphic up or down (9.188–9.189; 9.201).

Inline graphics —*continued*

9.178 Inline graphics, like paragraph rules or oversized initial caps, can hang outside of the text block. Whenever anything hangs outside the text block, it usually disappears until you redraw the screen. So if part of your graphic melts on you, either click in the zoom box (upper right of the window), change page views, re-choose the same page view (it's quick and easy to use the Command-key equivalent), or select the text block with the pointer tool and press Command F ("Bring to front").

9.179 In the **Story Editor** (Section 8), an inline graphic will appear as a little box (▓), as shown below. While in the Story Editor, to place a graphic inline you must "Import," not "Place"; see 9.194. The Story Editor is a good place to find all those inline graphics that were supposed to be independent graphics.

A Story Editor window, showing what an inline graphic looks like in a window view.

9.180 Because the graphic is actually part of the text block, when you place or paste it, the graphic drops in at the insertion point, just as with text. This means that you have to be conscious of whether and where the insertion point is flashing, even (and especially) if you are not *intending* to set an inline graphic.

9.181 Count how many times you accidentally place an inline graphic when you want an independent one, before you finally get in the habit of clicking the pointer tool before you paste or place. It's important to be conscious of where you are placing your graphics; if you accidentally place a large graphic inline that is too big for the text block, the text block rolls up and you don't see what happened. Or, what's really killer is leaving a flashing insertion point *on another page,* and pasting a graphic. You don't see the graphic anywhere, so you think maybe you did something wrong and you paste it again. Eventually you figure it out, but by then the text block on the other page has rolled up and you can't find the images. Or if the graphic was really big, you can't even unroll the text block big enough

to find the graphic and delete it. One of my favorite learning experiences was when I inadvertently placed my entire Scrapbook of 43 items into a text block. See 9.198 for some tips on how to get out of predicaments like that (use the Story Editor). Yes, as Mr. Cella said, "Experience is what you get—when you don't get what you want."

9.182 A most important tip: If the graphic is large and you need to significantly resize it, do the resizing *before* you paste it inline. If you don't, the graphic sometimes can't find room to squeeze in and so it keeps going deeper and deeper into the text block. I've lost 'em over 17 inches deep.

What to expect with inline graphics

9.183 Most of the images you see in this book are inline, especially the ones in the "If you want to do this" column, or the ones right in the text line itself, like this: . As the text gets edited, reformatted, cut and pasted, moved, etc., the graphic just goes right along with the flow. Amazing.

9.184 Even a little graphic, as the one in the paragraph above, usually carries with it a larger leading than in the text. As you know, the line will adjust to the larger

leading, creating this ☕ sort of look between the lines, which probably isn't quite what you want. The solution is exactly the same as with text that has a larger character in it: used fixed leading instead of auto leading (9.189).

9.185 If the graphic is significantly larger than the text, though, even the fixed-leading technique won't work because the graphic will overlap the text. On the screen at first it may look like the graphic is getting chopped off, but as soon as the screen redraws the graphic pops out in full. It may be transparent, or it may be opaque, depending on where it originated.

9.186 Because the graphic is basically a large text character, it's not so easy to put a couple of lines directly next to it, like a caption. This is what generally happens, even with the second line tabbed over:

        Alien creatures found

frolicking in the park.

9.187 You can, though, with intelligent use of the tabs and indents ruler, create a "hanging" graphic off the side of a paragraph (9.205), like so *(this greatest of tricks was invented by Olav Martin Kvern)*:

  The crow doth sing as sweetly as the lark, when neither is attended, and I think the nightingale, if she should sing by day, when every goose is cackling, would be thought no better a musician than the wren. How many things by season season'd are to their right praise and true perfection!

  A man may fish with the worm that hath eat of a king, and eat of the fish that hath fed of that worm.

William Shakespeare

9.188 When an inline graphic is in a text block, it is possible to adjust its baseline in connection with the other text on the line; that is, you can move it up and down to a certain extent. The following paragraph has an inline graphic with *auto leading:*

  I am a woman of the world, Hector;

and I can assure you that if you will only take the trouble always to do the perfectly correct thing, and to say the perfectly correct thing, you can do just what you like.

George Bernard Shaw
Heartbreak House

9.189 If you use *fixed leading* (triple-click on the paragraph before changing the leading; 4.25–4.26), you can use the pointer tool to press-and-drag on the graphic (9.201) up or down, above or below its natural baseline. Notice the difference in this version:

  I am a woman of the world, Hector; and I can assure you that if you will only take the trouble always to do the perfectly correct thing, and to say the perfectly correct thing, you can do just what you like.

George Bernard Shaw
Heartbreak House

If you want to do this:	Then follow these steps:	Shortcuts ▪ Notes ▪ Hints

Inline graphics

9.190 Paste a graphic inline

- This segment assumes you already have something on the Clipboard to paste (1.184–1.192).
- With the **text tool,** click in the text at the point where you want to insert the graphic. You can create a *new* text block for the graphic (click outside of any existing text) or create a bounding box (3.58).
- With the insertion point flashing, press Command V (*or* from the Edit menu, choose "Paste").
- You may need to adjust the graphic; see the following segments for resizing, replacing, moving, etc.

- If the graphic is fairly large, paste it on the page as an independent graphic first (simply by clicking on the **pointer tool** before you paste). Resize the graphic to approximately the size you will need (9.101), cut it, *then* follow these steps to paste it in.

9.191 Place a graphic inline

- With the **text tool,** click in the text at the point where you want to insert the graphic. You can create a *new* text block for the graphic (click outside of any existing text) or create a bounding box (3.58).
- From the File menu, choose "Place...."
- Find the graphic file you want to place and click once on it.
- Select the button "As inline graphic."
- Click OK, **or** double-click on the file name. It will appear at the insertion point.

- Placing a graphic inline involves exactly the same process as placing a graphic independently, or as placing text. If the graphic is fairly large, you might want to take note of the tip directly above (9.190).

If you want to do this:	Then follow these steps:	Shortcuts ▾ Notes ▾ Hints
9.192 Replace an existing inline graphic with another graphic file	■ With the **pointer tool,** click once on the inline graphic; **or** with the **text tool,** double-click on the inline graphic. If you have more than one graphic *in a row* to select, you must press-and-drag with the text tool, as you cannot use the Shift-click technique to select more than one inline graphic at a time. ■ From the File menu, choose "Place...." ■ Find the file you want to place, and click once on it. ■ Click in the button "Replacing entire graphic." ■ Click OK, or double-click on the file name. ■ The new graphic will replace the old one, and will take on all its formatting—size, image control, cropping, etc.	■ Please note an important distinction between replacing an existing inline graphic by *placing* a graphic file or by *pasting* an item from the Clipboard or Scrapbook (9.95): when you *place,* the new graphic takes on the size and formatting of the old one. When you *paste,* the new graphic just drops in, ignoring any specifications of the old one, including its size and cropping.
9.193 Replace an existing inline graphic with another graphic from the Clipboard	■ In order to replace the inline graphic with a graphic from the Clipboard, you must select the existing one with the **text tool,** not the pointer tool. Either double-click on it or press-and-drag over it. ■ From the Edit menu, choose "Paste," *or* press Command V. ■ When you *paste* the new graphic, it does *not* take on the formatting of the one it replaces.	■ See the note above.

If you want to do this: ■	Then follow these steps: ■	Shortcuts ▾ Notes ▾ Hints ■
9.194 Import (place) an inline graphic into the Story Editor	■ While in the Story Editor (Section 8), click in the text at the point where you want the graphic to be placed.	■ See Section 8 for full details on the Story Editor.

Table continued:

9.194 Import (place) an inline graphic into the Story Editor

```
≡□≡≡ To the right you se:1 ≡≡≡□≡
Body      To the right you see
          the charming face of
          Charles Lindberg:  ■
Body      What a cutie-patootie.
```

■ While in the Story Editor (Section 8), click in the text at the point where you want the graphic to be placed.
■ From the Story menu (not the File menu!), choose "Import...."
■ You will get what looks like the Place dialog box. Find the file you want to import and click once on it.
■ The button "As inline graphic" will be selected. That's your only choice.
■ Click OK, *or* double-click on the file name. You won't get the loaded graphic icon— you will just see the little box appear at the insertion point. When you go back to layout view you'll see the graphic in all its splendor. Which may surprise you.

■ See Section 8 for full details on the Story Editor.

9.195 Resize an inline graphic

■ With the **pointer tool,** click on the graphic.
■ Resize an inline graphic just as you resize any graphic (9.101–9.103). It will respond to Shift-resizing to keep its proportions. If the graphic is a TIFF, you can Command-Shift-resize to adjust the resolution to match your printer (9.103).

If you want to do this:	Then follow these steps:	Shortcuts ▾ Notes ▾ Hints
9.196 Cut or copy an inline graphic	■ With the **text tool,** double-click on the graphic, or press-and-drag over it; **or** with the **pointer tool,** click once on the graphic. ■ From the Edit menu, cut or copy as usual.	■ No matter which tool you use, the graphic will paste back in at the size it was when you cut or copied. It will even keep your cropping changes.
9.197 Delete an inline graphic	■ With the **text tool,** double-click on the graphic, or press-and-drag over it; **or** with the **pointer tool,** click once on the graphic. ■ Hit the Backspace/Delete key.	■ You cannot Shift-click with the pointer tool to select a group of inline graphics. It *is* possible to press-and-drag over several of them in a row with the text tool.
9.198 Delete an inline graphic you can't see because it is too big or it disappeared somewhere or there's so many of them you can't select them all at once	■ You can try widening the text block to find the graphic, and then delete it as above. **Or,** if that's not possible, do this: ■ With the **pointer tool,** triple-click on the text block, just above where you think the graphic disappeared; **or** with the **text tool,** click the insertion point in the text and press Command E. Either method will bring up the Story Editor. ■ In the Story Editor you will see little boxes (▓). Each one represents an inline graphic. ■ Select the graphic by double-clicking on it, or pressing-and-dragging over a group. Unfortunately, you can't tell one graphic from another in the Story Editor. But by the time you resort to this trick, you often don't care. Get rid of 'em all and start over. ■ Press Command E to get back to the publication page.	■ I must be sadistic. I love to see a roomful of people going nuts because they keep accidentally pasting graphics inline. It just cracks me up to see those bewildered and sometimes panic-stricken faces. I guess I enjoy seeing it because I have done it myself so many times that I find it satisfying to know it's not really stupidity that causes that to happen.

If you want to do this:	Then follow these steps:	Shortcuts ▾ Notes ▾ Hints

9.199 Move an inline graphic horizontally	■ You can't *drag* the graphic horizontally with the pointer tool, but you can *push* it over with hard spaces (4.207–4.216).
	  □ If the graphic is left-aligned and you want to move it to the right, insert hard spaces *before* the graphic.
	  □ If the graphic is right-aligned and you want to move it to the left, insert hard spaces *after* the graphic.
	■ You can also use tabs; in fact, you can get incredibly precise placement with tabs, since the tabs/indents ruler allows you to type in exact measurements (5.55).
	■ If you place the graphic in its own paragraph (hit a Return before and after you place it), you can then align it left, right, or centered (9.203), between the text block handles.
		■ Each graphic has a boundary around it. Some graphics have quite a bit of excess boundary area, while others have handles directly on the edges of the image itself (9.176). It is the *boundary* that is aligned on the left or right or top or bottom, *not* the actual image that you can see (9.202). If there is too much space around your graphic, use the cropping tool and crop that excess away (9.104; 9.202).

"Printing has been styled 'The telescope of the soul.'
As the optical instrument brings near and magnifies
objects remote and invisible, so printing puts us in
communication with minds of the past and present,
and preserves the thoughts of this age for future
generations."   —Emily C. Pearson, 1871

| **If you want to do this:** | **Then follow these steps:** | **Shortcuts ▼ Notes ▼ Hints** |

9.200 Step-and-repeat inline graphics horizontally, like so:

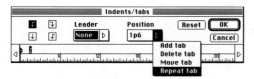

When you choose to repeat a tab, it is repeated across the ruler, either the distance from the selected tab to the next tab to its left, or the distance from the selected tab to the left margin, if there are no other tabs in-between.

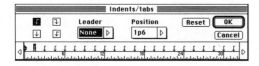

When you repeat a tab, any existing tabs to the right are removed. Any existing tabs to the left will remain.

- Actually, the rows of ducks were created simply by pasting the images in at repeated tabs. First resize your image small enough (9.101), and crop the excess boundary, if necessary (9.104; 9.176). Copy the graphic to the Clipboard (click on it with the **pointer tool** and press Command C).
- With the **text tool,** click to set an insertion point where you are going to paste.
- Press Command I to get the indents/tabs ruler.
- Click in the ruler where you want the first graphic to align. Click in the ruler where you want the second graphic to align, making sure to leave enough room between the two for the graphic.
- In the Position edit box, press on the little arrow to get the submenu; slide down and choose "Repeat tab." Tabs will repeat across the ruler in increments identical to the distance between the first two. Click OK.
- Hit the Tab key; press Command V. Repeat the Tab key and the Copy command until you have your row of inline graphics. If you hit a Return at the end of the line, you can continue to paste at the same tabs. Or just copy the first line and paste it in repeatedly.

- See Section 5 on Indents and Tabs for full details on using the tabs ruler.
- You *could* use power-paste to create a single step-and-repeat graphic (1.194–1.195), group the objects into one single image (9.108), then paste *that* graphic inline. An advantage to using a step-and-repeat with tabs, though, is that after you have the rows of them you can adjust the space between, above, or below them; you can eliminate some of the graphics, enlarge or reduce others, etc. Which method you use depends on your final objective.

If you want to do this:	Then follow these steps:	Shortcuts ▾ Notes ▾ Hints

9.201 Adjust the baseline of an inline graphic

WORK HARD. THERE IS NO SHORTCUT.

Alfred P. Sloan, Jr.

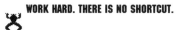

WORK HARD. THERE IS NO SHORTCUT.

Alfred P. Sloan, Jr.

WORK HARD. THERE IS NO SHORTCUT.

Alfred P. Sloan, Jr.

■ With the **pointer tool,** press on an inline graphic. You will see the pointer turn into this cursor: ↕

■ This cursor symbolizes the graphic, with the baseline positioned two-thirds of the way from the top. As you press, you can drag the graphic up and down on its baseline.

■ Play with this for a while to see how adjoining text reacts to the graphic as it moves—sometimes it goes up, sometimes it goes down, sometimes it seems like it bounces right back where it came from. The examples on the left all have exactly the same text formatting—same leading (Auto), size, paragraph space, etc.; the only difference is that the frog has been moved up or down.

The frog graphic is seen as one large character on the line, and its Autoleading takes over. When you use an inline graphic in a body of text, you will usually want to use fixed leading, rather than Autoleading (4.19–4.26). The examples in 9.189 and 9.205 both use fixed leading.

■ Remember, the baseline is determined by the size of the graphic *boundary* (9.176). If there is excess white space inside the boundary of the graphic, you may want to crop it away (9.104).

If you want to do this:

9.202 Precisely adjust the space above and below an inline graphic *that is in its own paragraph*

a) *An inline graphic showing its boundary handles, and the leading slug that adds the Autoleading value (in this example, 120%) onto the graphic.*

b) *The same inline graphic with its excess boundary cropped, and with the auto leading changed to 100%.*

Then follow these steps:

- An inline graphic has its own baseline. Its baseline, as with text, is determined by the leading slug (4.32). In a graphic, the leading (autoleading of 120%; 4.20) is added onto the outer boundary (9.176). The outer boundary may be larger than the image itself, as shown on the left. Thus it is difficult to determine the precise baseline, and to add or delete specific amounts of linespace above or below the image.
- So, there are two things you can do for yourself. I'd advise you to do both.
  □ One, crop the boundary down to as close to the actual image as possible (9.104; 9.176).
  □ Two, change the autoleading value, from the default 120%, to 100%:
    ▾ With the **text tool,** select the graphic.
    ▾ From the Type menu, choose "Paragraph...," *or* press Command M.
    ▾ Click on the "Spacing..." button.
    ▾ In the "Autoleading" edit box, type in the number 100. Press Option Return to close both dialog boxes.
- Now the leading slug will be the exact size of the graphic. You can then add paragraph space before and after (4.63–4.87) to create exactly as much space above and below your graphic as you like.

Shortcuts ▾ Notes ▾ Hints

- If you find you need to use this technique on a regular basis, create a style (Section 7) with an autoleading of 100% that you can apply to the paragraph containing the graphic. You will still have to crop any excess boundary space yourself.
- When you create the graphic in whatever program, push the image into the upper left corner before you save. This simple move will often save you the trouble of having to crop off the excess boundary space later.

This "feature" was first discovered by Olav Martin Kvern. Thanks, Ole!

If you want to do this:

Then follow these steps:

Shortcuts ▾ Notes ▾ Hints

9.203 Perfectly center an inline graphic in a text block

Remember, this is centered between the text block handles. *If you want to center it on* a column *you must stretch the text block handles to align with the column guides.*

- Simply paste the graphic into its own text block (or its own paragraph in an existing text block, if that will work). Make sure both the left and right handles of the text block are on the guidelines between which you want to center the image.
- Crop (9.104) any excess boundary space (9.176), as it will affect the centeredness.
- With the insertion point flashing in the graphic's paragraph, press Command M to get the Paragraph dialog box.
- Make sure the "Indents" edit boxes all have zeros in them. If not, enter zeros.
- Next to "Alignment," press to get the submenu; choose "Centered." Click OK.
- If the graphic still doesn't look quite centered, check to make sure you haven't added any spaces in front of or following the graphic, as PageMaker will center those along with the image itself.

- It's frustrating to try to center a graphic horizontally on the page, isn't it? Those nice little centered handles that show up when you select a graphic always disappear when you try to move the image. Whenever it's possible to use this technique, it sure works great.
- As with any centered alignment, PageMaker centers the item *between the text handles,* not between any guidelines or column guides.

9.204 Use image control on an inline graphic

- Use image control on an inline graphic just exactly as you would on an independent graphic (9.118–9.168). The same limitations and restrictions apply.

If you want to do this:

9.205 Set an inline graphic to the side of a paragraph

Aldus Manutius
The dictionary defines this man as "an Italian printer and classical scholar." See page 131 for an in-depth account of this interesting human being.

Claude Garamond
You probably thought Claude designed the typeface *Garamond,* which is the official typeface of Apple Computer, Inc. Wrong again, dear. Beatrice Ward successfully proved, in 1926, that Jean Jannon was the artful designer, 80 years after Claude himself died in 1561.

Scarlett Williams
Isn't she the cutest little thing you ever did see? And she is just as sweet as she is cute.

Then follow these steps:

- Each of the examples to the left have the same tab and indent setup. The inline graphic has been moved up or down (9.201). The first example uses auto leading; the other two use fixed leading (4.19–4.26).
- This paragraph is set up with a hanging indent (5.52). If you want a similar effect, this is how to arrange the ruler:

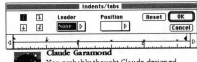

- Set the first-line indent (top triangle) at the far left margin.
- Set the left indent (bottom triangle) where you want the text to align.
- Position a tab directly on the left indent (½").
- Paste in the graphic at the first-line indent (at zero). Hit a Tab to move the insertion point to the left indent. Then type the text, and as it word wraps, it will align at the left indent. Fix the leading and adjust the baseline, if necessary. Piece of cake.

Shortcuts ▾ Notes ▾ Hints

- Re: auto and fixed leading:
  When a line uses auto leading, the space between the lines will adjust to accommodate the largest character; in the case of mixing inline graphics with text, the graphic is generally the largest character. When you paste a graphic inline, the larger auto leading of the graphic will override any existing fixed leading *(any leading value other than "Auto")* that may be attributed to the rest of the text. *So,* the thing to do is fix the leading *after* you place or paste the graphic: get the graphic into the paragraph, then triple-click on the paragraph with the text tool; apply the leading value (4.25).

10 ▾ Linking Text & Graphics

10.1 Minimums and maximums:

Item	Minimum	Maximum
Number of files that can be linked	0	32,767
Size of files that can be linked	Unlimited	

Note: Text files and EPS graphic files are always stored in the publication.

10.2 PageMaker 4.0 automatically **links** all text and graphics that you place in your publication. They are linked to their original, external files. Through the link, PageMaker keeps track of any changes that you make in the original text or graphic file and generally gives you a *choice* (10.59) of whether to update the publication version with the original, changed version.

10.3 If you choose, you can completely ignore the linking function and everything will operate as if linking didn't exist. If you don't change the link defaults (10.64), you'll never know it's working and it will never bother you. If you are just starting to work with PageMaker and are having trouble coping with its magnitude, this section is one you can return to later, after you've gotten a handle on everything else.

10.4 If you are working in a group, where several writers are revising text, several artists are working on graphics, and others are laying out the publication, this linking feature can be invaluable. With sensible use of it, you can keep track of which versions of the text or graphics have been updated, which have been modified but are not updated, which are missing their original versions, and other link management tasks.

About linking

10.5   You can link files that you bring into PageMaker through the "Place..." dialog box *or* in the Story Editor through the "Import..." dialog box (both commands are found in the File menu).

10.6   All placed text and graphics are *automatically* linked as you drop them into PageMaker. As soon as the placed document is in PageMaker, she sees it as having two parts: an internal file that is on the publication page, and an external file that is tucked away on a disk somewhere. Page-Maker keeps track of the *name* and the *location* of each external file (that is, in which folder and on which disk, whether hard or floppy). It's important to remember that PageMaker keeps track of the name and the location: if you change the name of the external file or if you move it, the link is broken. You can always re-establish a broken link (10.56).

10.7   Graphics or text that you *copy* from any other program or from the Scrapbook, then *paste* into PageMaker, will *not* have links established. The original must be a separate file stored on a disk in a definable location.

10.8   However, if you cut or copy graphics or an entire story from your PageMaker publication—*graphics or stories that already have links established*—the link information will also transfer when you paste them; that is, the pasted text or graphics will also be linked to the *original,* external files.

10.9   You can also *change* the links (10.44; 10.57). PageMaker doesn't really care what you link to what; if you say, "Link this to that," she'll do it (as long as you connect a graphic to a graphic and text to text). The link is only connected to a file with that particular name in that particular folder on that particular disk. If you put another file in the same location with the same name, then *that* new file is the one that will be linked to the publication. When you open the publication, PageMaker will notice that something has been changed and will ask if you want to update to the new version.

10.10   Text originally typed directly in PageMaker has no link to any external file. However, you can *create* a link, in case you may need to use that text in other publications. You need to export the story as a word-processing file (10.51). Then you can place it into the other publications, if you like. PageMaker will establish the link to the *external text file,* not to the original, internal PageMaker story.

10.11   If you happen to remove or lose or throw away an external file that is linked to a PageMaker publication, in most cases it is not a big deal (as long as you don't need the external changes). All text files and all EPS graphic files have their complete copies stored within the publication anyway (10.15–10.22), so what you see in the publication will print. Any other (non-EPS) graphic that is stored in the publication will also print as you see it. So the only problem you may run into is if you lose the external version of a high-resolution graphic file that is *not* stored in the publication—all you will be able to print is the low-res screen version.

Updating links

10.12 When you open a publication in 4.0, PageMaker looks for any links that have been established and then follows your instructions on how to deal with them. If you have never gone into any of the Links dialog boxes and fiddled around, then you won't notice any difference between opening a publication with links and opening one without links. See also 10.15–10.22.

10.13 If you do want to be in control of the links and take advantage of their power, you need to establish a *management system* (which is only a fancy term for deciding whether to update the files or not). You can choose to update the internal file in one of several ways:

a You can set an **application default** (10.64) that will check every link whenever a publication is opened and, if there are changes to an external file, will update the internal file. You can choose to have this done automatically upon opening a publication, or you can choose to have PageMaker ask if you really do want each update. As an application default, it will apply to every publication you create *from that point on.*

b You can set a **publication default** (10.65) for the link update options that will do the same as an application default, but it will only apply to the current publication. That is, the next time you open that particular publication, all links will either be automatically updated, or you will be asked for permission to update. A publication default will override any application default.

c You can set **separate** link update options for each text or graphic file (10.53) within the publication. When the publication is next opened, these options instruct PageMaker whether to update the link automatically, or to let you know before it gets updated. Individualized options will override any defaults.

d While you are working within a publication, you can choose to instantly update any or all files that you know (or you discover) have been changed externally (10.59).

e Also while you are working within a publication, you can choose to link an internal file to a *different* file altogether. This not only changes the link, it changes the internal file itself, right in front of your very eyes (10.57). Keep in mind, though, that as soon as you change the link, the new text or graphic file drops into the place of the first one. If it is a story, the new file takes on all the exisiting text attributes of the one it is replacing in the publication (unless you "Retained the format" when you originally placed it; 3.51). If it is a graphic image, the new file takes on the size and proportions of the one it is replacing.

10.14 Important note: If you made changes to the *internal version* of a Page-Maker story while in the publication, and then updated it with the changes that came from the *external version,* any alterations you made to the *internal version* will be lost. There is no automatic way to combine the revisions made within PageMaker with the revisions in the external file—the *external file* will always override the *internal file.* (See 10.61 to update the external version with the internal version.)

"Store copy in publication": updating links and missing links

10.15 PageMaker always stores complete copies of any text file or any EPS graphic file directly in the publication; that is, they just become part of the publication itself. If you copy the publication to another disk, all the text and EPS files that are part of it will be included in that copy. PageMaker maintains a link to their external files, though, in case you want to make any updates.

10.16 You can choose, through the "Link options" dialog box, whether or not to store a complete copy of other graphic files in the publication (10.47). If you do choose to store them, the publication size will grow that much larger, which can cause PageMaker to slow down, as well as cause the pub to become so large you would have trouble backing it up conveniently. (Remember to compress TIFF files before you place them; 9.109–9.110).

10.17 If you choose *not* to store graphic files, you will see the low-resolution version on the screen (to view a temporary high-res version of grayscale TIFFs, see 9.115). When you print, PageMaker will find the external, linked, complete version and use that data for printing, regardless of the screen version. So make sure you keep all your links

connected by not renaming them or removing them from their folder. If you do have to rename or move them, be sure to re-establish the links (10.56).

10.18 Now, there seems to be a Catch-22 here. As PageMaker opens the publication, any file that is stored *within* is left as is. If there is a file that has its only copy stored *outside* the publication (a non-EPS graphic file), that external file is the only one PageMaker can use to open the publication. Thus, any revisions to the original, external file *are automatically transferred to the publication version, without even asking your permission!* If you do not store a copy in the publication, you cannot *choose* to update and be alerted. As the pub opens, you will see a tiny, brief message flash by, then lo and behold, your image is changed. The response to this can range anywhere from surprise to irritation to homocidal threats.

10.19 There are two ways to prevent surprise revisions. One is to store the copy in the publication, then choose to update and be alerted before the update. But storing all of the graphics in the pub can create gargantuan files (in this book, Section 9 alone, without storing the files, with every

TIFF compressed, and without including fonts, is almost five megabytes—aack!).

10.20 A second way to prevent surprise revisions is to store the copy outside the publication, then make sure that any revisions that are not final do not *replace* the original, external version. You can do this by naming them something different, like "Graphic 2.1" and "Graphic 2.2." When you decide you *do* want to update, change the link to the new version (10.57).

10.21 As PageMaker opens the publication, she looks for the links. If she **cannot find a link** to a file that is **stored** in the publication, she quietly puts a question mark next to the file name in the "Links" dialog box (10.28). If you previously selected an automatic update on that file (10.53), PageMaker will ask you to find the missing link. When you establish a new link by selecting a file in the list, the internal file gets updated.

10.22 If PageMaker **can't find a link** to a file that is **not stored** in the pub, she gives you an alert box informing you that the link can't be found, asking you to ignore or re-establish the link. If you previously selected the update option, the file will be updated automatically as the link is re-established.

Printing linked files

10.23 When you choose to print, Page-Maker first looks for all the linked files in the places where they are supposed to be. If they are not there, she then checks the folder that holds the publication itself. If they are not there, she gives you a warning:

10.24 You can Cancel the printing and go back to re-establish the missing links (10.56) or update the file (10.59), and try printing again. Or you can ignore the warning and print anyway. You will see this warning even if you are printing only one page out of a multi-page publication. *It doesn't necessarily mean that the page you are printing is missing a link;* it just means that somewhere in the entire publication some link is amiss.

10.25 If you are taking your publication to another printer for output, either to a service bureau or to a do-it-yourself place, you must make sure to bring all the linked files. If PageMaker cannot find the external version of a high-resolution graphic, the printer will only print the low-resolution screen version. (Actually, the only linked files that are critical are the non-EPS graphic files that do not have copies stored in the publication.)

10.26 See 10.62 for an easy way to make sure you get all the linked files into one place so you can take them to the remote printer. You can choose to copy all the linked files, or just those linked files that are not stored in the publication. If you are going to a service bureau (18.122–18.133), ask them what they need from you.

Avoiding trouble in workgroups

10.27 One of the biggest problems that seems to arise in workgroup publishing is keeping track of all the versions of the stories and graphics and knowing which one is, or should be, in the current publication. If one person takes a copy of the linked word-processing file and tweaks it, then another person takes a different copy of the same file and tweaks it, pretty soon you have an incredible mess. There is undeniably a lot of cooperation and organization that must evolve in any group, and groups must work it out among themselves. But one tip regarding links management can help any group, and that is based on the Conch System. Remember *Lord of the Flies*? "He who has the Conch, speaks." In this case, "S/He who holds the File Folder containing the hard copy of the document, can tweak." If you don't have that file folder in your hand, you can't touch the document. If you do, then you and you alone are authorized to make changes. Put the hard copy for the current changes in the Conch folder, preferably with name, date, time, and notes. The person working on the PageMaker publication cannot update changes unless the appropriate Conch folder is in their hands.

10.28 The "Links" dialog box   *(from the File menu, choose "Links…"; or press Command =)*

10.29 *This dialog box gives a list of the text and graphic documents in the publication. The symbol in the margin indicates their link status (see 10.36–10.42).*

Items pasted from the Scrapbook or Clipboard are included in the list, in case you want to link them to external files.

Text or graphics that have been created within PageMaker are not included (text can be linked if you export it; 10.51).

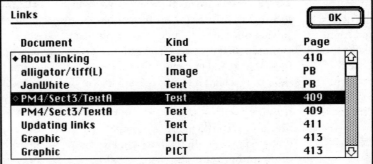

Links

Document	Kind	Page
◆ **About linking**	**Text**	**410**
alligator/tiff(L)	**Image**	**PB**
JanWhite	**Text**	**PB**
◇ **PM4/Sect3/TextA**	**Text**	**409**
PM4/Sect3/TextA	**Text**	**409**
Updating links	**Text**	**411**
Graphic	**PICT**	**413**
Graphic	**PICT**	**413**

Status : The linked document has been modified since the last time it was placed. However, automatic updates have not been requested.

OK

[Link info…] [Link options…] [Update] [Update all]

10.30 *This button will show the "Link info" for the selected file; 10.43–10.46.*

10.31 *This button will show the "Link options" for the selected file; 10.47–10.49*

10.32 *This button will immediately update the selected internal file with its current external version.*

10.33 *OK does not make anything happen in this dialog box! It will just close the box for you— nothing will be updated or changed unless you have clicked any of the buttons (or buttons within buttons) below. Notice you cannot Cancel any updates you made. If you make a mistake, you can Revert (16.26– 16.27).*

10.34 *In addition to the symbol denoting the status for the selected file (10.29), that status is also spelled out for you here.*

10.35 *This button will immediately update all files that have modified links **and** that have the option "Update automatically" checked in their "Link options" dialog box. (When you open the publication, you know, the files will be updated. But these Update buttons allows you to update the files without having to close the publication.)*

Status indicators

10.36 The narrow space, or column, to the left of the list of file names, displays the symbols that indicate the current status of all files in the publication. It's a guide to the publication at a glance. You can always click once on a file to get more detailed information in the "Status" info bar (10.34).

10.37 If the status column is **blank,** you have no problems—all the external, linked files are the same as the ones in the publication (or they are not even linked).

10.38 If the status column shows a **hollow diamond** (◇), it means that the external file (the source file) has been changed, but the link options for that file have *not* been set to update it automatically. You may want to check with whoever made the changes and see if they are really meant to be included in your publication. If they are, you can click the "Update" button to make the changes.

10.39 If the status column shows a **black diamond** (◆), it means that the external file (the source file) has been changed, and the link option has been set to automatically update it. Again, you may want to check to make sure the changes are really meant to be included in the pub. If they are, you can click the "Update" button, or you can just

wait until the next time you open the publication, as the changes will be made automatically at that time.

10.40 If the status column shows a **hollow triangle** (△), you may have a problem. This means that *both* the internal file and the external file have been changed. (If you have rewritten copy, reformatted, or even kerned characters in the publication itself, the internal file is considered changed.) If you ask for an update, the external changes will override any internal changes. It's a good idea to remove any "Update automatically" links from that file, then find out which set of changes (internal or external) takes precedence. If both, you have some manual work to do combining the changes.

10.41 If the status column displays a **question mark (?),** it means the linked, external file can't be found. It may have been moved from its folder, or the name may have been changed. If it is a text or EPS file and you never find it, it only means you won't be able to update any changes that may have been made in the external file; you will print what you see in the pub. If it is a high-res graphic and the link is missing, you will only be able to print a low-res screen version.

10.42 Status chart

Link status indicators

blank	This item is not linked, or the link is up-to-date *(check the comments; 10.34; 10.37).*
◇	The external file has been modified, but you haven't requested an automatic update (10.38).
◆	The external file has been modified; the internal version will be updated automatically the next time you open the publication (10.39).
△	Both the external file and the internal file have been modified (if it is updated, the internal changes will be lost) (10.40).
?	PageMaker cannot find the external, linked file (10.41).

These indicators are intended to provide at-a-glance info. For more specific info, click on the name of the file; below the list box you will see the precise, current status (10.34).

(x)	This symbol is listed in the PageMaker manual as indicating that the publication does not contain the complete copy of the named file. The manual is just kidding—Aldus never actually included this symbol in the code.

417

10.43 The "Link info" and "Link options" dialog boxes

(With the pointer tool, click on a text block or graphic, then from the Element menu choose "Link info…" or "Link options…." Or in the "Links" dialog box [10.28], click the buttons)

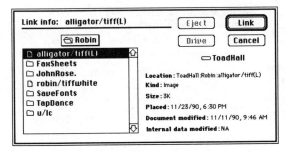

10.44 *Use the "Link info" dialog box to:*
1. ***Find information about an item.***
    NA stands for "Not applicable."
    "Image" means the item is a TIFF (tagged image file format; 9.22–9.28).
2. ***Change the link (10.57).***

10.45 *If you are just checking the information, click Cancel (or press Command Period) instead of hitting the Return key, as Return will activate the "Link" button, linking the item to whatever file is selected in the list box (if you do accidentally hit Return, you will have a chance to cancel, though).*

10.46 *If the "Link info…" command from the Element menu is gray, it means either nothing has been selected with the pointer tool or the text tool, or the item selected is not linked to anything because it was created within PageMaker.*

10.47 *Use the "Link options" dialog box to customize the options for the one selected item. Each option is dependent on the one above it being selected; that is, you cannot update automatically unless you first choose to store a copy in the publication (10.15–10.16). This does not mean you can't update the file—it just means the process won't take place automatically; you will have to request it (10.53).*

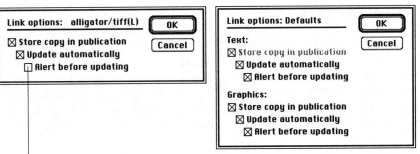

10.48 *If you choose to "Alert before updating," the next time the publication is opened and PageMaker notices that the original version has been altered, PageMaker will first ask you if you really do want to update the file.*

10.49 *If there is nothing selected and no insertion point flashing, the "Link options" dialog box (above; from the Element menu only) allows you to set the defaults (10.64; 10.65). "Store copy in publication" for text is gray because text is always stored in the publication (10.15).*

If you want to do this:	**Then follow these steps:**	**Shortcuts ▾ Notes ▾ Hints**
10.50 Establish a link to a file that has been placed or imported	▪ You already did. Really. To prove it, choose "Link…" from the File menu. Every text and graphic file you placed or imported into the publication is listed (10.28).	▪ Actually, the *link* itself is automatically established as soon as you place the file into PageMaker. What is *not* automatically established is how you want to deal with that link: whether you want any revisions in the external file to be incorporated into the publication version of the file, and whether you want to be asked before they are incorporated. See 10.47.
10.51 Establish an external link to text that was typed directly in PageMaker	▪ In order to establish an external link, you need to **export** the PageMaker file: ▪ With the **text tool,** click once anywhere in the story. ▪ From the File menu, choose "Export…." ▪ Choose a file format from the list of word processors (15.14–15.16). ▪ Make sure the Export button "Entire story" is selected. ▪ Click "Export tags" if you like (7.66). ▪ Make sure you are saving it into the folder you want to keep it in (16.6–16.9). Name it with a title that identifies the file. ▪ Click OK, *or* press Return. You now have an external version and it is linked.	▪ The internal version will be linked to the external version from now on. Any changes you make in the *internal* version will not be recognized by the *external* version, though. If you choose to update, the *external file* will replace the *internal file.* ▪ You can place the external version into other publications. Many different publications can all have files linked to the same external file. ▪ See Section 15 for detailed info on exporting; see 15.36 in particular.
10.52 Establish an external link to a graphic that was created directly in PageMaker	▪ You can't.	

If you want to do this:	Then follow these steps:	Shortcuts ▾ Notes ▾ Hints

10.53 Set the link options for a file

- With the **text tool,** click anywhere in the story, **or** with the **pointer tool,** click on any text block in the story or on any graphic.
- From the Element menu, choose "Link options...."
- If the selected file is text or an EPS graphic, the first option "Store copy in publication" is gray because those files are always stored in the publication. If the selected file is another sort of graphic, you can choose to have its copy stored in the publication (10.15–10.22).
- If the copy is stored in the publication, the next option becomes available to you: "Update automatically." If you check this box, any changes that are made in the original, external file will be automatically transferred to the internal file when the publication is next opened. If you do not check it, you will still be able to update the internal file (10.59)—it just won't happen automatically.
- If you choose to update automatically, the next option becomes available to you: "Alert before updating." If you select it, the next time you open this publication you will get a warning before the file is updated automatically, with an option to ignore the update.

- If "Link options..." is gray, the object (text block or graphic) you selected was created within PageMaker and has no external link. You can create an external link for the text (10.51); you cannot create an external link of a PageMaker graphic.
- The "Link options" dialog box looks slightly different for text and EPS graphics than it does for other graphics: the option "Store copy in publication" is gray and already chosen for text and EPS files, because they are *always* stored in the publication (10.15; 9.88; EPS: 9.29–9.35).

If you want to do this:	**Then follow these steps:**	**Shortcuts ▾ Notes ▾ Hints**

10.54 Determine the status of a file

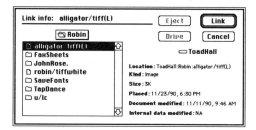

- With the **text tool,** click anywhere in the story, **or** with the **pointer tool,** click on any text block in the story or on any graphic.
- From the Element menu, choose "Link info...."
- The "Link info" dialog box will tell you all about your file (10.43–10.46).
- You can also get this dialog box for any individual file by following the steps in 10.55.

- Be careful about hitting the Return key to get out of this dialog box—the default button here is "Link," which will link the file that is selected on the publication page with the file that is highlighted in the list box. If you accidentally hit Return (and therefore "Link"), and the selected file is not the one you want to link to, an alert box will appear and offer you a chance to Cancel the link change.

10.55 Determine the status of any and all files

- From the File menu, choose "Links...," *or* press Command = .
- Check the status code for any file (10.36–10.42).
- Click once on any file name to see the exact status of the file spelled out for you at the bottom (10.34).
- Click once on a file, then click the "Link info..." button to get the "Link info" dialog box for further details about the file (10.43–10.46); *or* just double-click on the file name to get that dialog box.
- Click once on a file, then click the "Link options..." button to get the dialog box to change your storing and updating options (10.47–10.48).
- Click OK, or press Return.

- You can't Cancel out of this box; although the keyboard shortcut for canceling (Command Period) will close it, any changes you made in the Link dialog boxes will be retained. Clicking OK is a little disturbing in this dialog box, because we are used to OK buttons making things happen. In this case, nothing happens—the box just goes away.
- If you accidentally update or change something you really didn't mean to, you can Revert (16.26–16.27).

If you want to do this:

10.56 Re-establish a broken link

Then follow these steps:

- From the File menu, choose "Links...," *or* press Command = .
- Any file that has a question mark to the left of its name is missing its link (10.41). Double-click on the file name (**or** click once on it, then click the "Link info..." button); you will get the "Link info" dialog box.
- You can navigate through this dialog box just as you navigate through any other "Place" or "Save as" dialog box—open folders, switch disks, etc.—to find the external file to link up with. When you find the external file name, double-click on it (**or** click once, then click the "Link" button or hit Return).
- Click OK, or press Return.

Another method:

- If you know which file is missing its link, click once on it with the **pointer tool.**
- From the Element menu, choose "Link info...."
- Navigate through the folders and disks to find the missing link (the external file). When you find it, double-click on the file name (**or** click once, then click the "Link" button or hit Return).

Shortcuts ▾ Notes ▾ Hints

- If the link is missing because the external file has been renamed, you can simply name that external file with the original, linked name again. If the link is missing because the external file has been moved, put the file back into the folder in which PageMaker keeps looking for it. Or you could put it in the same folder as the publication, as PageMaker always looks there for linked files if she can't find them where they belong.
- You can also re-link any internal file to the external file with the new name or the new location. You can also change the link altogether and link the internal file to any other external file you want. See 10.57 to change a link.

If you want to do this:	Then follow these steps:	Shortcuts ▾ Notes ▾ Hints
10.57 Change a link	■ The process of changing a link is the same as that of re-establishing a link (10.56); the only difference is that you connect the link to a *different* file. Simply double-click on the file name you want linked to your internal file. ■ You must connect a graphic file to a graphic file, and a text file to a text file. Other than those parameters, you can switch any internal file to link up with any external file. ■ If the newly-linked file is different than the file in the original link, PageMaker will ask you if you want to change the linkage. If you click "Yes," the new link is established and the file in the publication is instantly updated to the new, external file.	
10.58 Establish a link to a graphic that came in through the Clipboard	If the graphic that came in through the Clipboard has an external version of its own (a MacPaint file, an ImageStudio file, etc.), then you just need to establish a link: ■ With the **pointer tool,** click once on the graphic. ■ From the Element menu, choose "Link info…." ■ Find the external file you want to link the graphic to; double-click on it. It will be updated to the new link instantly!	■ If the graphic has no original, external version, copy and paste the image into a graphic program and save it in a file format PageMaker can read (9.76–9.81). Go back to the PageMaker publication and place the new file you just created. This is particularly easy if you have the great little program DeskPaint.

423

If you want to do this:	Then follow these steps:	Shortcuts ▾ Notes ▾ Hints
10.59 Update one file immediately	■ With the **text tool,** click anywhere in the story, **or** with the **pointer tool,** click on any text block in the story or on any graphic. ■ From the Element menu, choose "Link info...." ■ Find the name of the external file in the list box. Double-click on it; *or* click once on it and click the "Link" button or hit Return. The internal file will immediately be revised to the external version. **Another method:** ■ From the File menu, choose "Links," *or* press Command = . ■ If the file has an external version that has been changed, you will see a black or a hollow diamond to the left of its name (10.36–10.32). Click once on the file name, then click the "Update" button. ■ Click OK.	■ Read 10.12–10.14 on all the ways to automatically update files each time the publication is opened. ■ If you update a file and then realize you really didn't want to do that, you can Revert (16.26; 16.27).
10.60 Update all files immediately	■ From the File menu, choose "Links," *or* press Command = . ■ If any file has an external version that has been changed, you will see a black or a hollow diamond to the left of its name (10.36–10.42). Click the "Update all" button. ■ Click OK.	■ Read 10.12–10.14 on all the ways to automatically update files each time the publication is opened.

If you want to do this:	**Then follow these steps:**	**Shortcuts ▾ Notes ▾ Hints**
10.61 Update the external version of a text file with the internal version	■ With the **pointer tool,** click once anywhere in the story. ■ From the File menu, choose "Export...." ■ Under "File format," choose the word processor that you typically work with. ■ Under "Export," click "Entire story." ■ In the list box, find the name of the external version you want to update. ■ Where the insertion point is flashing, type in the *exact* name of the external version you want to update. ■ Hit Return or click OK. ■ In response to the alert "Replace existing "_____"?," click "Yes." The external version is now the same as the internal version. ■ If you didn't get the "Replace . . ." alert, either you did not type the exact name, or the file you want to update was not in the list box. Either way, you did not *update* the external version, but created a *new* external version. The internal file is still linked to the *first* external version.	■ This procedure is actually *exporting* the internal text with the same name as the external file you want to update/replace. ■ See Section 15 for more details on importing and exporting.

If you want to do this:

10.62 Copy the files linked to your publication for remote printing (taking it to a service bureau or laserprint shop)

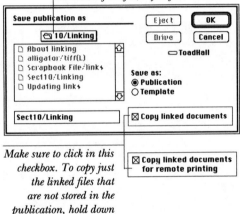

This is the label where you should see the name of the folder you just created.

Make sure to click in this checkbox. To copy just the linked files that are not stored in the publication, hold down the Option key before you click in the checkbox.

Then follow these steps:

- At the Finder/Desktop, *before* you open PageMaker, create an empty folder (Command N) and name it something appropriate to your project.
- Open your publication. Make sure there are no missing links (10.54; 10.56).
- I hope you've been using "Save as..." to compress the publication size all this time (16.25). Choose "Save as..." one more time. This time, click a checkmark in the "Copy linked documents" checkbox.
- In the list box, find the name of the new *folder* you just created. Double-click on it; you will see the folder's name in the label, as shown in the example to the left.
- Click OK, *or* hit Return. This will copy the publication *and all the linked files into that folder.* Quit PageMaker.
- If you are sending the publication through a modem, send the entire folder. If you are taking a disk to a service bureau and that folder will fit onto one disk, do it. If you need more than one disk, go ahead and split up the files. The service bureau will copy all the files into one folder on their hard disk and print from there.

Shortcuts ▾ Notes ▾ Hints

- **Important note:** This procedure copies all external, linked files, whether they are stored in the publication or not. Your service bureau may need only the linked files that are *not* stored in the publication. Call and ask. To copy only the linked files that are *not* stored in the publication, make sure there is no X in the "Copy linked documents" checkbox. Then hold down the Option key and click in that same checkbox; the button changes to "Copy linked documents for remote printing."
- If all the files are in the same folder as the publication, it doesn't matter where you initially set up the links. PageMaker will look for them where you said they would be; but if they are not there, she will look for them in the same folder as the publication, which is where the service bureau will put them.

If you want to do this:	**Then follow these steps:**	**Shortcuts ▾ Notes ▾ Hints**
10.63 Create a template with linked files that will automatically update	■ Let's say you created a membership directory of names and phone numbers. Someone typed all the names and numbers in a word processor and you placed that file in the publication. When you are finished with the first publication, make a template out of it (which is just the same as creating a publication, but when you choose to "Save as...," click the "Template" button; 12.14).	■ This comes in handy in repetitive projects like directories or parts lists, where everything but specific data stays the same.

■ Now it's time to do the quarterly update on the membership list. You can do either of two things:
  □ Open the original word processing list of names and numbers and revise it.
  □ Then open the PageMaker template. As it opens, PageMaker will ask if you want to update the internal stories. Yes you do. All the new names and numbers appear and you just have to fine-tune the publication.

OR:
  □ You can create a *new* word-processing file with updated names and numbers.
  □ Open the PageMaker template. Change the link of the existing text; link it to the new list of names and numbers (10.57). The new names will pour right onto the page.

If you want to do this:

Then follow these steps:

Shortcuts ▾ Notes ▾ Hints

10.64 Set link option **application** defaults

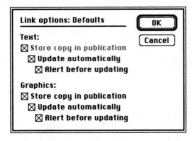

- Have PageMaker open, but no publication on the screen. All you should see is the PageMaker menu across the top.
- From the Element menu, choose "Link options...."
- Click checkmarks in the commands you want to set as defaults.
- Click OK.

- As application defaults, the commands you set here will affect every *new* publication you create. Application defaults will be overriden by any publication defaults (10.65).

10.65 Set link option **publication** defaults

- Open the publication for which you want to set defaults.
- From the Element menu, choose "Link options...."
- Click checkmarks in the commands you want to set as defaults.
- Click OK.

- As publication defaults, the commands you choose here will affect only the publication you set the defaults in. The new defaults will only affect files that are placed on the page *after* the defaults have been set; they will not affect any files already on the page.
- Individual link options (10.53) will override any publication defaults.

11.1   Minimums and maximums:

Item	Minimum	Maximum
Handles	3	As many as you can squeeze in
Standoff	-22.75 inches (.01 increments)	22.75 inches

Through
typographic
means, the designer now
presents, in one image, both
the message and the pictorial
idea. Sometimes, this 'playing'
with type   has resulted
in the loss of   a certain
amount of   legibility.
Researchers   consider this
a deplorable   state of affairs;
but, on the other hand, the
excitement created by a novel
image sometimes more than
compensates for the slight
difficulty in readability.

—Herb Lubalin

An example of wrapped text.

11.2   Text wrapping is the process of forcing text to wrap around certain boundaries of a *graphic* element. Without text wrap applied to a graphic, text will flow right over the top of the image.

11.3   You can apply a text wrap to any graphic you draw with the PageMaker drawing tools, to any image you paste in from the Scrapbook or the Clipboard, and to any graphic file you place from any other program. You can even create a *space*, or a placeholder, with a text wrap by making an *invisible* box (using a line of "None") with the Page-Maker drawing tools. One thing you *cannot* do is apply a text wrap to *text*, like an initial cap (but see 11.40).

11.4   When you apply a text wrap to a graphic, it sets up *boundaries*. You can control how far from the edge of the graphic these boundaries appear (11.9), and the text will wrap around the outside of them. The boundary initially appears as a rectangle, but you can customize its shape endlessly (11.30). In addition, you can put a text wrap on a master page, and all text on the publication pages will wrap around it (11.38). And it is even possible to turn the wrap inside out and have the text wrap *inside* the boundaries (11.41).

11.5   Text wrapping does slow down the process of redrawing the screen every time you change views or scroll. Small price to pay.

11.6 The "Text wrap" dialog box *(from the Element menu, choose "Text wrap…")*

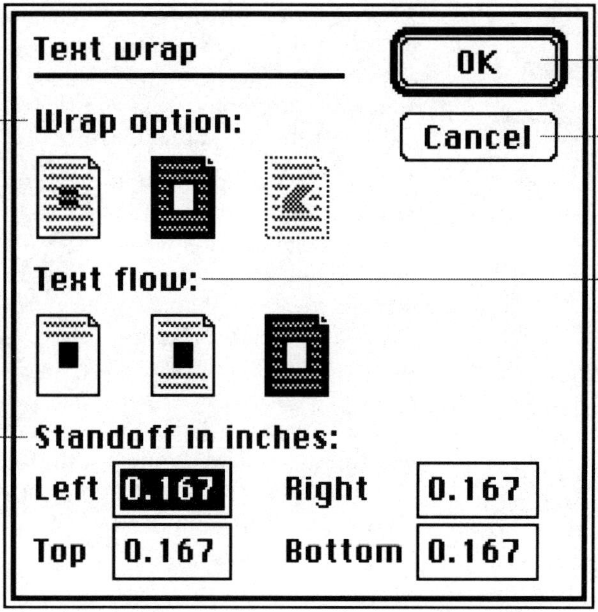

11.7 *The "Wrap option" provides a choice of whether the text will flow right over the top of (11.10)* **or** *around (11.11) the selected graphic. You cannot choose the third icon; it will be automatically selected when you customize a boundary (11.12).*

Text wrap

OK

Cancel

Wrap option:

Text flow:

Standoff in inches:

Left 0.167   Right 0.167

Top 0.167   Bottom 0.167

You can press Return or Enter instead of clicking OK.

Press Command Period to shortcut

11.8 *The "Text flow" option provides choices as to how the text will flow around the graphic (11.13–11.15). If the "No wrap" icon (the first of the three icons above; 11.10) is selected, these icons will be gray and inaccessible.*

11.9 *If the "Standard wrap" icon (the middle wrap option icon; 11.11) is selected, as shown above (11.7), you will be able to input values here to determine how far from the edge of the graphic the text wrap boundary will appear (11.16–11.20). The measurement system (here it is inches) is determined by your choice in "Preferences…"; see 1.211). The value .167 is one pica (4.6–4.7).*

Wrap option   ## Text flow

Wrap option:

11.10 The first icon, which is the default selection, indicates there is **no text wrap** applied. If you ever want to remove a wrap from an object, this is the icon to select (11.42). Since this icon means no text wrap, when it is selected the "Text flow" icons are blank.

Wrap option:

11.11 The second icon indicates the **standard rectangular text wrap.** If you select this icon, you can then choose a "Text flow" option and can insert values for the standoff (11.00–11.00).

Wrap option:

11.12 The third icon indicates a **customized wrap.** You cannot *select* this icon. After you have customized a standard wrap (11.30), this icon will be automatically selected.

Text flow:

11.13 The first text flow icon indicates a **column break.** When the text reaches an object that has this column break applied, the text will stop flowing and will jump over to continue at the top of the next empty column (11.38).

Text flow:

11.14 The second text flow icon is the **jump-over** icon (example: 11.23). When text reaches a graphic that has the jump-over wrap applied, the text will jump over it and continue on below it, leaving white space on both sides. The values you enter as the top and bottom standoff (11.16–11.20) determine how far above and below the graphic the text will stop and then continue.

Text flow:

11.15 The third text flow icon is the **wrap-all-sides** icon. Text will flow around all sides of an object with this wrap, whether rectangular or customized. The values you enter as the standoffs (11.16–11.20) determine how close the text will get to the graphic. See the example of the fish on page 429, and other examples in 11.19, 11.25, and 11.30.

Standoff

Standoff in inches:

Left [0.167]   Right   [0.167]

Top   [0.167]   Bottom [0.167]

11.16 The **standoff** boxes are where you determine how close you want the text to get to the object. You can enter a value from -22.75 inches up to 22.75 inches, in .01 increments. You can input a different value in each box. Specify 0 (zero) if you want the text to bump up right against the edge of the graphic boundary, or specify a negative value if you want the text to overlap the graphic. If you resize the graphic, the standoff remains the same.

11.17 The standoff is measured *from the edge of the rectangular **graphic** boundary.* Most often a graphic has a boundary that is larger than the actual graphic itself, especially if the graphic itself is not rectangular.

11.18 *The eight inner, unconnected handles belong to the graphic object. The dotted line is the text wrap boundary (its handles are diamond-shaped); the distance between the two sets of handles is the* **standoff** *(11.9).*

11.19 *I added more of the diamond-shaped handles to this text wrap boundary, and customized its shape (11.30). Notice the graphic still has its eight square handles in their original places.*

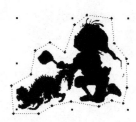

11.20 Since the standoff can be anywhere from -22.75 to 22.75 inches, you can actually create a text wrap that is on a completely separate part of the page than the actual graphic, or even across the other side of a two-page spread. I can't imagine why you would ever need to do that, but it's possible.

Listed below are the standoff values for this graphic, values that place the text wrap over there: ———

Left: -3   Right: 4

Top: 1.5   Bottom: -1

(using inches)

Examples of text wrapping

11.21 Standard rectangular text wrap on all sides (11.11)

In graphic design, as in all creative expression, art evolves from craft. In typographic design, craft deals with points, lines, planes, picas, ciceros, leads, quads, serifs, letters, words, folios, pages, signatures, color, printing, and binding. Just as there is no art without craft and no craft without rules, so too there is no art without fantasy, without child's art is much ideas. A fantasy but little craft. It is the fusion of the two that makes the difference.

—*Paul Rand*

11.22 Inside-out text wrap (11.41)

In graphic design, as in all creative expression, art evolves from craft. In typographic design, craft deals with points, lines, planes, picas, ciceros, leads, quads, serifs, letters, words, folios, pages, signatures, paper, ink, color, printing, and binding. Just as there is no art without craft and no craft without rules, so too there is no art without fantasy, without ideas. A child's art is much fantasy but little craft. It is the fusion of the two that makes the difference.

P A U L ✍ R A N D

11.23 Standard rectangular text wrap jumping over the graphic (11.14)

In graphic design, as in all creative expression, art evolves from craft. In typographic design, craft deals with points, lines, planes, picas, ciceros, leads, quads, serifs, letters, words, folios, pages, signatures, paper, ink, color, printing,

and binding. Just as there is no art without craft and no craft without rules, so too there is no art without fantasy, without ideas. A child's art is much fantasy but little craft. It is the fusion of the two that makes the difference.   —*Paul Rand*

11.24 Text wrap around an initial cap (11.40)

*I*n graphic design, as in all creative expression, art evolves from craft. In typographic design, craft deals with points, lines, planes, picas, ciceros, leads, quads, serifs, letters, words, folios, pages, signatures, paper, ink, color, printing, and binding. Just as there is no art without craft and no craft without rules, so too there is no art without fantasy, without ideas. A child's art is much fantasy but little craft. It is the fusion of the two that makes the difference.   —*Paul Rand*

11.25 Custom text wrap (11.30)

In graphic design, as in all creative expression, art evolves from craft. In typographic   design, craft deals with points, lines, planes, picas, ciceros, leads, quads, serifs, letters, words, folios, pages, signatures, paper, ink, color, printing, and bind- ing. Just as there is no art without craft and no craft without rules, so too there is no art without fantasy, without ideas. A child's art is much fantasy but little craft. It is the fusion of the two that makes the difference.

—*Paul Rand*

11.26 Text wrap around a placeholder with room for a caption (11.36)

In graphic design, as in all creative expression, art evolves from craft. In typographic design, craft deals with points, lines, planes, picas, ciceros, leads, quads, serifs, letters, words, folios, pages, signa- tures, paper, ink, color, printing, and binding. Just as there is no art without craft and no craft without rules, so too there is no art without fantasy, without ideas. A child's art is much fantasy but little craft. It is the fusion of the two that makes the difference.

photo caption

—*Paul Rand*

This page, with six text wraps on it, would not print. I kept getting an error message of "LimitCheck" because my LaserWriter IINT doesn't have enough memory to deal with this many text wraps. How did I finally print it? Two passes through the printer, once with half the text wraps, then again with the other half. The lino, with its larger memory, had no problem.

If you want to do this:	Then follow these steps:	Shortcuts ▾ Notes ▾ Hints
11.27 Create a standard rectangular text wrap around an object or around a group of objects 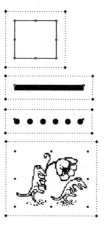	• With the **pointer tool,** select the object(s). • From the Element menu, choose "Text wrap…." • Under "Wrap option," click on the middle icon (standard rectangular wrap; 11.11). • Under "Text flow," click on the flow of your choice (see 11.13–11.15). • If you want space between the boundary of the object and the boundary of the text, type a value into the "Standoff in (measurement)" boxes (11.17). Remember, you can override the current measurement system (1.221), you can insert values from –22.75 inches to 22.75 inches, and you can always adjust the standoff manually on the screen or return here to change it. • Click OK.	• You can select more than one object and apply a text wrap to them all simultaneously. They will all have the same text wrap specifications. • You can pick up and move any object with a text wrap applied. The text the object leaves behind will word wrap back into place. The text the object drops into will wrap around the standoff you set.
11.28 Change the text wrap standoff *from the dialog box (also see 11.29)* **Standoff in inches:** Left `0.167` Right `0.167` Top `0.167` Bottom `0.167`	• With the **pointer tool,** select the object(s). • From the Element menu, choose "Text wrap…." • Under "Wrap option," click on the middle icon (11.11). If either the "no wrap" or "custom wrap" icon is chosen, you cannot change the standoff from the dialog box. • Type in new values in the "Standoff" boxes. • Click OK.	• You can enter values from –22.75 inches to 22.75 inches. You can override the current measurement system (1.221). • If the "Custom wrap" icon is selected, the "Standoff" boxes delude you into thinking you can change them—they are blank and the insertion point is flashing. If you enter values in them and click OK, PageMaker will completely ignore you. If you go back to the dialog box you will see the boxes are empty again.

If you want to do this:	Then follow these steps:	Shortcuts ▾ Notes ▾ Hints

11.29 Change the text wrap standoff *on the object itself (also see 11.30)*

a)

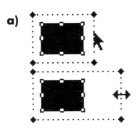

b)

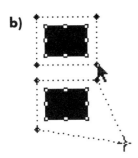

c)

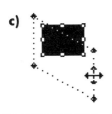

■ With the **pointer tool,** select the object.

To move one boundary edge (a):
■ Point the tip of the pointer directly on the dotted boundary line; don't click!
■ *Press*-and-drag; you should see the double-headed arrow (↔), pointing in the direction you are dragging (vertical or horizontal).

To move a corner (b):
■ Point the tip of the pointer directly on any corner handle.
■ *Press*-and-drag; you should see the crossbar cursor (+).

To move two sides and keep them parallel (c):
■ First you must press-and-drag any corner handle at least a pixel (which is just a teeny bit). Let go.
■ Now point to any edge with the **pointer tool;** *press* (don't click!) and it will become the four-headed arrow (✛).
■ Press-and-drag that four-headed arrow; you can even move it beyond the opposite side.

■ Every time you move a boundary, the text on the screen will reflow. This can get boring. Hold down the Spacebar while moving the boundaries; when you want to see the text reflow, let go of the Spacebar.
■ As soon as you move a boundary, even if you put it back right where it came from, PageMaker labels it "customized." If you go back into the text wrap dialog box while that graphic is selected, you will see the "custom" icon selected.
■ If you don't like how you moved the boundaries and you want to return it back to a rectangular wrap, select the graphic, get the text wrap dialog box, and click the middle wrap option again (11.11).
■ To create more handles so you can tug the boundary in a greater variety of ways, see 11.31.

435

If you want to do this:

11.30 Customize the text wrap to an odd shape

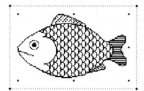

Graphic with a standard text wrap, standoff of .1 inch.

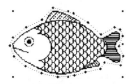

The same graphic with a customized text wrap. This is how the fish on page 429 were wrapped.

Then follow these steps:

- Follow the steps in 11.27 to select a graphic object and apply a standard rectangular wrap with any width of standoff you choose. Then:
- See 11.29 for changing the boundaries, using the sides and the four handles that already exist.
- Now you need to **create more handles** on the text wrap boundary so you can push and pull at other points besides the corners: with the **pointer tool,** click once on the dotted line at the spot where you want a new handle. *Do not press-and-drag,* as that will move the entire segment, not create a new handle. **Click, and then let go.**
- When you let go, you will see a new diamond-shaped handle. *Now* you can press-and-drag on that handle (vertex) to move that segment. You can press-and-drag the handle to move it *along* the segment, or you can move it out and about to *pull* the segment along with it.
- **To get rid of a handle,** press-and-drag it onto the top of another handle.
- **To get rid of all extra handles** and take the wrap back to a plain ol' ordinary rectangle: select the object, get the text wrap dialog box from the Element menu, and choose the middle wrap option (11.11).

Shortcuts ▾ Notes ▾ Hints

- As soon as you make any adjustments to the text wrap boundary, it becomes "customized." If you take a peek at the dialog box, you will see the "Custom wrap" option selected.
- At the risk of being repetitious, I want to remind you that you can hold the Spacebar down while you add handles and move them. This will prevent the text from reflowing every time you make a change. Let up on the Spacebar to reflow the text when you are done or when you just want to check out the wrap and see how it's doing.

If you want to do this:	Then follow these steps:	Shortcuts ▾ Notes ▾ Hints
11.31 Add handles (vertices) to a text wrap boundary	■ Follow the steps in 11.27 to get a standard rectangular text wrap. ■ With the **pointer tool,** *click* once at any point along the dotted line. *Do not drag*—just click. Click as many handles as you want.	■ There seems to be no limit to the number of handles you can have, except for the limit of space along the dotted boundary. Of course, the more handles, the more memory the graphic takes up.
11.32 Move the handles (vertices) on a text wrap boundary	■ With the **pointer tool,** press-and-drag on any *wrap boundary* handles and you will be able to move it right along the line segment. A corner handle won't slide along the line until you add a new handle to either side of it.	■ The movement depends on the direction you drag the pointer. If you move it *in* or *out,* you'll drag the boundary with it. If you move the handle *along* the line segment, it just runs right up and down the dotted line.
11.33 Delete the handles (vertices) on a text wrap boundary	■ With the **pointer tool,** press-and-drag on a handle and place it right on top of another handle. That will make it disappear.	■ **If you want to delete *all* the handles,** except for the original four corners: select the object; go back to the dialog box; choose the standard rectangular wrap (the middle option).
11.34 Delay the text reflowing until you finish changing the boundary	■ Hold down the Spacebar while you add, delete, or move the handles. The text will not recompose until you let go of the Spacebar.	■ Indispensable trick.
11.35 Resize the graphic object without affecting the text wrap boundary	■ With the **pointer tool,** press-and-drag on any of the *graphic* handles (any of the eight *square* handles) as you would normally (9.101). The standoff and custom wrap will resize in proportion.	■ Using the Shift key to keep the graphic proportional (9.101) and the Command key to magic-resize a bi-level graphic (9.103) has the same effect as on any graphic without a text wrap.

If you want to do this:	**Then follow these steps:**	**Shortcuts ▾ Notes ▾ Hints**

11.36 Put text, such as a caption, inside a text-wrapped object

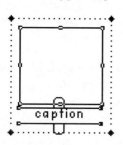

- As long as the handles *on both ends of the text block* are tucked *inside* the text wrap boundary, the text will just sit there patiently. Either enter a standoff value (11.28) that gives you enough space for the text, or drag the boundary to the size you need (11.29).
- Then, either create a little bounding box (1.206; 3.25) in the space provided and type in the text, **or** create the text outside the text wrap, size it small, and move it in.

- This is great for putting the captions running up the side of the photo—just specify a standoff wide enough, rotate the caption (3.186), and slide it in.

11.37 Set a tabbed leader that goes right over the top of a wrapped object

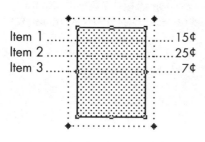

Item 1	15¢
Item 2	25¢
Item 3	7¢

- See Section 5 (5.63–5.67) on Indents and Tabs to create the tabbed leaders.
- As long as the beginning and end of the leaders *are outside the wrap boundary,* the leaders will ignore the wrap and just march right over the top of the graphic.
- If the leaders disappear, the graphic is probably just sitting on top of them. To make the leaders visible again, click once on the wrapped graphic with the **pointer tool** and send it to the back (press Command B; 1.178).

- "Leaders" are the little dots or bullets or dashes that lead from one item to the next, as in a table of contents. They're explained fully in Section 5.

11.38 Scenario #12: Using text wrap on master pages

Besides the obvious technique of wrapping a graphic that will appear on every page, you can take advantage of text wrapping on a master page in several other ways, some of which are yet to be discovered. Remember: anything you are able to do on a publication page, you can apply to all pages by doing it on your master page(s) (1.122–1.142).

Column breaks

Maybe you have a thin outer column on each page that you don't want text to flow into. Draw an invisible line or box at the top of the thin column. Apply the "Column break" text wrap to it. As you autoflow text (3.86–3.87), the text will bump into that line or box and immediately jump over to the top of the next column.

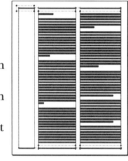

Perhaps the right-hand page on your two-page spreads is strictly for illustrations. Use the column-break text wrap to force text to ignore the entire page as it flows.

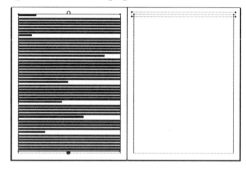

Invisible text wraps to manipulate white space on pages

Let's say you have several columns that you will be flowing text into, but you want to leave a four-inch spot at the bottom of the left column on every left page. So create an invisible box, or even a visible one if you prefer, and apply a rectangular text wrap to it. The text will flow around that box on every page, leaving you with four inches to do with what you will, including manually place text.

Carrying the previous example a little further, you can create several text-wrapped boxes to control the text in interesting ways.

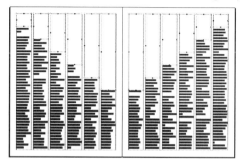

Create inside-out text wraps (11.41), or set up a master page text wrap for angled margins (11.39). Oh, there are so many possiblities. It's too much fun.

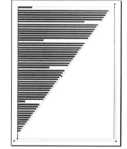

If you want to do this:	**Then follow these steps:**	**Shortcuts ▾ Notes ▾ Hints**

11.39 Use text wrap to create angled margins

Notice the text block handles are all the way out to the sides. Select the boxes and give them a line of "None" so they are invisible.

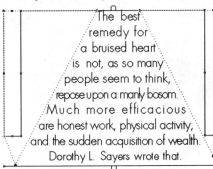

The best remedy for a bruised heart is not, as so many people seem to think, repose upon a manly bosom. Much more efficacious are honest work, physical activity, and the sudden acquisition of wealth. Dorothy L. Sayers wrote that.

- Use PageMaker's drawing tools (Section 2) to draw a thick line or a small box.
- Follow the steps in 11.27 to apply a text wrap to the line or box.
- Follow the steps in 11.30 to customize the text wrap boundary. Shape it into the angle you need. If necessary, create another shape on the other side at the same angle.
- Place the text next to the angled object. Make sure the top left of the text block is over far enough to allow all the text to flow along the angle (see note at left). when the text is all placed, select the line or box and choose "None" from the Line submenu (under Element).

- Once you know this trick, you may wonder why you hadn't used it many times before. It comes in handy regularly, and it's so easy.

11.40 Text wrap an initial cap

Once upon a time there was a mother and her three children. They lived in a little house and were very happy.

- You cannot create a text wrap around text, so you must turn the text into a graphic:
- Type the letter into a single text block. Size it close to what the final size will be.
- Select the letter with the **pointer tool;** put it on the first page in the Scrapbook (1.201).
- **Place** the first item in the Scrapbook (1.205; 9.96), then click on the pointer tool to absorb the rest of the items.
- The text is now a graphic and can be text wrapped as usual (11.27–11.30).

- Some third-party scrapbooks, such as Smart-Scrap, allow you to select *portions* of the scrapbook item. This makes the text-into-graphic process so easy. In SmartScrap, if text is just copied from the Scrapbook and pasted onto the PageMaker page, it is editable text. But if the text is *selected* with the little SmartScrap selection tool and *then* copied, when it is pasted on the page it is a graphic. Neato.

If you want to do this:

11.41 *Wrap* text *inside* a graphic object (also known as an *inside-out text wrap*)

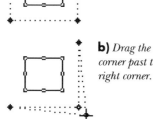

a) *Set up a text wrap around an object.*

b) *Drag the top left corner past the bottom right corner.*

c) *Drag the bottom right corner up to where the top left handle used to be.*

d) *If you have made some wild and crazy shape, make sure there is a little trap for the top left text block handle. Notice the trap here, and the little pathway that is too small for the actual text.*

Then follow these steps:

- Follow the steps in 11.27 to create a rectangular text wrap that flows on all sides of an object. You don't really need any standoff (11.16) for this, but that's up to your particular project.
- Press on the **top left corner handle** and drag it a bit beyond the diagonally opposite corner handle (bottom right).
- Press on the **bottom right corner handle** and drag it back to where the top left handle used to be. (Actually, it doesn't matter which corner you drag, as long as you reverse two opposite corners.)
- Now the wrap is inside out and the text will flow *within* the borders. If you drew a box and don't need to see it anymore, just change the Line weight to "None" (2.19).
- The only limitation is that the top left text block handle *must be inside the wrap somewhere.* This sometimes necessitates creating a little trap for it, a trap large enough to hold the corner handle, but too small for the text to flow into; see **d.**

Shortcuts ▾ Notes ▾ Hints

- This is a great trick. Typically a text wrap *repels* the text *away* from its borders. If you turn it inside out, the wrap will *contain* the text *inside* its borders.
- The Herb Lubalin quote on page 429 is an inside-out text wrap, with an inner, oval, regular text wrap. The example in 11.22 is an inside-out wrap also.
- This kind of wrap is also a good alternate method for creating those angled margins, as in 11.39.
- If you ever find that you have "lost" the invisible text wrap, there are a few tricks mentioned in 1.175–1.176 or 2.36 that can help you find it.

If you want to do this:	Then follow these steps:	Shortcuts ▾ Notes ▾ Hints

11.42 Remove all text wrapping from an object or group of objects

 This is the "No text wrap" icon

- With the **pointer tool,** select the object(s) you wish to remove the wrap from.
- From the Element menu, choose "Text wrap…."
- Click on the first "Wrap option" icon, which is the "No text wrap" icon.
- Click OK.

- As soon as you click OK, any text that was surrounding or inside the object(s) will reflow. If the graphic is now under a layer of text and you need to grab it, hold down the Command key and click to select the layer underneath (1.172; 2.36).

11.43 Set text wrapping as a default (defaults: 1.11–1.15)

- Click once on the **pointer tool,** even if the pointer is already selected.
- From the Element menu, choose "Text wrap…."
- Click on the middle "Wrap option" icon, which is the "Standard rectangular text wrap" icon.
- Fill in values for the standoff (11.16–11.20).
- Click OK.

- Once you have set a text wrap as a default, every time you *paste* a graphic from the Scrapbook or Clipboard, every time you *place* a graphic file, and every time you *draw* any line or shape, the image will appear with a text wrap around it.
- This procedure sets a **publication** default. To set the **application** default, follow the same steps *when there is no publication open* (1.12)..

11.44 Delete the text wrapping default

- Click once on the **pointer tool,** even if the pointer is already selected.
- From the Element menu, choose "Text wrap…."
- Click on the first "Wrap option" icon, which is the "No text wrap" icon.
- Click OK.

- To delete an *application* default, follow the same steps *when there is no publication open* (1.11–1.12).

Containing much Matter to exercise the Judgment and Reflection of the User.

12 ▾ TEMPLATES

12.1 This is a list of the templates PageMaker provides for you.

12.2 A **template** is a fake (or dummy) publication that is already set up with the specifications necessary for production. PageMaker provides over twenty pre-made templates, and you can turn any of your own publications into a template at any time.

12.3 A template may include formatted text, guidelines, columns, style sheets, graphics, etc. The text and graphics act as **placeholders.** When you use one of the pre-made Page-Maker templates, it is up to you to replace the existing text with new stories, adjust the style sheets and guides to suit your own style, replace the existing graphics with your own graphics, or eliminate items altogether. When you use a template you created for yourself, you'll be basically replacing your old text with your new text (12.17–12.18), and leaving the format the way you previously arranged it.

12.4 When you open a template, the original template document *stays intact on the disk;* PageMaker opens a **copy** of the original, and you save and work on the *copy.* This protects that original template from being changed inadvertently. Next time you need the template, it is still there, intact.

12.5 There are two advantages to using a template. One is that all the work that goes into the initial setup of a project— the design decisions, typographic decisions, guidelines, columns, style sheet specs, layout, masthead, logo placement, etc.,—are already done for you. You just need to come in and modify details, change text and graphics, et voilà—on to the next project. Or lunch.

12.6 The second advantage is that a template provides a way to keep all similar documents consistent. For instance, if you create a four-page newsletter every month, you may think, "Why create a template? I'll just take last month's, since we don't need it anymore, and replace the text." The problem here is that soon you lose the consistent look of the publication. Some months the four pages turns into five pages, or perhaps two pages. Some months there is too much text or too little text and so point sizes and leading are adjusted. If you keep changing one publication over and over again, even with those minor changes, you soon forget what the original specifications were. With a template, no matter what adjustments you need to make monthly, you can consistently start with an intact original.

12.7 Scenario #13: When, why, and how to create your own template

12.7   Create your own template for any project that you will be repeating more than once. For instance, this book was created in 24 separate publications. I set up the first section; I created the layout and the page design, put the guidelines in place, made a style sheet, and built the master pages. Then I saved it as a template. Every time I started a new section of the book, I opened a copy of the *template* and built from there. Thus each chapter is consistent, and I didn't have to repeat the same work 24 times.

12.8   If you write memos regularly, you'll want to set up a template with the standard memo information on the master page. The easiest way to do it is to just *do* the first one; that is, just put the memo together as you normally would, print it up, and send it off. But before you quit PageMaker, go back to "Save as..." and save it again, this time as a **template** (12.14; I'm assuming you previously saved it as a publication earlier in the process).

12.9   Another appropriate time to make a template is when you need to create multiple documents all based on the same design and layout. Let's say you work for a travel agency that sends people to various fly-fishing spots all over the world, and you are in charge of promoting those spots. You need to make a four-page brochure for each of them. Just like with the memo, go ahead and create the first one. When it's complete, save it again, this time as a template (12.14). For the next fly-fishing hot spot, open the *template* and just change the items necessary. Often in a case like this, much of the information is the same and does not even need re-keyboarding.

12.10   Several reports that are going to more than one office that may perhaps contain generally the same information (with just a different cover sheet, letter, and some data, for instance) would best be done as a template. Calendars, forms that are constantly changing, letterhead, invoices, literally anything you are creating more than one of, can easily be done as a template, saving you many hours of work.

12.11   I have suggested several times in this series of Scenarios to go ahead and build the first publication and *then* save it as a template. Another method is to create a template specifically as a template; that is, know what you want, put it together, and then use the template to build even the first publication.

12.12   The reason I have come to prefer the first method is that even though you may think you know exactly what you want, many finely-tuned design and typographic decisions are made during the process of creating an actual publication. Many of these decisions are not necessary when you are just setting up a style sheet, putting in guidelines, and placing phony text. When it comes to creating the actual publication, you will probably find (as I do every time) that some slight adjustments should be made in the template itself. And adjusting them in the *template* is much preferable to (and more efficient than) having to slightly adjust things every time you create a new publication based on this template. Working through the process of bringing a project to completion allows you to tighten up all the details *before* making the template. You can always, of course, go back to the original template and adjust it.

If you want to do this:

12.13 Open a copy of a template

Template Icon   Publication Icon

Then follow these steps:

- **If you are at the Desktop** (the finder), *and you are not using MultiFinder,* find the white template icon. (If you are not viewing the window by icon, then you will have a difficult time distinguishing between templates and regular documents. It is a good idea, whenever naming a template, to include the word "template" in its name to prevent this problem.)
- Double-click on the icon; this will put an *Untitled* copy on the screen. Be sure to save it as a *publication,* with a different name than that of the template.
- **If PageMaker is already open,** from the File menu, choose "Open...."
- Find the name of the template. If you can't remember whether a document is a publication or a template, click once on the file name; if it is a template, the little button in the lower right will switch from "Original" to "Copy."
- Either click once on the template name, then click OK, **or** double-click on the template name. This will put an *Untitled* copy on the screen. Be sure to save it as a *publication,* with a different name than that of the template.

Shortcuts ▾ Notes ▾ Hints

- **Note:** Under MultiFinder, double-clicking on the white template icon will usually open the template itself, *not an untitled copy* like it is supposed to. If the publication is not labeled "Untitled" after it opens, then you have opened the original template, not a *copy* of the template. To open a copy of the template under MultiFinder, open PageMaker first and follow the instructions for that method (see left).

- To save the file as a publication, just make sure the "Publication" button is checked when you "Save as...."

If you want to do this:	Then follow these steps:	Shortcuts ▾ Notes ▾ Hints
12.14 Save your PageMaker document as a template 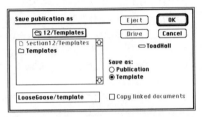	▪ From the File menu, choose "Save as...." ▪ In the mid right portion of the dialog box, click on the "Template" button. ▪ Give the template a name that will tell you it's a template, even if you can't see its icon (e.g., LooseGoose.tmp). *Remember, as when saving any publication, if there is already a publication with the same name, you will be* replacing *the first one (Section 16).* ▪ Click OK.	▪ You can choose to save a document as a template at any point, even if it has previously been saved as a publication. ▪ If you are working on a previously-saved publication and now save it as a template *with a different name,* PageMaker will put the *publication* away, safe on the disk, and the *template,* with its new name, will be on your screen. If you save it as a template *and give it the same name as the publication,* then PageMaker will *replace* the publication with the template (if they're in the same folder). You will get an alert box to verify the save.
12.15 Open the original template	▪ You cannot open the *original* of the template from the Desktop; you can only open a *copy.* So, first you must open PageMaker. Then ... ▪ From the File menu, choose "Open...." ▪ Find the name of the template in the list box. (If you can't remember whether a document is a publication or a template, click once on it; if it is a template, the little button in the lower right will switch from "Original" to "Copy.") ▪ Click *once* on the name. On the right, the button will automatically jump to "Copy"; click on "Original." ▪ Click OK.	▪ *It's not possible to shortcut this procedure!* That is, you can't use the double-click-on-the-file-name trick: you can't click on the file name, click the "Original" button, and then double-click on the file name, because as soon as you click on the file name again, the button switches back to "Copy." So you must use the OK button. ▪ You can usually open the original from the Desktop if you are under MultiFinder. You can always tell if you opened the original or a copy— if it's a copy, the title bar at the top of the window will show "Untitled."

If you want to do this:	**Then follow these steps:**	**Shortcuts ▾ Notes ▾ Hints**
12.16 Replace a template headline with your headline	▪ Just as you replace text anywhere, select the text with the **text tool** by pressing-and-dragging over it. ▪ While the type is highlighted, type in your own headline. You do not need to delete the existing text first; it will disappear as soon as you type the first letter.	▪ If the headline uses text in two different styles, such as bold and light, select just the bold text and type the replacement; then select just the light text and type the replacement.
12.17 Replace an entire template story with your story 	▪ With the **text tool,** click anywhere in any text block of the story you want to replace. ▪ From the File menu, choose "Place...." ▪ Find the name of the story in the list box; click *once* on it. ▪ On the right, click in the button for "Replacing entire story." ▪ Make sure there are no checkmarks in "Retain format" (3.51) or "Read tags" (3.48). Click OK.	▪ Make sure you understand the difference between a *text block* and a *story* (3.106). ▪ This procedure is exactly the same as replacing any story in any publication. See 3.53 for full details. ▪ Replacing the entire story without retaining the format ensures that the story you are bringing in will pick up all the text formatting of the story it is replacing.
12.18 Replace a selected portion of template text with new text 	▪ With the **text tool,** select the text you want to replace (use any of the selection methods detailed in 3.137–3.138). ▪ Then either simply retype text, as in 12.16 above; **or** use the "Place..." dialog box, as in 12.17, to replace it with an outside file, making sure you click the "Replacing selected text" button (3.55).	▪ The new text will retain the format of the text it is replacing.

447

If you want to do this:	**Then follow these steps:**	**Shortcuts ▾ Notes ▾ Hints**

12.19a Replace an **independent** graphic with another graphic from the Clipboard or the Scrapbook *(see 9.89–9.91 re: independent vs. inline graphics)*

- First you need to *eliminate* the existing graphic: click once on it with the **pointer tool,** then hit the Backspace/Delete key.
- After it is gone, copy and paste the new one in as usual (Command V) and move it into position, cropping and resizing as necessary (see notes at right).

- If there was a text wrap applied to the existing graphic, when you delete it you will also delete the text wrap, which will make the text reflow. You may want to first paste the new graphic, resize it, apply a new text flow, put it in position, and *then* delete the existing graphic underneath. To get rid of the one underneath, hold the Command key down. With the pointer tool, click in the graphic area until you see the handles that belong to the graphic underneath. Then hit the Backspace/Delete key.

12.19b Replace an **inline** graphic with another graphic from the Clipboard or the Scrapbook

- To replace an *inline* graphic, select it with the text tool. When you paste, the new graphic will replace the existing one and will also be inline (see 9.170–9.205 for detailed info about inline graphics).

12.20 Replace a template graphic with a graphic file

- If the graphic has its own file on disk, such as a MacPaint file or a TIFF file, then it is possible to *replace* the existing graphic, dropping the new one into its place. The new graphic will take on the same size, placement, proportions, and text wrap as the graphic currently on the page.
- With the **pointer tool,** click once on the graphic to be replaced.
- From the File menu, choose "Place...."
- Find the graphic file in the list box. Click once on the file name.
- On the right, click in the button "Replacing entire graphic."
- Click OK, or double-click the file name.

- You won't get a loaded graphic icon with this procedure (9.92); the graphic on the page will just instantly be replaced with the new graphic file.
- You may not want the exact same size and proportions as the graphic already on the page. But once it is there in position, you can easily adjust it (see Section 9).

You think you have trouble with points and picas?

The points-and-picas measuring system often confuses people who are just beginning to work with type. But take a look at what typographers had to work with until just before the 20th century—they used *names* to denote the sizes of type and the spaces between. ➥

Can you imagine pulling down a menu and setting your headline text as Double English with a Double Pica line spacing, an extra Minion after, and a Nonpariel-plus-a-German for the space before?

My goodness. Thanks, Nelson!
(Nelson Hawks, that is, who conceived of the points-and-picas system; see page 387.)

point size (approximately)	name
1	American
1.5	German
2	Saxon
2.5	Norse
3	Brilliant
3.5	Ruby
4	Excelsior
4.5	Diamond
5	Pearl
5.5	Agate
6	Nonpareil
7	Minion
8	Brevier
9	Bourgeois
10	Long Primer
11	Small Pica
12	Pica
14	English
16	Columbian
18	Great Primer
20	Paragon
22	Double Small Pica
24	Double Pica
28	Double English
32	Double Columbian
etc.	etc.

How to use the templates that PageMaker provides

12.21 The basic process for using the templates is this: Replace the existing "greek" text with your own stories; replace the "Title" with your own title (12.16); replace the masthead or logo with your masthead or logo (12.19); replace the boxes representing graphics with graphics and photographs of your own (12.19); delete pages or add pages as necessary (1.118–1.119); change the style sheets (Section 7) to take advantage of your own great collection of fonts (rather than use Times and Helvetica and thus scream to the world that your publication was created on a Mac).

12.22 The idea behind these PageMaker-provided templates is that since they have been professionally designed, people with little or no design background can easily put together nice-looking publications. Supposedly, you don't need to know Page-Maker intimately, either, in order to use the templates. That's true *to some extent.* But I found many instances in these particular templates where a beginner could get into major trouble if she didn't know all the ins and outs of text blocks and story continuity, or of adapting style sheets. I have tried to point out potential problems in each template.

12.23 There is a nice little book that is supplied with PageMaker, showing nice pictures of most of the template pages. The examples on the following pages show the guidelines and all the handles on each template. It's very important to see those, because they tell you a lot about how the publication is built and what you can expect when you start replacing things. You can see how many separate stories are in a publication or how long the story is that you may be replacing. You can see any blank text blocks that may get you into trouble (and there are several). You can see which graphics have a text wrap applied, and where the template has ignored the guidelines. I've tried to give a few suggestions for working with these particular templates.

12.24 Application template

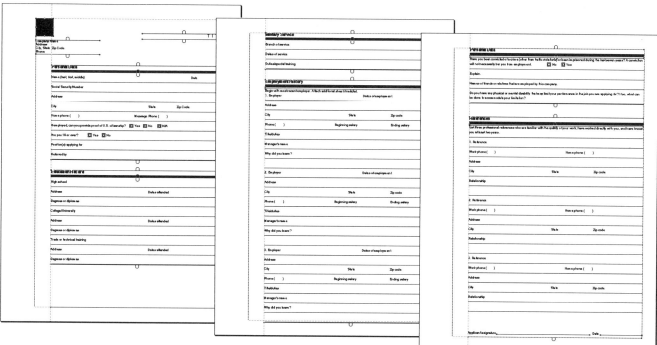

- Address
- Heading
  (includes rule)
- Question 1
  (includes rule)
- Title

Specs:
- 8.5 x 11 page size; tall
- Single-sided
- 3 pages in template

Master Pages:
- Guidelines

This template is a basic job application form. There are a few potentially confusing things on it: The checkboxes are each a tiny *drawn* box, rather than a dingbat embedded in the text, or at least an inline graphic. Since the boxes are separate, as you change the text you will have to move them, trying to keep them aligned without resizing them.

The rules, both thick and thin, are part of the style sheets, which is wonderful. But each group of questions is a separate text block from the head. If the space before and after the heads had been incorporated into the style sheet, you would not have to spend time measuring the spaces above and below the heads to keep the distances consistent. As it is, you will have to measure.

Check for real apostrophes (3.240).

12.25 Avery label templates

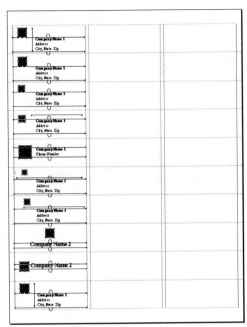

Style 5160

Style Sheet:
- Address
- Company Name 1
- Company Name 2
- Phone Number

  (Address and Phone Number styles are exactly the same. I wonder why.)

Specs:
- 8.5 x 11 page size; tall
- 3 columns
- Guides for 30 labels; 1" x 2⅝"
- Single-sided
- 1 page in template

Master pages:
- Guidelines

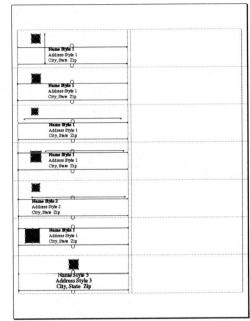

Style 5161

Style Sheet:
- Address Style 2
- Address Style 6
- Body Text
- Name Style 1 (also Name Styles 2–6)

  (I can't figure out what Body Text is for.)

Specs:
- 8.5 x 11 page size; tall
- 2 columns
- Guides for 14 labels; 1" x 4"
- Single-sided
- 1 page in template

Master pages:
- Guidelines

These four Avery label templates are customized to the standard Avery label sizes. They each match the pressure-sensitive photocopier paper of the same number.

In your copy of the template, find an address style you like and personalize it with your own logo and names. Get rid of the other variations, and paste your version into each label space (use power-paste! see 1.194–1.195).

These labels do not have to be used just for mailing purposes. Use them to label file folders, homemade jam, frozen foods, disks, binders, etc. Put some fancy little Christmas clip art on them and use them for package labeling or gift baskets. On the big labels, add "Hello, my name is _____. When I grow up I want to be _____." and use them for name tags.

12.26 Avery label templates

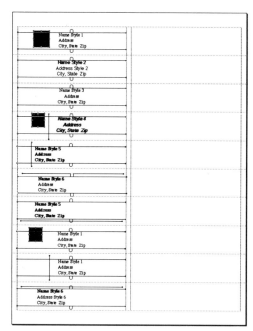

Style 5162

Style Sheet:

- Address Style 1
- Address Style 2
- Address Style 3
- Name Style 1
- Name Style 2
- Name Style 3

(Address Style 3 and Name Style 3 are exactly the same.)

Specs:

- 8.5 x 11 page size; tall
- 2 columns
- Guides for 14 labels; 1¼" x 4"
- Single-sided
- 1 page in template

Master pages:

- Guidelines

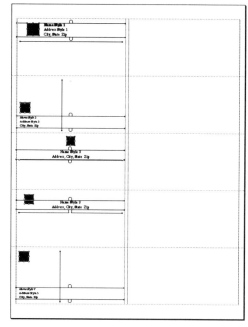

Style 5163

Style Sheet:

- Address Style 1
- Address Style 2
- Address Style 3
- Name Style 1
- Name Style 2
- Name Style 3
- Name Style 4

Specs:

- 8.5 x 11 page size; tall
- 2 columns
- Guides for 10 labels; 2" x 4"
- Single-sided
- 1 page in template

Master pages:

- Guidelines

In the template above, the address for the third and fourth labels is centered. However, the style sheet applied to them (Address Style 3) is flush left. So whoever designed it had to override the style sheet. I can't figure out why they didn't simply adjust the style sheet.

12.27 Brochure 1 template

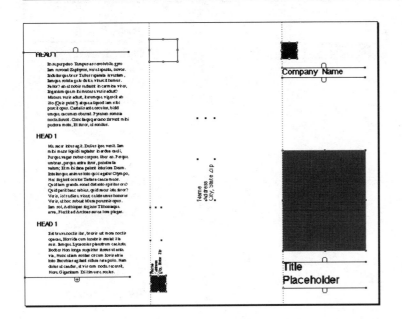

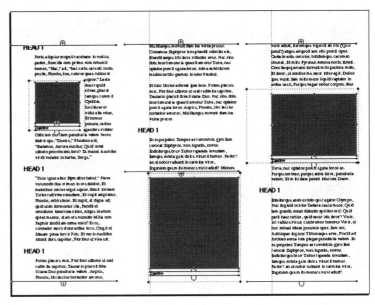

This template is set up as a mailer, although of course you can change that middle panel. The mailing information is rotated text (3.180–3.184).

Notice the text blocks—the entire brochure is one long *story* (3.106). And notice where the story begins (3.100)—the left panel on the outside of the brochure.

So you need to be careful about how you replace text; if you have several stories you are bringing in from an outside word processor, replace *selected* text (3.55), not the entire story. Or select text and create the copy directly in the Story Editor (Section 8) or on the page.

Watch out for the text wraps on the graphics.

Style Sheet:
- Body Copy
- Caption
- Company Name
- Head 1
- Mailing Address 1
- Mailing Address 2
- Title

Specs:
- 8.5 x 11 page size; wide
- 1 column *(why not 3?)*
- Double-sided
- 2 pages in template

Master pages:
- Nothing, not even guidelines

454

12.28 Brochure 2 template

Again, notice the text block connections in this brochure—the entire brochure is one long *story* (3.106). This may or may not be a problem, depending on whether your brochure text is in one long story or is broken up into several chunks to make it easier to manipulate on the screen. However you plan your brochure, just be aware of the format of this template.

A brochure like this would typically be printed from a laser printer or imagesetter, taken to a commercial printer for multiple copies on 11" x 17" paper, then folded down the middle.

But this is a five-page brochure. Really, to make sense you need to add a page or delete a page (1.118–1.119). Otherwise, if you use this format as is, you will have to staple the first page onto the rest of the brochure. A fifth page, if you really need one, should be inserted in the middle of the folded brochure, not plopped on top as the first page.

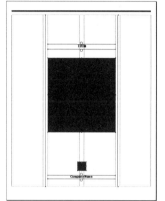

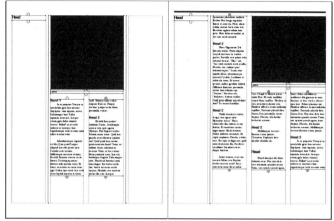
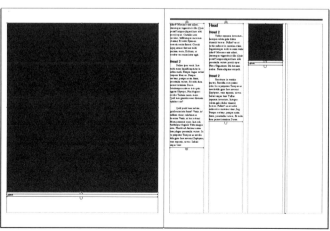

Style Sheet:
- Body Text
- Caption
- Company Name
- Head
- Head 2
- Title

Specs:
- 8.5 x 11 page size; tall
- 4 columns
- Double-sided
- 5 pages in template

Master pages:
- 6-point rule at top of right-hand page

12.29 Business cards template

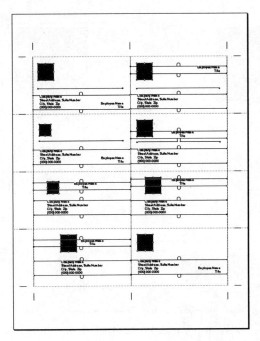

Style Sheet:
- Address 2
- Address 3
- Address1 *(notice it's not in numerical order because of the typo)*

Specs:
- 8.5 x 11 page size; tall
- 2 columns
- 8 options shown
- Single-sided
- 1 page in template

Master pages:
- Guidelines
- Tick marks

This is the same template without all the handles showing.

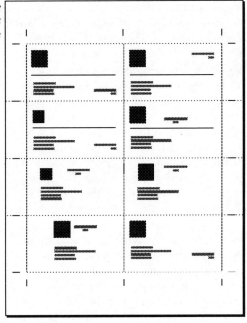

You can replace existing text and graphics with yours in each of these variations to see what you like best. When you decide on one format, pick a layout of your choice on one of the business cards and eliminate the rest. Copy-and-paste your favorite format into the other spaces on the template, and print it up. Take it to your commercial printer for multiple copies on card stock. The tick marks indicate where the cards will be cut after they are printed.

12.30 **Calendar template**

There are supposed to be 14 months' worth of dates provided to drop into this calendar template. I only found 11 in my folder (February, March, and April are missing), but the dates expired in January 1991 anyway. Oh well. The small months are in 5-point text, so unless you have a PostScript printer, you must make sure you have a 5-point font installed.

To update the numbered dates:

- With the **text tool,** click anywhere in the dates area on the large calendar.
- From the File menu, choose "Place...."
- In the Templates folder, find the folder called "Calendar Dates." Double-click to open it, and click on the month you want to change into.
- Click the button "Replace entire story."
- Click OK. In the "Smart ASCII" dialog box, click OK *(this assumes you installed the Smart ASCII import filter; 15.24, 15.25).*
- The dates are all scrunched up, right? With the **text tool,** click anywhere in the dates. From the Edit menu, choose "Select all."
- From the Style palette (or the Style submenu, under Type), click on the style "Dates" ("Small Dates" for the tiny calendars).

Style Sheet:
- Dates
- Days of Week
- Month
- Small Dates
- Small Month

Specs:
- 8.5 x 11 page size; wide
- 1 column
- Single-sided
- 1 page in template

Master pages:
- Guidelines
- Lines/rules

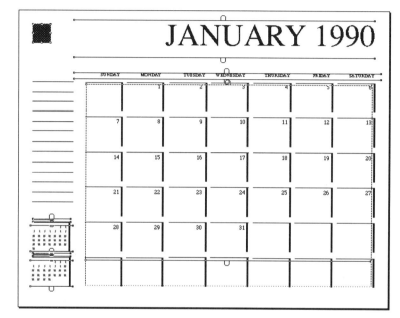

Notice that the dates all belong to one large text block. If you're going to print the template and write in it by hand *(what? use a pen?),* this presents no problem. But if you try to keyboard info into the little squares, that large text block presents a big problem, because typing in it causes all the numbers to move. Here is a good solution:

- With the **pointer tool,** click on the text block of numbers.
- Press Command X to cut the text block.
- Click on the master page icon (the R page).
- Press Option Command V to paste the text block into exactly the same position it was cut from.
- Now, on the publication page, you can type in the calendar boxes.

12.31 Catalog template

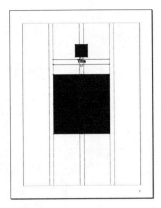

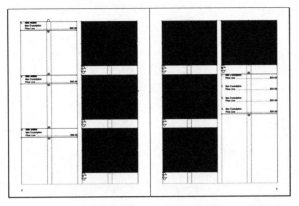

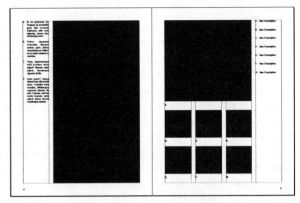

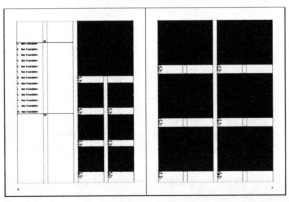

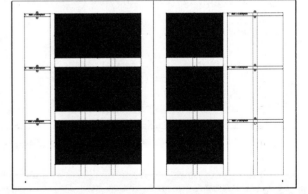

Style Sheet:
- Item Description
- Item Name
- Price Line
- Title

Specs:
- 8.5 x 11 page size; tall
- 4 columns
- Double-sided
- 9 pages in template

Master pages:
- Guidelines
- Column guides
- Page numbers

This catalog is handy for any collection that needs a number of photos. You need to add or delete a page to make it useful (see 12.28). You will probably want to get rid of the page number on the first page (why is it there?). Either cover it with a white box, or hide the master items (from the Page menu, choose "Display master items" to remove the checkmark).

12.32 **Directory template**

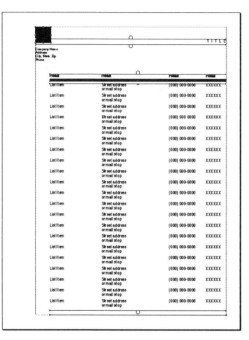

Style Sheet:
- Address
- Column Head
- Head
- List Item
- Title

Specs:
- 8.5 x 11 page size; tall
- 1 column
- Single-sided
- 1 page in template

Master pages:
- Logo and address spaceholders

12.32a *There's a funny thing with all these "Title" blocks in every one of these templates. They all are tagged with the style sheet "Title," and so it would be logical to suppose that if you select the text and retype your own title, the text would be widely letterspaced and all caps. But it isn't; what* you *type will be lowercase with regular letterspacing. I can't figure out why they didn't include all caps and letterspacing in the style sheet so that what you type in will be formatted the same as what you see.*

This can be used as a church mailing list, an employee mail stop list, a student class list, etc. (I don't know why the list copy is in a separate text block from the headline.)

The PageMaker manual suggests importing information from a large database to fill in the blanks. But when you import from a tab-delimited file, such as a database where you tab to each column, each field puts itself into a separate column: the city, state, and zip will not put itself *under* the street address; instead, each item will go looking for its own column. And in your database you *don't* want to put all that information into one field (which would then permit it all to go under the same address column in this template), because then you won't be able to sort by zip code or state, etc. So you're just going to have to type the info. See 3.137–3.138 for lots of text-selecting tips using with the keyboard.

12.33   Envelope templates (LW/LW+ *and* LWII)

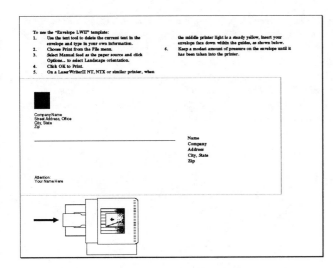

Style Sheet:
- Address
- Return Address

Specs:
- 8.5 x 11 page size; wide *(the instructions call it "landscape")*
- Single-sided
- 1 page in template

Master pages:
- Guidelines

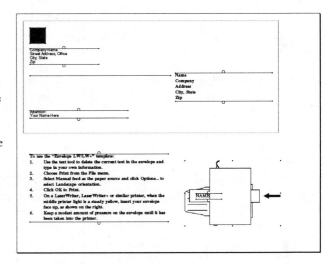

This is the Envelope LWII template, designed for use on the LaserWriter II models. Instructions for printing the envelopes are included on the template page.

This is the Envelope LW/LW+ template, designed for use on the LaserWriter or the LaserWriter Plus models. Instructions for printing the envelopes are included on the template page.

12.34 **Financial sheet template**

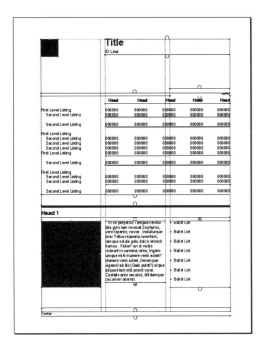

Style Sheet:
- Body
- Bullet List
- Caption
- Footer
- Head
- Head 1
- ID Line
- Listing, first level
- Listing, second level
- Title

Specs:
- 8.5 x 11 page size; tall
- Single-sided
- 1 page in template

Master pages:
- Guidelines
- 3 columns

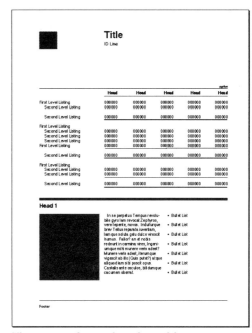

The same template, without the guidelines and handles.

The columns in this template are set up with decimal tabs for working with numbers. You might want to adjust the Bullet List style in the style sheet; the tab and the first-line indent don't quite line up (see their Indents/tabs ruler). Notice the bulleted list is a continuation of the paragraph of body copy on the left.

12.35 Invoice template

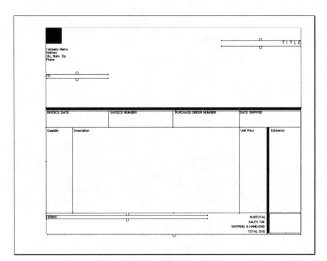

This is a nice, straightforward, standard invoice. You can insert your name and logo, then give a copy to your commercial printer, who can print it onto NCR paper for you, with sequential numbers even.

Don't try to type directly on the template, because there is one large text block covering the entire bottom portion. I'd suggest cutting the entire page and pasting it onto the master page, as described in 12.46.

Style Sheet:
- Address
- Title *(see 12.00)*

Specs:
- 8.5 x 11 page size; wide
- 1 column
- Single-sided
- 1 page in template

Master pages:
- Logo and address placeholders

12.36 Letterhead template

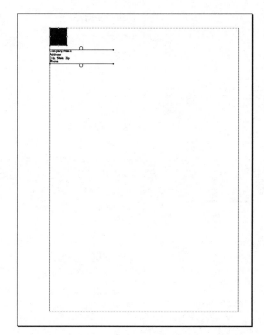

Style Sheet:
- Address
- Body text
  (for typing letters)

Specs:
- 8.5 x 11 page size; tall
- 1 column
- Single-sided
- 9 pages in template

Master pages:
- Guidelines

You can use this either to create your own letterhead, print a master copy, and give it to a commercial press for duplication in color; or to set up a simple letterhead and just use it in your laser printer. I would suggest placing the upper left elements onto the master page (cut, then Option Command V on the master page). Also add guidelines for the letter text. That way you can make more pages, write a bunch of letters, and just send them through on nice paper. Use a pretty marker to color in your logo after the letter is printed.

12.37 Manual 1 template

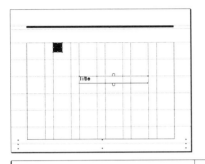

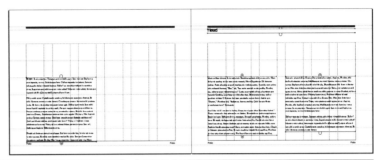

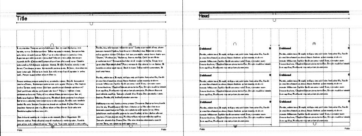

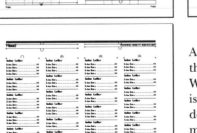

Style Sheet:

- Body Text
- Caption
- Folio
- Head
- Index Entry
- Index Letter (I & II)
- Notes
- Numbered List
- Running Head (L&R)
- Subhead 1
  (with hairline rule above)
- Subhead 2
  (with 8-point rule above)
- Subhead 3
- Title

Specs:

- 8.5 x 11 page size; wide
- 6 column grid
- Double-sided
- 9 pages in template

Master pages:

- Guidelines
- Folio placeholders
- Top rule, both left and right

At least there are several separate stories in this manual (unlike many of the others). Watch those master page "Folios" (a *folio* is a page number); I don't know why they don't include actual page numbers. This manual has a nice grid, but the layout ignores it in some odd ways.

12.38 Manual 2 template

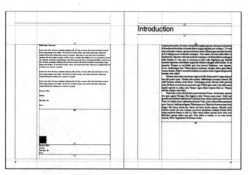
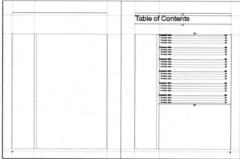

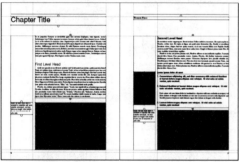
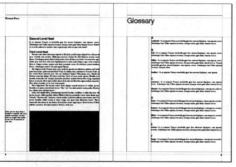
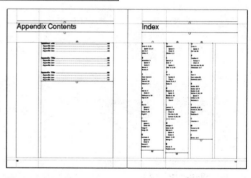

Style Sheet:
- Appendix Item
- Appendix Title
- Body Text
- Body text, first para
- Caption
- Contents item
- Contents title

- Credit address
- Credits
- Glossary Entre
- Glossary Letter
- Head 1 (also 2 & 3)
- Index 1 (also 2)
- Index letter
- Intro

- Intro first paragraph
- List Head *(with rule)*
- List item
- List paragraph
- Running Head
- Title

Specs:
- 8.5 x 11 page size; tall
- 1 column
- Double-sided
- 11 pages in template

Master pages:
- Guidelines
- Hairline rule at top of left and right pages

12.39 **Manual 3 template**

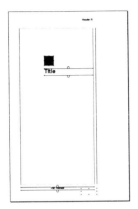

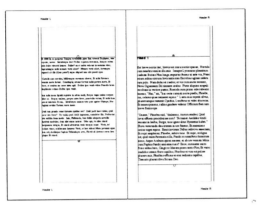

This manual template is actually half-size; the page size is 5.5 x 8.5, (8.5 x 11 folded in half), making a tall, slender manual. Each page that comes out of the printer will have this smaller size centered on it, so be sure to choose crop marks (18.82–18.83). You can then paste up two pages on each 8.5 x 11 for printing at your commercial printer or copying on your copy machine.

Style Sheet:
- Body Text
- Caption
- Caption Title
- Copyright
- Glossary Entry
- Head 1
- Head 2
- Header L
- Header R
- Index Entry
- Index Letter
- Part Number
- Subhead
- Table of Contents
- Title

Specs:
- 8.5 x 11 paper size; wide
- 5.5 x 8.5 page size; 2-up on one sheet
- Double-sided
- 8 pages in template

Master pages:
- Margin guides
- Vertical hairline rules
- Headers and footers
  (they are named Header and Header)

12.40 Memo template

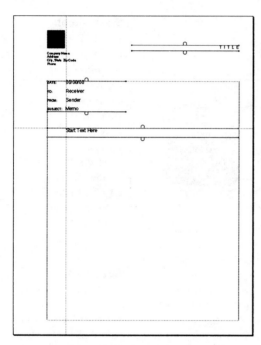

Style Sheet:
- Address
- Body Text
- Header Text
- Memo
- Title *(see 12.32a)*

Specs:
- 8.5 x 11 page size; tall
- 1 column
- Single-sided
- 1 page in template

Master pages:
- Margin guide
- Logo and address placeholders
- Date:
  To:
  From:
  Subject

From this template you can either create a customized memo form to copy on your copy machine or at your commercial printer, or create an on-line memo and send it through your modem or fax.

12.41 Newsletter 1 template

Style Sheet:
- Body Text
- Caption
- Drop Cap
- First Level Head
- Header
- Masthead
- Page Number
  (I don't know why this has a style tagged to it. Also, where is the number?)
- Second Level Head

Specs:
- 8.5 x 11 page size; tall
- 3 columns
- Double-sided
- 4 pages in template

Master pages:
- Column guides

Be careful when replacing text in this newsletter—this is one long, connected *story* (3.106). There is a text wrap applied to each graphic placeholder, also.

Watch those initial caps—initial caps *should* always sit on the same baseline as one of the lines of text, which these don't. Notice the text blocks are split to wrap around the caps; as you change the text, make sure you keep consistent linespacing between the two text blocks (see 19.8).

The First Level Heads, as you can see, are in their own text blocks, *but the text blocks are connected both at the tops and bottoms,* which means as you edit text, the heads will reflow into other text blocks. They didn't make this easy on you. I do hope you are more conscientious about making the top and bottom baselines in the columns align, as well as making the space above heads consistent (had they all been part of their stories, you could have relied on paragraph space before and after [4.63; 4.87] to set uniform space between Heads and Body).

12.42 Newsletter 2 template

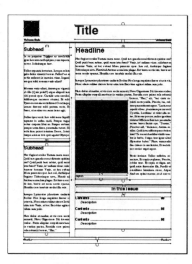
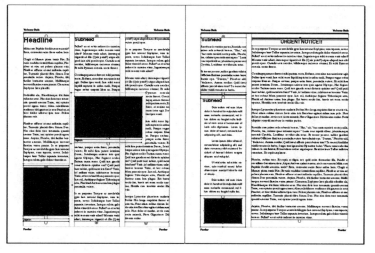

Style Sheet:
- Body Text
- Boxed Subhead
- Boxed Text
- Caption
- Contents
- Continued
- Description
- Footer
- Headline
- Subhead
- Title
- Volume–Data

Specs:
- 8.5 x 11 page size; tall
- 3 columns
- Double-sided
- 4 pages in template

Master pages:
- Header
- Footer, left and right
- Column guides

Check carefully to see where stories in this newsletter are threaded (3.95–3.106). Notice that the first two news stories are actually *one* PageMaker story—from Subhead through Headline. I don't know why they did that. The second page is all one story, continuing into the Subhead on the third page. The fourth page is all one story, except for the story that is "continued from page 00": that little story is not connected to anything!

For some unknown reason there is a superfluous text block on page one for a page number. On the other pages, watch out when you replace that very first Subhead —there is a blank, invisible text block sitting right on top of it, just waiting to trip you up.

12.43 Newsletter 3 template (tabloid size)

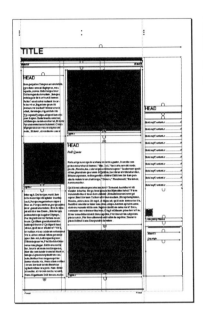
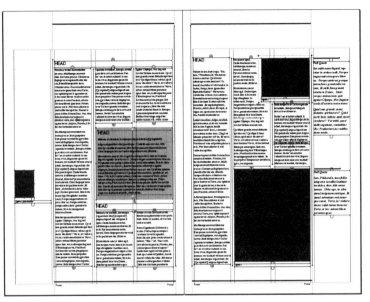
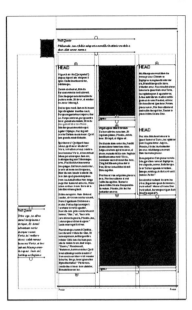

Style Sheet:
- Body Text
- Caption
- Company Name
- Copyright
- Footer L
- Footer R *(which is exactly the same as Footer L)*
- Head
- Head 2

- Header
- Note
- Pull Quote
- Table of Contents
- Title

Specs:
- 11 x 17 page size
- 8.5 x 11 paper size; tall
- 4 columns

- Double-sided
- 4 pages in template

Master pages:
- Column guides
- Footers
- Rules (lines) at top and bottom of pages *(notice the white bar covering the top rule on the first page)*

I can't believe this entire four-page, tabloid size newsletter is made of one story (with the exception of a few little stories on the sides). Even all those heads are just little text blocks separated from the one story. That makes it so very difficult to edit and rearrange. And watch out for that empty text block that is sitting on top of the other text in the third column on the third page.

If your printer doesn't print tabloid-size paper, you will need to manually tile this newsletter (18.90–18.93) onto regular paper and then paste up the sections.

12.44   **Price list template**

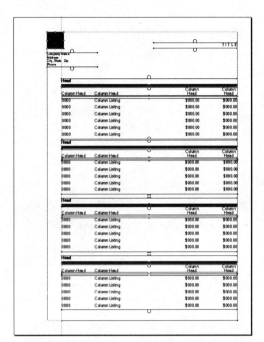

Style Sheet:
- Address
- Column *(although nothing is tagged as Column)*
- Column Head
- Column Listing
- Head
- Title *(see 12.32a)*

> *These three styles are overridden every time they are used on this page. I'm not sure why the style sheet itself wasn't just changed.*

Specs:
- 8.5 x 11 page size; tall
- 1 column
- Single-sided
- 1 page in template

Master pages:
- Guidelines

The tabloid-size newsletter on the previous page was one continuous story, making it difficult to work with. Now this price list, which *should* be one story, is made up of lots of stories, as you can see. This makes it difficult to keep the spacing consistent; that is, the spacing above and below the heads and the subheads. The original template

you see here doesn't even have consistent line spacing itself. I'm very surprised the designer didn't take advantage of the style sheets to make this entire page a piece of cake to work with. But at least the Head and Column Head styles contain paragraph rules.

A couple of funny things happen with

this template. When you open it, it doesn't appear in the middle of the screen, but half off the screen. And the super- and subscript positions (3.163–3.170) in the defined styles are still 66%, which are the positions they were mistakenly given early in the Page-Maker 4.0 development stage, before being changed to 33%.

12.45 Proposal template

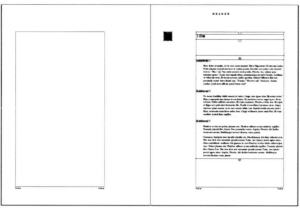

Style Sheet:
- Address&Date
- Body Text
- Caption
- Company Name
- Endnote
- Footer
- Header
- Letter
- Subhead 1 (& 2)
- Table Head
- Table Item
- Title

Specs:
- 8.5 x 11 page size; tall
- 1 column
- Double-sided
- 7 pages in template

Master pages:
- Margin guides
- Header and footers

For some unfathomable reason, all the text is assigned the color "Registration." This means if you were to use color in this publication and print spot color overlays, all the text would appear on every overlay for every color.

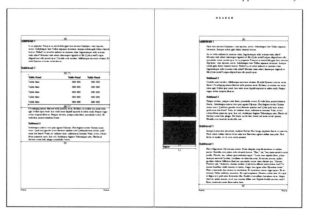

As with most of the other templates, you'll want to be careful when replacing text, as the main body copy on these seven pages is one long text block.

12.46 Purchase order template

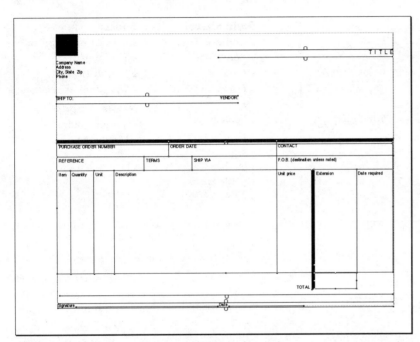

Style Sheet:
- Address
- Title *(see 12.32a)*

Specs:
- 8.5 x 11 page size; wide
- 1 column
- Single-sided
- 1 page in template

Master pages:
- Margin guides
- Logo and company name placeholders

I would suggest that you make any of the changes you find necessary, then cut the entire page (with the pointer tool, press Command A; then Command X). Go to the master page and power-paste the entire page (Command Option V; 3.194). That way you won't accidentally move any lines out of place or inadvertently change any of the text you want to be permanent.

Putting the form on the master page will also allow you to type directly onto the publication page if you want to. As it is, with that one big text block, you can't really type on the page or it will move all the headings around.

Notice in that thick vertical rule there is a hairline rule stuck under it. You might want to remove the hairline so it won't cause problems later (Command-click until you see its handles, then backspace; 3.176).

12.47 **What is a grid?**

A **grid** is a framework of guidelines that provides a structure upon which to build a publication. Grids can be simple or quite involved and technical. A well-thought out grid is really the only solution when designing a lengthy, complex project, such as an encyclopedia or informational atlas, that involves a number of different elements. But you will also find it invaluable for any publication of more than one page that needs a unified, professional appearance.

A well-designed grid is based on an interplay between all the possible demands of the text and the graphics. That is, a grid is based on the point size of the text type and its leading. The point size and leading of the headlines, subheads, captions, and pullquotes should all be based on multiples of the body text. For instance, if the body text is 10/12, the grid will be based on 12-point units of space. So headlines, in order to fit the grid, will work at sizes such as 24/24, or perhaps 34/36. Captions could be italic, 9/12, etc. Text blocks should always align with the grid. Graphics should be cropped or scaled to fit within the grid.

Take a look at 12.37 and 12.38 to see how those publications make use of the underlying grid. (But notice also how the captions are placed, ignoring the grid in some inappropriate and incomprehensible ways.)

Really, the secret to creating a successful, dynamic publication with a grid is knowing how and when to override the grid, while still keeping the continuity, the unity, the clarity, and the organization that the framework of the grid provides.

Grid theory is one of the most fascinating studies in graphic design. If you have any interest in pursing this topic, I strongly recommend you read these classics:

Grid Systems in Graphic Design, Josef Müller-Brockmann. Second revised edition. New York: Hastings House Publishers, Inc. 1985.

The Grid, Allen Hurlburt. New York: Van Nostrand Reinhold Company, 1978.

Use a grid the same way you use a template. Take advantage of the framework that is already provided for you, and place your own text and graphics within the framework. Align text along the top of the rectangles, scale and crop graphics to fit within the rectangles, align captions and pull quotes to match body text baselines, etc.

12.48 **The grid templates**

The following pages show grid templates that PageMaker has provided for you to work with. They are all based on 12 points of leading. The gutters between the horizontal grid units are also 12 points, as you would expect. With each grid there are myriad possibilities for layout. You need to use your aesthetic sensibilities to limit yourself to a basic format and work within it.

All the grids provided have the guidelines on the master page. The guides are all locked (1.66), and the zero point is locked (1.72). "Snap to guides" (1.64) and "Snap to rulers" (1.55) are turned on. The measurement system (1.211) is in picas (4.6–4.7), and the vertical ruler is customized (1.54) to 12 points. Oddly enough, "Align to grid" is not on (4.89; 4.103).

The grids shown are from the master pages of each template. The page setup has been set to double-sided, but each template, when you open it, will only show one page in the publication. It is just waiting for you to add the rest.

12.49 **Grids**

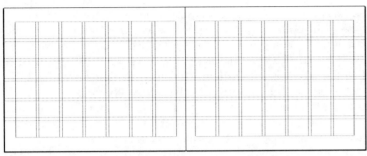

a) *11 x 8.5 (A4); 7 columns x 6 rows*

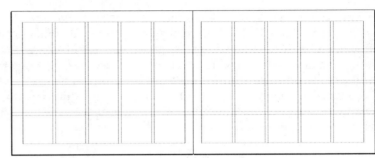

b) *11 x 8.5 (A4); 5 columns x 4 rows*

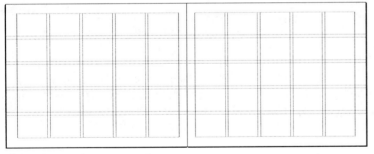

c) *11 x 8.5 (A4); 5 columns x 5 rows*

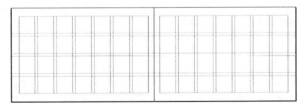

d) *8.5 x 5.5 (A5); 7 columns x 4 rows*

Grids —*continued*

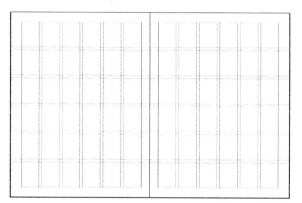

e) *8.5 x 11 (A4); 6 columns x 6 rows*

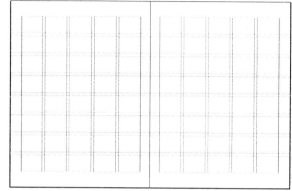

f) *8.5 x 11 (A4); 5 columns x 8 rows*

g) *5.5 x 8.5 (A5); 7 columns x 3 rows*

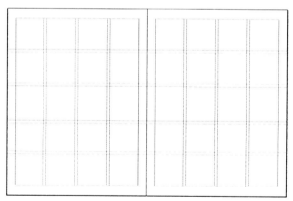

h) *8.5 x 11 (A4); 4 columns x 5 rows*

Grids   *—continued*

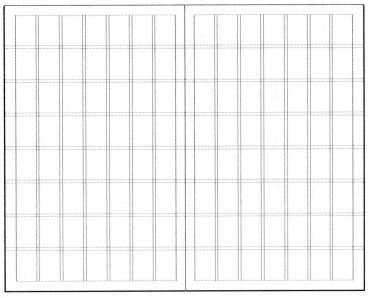

i) *11 x 17; 7 columns x 8 rows*

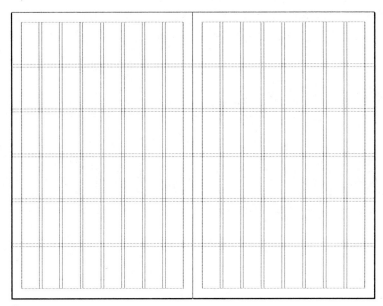

j) *11 x 17; 8 columns x 6 rows*

13 ▾ BOOK PUBLICATIONS

13.1 Minimums and maximums:

Item	Minimum	Maximum
Number of books in a book list	1	Unlimited
Index entry	1 char.	50 char.
Table of Contents entry	1	over 4,000
Table of Contents or Index titles	0 char.	30 char.

Changes in version 4.01: Most of the changes in the update from 4.0 to 4.01 take place in the book publication features. In 4.01 you can:

- Copy the entire Book List into each publication in the List (13.24).
- Automatically renumber the pages consecutively when printing the Book List (13.27).
- Automatically capitalize all index entries (13.147).
- Automatically index all the names in a list, all at once (13.146).
- Add multiple entries without leaving the dialog box (13.134–13.143).
- Accept entries that will stay when you Cancel others (13.132; 13.149).
- Undo index entry additions and deletions (13.150).
- Suppress the page range (13.102).

13.2 PageMaker 4 has several features specifically geared toward the publication of long documents: the Book, Table of Contents, and Indexing features.

13.3 In order to create either a Table of Contents or an Index for a book that is comprised of more than one PageMaker publication, you need to know how to create and use a Book List. It'll take you about five minutes to learn.

13.4 The Table of Contents feature is very straightforward and easy to use. If you take advantage of your style sheets as you create the Table of Contents, you can whip up a great Table in no time, with all your headings and subheads referenced to their appropriate page numbers. As you edit, add, or delete pages, PageMaker keeps track of the changes and allows you to instantly update to the new page numbers.

13.5 The Indexing feature is not so straightforward, but it is really remarkable, once you figure out how to use it. You can just buzz through your publications (thoughtfully, of course), entering index entries, many with just a keystroke. After you've created indices for all the publications that make up your entire book, you can then create one major index for the whole thing, complete with cross-references and subentries. The index drops in fully formatted, complete with editable style sheets, one- and two-em indents for subentries, en dashes between page ranges, etc. It's too cool. As you edit, add, or delete pages, PageMaker keeps track of the entries and allows you to instantly update to the new page numbers.

Note: When either the Table of Contents or the Index becomes large, PageMaker can take an incredibly long time to create and show it. I mean seriously long, like half an hour for an index consisting of a couple thousand entries. Even editing in the "Show index" dialog box becomes tedious.

The Book List

13.6   You can create a single PageMaker publication up to 999 pages. Big deal—you would never want to create one file that large. It would get awkward and ungainly, and would be difficult to back up, maneuver, keep track of, etc., etc., etc. This book in your hands has fewer than 800 pages, but weighs in at 40 megabytes, not including the fonts necessary to print it.

13.7   You will probably want to divide any book or document longer than about fifty pages into sections or chapters. For these lengthy works it's better to create a separate PageMaker file for each of its sections, plus a separate file for the table of contents and the index sections (some people like to combine those two into one file; I like to keep a separate file for each). You can then create a **Book List** to connect all the separate files and work with them as one publication for printing and generating an index and a table of contents.

13.8   The Book List contains a list of all the publications that belong to the entire book, listed in the order you want them to print. (Any publication may be listed in more than one Book List.) Typically you will set up your Book List in only one of the separate publications, most likely in the table of contents pub. If you would like to have it in any of the other separate publications, PageMaker version 4.01 has a keyboard command to copy the existing Book List into every publication in the list (13.24).

13.9   You can then print every publication in the Book List, one after another, without having to open each one separately. You can generate a table of contents (13.28–13.63) and an index (13.64–13.190) that encompass every section. The table and the index will automatically include the page number of each item. As you add or delete pages in the publication, the page numbers recorded in the internal table of contents and the index will change accordingly.

13.10   In PageMaker version 4.0, the separate sections cannot be automatically numbered consecutively as you print the entire Book List; you must open each section and set the "Start page #" yourself (1.29) before you print the list. PageMaker 4.01, though, has a few extra buttons in the "Book publication list" dialog box (13.18). These buttons allow you a variety of ways to automatically and consecutively number your publications as they print (13.27).

13.11   The Book List is actually just a list that tells PageMaker where to *find* the publication. If you move or rename the publication after you have added it to a Book List, PageMaker will ask you to find it when you try to print or generate a table of contents or an index.

13.12   Be sure to take advantage of creating templates (Section 12) and copying style sheets (7.19; 7.50) to keep each publication in the book consistent. That is really one of the secrets of a professional-looking piece—consistency—because it creates a unified work that looks like the creators knew what they were doing.

"Book publication list" dialog box *(from the File menu, choose "Book...")*

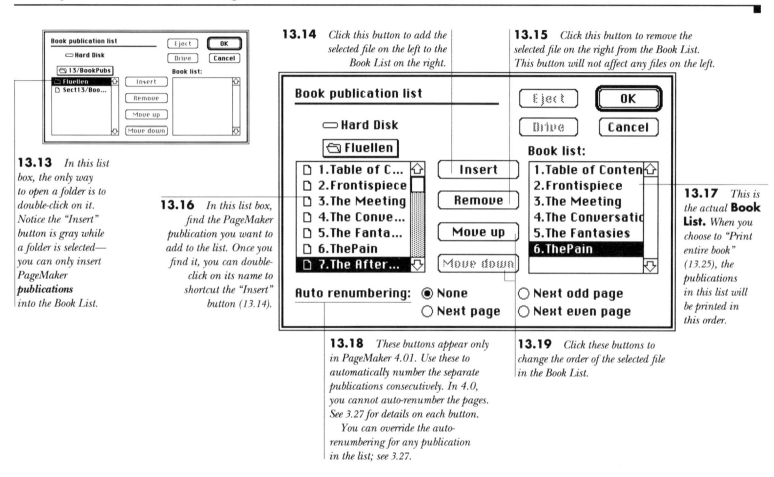

13.14 *Click this button to add the selected file on the left to the Book List on the right.*

13.15 *Click this button to remove the selected file on the right from the Book List. This button will not affect any files on the left.*

13.13 *In this list box, the only way to open a folder is to double-click on it. Notice the "Insert" button is gray while a folder is selected— you can only insert PageMaker* **publications** *into the Book List.*

13.16 *In this list box, find the PageMaker publication you want to add to the list. Once you find it, you can double-click on its name to shortcut the "Insert" button (13.14).*

13.17 *This is the actual* **Book List.** *When you choose to "Print entire book" (13.25), the publications in this list will be printed in this order.*

13.18 *These buttons appear only in PageMaker 4.01. Use these to automatically number the separate publications consecutively. In 4.0, you cannot auto-renumber the pages. See 3.27 for details on each button.*
You can override the auto-renumbering for any publication in the list; see 3.27.

13.19 *Click these buttons to change the order of the selected file in the Book List.*

479

If you want to do this:

13.20 Create a Book List

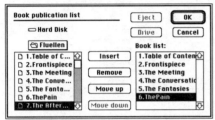

The dialog box in version 4.0.

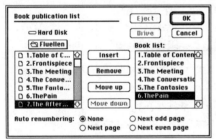

The dialog box in version 4.01.

Then follow these steps:

- Open any one of the publications that comprise the whole book (preferably the first publication in the group, just so you always know where the Book List is).
- From the File menu, choose "Book...."
- In the "Book publication list" dialog box, there are two list boxes. On the left, navigate through your disks and folders to find the publication you want to add to the Book List (the publication you are currently in will already be visible in this list). *The only way to open a folder in the left-hand list box is to double-click on it.*
- Once you find the publication that you want to include in the List, click once on its name, then click the "Insert" button (or double-click on its name). The publication will be added to the Book List on the right side.
- Once it is on the Book List, you can move the publication up higher on the list: select it (click once on its name); click the "Move up" button as many times as necessary. Click the "Move down" button to move the publication below any other file in the List.
- Before you click OK, you can navigate through your folders to find any other publications to add to the list.
- Click OK.

Shortcuts ▾ Notes ▾ Hints

- Actually, the publication is not always added to the *end* of the Book List; it is added directly after whichever publication in the Book List is *selected* (highlighted). So if you want to control the order of the publications without the extra steps of moving them up or down, simply select the name in the Book List that you want the new publication to *follow* (click once on it; see the illustrations in 13.21). When you insert the next publication, it will appear directly after the selected name.

If you want to do this:

Then follow these steps:

Shortcuts ▾ Notes ▾ Hints

13.21 Add a publication to the Book List

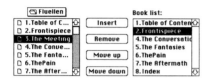

If you want to add a new publication directly below one that is already in the list, click once on the pub in the Book List.

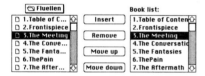

When you insert the new pub, it will appear directly below the one that was previously selected.

- Open the publication that contains the Book List.
- From the File menu, choose "Book...."
- Just as in 13.20, navigate through the disks and folders in the left-hand list box to find the publication you want to add to the list.
- The existing Book List is in a particular order—you will probably want it in the order in which the book is to be read. If you want to add a publication to that list in a certain spot in the order rather than at the bottom, do this:
  - ☐ In the Book List on the right, click once on the name of the publication that you want the new one to *follow*.
  - ☐ In the publication list on the left, double-click on the pub you want to add (or select it and click the "Insert" button). The new publication will be added to the Book List directly *after* the one that was selected.
- If the publication is added to the *bottom* of the Book List and you want it in a different order, you can move the selected publication up or down in the list order by clicking the "Move up" or "Move down" buttons.
- Click OK.

If you want to do this:	**Then follow these steps:**	**Shortcuts · Notes · Hints**
13.22 Remove a publication from the Book List	■ Open the publication that contains the Book List. ■ From the File menu, choose "Book...." ■ In the Book List shown on the right, click once on the publication you want to remove. ■ Click the "Remove" button. You will not get an alert box asking if you really want to do this. If you didn't want to remove it, but you did, you can either Cancel this dialog box (which will cancel any other changes you made here), or you can simply find the publication and insert it again. ■ Click OK.	
13.23 Change the order of the publications in the Book List	■ Open the publication that contains the Book List. ■ From the File menu, choose "Book...." ■ In the Book List shown on the right, click once on the publication of which you want to change the order. ■ Click either the "Move up" or "Move down" buttons. Click OK.	
13.24 Copy the Book List into every other publication in the list  Copying book publication list. ☐☐☐☐ [Cancel] Copying book publication list. Publication: 5.The Fantasies	■ You can only do this in version 4.01. Press the Command key as you choose "Book..." from the File menu. You won't get the actual dialog box; you will just see a progress report of the copying process.	■ The current publication must have a Book List, of course, and the pub must be titled (not "Untitled"). This process will replace any existing book lists that may already be in the other publications.

If you want to do this:

13.25 Print all the publications
on the Book List

Book: ○ **Print this pub only** ● **Print entire book**

Then follow these steps:

- Open the publication that contains the Book List.
- If you have PageMaker 4.01 and you want to automatically renumber each publication in the Book List, see 13.27.
- From the File menu, choose "Print...," *or* press Command P.
- Click the button "Print entire book" (this button is only available in publications that contain a Book List).
- Set up the "Print to" dialog box and the "Options" dialog box the way you like. You cannot:
  - □ Print more than one copy.
  - □ Tile.
  - □ Print in reverse order.
  - □ Collate.
  - □ Print PostScript to disk.

  PageMaker will let you *think* she will do these functions; you can check the boxes and enter a number in the "Copies" edit box, but you will just be ignored.

  You can choose any of the other options. All the specs you choose here will apply to every publication in the list, regardless of their individual print specifications (see the note to the right!).
- Click "Print," or hit Return.

Shortcuts ▾ Notes ▾ Hints

- The publications are printed in the order they are listed, even if the one on the screen is not the first in the list (even if the one on the screen is not even in the List). They will print with the page number of their own publication, though, not the page number of the order they pop out of the printer (unless you choose to automatically renumber them, using PageMaker version 4.01; 3.27).
- **Important note:** All the pubs will print with the print specifications that are in the publication you are printing from, even if the current publication is not in the List.

  If you hold down the Option key when you click the Print button, each publication will print with the specs that are stored with each separate publication. But the only way the specs will have been stored is if you previously printed the publication all the way through; if you canceled the printing the specs were not stored.

If you want to do this:

13.26 Print just some of the publications on the Book List

Book: ◯ Print this pub only ◉ Print entire book

Then follow these steps:

- If you don't want to print every pub on the List, change the List. You can always change it back later.
- **Or** move the publications that you do want to print into the first positions (13.23). After those pages come out of the printer, Cancel the printing (click on the "Cancel" button, or press Command Period).
- **Or** open another publication and create another Book List that contains just the pubs you want to print. Any publication can be in any number of Book Lists, because the Book List is just a list that tells PageMaker where to *find* the actual pub.

Shortcuts ▾ Notes ▾ Hints

- Remember, no matter which publication contains the Book List, when you print the entire book, the printing proceeds only in the order on the List and includes only those publications listed there. So you can actually have a publication open that contains a Book List that doesn't even list the pub that is open! But from within this publication, you can print any other PageMaker file on your disk. That's a good trick.

If you ain't the lead dog, the scenery never changes.
— E. Wilson

If you want to do this:

13.27 Automatically renumber, consecutively, all the pages in the publications printed from the Book List

Auto renumbering:

⦿ None ○ Next odd page
○ Next page ○ Next even page

Then follow these steps:

- This is only available in version 4.01.
- Before you print, from the File menu, choose "Book...."
- Click one of the buttons for "Auto renumbering":
  - □ **None:** This is the default setting. Page-Maker will not renumber the pages.
  - □ **Next page:** The following publication will begin with a page number that is in exact sequence with the previous publication in the list.
  - □ **Next odd page:** This is just like "Next page" except that it forces each new publication to begin printing on an odd page (which is a right-hand page). The publication will end on an even-numbered page (left hand). PageMaker will insert pages, if necessary, at the beginning and end to accomplish this. Since she is inserting blank pages, they will not print unless you check the "Print blank pages" box in the Options dialog box before you print (18.94). They won't print with any page number on them.
  - □ **Next even page:** This works exactly like "Next odd page" above, except that the first page will always be even.

Shortcuts ▾ Notes ▾ Hints

- This automatic renumbering feature actually changes the page numbers on the publication pages. That is, if you had five publications of 6 pages each, each numbered from 1 to 6, after you print with this automatic renumbering in effect, those pages will be numbered 1 to 6, 7 to 12, 13 to 18, etc.
- **If you want to override the auto page numbering for any publication in the Book List,** you need to click the "Restart page numbering" checkbox in that particular publication's "Page setup" dialog box (from the File menu). This will cause the pub to retain its own numbering.

Tables of Contents (TOC)

13.28 PageMaker makes it incredibly easy to generate a table of contents. It does involve foresight and planning, however, and you really should have a working knowledge of style sheets (Section 7) in order to use this feature without frustration.

13.29 The **Table of Contents** (**TOC**) feature works in this way: In any publication, whether it is complete in itself or part of an entire book, you choose which *paragraphs* you want to include in a table of contents. Remember, on the Mac any text that ends with a Return key is one *paragraph;* each separate one of your chapter titles, headings, subheads, etc., is considered a separate *paragraph.* PageMaker can compile all the paragraphs you choose and create a table of contents for the current publication, or for the entire Book List, all accurately paginated and set up with leader tabs (see the examples on page 490).

13.30 You can choose whether a paragraph should be included in the table of contents in either of two ways:

- You can select the individual paragraph (just click in it with the text tool), then bring up the "Paragraph specifications" dialog box (from the Type menu, choose "Paragraph..."). Click in the checkbox, "Include in table of contents."

- Or you can include the option, "Include in table of contents," right into your style sheet so it will automatically build every instance of that style (be it headline, subhead, etc.) into your table of contents.

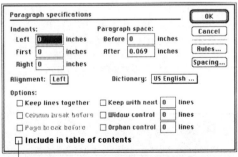

Click this checkbox, whether individually or through your style sheet definitions (Section 7).

13.31 It is best, really, to plan on using your style sheets to help define the table. Then you know nothing will be forgotten; plus, it keeps everything consistent. It does mean you have to be aware that every time you apply that particular style, the tagged paragraph will be added to the table of contents *(which is editable, though).* And if you base any other styles (7.20–7.26) on that particular style, those paragraphs will also be included in the table of contents.

13.32 That's not the only reason you need to understand your style sheets: When the table of contents is generated, PageMaker creates and applies a style to each level (see 13.38–13.39). It will rarely look exactly like you want, so you need to know how to edit the style sheet to your satisfaction.

The process of creating a Table of Contents

13.33 First, you must tag all the paragraphs that you want included in the table of contents (13.30; 13.55). You can create a table for just one individual publication, or you can create a table that spans every publication in the Book List (13.58–13.59). Or you can do both, as I did in this book.

13.34 You can apply a prefix to the page numbers; the prefix will appear only in the table of contents and the index (not on the pages themselves). For instance, you may have your publication divided into sections A, B, and C. You can set up a prefix, using the "Page numbering" dialog box (13.57), that will precede each number with the section letter; e.g., A1, A2, A3, etc. Or perhaps you want to label your appendix pages or your front matter pages differently than the regular pages. These prefixes are specific to each publication.

13.35 If you are working with one individual publication, after you are finished and everything has been tagged, you can choose "Create TOC..." from the Options menu and create the table (13.58).

13.36 If you are working with several publications as part of a book, there are several other factors to deal with:

a) You can choose to include all the publications that appear in the Book List contained within the open publication.

b) If you decide to include the entire Book List, the items in the table of contents *will be in the order of the Book List,* not in their page number order. That is, if your Book List shows Sections 1, 2, 4, 3, your table of contents will reflect that same order.

c) Unless you have version 4.01,* PageMaker does not automatically number your pages in consecutive order just because they are in a Book List. You have to go into the "Page setup" dialog box of each publication and change the "Start page #" appropriately (1.29; 13.10).

(If you have version 4.01, see 13.27).

13.37 When you choose "Create TOC...," PageMaker gathers up all the paragraphs that have been tagged, whether in the individual publication or in all the pubs in the Book List. She arranges them in the order they appear in the publication and in the order the publications appear in the list.

13.38 Each item in the table is tagged with a style that PageMaker creates; these styles are automatically added to your style sheet. Each style is named with the prefix "TOC," followed by the name of the style the item is already tagged with. That is, if Subhead 1 is checked to include table of contents items, then when those tagged items are generated into a Table of Contents, each will then be tagged with the style "TOC Subhead 1."

13.39 All TOC styles default to a tab with a dot leader (which you can change; 13.61) leading over to the page number. The size, type style, other tab stops, and the alignment are the same as they are in the style they were generated from.

—continued

The process   —*continued*

That is, if the style "Subhead 1" is 18-point Garamond Bold, then in the generated Table of Contents the corresponding "TOC Subhead 1" will use 18-point Garamond Bold. That's why it is important for you to know how to work with and edit your style sheets. Change the style sheets to your heart's content, *but don't change the style names!! (13.41)*

13.40 When you click OK in the "Create table of contents" dialog box (13.58), Page-Maker generates the table.

- If you are on a publication page, you will get a loaded text icon. Click on the page to place the table of contents story.
- If you are in the Story Editor (Section 8), you will get a new story window displaying the table of contents. Press Command D to get the loaded text icon; click to place the story on the publication page.

13.41 You will undoubtedly need to edit the TOC style sheets to arrange the text aesthetically and legibly. Edit the styles all you want, *but don't change the style names!!* When you update the Table of Contents, you can choose to have PageMaker replace the current version with the new version; the new version will reuse the customized style sheet *if the styles have the same names as PageMaker originally gave them.*

13.42 If a paragraph that is included in the table of contents is not tagged with a style, PageMaker will format it, but will not assign it a style (it will be "No style").

13.43 In the "Create table of contents" dialog box (13.47), you have an option of creating a title for the table of contents page. The standard title is "Contents," and that is the default PageMaker supplies. You can change that edit box (13.48), though, to any title you choose, up to 30 characters in length. Or you can just leave it blank.

13.44 If you decide to have a title, Page-Maker will assign it a style, "TOC title." Because of this, it is best not to name any of your own styles *(ones that will be included in the table of contents)* with the name "Title," or you may end up confused.

13.45 If you will be adding the Table of Contents to the beginning of an existing publication, be sure you allow enough pages for it. Take into consideration the fact that, as you add pages, your page numbers will all change, including the first page of your first chapter. That may or may not be a problem for you.

13.46 If you really want the TOC to be included in the same publication as the rest of the pages, consider adding the Table of Contents at the end of the publication, without page numbers. That way the first chapter can start on page one, yet your Table of Contents can expand as necessary.

13.47 The "Create table of contents" dialog box *(from the Options menu, choose "Create TOC...")*

13.48 *You can enter up to 30 characters in the "Title" edit box. This will be the title at the top of the table. You do not have to have a title at all, if you so choose; you can just leave it blank See 13.43.*

13.49 *This is only available if there is an existing table of contents; see 13.62.*

13.50 *This is available only if the current publication contains a Book List (13.6–13.27); see 13.59.*

13.51 *You can choose the basic format of the number placement, or even whether to have numbers at all; see 13.60.*

Create table of contents

OK

Cancel

Title: **Contents**

☐ Replace existing table of contents

☒ **Include book publications**

Format: ○ No page number
○ Page number before entry
◉ Page number after entry

Between entry and page number: `^t`

13.52 *You can specify how you want the space formatted between the entry and its page number. You can enter up to seven characters here. What is shown is the default, a code for creating a tab; the style sheet contains a right-aligned leader tab to match. See 13.61 for more information on this option. See 13.183 and Appendix D for entering other formatting codes.*

Examples of Tables of Contents

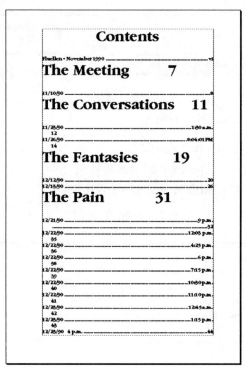

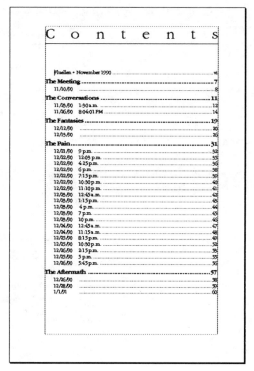

13.53 *This is an example of a typical table of contents for a Book List, using PageMaker's defaults (13.59), including "Page number after entry." Notice the Table needs some adjusting.*

13.54 *This is the same table as in 13.53 (left), but the style sheets have been customized to my specifications. When I update (replace) this table of contents, PageMaker will re-use my customized style sheets.*

If you want to do this:	Then follow these steps:	Shortcuts ▾ Notes ▾ Hints

13.55 Tag individual paragraphs to be included in a table of contents

- With the **text tool,** click in the paragraph you want to include.
- From the Type menu, choose "Paragraph...," *or* press Command M.
- At the bottom of the "Paragraph specifications" dialog box, click in the checkbox "Include in table of contents" (13.30).
- Click OK.

- Remember, a **paragraph** on the Mac is anything that has a Return after it. Paragraphs can be single words on one line, or they can even be blank lines.

    The kinds of items that typically go into Tables of Contents, such as Headlines, Subheads, etc., are one line.

13.56 Use a style sheet to tag paragraphs to be included in a table of contents

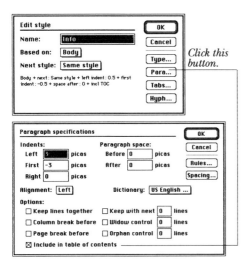

Click this button.

- Go to the "Edit style" dialog box for the style you want to include by one of these methods. Either:
  - □ From the Type menu, choose "Define styles...," *or* press Command 3. Double-click on the style name you want to edit.
  - □ **Or:** Hold down the Command key; from the Type menu, slide down to "Style," then out to the submenu and choose the style you want to edit.
  - □ **Or:** Show the Style palette (choose it from the Windows menu, or press Command Y). Hold down the Command key; click once on the style you want to edit.
- Click on the "Para..." button.
- In the "Paragraph specifications" dialog box, click in the checkbox "Include in table of contents" (see left).
- Press Option Return to close both boxes.

- Be careful: if you "base" any other styles on this one (7.20–7.26), the other styles will also be included in the table of contents. It doesn't matter how many characters are in the paragraph— I created a table of contents entry that had over 4,000 characters in it. Use "Based on" wisely.
- See Section 7 for complete details on Style Sheets.

If you want to do this:	**Then follow these steps:**	**Shortcuts ▾ Notes ▾ Hints**
13.57 Define a prefix for the page numbers in a table of contents *(optional)* 	■ Open the publication with the table of contents to which you want to add a page number prefix (such as the appendices, index, or perhaps volumes). ■ From the File menu, choose "Page setup." ■ Click on the button "Numbers...." ■ In the "TOC and Index prefix" edit box, enter the characters that you want to precede the page number (you can enter up to 15 characters). Be sure to also type any spaces you need, such as the space directly before the number. ■ Hit the Return key twice, or press Option Return to close both dialog boxes.	■ This optional format is *publication-specific;* that is, it will apply only to the page numbers from this one publication. If you are creating a table of contents for an entire Book List, then you must follow this procedure for every separate publication that you want prefixes for. ■ You can always press Command Option Period to Cancel out of nested dialog boxes.
13.58 Create a table of contents for just the current publication, using PageMaker's defaults 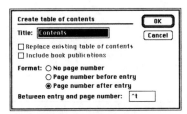 *If the publication does not contain a Book List, the option to "Include book publications" is not even available.*	■ Go to the page where you want to set up the Table of Contents. ■ If you have tagged paragraphs (13.33; 13.55–13.56), then from the Options menu choose "Create TOC...." ■ If you are updating or replacing a table, see 13.62. If you want to change any of the defaults shown, see 13.60 and 13.61. Then simply click the OK button. You will get a loaded text icon; click on the page to place the story, just as you would place any story. ■ Edit the style sheets as necessary (13.63).	■ If you have not tagged any paragraphs to be included in the table of contents (13.55; 13.56), then your table of contents will be empty except for the title "Contents." ■ You can also do this while in the **Story Editor** (Section 8). Instead of a loaded text icon, you will get a new story window displaying the table of contents. Press Command D to place this story on the page. You will get the loaded text icon; click with the icon to pour the story onto the layout page, just as you place any story.

If you want to do this:

13.59 Create a table of contents for an entire Book List, using PageMaker's defaults

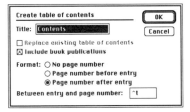

Then follow these steps:

- Open the publication in which you want to set up the table of contents. The publication must contain a Book List. If there isn't one there already, create one now (13.6–13.12; 13.20).
- If you have tagged paragraphs (13.55–13.56) in each publication in the Book List, then from the Options menu, choose "Create TOC...."
- The checkbox "Include book publications" should be checked on.
  - ☐ If you are updating or replacing a table, see 13.62. If you want to change any of the defaults shown, see 13.60 and 13.61. Then simply click the OK button.
- PageMaker will collect all the entries, and you will eventually get a loaded text icon. Click on the page to place the story, just as you would place any story.
- Edit the style sheets as necessary (13.63). If you edited them in another publication and want to use the same format, just "Copy" the style sheet (7.19; 7.50).

Shortcuts ▾ Notes ▾ Hints

- If you have not tagged any paragraphs to be included in the table of contents (13.30; 13.55-13.56), then your table of contents will be empty except for the title "Contents."
- You can also do this while in the **Story Editor** (Section 8). Instead of a loaded text icon, you will get a new story window displaying the table of contents. Press Command D to place this story on the page. You will get the loaded text icon; click with the icon to pour the story onto the layout page, just as you place any story.

| **If you want to do this:** | **Then follow these steps:** | **Shortcuts ▾ Notes ▾ Hints** |

13.60 Change the presentation of the page numbers

Format: ⦿ No page number
○ Page number before entry
○ Page number after entry

Between entry and page number: [^t]

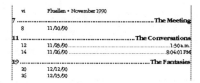

If you choose "No page number," you will get a nice list of the contents.

If you choose "Page number before entry," the page numbers will be on the left, with the default tab leader leading to the item. You will need to do some editing.

■ Follow the steps in 13.58 or 13.59 to create a table of contents. Before you click OK, decide what format you want the numbers to have.

▫ If you choose "No page number," then of course you will see no page number. This is handy when you just want to generate a list of items. When you choose this option, the "Between entry and page number" option is gone.

▫ If you choose "Page number before entry," then the page number will be on the left side of the page, left-aligned (numbers really should be right-aligned). You will need to edit your style sheet and will probably need to insert tabs (Section 5) to align the numbers.

▫ The default option is "Page number after entry," which gives you the standard look, as shown in 13.53.

■ I created the list of tasks in Appendix B by using this TOC feature with no page numbers.

If you want to do this: ■	Then follow these steps: ■	Shortcuts ▾ Notes ▾ Hints ■

13.61 Format the space between the entry and the page number

Between entry and page number: `^t`

The Conversations page 11
11/23/90   page 12
11/26/90   page 14

In this example, "page " was entered in the edit box.

The Fantasies ·······19
12/12/90 ·······20
12/13/90 ·······26

In this example, the centered period was entered (Option Shift 9).

The Pain ·•·•·•·31
12/21/90 ·•·•·•·32
12/22/90 ·•·•·•·35
12/22/90 ·•·•·•·36

In this example, periods and bullets (Option 8) were entered.

- Prepare to create a table of contents as in 13.58 or 13.59.
- In the "Create table of contents" dialog box, enter up to seven characters in the "Between entry and page number" edit box. You can enter more, but they will be ignored.
  - The default character (^t) is a tab; the style sheet sets it as a right-aligned leader tab. Even if you change this existing tab character, the tab ruler in the corresponding style sheet still retains a right-aligned tab marker. (That tab marker is difficult to see in the ruler because it is directly on top of the right margin marker.)
  - See 13.183 and Appendix D for a list of the codes to enter to create the special characters, such as Returns, tabs, non-breaking spaces, line breaks, etc.
- When you click OK, the table of contents will be created using those characters before the page number. To the left are several examples. Be sure to enter any spaces you also need; e.g., in the first example, five characters were entered: "page " (the four letters in *page*, plus a space).

- Anything you enter in this entry box will apply to every page number in the table of contents. Notice the text formatting of the characters is the same as that of the text itself. You can even use the Change feature in the Story Editor to change the formatting (8.63–8.73). I'd advise you to wait until you are sure the current table of contents is the final version before you do this, because if you update the table later all the changes will be replaced.
- If you want to add characters to the page numbers of just certain publications, such as "Volume A," define a prefix in the "Page numbering" dialog box (13.57).
- Remember, you can also customize those leaders; see 5.63–5.65.

495

If you want to do this:	Then follow these steps:	Shortcuts ▾ Notes ▾ Hints

13.62 Update (replace) an existing Table of Contents

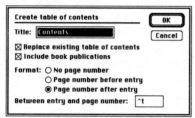

- Open the publication that contains the existing table of contents. You don't have to actually be viewing the page that the table is on, although it is nice to see what you're doing. If you are not on the TOC page, PageMaker will take you to it when she replaces the text, anyway.
- From the Options menu, choose "Create TOC...."
- Click in the checkbox "Replace existing table of contents."
- Change the other specs in this dialog box as you wish.
- Click OK. You won't get a loaded text icon. PageMaker will recreate the table, removing the one that is currently on the page and automatically replacing it with this new one. The new one will pick up all the style sheet changes that you have made. *But the new one will not pick up any editing changes or revisions that were made in the previous table!* That's why it's a good idea to leave the editing until you create the final version.

- There can only be *one* Table of Contents story in the publication. You can create what looks like more than one; I mean, you can place two or three or four on the page, but PageMaker will consider only the very latest one the *actual* Table of Contents. It is the latest one that will be updated; the rest are just plain ol' text blocks.

13.63 Edit the TOC styles to format the Table of Contents

- Press Command Y to get the Style palette. Hold the Command key down and click on the style name to get the "Edit style" dialog box. See 7.48 for details.

- Section 7 explains Style Sheets in detail. Style sheets are probably the most important thing you could learn to master in PageMaker. And paragraph rules.

Indexing

13.64 This is a pretty amazing feature. You can quickly and easily compile a great index, either as you write or at the very end of the publication. PageMaker will alphabetize it for you, indent for secondary and tertiary entries, create bold headings, and even set up cross-referencing cues. PageMaker keeps track of the pages on which each entry is found; as you edit text and as page numbers change, you can instantly update the index to include the changes automatically. You can create an index for just the current publication, or you can combine the indices from each publication in the Book List (13.6–13.12) into one large index.

13.65 This is not just a search-and-add process, where every occurrence of a word or phrase is added to the index; *you* control which occurrences of each item are entered into the index by selecting an item and then entering it (13.133). PageMaker relies on your intelligence and simply provides you with a tool, replacing a typewriter and thousands of index cards.

13.66 You can use the index feature on several different levels, from simple to complex; that is, if you have just a small, simple indexing job to complete, don't be scared away by the complexity and potential power of this feature. I completed the index on the right in less than fifteen minutes, using only one keyboard command and never looking at a dialog box. I just repeatedly selected text and hit a keystroke; when I finished entering items, I chose "Create index..." and hit Return; the index you see on the right appeared on the page. I did some minor editing. For this quick, easy method, see the ultra-zippy shortcut in 13.133.

13.67 Just as when you generate a table of contents (13.33–13.46), PageMaker adds styles to your style sheet to format the index. The styles are preceded with the identifying label "Index"; e.g., "Index level 1" or "Index section." You do need to know how to work with style sheets in order to take advantage of this most important convenience.

(Unfortunately, the index in this book could not be compiled using this index feature. PageMaker supplies the page number for each entry, but most index entries in this book are located by paragraph number, not by page. Mary spent hundreds of painstaking hours creating the index manually—well, manually using a computer.)

Index

A
abdominal pain 21
acute pediatric illness 12
acute surgical abdomen 20
Artificial Intelligence 12
B
bronchiospasm 20
C
collapse 20
conclusion 22
D
data collection 18
de novo 19, 22
DeDombal 21
double-blind 19
E
ear infection 20
educational tool 12
EKG 21
emergencies 19
encyclopedia 14
expert systems 21
F
fever 15
First Opinion 12
FORTH 13, 15
G
glitches 20
H
HyperCard 17
I
IBM PC 17
"if/then" rules 16
K
knowledge base 20, 13

L
lab tests 19
M
Macintosh 17
medical expert systems 12
N
nasal stuffiness 20
non-emergency 20
O
otitis media 15
P
physical exam 19
post-history 20
pulmonary function 21
R
references 23
respiratory distress 20
results 20
S
SA-4 inference engine 13, 15
self-resolving situations 19
sore throat 20
Sphinx 21
study methods 19
surgical findings 21
symptom-based indices 14
symptomatology 20
T
Torasso 21
triage 12, 20, 21
Triage Assessment option 19
W
well-child care 19
Y
yes/no questions 18

The basic process

Note: The indexing features in versions 4.0 and 4.01 have some major differences. The basic process is the same, but I mention the differences along the way. Version 4.01 is a little more sophisticated; if you are doing a serious index, I would suggest you make sure you have the upgrade.

13.68 The index commands are found in the Options menu. They can be rather intimidating, and they are definitely not intuitive: the "Index entry..." command has three dialog boxes; the "Show index..." command has five dialog boxes, some of which look the same as those in "Index entry"; the "Create index..." command has two dialog boxes. Each dialog box has a very specific and different function, even though several of them look exactly alike.

13.69 Use the "Index entry..." command to create the list of entries, to add to the list of entries, to create topic references, and to set up cross-references.

13.70 Use the "Show entry..." command after the list is created, to review the existing list, or to edit, cross-reference, or remove entries. You cannot add new entries to the index with this command (*well, you can add them, but they won't have a page number locator*).

13.71 If you are creating a book that is comprised of several separate publications, build an index for each publication (you don't even need to place it on a page). Make a new publication just for the index pages (or perhaps for the index and the table of contents pages). In that new pub, make a Book List of all the publications whose indices you want to include (13.20). Now when you create the index you can choose to include the book publications, and you will have one cohesive index covering the entire book (13.169). Wow.

13.72 Use the "Create entry..." command to generate the actual index in story form to place on the page. This is also where you will format the look of the index, defining how many spaces between the entry and the number, whether the secondary entries nest or run-on into each other, etc. As you add or edit entries, use the "Create index..." command to automatically update the index on the page.

13.73 Once an entry is made into the index, it is keyed to the text on that page. If the text on that page is moved to another page, the index will change to reflect the new page number. If the text is deleted, the index entry will disappear. (If you have already placed the index on the page as a story, you will not see the changes in that story; the changes are made to the *internal* index. When you *update* the index story, you will see the revisions; 13.165; 13.185).

13.74 Once you place the index as a story on a page, you will undoubtedly find things you want to change. *Don't spend any time editing the index on the page, since all changes will be lost as soon as you update it!*

Instead, **edit the internal index:** Edit the index entries through "Show index..." (13.149). Edit the format of the index through "Create index..." (13.171–13.183). Edit the text specifications through the style sheets (Section 7).

When you are completely finished with the book and the index entries and you have the final version on the page, *then* it is worthwhile to spend time revising the index story directly on the publication page.

13.75 *"Create index entry"* **dialog box** (version 4.0; see next page for version 4.01)   *(from the Options menu, choose "Index entry…," or press Command ;)*

13.76 *This is an example of the formatting for first, second, and third level entries.*

> **F** *(index section marker)*
> Primary entry (first level)
>   secondary entry (second level)
>   tertiary entry (third level)
> Primary again (first level)

13.77 *To make a primary entry into a secondary entry, or a secondary into a tertiary, or a tertiary into a primary, click this button. It just moves the entered text into the next box in line (13.119).*

13.78 *Use "Sort" to alphabetize an entry under separate characters, such as "St." under "Saint." See 13.120–13.135; 13.155–13.156.*

13.79 *The OK button is only available if there is text selected on the page, or if the insertion point is flashing in an* **existing** *text block. If OK is gray, no text is selected and no insertion point is flashing within text; you can enter a topic, but PageMaker will not locate a page number. If OK is gray, the only thing you can do is create a cross-reference to an existing topic (13.101; 13.157–13.158).*

13.80 *If text was selected before you pulled up this dialog box, it will be entered here. This first box is for primary entries (also known as first level); 13.133*

Secondary entries (second level); 13.138; 13.139

Tertiary entries (third level); 13.141–13.142

Create index entry

Topic:
> Book Publications

Sort:

OK

Cancel

Topic…

X-ref…

Press Command Period to shortcut.

13.82 *This will bring up the "Select topic" dialog box; see 13.103–13.110.*

13.81 *The range refers to the expanse of text where the new entry is the topic. If the range spans several pages and you indicate that expanse here, PageMaker will list all the appropriate pages in the index (e.g., 37–43). See 13.94–13.100.*

Range: ● **Current page**
   ○ **To next style change**
   ○ **To next occurrence of style:** Body
   ○ **For next** 1 **paragraphs**
   ○ **Cross-reference (x-ref)**

Reference override: ☐ **Bold** ☐ **Italic** ☐ **Underline**

13.83 *After you click in the "Cross-reference (x-ref)" radio button, the "X-ref…" button above will be available. Clicking the "X-ref…" button will bring up the "Select cross-reference topic" dialog box. See 13.103–13.110.*

13.84 *When you choose to cross-reference (13.101), PageMaker inserts either "See also…" or "See…," depending on the entry. This "Reference override" option allows you to format those cross-referenced topics. See 13.159.*

13.85 "Add index entry" dialog box (version 4.01; see previous page for version 4.0)

(from the Options menu, choose "Index entry…," or press Command ;)

13.86 Although this 4.01 dialog box initially looks very different than that in 4.0, it operates in the same way, with a few minor additions. Only the differences and additions are noted here.

13.87 *If text has been selected or if the insertion point is flashing when you choose the "Index entry…" command, then you will see this dialog box, ready to accept your topic entry. You can click the "Cross-reference" button to get the dialog box you see below, which gives you access to the "X-ref…" button.*

Add index entry

OK

Cancel

Type: ● Page reference ○ Cross-reference

Add

Topic: **Sort:**

Topic…

Page range: ● Current page
○ To next style change
○ To next use of style: [Body]
○ For next [1] paragraphs
○ Suppress page range

Page # override: □ Bold □ Italic □ Underline

13.92 *The "Add" button (which is black when there is text in a "Topic" edit box) allows you to index multiple entries, without having to leave and enter the dialog box each time. This is great for sorting with several different entries and for cross-referencing. Anything you add will all be referenced to the same page number. "Cancel" does not cancel anything you have added. See 13.132.*

13.88 *You can override the format for page numbers just as you can override the cross-reference formatting; 13.84; 13.159.*

13.89 *If no text has been selected and there is no insertion point flashing when you choose the "Index entry…" command, you will see this dialog box, because then the only thing you can do is cross-reference. You can enter text as a topic, but PageMaker will not be able to give it a page number location.*

Add index entry

OK

Cancel

Type: ○ Page reference ● Cross-reference

Add

Topic: **Sort:**

Topic…

X-ref…

Denoted by: ● See [also]
○ See
○ See also
○ See herein
○ See also herein

X-ref override: □ Bold □ Italic □ Underline

13.93 *This is the same as the "Add" button in 13.92, above. Also see 13.132.*

13.90 *You can choose your "See…" preference for cross-references.*

13.91 *This is the same as "Reference override"; 13.84; 13.159.*

Range (4.0) *or* Page range (4.01)

13.95 The **Range** option tells PageMaker which pages to reference in the index. The range *applies to the newest entry in that dialog box.*

Say you entered "Dogs" at one point, and you gave it a range of "To next style change," which covers several pages. Later, you add a secondary entry of "Labradors" under the same topic of "Dogs" (13.138). When you are in the dialog box for the *second* time, creating that *secondary* entry of "Labrador," the range you now select will apply to that *new* entry "Labrador." "Dogs" will retain its original page range, and "Labradors" will pick up the *new* page range.

13.96 In 4.0, if all the range buttons are gray except "Cross-reference," it means you have not selected text or placed an insertion point within an existing text block. Thus your only option is to cross-reference an existing topic (13.101; 13.157–13.158).

13.97 Current page: This is the default choice. If this button is on, the entry in the completed index will reference just the one page that contains the **paragraph** in which the entry is mentioned.

13.98 To next style change: Click this button if you want the entry referenced to all the pages of information that continue until the *style* (as in Style Sheet; Section 7) changes. For instance, perhaps "Labradors" is mentioned several times under a subhead of "Working Dogs." The text that talks about Labs is tagged with the style Body Text. You know that when the next subhead appears, the text of which is tagged Subhead 1, the topic moves on to "Froofroo Dogs," thus ending the discussion on Labradors. By clicking the "To next style change" button, PageMaker will list all the pages with the relevant information, starting from the page number on which you initially created the entry, and ending on the page number where the style sheet changes.

13.99 To next occurrence/use of style ___: Click this button if you want the reference to continue on past other style changes (see above, 13.98) until it meets text that has been tagged with the *particular* style that you choose here from the mini-menu of your style sheet, such as a "Headline."

13.100 For next ___ paragraphs: Click this button if you want the reference to cover a certain length of text, regardless of style changes. You can enter a number from 1 through 255.

13.101 Cross-reference (x-ref): Click on this button if you want to cross-reference the entry. Remember, as in any of these range buttons, you are applying the cross-reference to the entry for which you set up this dialog box. That is, if you are creating a *secondary* entry (13.138), that secondary entry is what the cross-reference will apply to, not to the primary (first-level) topic. See 13.157–13.159 for complete details on cross-referencing.

13.102 Suppress page range (4.01 only)**:** If you click this button, the index will not display the page number. You will see the number in the dialog box with parentheses around it, but it will not print in the index.

"Select topic" and "Select cross-reference topic" dialog boxes (v.4.0)

*(from the Options menu, choose "Index entry...";
click the "Topic..." or the "X-ref..." buttons)*

13.103 In the "Create index entry" dialog box, there are two buttons, "Topic..." and "X-ref...." They bring up dialog boxes that appear to be exactly the same; they both have a list of all the topics that have been entered into the index or that have been *imported* (13.106; 13.115–13.117; 13.145). You can use the "Select topic" list to select primary-level topics that you want to enter as secondary or tertiary entries (13.138; 13.141). Use the "Select cross-reference topic" list to establish a cross-reference to an existing topic (13.157–13.158).

13.104 Topic section: This is a little menu that lists the alphabet. Slide up or down to choose the letter representing the particular *section* of the index you want to view. Topics starting with the letter you choose will appear in the list.

From the "Show index..." (13.111) command, this same mini-menu is called **Index section.** They are exactly the same.

13.105 Go to next: This button presents the next alphabetical *section* of the index that has any entries, skipping all those alphabetical sections that are empty. It's a shortcut to the "Topic section" or "Index section" mini-menus.

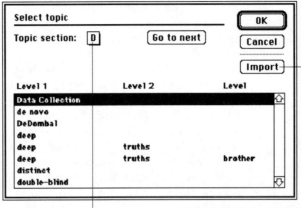

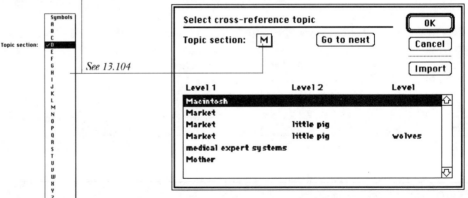

13.106 *If you have created a Book List for this publication (13.6–13.20), then when you click the "Import" button all the index topics from every other book in the Book List will appear in both of these dialog boxes.*

Notice there is no ellipsis on the button; that means you will not get a dialog box asking you from which publications to import; PageMaker just imports them all, instantly. Once topics are in either of these two lists, there is no way to remove them. Ever. See 13.115–13.117; 13.145.

☞ The same dialog boxes, but as seen in version 4.01

13.107 These dialog boxes are essentially the same as those in 4.0, on the previous page, except for the addition of the topic edit boxes and the "Add" button. Everything works the same, but now it is easier to add secondary and tertiary references, without having to retype the other levels (13.132).

13.108 *These topic edit boxes are only in version 4.01.*

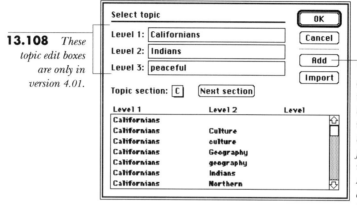

13.109 *This "Add" button allows you to add other entries without having to leave and enter the dialog box each time. Just remember, as long as you don't leave the dialog box to enter something from another page, all the page number locators will be the same. Anything you "Add" will be saved even if you click "Cancel." See 13.132.*

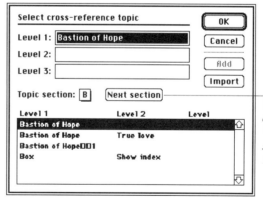

13.110 *This is exactly the same as the "Go to next" button you see on the previous page; 13.105.*

"Show index" dialog boxes   (from the Options menu, choose "Show index...")

13.111   Do you find this confusing? It is. Just follow the directions for the task you want to complete—they'll take you through step-by-step. The "Show index" dialog box shown here is from version 4.01 to display the new "Accept" button. All the other dialog boxes are from version 4.0, since they are essentially the same.

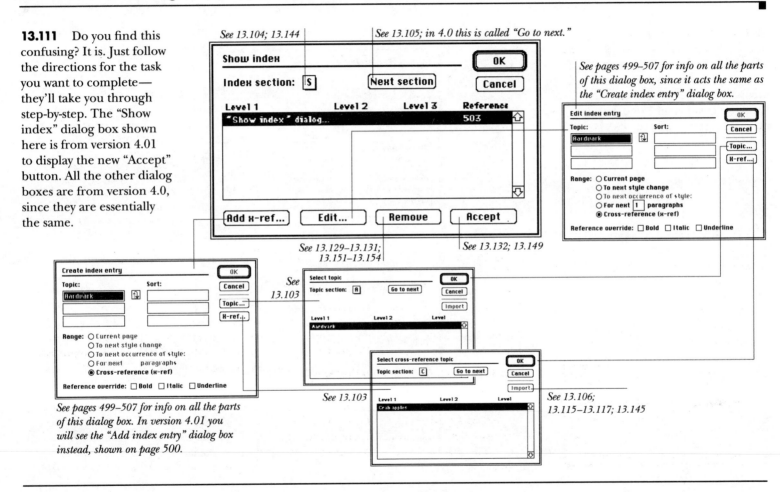

See 13.104; 13.144

See 13.105; in 4.0 this is called "Go to next."

See pages 499–507 for info on all the parts of this dialog box, since it acts the same as the "Create index entry" dialog box.

See 13.129–13.131; 13.151–13.154

See 13.132; 13.149

See 13.103

See 13.103

See 13.106; 13.115–13.117; 13.145

See pages 499–507 for info on all the parts of this dialog box. In version 4.01 you will see the "Add index entry" dialog box instead, shown on page 500.

Topic vs. entry

13.112   There is a subtle distinction between the terms *topic* and *entry*. **Topic** always refers to a primary-level entry. It is often a general category that has subentries below it. The Topic Lists and the Cross-Reference Lists are organized by these topics.

13.113   An **entry** is anything you have entered into the index. All primary-level, secondary, and tertiary information that you input is considered an entry. Primary-level text, then, can be referred to as an entry *or* as a topic.

13.114   In the Dialog boxes, you will see the topic entered a separate time for each subentry connected with it. As long as the topic is spelled exactly the same (including capitals), they will all combine into one group. The page number you see in the "Show index" dialog box is the page number for the lowest-level entry.

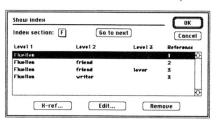

Import

13.115   **Import:** If you look at the Topic or Cross-Reference Lists from the "Index entry..." command (13.85), you will see the "Import" button (13.106). This button imports all the indexed topics from every other publication that is *listed in the current publication's Book List (13.106).* You only need to import once, even though the button is available (black) every time you open this list, because once you have imported topics they never leave. The only time you will need to click it again is if you have added another publication to the Book List, or if you have added other entries to the other publications.

13.116   If you look at the Topic or Cross-Reference Lists from the "Show index..." command (13.111), you will also see the "Import" button, but it is always gray. This is because the "Show index" dialog box and topics lists *automatically* display all topics from every publication in the Book List.

13.117   It's possible to limit the "Show index" dialog box to just the entries that you created in the current publication (hold down the Command key while you select "Show index..." from the Options menu). If you do this, the "Import" button will be available.

Index prefix

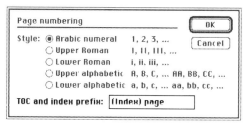

To get this dialog box, from the File menu choose "Page setup." Click on the "Numbers..." button.

13.118   From this dialog box, you can apply a prefix to the page numbers in the index or in the table of contents (not the numbers on the layout pages themselves).

For instance, you may have divided your book into three segments: A, B, and C; each segment is set up as a separate publication. Using the dialog box shown above, you can create a prefix in each publication. Then each page number in the index or table of contents in that publication will be preceded by the segment letter; e.g., A1, A2, A3, etc. (13.57).

Or you can use this feature to label your appendix pages or your front matter pages (in the index or table of contents) differently than on the layout pages. These prefixes are specific to each publication.

⬍ **Move-down button**

13.119 You will sometimes use this button when creating secondary and tertiary entries (13.138; 13.143). It moves entries up or down in the three-level edit boxes. Actually, it won't move anything *up;* it just keeps moving the text down until it cycles back up into the top edit box again.

Topic:

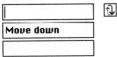

With one click, the first-level entry becomes a second-level (secondary) entry.

Topic:

Now you can type a first-level entry into the edit box, and the secondary entry will still be referenced to its page number (13.139).

p.s. If you call Aldus Tech support, don't refer to this button as the "Move-down" button. I had to make that name up because its actual title is not in any documentation, and no one in Tech Support knew what it is called. The manual doesn't even mention it.

Sort *(alphabetize)*

13.120 In an index, sometimes words need to be alphabetized (sorted) by characters other than the first several characters in the entry itself. For instance, "St." is usually sorted as if it was spelled out "Saint"; "Mt." is usually sorted as "Mount." PageMaker gives you the option of assigning different sorting characters to each entry (also see 13.155).

13.121 Use the edit boxes under "Sort" to change the characters used to alphabetize an entry. Each Sort edit box refers only to the entry in the Topic edit box to its left.

- If there is nothing in the Sort edit box across from the entry, then the entry will be sorted as usual, by its own characters as entered in the Topic box.

- If there *is* an entry in the Sort edit box, then the entry will be alphabetized by what is in the Sort box, not by its own characters. **In the index, it will still be *spelled* as it is in the Topic box, though.**

13.122 For instance, in the example above right, the number 11 would be sorted in ASCII order (13.125), before letters. By typing "eleven" into the Sort box, it will be entered in the index under "E."

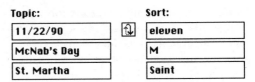

Topic:		Sort:
11/22/90	⬍	eleven
McNab's Day		M
St. Martha		Saint

13.123 You can have one entry sorted in several different ways, to make sure a reader will find it, but you have to create each entry separately; see 13.156.

13.124 Characters sort in this order:
- Blank spaces always come first.
- Symbols next (%$#*), in random order.
- Numbers, in ASCII order (13.125).
- Letters in alphabetical order.

13.125 When dealing with numbers, take note that *ASCII sort order is not numerical!* It's more like alphabetical: it will list all the numbers that start with 1, then all the numbers that start with 2, etc. For example, these numbers are sorted in ASCII order: 1, 100, 11, 110, 111, 2, 20, 207, 22, 3, 30, etc. If you need numbers in numerical order, use the Sort edit boxes to alphabetize them this way: 001, 002, 003, 011, 020, 022, 030, 100, 110, 111, 207, etc. Use as many place holders as the largest number (e.g., if there are numbers in the thousands, use 0001).

"Show index"

13.126   Use the "Index entry..." command (13.133–13.143) to enter topics and subentries; use the **Show index...** command to edit and cross-reference those entries.

13.127   The "Show index" list box will show you the entries that will actually print in the index; it includes all the entries from every publication in the Book List. You can choose to edit, cross-reference, or remove any entry. You cannot *add* new entries here, even though you get a dialog box similar to the one in which you created entries. You *can* add *cross-references* to existing topics (13.101). You can add *words* to the index here, but the words will not be referenced to page numbers (13.135).

13.128   You may notice that the "Topic" list and the "X-ref" list appear to be the same. And you may notice that they *appear* to be the same ones you had from the "Index entry..." command. And the "Edit index entry" dialog box looks just like the "Create index entry" dialog box. Yes. It can be terribly confusing. The safest thing to do is to find the task you want to complete (enter an entry, delete an entry, add a secondary entry, cross-reference, etc.) and then just follow the directions for that task *(tasks begin on the next page).*

Remove

13.129   You can remove any topic from the index by selecting it in the "Show index" list and clicking the **Remove** button. This will also remove it from both the "Topic" list and the "X-ref" lists after you click OK.

13.130   In version 4.01, you can remove, or undo, the most recent index entry additions. You can also undo the index entries you recently removed (see 13.150).

13.131   Please note: "Remove" does not remove any entries from the "Topic" or "X-ref" lists *in the "Index entry..." command!* Right now, there is no way to remove any unwanted entries from the lists in the "Index entry..." command (which, as you recall, look exactly like the lists in the "Show index..." command). It seems to be an oversight in the program. The problem this presents is that it becomes possible for you to cross-reference an entry to a topic *that has actually been removed from the index.*

Add and Accept (4.01 only)

13.132   PageMaker 4.01 adds two new buttons to the index dialog boxes: **Add** and **Accept.** They both function in the same way. As you enter or edit entries, you can click whichever of these buttons you see in the dialog box to add your entry to the index. This allows you to add multiple entries or cross-references without having to close the dialog box each time. If you Cancel, anything that has been "Added" or "Accepted" will not be canceled.

507

| **If you want to do this:** | **Then follow these steps:** | **Shortcuts ▾ Notes ▾ Hints** |

13.133 Create an index entry: enter an existing, selected word

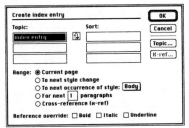

4.0 dialog box (see 4.01 below)

- With the **text tool,** select the text you want to enter into the index. If it is just one word, simply double-click on the word.
- From the Options menu, choose "Index entry…," *or* press Command ; *(semicolon).*
- In the "Create index entry" dialog box, you will see the selected word in the *primary level* edit box. If you need to capitalize it or change the spelling (e.g., *Fox hunting* to *Fox hunt*), do so now.
- Choose the "Range" for which you want PageMaker to reference a page number (see 13.95–13.102).
- Click OK.

- **Ultra-zippy shortcut:** If you want the "Current page" range and you don't need to edit the text at this moment, then you can do this: Select the text (double-click if it's one word). Press Command Shift ; *(semicolon).* You won't even see a dialog box—the text simply gets entered straight into the index.
- Use this method to enter into the index words that you have directly located.
- If you have PageMaker version 4.01, see 13.147 for a way to automatically capitalize entries.

13.134 Create an index entry: enter your own word that you want referenced to this paragraph

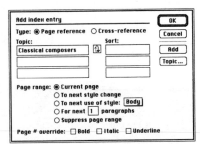

4.01 dialog box (see 4.0 above)

- With the **text tool,** click once in the paragraph that contains the information you want to reference.
- From the Options menu, choose "Index entry…," *or* press Command ; .
- In the "Create index entry" dialog box, type the text you want to reference to the information in this paragraph; type it into the *primary level* edit box (the top one; 13.80).
- Choose the "Range" for which you want PageMaker to reference a page number (see 13.95–13.102).
- Click OK.

- Use this method to enter words that *refer* to a topic in a paragraph, but where the word itself isn't directly mentioned in the paragraph. For instance, the paragraph may discuss Chopin's music, and you want to enter a general index reference locating "Classical composers."
- In version 4.01, you can click the "Add" button to add the current entry, then retype and add another without having to close the dialog box. Remember, though, any other entries you add will still be referenced to the same paragraph you originally started from.

If you want to do this:	Then follow these steps:	Shortcuts ▾ Notes ▾ Hints
13.135 Enter a list of topics with no page numbers *(useful as an outline, or to be used later for topics and cross-referencing)* *(Also see 13.137.)*	■ With the **text tool,** type a list of the topics you want to enter. ■ With the **text tool,** select one topic (if the topic is only one word, double-click on it). ■ Press Command Shift **;** *(semicolon)*. This enters the entry. ■ Repeat those two steps with the next word on the list. ■ When the list is completely entered, choose the **pointer tool.** Click on the text block that contains the list, and delete it (hit the Backspace/Delete key). ■ The topics are now in the Topic List and the Cross-Reference List that you find in the "Index entry..." command (from the Options menu). The topics will not appear in the "Show index" lists. Only the topics that you choose to place in the primary topic edit box (13.80) or that you cross-reference with another entry (13.101) will actually appear in the final index.	■ You can enter topics of up to fifty characters. ■ In version 4.01, if you delete the text block, the entries will be deleted from the "Show index" dialog box Topic and Edit lists. They will still be in the "Add index entry" dialog box Topic and Edit Lists. ■ See 13.136 for creating an index entry with no page number reference.
13.136 In version 4.01, create an index entry with no page number reference	■ Follow the steps in 13.133 or 13.134 to create an index entry. ■ Click the "Suppress page range" button. ■ Click OK. The entry will appear in the index when you place it on the page, but it will have no number locating it.	■ The page number will appear in parentheses in the "Show index" dialog box list, but the number will not appear in the actual index when you place it on the page.

If you want to do this:	Then follow these steps:	Shortcuts ▾ Notes ▾ Hints
13.137 In version 4.0, create an index entry with no page number reference *(Also see 13.137.)*	■ Follow the steps in 13.133 or 13.134 to create an index entry. ■ Hold down the Command and the Shift keys; click on the "Current page" radio button. Yes, I know, it is already highlighted. Click on it anyway. ■ Click OK. This entry will appear in the index, but will have no number locating it.	■ The page number will appear in parentheses in the "Show index" list, but the number will not appear in the actual index when you place it on the publication page.

Level 1	Level 2	Level 3	Reference
no page number			(505)

13.138 Create a secondary (second-level) entry *(one method)* 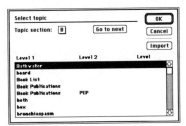 **a** *The "B" section of the Topic List.* **Topic:** Bathwater babies in **b** *Type in the secondary entry.*	■ With the **text tool,** click once in the paragraph you want to reference. ■ From the Options menu, choose "Index entry…," *or* press Command ; *(semicolon).* ■ Click the "Topic…" button to get the list of topics that you have already entered. ■ Press on the "Topic section" mini-menu (13.104) to choose the alphabetical section you wish to view. Or click the "Go to next" button to view the next section that contains topic entries. ■ In the list, find the topic (**a**) for which you want to create the secondary entry. Double-click on the topic (or click on it once, then click OK or hit Return). ■ Now *that* chosen topic is in the primary topic edit box (**b**). Type the second-level entry into the next edit box. Don't try to type a third-level entry; see 13.141–13.143. ■ Click OK.	■ This method involves manually typing the second-level entry. The second method (13.139) involves manually typing the primary topic. *Either way, the primary topic must already have been entered into the index.* ■ The advantage to this first method is that you never have to worry about misspelling the primary topic. If you do misspell it, you will have separate topics, each with its own subentry, rather than one primary entry with a combined list of subentries. ■ If you have removed topics from the list through the "Show index" command, they are not removed from this topic list! Thus it is possible to create subentries and cross-references to topics that are non-existent. This is a bug. A cockroach.

If you want to do this: ■

Then follow these steps: ■

Shortcuts ▾ Notes ▾ Hints ■

13.139 Create a secondary (second-level) entry (*another method*)

Topic:

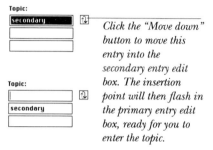

Click the "Move down" button to move this entry into the secondary entry edit box. The insertion point will then flash in the primary entry edit box, ready for you to enter the topic.

S
Show   503
    secondary   504

This is what a secondary entry looks like when the index is placed on the page.

- You must know the exact spelling of the primary topic under which you want to create this secondary entry.
- With the **text tool,** select the text you want to enter into the index, *or* click once in the paragraph you want to reference.
- From the Options menu, choose "Index entry...," *or* press Command **;** *(semicolon).*
- If the insertion point is flashing, hit the Tab key to send it to the second-level edit box; if the selected word appears in the first-level edit box, click on the "Move down" button (see left; also see 13.77).
- Now this is the trick: you have to manually *type* the primary-level topic into that edit box. If it's not exactly correct, that's okay, because you can always edit it later (13.149). Don't try to enter a third-level entry at this point; see 13.141–13.143.
- Click OK.

- PageMaker can only locate one page number per entry in the dialog box. Thus there is no way to simultaneously reference a primary-level entry *plus* a secondary entry, or a secondary *plus* a tertiary. You just have to accept the fact that you need to OK this dialog box and come back again to create the next entry.
- In version 4.01, you can click the "Add" button to add the current entry, then retype and add another without having to close the dialog box. Remember, though, any other entries you add will still be referenced to the same paragraph you originally started from.
- If you try to add entries into more than one level in this dialog box, only the lowest-level entry will have a page number attached. The other words will be entered into the index, but they won't have page references.

13.140 Create another secondary entry under the same primary topic

- Repeat the steps in 13.138 or 13.139. If the primary topic is the same each time, all the secondary entries will be listed under the one primary topic. *That's why you need to spell all the primary topics the same way!* (See 13.149 for editing existing entries.)

- In version 4.01, you can click the "Add" button to add the current entry, then retype and add another without having to close the dialog box. Remember, though, any other entries you add will still be referenced to the same paragraph you originally started from.

511

If you want to do this:

13.141 Create a tertiary (third-level) entry *(one method)*

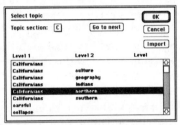

a *The "C" section of the topic list.*

b *Type in the tertiary entry.*

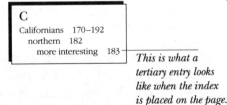

This is what a tertiary entry looks like when the index is placed on the page.

Then follow these steps:

- With the **text tool,** click once in the paragraph you want to reference.
- From the Options menu, choose "Index entry...," *or* press Command **;** *(semicolon).*
- Click the "Topic..." button to get the list of topics that have already been entered.
- Press on the "Topic section" mini-menu (13.104) to choose the alphabetical section you wish to view. Or click the "Go to next" button to view the next section that contains topic entries.
- In the list, find the topic (**a**) for which you want to create the tertiary entry. *The topic you choose must already have a secondary entry.* Double-click on the topic (or click on it once, then click OK or hit Return).
- Now *that* chosen topic is in the primary topic edit box (**b**), with the secondary entry in its own edit box. Type the third-level entry into the last edit box.
- Click OK.

Shortcuts ▾ Notes ▾ Hints

- You can type any other words into the primary and secondary edit boxes, rather than choose a topic from the topic list, but anything you type in will not be located to a page number.
- If you choose a topic that does not have a secondary entry, you will have to type a secondary entry before PageMaker will accept it; it is not possible to have only a primary plus a tertiary entry. If you *type* a secondary entry, though, that entry will not be referenced to any page number. *PageMaker will only reference the lowest-level entry* (primary level being the highest).
- In version 4.01, you can click the "Add" button to add the current entry, then retype and add another without having to close the dialog box. Remember, though, any other entries you add will still be referenced to the same paragraph you originally started from.

If you want to do this:

Then follow these steps:

Shortcuts ▾ Notes ▾ Hints

13.142 Create a tertiary (third-level) entry *(another method)*

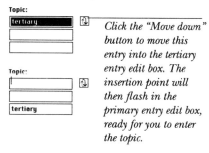

Click the "Move down" button to move this entry into the tertiary entry edit box. The insertion point will then flash in the primary entry edit box, ready for you to enter the topic.

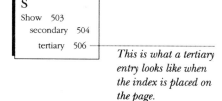

This is what a tertiary entry looks like when the index is placed on the page.

- With the **text tool,** select the text you want to enter into the index, *or* click once in the paragraph you want to reference.
- From the Options menu, choose "Index entry...," *or* press Command ; *(semicolon).*
- If the insertion point is flashing, hit the Tab key to send it to the third-level edit box; if the selected word appears in the first-level edit box, click twice on the "Move down" button (see left; also 13.77).
- You have to actually *type* the primary-level topic *and* the existing secondary entry into that edit box. You *must* enter a secondary entry. (If the spelling is not exactly correct, you *can* edit it later; 13.149.)
- Click OK.

- You must know the exact spelling of the primary topic *and* the secondary entry under which you want to create this third-level entry. You can click the "Topic" button to look it up (13.82).
- This is handy for those times when you need to enter a complex word and you are sure you will misspell it if you have to retype it, like diethymethoxylate-19-psq.
- In version 4.01, you can click the "Add" button to add the current entry, then retype and add another without having to close the dialog box. Remember, though, any other entries you add will still be referenced to the same paragraph you originally started from.

13.143 Create another tertiary entry under the same secondary topic

- Start all over again and repeat the steps in 13.141 or 13.142. If you enter the same primary and secondary entries each time, all the tertiary entries will be listed under the one primary topic. *That's why you need to spell all the primary and secondary entries the same way!*

- See the note directly above, regarding adding multiple entries in 4.01.
- See 13.149 for editing existing entries.

513

If you want to do this:	**Then follow these steps:**	**Shortcuts ▾ Notes ▾ Hints**

13.144 Check the Topic List to see what's available

Anything you select in the topic list will be placed in the edit box:

Topic:

- In the "Create/Add index entry" dialog box, just click on the "Topic..." button to get the list of topics.
- Press on the "Topic section" mini-menu to choose the letter under which you want to view the entries. Or you can click the "Go to next" button to jump to the next section that contains entries.
- The entry that is selected when you click OK will be entered in the primary topic edit box. Any accompanying secondary and tertiary entry will also be entered. *Anything already existing in those edit boxes will be replaced.* So if you don't want to actually put the selected topic into the dialog box, click Cancel.

- The topics are alphabetized by the primary-level entry.
- This topic list is especially handy when you are entering secondary or tertiary entries, when you need to go get a topic, or when you need to check to see how the primary topic was actually spelled; e.g., to see whether you spelled the entry *Pharaoh* or *Pharoah,* or whether the topic is *Create entropy* or *Creating entropy.*

13.145 Import topics
(also see 13.105; 13.115–13.117)

Select topic

Topic section: [C] [Go to next]   [OK] [Cancel] [Import]

The "Import" button is in both the "Select topic" dialog box (Topic List) and the "Select cross-reference topic" dialog box (Cross-Reference List).

- You can only import topics from the indices belonging to the other publications that are in the current publication's Book List (13.6–13.12). Create a Book List, if necessary (13.20).
- To import topics into either the Topic List or the Cross-Reference List, click the "Import" button. Only the topics that you actually create subentries for or that you cross-reference will appear in the final, placed index.

- The purpose of importing is to give you access to the other topics in the other publications that are part of the book, topics you may need for cross-referencing or for creating subentries.
- Once you click the "Import" button, those topics are in the lists forever. Even if you Cancel both dialog boxes, *even if you eliminate the topics from the original publication,* they are in the lists. Which means there is potential for cross-referencing to topics that aren't really there. Uh oh.

If you want to do this:	**Then follow these steps:**	**Shortcuts · Notes · Hints**

13.146 In version 4.01: Automatically index proper names

- All words in the selected text are names.
- All names are in either of these formats: "FirstName LastName" *or* "LastName, FirstName."
- If there is no comma between FirstName LastName, the second name is considered the last name.
- If a first or last name is a multiple word, the two parts of the name must be connected with a non-breaking space (Option Spacebar) or a non-breaking hyphen (Command Option Hyphen).
- A unique character (such as a comma, a semicolon, or a return) must separate the names in a list.

- You can select any single name or a lengthy list of names and instantly enter the entire list. Each name will be a separate entry, and will be formatted as LastName, FirstName. The single name or the list of names must abide by the rules as noted in the left column.
- Select the name, or the entire list of names.
- Press Command Shift Z. You won't *see* anything happen (the dialog box will not appear) but if you check out the Topic List, you will see all the names. Wow.

- Each name is indexed separately as a primary-level entry.
- Each entry will have a page range of "Current page" (13.97).
- PageMaker handles some name extensions properly, like Jr. or Sr., but you should check.
- PageMaker will consider titles after names as separate names, so you need to index (or at least edit) those manually.

13.147 In version 4.01: Automatically capitalize index entries

- From the Options menu, choose "Index entry...," or press Command ; .
- Click on the "Topic..." button on the right.
- To capitalize the first letter of all existing **primary** topics, press the Command key and click the "Next section" button.
- To capitalize the first letter of **all levels** of existing entries, press the Command and Shift keys and click the "Next section."
- Click Cancel to put the dialog boxes away; the changes will be retained.

- This will only capitalize the existing entries; it will not affect any other entries you add in the future.
- If you have already placed your index on the page, you will have to update it in order to see the capitalization changes.
- This won't work in the Topic List that you access while in the "Show index" dialog box.

515

If you want to do this:

13.148 Show all the entries before generating the actual index

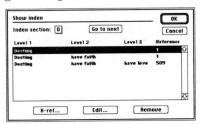

The section shown above will produce the index entries shown below:

Then follow these steps:

- From the Options menu, choose "Show index...." This command shows what is in the index for all the publications *that are in the Book List,* so if the current publication is not in the List, you will not see its index!

    You can *add* the current publication to the Book List (13.21), or you can choose to *view just the index for the current publication:* hold down the Command key before you choose "Show index..." from the Options menu.
- What you see in the "Show index" dialog box is what you will get in the final index. In the example to the left, you see *Destiny* three separate times: once with a page number, once with a secondary entry and its page number, once with a tertiary entry and its page number. *Destiny* will appear as one entry with its corresponding secondary and tertiary entries, as shown, *if* *all primary and secondary entries are spelled exactly the same, including capital letters.*
- If you need to edit entries so they are the same, see 13.149.

Shortcuts ▾ Notes ▾ Hints

- Use the "Show index..." command when you want to review and edit the index.
- What you see in that first dialog box is what will print. What you see in the Topic List and in the Cross-Reference List is not what will be in the final index; they are just the possible topics you can cross-reference to, or add secondary and tertiary entries to. If you choose to remove entries (13.151), they will be removed from the "Show index" dialog box, not from the Topic or Cross-Reference Lists.

If you want to do this:

13.149 Edit entries

(especially necessary to amalgamate all primary topics with their respective secondary and tertiary entries; 13.76)

Then follow these steps:

- From the Options menu, choose "Show index...."
- In the dialog box, press on the "Index section" mini-menu; choose the letter of the alphabetical section that contains the entry you wish to edit.
- Click once on the entry you want to edit, then click the "Edit..." button, *or* just double-click on the entry itself.
- This is the "*Edit* index entry" dialog box; you cannot enter *new* entries here! (Well, you can type them in, but they won't have page numbers.) Check spelling, etc.
- Click OK. If you want to edit others, find and edit them in the same way. When you are finished, close all the dialog boxes and PageMaker will update the entries.
  - ☐ In PageMaker 4.01, there is an "Accept" button (13.132). After each edit, you can click this button to add it to the index immediately, without having to wait until you click the OK button. If you later Cancel, you will only Cancel the editing that occurred after the last time you clicked "Accept."

Shortcuts ▾ Notes ▾ Hints

- You do need to go through the entire index and combine all those like items that may be phrased slightly differently, or perhaps capitalized differently. Otherwise each entry will be completely separate; e.g., *horses* will be separate from *Horses*.
- You can also edit entries through the "Index entry..." command from the Options menu, but I suggest you do your editing through "Show index...." The "Show index" dialog box (13.14) is the only place where you see a true account of the actual *entries*. Keep in mind that the Topic and Cross-References Lists can all contain *topics* that will not appear in the index itself when it is placed on the page (*topics vs. entries*, see 13.112–13.114).

If you want to do this:	Then follow these steps:	Shortcuts ▾ Notes ▾ Hints

13.150 In version 4.01: Undo the latest index additions or deletions	■ This trick will only undo the editing changes you have made in the "Show index" dialog box. It will not affect any changes that you have added to the index by clicking the "Accept" button or that were already in the index when you opened the dialog box.
	  ■ **To undo additions:** hold down the Option key and click "Add x-ref...."
	  ■ **To undo deletions:** hold down the Option key and click "Remove."	

13.151 Remove entries from the index	■ From the Options menu, choose "Show index...."
	■ In the dialog box, press on the "Index section" mini-menu; choose the letter of the alphabetical section from which you wish to remove an entry.
	■ Click once on the entry you want to remove.
	■ Click the "Remove" button. You will not get an alert button asking if you really want to do this.
	  □ In 4.0: if you change your mind, Cancel.
	  □ In version 4.01: if you change your mind, press the Option key and click "Remove." All index entries you have deleted since the last time you clicked OK or "Accept" will be reinstated.
		■ "Remove" automatically removes the entry from the Topic and the Cross-Reference Lists that are accessed through the "Show index..." command (after you click OK). It will *not* remove entries from the similar-looking Lists of the same names that are accessed through the "Index entry..." command.
		■ Also see 13.152 and 13.154.

If you want to do this:

13.152 Remove all page-referenced entries from the entire index
(read the warning on the right!)

13.153 Remove all cross-referenced entries from the entire index
(read the warning on the right!)

13.154 Remove all cross-referenced entries, as well as all entries with page references, from the entire index (which means eliminating the entire index)
(read the warning on the right!)

Then follow these steps:

- From the Options menu, choose "Show index...."
- Hold down the Command and the Option keys while you click the "Remove" button.
- If you change your mind, immediately click the "Cancel" button.

- From the Options menu, choose "Show index...."
- Hold down the Command and the Shift keys while you click "Remove."
- If you change your mind, immediately click the "Cancel" button.

- From the Options menu, choose "Show index...."
- Hold down the Command, Shift, and Option keys while you click "Remove."
- If you change your mind, immediately click the "Cancel" button.

Shortcuts ▾ Notes ▾ Hints

- **Warning!!** Each of these tasks (13.152–13.154) eliminates the entries *from every publication in the Book List!* Really. If you do one of these removals and then open up another of the publications that is on the Book List, you will find that it is missing its entries. **Task 13.154, then, eliminates the entire index from the entire book.** Be careful.

If you want to do this:	Then follow these steps:	Shortcuts ▾ Notes ▾ Hints

13.155 Sort an entry by characters different than the entry's original characters

Topic:		Sort:
11/22/90	⬆⬇	eleven
McNab's Day		M
St. Martha		Saint

In these examples, 11/22/90 will be alphabetized as "eleven"; McNab will be alphabetized as the letter M, meaning it will be placed before Mac, since empty spaces come before letters; "St." will be alphabetized as "Saint," rather than being placed towards the end of the list as St.

- Read 13.120–13.125 to understand what "Sort" accomplishes.
- Simply type the characters you want the entry to be alphabetized by in the edit box directly across from it. That is, the primary topic will be sorted by what is in the first edit box under "Sort"; the secondary entry will be sorted by what is in the *second* Sort edit box; the tertiary entry will be sorted by what is in the *third* Sort edit box. You are not allowed to have a sort character in the Sort edit boxes unless there is a corresponding entry on the left.

- Whenever there is an entry in any edit box, in either the "Create index entry" or the "Edit index entry" dialog boxes, you can apply a new sort character. So you can do this at any time, either right when you enter it or later.

13.156 Sort an entry by several different sets of characters

Topic:		Sort:
11/22/90	⬆⬇	

Topic:		Sort:
11/22/90	⬆⬇	November

Each separate sort must be entered into the index separately.

- To sort an entry by its own first character, leave the Sort edit box blank; click OK.
- Then, to sort the same entry by another character, *as well as* by its own first character, you must enter it a *second* time: in its corresponding "Sort" box, type the other characters you want the entry alphabetized by; click OK.
- To sort the entry by a third category, enter it a *third* time: in its corresponding "Sort" box, type the next set of characters you want the entry alphabetized by; click OK (or "Add," if you have 4.01).
- Get it? Just keep entering them separately.

- In version 4.01 you can click the "Add" button to add the entry to the index, rather than closing the dialog box each time.
- If there is no character in the Sort edit box, then the entry will be sorted as usual, in ASCII sort order (13.125). If you want to sort the entry by other characters, *as well as* by its own first character, you must create a separate entry for each one.

If you want to do this:

13.157 Cross-reference an entry

a
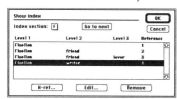

b

c
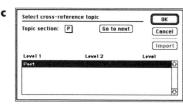

d

Then follow these steps:

- From the Options menu, choose "Show index...."
- Using the "Index section" mini-menu (13.104), find the topic to which you want to attach a cross-reference. Click once to select it (**a**).

  Note: Notice in this section that *Fluellen* is listed four times. It will actually print in the index only once, with its corresponding page number (**a**). The second *Fluellen* listed indicates a secondary entry and its page number. The third *Fluellen* listed indicates a tertiary entry, under *friend*. The fourth *Fluellen* listed indicates another secondary entry. **The cross-reference will apply to the lowest entry in the topic you select.** That is, if you select the first *Fluellen,* the cross-reference will apply to the primary topic. In the example, the topic selected has a *secondary* (lower) entry, so the cross-reference will apply to the *secondary* entry.

- Click the "X-ref..." button to get the "Edit/Add index entry" dialog box.* The entry you just selected will be in the edit box(es) and the "Cross-reference (x-ref)" radio button will be selected already (**b**).

—continued

Shortcuts ▾ Notes ▾ Hints

- It is best to have all or at least most of the entries entered into the index before you start to cross-reference.
- If the topic has a page number next to it, the cross-reference will state *"See also...."* If the topic has no page number, the cross-reference will state *"See...."* Version 4.01 offers more options for *"See...."*
- "Show index" will show you all index entries that are included in every publication that is listed in the current publication's Book List (13.6–13.11). It is possible to remove entries from the "Show index" list. But keep in mind that removing them from the "Show index" list *does not remove them from the Cross-Reference List!* Thus it is possible to cross-reference entries to topics that are no longer in the index. For instance, maybe yesterday you eliminated all mentions of Fluellen's poetry from the book and also from the index. *Poet* is still in the Cross-Reference List. In the example to the left, *Fluellen* is cross-referenced to *Poet.* But if someone were to look up *Poet* in the index, she would find no such entry.
- See 13.159 regarding the text format for the cross-reference.

* In version 4.0, the dialog box is "Edit index entry"; in version 4.01, the dialog box is "Add index entry."

If you want to do this:	**Then follow these steps:**	**Shortcuts ▾ Notes ▾ Hints**

—continued

```
┌──────────┐
│ Topic... │
└──────────┘    The "X-ref..." button
┌──────────┐
│ X-ref... │
└──────────┘
```

e
```
┌─────────────────────────────┐
│ F                           │
│ Fluellen  1                 │
│   friend  2                 │
│     lover  3                │
│     writer  3.  See also Poet│
└─────────────────────────────┘
```

■ Click the "X-ref..." button (on the right).
■ In the "Select cross-reference topic" list, find the topic you want cross-referenced to the entry. Select it and click OK; you will return to the "Edit index entry" dialog box. Click OK again to get back to the "Show index" dialog box, in case you want to add another cross-reference to this or to another entry. If you are done, click OK.
■ Now in "Show index" you can see the cross-reference listed (**d**). If you are done cross-referencing and editing, click OK.
■ When you generate the index and place it on the page, the cross-referencing will appear as shown on the left (**e**).

■ Instead of clicking OK, you can shortcut by double-clicking on the topic entry.
■ In version 4.01, the "Edit index entry" dialog box is called "Add index entry."

■ In version 4.01, you can click the "Accept" button. That will enter the new information yet leave you in the dialog box if you want to continue working there.

13.158 Cross-reference a secondary or tertiary entry *as you create the entry* (*another method, similar to 13.157*)

■ Create a secondary **or** a tertiary entry (see 13.138–13.143). After you have entered the subentry, but before you click the final OK, select the "Cross-reference (X-ref)" radio button (in version 4.0, it's under "Range"; in 4.01, it's above the "Sort" boxes).
■ Then click the "X-ref..." button (on right).
■ From the list, find the topic to which you want to cross-reference. Double-click on it.
■ If you like, override the current cross-reference format (13.159).
■ Click OK in the "Edit/Add index entry" dialog box.*

■ You cannot cross-reference both a secondary *and* a tertiary entry in the same listing; each one needs to be entered and cross-referenced separately.
■ In version 4.0, if the topic has a page number next to it, the cross-reference will state *"See also...."* If the topic has no page number, the cross-reference will state *"See...."* In 4.01, you can choose which version of *"See..."* you wish to use.
■ Be careful about cross-referencing to topics that no longer exist in the index (see notes in 13.131; 13.138).

---

* In version 4.0, the dialog box is "Edit index entry"; in version 4.01, the dialog box is "Add index entry."

If you want to do this:

13.159 Format the cross-reference
(or in version 4.01, the page numbers)

Reference override: ☐ **Bold** ☐ **Italic** ☐ **Underline**

| E | *No override* |
| Entropy 1. *See also* Xanadu | |

| E | *Bold override* |
| Entropy 1. *See also* **Xanadu** | |

| E | *Italic override* |
| Entropy 1. *See also Xanadu* | |

Page # override: ☐ **Bold** ☐ **Italic** ☐ **Underline**

*In PageMaker version 4.01 you can
override the page numbers in the same way.*

Then follow these steps:

- In either the "Create index entry" or the "Edit index entry" dialog boxes, you can format the cross-reference text. These buttons only apply to cross-references. After you have created the cross-reference, simply click in the override of your choice. It will override whatever type style you've defined in the style sheet for this paragraph. Notice in the examples on the left that the override affects just the text following *See* or *See also.*
- The choices are cumulative; you can choose one, two, or all three of the options (but see the note to the right).
- If you change your style sheet so the entries are already formatted in bold, then clicking the "Bold" checkbox will have just the opposite effect: the cross-reference will be Normal. The same holds true for the italic and underline overrides.

Shortcuts ▾ Notes ▾ Hints

- In version 4.01 you can also choose to override the type specifications for the page numbers, as well as the cross-references.
- Although one choice for the override is underline, I do hope you realize that text never looks good when it has an underline style applied. I don't know why that is even an option. The underline bumps into the descenders and it is too heavy for the small text in an index. Besides, underlining is a primitive holdover from typewriters, where it was one of the few options available for emphasizing words. An underline's actual purpose is to indicate that the underlined words should really be italiziced, since the typewriter couldn't create italics. Knowing that, you can see how redundant it would be to check underline *and* italic.
- There is no way to create a default for a reference or page number override. That means you must religiously click the override button for each entry if you want the index to be consistent.

If you want to do this:	Then follow these steps:	Shortcuts ▾ Notes ▾ Hints
13.160 Show all the index entries	■ From the Options menu, choose "Show index...." The entries you see in *this* dialog box are the entries that will actually place on the page. It includes all entries from each publication listed in the Book List (13.6–13.11) in the current publication. ■ Click the "Go to next" button to view each section.	■ Remember, it is possible to have topics in both the Topic List and the Cross-Reference List that are not actually entries in the index. The actual entries are only what you see in the "Show index" dialog box list. ■ If the current publication is not listed in the Book List, its index will not be included in the "Show index" dialog box.
13.161 Show the index for just the current publication only	■ Hold the Command key down. ■ From the Options menu, choose "Show index..." while still holding the Command key.	■ If you have established cross-references to topics in other publications in your Book List, those topic entries are considered to be part of this publication now.
13.162 Get rid of all those useless topics that you don't need anymore in the "Index entry..." Topic and Cross-References Lists	■ You can't.	■ This is an oversight in the program. ■ See the notes in 13.131; 13.151.

Formatting and placing the actual index

13.163 As you place the index for the first time, PageMaker creates style sheets for each level, as well as for the section headings (the letters defining each alphabetical section) and for the index title. You can edit the style sheets; when you update the index, PageMaker will re-use your customized style sheets *as long as you haven't renamed them.*

13.164 PageMaker offers you a lot of control over the appearance of your index through the "Index format" dialog box (see next page). You also have control over which parts of the index you want to show up, as indicated below:

13.165 Replace existing index: If there is no existing index in the publication, this option is not available (it's gray). If this box is checked and there is an index somewhere in the publication, even if only one character of it is visible, PageMaker will replace that existing index with this newer version.

13.166 You can *place* more than one index in the publication, but PageMaker will only recognize the latest version as the true index. It is the latest version that will be updated.

13.167 "Create index" dialog box *(from the Options menu, choose "Create index...")*

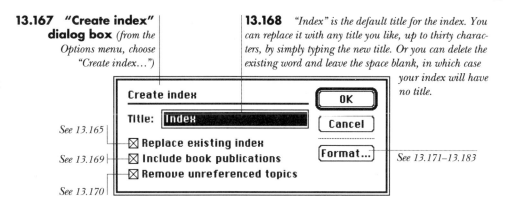

See 13.165
See 13.169
See 13.170
See 13.171–13.183

13.168 *"Index" is the default title for the index. You can replace it with any title you like, up to thirty characters, by simply typing the new title. Or you can delete the existing word and leave the space blank, in which case your index will have no title.*

13.169 Include book publications: If the current publication does not contain a Book List (13.6–13.11), this option is not available (it's gray). If there is an existing Book List, you can check this box to include the index entries from all the other publications in the List. If this box is not checked, only the entries from the current publication will be included in the printed index.

13.170 Remove unreferenced topics: If you check this box, PageMaker will not place any primary topics that have no page locators, no subentries, and no cross-references. This does not remove the entries from the *internal* index, it just prevents them from appearing in the *printed* index.

"Index format" dialog box *(from the Options menu, choose "Create index..."; click the "Format..." button)*

13.171 With a few simple clicks in this "Index format" dialog box, you can format the entire index consistently. You only need to set these specs once. If you decide you don't like something, you can always change it and simply update the index (13.185) to show the changes.

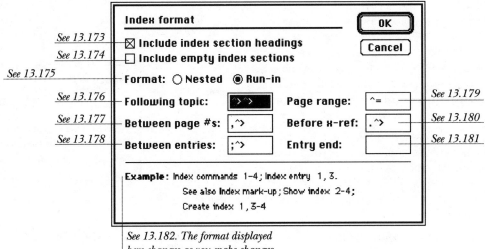

See 13.173
See 13.174
See 13.175
See 13.176
See 13.177
See 13.178
See 13.179
See 13.180
See 13.181

See 13.182. The format displayed here changes as you make changes in the edit boxes above. It displays how the index will appear with your chosen specifications.

The whole world admits
unhesitatingly,
and there can be no doubt about this,
that Gutenberg's invention
is the incomparably greatest event
in the history of the world.

Mark Twain

Index format specifications

13.172 As you change any of the specifications in the "Index format" dialog box, you will see the changes reflected in the bottom portion of the box, under "Example." Those cryptic symbols in the edit boxes are codes for entering special characters; you will find a complete list of the codes in Appendix D. In 13.183 I've detailed several of those you're most likely to use.

13.173   Include index section headings: The "index section headings" are the large capital letters that break the index into alphabetical sections. If you uncheck this box you won't see any letters, but there will still be extra space to separate the sections.

13.174   Include empty index sections: If this box is not checked, PageMaker will only place section headings over the sections that actually contain entries. If this box is checked, all 27 section headings (the alphabet, plus "Symbol") will appear in the index, whether or not they contain entries. If the section is empty, PageMaker will insert *"no entries."*

V
no entries

An empty index section

13.175   Format (Nested or Run-in): A **Nested** index lists all the subentries on their own indented lines, one per line. It is much easier to find items this way. (The index in this book is nested.)

A **Run-in** index lists all the subentries in paragraphs, one entry after another. As you click in either button in the dialog box, you can see an example of the format reflected in the bottom portion of the dialog box.

13.176   Following topic: Whatever is entered in this edit box will separate any index entry from its first page number. The code ^> indicates an en space (4.207–4.214), so the default you see is two en spaces (*I don't know why they didn't just use one em space*). En spaces, remember, don't break, so the entry will never be separated from its page number.

13.177   Between page #s: When an entry is referenced to more than one page number, the page numbers will be separated by whatever is entered in this edit box. The default is a comma and an en space. Remember, the en space won't break (PageMaker will think all the numbers are one word), so if you have a lot of numbers for an entry, I would suggest using a comma and a regular space. Just type "**,** " (Comma Spacebar).

13.178   Between entries: Whatever is entered in this edit box is what will separate the multiple secondary entries in the "Run-in" format, as well as any multiple cross-references in either format. The default is a semicolon and an en space. Again, I would suggest using a regular space to make it easier on PageMaker to break the lines at reasonable places, especially considering that index columns are generally rather narrow. (To separate the secondary entries in a "Nested" format, use "Entry end"; see 13.181.)

Index format specs —continued

13.179   Page range: Sometimes index entries have a *range* of pages where the information can be found, such as "35–39" (13.95–13.100). Whatever is in the "Page range" edit box is what will separate those numbers. The default is an en dash, which is the appropriate mark to show a range of information.

13.180   Before x-ref: Whatever is in this edit box is what will separate an index entry from its corresponding cross-reference. The default is a period and an en space. Again, you might want to consider a normal space rather than an en space, which will make it easier for PageMaker to break the lines.

13.181   Entry end: Whatever is in this edit box is what will appear at the end of every entry in a "Nested" format. In a "Run-in" format, this character will appear at the end of the last reference in each topic. The default is no character at all, because we typically see the end of the line as denoting the end of the information. But you may want to have a stronger visual marker for the end of the entry, such as a bullet of some sort. See the examples in 13.182.

13.182   Remember, you can enter characters in these edit boxes and instantly see how they will affect the index. You'll see an example of the proposed format in the bottom portion of the dialog box:

Example : Index commands 1-4 ●
   Index entry 1, 3. See also Index mark-up ●
   Show index 2-4 ●

This is an example of a Nested format with a thin space and a bullet used in "Entry end."

Example : Index commands 1-4; Index entry 1, 3.
   See also Index mark-up; Show index 2-4;
   Create index 1, 3-4 ●

This is an example of a Run-in format with a thin space and a bullet used in "Entry end."

Character codes

13.183   Here is a brief list of some of the codes you can enter into the edit boxes in order to create special characters within the index. Notice that these are different than what you type to put that same character on the page. You'll find a complete chart in Appendix D. *(Type the caret [^] by pressing Shift 6.)*

To get a:	Type:
Normal space	Spacebar
Non-breaking space	Option Spacebar *or* ^s *or* ^S
Em space	^m *or* ^M
En space	^> (> *is above the period*)
Thin space	^< (< *is above the comma*)
Em dash	^_ (_ *is next to zero*)
En dash	^=
Tab	^t *or* ^T
Return	^p *or* ^P
Line break	^n *or* ^N
Non-wordbreaking slash	^/
Non-wordbreaking hyphen	^~
Bullet	Option 8
Raised period	Option Shift 9
Apple	Option Shift K

If you want to do this:	**Then follow these steps:**	**Shortcuts ▾ Notes ▾ Hints**
13.184 Create/place the index for the first time *(actually put it on the page)*	■ Open the publication that you want to place the index in. It would be easiest if you are on the correct page, also. ■ If there is no Book List in this publication, create one (see note to the right). Include all the publications that have entries you want to include in this index. ■ From the Options menu, choose "Create index...." ■ Read 13.169–13.170 and decide if you want to include the entries from all publications in the Book List or if you want to remove all unreferenced topics. ■ If you want to change the title, type the change. ■ Click the "Format..." button and format the index entries (see 13.172–13.183). Click OK. If you just want to accept the defaults, you can skip this step. ■ Click OK in the "Create index" dialog box. ■ If you are on a layout page, you will get a loaded text icon, just as if you were placing an outside text file. Click on the page to place the text. ■ If you are in the Story Editor, PageMaker will create a new story window with the index in it. To get the loaded text icon to place the index on the layout page, press Command D.	■ Of course, you only need to have a Book List (13.6–13.11) if you are compiling one comprehensive index that includes entries from more than one PageMaker publication.

If you want to do this:	**Then follow these steps:**	**Shortcuts ▾ Notes ▾ Hints**
13.185 Update an existing index, *replacing* the existing one	▪ You must be in the publication that contains the existing index that you want to update. You don't have to be on the same page as the existing index; Page-Maker will automatically take you there as soon as you update it. ▪ From the Options menu, choose "Create index...." ▪ Put a check in the checkbox, "Replace existing index." ▪ Set up the rest of this dialog box and the "Format" dialog box as you like. Any changes you make here will override whatever is in the existing index. ▪ Click all the OK buttons you find. You won't get the loaded text icon this time; PageMaker will wipe out the existing index and replace it with the updated version, using the same style sheet.	▪ It is entirely possible to place the up-dated index on the page without *replacing* the existing index. Just don't check the "Replace existing index" button (13.165). ▪ If you have placed more than one index on the page without *replacing* (updating) any, then PageMaker will update the last one you placed. If by chance you have eliminated the last one, then PageMaker thinks you don't have an index at all and the "Replace existing index" option will be gray (unavailable).
13.186 Update an existing index, *without* replacing the existing one	▪ Follow the steps in 13.185, above. But this time, do *not* put a check in the "Replace existing index" checkbox. Click all the OK buttons you find. ▪ You will get a loaded text icon if you are on a layout page, or a new story window if you are in the Story Editor, just as you did the first time (13.184).	▪ It is not possible to have more than one index that PageMaker recognizes; that is, as you place more than one index on the page, only the latest version will be considered the actual index. The others simply become plain ol' stories that can never again be updated, even if you delete the latest version.

If you want to do this:

13.187 Search the index for an entry

Then follow these steps:

- First you must place the index in the publication (13.184).
- If you are not already in the Story Editor, viewing the index story, then get there:
  - □ With the **pointer tool,** triple-click on the index story; **or**
  - □ With the **text tool,** click once in the story, then press Command E.
- From the Edit menu, choose "Find...," *or* press Command 8.
- In the "Find" dialog box, type the word, or at least several characters of the word you want to find. If you know which style it is tagged with, you can narrow the search by applying that attribute to the word (click the "Attributes..." button and choose the style from the mini-menu).
- Click the "Find" button. If PageMaker finds a word that is not the precise word you were looking for, click the "Find next" button. Keep clicking until you find it.
- See Section 8 on the Story Editor for full details on using "Find."

Shortcuts ▾ Notes ▾ Hints

- The basic idea here is to go into the Story Editor, view the index story window, and then use "Find." The directions here are very abbreviated; for detailed info on the Story Editor, see Section 8. For specifics on the Find command, see 8.46–8.62. For details on using Find-and-Change, see 8.63–8.78.

If you want to do this:	Then follow these steps:	Shortcuts ▾ Notes ▾ Hints
13.188 Define a prefix for the page numbers in the index *(optional)*	▪ Open the publication in which you want to add a prefix to the index page numbers (such as the appendices, charts, or perhaps volumes; see 13.118). ▪ From the File menu, choose "Page setup." ▪ Click on the button "Numbers...." ▪ In the edit box, enter the characters (up to 15) that you want to precede the page numbers. Be sure to type any spaces you need, such as the space directly before the number. ▪ Hit the Return key twice, *or* press Option Return to close both dialog boxes.	▪ Remember, if you want appendices, charts, volumes, etc. to have separate prefixes, they each need to be a separate publication. ▪ This optional format is *publication-specific;* that is, it will apply only to the page numbers from this one publication. If you are creating an index for an entire Book List, then you must follow this procedure for every separate publication that you want prefixes for. ▪ You can press Command Option Period to Cancel out of both boxes.
13.189 Eliminate the entire index *(the internal index, not the index that has been placed on the page)* **Caution! Read the notes** ➡	▪ From the Options menu, choose "Show index...." ▪ Hold down the Command, Option, and Shift keys while you click the "Remove" Button. Click OK.	▪ This will remove all entries *from every index in the current Book List.* I mean, seriously—when you return to another publication (in that Book List) for which you laboriously created entries, those entries will be **gone.** ▪ See also 13.129–13.131 and 13.152–13.154.
13.190 Eliminate the index in the current publication *(the internal index, not the index that has been placed on the page)*	▪ Hold down the Command key. From the Options menu, choose "Show index...." ▪ Hold down the Command, Option, and Shift keys while you click the "Remove" Button. Click OK.	▪ When you hold the Command key down, PageMaker assembles only the entries from the current publication into the "Show index" dialog boxes. If you remove these entries, no other publication will be affected.

14 ▾ COLOR

14.1 Minimums and maximums:

Item	Minimum	Maximum
Colors in Color palette	3	65,280
Hue (measured in)	0°	359°
Values in Color Wheel edit boxes	0 low intensity	65535 high intensity

14.2 There are several ways of working with color in PageMaker. Even on a black-and-white monitor, you can apply certain types of color and print spot color overlays.

14.3 PageMaker offers you the option of working with one of four different color *models* (14.12–14.19). The one you choose to work with depends on the reproduction process you will use to produce the publication (14.37–14.41). Color is a very complex creature, in both color theory and how to design *with* it, as well as in color technology and how to design *for* it. It is beyond the scope of this book to provide theory or technology. In the next few pages I cover the very basics of how to work with color presses to reproduce your job, and how to prepare your PageMaker publication appropriately.

14.4 If you have no idea what the terms *four-color process* or *color separations* mean, you probably will not be using them and can ignore all references to that information, if you so choose. Sometimes our brains just get full.

The basics of color reproduction: one color

14.5 To work with color in PageMaker, you will find it helps to have an understanding of how the color will be put on the paper when it is reproduced. This is a ten-minute rendition of a complex topic, geared to people with no previous background in any type of printing technology.

14.6 Let's start with **one color.** When a job is termed a "one-color" job, that means it will go through the printing press one time. One color of ink will be loaded onto the press; the paper will go through the press one time to print one side (it may, of course, go back through on the other side later). It doesn't matter what color of ink is on the press—it may be black, it may be purple, it may be a PMS color (14.49). The point is, *there is only one color of ink.* You may use a different color of paper, so when the job is finished, it *looks* like it is two color (e.g., brown ink on pink paper). But the color of the paper is entirely irrelevant; **a one-color job uses one color of ink.** If you are using a copy machine, the concept is equivalent: there is only one color of toner being laid onto the page; the paper goes through the machine only once.

14.7 One way to get variations out of a single color is to apply a **tint screen** (often called a **percentage value**) to objects or to text. These screens, or values, will create the *appearance* of a lighter shade. A percentage value means you are only getting a percentage of the full color. For instance, if you create and apply a 50% screen to a black shape, PageMaker breaks up the black area into dots in such a way that only 50% of the black is still there. The other 50% is the white space around the dots. This is an enlarged example:

Below, the box on the left is black. The box on the right has been assigned a 20% screen. It *appears* to be gray, because the tiny black dots it was printed with are blending with the white paper, making your eye think it is gray.

If these two boxes had been printed with red ink, the left box would be red and the right rule would appear to be pink.

See 14.113 for the steps to create and apply a tint screen.

14.8 You can assign various percentage values to text or objects in a one-color job, giving that job the appearance of having been created with more colors. The color of the paper will affect any tint screens, remember, because in your eye the paper color blends with the ink color. A 40% red on white paper will appear to be a different color than a 40% red on purple paper.

14.9 If you are creating a one-color job and you know it will be printed in, say, blue ink, *it is entirely unnecessary* to assign a blue color to everything in the publication! The laser printer or the imagesetter (18.5–18.10) can only output your publication in black, anyway. You take your black-and-white pages to the press, and the press person uses the black-and-white pages to make the *printing plates* that get put on the press. The press person then puts the color of ink you choose on the press and applies that ink to the paper. So no matter what color you want the finished product to be, if you're planning a one-color job you can just leave everything black-and-white.

The basics of color reproduction: multi-color, spot color

14.10 This brief intro discusses **two- or three-color jobs.** The information also applies to publications with four, five, or six colors, as long as they are *spot colors* rather than *four-color process.* **Spot color** is when you select text or an object and apply a color to it, using the Color palette found in the Windows menu, or when you place or paste a one-color image. *Four-color process* is the technology the press will use when you reproduce color photographs or illustrations. This will be explained on the next page.

14.11 There is one abiding rule about printing multi-color jobs: **talk to the printer first.** I don't mean talk to your laser printer; I mean talk to the commercial press printer who will reproduce the publication for you. Ask how they would like you to prepare the *mechanical,* or the *boards* (which means the pages of your publication, usually pasted onto illustration board so they don't flop around), so the press can print the job most efficiently. Depending on where the colors are, whether or not they bump into other colors, and a few other factors, the printer may want you to prepare *overlays, knockouts,* or *traps,* or they may just want you to point out where the other colors go. Whatever they want,

prepare it that way. Different presses may require slightly different preparations, so make sure you prepare it for the press that will actually be reproducing the job.

14.12 When a multi-color job is printed on a one-color press, the paper goes through the press once for each color. The printer (a person) has to wash the ink off the roller and prepare it for printing the next color. A multi-color press has more than one roller; each roller can have a different color ink.

No matter what kind of press is used in a multi-color job, the press person must make a separate printing *plate* with which to print each color. To make those plates, the printer may ask you to provide an *overlay* for each color. In PageMaker, you can print overlays automatically; each color will print on a separate page (14.16–14.22; 14.107). For instance, the red objects will come out of the laser printer on their own pages, the green objects will be on their own pages, etc.

14.13 If the separate colors **do not** *touch each other,* it is entirely possible your commercial printer would not need or want separate overlays. For instance, if all the headlines are to be pale blue and all the

body copy is to be dark gray, the two colors won't touch each other. Many presses won't need you to provide separate overlays in this case. This is especially true if you are not going to a "quick" printer (a "quick" printer is any press with the word speedy, quick, fast, instant, etc., in its name). **Talk to your printer first.**

14.14 If the separate colors **do** *touch each other* (a red box overlapping a green circle, for instance), then you must create overlays. Also, the printer may ask if you can provide a *knockout* and perhaps even a *trap* (14.23–14.30). You should mention that although PageMaker can do this, it is still better (at this point in technology) for the printer to do it him/herself.

14.15 With multi-color, you can use varying screen percentages (tint screens, percentage values; 14.7–14.9) to give the appearance of even more colors, or you can overlap a percentage of one color on an area of a solid, different color. You must be careful when you overlap two different screen percentages, though; you will end up with *moiré* patterns (9.11–9.12).

Overlays   *(please read the next page, also, for information very related to overlays)*   ✐   ✐   ✐

14.16   When you take your pages to a commercial print shop, they print multiple copies on a press: they take the pages of your publication, make a *plate,* and put that plate on a roller on the press. Each roller on a printing press can print only one color at a time.

14.17   If you have a multi-color job, each of the colors in the job must be on its own separate roller. If it is a one-color press (with only one roller), that means the printer has to clean off one color of ink, put the next plate on, and put the next color of ink on. That's one of the reasons why printing more than one color is costly.

14.18   Each printing plate that goes on each roller must have just the elements on it that will all be printed in the same color. Since the printing plates are made from the pages you give the press, each of the elements of like colors must be on its own page. For instance, let's say all the text is going to print black, and all the headlines and rules are going to print light blue. Then all the black text must be on one page *without* the headlines and rules. All the headlines and rules must be on another page, *without* the text.

14.19   PageMaker makes this easy for you through the "Spot color overlays" option when you print (14.12; 14.107; 18.79). Page-Maker will separate the colors for you (say the black and the light blue I just mentioned), and put each color on a separate page; the pages are considered **overlays.** (The term is a holdover from traditional paste-up, when we actually used to have to put everything of one color onto a separate piece of acetate and tape it down to the board, overlaying the color that was already on the board.)

14.20   Now, when your laser printer or the imagesetter prints the separate overlay pages, they always come out of the printer black, right? It doesn't even matter what color they were on your screen. It doesn't matter what color you specified. They are always black, and that makes the commercial printer happy because he can only make a plate from a black-and-white original. After the plate is on the roller, he can put whatever color of ink that you like on the roller. Or, when you put it in the copy machine, you can set the machine to print any color of toner you like.

14.21   Remember, we are talking about *spot colors:* text or objects that you have applied a solid color to, such as Red, Green, Blue, or a PMS color. When working with spot color, you typically don't want to use more than two or three different colors because of the expense (see 14.7–14.8 for some tips on how to make it *appear* that you are using more colors). If you need more than three or four colors, you need to learn how to use *process colors* (14.31–14.36) and how to build specific colors out of the four process ones. Which is beyond the scope of this book. Thank goodness.

14.22   You know what? If you are going to reproduce the job at a higher-quality commercial press (as opposed to a "quick" printer), *you do not need to make overlays if the two (or more) colors do not touch each other.* For instance, headlines and rules generally do not touch the body text. Just tape a piece of translucent tissue paper over the top of the page and neatly indicate the items that you want inked in a second or third color. **Talk to your printer about it first!**

Knockouts and traps   *(if you don't know the purpose of overlays, please read the previous page first)*

14.23 If your publication consists of more than one spot color, and those colors touch each other, then you need to create overlays (14.107).

14.24 If the colors overlap each other at any point, you have two choices regarding those overlays:

a You can let one color print on top of the other color, called **overprinting.** This usually results in a mismatched effect, where the color underneath discolors the one above (14.26). (You won't see the discoloration on the screen because the PageMaker objects are opaque.)

b Or you can remove the portion of whatever is beneath the first color, which is called a **knockout.** The color underneath is being knocked out of the color above (14.27).

14.25 For instance, let's say you are printing a yellow square that is partially on top of a red rectangle, sort of like this:

14.26 If you were to *overprint,* the final product would look like this:

14.27 A commercial printer would *knock out* the portion of the red rectangle that is overlapped by the yellow square, so the yellow square will print onto the white paper and the red "rectangle" will print right up next to it. PageMaker can create knockouts for you. These two shapes, printed on two separate overlays with a knockout, will show up on their respective pages like this:

first overlay   *second overlay*

14.28 The problem inherent in Page-Maker's knockouts is that this image is now dependent on the press registering these two colors to each other *perfectly;* that is, these two colors must now be *exactly* lined up with each other on the press or a white line will show where the colors didn't quite connect.

14.29 A commercial printer never creates a knockout without a **trap.** A trap is the thin line where the two colors overlap, giving the press a tiny bit of leeway where the two colors abut. A camera person at the printshop puts the images through photographic contortions like "chokes" and "spreads" to create the trap. They like to do that because it makes printing the job much easier. Commercial printers will most likely not be very happy with you if you try to give them overlays with PageMaker's knockouts. *Talk to your printer first!* Ask if they want the knockouts, being sure to explain that there are absolutely no traps provided.

14.30 You can put *yourself* through contortions to create your own trap, making this a touch bigger and and that a touch smaller and aligning everything just perfectly. Personally, I think you and everyone else will be happier if you let the commercial press prepare them for you.

The basics of color reproduction: four-color process

I must remind you once again that this is an extremely brief introduction to a very complex subject.

14.31 *Spot color* refers to objects that have been assigned one color. A color photograph or multi-color illustration is not spot color; it is *full color*. Full-color images cannot be separated into spot color overlays; that is, you cannot tell PageMaker to print the orange on one page, the mauve on another, the peach on another, etc. There are too many millions of possible colors. So, traditionally, full-color images have always gone through the **four-color separation process.**

14.32 In this process, powerful, high-tech machines scan the image and separate all those millions of colors into the three process primary colors, plus black, that together make up the full-color image. The process colors are Cyan (blue), Magenta (the closest thing to red in process colors), Yellow, and Black (which provide the initials for CMYK). The machine finds all the cyan, for instance, in the image, whether it is embedded in the color purple or green or violet or whatever, and represents that layer on a piece of film in varying degress of dark to light blue. It then finds all the magenta,

all the yellow, and all the black, and separates each layer of color onto a separate piece of film. The colors are transparent, so when these four layers of film are laid over one another, the full-color image appears. Where dark cyan overlaps dark magenta, the image is dark purple; where light yellow overlaps a mid-blue with a touch of magenta, the image is a rich green.

14.33 The full-color image is reproduced by printing these four colors onto paper, one color at a time (one color per roller, anyway). By combining these four colors in millions of varieties, virtually any color can be reproduced. If you use a magnifying glass (printers use a special *loupe*) to take a look at any color photo in any magazine, you will see combinations of the four colors overlapping each other to produce the colors your naked eye sees. You will see little *dots* of color, because the principle is the same as printing various tint screens (14.7) in one color—the press can lay down only a solid layer of ink, so by using dots we can make the colors *appear* to be lighter.

14.34 Four-color process printing is a very exacting procedure. Each of the four colors is printed on the paper as miniscule dots.

The dots are lined up in rows. Each color must have its rows of dots lined up at a very precise angle to avoid a *moiré* pattern. A moiré pattern is the strange pattern that appears when the lines of dots overlap each other at random angles. Although the patterns may be very interesting, generally they are undesirable (9.11–9.12).

14.35 The four-color process recreates most colors. It does not make a very good red, though, so oftentimes a true red is added as a fifth, PMS color. Metallics (silver, gold, etc.) or other PMS colors are also often added as fifth or sixth colors.

14.36 You can place full-color images, such as color TIFFs or EPS graphics, into Page-Maker publications. But PageMaker does not create the four-color separations for printing. Within PageMaker, you can *prepare* the publication to be separated by another program, such as Aldus PrePrint (14.109). Color separations by personal computers, though, can provide only medium-quality work at this time. For high-quality, professional seps, many color images should still be traditionally scanned.

Color models: which one to use *(the color models are explained on the following pages)*

14.37 PageMaker offers several different **color models** (14.42–14.49) to work with. A color model is a method of describing the type of color you want to apply. The model you choose to work with depends on how you are going to reproduce the publication. You have a choice of RGB, HLS, CMYK, or PMS (Pantone), all of which are explained on the next few pages.

14.38 If you know you will be reproducing the publication either on a **slide recorder** or on a **color printer,** use the RGB or HSB color model (including the Apple Color Wheel, if you like; 14.54–14.61). For instance, perhaps you will be printing directly to a color printer to get a full-color comp to show a client, or because you only need six printed copies of this job. Or perhaps you are designing a presentation that will be output onto color slides.

14.39 If you are going to take your PostScript-printed pages to a **copy machine** or a **commercial press** to have one, two, or three different colors of ink or toner applied, you can use any color model you like, *except* CMYK. Just make sure you make a spot color overlay for each separate color (14.16–14.22; 14.107). This method will also work for four, five, or six colors, as long as you are not trying to separate a full-color photograph or illustration.

14.40 If you will be taking your publication to a **commercial press** and you want to use specific **PMS** colors (14.49), then specify your colors using the PMS model. If you will be working with any fills, stick to the ones you find in the Fill menu (as opposed to creating tints yourself). When you print, create spot color overlays for each color.

14.41 If you have a publication with **full-color photographs** or **illustrations** in it, which of course will be going to a commercial press, use the CMYK color model (these are called *process colors*). If you use fills for PageMaker-drawn shapes, make them solid and apply the percentage tint with a process color or combination of process colors. You will need to print the publication to disk (14.109; 18.134–18.156) in order to have the four-color separations made.

E X P E R I E N C E
teaches you
to recognize a mistake
when you've made it again.

See 14.76–14.83 for editing colors using any of these models.

RGB

Edit color

Name: purple

Model: ⦿ RGB ○ HLS ○ CMYK

Red:	22	%
Green:	0	%
Blue:	75	%

OK

Cancel

PANTONE®...

HLS

Edit color

Name: purple

Model: ○ RGB ⦿ HLS ○ CMYK

Hue:	257	°
Lightness:	37	%
Saturation:	100	%

OK

Cancel

PANTONE®...

CMYK

Edit color

Name: purple

Model: ○ RGB ○ HLS ⦿ CMYK

Cyan:	78	%
Magenta:	100	%
Yellow:	25	%
Black:	0	%

OK

Cancel

PANTONE®...

14.42 RGB stands for **Red, Green,** and **Blue.** The RGB model is actually not a color standard for printing to paper, but comes from the balance of colors used to create color photographic prints from color negatives and for creating video and television displays. Color Mac monitors use the RGB model to display. In PageMaker, RGB works interactively with HLS (see the next column, and the Apple Color Wheel info, next page).

14.43 If you are going to print straight to a color printer for a tight comp, or if you are going to reproduce your screen through a slide recorder, RGB is a fast, easy way to create colors on the fly. If you are going to need to separate those colors for printing on a press, just go straight to the CMYK and/or the Pantone color model, instead.

14.44 HLS stands for **Hue, Lightness,** and **Saturation** (also known as HSB for Hue, Saturation, and Brightness; same thing).

14.45 Hue refers to the color itself, such as whether the color is blue or green or orange, etc. **Lightness** refers to how much white is added to the color; the more white, the lighter the color. **Saturation** refers to the intensity, or purity, of the color. Typically, the more saturated the color is, the richer and deeper it appears.

14.46 Notice that the color purple as defined in RGB (top left) automatically translates into certain values here in HLS. If you change the HLS values, you will find that the RGB values for the same color have also changed.

14.47 CMYK stands for **Cyan, Magenta, Yellow,** and **Black** (see 14.32). This model uses what are called the *process colors* and is the standard for printing full-color jobs (14.33–14.36).

14.48 Notice that no matter which model you use to define a color, all the other models enter their appropriate values for that color. The example above shows the CMYK values for the color purple that I originally defined in RGB. Fortunately, PageMaker keeps track of those colors in its process palette, so if you initially defined colors using RGB and/or HLS for color proofs, and then you change your mind and want to print it four-color process, just change the color model in its edit box: switch it from one model to CMYK.

Pantone (PMS)

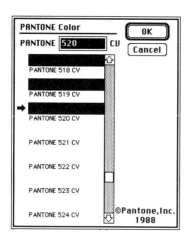

14.49 **PMS** stands for the **Pantone Matching System,** which is an internationally-recognized color identification system used by ink manufacturers, designers, and commercial printers. Color names such as teal, forest green, or sky blue, are always open to misinterpretation. But with the Pantone Matching System a designer can identify the exact color she wants by checking a Pantone color swatch book or catalog. Each color is identified with a number. She can then specify that PMS number to almost any printer in the world and be guaranteed the color will match what she had in mind.

14.50 PageMaker displays over 700 Pantone colors, listed in the same order as in the *Pantone Color Formula Guide 747XR.* Even if you have a black-and-white monitor, you can choose the color from the *Formula Guide* (available at most art supply stores and sometimes from your commercial press), then find the corresponding color in PageMaker and add it to your Color palette (14.91). When you print with spot color overlays (14.107), each PMS color will print on a separate overlay.

14.51 As you define RGB, HLS, or process colors (CMYK), you will notice that you can always click on the "Pantone®..." button. PageMaker automatically selects the Pantone color that most closely approximates your definition.

14.52 In a Pantone swatchbook, the numbers have a letter after them, usually a "C" for "Coated," or a "U" for "Uncoated." This letter refers to the kind of paper on which the ink is to be printed. In PageMaker, you see the letters "CV," which stand for "Computer Video." *Because computer monitors use RGB to display, the color you see on your screen is not an exact match to the color that will output from a color printer, which is not an exact match to the true PMS color of that same number*

that the press will use to reproduce your job. It is critical that you accept this fact. If you are accustomed to working with PMS color and process colors, you are probably accustomed to having color proofs and chromes made before going to press. Don't skip that process now! In fact, it's even more critical now, since the RGB color computer screen can delude you.

14.53 A note for people who regularly work with process and PMS colors: As you already know, process inks (CMYK) cannot create certain colors (14.35). If you use the PMS color model in addition to the four process colors in your publication (a five- or six-color job), you need to make that fact clear to the service bureau that will be making the separations. Give them a list of the inks and tell them which ones need to be converted to process and which ones should be left as spot color (people who work with Aldus PrePrint will understand). If you don't make sure that the PMS colors are left as spot color, they will be separated into the four process colors to create as close an approximation as possible to the color you wanted, which of course defeats the whole purpose of using PMS colors in the first place.

14.54 Apple Color Wheel *(also known as the Apple Color Picker; press the Shift key as you click "Edit" in the "Edit color" dialog box, or hold both the Command and the Shift keys down as you click on a color [not Black, Paper, or Registration] in the Color palette)*

14.55 If you have a grayscale or color monitor, you can tap into the Apple Color Wheel (hold the Shift key down when you click on the "Edit…" button in the "Define colors" dialog box; 14.74). With the color wheel, you can just buzz around and pick up the color you want. The specs for it will automatically drop into both the HLS and the RGB models, and the closest Pantone color will be selected. (Notice the Apple

Color Wheel uses HSB while PageMaker uses the comparable HLS; see 14.44).

14.56 The color wheel can display 16.8 million colors (who counted them, I want to know). You can view the color wheel on a black-and-white monitor; you get little initial letter clues (shown below) telling you where each color would be if you could see it. That's not a whole lot of help.

14.57 *This is the name of the color that was selected when you clicked the Edit button.*

14.58 *The bottom half of this Color Box shows the original color. The top half shows how the color changes as you edit it. Click on the bottom half of the Color Box to return to the original color.*

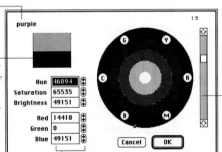

14.59 *To adjust the brightness (lightness), press on the scroll arrows, drag the scroll box, or click in the grey scroll bar.*

14.60 *You can press the arrows to change any of the specs; the color wheel will change right before your eyes.*

You can also **type** *a value from 0 (low intensity) to 65535 (high intensity). You will not see the color change until you click somewhere in the dialog box; click anywhere except in the bottom half of the color box (14.58).*

14.61 To define the color values:

Hue *(the color)* **:** Press the mouse button and move the pointer around on the color wheel. The selected color will appear in the top half of the Color Box (14.58)

Saturation *(the purity or intensity of the color)* **:** Click toward or away from the center of the wheel. There is actually a very thin line running from the outer edge of the circle towards the center, along which the hue stays the same. For example, you can click on the outside edge and pick up hue 35944, and then click towards the center and pick up the same hue with less saturation. It's easier, though, to pick a hue in the color wheel, and then use the arrows (14.60) to control the saturation and brightness.

Lightness (brightness)
(how much white is in the color) **:**
Use the scroll bar on the right. The up arrow lightens/brightens the color; the down arrow darkens/shades the color, all the way down to black.

Also see 14.60.

The color Registration, the color Paper, and the fill Paper

14.62 "Registration" isn't even a color, actually; it is a *tag*. When you are printing separations or spot color overlays, any text or object that has had **Registration** applied to it (*tagged*), will appear on *every* overlay. For instance, if you created one page with six different multi-color business cards on it, you probably made tick marks to define the boundaries of the cards. If you apply the color "Registration" to the tick marks, the marks will show up on every page when you print the separate color overlays.

14.63 The **color Paper** (from the Color palette) actually is the color of the paper you are working on. Usually it is white, because PageMaker gives you a white page whenever you create a new publication. You can change the color of Paper, though, to anything you like! If you have a color monitor and will be printing the job on a pale peach stock, you can change Paper to pale peach. The pages on your screen will be pale peach, giving you a clearer indication of how all the various colors will react together. On a black-and-white laser printer or imagesetter, Paper will always print as white, though (because you don't want a solid black sheet from the printer showing where to print pale peach).

14.64 When you change the *color* Paper, the **fill Paper** (from the Fill submenu in the Element menu) also changes to that color. But the two Papers function a little differently.

14.65 If you draw a box with a black border and **fill** it with Paper, the inside of the box is Paper colored and the border is black. Right.

If you select that box and apply the **color** Paper, then both the inside *and* the border become Paper colored; if the box is on the page, it essentially becomes invisible.

14.66 When you print separations or spot color overlays, an object with a **fill** of Paper will appear on only one overlay (the overlay of the border color). It will obscure only other Paper-*filled* objects on any layer beneath it.

If the *border* of a Paper-*filled* object is Registration colored, the object will print as white on every overlay, and will obscure anything behind it on every overlay (the border, of course, will print black).

14.67 An object that has been assigned (tagged with) the **color** Paper will print on *every* color overlay. Unlike a Paper-*filled* obect, a Paper-*colored* object will obscure *all* objects behind it on every overlay, no matter what color they are.

This can come in very handy. Say you want a crescent shape, so you overlay one dark circle with a white circle. If you print overlays, the entire dark circle will print if the white circle overlay is Paper-*filled*. But if the white circle overlay is Paper-*colored*, then it will obscure that portion of the dark circle, even on the overlay.

Black circle with white circle on top to create a crescent.   *Overlay result if white circle is Paper-filled.*   *Overlay result if white circle is Paper-colored.*

14.68 If you change the Paper *color* in the Color palette, the new color *does* affect every object already in the publication that has a *fill* of Paper, as well as objects with the *color* Paper already applied.

The "Define colors" dialog box *(from the Element menu, choose "Define colors...")*

14.69 The style sheet for colors works the same as the style sheet for text. To apply a color to a graphic object or to text, simply select the object or the text with the appropriate tool, then click on the color shown in the Color palette (graphic: 14.104; text: 14.102). This is also called *tagging* an object with a color. If you edit (change) that color in the color style sheet, then everything that has had that color applied to it will automatically and instantly change throughout the publication.

14.70 *On a color monitor, this bar will display the selected color.*

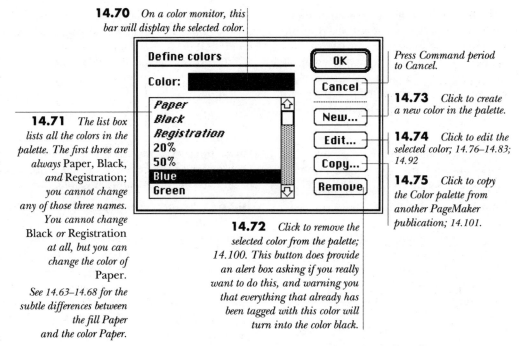

14.71 *The list box lists all the colors in the palette. The first three are always* Paper, Black, *and* Registration; *you cannot change any of those three names. You cannot change* Black *or* Registration *at all, but you can change the color of* Paper.

See 14.63–14.68 for the subtle differences between the fill Paper and the color Paper.

14.72 *Click to remove the selected color from the palette; 14.100. This button does provide an alert box asking if you really want to do this, and warning you that everything that already has been tagged with this color will turn into the color black.*

Press Command period to Cancel.

14.73 *Click to create a new color in the palette.*

14.74 *Click to edit the selected color; 14.76–14.83; 14.92*

14.75 *Click to copy the Color palette from another PageMaker publication; 14.101.*

You look rather rash my dear your colors dont quite match your face. —Ms. Daisy Ashford

The "Edit color" dialog boxes

14.76 This example shows the CMYK edit box, but the edit box for each color model works exactly the same.

14.77 If the Color palette is showing on your screen (press Command K if it is not), you can shortcut to the edit box of any color on it: hold down the Command key and click once on the color name. The only limitation of the "Edit color" dialog box is that it doesn't allow you to change the name of the color; to do that you must go through the "Define styles..." command (14.93).

14.78 Remember, these colors are a style sheet. If you have assigned a color to an object or to text, that object or text is considered *tagged*. If you edit any color, all objects or text with that color tag will be changed to the new version of that color.

14.79 *Type the name of the color here. It's a good practice to give an identifying clue to the name to let you know which color model you used. For instance, "p.purple" would tell me I used process colors; "pms.purple 520" would tell me it's a Pantone color. Adding the code to the beginning of the name forces like models to group together in the Color palette.*

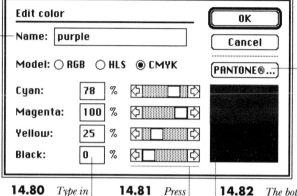

14.80 *Type in a value in any of these boxes. To see the new color, click on the top portion of the Color Box on the right (14.82).*

14.81 *Press on the arrows, drag the box, or click in the gray area to change the values. You will see the changes reflected in the Color Box on the right (14.82).*

14.82 *The bottom half of this Color Box displays the original color. The top half displays the new color you create as you change the values. To return to the original color, click on the bottom half.*

14.83 *Click to get the Pantone color model dialog box (14.49–14.53). The Pantone color you see selected there (the one with the arrow) is the closest approximation to the specs shown in this dialog box.*

Color defaults

14.84 You can add any color in the Color palette to any paragraph style in your style sheet (14.103; see Section 7 on Style Sheets). For instance, you may want all your Headlines to be Purple. Just remember that before you can add a color to a style, you first need to define it so it appears in your Color palette (14.91).

14.85 You can set a default color that will automatically apply to text.

You can set a *separate* default color that will automatically apply to objects.

14.86 Step-by-step directions for setting a text default color are found in 14.112. The basic concept is that you are just adding a further specification to the text defaults that already exist (3.35). The current text color default is probably Black; you can change it to any color in the Color palette. Then whenever you type using the default style "No style," your text will be in that particular chosen color.

14.87 You can always temporarily override a paragraph style sheet by simply selecting text and choosing a color, or by choosing a color while the insertion point is flashing (see 7.36–7.41 regarding overrides). This temporary override will be in effect only until you click the insertion point somewhere else. Removing these colorful temporary style sheet overrides is easy: with the insertion point flashing in the paragraph, click on the style name again (7.58).

14.88 You can set a default color that will apply to any graphics you draw in Page-Maker (that is, any line, box, or oval; 14.111). This default will also automatically apply to any graphic you paste in from the Clipboard (as long as it did not come from the Scrapbook), and also to any external graphic file you *place,* **if** the graphic has not had a color assigned to it previously.

There is a strange thing that happens to many people in PageMaker: On some machines, anything you paste from the Scrapbook defaults to the "Registration" color. This is not a problem if you are printing only one color. But if you create overlays, anything that is tagged with "Registration" will appear on every overlay!

14.89 It's important to know about color defaults because it is so easy to change them inadvertently, and if your screen is black-and-white you won't even know the color has changed. On my grayscale monitor (which is set to black-and-white so it will redraw faster), I unknowingly pasted in every screen shot in the entire publication with a 20% tint. I didn't catch it until I printed the pages.

It's a very good idea, when you are working with colors on a monochrome monitor, to leave your Color palette visible on the screen (press Command K). That way you can see the color selection jump from one to another as you place, paste, and create.

If you want to do this:	**Then follow these steps:**	**Shortcuts ▾ Notes ▾ Hints**
14.90a Show the Color palette	■ From the Windows menu, choose "Color palette," *or* press Command K.	■ If there is a checkmark in the Windows menu next to the command "Color palette," it means the palette is on the screen. If you don't see it, check behind the Style palette.
14.90b Hide the Color palette	■ From the Windows menu, choose "Color palette," *or* press Command K.	
14.91 Create/define a new color	■ From the Element menu, choose "Define colors...." ■ Click the "New..." button. The specifications you see in the edit boxes are those from whichever color in the palette was highlighted when you clicked "New...." Changing the specs will not affect any existing color. ■ Name the color. It's a good idea to set up a system of naming colors that gives you an indication of which model the color was created in (14.79). ■ In the "Edit color" dialog box, click on the radio button to choose the color model you want to use (see 14.37–14.53 to decide on the appropriate model). ■ Adjust the specifications: type in values, (14.80), use the scroll bars (14.81), or choose a Pantone color (14.83). See 14.76–14.83 for detailed info on using the "Edit color" dialog box. ■ Click OK, click OK; *or* press Option Return to close both boxes.	■ **Extra-zippy shortcut:** □ If the Color palette is not already on the screen, press Command K (14.90a). □ Hold the Command key down and click on "Black" or "Registration." This brings up the "Edit color" dialog box. □ Define the color. Click OK. □ This extra-zippy shortcut does not *apply* the color to anything on the page. You can just keep Command-clicking "Black" to create new colors. ■ If the OK button in the "Edit color" dialog box is not black, it means you have not named the color. ■ If you click on the bottom half of the Color Vox (14.82), you cancel your new specs and remove the name. The dialog box stays, though. ■ Any new color you define will appear in the Color palette, in the "Type specifications" dialog box, and in the "Paragraph rules" dialog box.

If you want to do this:	**Then follow these steps:**	**Shortcuts ▾ Notes ▾ Hints**

14.92 Edit (change) a color in the Color palette

- From the Element menu, choose "Define colors...."
- Click once on the name of the color you want to edit, then click the "Edit..." button; *or* just double-click on the color name.
- Editing a color is basically the same as creating a new color. You can change its name, any of the values, or even the color model. See 14.76–14.83 if you need further help on using the "Edit color" dialog box.
- Click OK, click OK; *or* press Option Return.

- **Extra-zippy shortcut:**
  - □ If the Color palette is not already on the screen, press Command K (14.90a).
  - □ Hold the Command key down and click once on the color name to bring up its "Edit color" dialog box.
  - □ Edit the color. Click OK.
    (You can't change the name of the color this way; see 14.93.)
- Any changes you make to this color will then instantly be applied to all text or objects that have been tagged with this color (14.69; 14.78).

14.93 Change the name of a color

- From the Element menu, choose "Define colors...."
- Double-click on the color name that you want to change.
- In the "Edit color" dialog box, type in the new name.
- Click OK, click OK; *or* press Option Return.

- You cannot use the extra-zippy shortcut (mentioned above) to change the name of a color. If you Command-click a color in the Color palette, you will be able to edit any of the specifications *except* the name.

T i m e   i s   w h a t   k e e p s   e v e r y t h i n g   f r o m   h a p p e n i n g   a t   o n c e .

If you want to do this:	**Then follow these steps:**	**Shortcuts ▾ Notes ▾ Hints**
14.94 Use the Apple Color Wheel to edit an existing color	■ The Apple Color Wheel is only accessible if you have a grayscale or color monitor. ■ From the Element menu, choose "Define colors...." ■ Click once on the name of the color you want to edit; hold down the Shift key and click on the "Edit..." button; **or** hold the Shift key down and double-click on the color name. ■ See 14.54–14.61 for specifics on how to choose and change the values. ■ Click OK to get back to the "Edit color" dialog box. Continue editing, if necessary, or press Option Return to close both dialog boxes.	■ **Extra-zippy shortcut** to the color wheel: If the Color palette is not showing, press Command K to show it. Then hold down the Command and Shift keys and click once on the name in the Color palette. ■ You can only use the Color Wheel to *edit* an existing color—you can't get to the wheel through the "New..." button. You *can* create a new color and click OK in the "Edit color" dialog box. Then hold the Shift key down and double-click on the name of that new color to get the Color Wheel.
14.95 Use the Pantone Matching System color model	■ From the Element menu, choose "Define colors...." ■ Click the "New..." button to define a new color, or double-click on an existing color to change it to a PMS color. ■ It's best to click on the CMYK button, just to maximize your options. ■ Click on the "Pantone®..." button. ■ Scroll to find the color you want, or type in the number, if you know it. Click OK.	■ It is entirely possible to define a color as a PMS in any color model and then change its values. This means the PMS color you see on the screen is *really* not going to match the printer's PMS ink (14.49). *Make sure you rename the PMS color if you change its values!!!* ■ If you will be printing four-color process, you can tell the service bureau doing the separations to separate the PMS colors, as well as the CMYK, **or** to separate just the CMYK and leave the PMS as spot color overlays (14.53).

If you want to do this:	**Then follow these steps:**	**Shortcuts ▾ Notes ▾ Hints**
14.96 Change the color "Registration"	■ You can't.	■ "Registration" isn't even a color, really. It is just a tag to apply to those items that you want to show up on every page of the spot color overlays or the four-color separations (14.62).
14.97 Change the color "Black"	■ You can't.	■ You may have noticed that if you Command-click on either "Registration" or "Black" in the Color palette, as if to edit the color, the name is missing. If you make any changes in this "Edit color" dialog box, you will not be changing "Black" or "Registration," but you will be defining a new color.
14.98 Change the color "Paper"	■ You can get the "Define colors..." dialog box and edit "Paper," just as you would any other color (14.92). **Or:** □ If the Color palette is not showing, press Command K to show it. □ Hold the Command key down and click once on the color "Paper." □ In the resulting "Edit box," change the color using any of the color models you like (14.37–14.53). □ Click OK.	■ Changing the color "Paper" *actually changes the color of your paper on the screen!* "Paper" is a color you can apply to text or ojbects, but it also refers to the color of the paper you are creating your publication on (your page itself doesn't show up as an overlay, though). See 14.63–14.68. ■ Whatever color you change "Paper" to will also apply to the *fill* "Paper" in the Element menu. There is a slight difference, though, in how PageMaker prints objects that have been *filled* with "Paper" and objects that have been *colored* "Paper." See 14.64–14.68.

If you want to do this:	**Then follow these steps:**	**Shortcuts ▾ Notes ▾ Hints**

14.99 Change the color "Paper" back to its original color (white)

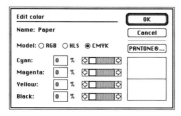

- From the Element menu, choose "Define colors...."
- Click once on "Paper," then click the "Edit..." button, *or* double-click on "Paper."
- In the "Edit color" dialog box, click on the "CMYK" button.
- Change the values in all the edit boxes to 0 (zero), either by typing the number or by dragging the scroll boxes to the left.
- Click OK.

- If the Color palette is visible on your screen (press Command K to show it), Command-click on "Paper" to get the "Edit color" dialog box.
- If you type 0 (zero) and you don't see the change reflected in the Color Box on the right, click in the top half of it (14.82).

14.100 Remove a color from the Color palette

- From the Element menu, choose "Define colors...."
- Click once on the name of the color you want to remove, then click the "Remove" button.
- Thoughtfully, PageMaker asks if you really want to do this, even warning you that any objects that have had this color applied will turn black. Click OK, if you really do want to remove it.
- Click OK to close the "Edit color" dialog box (Cancel, of course, if you have changed your mind).

- Since you probably read *The Little Mac Book,* you know that Rule Number One on the Mac is Save Often. You really should be especially conscious of saving just before you do something potentially drastic, like removing something. That way you can always Revert (16.26).

If you want to do this:	**Then follow these steps:**	**Shortcuts · Notes · Hints**

14.101 Copy a Color palette from another publication

The dialog box allows you to choose the publication that contains the color styles you want to copy into the current publication.

PageMaker will warn you before replacing any existing colors.

- From the Element menu, choose "Define colors...."
- Click the button "Copy...." This takes you to a dialog box where you can look for the PageMaker publication that contains the Color palette you want to copy into the current publication. Switch disks and/or open folders to find it.
- When you find the PageMaker publication, double-click on it. All the colors in that file's Color palette will be added to the current Color palette. (You could, of course, single-click on the file name and then click the OK button.)
- If the palette you are copying from has a color with the same name as a color in the current palette, PageMaker will ask if you want to replace the current color. If you click the Cancel button here, you will just cancel that one replacement; you will not be canceling the entire copy process. You will get a separate little alert box for every color with the same name (regardless of caps and lower case).
- Click OK if you are done. You can Copy a palette from another file; you can Cancel if you decide this was not a smart thing to do; you can Remove any colors that you now see need to be removed (14.100).

- When you copy a Color palette from another PageMaker publication, the other colors are *added* to the current Color palette. If any colors have the same name (regardless of capital letters), PageMaker will ask if you want to replace the current one with the copied one. If you *replace* a color, remember, all objects that have had that color applied will change into the new, copied version of that color.
- Copying colors comes in very handy when you are working on several publications in which you want similar colors.
- Since the color you see on the screen is not what prints on the color printer, nor is it what will print on the press, you may want to create a template (Section 12) that contains a set of colors you have adjusted to specifications that you know will print. For instance, maybe your company uses a particular color for its logo. After much trial and experimentation and frustration, you finally found exactly the right combination of CMYK that creates exactly that color on the press. If you store it in a template, you can always copy that color into any other publication, even if you don't want to use the template pages.

If you want to do this:

Then follow these steps:

Shortcuts ▾ Notes ▾ Hints

14.102 Apply colors to text

You can only *apply* colors that you have previously *defined* (14.91).
- Get the Colors palette, if it isn't already visible: from the Windows menu, choose "Color palette," *or* press Command K.
- With the **text tool,** select the text you want to color.
- Click on the color in the Color palette.

Or:

Select the text, then get "Type specs..." from the Type menu. Choose the color from the "Color" submenu. Click OK.

- If the insertion point is flashing, any color you choose will be poured into that insertion point; text you type from that point on will be in color.
- All colors you define will also appear in the "Type specifications" and the "Define styles" dialog boxes, and from either of these boxes you can apply color to text. All colors you define will also be available in the "Paragraph rules" dialog box for coloring rules (lines).

14.103 Add colors to paragraph styles

- If your Style palette is showing, just Command-click on the style you want to add color to. If the Style palette is not showing, from the Type menu, choose "Define styles..." and double-click on the style name.
- Click the "Type..." button.
- From the Colors submenu, choose the one you want. All colors from the Color palette will show up here.
- Click as many OK buttons as necessary.

- To show the Style palette, you can choose it from the Windows menu, or press Command Y.
- Of course, if you are starting a new style from scratch (7.43; 7.44), you can just build color into it from the beginning. See Section 7 on Style Sheets.
- If you sometimes see a white box behind the colored text, don't worry about it— simply redraw the screen (resize the view, click in the zoom box, etc.) and the white box will go away.

If you want to do this:	**Then follow these steps:**	**Shortcuts ▾ Notes ▾ Hints**
14.104 Apply colors to graphics	■ You can only *apply* colors that you have previously *defined* (14.91). ■ Get the Colors palette, if it isn't already visible: from the Windows menu, choose "Color palette," *or* press Command K. ■ With the **pointer tool,** select the graphic you want to color. ■ In the Color palette, click on the name of the color you want to apply.	■ You can apply color to any object on the page, except graphics that have color built into them, such as color TIFFs (like color photographs) or color EPS files. Even on a color monitor, though, you will not *see* PICT or EPS graphics in their color. You *will* be able to see the color you apply to black-and-white TIFFs and paint-type graphics (see Section 9 on Graphics).
14.105 Create a box with a colored border and a fill of a different color  *You can get double colored borders, even, by making the None-filled box a thinner border, smaller box, etc.*	■ Create a box with the border and the fill you want, regardless of color. ■ Apply a color to it for the fill (14.104). ■ While the box is still selected, press Command C to copy it. ■ Press Option Command V to paste the box directly on top of the first one. ■ While the top box is still selected, from the Element menu choose "Fill" and change the fill to "None." ■ While the box is still selected, change the border color by clicking on the color name from the Color palette.	■ You can get some interesting effects this way, by doing things like resizing the box on top so it is just a touch smaller than the box behind, thereby creating a box that appears to have an outer border and a fill of one color, with an inner border of another color. *This box has a border and* *fill of one color, then a box on top of it with a double-border of another color and a fill of None. The opaque area in the double-border will print as Paper.*
14.106 Change the color of text or graphics	■ To change a color, go through the process of applying a color (14.102; 14.104) again. ■ **Or,** if you change a color in the Color palette (14.92), all text or objects that had been tagged with that color will change.	

If you want to do this:	**Then follow these steps:**	**Shortcuts ▾ Notes ▾ Hints**
14.107 Print spot colors on separate overlays	▪ From the File menu, choose "Print...," *or* press Command P. ▪ Set up this dialog box the way you need. Click on the "Options..." button. ▪ Click in the checkbox "Spot color overlays." ▪ Press on the submenu directly across from the "Spot color overlays" checkbox; choose the color layer you want to print. ▪ Click "Crop marks" (18.82–18.83). ▪ The laser printer or imagesetter will print a separate piece of paper for each color; all items of the same color will print on the same sheet of paper (14.12–14.14; 14.19). If the page size is smaller than the paper size, each piece of paper will have the color name identifying the page so you won't get mixed up. Also, if there is room, PageMaker will provide registration marks to help line up the separate overlays. ▪ Click the OK buttons to start printing.	▪ See Section 18 for in-depth info on all sorts of printing. ▪ You cannot print the color "Paper" as a separate overlay. ▪ On a laser printer that uses 8.5 x 11 paper, you won't see the crop marks (18.82–18.83), the registration marks, or the color overlay identification. These items *will* show up on an imagesetter (usually), because the paper size is larger. ▪ Most commercial printers ignore the registration marks that are provided on any job, so don't worry too much about them. *Talk to your printer* (14.11–14.13).
14.108 Print spot color overlays with knockouts	▪ Print as you normally would print spot color overlays (14.107, above). But put a checkmark in the "Knockouts" checkbox (which is only available if "Spot color overlays" has been checked on). See 14.16–14.30 for details on spot color overlays and knockouts.	▪ If you are going to make a few copies on a copy machine, you might want to try this, although it doesn't work very well because the paper doesn't go through the machines precisely enough. I don't know a commercial press that wouldn't rather create the knockouts in-house. Be sure to read 14.10–14.22.

If you want to do this:

14.109 Prepare a file for four-color separations of process colors
(also see 18.162)

Then follow these steps:

☛If you want to have the full-color publication separated into the four-color process overlays, you must **print the file to disk.** A PostScript printer (18.6) must be selected in "Chooser" (18.13–18.14). See the notes to the right if you don't have a PostScript printer.

■ When you are *completely finished* with the publication, choose "Print..." from the File menu.

■ Set up the "Print to" dialog box as usual. Be sure to enter **1** copy, and enter the exact pages to print, if not "All."

■ Click the button "Options..." and set up the dialog box. Do *not* check "Spot color overlays" or "Proof print." Click OK.

■ Click the button "PostScript...."

■ Check the box "Print PostScript to disk."

■ Click the button "For separations." You don't need to check "Include images," as Aldus PrePrint always reads the links.

■ Click the button "File name...."

■ Notice PageMaker has already named the file with the extension ".sep" *(pronounced dot sep)* after the name, so it will be clear what this file is intended for. If that name is fine, click OK.

■ Click "Print." PageMaker will put a new file icon on your disk when it is finished.

Shortcuts ▾ Notes ▾ Hints

■ You don't need to be *hooked up* to a PostScript printer, or even have one in your office or home; you just need to have a PostScript printer icon sitting in your System folder. As long as the icon is in your System folder, you can select it in Chooser and then print to disk.

■ To print a four-color separation file to disk with the Apple driver, see 18.163 (see 18.20–18.28 for info on the Apple vs. the Aldus driver).

■ You will find detailed information on printing to disk in Section 18 on Printing, 18.134–18.156.

■ When you take the printed-to-disk file to the service bureau, be sure to include all companion files, as PrePrint reads the links (see 10.2–10.22 for info on links; see 18.129 for info on companion files; see 18.122–18.133 for info on how to take the files to your service bureau).

If you want to do this:	Then follow these steps:	Shortcuts ⋅ Notes ⋅ Hints
14.110 Print a color comp on a color printer	▪ If all you want is a full-color comp, you don't need to do anything special, just print as usual. If you are taking the publication to a service bureau for the comp, be sure to tell them you want a **color comp, not color separations!** Never assume they know what you want.	▪ *Never ever forget that a color comp (comprehensive) created on a computer video screen and printed to a color printer is not going to give you an accurate representation of the color of the actual printed piece.* For accurate color, always have a traditional Matchprint or Chromalyn made. See your commercial press for details.
14.111 Change the default color for graphics	▪ If the Color palette is not showing, press Command K (or choose it from the Windows menu). ▪ Click once on the **pointer tool.** ▪ Click once on the color you want as a graphic default. The color you choose is the color in which all PageMaker-drawn objects will automatically draw, all graphics from the Clipboard or the Scrapbook will paste, and all graphic files will place (as long as the graphic was not assigned a color previously, either in PageMaker or in another program).	▪ If you read the section on defaults (1.6–1.16), you know there are two levels of defaults for most items in PageMaker: *application* defaults that apply to the entire program, and *publication* defaults that apply just to the current publication. The color choice default can be applied only to the current publication; you cannot set the application default. That's probably a good, safe thing.

If you want to do this:	Then follow these steps:	Shortcuts ▾ Notes ▾ Hints
14.112 Change the default color for text	<ul><li>If the Color palette is not showing, press Command K.</li><li>If the Style palette is not showing, press Command Y.</li><li>Click once on the **text tool.**</li><li>In the Style palette, click once on the style "No style." (If any other style is selected, you will set a temporary override in that particular paragraph style.)</li><li>Click once on the color you want as a text default. When you type with the style "No style" selected, the text will be that color.</li></ul>	<ul><li>If you find you have inadvertently set a color *override* (7.34–7.41) in a paragraph style, rather than a new text default color, simply click on the text tool and then click in the style name.</li><li>If text is on the page that has a paragraph style applied, but you accidentally changed its color, simply click inside the paragraph with the text tool, then click on the style name in the Style palette. The original color will be returned.</li><li>See 3.242–3.244 re: text defaults in general.</li></ul>
14.113 Create and apply a tint screen (percentage value) *I applied a PMS color to this PageMaker-drawn box. Then I chose a 30% **fill** from the Shades menu. The 30% fill applies only to the inside.* *In the left-hand example, I applied a 25% **tint screen** of Magenta (pretend) to the same box as above; the 30% **fill** is now even lighter. In the right-hand example, the box has a shade (fill) of Solid, so the entire box is really 25% Magenta.*	<ul><li>From the Element menu, choose "Define colors...."</li><li>A tint screen is any *solid* color, screened back; that is, you must first enter zeros in the edit boxes of any other color values (otherwise you are just making up a new color). For instance, if you want a 45% tint of Magenta, click the CMYK button. Enter 0 (zero) in all the boxes, except Magenta, where you enter 45. Click OK.</li><li>Apply the tint just as you would any other color: select the text or the object, and click on the color name in the Color palette.</li></ul>	<ul><li>Talk to your commercial printer before you use tint screens. They may want you to provide the objects as solid black, and they will screen it back—it entirely depends on the project. If you are just printing a one-color job at a quick printer or on a copy machine, go ahead and make all the black-and-white tint screens you like.</li><li>PageMaker tints are all opaque. If you overlap a tint onto a solid object on the screen, you won't see the colors blend. Commercial printers, though, can print the same objects with transparent inks.</li><li>If you make several different tints, even though they are of the same color, *PageMaker will print each tint on a separate color overlay.*</li></ul>

15 ▾ IMPORTING & EXPORTING

The invention of printing

is the greatest event in history.

It is the mother of all revolution,

a renewal

of human means of expression

from its very basis.

Printed thoughts are everlasting,

provided with wings,

intangible and indestructible.

They soar like a crowd of birds,

spread in all four directions

and are everywhere at the same time.

»«

Victor Hugo

15.1 **Importing** in PageMaker is actually the same as *placing*, which is covered in great depth in Section 3 on Text (placing text, 3.27–3.58), Section 8 on Story Editor (importing text files into a story window, 8.34–8.35), and in Section 9 on Graphics (placing varieties of graphic files, 9.92–9.96).

15.2 The command for importing is "Place..." from the File menu. When you place a file, you get a loaded icon; when you click, the text or graphic pours onto the page.

15.3 In the Story Editor (Section 8), the command for importing is "Import..." from the File menu. When you import a text file into the Story Editor, PageMaker puts the text into a story window for editing before you place it on the layout page. You can import *inline* graphics (9.170–9.182) into the Story Editor as well (8.37; 9.194).

15.4 You can also import text or graphics by *pasting* the items from the Clipboard (1.184–1.193) or the Scrapbook (1.200; 1.204).

15.5 PageMaker is able to import and export text files to and from almost any word processing program through the import and export filters you installed when you first installed the program (15.6–15.16). The Story Importer is another important filter which allows you to import stories from other PageMaker 4 publications (15.35).

Import and export filters

15.6 Many software programs have problems importing files from other programs because developers are always changing the darn things. For instance, just after PageMaker 3.0 was released, Microsoft released version 4.0 of Word and version 2.0 of Works. Since PageMaker 3.0 was invented before those new word processing releases, PageMaker couldn't read any of those new files. So they updated PageMaker to 3.01 and 3.02 to fix that (and a couple other minor things).

15.7 PageMaker 4.0 has solved this problem with the **import** and **export filters.** These filters let you import and export files to and from the most popular word processing software packages. If a new or upgraded word processing software program is now released, Aldus will just create a new filter for it, rather than update the PageMaker program itself.

15.8 When you install PageMaker, you are offered a list of import and export filters. The list, to the uninitiated, looks a bit intimidating. You are asked to choose which ones you want to install. If you have disk space and you don't want to waste brain time trying to decipher the list, go ahead and install all of them (390K worth of space) and you will be ready for anything anybody wants you to place into PageMaker. If you need to conserve disk space, then take a close look at the list. You will notice it is nothing more than the names of word processing programs and their version numbers. Just select the filters for the word processing programs you use.

15.9 You can choose to **import** from these Mac programs *(see 15.33 for info on PC import filters)*:
- Acta Advantage 1.0
- MacWrite 1.0 through 5.0; MacWrite II
- Microsoft Word 1.05, 3.0, and 4.0
- Microsoft Works 1.0 and 2.0a
- WordPerfect 1.0 through 1.03
- WriteNow 1.0 and 2.0

Also: RTF (Rich Text Format; 15.10) and Smart ASCII (pronounced *askee;* 15.10) text-only format.

15.10 In addition to the filters for the word processing programs you use, also install these:

- **ASCII export** and **Smart ASCII** import filters. ASCII (pronounced *askee*) is the simplest and most universal file format for text. "Smart" ASCII is an import format used specifically by PageMaker that allows you to retain more of the formatting of imported text than does a regular ASCII filter. These filters allow PageMaker to read almost any text file and to export PageMaker stories in a format that can be read by almost any other program.

  "Text only" = ASCII.

- **RTF** filters. RTF is similar to ASCII, but it holds onto more of the typeset formatting.

- **Story Importer.** Don't forget to install this. It allows you to import any other PageMaker story from any other PageMaker 4 publication. Great tool.

Filters —continued

15.11 When you choose to import or place a file, you don't need to know which filter to use—PageMaker automatically gets the one it needs. If the necessary filter is not installed, you will get this alert box:

15.12 If you get this alert, you will have to install the filter for that document before you can place or import it into PageMaker (15.25). If that is not possible for some reason, you can try opening the file in the program it was created in and save it in a different format, one for which you have a filter.

15.13 There may be some formatting in the imported file that PageMaker cannot deal with, such as hidden text or vertical tab rules. These will be lost in the version you see in PageMaker. However, if you export it back to its word processing program, the formatting will usually be returned to it, *depending* on the program it came from and what the formatting is.

15.14 You can choose to **export** any story in PageMaker. You can export it in any of several different file formats, depending on which program you want to be able to read it. PageMaker provides these export filters:

- MacWrite II
- Microsoft Word 3.0/4.0
- WriteNow
- Rich Text Format (RTF) (PC or Mac)
- ASCII (text-only) format (PC or Mac)
- DCA (Document Content Architecture; for PCs)
- XyWrite III (PC)

15.15 If you are exporting a story to be read by a program other than these listed, then export it as "Text only." That turns the story into an ASCII file that almost anything can read (15.10).

15.16 When you export text, you are actually creating a new file that will have its own icon on your disk. It does not affect or remove the text in your publication, nor does it change any established link (10.2–10.11); it simply makes a copy of the story.

The brain is a wonderful organ; it starts working the moment you get up in the morning and does not stop until you get to the office.
Robert Frost

"Smart ASCII import filter" dialog box *(this dialog box automatically appears when you import or place a text-only file)*

15.17 When you choose to import a text-only file, either onto your publication page or into the Story Editor, PageMaker automatically displays this dialog box, allowing you some control over the formatting. This is especially useful when you're importing a file that has been converted from a PC.

15.18 *A typical ASCII file puts a carriage return at the end of every line, not just at the end of paragraphs. This option gives you a choice of retaining or deleting those returns (usually you do **not** want a return at the end of every line).*

15.19 *If you check "Between paragraphs," this filter will remove all but one carriage return between paragraphs.*

15.20 *If you have checked either of the first two options, this option becomes available. If there are lines of text that begin with spaces or tabs, or if a line contains embedded tabs, PageMaker will not remove the carriage returns from them.*

15.21 *If the person who input the text used spaces instead of tabs, you can turn those spaces into tabs with this option. You can input a value from 3 through 80.*

Some programs, in converting text from one format to another, automatically replace tabs with spaces. This option will turn them back into tabs.

15.22 *This option turns all your text into Courier, a monospaced PostScript font that looks like typewriter text. I don't know why you would want to do that.*

Smart ASCII import filter, v1.2   OK

Remove extra carriage returns: Cancel
  ☐ At end of every line
  ☐ Between paragraphs
  ☐ But keep tables, lists and indents as is

☐ Replace **3** or more spaces with a tab
☐ Monospace, import as Courier
☒ No conversion, import as is

This will cancel the importing procedure.

15.23 *This is the default option. You cannot manually click it off. As soon as any other box is checked, this option automatically becomes unavailable.*

If you want to do this:	Then follow these steps:	Shortcuts ▾ Notes ▾ Hints
15.24 Check to see which import and export filters are installed 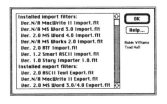	▪ Hold down the Command key. ▪ From the Apple menu, choose "About PageMaker®...." ▪ You will see a list of all the installed import filters, export filters, dictionaries, and a few other odds and ends.	▪ Trivia: If you hold down the Shift key when you choose "About PageMaker®..." you will see the names of the people who developed PageMaker.
15.25 Install a filter that was not originally installed *Filter icon.* MacWrite II Import.flt *Click "Drive" until the name of your hard disk appears here.* 	▪ Insert Disk 1 of the original PageMaker disks. ▪ If the "Utilities" window is open, close it. ▪ Double-click on the "Aldus filters" folder. ▪ There are 25 filters in this folder, all compressed. Find the one you want to install and double-click on it. You will get a dialog box (shown left). ▪ Single-click the "Drive" button (or press the Tab key) until you see the name of your hard disk in the label at the top. ▪ Double-click on the "System Folder" (scroll, if necessary, to find it in the list). ▪ Double-click on the "Aldus" folder. ▪ Double-click on the "Aldus filters" folder. ▪ Click the "Save" button. ▪ When you're done, close the windows and eject the disk (drag it to the trash *or* press Command Option E).	▪ You cannot install a filter by dragging it into the folder. All that will happen is that you will copy the *compressed* file onto your hard disk. You must go through this mini-install process. ▪ Actually, you can install more than one filter at a time. Shift-click or use the marquee (1.168–1.169) to select all the filters you want to install. When you click the "Save" button, PageMaker will install the first one, then bring you back to that dialog box so you can click "Save" again. This will be repeated until all the filters you chose are installed.

If you want to do this:	Then follow these steps:	Shortcuts ▾ Notes ▾ Hints
15.26 Import a word-processed file into the layout view *(the layout view is the normal publication page, as opposed to the story window [view] in the Story Editor)*	▪ "Import" is just another word for "Place." From the File menu, choose "Place...." ▪ In the list box, find the file you want to import into PageMaker. You may need to scroll to find it. Double-click on the file name (*or* single-click and click OK). ▪ You will get a loaded text icon. Click on the publication page to pour the text onto the page.	▪ This is an extraordinarily brief synopsis of the process. It is covered in great depth in Section 3 on Text, 3.27–3.58. You really should read that section, because there is much more involved than just clicking.
15.27 Import a word-processed file into the Story Editor 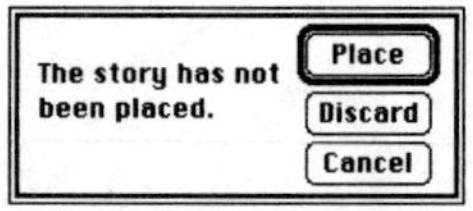	▪ First you must be in the Story Editor (press Command E). It doesn't matter which window appears on your screen. ▪ From the Story menu, choose "Import...." ▪ In the list box, find the file you want to import into PageMaker. You may need to scroll to find it. Double-click on the file name (*or* single-click and click OK). ▪ PageMaker will create a new story window for the file, where you can edit it. When you are ready to put it on the layout page, either choose "Place..." from the File menu, *or* press Command D. You will get a loaded text icon and you can place the text as usual (3.27–3.58). **Or** you can press Command W to close the story window. You will get the alert box shown on the left. Click "Place" or hit Return to get the loaded text icon.	▪ Again, this is an extraordinarily brief synopsis of the process. You really must read Section 8 on the Story Editor, 8.6–8.19.

The story has not been placed. | Place | Discard | Cancel |

If you want to do this:	**Then follow these steps:**	**Shortcuts ▾ Notes ▾ Hints**
15.28 Import a graphic ▨ *This is what an imported graphic looks like in the story view.*	▪ Importing a graphic **in the layout view** is just another term for "placing" the graphic. See Section 9, 9.92–9.96. ▪ Importing a graphic **in the story view** is the same as importing text (15.27). The difference is that in the story view you can only import a graphic as an *inline* graphic (9.170–9.182), not as an *independent* graphic. The inline graphic will appear in the story window as a little box (see left). When you place the story itself on the publication page (15.27; 8.79) you will see the actual graphic.	
15.29 Import a text-only file	▪ From the File menu, choose "Place..."; (if you are in the Story Editor: from the Story menu, choose "Import..."). ▪ Double-click on the file name you want to import/place. ▪ You will get the Smart ASCII import filter dialog box. See 15.17–15.23 for details on the available options. Check the boxes of your choice. Click OK. ▪ Place the file as usual (see 15.26; 15.27).	▪ You don't have to know beforehand whether the file is text-only or not; PageMaker knows. You will know it, too, when you see the Smart ASCII import filter dialog box appear.

If you want to do this:	Then follow these steps:	Shortcuts ▾ Notes ▾ Hints

15.30 Import a Microsoft Word 4.0 file, with control over the Table of Contents entries, index entries, character spacing, and "Page break before" setting

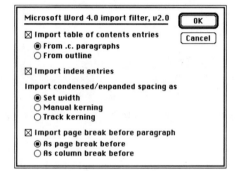

- From the File menu, choose "Place…"; (if you are in the Story Editor: from the Story menu, choose "Import…").
- Locate the file you want to import. Click once on it. Hold the Shift key down while you click OK (or while you double-click the file name). You will get the dialog box shown on the left.
- To import table of contents entries, click the box and specify how you entered them ("From .c. paragraphs" or "From outline").
- Check "Import index entries" if you want.
- If you condensed or expanded any letter spacing in Word, you need to translate it into something PageMaker can format:
  □ "Set width" retains Word's line length, and expands or condenses the *characters* to fit (4.200–4.206).
  □ "Manual kerning" tries to match Word's letter spacing with PageMaker's pair-kerning values (4.176–4.179).
  □ "Track kerning" tries to match Word's letter spacing with one of PageMaker's six tracking values (4.187–4.192).
- PageMaker does not retain Word's automatic or forced page breaks inserted in the text; she will only read "Page break before" specified from Word's "Paragraph"

- How come only Word gets this special, secret little filter?
- The reason you have to convert the letter spacing when you import is because Word measures spacing between letters in *points*, and PageMaker measures it in percentages of the font size.

—*continued*

If you want to do this:	**Then follow these steps:**	**Shortcuts ▾ Notes ▾ Hints**
—continued	dialog box. You can choose to import these page breaks either "As page break before," in which case text will jump to the top of the next available page (3.218), or "As column break before," in which case the text will jump to the top of the next available column (3.217). ■ Click OK, and you can continue to place as usual (15.26; 15.27).	■ Really, paragraphs specified with "As page break before" absolutely *cannot* physically be placed on the same page as the previous text. The text block will "exhibit puzzling behavior," such as roll itself up and refuse to unroll.

15.31 Import a Microsoft Word 4.0 table as a graphic (PICT)

On Government	On Politicians	On Diplomacy
It is dangerous to be right when the government is wrong.	Ninety percent of the politicians give the other ten percent a bad reputation.	Diplomacy is the art of saying "Nice doggie" until you can find a rock
Voltaire	*Henry Kissinger*	*Will Rogers*

A Word table imported as a PICT graphic.

■ In Microsoft Word, after you have created and saved the table, go to the Edit menu and choose "Preferences."
■ Turn off "Show Hidden Text" and "Show Table Gridlines." Click OK.
■ Select the entire table (press-and-drag from one corner to the diagonally-opposite corner). Don't select any lines above or below the table, even if they are blank.
■ Press Command Option D; this puts the table into the Clipboard.
■ Quit Word and open your PageMaker publication.
■ Click once on the pointer tool, then press Command V to paste the table. If the insertion point is flashing, you can paste the table as an inline graphic (9.170–9.182). The table is a PICT graphic (9.14–9.21), so you cannot edit it in PageMaker.

■ This procedure puts the table in the Clipboard, which is only a temporary holding place (1.184–1.190). If you want to copy more than one table from Word to PageMaker, or if you want to store a copy of the table more permanently, paste it into the Scrapbook (1.200).
■ Once the table is in PageMaker it is a graphic, so you can resize or stretch it as any other graphic.
■ If you need to make changes to the table you will have to return to Word, make the changes, then copy the revised version into PageMaker again, replacing the existing one. You cannot link a graphic (10.2–10.11) to something that came in through the Clipboard or the Scrapbook.

If you want to do this:

Then follow these steps:

Shortcuts ▾ Notes ▾ Hints

15.32 Import a Microsoft Word 4.0 table as text (tab-delimited)

Actor	Role	Year
David Garrick	Richard III	1783
Charlotte Cushman	Romeo	1852
Sarah Bernhardt	Hamlet	1899

◄ *The original table in Word.*

◄ *The table, imported into PageMaker.*

◄ *The same table, showing the Tabs and Returns.*

Actor	Role	Year
David Garrick	Richard III	1783
Charlotte Cushman	Romeo	1852
Sarah Bernhardt	Hamlet	1899

▲ *The same table, with the Tabs customized in PageMaker.*

- In Microsoft Word, open the document that contains the table.
- Insert a new line right before the table, and type a capital letter **T** in the line.
- Select the **T.**
- From the Format menu, choose "Character...."
- In the "Style" section of the dialog box, check "Hidden." Click OK.
- Save the document. Quit Word.
- Open the PageMaker publication.
- Place or import the file as usual (15.26; 15.27).
- The placed file will not look like the original table (see left).
  - □ Borders are eliminated
  - □ The type style in the first cell in each row is applied to the entire row.
  - □ The left edge of each column comes in as a left-aligned tab (including the first column), and other text in the cell is aligned to that tab.
  - □ The rows are separated by paragraph Returns.

- Obviously, the text from this kind of importing needs some editing.

If you want to do this:

15.33 Import a text files from a PC
(except from Microsoft Word; see 15.34)

Available filters:

■ **DCA** (for programs that create
Document Content Architecture, such
as Samna Word, IBM DisplayWrite 4,
WordStar 3000, Volkswriter 3)
extension: .DCA

■ **WordPerfect** 4.2
extension: .WP

WordPerfect 5.0 (and 5.01)
extension: .WP5

■ **XyWrite III (Plus)**
extension: .XY3

■ **RTF** (for programs that save files in
Microsoft Rich Text Format)
extension: .RTF

■ **Smart ASCII** (for programs that
save files in ASCII format from
PC AT-compatible computers)
extension: .TXT

Then follow these steps:

■ Make sure you have installed the filter
for the program from which you want
to import (see list at left).
■ The file you want to import must have
the correct filename extension (see list).
■ Use a communications bridge (such
as TOPS, Daynafile, PC MacBridge, or
MacLink) to transfer the document as
a binary file. *If* your PC can write to a 3.5"
floppy disk, and *if* your Mac has a Super
drive (FDHD), transfer the file with the
Apple File Exchange utility and translate
it into a Macintosh-readable format.
■ Once you have done all that, import the
file as you would any other (15.26; 15.27).

Shortcuts ▾ Notes ▾ Hints

■ The PC character sets are different than
the Mac characters sets, so some of the
special characters you inserted in the PC
file may not duplicate properly. If you
don't change them, they will be retained
if you transfer the file back to the PC.

If you want to do this:	**Then follow these steps:**	**Shortcuts ▾ Notes ▾ Hints**
15.34 Import a Microsoft Word text file from a PC *Import from:* MS-DOS: Microsoft Word 3.0, 4.0, 5.0 OS/2: Microsoft Word 5.0	■ **If** you have saved the Word file as ASCII (text-only), or as ASCII with line breaks (both with the extension .TXT), or as RTF (.RTF): □ Transfer the file to your Macintosh. □ Import as usual (15.26; 15.27). ■ **If** you have saved the DOS or OS/2 Word file in Normal format: □ Transfer the file to your Macintosh. □ Open the file in Word 3.0 or 4.0 for the Mac. Save it. Quit. □ Import as usual (15.26; 15.27).	■ When you save DOS or OS/2 Word files as RTF or Normal, they retain almost all their formatting when you import them into PageMaker.
15.35 Import stories from another PageMaker 4 publication	■ You must have the Story Importer filter installed to do this (see 15.24 to check). ■ From the File menu, choose "Place..."; **or,** if you are in the Story Editor, from the Story menu choose "Import...." ■ Find the name of the PageMaker publication and double-click on it. ■ From this list, select the stories you want to place/import. You can Shift-click to select more than one, or Shift-and-drag. ■ Click OK. You will get a loaded text icon if you are in the layout view, **or** the stories will put themselves into a new story window if you are in the Story Editor. All the stories will be combined into one story, with paragraph returns between them.	■ This is a brief synopsis of the procedure. You will find great detail in 3.59–3.80. ■ The Story Importer can only import other PageMaker stories that are in version 4.0 or above (4.01, etc.). If you want to import a 3.0 story, you must first convert it to a 4.0 publication (15.38).

If you want to do this:

15.36 Export a PageMaker story
as a text document

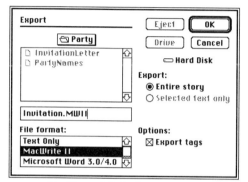

*The "Export" dialog box. Notice the name of
the file has an extension so I can remember
which file format I saved it under.*

Then follow these steps:

- You can export a story in any file format
  for which you have a filter (15.6–15.16).
- Click once on the **text tool.**
  - □ To export the entire story, click once
    anywhere in any text block of the story.
  - □ To export a selected portion of the
    story, select the portion.
- From the File menu, choose "Export...."
- Name the file. You may want to add an
  extension to the name so you know which
  file format it is saved under.
- In the "File format" list, select the format
  in which you want to export this file.
- Under "Export," choose the appropriate
  option ("Selected text only" is available
  only if you selected a portion of text
  before you brought up this dialog box).
- If you have applied paragraph style tags
  from your style sheet, you may want to
  click the checkbox "Export tags." If the
  program you are exporting to supports
  style sheets, it will be able to read *most*
  of the formatting. Also, if you export the
  tags, PageMaker will be able to read them
  and re-apply the style formatting if the file
  is imported back into PageMaker.
- Make sure you are about to save into the
  proper folder so you will be able to find
  this file again (16.6–16.13); then click OK.

Shortcuts ▾ Notes ▾ Hints

- I am sad to report that when a file is
  exported to MacWrite II (my favorite
  word processor), all the em and en
  dashes (3.240) are turned into hyphens.
  (I wonder if someone did that on purpose
  to coerce us into using Word.)
- If you export tags and the word processor
  cannot translate them, they will appear
  as text: `<Body text>`. If you place this
  file back into PageMaker, PageMaker will
  read those tags, eliminate them, and apply
  the style to the paragraph (see 7.64–7.65).

- Basically, PageMaker and the exporting
  program can read each other's common
  formatting. That is, PageMaker cannot
  import formatting she cannot do, such
  as vertical-line tabs or hidden text. The
  word processing program probably can't
  read the set widths or tracking values.

If you want to do this:	Then follow these steps:	Shortcuts ▾ Notes ▾ Hints
15.37 Export graphics	• You can only export inline graphics that are in the PICT format, and you can only export them to a program that can deal with inline graphics. • Place the graphic inline (9.191), even if it is the only item in the text block (to make it the only inline graphic in the text block, click the insertion point outside of any existing text block before you place or paste). • Export the graphic as if it were text (15.36). *But don't export it as "Text only."* Save the file in a Word or an RTF file format.	• Even though MacWrite II can accept graphics, the MacWrite filter won't catch them. MacWrite can open Word or RTF files, though, so you can save the file as Word or RTF, and then open it in MacWrite II.

If you want to do this:

Then follow these steps:

Shortcuts ▾ Notes ▾ Hints

Converting 3.0 Mac or PC to 4.0 Mac

15.38 Convert a Macintosh PageMaker 3.0, 3.01, 3.02, or 3.02CE publication (all hereinafter referred to as 3.x) into a PageMaker 4.0 (or 4.01) publication

- Open PageMaker 4 (the application itself).
- From the File menu, choose "Open...."
- Find the name of the 3.x publication. Double-click on it. It will open as an "Untitled" publication.
- From the File menu, choose "Save as...." Give the file a name.
  - ▢ If you name this file with exactly the same name as the 3.x publication and then click OK, you will get an alert box asking if you want to replace the other file of the same name. If you click "Yes," then the 3.x version of the publication will be eliminated.
  - ▢ If you name this file with a different name than the 3.x version (or save into a different folder), then you will have two copies, one in 4.0 and one still in 3.x.
- Click OK.
- You may want to recompose the text: Hold down the Option key; choose "Hyphenation..." from the Type menu. When you get the "Hyphenation" dialog box, click Cancel. *Save again.* This process adjusts any odd letter or word spacing that may have occurred in the conversion.

- PageMaker 4.0 calculates inter-character spacing and line spacing more accurately than 3.x, so you may find that your text blocks are shorter, and that your line breaks are not exactly as they were in the 3.x version of the publication.
- Usually, the 4.0 version will be smaller, especially if you never compressed the 3.x version (16.25).
- Publication defaults (1.9–1.11) are retained in the conversion, except the type specification defaults (3.242–3.247). Nothing already on the page will change, but any new text you type or paste or place will pick up the new defaults.
- If there are any text-wrapped objects on the master page, PageMaker 4 will wrap the text on the layout pages also. It won't wrap, though, until you edit or move the converted text.

  A text wrap on every page can seriously slow down page turning.

573

If you want to do this:

15.39 Transfer a PC PageMaker publication to Mac PageMaker 4.0

Then follow these steps:

- If the publication is PC PageMaker **3.0**, in either Windows or OS/2, you must first convert it to a PC PageMaker **4.0** publication (follow the Mac steps; 15.38).
- You will get the best type specification results if you set a PostScript printer as the target printer for both the PC and the Mac.
- Use a communications bridge (such as TOPS, Daynafile, PC MacBridge, or MacLink) to transfer the publication as a binary file. *If* your PC can write to a 3.5" floppy disk, and *if* your Mac has a Super drive (FDHD), transfer the file with the Apple File Exchange utility and translate it into a Macintosh-readable format.
- Then you can open the publication in Macintosh PageMaker as usual.
- Linked graphic or text files are not automatically converted; you must transfer them separately and re-link them (10.1–10.11).
- Draw-type (object-oriented) graphics are not transferred; they will appear in the Mac version as an X inside a box. Transfer the graphics to PICT format separately, and then replace them in the publication.
- Low-res screen versions of scanned graphics and graphics that have their complete copy stored in the publication (including EPS) will be transferred.

Shortcuts ▾ Notes ▾ Hints

- Once it has been transferred, you can open a PC PageMaker publication with the same version of Macintosh PageMaker.
- The PC character sets (ANSI) are different than the Mac characters sets, so some of the special characters you inserted in the PC file may not duplicate properly. PageMaker version 4.01 can re-create more of the special characters than can version 4.0.

  If you don't change those special characters, they will be retained if you transfer the file back to the PC.
- If the targeted printers for the PC publication and Mac PageMaker (you can set a printer default; 1.13) are not the same, or if they use different font names, then the PC type specifications will not be transferred. Mac PageMaker will use her own default specs. Supposedly the original specs are saved and will be returned to the publication if it is transferred back to the PC.

16 ▾ SAVE and REVERT

Read this, even if you think you know everything about Saving on the Macintosh!

16.1　Saving, of course, is the process of taking the pages of your publication out of their temporary holding place in RAM and storing them more permanently on the disk (hard or floppy). It is good practice to "Save as…" your publication to a disk immediately upon beginning, then Save the changes every few minutes—*literally, every few minutes*—to avoid losing any data in the event of a catastrophe of any considerable dimension.

Unlike most software applications, Page-Maker has this wonderful system built into itself that is very forgiving and advantageous in the event of a catastrophe. You see, Page-Maker actually saves *two* versions of each publication. One version is the regular one you create when you "Save as…," the version that is stored on your disk and updated each time you press Command S or choose "Save" from the File menu. It is this version that PageMaker will return to when you choose "Revert" from the File menu (16.26).

16.2　But PageMaker also creates a "mini-save" file. Every time you turn a page, insert a page, delete a page, change the page setup, click the icon of the page you are currently on, copy, or print, PageMaker updates the mini-save. It is this version that PageMaker will return to *when recovering from a power loss or malfunction!* Even if you never saved your document in the first place, even if it is still Untitled when the power goes out, you can usually retrieve it (16.29). You can also choose to Revert to this mini-version at any time (16.27).

16.3　Each version is a complete publication, which is one reason PageMaker files are so large. Even if you delete text, graphics, or pages, the files grow larger! But, thoughtfully, along with this problem of large files, there is a solution. Every time you use "Save as…," the current *mini-version* is deleted (16.25). **This significantly reduces the size of the publication—anywhere from 20 to 60 percent!** It's too wonderful.

16.4　The mini-version instantly creates itself again, as soon as you touch the page. **To keep the file small, to prevent Mac from crashing, and to prevent the file from getting so large that PageMaker can't even open it (which I have seen happen to two-page files), "Save as…" every half hour or so (16.25). Really.**

16.5　PageMaker version 4.01 has a new option in the "Preferences" dialog box:

Save option: ◉ Faster ◯ Smaller

If you click the **Faster** button, everything will function just as it always has. You will grow mini-versions and you can mini-revert back to them. When you press Command S, PageMaker will save the latest changes.

If you click the **Smaller** button, Page-Maker will automatically compress the file (by deleting the mini-version) every time you do a regular Save (from the File menu, *or* by pressing Command S). This takes longer than the regular, faster save.

The "Save as..." dialog box   *(from the File menu)*

16.6   *Always look here! This* **label** *tells you exactly which folder you will be saving into. Notice the open folder icon? If you were not in a folder, this icon would be a disk.*

16.7   *If there is a folder icon showing in this* **label,** *pressing on the name will drop down a* **menu** *with a* **list** *of all the folders and the name of the disk they are on (the "hierarchy," as shown to the right). Slide down the menu to go into another folder or back to the face of the disk itself (16.13).*

Save publication as

| Comedies |
| Shakespeare |
| WorkHard |
| Erro |
| Mer |
| Tempest |

The menu, as mentioned in 16.7

16.8   *This is the* **list box,** *showing you the folders and documents that are in the folder or on the disk that is named in the* **label** *(16.6; 16.7).*

16.9   *Folders are black in the list box showing that you can open them if you want to save something inside. Double-clicking on any folder opens it and allows you to save into it.*

Save publication as

📂 Shakespeare

▢ Comedies
▢ Histories
▢ Tragedies
▢ MerryWives

Tempest

Eject   **OK**

Drive   Cancel

▭ WorkHard

Save as:
● Publication
○ Template

☐ Copy linked documents

The Return or Enter key will shortcut OK; Command Period will shortcut Cancel.

16.13   *This shows the name of the disk you are working from.*

16.14   *Choose to save your work as a publication or as a template (see Section 12 regarding templates). If you don't know what a template it, save it as a publication and read Section 12.*

16.15   *If you have either text or graphic documents that are linked (Section 10) to this publication, you can choose to copy them into the same folder this file is being saved into (16.30; 16.31).*

16.10   *To* **save** *a document for the first time, type a name here in the* **name box,** *then click OK (16.18).*

16.11   *If you want to* **replace** *a document (16.19), or compress the file (16.25), click OK without changing the name. (*__Note:__ *this will only replace or compress the file of the same name* **if** *you can see that name in the list box!)*

16.12   *If you want to make a* **copy** *of a document, type a new name; click OK (16.24).*

16.16   *Click* **Drive** *to switch to a disk in another drive. If there is more than one drive, click here to cycle through them all. Shortcut: press Tab.*

16.17   *Click* **Eject** *to eject the floppy disk which is currently visible (16.13). This will allow you to insert a different disk on which to store your publication.*

If you want to do this:	**Then follow these steps:**	**Shortcuts ▾ Notes ▾ Hints**
16.18 Save a **publication** Publication Icon	▪ From the File menu choose "Save as...." ▪ You *must* name the publication; just type a descriptive name (no colons allowed). ▪ Check to make sure the button next to "Publication" is checked. ▪ Click OK, or press Return; your publication will now show its name in the title bar, and an icon will be on your disk when you quit. ▪ Be sure to update changes every few minutes (press Command S) and compress the file regularly (16.25).	▪ Be sure you are saving your document onto the right disk and into the right folder! If you don't get into that habit, documents end up all over the place and some may never be found again. If it's not clear to you how to save something into the folder you want, studying the previous page may help. ▪ If you haven't named the file, choosing "Save" *or* pressing Command S will give you the same dialog box as "Save as...."
16.19 Save changes to the **publication** *(if you have PageMaker version 4.01, also see 16.5)*	▪ From the File menu choose "Save," *or* press Command S. ▪ Once you've named your publication, you do not need to go back to "Save as..." again, unless you want to make other versions based on this publication (16.24) or unless you want to compress the file (16.25).	▪ You won't see much happen: the File menu will flash, and you may see the watch cursor. But any changes you created since the last save have been saved onto the original version. *Yes, this does replace the original.* If you want to make copies *without* affecting an original, see 16.23–16.24.
16.20 Save a **template** Template Icon	▪ From the File menu choose "Save as...." ▪ You *must* name the template; just type a descriptive name (no colons allowed). ▪ Click the button next to "Template." ▪ Click OK; your template will now have its name showing in the title bar, and a white icon will be on your disk when you quit.	▪ Read all about templates in Section 12. ▪ If you ever want to open the original template again, you must go through the "Open..." dialog box inside PageMaker (16.22).

If you want to do this:	Then follow these steps:	Shortcuts ▾ Notes ▾ Hints
16.21 Save changes to the **template** *before* it has ever been closed	■ Once the template has been given a name, you do not need to go back to "Save as..." again, unless you want to make other versions based on this template (16.12) or unless you want to compress the file (16.25). ■ From the File menu choose "Save" *or* press Command S.	■ You won't see much happen: the File menu will flash, and you may see the watch cursor. But any changes you've created since the last save have been saved onto the original template. *Yes, this does replace the original.* If you want to make copies *without* affecting an original, see 16.23–16.24.
16.22 Open the original **template** again in order to create and save changes	You must open the *original* template in order to make changes in it. Once the template has been closed there is only one way to open the original again: ■ Open PageMaker. ■ From the File menu choose "Open...." ■ Find the name of the template to open; click **once** on its name. ■ "Copy" is already selected—click on "Original"; click OK.	■ The trick here is not to shortcut by double-clicking. Double-clicking on the template icon at the Desktop (Finder) will open a *copy*. Double-clicking in the "Open..." dialog box will open a *copy*. You must use this OK method from inside PageMaker. (**Note:** if you double-click on the icon while in MultiFinder, PageMaker *will* open the *original*.) ■ Be sure to read Section 12 on Templates.
16.23 Save a copy of the **publication** or **template,** *with the same name,* into a different folder or onto a different disk	■ From the File menu choose "Save as...." ■ The current name of the publication is highlighted in the name box. Navigate to the other disk and/or folder. Click Drive to find the other disks, and double-click on folders, if necessary, to open them. ■ When you see the name of the disk you want (16.13) and the name of your folder in the label (16.6; 16.7), click OK.	■ This process leaves the original publication intact, with its icon right where you left it last time you saved. ■ After you click OK you will see the new name in the title bar—this is now a *different* publication with its own icon! ■ Any changes you make in this publication will have absolutely no effect on the one you started with.

If you want to do this:

Then follow these steps:

Shortcuts ▾ Notes ▾ Hints

16.24 Save a copy (a separate version) of the **publication** or **template,** *with a different name,* into any folder or onto any disk

- From the File menu choose "Save as...."
- The current name of the publication is highlighted. To prevent your new copy from replacing that original file, you must rename it. Typing any character after the current name, such as a period or a number *or even a blank space,* will effectively change the name.

- This process leaves the original publication intact, with its icon right where you left it last time you saved.
- After you click OK you will see the new name in the title bar—this is now a *different* publication with its own icon!
- Any changes you make in this publication will have absolutely no effect on the version you started with.

16.25 Reduce the size of a PageMaker publication *(if you have PageMaker version 4.01, also see 16.5)*

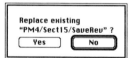

- While the publication is open on the screen, from the File menu choose "Save as...."
- Make sure you see the name of the current document in the list box! (It will be gray. If you don't see the name, change disks or folders until you see it listed.)
- The name of the current document should be in the name box. If for some reason it isn't (like you accidentally hit the spacebar), type the *exact* name again.
- Click OK; you will get an alert box asking if you want to *replace* the item with the same name; **click YES.**
- If you did not get the alert box, then you created a separate (and reduced) version because there was no file of that same name in the list box. When you get back to your Desktop, you can replace the larger publication with the smaller one.

- If you don't remember where the original is stored, use Find File (1.233).
- If the disk is already very full, PageMaker cannot "Save as...," even though doing so would reduce the file size (she has to have room to create another one, then replace the first one). Switch drives and save to another disk; back at your Desktop later, replace the large one with the smaller version. It's a good idea to label the reduced version (by renaming the second, saved-as one) so you don't get the two files mixed up.
- If the two files have the same name and you don't remember which is the larger, Get Info will give you the file size: at the Desktop, click once on the file icon; from the File menu, choose "Get Info." Or change the window views to "By size."

579

If you want to do this:	**Then follow these steps:**	**Shortcuts ▾ Notes ▾ Hints**

16.26 Revert to the last saved version

- From the File menu choose "Revert." You will get an alert box to verify your decision ("Revert" will be gray if you have just saved).
- Click OK.

- This reverts to the last time you saved the publication, either with "Save" or with "Save as…." Any changes made since that point will not be recorded: another good reason to save often.
- It is not possible to revert just a portion of the publication—it's all or nothing.
- This cannot be undone!

16.27 Revert to the last mini-save version

- Hold down the Shift key (you *must* press the Shift key *before* you go up to the File menu).
- From the File menu choose "Revert" while the Shift key is still held down. You will get an alert box to verify your decision.
  □ If the message doesn't say "mini-save" then you probably weren't holding down the Shift key before you went to the menu. Cancel and try again.
  □ It the message still doesn't say "mini-save" then perhaps you have not done anything to update the mini-version, such as turn a page, delete a page, copy, etc.; see the note on the right.
- In the alert box, click OK.

- This will revert to the last time you clicked on a page icon, turned a page, inserted or deleted a page, changed the page setup, copied, or printed.
- This is great, for several reasons. One is that if there was a power failure or system crash and you haven't saved for a while, you could bring back your document to the mini-save point (16.29). Another is that sometimes you want to revert, but not all the way back to the last time you saved. You could take advantage of the mini-save consciously, to develop various layout ideas along the way until you're ready for the Big One.

If you want to do this:	**Then follow these steps:**	**Shortcuts ▾ Notes ▾ Hints**
16.28 Close the publication or quit PageMaker *without* saving changes 	▪ To **Close,** simply click in the close box in the upper left of the publication window, *or* choose "Close" from the File menu. ▪ To **Quit,** from the File menu choose "Quit," *or* press Command Q. ▪ Either way, if you did not save your latest changes (even if you just clicked on another page icon or changed views) PageMaker will thoughfully remind you that you haven't saved those changes and ask if you would like to. ▪ Just click your choice. "Cancel" will take you back to your publication.	▪ Remember, Close just closes the current open publication, leaving you in Page-Maker. You will see the PageMaker menu. She is waiting for you to create a "New..." publication or to "Open..." an existing one. ▪ Quit will close the file, plus take you back to your Desktop (Finder).
16.29 Open a publication that was closed due to a power failure or system malfunction *(this will not work on a damaged disk)*	**If you did not have a chance to save the publication before the failure:** ▪ Restart the computer. ▪ In the System Folder you will see two files: one named PMF000; one named PMF001. ▪ Double-click on PMF001; this will start PageMaker and place the publication on the screen in the last *mini-saved* version. **If you did save the publication before the failure:** ▪ In the folder you were working from you will find your document. Double-click; it will open to the last *mini-saved* version. ▪ Save it immediately. In fact, do a "Save as..." just to be safe.	▪ Wow—can you believe this? Even if the document was Untitled because you never even got to "Save as...," you can salvage up until you last clicked a page icon, deleted or added pages, changed the page setup, printed, or copied. What a thoughtful feature. ▪ Of course, you can also start PageMaker and then open the PMF001 file from the File menu (find it in the System Folder). ▪ After you've re-opened it, you can also choose to "Revert" to the last real save.

If you want to do this:	Then follow these steps:	Shortcuts ▾ Notes ▾ Hints
16.30 Copy linked documents when saving a PageMaker file 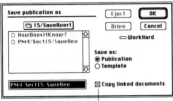 *Click in this checkbox*	■ From the File menu, choose "Save as...." ■ If there are stories or graphics in the publication that are linked to the original stories or graphics outside of PageMaker (see Section 10 on Linking Text and Graphics), then the checkbox "Copy linked documents" will be available. Click once in it. ■ Name the file, if necessary. Click OK.	■ If you choose to copy linked files, then PageMaker will find all the originals to all the linked text and graphics in your publication and put copies of them into the folder that is storing this PageMaker publication. The links will still be connected to the original linked file, not to the one you copied into this folder. ■ This is a handy technique for gathering up all the files in one place, as you may need to do to take the publication to a service bureau (18.122–18.133) or to give to a client.
16.31 Copy linked documents for remote printing when saving a PageMaker file 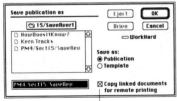 *Press the Option key and click in this checkbox*	■ From the File menu, choose "Save as...." ■ If there are stories or graphics in the publication that are linked to the original stories or graphics outside of PageMaker (see Section 10 on Linking Text and Graphics), then the checkbox "Copy linked documents" will be available (16.30). Make sure there is *no* checkmark in it; if there is, click again to remove it. ■ Hold down the Option key and the button will change to "Copy linked documents for remote printing." *Now* click once in the checkbox. ■ Name the PageMaker file, if necessary. ■ Click OK.	■ PageMaker must have access to any file (such as a graphic file) that is not stored in the publication; otherwise PageMaker cannot print it properly. When you hold the Option key down and check this box, PageMaker will copy into the same folder *only* those linked files that are *not* stored in the publication (10.15–10.22), including a file called "Kern Tracks" which some service bureaus may need. See 18.122–18.133 for details on using a service bureau.

Containing a Discourse on this separate
Contraption, which may afford a useful lesson
to all Users who happen to desire
clear and complete Documentation.

17 ▼ TABLE EDITOR

17.1 Minimums and maximums:

Item	Minimum	Maximum
Table size	8 pts. x 8 pts.	22.75" x 22.75"
No. of columns	1	80
No. of rows	1	80
Width of col.	8 pts.	22.75" *
Height of row	6 pts.	22.75" *
Gutter	0	5" *
Type size	4 (1-pt. increments)	127
Leading	4 (1-pt. increments)	127
Auto leading	100% (1-pt. increments)	200%

* Depends on the size of the table and the size
and number of the rows and columns.

17.2 PageMaker's Table Editor is a great little program. Use it to create lists, charts, schedules, statistical tables, graphic aids, worksheets, and forms of all sorts. It's a bit primitive yet and still a little buggy, but you can't let the seeds stop you from enjoying the watermelon. Learn to use it now, and then you can slip right into the upgrades as it gets better and better.

17.3 The **Table Editor** is a separate program from PageMaker. When you installed PageMaker onto your hard disk, the Table Editor was automatically installed into the same folder as the application. This is its icon:

Table Editor 1.0

If the Table Editor application is not there, you can copy it directly onto your disk from the original PageMaker disk. The Table Editor does not need to be in any special folder.

17.4 Once you have a table completed, you can export it as a PICT graphic or as a text-only file to *place* into a PageMaker publication (17.121–17.125); *a table cannot be printed from the Table Editor.*

17.5 Several functions in the Table Editor work a bit differently than the way you're accustomed to them working in PageMaker. I would suggest reading through the general info in the next several pages to get an idea of how things operate. Then dive right in and start creating. Scenario #13 on page 614 takes you through the process of building a small table in about ten minutes.

PageMaker's
Table Editor Contents

17.6
*A simple table
created in the
Table Editor.*

Advantages and Limitations

17.7   This is one of several examples of tables in this section. This one is fairly simple. The type is slightly condensed because I resized the table a bit after I brought it into PageMaker.

Advantages

Cells are easy to manipulate; you can make them wider or deeper, grouped or ungrouped, shaded or unshaded, bordered or unbordered.

If you are familiar with entering data in cells and working with rows and borders as in a spreadsheet, many of the Table Editor's functions will feel very comfortable to you.

You can move information in the cells from one place to another easily.

You can format each cell with a different font, style, size, leading, or alignment (both horizontally and vertically).

You can use arrow keys in the text. You can use the Shift-Return to break lines of text.

You can choose the pointer tool by pressing Command Spacebar.

You can manipulate and reformat borders (rules) easily. When you cut or copy a cell, you can choose whether or not to cut/copy its formatting, including rules, or to cut/copy just the text.

When you choose to clear the info from a cell, you have a choice of clearing just the text, just the rules, just the shades, or everything.

After you place the table in PageMaker, you can resize it just like a graphic.

Limitations

You cannot print from the Table Editor—the table must be exported and then placed into a PageMaker publication.

You can import the table as text, and then you can edit it in PageMaker, but you lose all the formatting (and the formatting is generally why you did it in the Table Editor). You can import the table as a PICT graphic, but then you cannot edit it in PageMaker (you can link the graphic to the original and update any changes, though).

Within a cell you can have only one font, style, size, leading, and alignment. You cannot kern nor use text spacing.

You cannot create more than one page at a time, nor can you create an actual template.

There seem to be a few bugs in the program yet. Just little annoying things.

About the Table Editor

17.8   In the Table Editor you create rows and columns that in turn create cells in which you input your text. Each cell can have its own variation of text formatting and borders. You can enlarge or reduce the rows and columns, rearrange cell text, and adjust formatting to your heart's content.

17.9   When you save a table you have created in the Table Editor, it is saved as a separate document, not as a PageMaker document. This is a table document icon:

Merry Wives

17.10   You cannot print from the Table Editor; the table must first be placed into a PageMaker publication, and then printed from there (17.125). In order to place the table into PageMaker, you must first export it, either as a text-only file or as a graphic (PICT) file (17.121–17.122). These are the corresponding icons:

MerryWives/Text   MerryWives/PICT

17.11   A **text-only table** will place into PageMaker literally as text only—formatting, shades, or borders will not appear.

A **PICT table** will place as a graphic and will retain all of its lines, shades, and text formatting. But it is not editable. See 17.89–17.90 for examples.

17.12   As you place the table into Page-Maker, a *link* is established (Section 10). If you make any changes to the original text or PICT file, the changes can be automatically updated to the table in the PageMaker publication (17.128). It's a good thing you can update the changes, because of course you never see the typos or the mismatched lines until it's printed.

17.13   You can import text into a table in the Table Editor (17.118–17.119) that has been created in other programs that have data separated by tabs (tab-delimited) or data separated by commas (comma-delimited). The Table Editor even gives you the option of flowing text vertically or horizontally, which enables you to turn column headings into row headings (17.120).

17.14 A quick overview on creating a new table:

- Open Table Editor from the Finder (double-click on its icon).
- From the File menu, choose "New...."
- In the "Table setup" dialog box (17.15–17.18), specify the number of rows and columns you want, the size of your table, and the width of the gutter. You can change any of these specifications at any time.
- Type your text into the cells (17.29–17.32; 17.105), grouping them as necessary (17.36–17.37; 17.103). Format the text (17.68–17.78).
- Resize your columns and rows to fit your developing table (17.97–17.102).
- Add or delete rows and columns as necessary (17.93–17.96).
- Add borders and shades to contribute to the organization and impact of the table (17.38–17.45; 17.108–17.110).
- You have, of course, already saved this table. Now export it (17.121–17.122) in order to place it into a PageMaker publication.
- In PageMaker, place the PICT as you would any other graphic (9.92).

The "Table setup" dialog box   *(when creating a "New" table, **or** from the File menu while working on an existing table)*

```
┌─────────────────────────────────────────────┐
│  Table setup _____     ┌─────────┐ │
│                                  │   OK    │ │
│  Number of columns:  [3    ]     └─────────┘ │
│                                  ┌─────────┐ │
│  Number of rows:     [3   ]      │ Cancel  │ │
│                                  └─────────┘ │
│                                              │
│  Table size: [6    ]  by [3    ]  inches     │
│                                              │
│  Gutter in inches:     Column: [0.1  ]       │
│                                              │
│                        Row:    [0.1  ]       │
│                                              │
└─────────────────────────────────────────────┘
```

17.15 *Enter the number of columns and rows you think you will need in the table, from 1 to 80. You can always add more or delete some later. Initially, the width of the columns will be determined by the space available. Every column will be the same width and every row will be the same height, dividing up the space with the gutters. You can customize columns and rows directly on the table.*

> ✋ **Cannot set up Table with these measurements and dimensions.**   [OK]

17.16 *Enter the amount of space you want between the columns and between the rows. You can override the measuring system (e.g., substitute picas for inches; see 1.221).*

You can enter any value from 0 (zero) to the maximum amount of space available for the number of rows and columns you request. If the space you request is too much, the Table Editor will let you know with a dialog box (see left), and the offending value will be highlighted in the dialog box.

*Gutter space is **cumulative.** That is, if you ask for a half-inch gutter between the rows, **each** row will have a half-inch space above **and** below it. Thus the rows of text cells will actually have **one inch** of space between them.*

17.17 *Enter values to set up the initial table size, **width by height,** up to 22.75 x 22.75 inches. While you are creating the table on the screen, though, you can make the table larger and smaller as suits the project.*

17.18 *If you need a specific table size to fit into a PageMaker publication, do this: in the publication, draw a rectangle the size of the space you want the table to fill. Cut it to the Clipboard. Quit PageMaker and open the Table Editor. Choose to create a new table; the dimensions in the "Table size" edit boxes will be the dimensions of the rectangle that is in the Clipboard. See 17.129.*

The initial table setup

17.19 To the right is a reduced version of what a table initially looks like. This one is based on the specs you see in the table setup on the previous page, these specs being the default settings.

17.20 The table is built on a page, similar to any page in a PageMaker publication, with rulers, scroll bars, and a mini-toolbox (17.28). The toolbox has a pointer and a text tool that function just as you are accustomed to: the pointer selects items and the text tool creates text. The scroll bars are only available if the table is larger than what will fit on the screen. It is a little irritating, when you're working at the bottom of the screen, not to be able to scroll the cells into the middle of the screen.

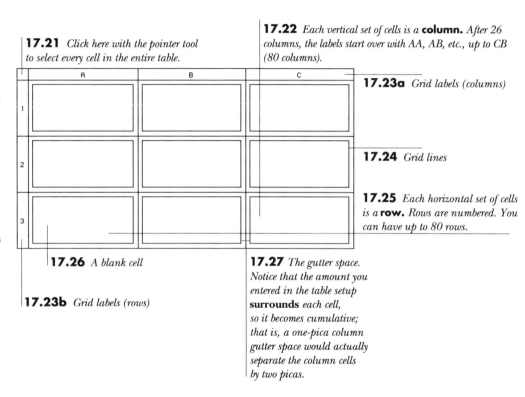

17.21 *Click here with the pointer tool to select every cell in the entire table.*

17.22 *Each vertical set of cells is a* **column.** *After 26 columns, the labels start over with AA, AB, etc., up to CB (80 columns).*

17.23a *Grid labels (columns)*

17.24 *Grid lines*

17.25 *Each horizontal set of cells is a* **row.** *Rows are numbered. You can have up to 80 rows.*

17.26 *A blank cell*

17.23b *Grid labels (rows)*

17.27 *The gutter space. Notice that the amount you entered in the table setup* **surrounds** *each cell, so it becomes cumulative; that is, a one-pica column gutter space would actually separate the column cells by two picas.*

17.28 *The Toolbox. The pointer and the text tool work just like their counterparts in PageMaker.*

Typing in the table cells

17.29 Typing in a table is very much like typing in PageMaker or any word processor: choose the text tool and click in the cell in which you want to type. The arrow keys on your keyboard will also work as usual within the cell.

17.30 There are some limitations to text, however. You cannot set tabs within a cell. You cannot kern, track, or use super- or subscripts. You can't even set type as small caps. You cannot insert em, en, or thin spaces, although you can use the hard space (Option Spacebar).

17.31 Each cell can have its own formatting, including its own horizontal and vertical alignment (17.76–17.78), font, style or combination of styles, size, and leading (17.73–17.75), *but* the formatting is all or nothing. That is, you cannot set *just one word* in the paragraph bold or italic. You'll have to set *the entire paragraph* bold or italic (or both).

17.32 As you type in a cell, the width is stable. Text will bump into the right edge and word wrap to the next line, just as in a text block. And also just as in a text block, the cell will expand downwards (expanding with it all the cells in that row).

17.33 If you press the Tab key, the insertion point bounces into the next cell to the right, just as in most spreadsheets or databases. If the insertion point is already in the last cell, it bounces into the first cell in the next row. Press Shift Tab to send the insertion point backwards; that is, into the cell to the left.

17.34 If you press the Return key, the insertion point bounces into the cell directly below. If the insertion point is at the bottom of a column, pressing the Return key will bounce it into the cell at the top of the next column. This means, of course, that you cannot press the Return key to break a line within a cell.

17.35 To create a line break within a cell, press Shift-Return.

Grouping cells

17.36 No matter how many rows and columns are in the basic table, you can choose any number of adjacent cells and group them together into one cell (17.103), as shown:

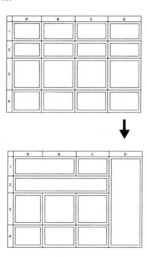

17.37 Each grouped cell then acts as a single cell. It can have one set of formatting specifications and one set of borders. Any grouped cell can be ungrouped at any time (17.104).

Cell borders

17.38 Every cell can have a set of borders. You can choose a border width or a style from the Lines menu, which contains a limited selection of the same Lines available in PageMaker.

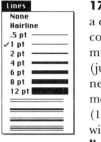

17.39 With sensitive use of these borders you can create sophisticated, well-organized, attractive tables with very little time and effort. You can choose to cut and copy the border along with the text of the cell, or just remove the text and leave the borders. As you increase the type size or change fonts or widen columns or delete rows, the borders adapt to the changes. Really, even with all the little bugs and minor inconveniences, creating tables in this Table Editor is addictive.

17.40 The lines (from the Lines menu) can be applied to any of the four sides of a cell, or to just the outer (perimeter) edges of a group of cells. Each side of a single cell or of a group of cells can have a different border, if you like. The cell does not need to have text in it in order to be set up with a border.

17.41 The process of applying a border to a cell is a bit convoluted. Not difficult, but convoluted. First, with the pointer tool you must select the cells that you want bordered (just press-and-drag over them). Next, you need to choose "Borders..." from the Cell menu and check the appropriate boxes (17.42). Then, you must choose the line width from the Lines menu. **If you want no lines, you must choose "None."** See Scenario #13 on page 614. Yes, it's a little awkward, but this is version 1.0.

17.42 In the "Borders" dialog box, you have six choices. You can choose any number of these. "Perimeter" is referring to the outside edges of the selected area. If you select a group of cells and check just the "Top" and "Bottom" boxes, then the border will appear on just the top and bottom of that *group,* not on the top and bottom of each cell in the group. If you do want a border on the top and bottom of *each cell* in the group, than you must check the "Interior Horizontals." Check out the examples in the next column.

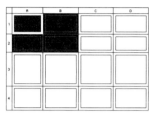

17.43 *The four cells in the upper left have been selected. (In this example, the grid labels and lines are "on," and thus visible.)*

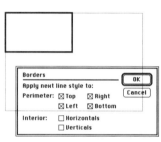

17.44 *With just the "Perimeter" edges checked, the border applies only to the outer edges of the **group** of cells. (Grid lines and labels have been turned "off.")*

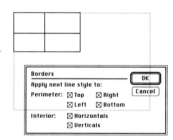

17.45 *With the "Interior" horizontal and vertical edges checked as well as the "Perimeter" edges, the border applies to the edges of each **single** cell.*

Cut and Copy

17.46 **Cut** and **Copy** work essentially the same way they do in PageMaker, cutting and copying information and placing it on the Clipboard, ready for pasting. What gets cut or copied, though, depends on which tool you use to select with.

17.47 If you select the text in a cell with the **text tool,** "Cut" will remove just the selected text. "Copy" will copy just the selected text.

17.48 If you select a cell or a group of cells with the **pointer tool,** then "Cut" will remove *all* the text in the selected cells, *as well as all lines and shades.* "Copy" will copy *all* the text in the selected cells, *as well as all lines and shades.*

17.49 See the notes in 17.60–17.66 regarding what happens when you paste back into the Table Editor. An interesting thing happens, though, when you take that information and paste directly into PageMaker itself: Whether you cut or copy with the pointer tool or the text tool, the entire cell(s) drops into PageMaker as a PICT with all of its formatting, including the borders and shades. If an insertion point is flashing, the cell becomes an inline graphic (9.91).

"Clear..." and Backspace/Delete

17.52 **Clear** (from the Edit menu) works essentially the same way it does in Page-Maker, clearing information from the page, *without* placing it on the Clipboard. If you choose "Clear..." from the Edit menu you will see a dialog box:

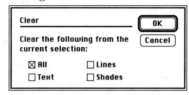

17.53 If you select the text in a cell with the **text tool,** "Clear..." from the Edit menu will remove just the selected text. The dialog box will give you the options shown above, *but this dialog box is just fooling you.* No matter what you check, only *the selected text* will clear.

17.54 If you select the cell or a group of cells with the **pointer tool,** the dialog box you get from choosing "Clear..." from the Edit menu will listen to you. You really can choose to clear just the lines, or the shades, or the text, or everything.

17.55 The Backspace or Delete key acts just like "Clear...," except that if you use the **text tool** to select text, and then Backspace/Delete, you won't see the dialog box. You *will* get the dialog box if you use the **pointer tool** to select text, and then Backspace/Delete.

Paste

17.56 **Paste** works essentially the same as it does in PageMaker, pasting information from the Clipboard into the table.

17.57 Read the previous page to understand exactly what you put on the Clipboard by cutting or copying with either the pointer tool or the text tool. It affects what will paste.

17.58 If you use the **pointer tool** to select the cell or cells to be pasted into, then *everything* on the Clipboard will paste— all the text, the lines, and the shades. If necessary, the depth of the row will expand to fit the text.

17.59 No matter what text is in the selected cells, and no matter what formatting, lines, or shades are applied, *everthing in the cell(s) will be replaced* by the text, lines, and shades that are on the Clipboard when you paste with the pointer tool selected.

> *Note: see 17.49 regarding pasting cut or copied data directly into PageMaker.*

17.60 If you use the **text tool** to select text to paste over, or if there is an insertion point flashing in a cell, then only the *text* that is on the Clipboard will paste.

17.61 If the selected cell is empty, then the text that is pasted will retain its own formatting. But if there is already text in cell, then the text pasted in will take on the formatting of the existing text.

17.62 If you cut or copied a number of cells into the Clipboard, then you must select that exact number of cells in which to paste. For instance, if there are three cells on the Clipboard but you only select two cells for pasting into, you'll get a dialog box asking if you want to do a partial paste or Cancel. If you choose a partial paste, then only the selected cells will fill, and the leftover cells are simply left out.

17.63 It is possible to do something like select two *rows* of six and paste it into two *columns* of six (17.120). You will get the dialog box alerting you that things don't match, but as long as there are the same number of cells, each cell will be filled in. If there are more cells selected than are on the Clipboard, any extra cells will just remain as they were.

Select all

17.64 **Select all** is found in the Edit menu. If any text has been selected with the **text tool** or if an insertion point is flashing, then "Select all" will select all the text *in that one single cell.*

17.65 If the **pointer tool** is chosen, then "Select all" will select *every cell in the table.*

17.66 You can also select every cell in the table with *either* tool by clicking once in the "Select all" box in the upper left corner of the table (17.21). This little box is only visible when the grid labels are showing (from the Options menu; 17.85).

Undo

17.67 You can't **Undo.** The Table Editor, version 1.0, does not have this function working yet.

Formatting text

17.68 Format text in a cell just as you format any text in PageMaker: select the text, then go up to the Type menu and choose your specs. Your choices are similar, but much more limited.

17.69 The biggest difference in formatting here in the Table Editor is the way you select the text—you can select it **with the pointer tool or with the text tool.** You do not need to press-and-drag over characters; just click in the cell with either tool. Using the text tool, you can select only one cell at a time. Using the pointer tool, you can select any number of cells.

17.70 Each cell can have only one set of specs; that is, it is not possible to have two different fonts or two different styles or alignments in one cell—it's all or nothing. The entire cell can have multiple *styles,* such as bold-italic-reverse, but it is not possible for all the text to be normal with one word in bold.

17.71 You are limited to type sizes from 4 to 127 points. The type size is also limited by the size of the table; that is, you can't make the font so large that it won't fit in the table size. Leading is limited to values from 4 to 127 points.

17.72 You can set application defaults for type specs, just as you do in PageMaker (17.129). To set the publication defaults, though, you must first *select* all the cells (click in the upper left of the table; 17.21), then choose the specs. Any new rows and columns you add will use the application defaults.

Leading

17.73 **Leading** operates in the Table Editor exactly as it does in PageMaker (4.12–4.18). You can assign a **fixed leading value** (4.25) through the "Type specs..." dialog box from the Type menu (Command T). The values are limited from 4 to 127 point.

17.74 You can change the **auto leading** value by choosing "Leading..." from the Type menu (17.73; also see 4.19–4.24 on auto leading). The values are limited from 100% to 200%.

17.75 Leading, like the other text formatting, is cell-specific; that is, it can be applied to one cell at a time, and it applies to the entire cell.

Alignment

17.76 The upper half of the **Alignment** submenu allows you to choose whether the text aligns horizontally Left, Right, or Centered, *within the cell* (17.107).

17.77 The second group of choices (Top, Middle, and Bottom) are vertical choices, again *within each cell.* That is, "Middle" would center the text vertically in the middle of the cell. As the cell gets larger or smaller, the text stays in the middle (17.78).

17.78 Each separate cell can have its own specific alignment, but the alignment applies to all text within the cell.

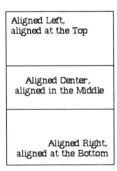

Shades

17.79 The Table Editor offers basic shades with which you can color a cell or a group of cells, typically to aid organization, or perhaps just to create an interesting look.

17.80 In order to apply a shade, you can select a cell with either the pointer tool or the text tool. If you use the text tool, you can only select one cell at a time, while with the pointer tool you can select a range of cells. Check out the tables on pages 583, 594, and 614 for examples of using shades.

17.81 *Wow. Instant, perfect checkerboards, using the Solid shade.*

Options menu

17.82 The Table Editor uses **Rulers** just as PageMaker does. From the Edit menu you can choose "Preferences..." and change your measuring system for those rulers (which would also change the measuring system in the column width, row height, and page setup dialog boxes). You can choose to have your vertical ruler different than your horizontal ruler as well (1.52–1.53).

17.83 If you choose **Snap to rulers,** then the column or row *boundaries* will snap to the ruler increments as you resize them. You can customize your vertical ruler (click "Custom" and type in a point value) to make it easy to lay out your grid.

17.84 The **zero point** can be moved as necessary, just as in PageMaker (1.69). **Zero lock** locks the zero point into position (1.72) so it cannot be moved accidentally.

17.85 The **Grid labels** must be showing if you want to resize columns or rows (press Command 8 to hide and show the labels). **Grid lines** display the non-printing guide lines (press Command 9 to hide and show the grid lines).

Number formats

17.86 The Table Editor allows you to format numeric values in a table (17.116). You can actually sum these values and place the total in a cell (17.117).

17.87 Below is a table showing how the different numbering formats (available from the Cell menu) affect the numbers you enter. Notice there are a few bugs yet, like you don't really get the whole number you would expect if you format the cell as **0**.

With this format:	If you type:		
	3798.7	-3798.7	.37987
General	3798.7	(3798.7)	0.37987
0	3799	-3799	0.4
0.00	3798.70	-3798.70	0.38
#,##0	3,799	-3,799	0.4
#,##0.00	3,798.70	-3,798.70	0.38
$#,##0 ; ($#,##0)	$3,799	($3,799)	$0.4
$#,##0.00 ; ($#,##0.00)	$3,798.70	($3,798.70)	$0.38
0%	3799%	-3799%	0.4%
0.00%	3798.70%	-3798.70%	0.38%

Importing

17.88 The Table Editor allows you to import tab-delimited or comma-delimited text-only files from other programs (17.118). A tab- or comma-delimited file is one that has its information separated by tabs or commas, as in many databases or spreadsheets. For instance, each column in a Microsoft Works database would drop into a column in a Table Editor table. You can even import PageMaker stories into the Table Editor, as long as you have exported it as text-only (15.36). Even if there are no tabs in the story, each Return character will start a new row (or column; 17.120), and each paragraph will be placed into its own cell.

Exporting

17.89 The only way to get a table into a PageMaker publication is to *export* it and *place* it into PageMaker. You can export it as a **PICT** graphic (17.122), in which case it retains all its text formatting, lines, and shades, like so:

**Great Words
I Have Known**

uxorious: *foolishly fond of one's wife*

quidnunc: *a busybody gossip*

17.90 You can export the table as **text-only** (17.121), and all that will place into Page-Maker is the text (below). Saving the file as text-only is more appropriate if you will be importing the information into a database or spreadsheet rather than into PageMaker.

Great Words

I Have Known

uxorious:

foolishly fond of one's wife

quidnunc:

a busybody gossip

If you want to do this:

17.91   Create a new table

Table Editor 1.0

The Table Editor application icon

 ⬧ File Edit Options View Cell Type Lines Shades

The Table Editor menu

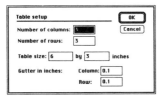

The "Table setup" dialog box (page 586)

Then follow these steps:

- Table Editor is a separate application, so you need to be at the Desktop (the Finder) in order to start a new table. If you use MultiFinder you can have both applications open at once, which makes the process much easier.
- When you are at the Desktop, double-click on the Table Editor icon. It was installed into the Aldus PageMaker 4.0 folder.
- From the File menu, choose "New...."
- You will get the "Table setup" dialog box (17.15–17.18). Enter the number of columns and rows you want in your table, the size of the table, as well as the amount of gutter space between the columns and rows (17.16); click OK. You can change any of these specifications at any time while you're creating the table.
- Enter text in the cells using the **text tool:** simply click in the cell and type (17.29–17.35; 17.105).
- To change text formatting, select a cell with the text tool, *or* select a range of cells with the pointer tool. Choose the specs from the menu *or* the "Type specs" dialog box (Command T).
- Add borders to cells or to a range of cells (17.38–17.45; 17.110).

Shortcuts ▾ Notes ▾ Hints

- This is just an outline of the process. See the references for each specific step.
- The maximum size of a table is 22.75 x 22.75 inches.
- The maximum number of columns is 80; the maximum number of rows is 80.
- The maximum gutter size is whatever will leave at least 8 points in the column itself.
- Type size can be anywhere from 4 to 127 points in 1-point increments. Leading can be specified from 4 to 127 point in 1-point increments.
- After you create the table, you must export it (17.121–17.122). Then you must open a PageMaker publication and place the table so you can print it (17.124).

If you want to do this:	Then follow these steps:	Shortcuts ▾ Notes ▾ Hints
17.92 Open an existing table Merry Wives *An icon for an existing table* MerryWives/Text MerryWives/PICT *Icons for an exported text-only file and for a PICT graphic file. You cannot open these.*	▪ If you are at the Desktop (the Finder), just double-click on the icon of the existing table. *You cannot open the PICT or the text-only export versions of a table.* ▪ If you are already in the Table Editor, you must close any table that may be open. Then from the File menu, choose "Open...." You may need to switch drives or folders to find the table you want. When you see the file's name in the list box (16.8), double-click on it.	▪ If you double-click on the text-only or the PICT versions, you will open the Table Editor, but no document will be on the screen.
17.93 Add rows  	You can add rows two ways: ▪ From the File menu, choose "Table setup...." ▪ Enter the total number of rows you want in the "Number of rows" edit box. ▪ You will usually get a dialog box warning you that the size of the table will increase, which you probably knew would happen. Click OK. All rows will be added onto the bottom of the table. *The new rows will be the height of the existing last row.* ▪ **OR** with either tool, select a row (click in the grid label) *or* select any cell in a row. ▪ From the Cell menu, choose "Insert...." ▪ Enter a number; click in the radio button for "Row"; click OK. ▪ The rows will be added directly *above* (and the same height as) the selected one.	▪ If the selected row has any borders, type specifications, or shades *consistent, or even predominant, throughout the entire row,* then the added rows will also have those same borders, shades, and type specs.

If you want to do this:	**Then follow these steps:**	**Shortcuts ▾ Notes ▾ Hints**

17.94 Delete rows

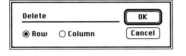

- With either tool, select the rows you want to delete by clicking in the grid label or by clicking in any cell in the row.
- From the Cell menu, choose "Delete...," *or* press Command K.
- In the dialog box, click the Row button; click OK.

- You cannot delete rows from the "Table setup" dialog box, nor can you select rows and "Cut" them.
- This process deletes the entire row. If you want to delete just the text in the row, or just the lines or shades, see 17.113; 17.115.

17.95 Add columns

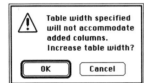

You can add columns two ways:
- From the File menu, choose "Table setup...."
- Enter the total number of columns you want in the "Number of columns" edit box.
- You will usually get a dialog box warning you that the size of the table will increase, which you probably knew would happen. Click OK. All columns will be added onto the right side of the table. *The new columns will be the width of the existing last column.*
- **OR** with either tool, select a column (click in the grid label) *or* select any cell in a column.
- From the Cell menu, choose "Insert...," *or* press Command I.
- Enter a number; click in the radio button for "Column"; click OK.
- The columns will be added directly to the *left* of the selected one and will be the same width as the selected one.

- If the selected column has any borders, type specifications, or shades that are *consistent, or even predominant, throughout the entire row,* then the added columns will also have those same borders, shades, and type specs.

If you want to do this:	Then follow these steps:	Shortcuts ▾ Notes ▾ Hints
17.96 Delete columns 	■ With either tool, select the columns you want to delete, either by clicking in the grid label or in any cell in the column. ■ From the Cell menu, choose "Delete…," *or* press Command K. ■ In the dialog box, click the Column button; click OK.	■ You cannot delete columns from the "Table setup" dialog box, nor can you select columns and "Cut" them. ■ This process deletes the entire column. If you want to delete just the text in the column, or just the lines or shades, see 17.113 and 17.115.
17.97 Change column width *(and thus change the table size)*	■ With either tool, select one or more columns (press-and-drag in the grid labels), *or* select even just one cell in a column. ■ From the Cell menu, choose "Column width…." ■ Type in a value and click OK. You can override the current system measurement, if you like (see 1.221).	
17.98 Change column width, *without changing the size of the adjacent column* *(This will also change the table size)*	■ Make sure the grid labels are visible, as shown in 17.43. If they are not, from the Options menu choose "Grid labels," *or* press Command 8. ■ Hold down the Option key; press-and-drag a column boundary in the grid label to make it wider or narrower (see the illustration in 17.99).	■ When you resize with the Option key pressed, the adjacent column will just move over to accommodate the new size. This will increase or decrease the overall table size.

If you want to do this:	**Then follow these steps:**	**Shortcuts ▾ Notes ▾ Hints**

17.99 Change column width, without changing the table size

To resize a **column,** *press on the boundary guide with either tool; the pointer will become a two-headed arrow. Drag left or right to resize it.*

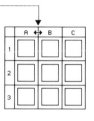

- Make sure the grid labels are showing, as you see on the left. If they are not, from the Options menu, choose "Grid labels," *or* press Command 8.
- Press-and-drag a column boundary in the grid label to make it wider or narrower. *The adjacent column will also change size; see 17.98 if you want to avoid that.*

- You can change *the space available* in every column by changing the gutter space in the "Table setup" dialog box.

17.100 Change row height *(thus changing the table size)*

Either:
- With either tool, select one or more rows (press-and-drag in the grid labels), or select even just one cell in a row or rows.
- From the Cell menu, choose "Row height...."
- Type a value and click OK. You can override the current system measurement, if you like (see 1.221).

Or:
- Make sure the grid labels are visible, as shown on the left. If they are not, from the Options menu choose "Grid labels," *or* press Command 8.
- Press-and-drag a row boundary in the grid labels to make it taller or shorter. The adjacent row will not change size, but the depth of the table will change.

To resize a **row,** *press on the boundary guide in the grid label with either tool; the pointer will become a two-headed arrow. Drag up or down to resize it.*

- You can change *the space available* in every row by changing the gutter space in the "Table setup" dialog box.
- Increasing or decreasing the leading and/or the point size of the type will also change the height of the row.
- *You cannot resize a row without changing the table size.*

If you want to do this:	**Then follow these steps:**	**Shortcuts ▾ Notes ▾ Hints**
17.101 Increase the table size without adding more rows or columns	■ From the File menu, choose "Table setup...." ■ Increase the values in either the width or the depth of the table ("Table size"; 17.17). *The last column or the last row will increase in size.*	■ It is not possible to *decrease* the size of the table from the "Table setup" dialog box (see 17.102).
17.102 Decrease the table size	■ You cannot decrease the table size from the "Table setup" dialog box. You must either delete entire rows or columns (17.94; 17.96), or decrease the size of existing rows or columns (17.100; 17.97).	
17.103 Group cells	■ With the **pointer tool,** select the separate cells that you want to group into one cell (see 17.36–17.37 for an example). ■ From the Cell menu, choose "Group," *or* press Command G.	■ If there is text in the selected cells, it will all disappear, *except* for the text in the top left selected cell. If you ungroup, all pre-existing text returns! ■ G for Group, right?
17.104 Ungroup cells	■ With the **pointer tool,** click in the cell you want to ungroup into separate cells. ■ From the Cell menu, choose "Ungroup," *or* press Command U.	■ U for Ungroup, right? I'm so happy they make it easy for me.
17.105 Type into a cell	■ With the **text tool,** click into any cell. This sets the insertion point within the cell, and you can just type as usual. Tab moves the insertion point to the next cell over; Return moves it down one cell. Shift-Return breaks a line of text in the cell.	■ There are no keyboard shortcuts for any of the type specs, unfortunately. ■ See 17.29–17.35.

If you want to do this: ■

Then follow these steps: ■

Shortcuts ▾ Notes ▾ Hints   ■

17.106   Change the type specs

- With the **text tool,** click in any single cell; **or** with the **pointer tool,** click in any cell *or* press-and-drag to select a range of cells.
  - □ To select an entire row or column, click in a grid label (17.23a) with either tool, *or* press-and-drag across grid labels.
  - □ To select every cell in the table, click in the little box in the upper left (17.21) with either tool. **Or** with the pointer tool choose "Select all" from the Edit menu, *or* press Command A.
- From the Type menu, choose your specifications either from the submenus or from "Type specs" just as you do in PageMaker.

- *All type specifications apply to the entire cell.*
- Unlike in PageMaker, type in the Table Editor can be selected with the pointer tool for formatting changes.

17.107   Change the alignment of the text within a cell

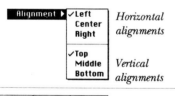

- Each cell offers you two separate alignment possibilities: horizontally within the cell, and vertically within the cell (see left).
- Select the cell(s) as in 17.106 above.
- From the Type menu, choose the "Alignment..." submenu and select the alignment of your choice. You will have to repeat the process if you want to choose both a horizontal *and* a vertical alignment.

- Also see 17.76–17.78.

If you want to do this:	Then follow these steps:	Shortcuts ▾ Notes ▾ Hints

17.108 Apply shades to a cell or to a range of cells

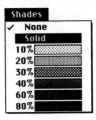

- With the **text tool,** click in any single cell; **or** with the **pointer tool,** click in any cell *or* press-and-drag to select a range of cells.
  - ☐ To select an entire row or column, click in a grid label (17.23a) with either tool, *or* press-and-drag across grid labels.
  - ☐ To select every cell in the table, click in the little box in the upper left (17.21) with either tool. **Or** with the pointer tool choose "Select all" from the Edit menu, *or* press Command A.
- From the Shades menu, choose a shade.

17.109 *The Top, Left, Right, and Bottom Perimeter of this table has a 1-point rule (line; border). The Interior Horizontals and Verticals have hairline rules.*

None	**Solid**	**10%**	**20%**
30%	**40%**	**60%**	**80%**

If you want to do this:

Then follow these steps:

Shortcuts ▸ Notes ▸ Hints

17.110 Apply borders to a cell
or to a range of cells

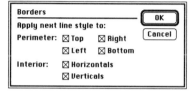

- With the **text tool,** click in any single cell;
or with the **pointer tool,** click in any cell,
or press-and-drag to select a range of cells.
  □ To select an entire row or column, click
  in a grid label (17.23a) with either tool,
  or press-and-drag across grid labels.
  □ To select every cell in the table, click
  in the little box in the upper left (17.21)
  with either tool. **Or** with the pointer
  tool choose "Select all" from the Edit
  menu, *or* press Command A.
- From the Cell menu, choose "Borders...."
- Click in the checkboxes for the edges you
  want to apply a border to. See 17.42–17.45
  for specific details on the difference
  between Perimeter and Interior.
    This dialog box does not **apply** *a border;*
    this just tells the Table Editor where to apply the
    border that you are going to choose in a minute.
    Click OK.
- Now from the Lines menu, choose a line
  width for the border. This line will be
  applied to all the edges you just checked
  in the "Borders" dialog box.

- Any checkboxes that are selected in the
  "Borders" dialog box will *stay* selected
  until you change them yourself or until
  you start another table. That is, you don't
  have to go to the dialog box every time. If
  you want to change a lot of bottom lines
  in cells that are not connected, check the
  "Bottom" checkbox. Then just select the
  separate cells one at a time and give
  them each a line width. The line width
  will be applied to the bottom of each cell
  until you return to the "Borders" dialog
  box and change the selection.
- **Note: if you want to get rid of any
  border,** you must get the "Borders"
  dialog box, select the edges from which
  you want to remove any border, and then
  choose "None" from the Lines menu.
  You can't just deselect the checkboxes in
  the dialog box—you must actually apply
  "None."

17.111 Remove existing borders

- Follow the steps above, but select a Line
  of "None."

- I strongly recommend setting an application default of no borders on any cell
  (17.129). Otherwise every time you add
  new cells they have a border already.

If you want to do this:	Then follow these steps:	Shortcuts ▾ Notes ▾ Hints
17.112 Copy or cut just the text from a cell	▪ With the **text tool,** select the text you want to cut or copy. You can use most of the selection tricks that are available in PageMaker, like double-clicking and Shift-clicking. ▪ Cut or copy from the Edit menu or with the keyboard commands, as usual.	▪ If you cut or copy text and then paste it into PageMaker, the text drops onto the publication page as a graphic (17.49). You will not be able to edit it.
17.113 Clear just the text from a cell 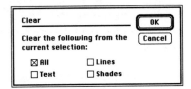	▪ If you select text with the **text tool** and choose "Clear..." from the Edit menu, you will get the dialog box shown on the left, pretending to give you choices. It is lying; you really have no choice. Just the text will be deleted, no matter which box you check. ▪ Another way to clear the text is to simply select it with the **text tool** and hit the Backspace/Delete key.	
17.114 Cut or copy the text, shades, and lines from a cell or from a range of cells	▪ With the **pointer tool,** click on a cell, *or* press-and-drag over a range of cells. ▪ Cut or copy from the Edit menu or with the keyboard commands, as usual.	▪ When you use the **pointer tool** to cut or copy, *everything* in the cell is cut or copied—all the lines, the type specifications, the shades, the alignment. After you *cut* from a cell, the type specs in that cell will return to the default specs.

If you want to do this:	**Then follow these steps:**	**Shortcuts ▾ Notes ▾ Hints**
17.115 Clear just the text, or just the shades, or just the lines from a cell or from a range of cells 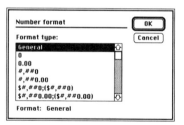	▪ With the **pointer tool,** click in a cell, *or* press-and-drag to select a range of cells. ▪ From the Edit menu, choose "Clear...," *or* hit the Backspace/Delete key. You will see the dialog box shown on the left. ▪ Make your choice as to what you want to delete. These are checkbox buttons, which means you can select any number of the options. Click OK.	
17.116 Change the number format of the numeric values in a cell	▪ With either tool, select a cell or a range of cells that have numeric values in them. **Or,** with the **text tool,** select just the numeric portion of the text in a cell. Each cell can have more than one number format in it—*the number format does not apply to the entire cell.* ▪ From the Cell menu, choose "Number format...," *or* press Command F. ▪ Scroll through the list of options. Check out 17.87 to see how the different formats affect your numbers. ▪ Click on the format you want, then click OK; *or* double-click on the format choice.	▪ Don't expect this number format option to operate as it does in a spreadsheet. That is, neither the cell nor the number itself holds onto that format. Once you have selected a number and changed it, you can select the same number and retype a new number (or even type text) into its place; the new number will *not* automatically transform into the format you previously chose.

605

If you want to do this:

17.117 Sum the numeric values from a range of cells

 The sum cursor

Then follow these steps:

- From the Cell menu, choose "Number format...." Select the format for the sum. Click OK.
- With the **pointer tool,** press-and-drag over the range of cells you want to sum; they do not all have to be in one column. To select one column or one row, click in its grid label (17.23a,b).
- After selecting the cells, from the Cell menu choose "Sum," *or* press Command = (equal sign, next to Backspace/Delete). You will get a new cursor, as shown on the left. *This cursor is only visible when the pointer is directly over the grid of the table.*
- Click in the cell where you want to place the answer and the answer will appear. If you click in a cell that already has a number or any text in it, the sum will replace the entire contents.

Shortcuts ▾ Notes ▾ Hints

- **Note:** The sum will not change if you change any of the numbers that were selected as part of the total sum. This is not a spreadsheet.

" Hot lead

can be almost as effective

coming from a linotype

as from a firearm."

John O'Hara, journalist

If you want to do this:

Then follow these steps:

Shortcuts ▾ Notes ▾ Hints

17.118 Import text into an existing table in the Table Editor

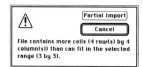

- Set up a new table as usual (17.91) or open an existing one (17.92). If you want to import into just a selection of cells, select them with the **pointer tool.**
- From the Edit menu, choose "Define flow...." The option you select here will determine whether the tab- or comma-delimited text flows in from left to right or from top to bottom. See 17.120.
- From the File menu, choose "Import...." You will get a dialog box similar to Page-Maker's "Place," with the option to replace the entire table or any selected cells (if you selected some). Click an "Import" option.
- Double-click on the file name to import it (*or* click once on it, then click OK).
- If the new text won't fit, the Table Editor will warn you. You will have a choice of canceling the operation or of pasting what will fit (see left).
- When you import the text, it will flow into the cells in the order you have chosen in the "Define flow" dialog box. Any existing text will be replaced.

- The only files the Table Editor can read are files that were saved as "text only." If the imported text has tabs, each unit that was separated by a tab will land in its own cell. Each Return key in the text will start a new column or a new row, depending on your defined flow (17.120).
- Even if the imported text has no tabs, each paragraph (Return) gets its own cell, again in columns or rows, depending on your defined flow (17.120).
- You can import any story you have in PageMaker *after* you export it as text-only (15.36).

17.119 Paste text into the Table Editor

- Follow the steps in 17.118 above; just skip the steps in the "Import file" dialog box. Instead, use text you cut or copied to the Clipboard.

607

If you want to do this:	Then follow these steps:	Shortcuts ▾ Notes ▾ Hints
17.120 Define the flow for pasting or importing text 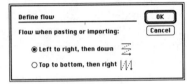	▪ From the Edit menu, choose "Define flow...." ▪ If you select "Left to right" then each time there is a tab in the text, that text flows into the next column to the right. Each time there is a Return, the text jumps down to the beginning of the next row. ▪ If you select "Top to bottom" then each time there is a tab in the text, that text flows into the cell in the row directly below. Each time there is a Return, the text jumps to the top of the next column.	▪ This comes in very handy for quickly transposing data. For instance, it is not an uncommon task to turn your spreadsheet column headings into row headings, or vice versa. ▪ This "Define flow" feature doesn't always work like you would think it should. If your data pastes in wrong, leave it all selected. Go back to the dialog box and change the flow and try again.
17.121 Export a table as editable text 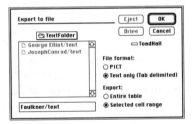	▪ Have the table you want to export open on the screen. If you want to export just a portion of the table, select cells with the **pointer tool.** ▪ From the File menu, choose "Export...," *or* press Command E. ▪ Under "File format" select "Text only." ▪ Under "Export," the button "Selected cell range" will be available only if you selected cells before getting this dialog box. Make your choice. ▪ Name the file. For easy identification later, it is a good idea to indicate in the file name whether this is an original table, a text-only file, or a PICT file. ▪ Click OK.	▪ Exporting your table as "text-only" removes any text formatting, lines, and shades that may have been in the table (17.90). When you place or import the exported text file into another program, each column from the Table Editor will align with a tab, and each row will be separated by Returns. If you import the text into a database, for example, the columns and rows will appear just as they did in the original table. ▪ If you import the text into PageMaker, the text will follow its own tabs (whatever they may be), *not* the default tabs or the tabs of the paragraph it is set into. You can change the tabs after the table is in PageMaker.

If you want to do this:	Then follow these steps:	Shortcuts ▾ Notes ▾ Hints
17.122 Export a table as a graphic (PICT format) 	■ Have the table you want to export open on the screen. If you want to export just a portion of the table, select cells with the **pointer tool.** ■ From the File menu, choose "Export...," *or* press Command E. ■ Under "File format," select "PICT." ■ Under "Export," the button "Selected cell range" will be available only if you selected cells before getting this dialog box. Make your choice. ■ Name the file. For easy identification later, it is a good idea to indicate in the file name whether this is an original table, a text-only file, or a PICT file. ■ Click OK.	■ This PICT file can be placed into any program that will accept a PICT (9.14–9.19). As a graphic, it is not editable. It will retain all the lines and shades and text formatting. ■ Of course, after you place the PICT into PageMaker and print it, you will find typos or other little points you want to change. After you go back to the Table Editor and change the original PICT, update the version in the PageMaker publication. See 17.128 for full details.
17.123 Save the table as a graphic in the Scrapbook	■ With the **pointer tool,** select the range of cells you want to copy. To select the entire table, click in the upper left select-all box (17.21); **or** with the **pointer tool,** choose "Select all" from the Edit menu. ■ From the Edit menu, choose "Copy," *or* press Command C. ■ From the Apple menu, choose "Scrapbook." ■ From the Edit menu, choose "Paste." ■ Close the Scrapbook by clicking in its close box (upper left).	■ Once the graphic is in the Scrapbook, you can paste it into any program, including PageMaker, that will accept a PICT. ■ If you need to know more about the Scrapbook, see 1.200–1.205. If you need to know more about PICTs, see 9.14–9.19.

If you want to do this: Then follow these steps: Shortcuts ▾ Notes ▾ Hints

17.124 In PageMaker, *place* the table as editable text or as a graphic (PICT format)

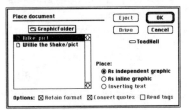

- Place the table just as you place any text file (3.51–3.52) or graphic file (9.92).
- Text will place with its own set of tabs, supposedly one tab for each column, although I didn't find that to be very consistent. The text will ignore any tabs you may have set up already, even if you insert the table into an already existing, tabbed story. Rows will place as separate paragraphs, separated by Return characters.
- A table placed as a graphic acts just like any other graphic. You can resize it, (9.101), crop it (9.104), text-wrap it (9.105), or insert it as an inline graphic (9.91; 9.190–9.191).

- Note that when you place a table, you are not placing the *original* table. You are placing the file you *exported*. Thus if you place a graphic, the PageMaker publication version is linked (Section 10) to the *exported* version, not to the original table. Any changes you make to the original table in the Table Editor will not update the PageMaker version; *you must update the exported graphic file* (17.128).

17.125 In PageMaker, *paste* the table as a graphic

- In the Table Editor, with the **pointer tool** select the range of cells you want to paste into PageMaker. To select the entire table, click in the upper left select-all box (17.21), *or* from the Edit menu, choose "Select all." **Or** if the graphic is in the Scrapbook, open the Scrapbook and find the image.
- From the Edit menu, choose "Copy," *or* press Command C. Now the table (or range of cells) is on the Clipboard. Close the Table Editor or the Scrapbook.
- Open the PageMaker publication. With the **pointer tool** selected, from the Edit menu choose "Paste."

- Pasting a table into PageMaker (or into any other application) is exactly the same as pasting anything from the Clipboard.
- A table pasted from the Clipboard *will not be linked to any form of the original table.* You will not be able to take advantage of the automatic updating of linked graphics that PageMaker provides. You'll be stuck with what you've got.

If you want to do this:	**Then follow these steps:**	**Shortcuts ▾ Notes ▾ Hints**
17.126 Remove the white line from around the PICT table, while in PageMaker ⛏ *The cropping tool*	• All you need to do is crop the table. • With the **cropping tool,** click once on the graphic image. • Center a corner handle in the inner space of the cropping tool. • Press-and-drag that handle. As you drag, part of the picture will be eliminated. See 9.104 for greater details.	• The white line that shows up around the table is the border that shows up around most PICT-type graphics. It will only be troublesome if the table is overlaying some other element. It is very thin, so you probably won't see it until you print.

17.127 Import a table into PageMaker's Story Editor	• Open a publication in PageMaker.
	• Open the Story Editor (8.30–8.31).
	• From the Story menu choose "Import...." You will see the typical "Import" dialog box, which is basically just like the "Place" dialog box (3.40–3.50) and functions in the same way.
	• Find the file you wish to import.
	  ▫ If the table is a graphic, your only choice will be to import it as an inline graphic (9.91). It will import into the Story Editor as a little icon: ▣. The graphic itself will appear in the layout view (see 8.37).
	  ▫ If the table is a text-only file, you will have the same choices as when you *place* a file (3.40–3.50). The table will import into the Story Editor as text, delimited by tabs of its own choice.
		• In order to import, you must have previously exported the file from the Table Editor as a PICT.
		• See Section 8 on the Story Editor.
		• See 9.170–9.182 for more info on inline graphics and how to deal with them.

If you want to do this:

17.128 Revise and update the graphic table that you placed into the PageMaker publication

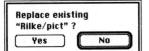

Then follow these steps:

- In the Table Editor, open the original table. You can't put the PICT version on the screen—you must get the table itself.
- Make the necessary changes.
- From the File menu, choose "Export...," *or* press Command E.
- Make sure the name of the original PICT is in the list box (16.8). Rename the file with *exactly the same name* as the PICT that is currently in the PageMaker publication.
- Click OK *or* press Return. You will be asked if you want to replace the existing file with the same name. Click Yes. *If you don't get the alert box asking if you want to replace the existing PICT, then you will not be able to update with this technique; you'll just have to manually replace the one in the publication.*
- Quit the Table Editor and open the PageMaker publication.
- From the File menu, choose "Links...," *or* press Command = . The name of the table should be in the list and it should have a white diamond symbol next to it (10.29; 10.34; 10.42). If there is no white diamond, it means you didn't change the original PICT. Maybe you just changed the original table?
- Click once on the name of the PICT. Click the button "Update" (10.32). Click OK.

Shortcuts ▾ Notes ▾ Hints

- For more info on linking text and graphics in the PageMaker publication to their original files, see Section 10 on Linking Text and Graphics.
- When re-exporting the table, you must make sure you are exporting it into the same folder the original graphic table is stored in, or PageMaker will not be able to implement the update. *If you do not get the little dialog box asking if you want to replace the existing file of the same name, then you will not update the PageMaker version.* You may need to navigate (search through folders and/or disks) to find that first one. Use that great Mr. Find File (1.232–1.233).
- You could also set up an automatic update so the next time you open the PageMaker publication the table will be updated as PageMaker opens. See 10.53.

If you want to do this:	**Then follow these steps:**	**Shortcuts ▾ Notes ▾ Hints**
17.129 Set the default specifications for the Table Editor application	Set default application specifications just as you do in PageMaker (1.12): ■ With the Table Editor open, but with no table open on the screen (you should see just the menu, no Table Editor window), choose anything from any of the menus and dialog boxes, including "Table setup." These become your defaults. ■ The only default you cannot specify is the table size in the "Table setup" dialog box (from the File menu). You will find that the table size may change often. That's because *it will automatically enter the size of any graphic that is in the Clipboard.*	■ You can use this changing table size phenomenon to your advantage. If there is a particular size space in your publication for which you want to create a table, use the rectangle tool to draw a box just that size. Cut it to the Clipboard. When you open the Table Editor, that size will already be entered for you.
17.130 Set the default specifications for the open table	■ With the **pointer tool,** select every cell in the table: either choose "Select all" from the Edit menu, or click in the select-all box in the upper left (17.21). ■ Now set specifications from any menu and from any dialog box. ■ If you add rows or columns, they will have these defaults. *But,* if you select any cell or group of cells and use the **Cut** command, you will also cut the current table default specs. The selected cells will revert back to the application defaults.	■ These defaults apply just to this table. When you open another table, that table will revert to its own defaults.

17.131 Scenario #13: Creating a table

This scenario is actually a mini-tutorial that will take you about ten or twelve minutes to complete. It's just to show you how easy it is to create these great tables. When you finish, you will have a table that looks like this:

Snails	What to do with snails.
1 Eat them.	
2 Squish them.	
3 Throw them.	
4 Sprinkle salt on them.	
5 Drop them into turpentine.	
6 Feed them beer.	
7 Introduce them to ducks.	

- Open the Table Editor.
- From the File menu, choose "New...."
- Enter these specs, then click OK:

  Number of columns: 6
  Number of rows: 10
  Table size: 4 x 6
  Gutter in inches: 0.05
                              0.05

Your table should look like this:

The select-all box

- Save the table before we go any further. Save it just as you always save any Mac file.
- Let's set some default specs for the entire table and get rid of all the default borders so we can create our own:
  - Click in the far upper left corner in the select-all box; the entire table should turn black.

- From the Type menu, choose a font. Also choose type size 14.
- From the Cell menu, choose "Borders...." Make sure every checkbox contains an X.
- From the Lines menu, choose "None."
- From the Type menu, slide down to Alignment and choose "Left." Repeat and choose "Middle."
- Now let's group some of the cells together to make a more interesting arrangment. With the pointer tool, press-and-drag over the cells you want to combine into one group, then press Command G. Follow this guide:

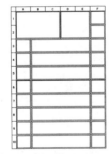

- Let's make column F narrower. Press-and-drag on the left boundary guide of column F; drag to the right.

—continued

Creating a table —*continued*

- Type in the headline **Snails**: With the text tool, just click in the cell. Type. Format the word to 30 point, bold, and align it center.
- Type in the numbers: with the text tool, click in cell A3. Type **1**, hit Return; type **2**, hit Return; etc.
- Oops—we have an extra row, right? So get rid of it. Click in the grid label (the number 10) and press Command K. Yes, we want to get rid of the row, so click OK.
- We want that entire column of numbers to align right. So with the pointer tool, press-and-drag through the cells with the numbers in them. From the Type menu, slide down to Alignment; choose "Right." Also from the Type menu, slide down to Type Style and choose "Bold." It should look like this now:

- Type the text into the large cell next to "Snails." Center it.
- Type the text into the cells next to the numbers: With the text tool, click in the cell to the right of the number **1,** type the words, then hit Return and type the next line. Continue to the end.
- Put the Shades in: Click in the grid label for **row 4** (not the *cell* that has the *typed* number 4 in it); the entire row 4 should highlight. From the Shades menu, choose 10%. Select every other row, one at a time, and apply the 10% shade.
- Apply the solid black shade to column F: Just click in the grid label (directly on the F) to select the entire column. From the Shades menu, choose "Solid" (it won't actually *look* solid until you deselect it). Your table should look like this:

- All we need to do now is put the borders in. Select the top portion—those two large cells and the narrow black one (you can ignore the narrow black one, if you choose).
- From the Cell menu, choose "Borders...."
- Uncheck boxes until you have only the box for "Bottom" checked. Click OK.
- From the Lines menu, choose the double line that has the thin line above and the thick below. (The Table Editor arranges them oddly, so you will actually get the double line with the thin line below and the thick line above; 17.110).
- Select the bottom row (click on the 9), and from the Shades menu, choose the opposite double border—the one with the thin line below and the thick line above. It should look like this:

615

Creating a table —*continued*

- Let's get rid of the grid labels and grid lines so we can see what we're doing: press Command 8 and Command 9.
- We need a thin line around the top and left perimeter of the table. So from the Cell menu, choose "Borders...." Put a check in only the Top and Left checkboxes; remove all others.
- Select the entire table: with the pointer tool, press Command A (notice you can "Select all" *after* you have chosen your borders; what you set in the "Borders" dialog box will stay and apply until you go in and change it).
- From the Lines menu, choose "Hairline." Your table should look like this:

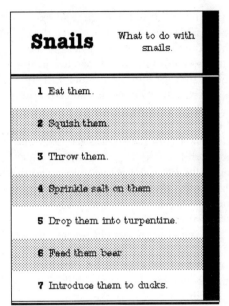

Now, you must admit, that was fun and easy. You've been saving your changes all along, right? Now you need to export the completed table so you can place it into your PageMaker publication and print it.

Just go to the File menu and **Export** the table as a PICT (17.122). Open your Page-Maker publication and **place** the table just as you place any other outside graphic (9.92). It will look like the table on page 614 (but larger).

When you decide you want to make changes to the table, you do have to return to the Table Editor. Follow the steps in 17.128 to update the link so the changes in the original PICT table will be reflected in the PageMaker publication with the least amount of fuss and bother.

On Love and Fools

Rosalind	Love is merely a madness, and, I tell you, deserves as well a dark house and a whip as madmen do; and the reason why they are not so punished and cured is, that the lunacy is so ordinary that the whippers are in love too.		Duke	Thou seest we are not all alone unhappy: this wide and universal theatre presents more woeful pageants than the scene wherein we play in.
Silvius	In thy youth thou wast as true a lover as ever sigh'd upon a midnight pillow.		Jacques	O that I were a fool! I am ambitious for a motley coat.
Rosalind	For your brother and my sister no sooner met but they looked, no sooner looked but they loved, no sooner loved but they sighed, no sooner sighed but they asked one another the reason, no sooner knew the reason but they sought the remedy.		Jacques	All the world's a stage, and all the men and women merely players: they have their exits and their entrances; and one man in his time plays many parts.
Touchstone	We that are true lovers run into strange capers; but as all is mortal in nature, so is all nature in love mortal in folly.		Celia	For since the little wit that fools have was silenced, the little foolery that wise man have makes a great show.
Rosalind	Men have died from time to time and worms have eaten them, but not for love.		Touchstone	The more the pity, that fools may not speak wisely what wise men do foolishly.
Celia	The oath of a lover is no stronger than the word of a tapster; they are both the confirmer of false reckonings.		Celia	But all's brave that youth mounts and folly guides.
Rosalind	The sight of lovers feedeth those in love.		Jacques	By my troth, I was seeking for a fool when I found you.
Touchstone	As the ox hath his bow, sir, the horse his curb and the falcon her bells, so man hath his desires; and as pigeons bill, so wedlock would be		Orlando	He is drowned in the brook: look but in, and you shall see him.
Rosalind	If I were a woman I would kiss as many of you as had beards that pleased me, complexions that liked me, and breaths that I defied not.		Jacques	And so, from hour to hour, we ripe and ripe, and then, from hour to hour, we rot and rot; and thereby hangs a tale.

As You Like It • William Shakespeare

17.132 This table was created in a very short time. Having items in rows and columns and cells makes it remarkably easy to rearrange and alter, yet stay consistent.

A few more examples

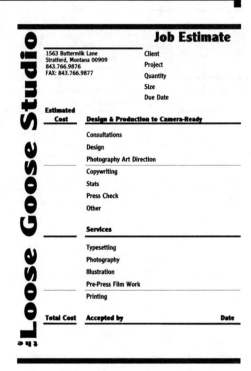

Readability and Legibility Ratings for Typefaces

Serif Fonts	Readability	Legibility
Benguiat	◆	◆
Bodoni	◆◆	◆
Baskerville	◆◆◆◆	◆◆◆
Garamond	◆◆◆◆	◆◆◆
Times	◆◆◆◆	◆◆◆

Sans Serif Fonts	Readability	Legibility
Avant Garde	◆	◆◆
Blippo Black	◆	◆
Franklin Gothic	◆◆	◆◆◆◆
Futura	◆◆	◆◆◆◆
Helvetica	◆◆	◆◆◆◆

Readability vs. Legibility

Readability refers to how easily a typeface can be read in extended text.

Legibility refers to how easily characters can be distinguished in a short burst of text.

17.133 This is what the table in 17.132 looked like in the Table Editor with its grid lines and labels showing.

17.134 This sweet little chart could develop into a very interesting and useful poster. Just what we need.

17.135 "The Loose Goose Studio" logo was created in PageMaker (using text rotation) and dropped into the completed estimate form in the publication.

Which treats of Matters
of a very different Kind
from those in the preceding Chapters.

18.1   Minimums and maximums:

Item	Minimum	Maximum
Page size	Depends on printer	
Print area	Depends on printer	
Number of publication pages to print	Limited only by the amount of memory in the printer	
Number of copies	1	100
Manual tile overlap	0 pts. 0 inches (.1 increments)	360 pts. 30 inches
Thumbnails per page	1 (increments of 1 or 2)	64
Scaling	25%	1000%

18.2   When you get right down to it, printing is the proof of the pudding. No matter how stunning your publication, you have to print it to be able to use it. Some of the decisions you make about your publication depend on the printer you will be using for your final output, so it is a good idea to be familiar with the printing aspect of PageMaker before you begin creating.

18.3   Laser printers use an immense amount of power, kind of like refrigerators. It's recommended that you let a laser printer have its own power source, rather than plug it into an outlet strip. If energy conservation or electric bills concern you, don't keep a laser printer on unnecessarily.

18.4   Every time you turn on most laser printers you get a printout, useful for checking the toner level and general print quality. The printout from the Apple LaserWriter also lets you know how many pages have been printed on that machine. If you don't want to waste that paper and toner every time the printer is turned on, then simply pull out the paper tray just before you switch it on. After a minute or two you can put the tray back in and begin printing.

Printers: Laser printers, Quickdraw printers, and PostScript imagesetters

18.5 Printers can be divided into three categories, each providing a different level of quality: PostScript laser printers, Quickdraw printers, and PostScript imagesetters.

18.6 PostScript laser printers, such as the Apple LaserWriter, TI OmniLaser, or QMS-PS, read **PostScript,** a page-description language. The visual images you see on the screen are sent to the printer in the Post-Script language. The printer interprets the information and creates the images on "plain paper" in resolutions of 300 to 600 dots per inch. This resolution is perfectly adequate for many publications, especially if you use smooth (not glossy) paper that has been specially formulated for laser printers. To prevent text from looking heavy and to keep the small areas (called "counters," such as inside the letter *e*) from filling in, keep the toner level down to the minimum necessary for good blacks.

18.7 QuickDraw printers, such as the Apple ImageWriter, Apple LaserWriter SC, or the HP DeskWriter, use the Mac's own **QuickDraw** drawing language to create the printed pages. Their resolution is generally between 72 and 300 dots per inch. The different printers can vary widely in what they require from a font in order to print text; you need to check your printer documentation.

18.8 Because QuickDraw printers cannot read PostScript, they cannot print EPS graphics very well, if at all (Encapsulated PostScript graphics; 9.29–9.35). They can usually print the PICT screen representation of an EPS image, though (9.30–9.31). It is up to you to decide whether the image quality of this version is satisfactory for your publication.

18.9 PostScript imagesetters, such as the Linotronic 300, Compugraphic 9700, or Varityper 4300P, read PostScript and print at resolutions of between 1000 and 2540 dots per inch. They use "resin-coated" paper, as traditional typesetters do, as opposed to the "plain paper" that is used by personal laser printers. Besides providing the best possible quality for text and graphics, output on resin-coated paper is much more durable if you are going to paste-up with rubber cement or wax.

18.10 Imagesetters are found in **service bureaus.** You can take your disk to a service bureau, leave it there for a few hours or overnight, and then return later and pick up your finished publication pages. Or you can send your file over a modem. Please see 18.122–18.133 for tips on how to prepare your publication for a service bureau.

EPS graphic printed on an Apple LaserWriter, 300 dpi. *EPS graphic printed on an HP DeskWriter, 300 dpi.*

EPS graphic printed on a Linotronic, 1270 dpi.

Illustrations by Tuan Pham

APDs  LaserWriter II NT.apd

18.11 An APD is an **Aldus Printer Description** file. Each printer must have its own APD, which looks (to mortals) like a text document. It is. It contains information about the printer that PageMaker reads before it sends the publication over to be printed (FreeHand and PrePrint read these same APDs). This information tells PageMaker such things as the name of the printer model, the paper sizes that particular printer can handle, the image area for each paper size, the paper trays that are available, the fonts that are resident (18.38–18.40) in the printer, and any other special features or options.

18.12 You can only print to printers whose APD is in the APD folder* (in the Aldus folder, which is in the System folder). The APD folder was created when you installed PageMaker. If you need to add an APD to the folder, see 18.168. Be sure to add the APD for the printer your service bureau uses. Without the APD, you will not see the printer listed in the "Print to" dialog box, and thus you will not be able to magic-resize to its resolution (9.11–9.13), or print to disk using its specifications (18.134–18.139).

If there is no APD for your printer, try using the "General" APD.

Before you print: Chooser

18.13 If you are going to print directly from your computer to the printer, you need to go to **Chooser** (from the Apple menu) before the very first time you print to that printer, or each time you switch printers. In the "Chooser" dialog box, click once on the printer icon (only those printers whose icons are in your System folder will appear here). Then click on its name in the list box on the right (with some printers, the name will be visible only if the printer is turned on). Close it by clicking in its close box (upper left). See 18.157 details.

The Chooser dialog box (actually, it's a window) from the Apple menu.

18.14 You need a System file printer icon (as shown in the Chooser, above) for each printer you are *connected* to. The icon must be in the System folder. You find printer icons on the disks that come with your printer.

You should have an APD file for each printer you may ever want to print to, *even if you are not connected to it.* The APD file must be in the APD folder (18.12).

Print spoolers

18.15 A **print spooler** is a software program that allows you to work on the screen while the job is printing.

18.16 Normally when you tell PageMaker to print, the Mac sends the information to the printer at a fairly rapid rate, but the printer processes the information at a much slower rate than it is received, thus tying up your screen while it figures out how to produce the page. If you use a spooler, the information goes to the spooler, which takes care of funneling the information to the printer at the printer's slower speed, and you get your screen back much faster.

18.17 There are two basic kinds of spoolers: computer-resident spoolers, which are installed in your System folder; or network spoolers, which run on separate machines.

18.18 Apple's "Background Printing" computer-resident spooler works only with MultiFinder, the Apple driver (18.20–18.28), and laser printers. Click the button in the "Chooser" to turn it on.

18.19 The Aldus driver works very well with network spoolers, which have their own icon in "Chooser." In the "Chooser," select the spooler icon instead of the printer icon.

Prep files, the Apple driver, and the Aldus driver

18.20 All Macintosh programs use a file called the **Apple driver** to send their pages to a printer. The Apple driver uses a printer preparation file for PostScript printers, called **Laser Prep,** which contains PostScript routines to tell the printer how to do things. You have probably seen the Laser Prep icon in your System folder.

Laser Prep

18.21 Well, Aldus wasn't happy with the way the Apple driver dealt with printing PageMaker documents on some of the PostScript printers, so Aldus invented its own driver: the **Aldus driver.** The Aldus driver is contained within PageMaker and uses its own prep file, called **Aldus Prep** (which you have also probably seen in your System folder). It is only used with Post-Script printers.

Aldus Prep

18.22 A word about **prep files** before we move on to drivers: Each driver sends its own prep file to the printer with the first printed job of the day. The prep file stays in the printer's memory until the printer is turned off. If the printer will be doing jobs for several Macintosh applications during the day, including PageMaker, then both the Aldus Prep and the Laser Prep will be taking up space. If insufficient memory is a problem, you may want to consider using the Apple driver to print PageMaker (18.25), so there will be only one resident prep file.

18.23 Also, Aldus Prep is revised every time PageMaker is revised. As usual, newer versions will support older versions, but not vice versa. If several different people are using several different versions of Aldus Prep with the same printer, you will get the message, before printing, that the printer is being "re-initialized." To avoid this, make sure every user has *only* the latest version of Aldus Prep in their System folder (find and trash all other versions; see 18.169).

18.24 Back to **drivers:** When you choose to print from PageMaker, the default driver is the Aldus driver *if a PostScript printer has been selected in the Chooser (18.6; 18.13–18.14).* If a non-PostScript printer (18.7) has been selected in the Chooser, you will automatically print with the Apple driver.

18.25 If a PostScript printer is selected in Chooser, but **you want to print with the Apple driver,** you must hold the Option key down while you choose "Print..." from the File menu (see 18.100–18.121).

18.26 Each driver has its own set of dialog boxes and options, all of which are explained in detail in this section. Each driver also has some advantages over the other, so the one you choose may depend on your job. Check out the chart on the next page to decide when you may be better off using either one.

18.27 If you have trouble printing a publication with the Aldus driver, try printing it with the Apple driver. One never knows. Also check out the trouble-shooting techniques, 18.170–18.172.

Advantages and disadvantages of the different drivers

18.28

	Downloadable fonts	APDs	Magic-resizing	Printing to disk	Print spooling	Printer memory
	18.41–18.55	18.11–18.12	9.11–9.13; 9.103	18.134–18.156	18.15–18.19	18.22; 18.38
Aldus driver	The Aldus driver leaves the downloaded font in the printer's memory in case you need it later. It will remove a font from memory when it needs the room to download a new one.	The Aldus driver can take advantage of any special features or capabilities of a printer by reading its APD.	The Aldus driver can change the resolution of bitmapped graphics to match the selected printer's resolution.	The Aldus driver is easier to use and is more consistent when printing files to disk.	You cannot use Apple's back-ground print spooler with the Aldus driver. However, the Aldus driver supports most network spoolers.	If you are printing only PageMaker files, the Aldus driver won't affect the memory.
Apple driver	If you check the "Unlimited fonts" option, the Apple driver downloads a font to create some text, then erases that font, downloads the next font, erases it, etc. This slows printing considerably.\n\nIf the "Unlimited fonts" option is not checked, the fonts are never erased and the print job will fail if the memory gets full.	The Apple driver does not read APDs.	Using the Apple driver, magic-resizing defaults to 300 dots per inch, no matter which printer is selected.	The support for printing to disk is not as good with the Apple driver. You can create a Normal file, but you cannot make an EPS file or separations.	The Apple driver provides better support for computer-resident print spoolers, especially Apple's own background spooler.	If you are printing from other Mac applications, both Laser prep and Aldus prep will be lodged in the printer's memory. To free up memory, use the Apple driver so only the Laser prep will be stored.

Fonts: Bitmapped and outline; screen and printer; resident and downloadable

18.29 The subject of fonts (or typefaces), on the Mac can be as confusing to people with a background in typography as it is to people with no type background. On these few pages is a brief synopsis of the font technology that you really need to know to work effectively in PageMaker. If you want to go beyond the basics, *The Macintosh Font Book* by Erfert Fenton is an excellent source of in-depth information.

18.30 There are two kinds of type formats for printing: **bitmapped** and **outline.**

18.31 **Bitmapped fonts** are created using the QuickDraw display language. They are built out of the little dots on the screen, and are designed to take advantage of the 72-dot-per-inch screen resolution. Bit-mapped fonts are always *(well, there are a couple of rare exceptions)* named for a city: Geneva, New York, Monaco, Athens, Cairo, etc., are all bitmapped fonts. Bitmapped fonts will look good on the screen if you use a size that is installed in your System (indicated by the outlined size in the menu; 3.141).

18.32 **Never use a font with a city name** unless you are printing to a QuickDraw printer. Laser printers and imagesetters cannot read bitmapped fonts. They will make substitutions for some fonts (18.84–18.85), freak out at others, and provide smoothed-out bitmaps for the lucky ones. Service bureaus will not be happy if you provide them with files that include bitmapped fonts.

18.33 **Outline fonts,** often called Post-Script fonts, have been designed with math-ematical formulas written in the PostScript language, rather than with little square dots. Reading the formula, any PostScript printer can create the fonts and scale them to any size and any resolution. They won't look as good on your screen (unless you are using Adobe Type Manager) because they are not built around the dots, but they will print beautifully. Outline fonts are never *(well, there are a couple of rare exceptions)* named for a city: Avant Garde, Bookman, Helvetica, Times, etc., are all outline fonts.

18.34 Outline fonts are actually made up of two parts: One part is a **screen font** that is actually *(now, don't get confused!)* a *bitmapped* version of the outline font. The *computer* uses the screen font to display the type on the screen (see 18.35). The Other part of an outline font is the **printer font,** which is the technical data that the *PostScript printer* uses to print the typeface on the page (see 18.36).

18.35 The **screen font** is what you see on the screen; it's the bitmapped portion of the outline font that the *computer* reads. Screen fonts are bitmapped because they must be represented with the dots on the screen. Even though they are just a visual represen-tation of the outline font that will actually print on your page, you must have the bit-mapped screen font installed to use the outline font for printing.

Screen fonts must be installed into your System using the Font/DA Mover. (See *The Little Mac Book* to learn how to use the Font/DA Mover.) Screen fonts reside in little suitcases with the letter A on them (see below); you can't really *see* the font itself.

ClassicText

*A **bitmapped** font (18.31) is stored in a "suitcase." Every **outline** font (18.33) has a corresponding bitmapped, or screen font, also stored in a suitcase. Some people inter-change the terms* bitmapped *and* screen *fonts. It's a tricky distinction.*

Fonts —*continued*

18.36 The **printer font** is the portion of the outline font that the *PostScript printer* reads in order to print the type on the page. Printer fonts have their own icons, and each font vendor's icon looks different:

Printer font:	Goudy	TypoUpr	BrushScr
Vendor:	*Adobe*	*Bitstream*	*LaserMaster*

18.37 Printer font icons must be stored directly in the System folder. They cannot be inside a folder within the System folder. When you choose to print, PageMaker gets the outline information and **downloads** it into the printer so the printer knows how to create the font.

18.38 If PageMaker needs to download outline printer fonts into the printer, do you wonder why you don't see printer font icons in your System folder for Times, Palatino, Bookman, etc.—all the fonts that are standard on the Apple LaserWriter (Plus and above)? It's because most laser printers have a *read-only memory* (ROM) that has certain fonts **resident** in it. The outline information for those fonts is stored in a chip in the printer so the printer can use them whenever it likes.

These fonts are **resident:** Avant Garde, Bookman, Helvetica, New Helvetica Narrow, Palatino, Times, Symbol, Courier, Zapf Chancery, and Zapf Dingbats. All other outline fonts are termed **downloadable,** and you must buy them from a font vendor.

18.39 Now, these names (Times, Palatino, Garamond, etc.) are actually *family* names; they denote a group of *related* fonts. The relations are variations such as Roman, Italic, Bold, Bold Italic, etc. Technically, each relation is a separate font; they have been completely redesigned, and they each have their own outline information. Italic is not simply slanted type. Notice the difference between the roman (straight, upright) letters and the corresponding italic letters in the same family: a *a* f *f* g *g*.

18.40 When you select *bitmapped* text (like Geneva) and hit the keyboard command to italicize it, the Mac just slants the type. But when you select *outline* text (like Times) and italicize it, the Mac actually switches to the italic *font*. Using the type style menu and the keyboard to create the style variations works fine for the *resident* fonts because all the information for printing them is in the printer's ROM.

18.41 When you buy and install **downloadable** fonts, though, you cannot use the keyboard or menu commands under "Type style" to change the style *(well, you can on some of them, but don't count on it)*. For example, if you buy the Goudy family you will get a disk with four printer icons (one each for the Roman, Italic, Bold, and Bold Italic fonts) and a suitcase containing the four corresponding screen fonts. When you use Goudy and you want an italic word, *you must choose the font Goudy Italic from the font menu.*

18.42 If you have a lot of downloadable fonts, your font menu becomes long and unwieldly. Plus there is a limit to the number of fonts the System will allow. If you get to that point, you really must invest in a font handler utility, such as Suitcase II™ (Fifth Generation Software) or Master Juggler™ (AlSoft, Inc.). These utilities allow you to organize and consolidate your font menu by families, thus enabling you to use the "Type style" menu or keyboard shortcuts to change styles. They also resolve font conflicts—if you have a lot of fonts, you run the considerable risk of the fonts having mistaken identity crises: Korinna thinks it is Lubalin Graph, etc.

Downloading the downloadables

18.43 If you never use any other fonts except the standard residents (18.38), you needn't bother reading these two pages, except for this note: if you use only the resident fonts, your work will scream THIS WAS DONE ON A MACINTOSH! That's perfectly okay for exams you are giving to your high school geography class, for English term papers, letters to the folks back home, recipes for the bridge club, or any of the wonderful, myriad uses we all have for the Mac. Many, many people need never go beyond Times and Helvetica. However, if you want to give your work a professional, creative appearance, you really should invest in downloadable fonts. You also should read *The Mac is not a typewriter* or your work will still scream of the Mac.

18.44 You know what downloadable fonts are (18.33–18.37). Now you need to know how PageMaker and the printer deal with them so you can work most efficiently. Downloadable fonts have to be downloaded into the printer's *random-access memory* (RAM). Resident fonts, remember, are stored in the printer's ROM, which is *permanent* (18.38–18.40). RAM is a *temporary* storage place that is emptied whenever you turn off the power.

18.45 Font downloading is only necessary when you print to a PostScript printer (18.5–18.10). Other printers just print the bitmapped screen fonts or their own specially-developed printer fonts. For those printers, the Adobe Type Manager program (ATM, from Adobe, Inc.) can significantly improve the look of the printed pages, as well as how the type looks on the screen.

18.46 Font downloading can be handled **automatically,** which is probably what has been happening all this time. If your printer font icons are in your System folder, then when you choose to print using the Aldus driver (simply by choosing "Print..." from the File menu; 18.158), PageMaker goes into the System folder, gets the font, and downloads it into the printer's memory. If the memory gets full because you used a lot of fonts in your publication, PageMaker has to remove a font (flush it from memory) to make room for the new one.

18.47 Automatic downloading with the Aldus driver works quite well, particularly if your printer has two or three megabytes of RAM available and your publication doesn't use more than three or four fonts. *Remember,* Goudy is one font, Goudy Italic is another font, Goudy Bold is another font, etc. etc. etc. However, if your printer has only 1 or 1.5 megs of RAM, then PageMaker has to keep flushing out one face and downloading another and it can get quite boring, as well as time-consuming.

18.48 If you use the Apple driver (by holding the Option key as you choose "Print..." from the File menu; 18.24–18.25), you have an option of "Unlimited downloadable fonts" (18.105). If you check it, the Apple driver will erase each font from memory before downloading the next one. But that means every time it comes across an italic word or a Zapf Dingbat or a bold subhead, etc., the existing font is flushed and the new one is loaded. This is *really* boring.

18.49 However, if you do *not* check that "Unlimited fonts" box, then the Apple driver never erases the fonts from memory. When the memory gets full (which it will do if there are more than three or four fonts or if it's a long publication) the print job will just go belly-up. Of course, the more RAM you have, the less this is a problem.

Downloading —*continued*

18.50 If you have had no trouble with automatic downloading and you don't find that it takes an interminable length of time, then you needn't worry about doing it any other way. You can stop reading this and go back to work. If, however, you would like to speed up the process, you can **manually download** the printer fonts. Read on.

18.51 When you buy downloadable fonts, the font vendor always sends you a *font downloader utility.* You just double-click on the downloader icon and it will walk you through the process. This is what the Adobe downloader looks like:

Font Downloader

18.52 If your printer memory is limited (which it probably is if you are having to manually download fonts), then make sure you turn off the printer, then turn it back on again just before you download. This empties the RAM so you will have the maximum space available. If other people are working on the same printer, be sure you ask before you turn off the printer in the middle of their job.

18.53 If the printer has only 1 or 1.5 megs of RAM, you can download only about three fonts (e.g., Goudy, Goudy Italic, Goudy Bold). You might be able to squeeze in a fourth (Goudy Bold Italic), but then you often won't have enough memory to print the publication. Download the font(s) your publication uses the most. As long as the printer font icons are in the System folder, PageMaker will be able to find and use the fonts that occur only occasionally.

18.54 Printer fonts that are manually downloaded are **temporary.** As soon as RAM is emptied (by turning off the printer, by a power failure, or by RAM getting too full, in which case the printer tells you to turn itself off and on), everything stored in RAM disappears. So tomorrow, after the publication gets proofed and all the errors show up, you must download the fonts again when you come in to make corrections. After a few weeks of trying to print complex jobs you will be ready to add more RAM to your printer.

18.55 There is one **permanent** way of downloading fonts to your printer, and that is buying a PostScript printer that allows you to connect a hard disk that holds all your downloadable fonts (printers such as the Apple LaserWriter II NTX, the GCC Business Laser Printer, or any imagesetter). Once on that special hard disk, all your fonts will act just like resident fonts (18.38–18.40).

My plan was to kiss her with every lip on my face.
Steve Martin, in Dead Men Don't Wear Plaid

18.56 "Print to" dialog box   *(from the File menu, choose "Print..." or press Command P; this is the Aldus driver print dialog box; see 18.57–18.58)*

18.57 If a Post-Script printer has been selected in "Chooser" (18.13–18.14), this is the dialog box you will see when you choose "Print..." from the File menu.

18.58 If a Quick-Draw printer (18.7) has been selected in "Chooser" or if you use the Apple driver by holding down the Option key when you choose "Print...," you will get a different series of dialog boxes; see pages 638–639.

See 18.72

See 18.62 | See 18.63

Hit the Return key to shortcut.

Press Command period to shortcut. **Canceling does not cancel any changes you made for "Printer" or "Paper."**

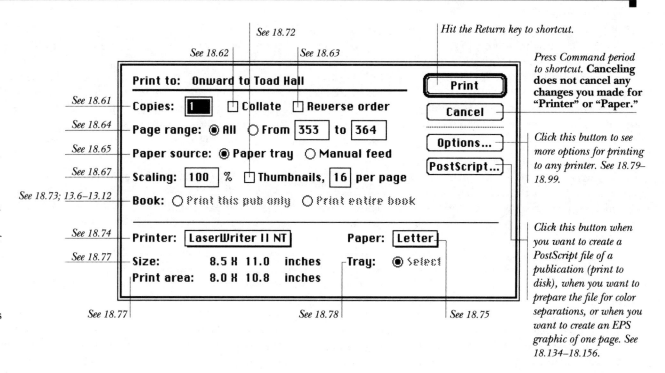

See 18.61
See 18.64
See 18.65
See 18.67
See 18.73; 13.6–13.12
See 18.74
See 18.77

Print to: Onward to Toad Hall

Copies: 1   ☐ Collate   ☐ Reverse order

Page range: ◉ All   ○ From 353 to 364

Paper source: ◉ Paper tray   ○ Manual feed

Scaling: 100 %   ☐ Thumbnails, 16 per page

Book: ○ Print this pub only   ○ Print entire book

Printer: LaserWriter II NT   **Paper:** Letter

Size: 8.5 H 11.0   inches   **Tray:** ◉ Select
Print area: 8.0 H 10.8   inches

[Print]
[Cancel]
[Options...]
[PostScript...]

Click this button to see more options for printing to any printer. See 18.79–18.99.

Click this button when you want to create a PostScript file of a publication (print to disk), when you want to prepare the file for color separations, or when you want to create an EPS graphic of one page. See 18.134–18.156.

See 18.77 | See 18.78 | See 18.75

"Print to" specifications

18.59 First of all, take notice that the name of the designated printer is showing at the top of the dialog box, after "Print to." Make sure that it's the correct printer (in the example on the previous page, the name of my printer is "Onward to Toad Hall").

18.60 All specifications you select in this dialog box will remain selected for this publication until you choose to change them (unless you cancel before the print job is complete).

After your first printing, you can buzz into your next printing in the same publication by hitting Command P, then instantly hitting the Return key. You won't even see the dialog box. If you need to specify a range of pages, do this: Press Command P; hit Tab; type the number of the first page to print; hit Tab; type the number of the last page to print; hit Return. It's very satisfying when you can do it so fast the dialog box doesn't even appear.

18.61 Copies: In this little edit box, type the number of copies of each page that you want to come out of your printer. You can enter a value up to 100 copies, but if you need more than a few copies it is much more cost-effective and efficient to print just one original and then duplicate the original on a copy machine.

18.62 Collate: Check this box if you are making more than one copy of multiple pages and you want the printer to collate the pages for you. To collate a publication, though, the printer has to build a page, print it, build the next page, print it, etc., for the entire publication, then repeat the process for the next collated collection. *Without* collating, the printer builds the page, then prints the number of desired copies; then it builds the next page and prints those. Checking the collate button will slow down printing significantly. If you do collate, make sure you know which order your designated printer will print: last page first, or first page last, and check the "Reverse order" button accordingly.

18.63 Reverse order: The printer's APD (18.11–18.12) determines in which order the pages are printed—back to front or front to back. Whichever order your printer normally prints, checking this button will reverse it.

18.64 Page range: To print just a few select pages, type in the range of page numbers *including* the pages to print. If you click the "All" button to print every page in the publication, the numbers for the full page range will be filled in for you.

18.65 Paper source: Obviously, if you're printing from a paper tray, you want to leave "Paper tray" selected. If you want to manually feed in odd-sized paper, envelopes, card stock, etc., you can click "Manual feed," but I have never found the need to actually select the button. If the printer finds paper in the manual feed tray, it takes *that* paper first, rather than the paper that is in the paper tray itself. If you are feeding paper or envelopes in one at a time, be sure to wait exactly three seconds between the time the one in front disappears and the time you feed in the next one. It takes a little bit of practice to get the timing just right. If you will be using legal-sized paper occasionally, you really don't need to buy a separate paper tray for it—just choose "Legal" in the "Paper" option (18.75) and feed the pages in manually.

—continued

"Print to" specifications —*continued*

18.66 "Card stock" is paper that is heavier than normal; it often has problems wrapping around the drum as it goes through the printer. Most printers have a tray that opens out the back end, especially made to solve that problem. With that tray open, the paper rolls right on through, flat, out into the flat tray (envelopes and transparencies work well with the back end open, also). Note that this will reverse the order, though! Pages that would otherwise wrap around the drum and come out face down on the bottom of the pile, will now come out face up on the bottom of the pile.

18.67 Scaling: You can enter a value from 25 to 1000 (in 1% increments) to reduce or enlarge the printed pages. If a page is **reduced** it will be centered on the paper, in which case you should choose to show the "Crop marks" (18.79). If you don't show the crop marks, you won't know where the boundaries of the reduced page are (18.82).

18.68 If you **enlarge the page** and it exceeds the width or depth of the paper size, you may need to "Tile" in order to print all of the image. The page will be printed

onto several sheets of paper that you will need to paste together (under "Options..."; see 18.90–18.93). If you only need to **enlarge a portion** of the page and don't care about printing the rest of it, you still might want to read the tiling information to make sure that the image you want enlarged will show up on the paper when you print.

18.69 If you only want to **enlarge a portion** and don't want to bother tiling, place the image in the center of the page.

18.70 If you want to fit a single, tabloid-sized page onto a letter-sized piece of paper, scale it to 62 percent. To fit a tabloid-sized page onto legal paper, scale it to 80 percent.

18.71 Some people like to print their pages slightly enlarged, say 125 percent, and then have the commercial press reduce the pages when they make the printing plates for reproduction. This gives the effect of a higher resolution.

18.72 Thumbnails: Thumbnails are small, "thumbnail"-sized reproductions of the pages, useful for viewing the layout of the overall project to check for consistency, concept, missing elements, etc. You can ask for anywhere from 1 to 64 thumbnails per

page, bearing in mind that the size of the thumbnail will depend on how many you request per page (the fewer the number, the larger the images); if you request 16 per page, but you only print 4 pages, the 4 thumbnails will be as small as if there were 16. Each thumbnail representation of a page is numbered for you and has a nice border with a drop-shadow to define it. Thumbnails are really a neat way to view your project.

PageMaker will print all the pages in the publication, or just the range you specify. Blank pages will be included, even if you don't check that box (18.94). It takes just as long to print thumbnails as it does to print full-sized pages!

18.73 Book: This option is only available if there is a Book List (13.6–13.12) in *this* publication. If you check the button "Print this pub only," printing will proceed as usual. If you check "Print entire book," every publication that is listed in the book list will print, in the order you have arranged. You will only be allowed to make one copy, and certain options will not be available to you. See Section 13 on Book Publications for more in-depth information on this feature (13.25–13.27 for printing a whole book).

"Print to" specifications —continued

18.74 Printer: If you press in the box next to "Printer" you get the pop-up menu listing all the printers whose APDs are in the APD folder (18.11–18.12). The printer you choose from this menu affects some of the other options, such as the print area or the paper sizes available. Typically you choose the same printer here that you have selected in the "Chooser," unless you are setting up the "Print to" dialog box for magic-resizing (9.11–9.13) or for remote printing at a service bureau (18.161–18.162).

```
Printer: │LaserWriter II NT│      Paper: │✓Letter        │
                                          │ Lettersmall   │
Size:      8.5 H 11.0  inches     Tray:   │ A4            │
Print area: 8.0 H 10.8  inches            │ A4small       │
                                          │ B5            │
                                          │ Legal         │
```

```
Printer: │Linotronic 100/300│     Paper: │✓Letter         │
                                          │ LetterExtra    │
Size:      8.5 H 11.0  inches     Tray:   │ A4             │
Print area: 8.5 H 11.0  inches            │ A4Extra        │
                                          │ Legal          │
                                          │ LegalExtra     │
                                          │ A3             │
                                          │ Tabloid        │
                                          │ TabloidExtra   │
                                          │ LetterTransverse│
                                          │ A4Transverse   │
```

Notice how the relative print area and the possible paper sizes change with the different printers.

18.75 Paper: This pop-up menu allows you to choose the paper size you want to print onto. Notice in 18.74 that the choices of size depend on the printer selected. Also notice that when you choose a paper, its actual size is indicated on the bottom left (18.74–18.77). This *paper size* is different than the *page size* you specified in the "Page setup" dialog box. Whatever *page size* you set up will be centered on the *paper size* you select here. The unit of measure you see here is based on the measurement system you chose in the "Preferences" dialog box (1.210–1.2111).

18.76 Imagesetters don't use single sheets of paper—they print onto *rolls* of resin-coated paper. If you are printing to an imagesetter using the "Tall" orientation (18.96) for letter-sized pages or smaller, you can get more pages in less space on the roll if you choose the paper size option "Letter transverse." This makes the pages print perpendicular to the roll, wasting much less paper. ***Check with your service bureau, though, before you change any of the print options for an imagesetter!*** *(service bureau tips: 18.122–18.133)*

18.77 Size and **Print area** tell you the exact *size* of the paper you selected in the "paper" pop-up menu, and the *area that can actually be printed* for that paper in that printer. Notice in 18.74 that the print area per letter size varies between the LaserWriter and the Linotronic. Most laser printers cannot print all the way out to the edge of the paper, while imagesetters, because they print on a roll, can use the entire space, even beyond the actual image area specified. See 18.159 for a nice trick for getting things printed on the sheet, but outside the actual page size.

18.78 Tray: Depending on the APD you have selected, you may have options for selecting another paper tray, such as Legal, Upper, or Lower. If there are no options, the choice is usually a gray "Select." If you have just a few legal-sized pages to print, you really needn't change paper trays: simply slip the paper into the manual feed tray of the tray that is already in. You don't even need to choose "Manual feed" because the printer takes a page from the manual feed first.

18.79 "Aldus print options" dialog box *(from the File menu, choose "Print..."; click on the "Options" button)*

See 18.86

See 18.82–18.83

Hit Return to shortcut OK; this takes you back to the "Print to" dialog box. Press Option Return to OK both this dialog box and the Print dialog box.

Aldus print options

OK

Cancel

As usual, Command Period will shortcut this button. Changes will not be saved.

See 18.81 ☐ **Proof print**   ☒ **Crop marks**

See 18.84 ☐ **Substitute fonts**   ☐ **Smooth**

See 18.87 ☐ **Spot color overlays:** [All colors]   *See 18.87*

See 18.88–18.89 ☐ **Knockouts**

See 18.90–18.93 ☐ **Tile:** ◉ Manual   ○ Auto overlap [0.65] **inches**   *See 18.90–18.93*

See 18.94 ☐ **Print blank pages**

See 18.95 **Even/odd pages:** ◉ **Both** ○ **Even** ○ **Odd**

See 18.96 **Orientation:** ○ **Tall** ◉ **Wide** ┌**Image:** ☐ Invert ☐ Mirror

See 18.97–18.99

18.80 If you click OK in this dialog box and then Cancel the "Print to" dialog box, any changes you made here will also be canceled.

If you click OK in this dialog box, then click OK to print in the "Print to" dialog box, any changes you made here will stay with the publication for any subsequent printing (as long as you don't cancel the printing before it's finished).

"Aldus print options" specifications

18.81 Proof print: With this option checked, only the text prints. Graphics show up as boxes with Xs slashed through them. If your publication contains a lot of graphics but you just want to proofread the text, check "Proof print" to speed up the printing process immensely.

18.82 Crop marks: If the *page size* you defined in the "Page setup" dialog box (from the File menu) is smaller than the *paper size* it will be printed on, your page will be centered on the paper when it is printed (**b**). Since the page boundaries that you see on the screen don't show up on the paper when you print, you have no way of knowing where your actual page begins and ends. For instance, in the example to the right (**b**), I specified a 4" x 6" *page setup.* It was printed on an 8.5 x 11 *page,* but I can't tell where my 4 x 6 space really is.

But when I chose "Crop marks," the 8.5 x 11 paper came out of the printer with marks defining that 4" x 6" boundary (**c**).

18.83 Crop marks will only appear on the printout if the boundary of the specified *page size* is at least ½ inch smaller than the *paper size.*

a) *The 4x6 page on the screen.*

b) *The 4x6 page printed on 8.5x11 paper with no crop marks.*

c) *The 4x6 page printed on 8.5x11 paper with crop marks.*

18.84 Substitute fonts: You will never need to use this option because you know better than to use city-named fonts (18.31–18.32) in any publication that will be printed on a PostScript printer. If you do happen to check it, then when PageMaker finds the font New York she will substitute Times for it (do you see the intellectual connection between New York and [The] Times?). When Page-Maker finds Geneva, she will substitute Helvetica (Helvetica was named after the country Confederatio Helvetia, or Switzer-land). And Monaco gets turned into Courier (if anyone has figured out the *intellectual* connection in the names, please let me know).

18.85 Actually, any other font for which PageMaker can't find a corresponding *printer* font (18.33–18.36) will be turned into Courier (which looks and spaces like a type-writer). No matter what kind of font Page-Maker substitutes (or even if you *don't* check the "Substitute fonts" box and *nothing* gets substituted), if you don't have the correct printer fonts your publication is going to look different than you expect. Some of your text will either turn into Courier or it will turn into gibberish because there is no printer font with which to create it.

"Aldus print options" specifications —*continued*

18.86 Smooth: This option smooths the edges of bitmapped, paint-type graphics and bitmapped fonts. This does not necessarily improve the image, and it definitely slows down the printing speed.

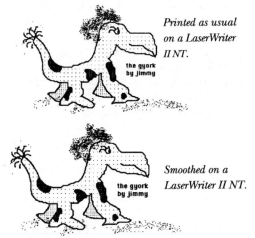

Printed as usual on a LaserWriter II NT.

the gyork by jimmy

Smoothed on a LaserWriter II NT.

the gyork by jimmy

18.87 Spot color overlays: You may have applied color to text or (14.102–14.105). If so, you can check this box (and use the sub-menu to its right) to have each tagged color output on a separate page. See 14.10–14.15 for info on multi-color printing; 14.16–14.22 for info on overlays; 14.107 for the steps to print spot color overlays.

18.88 Knockouts: If you checked "Spot color overlays," you then have the option to check "Knockouts." If the objects that are tagged with spot color do not touch any other objects of a *different* color on the page, then you don't need to worry about knockouts. If two different colors are overlapping, though, you will get a third color where they overlap. For instance, if you have a fat red line overlapping a blue circle, the line will be purple where it overlaps.

18.89 But often you don't want that third color—you want the red line to stay red as it crosses the blue circle. That's when you use "Knockout": the blue layer will then print with a blank area in the exact space where that fat red line overlaps the blue circle. It leaves you no *trap line,* though; the two images will be perfectly abutted. For greater details on trapping and knockouts, see Section 14 on Color (14.24–14.30).

18.90 Tile: You have to use this option when the *page size* of your publication is greater than the *paper size* that comes out of your printer, or if you *scale* the page to print larger (18.67–18.69). For instance, if you are creating a tabloid-sized newsletter (11" x 17") and printing to an Apple Laser-Writer, you must *tile* in order to print each 11 x 17 page. The 11 x 17 page will be divided into equal sections, and PageMaker will print each section on a separate 8.5 x 11 piece of paper. After the pages come out of the printer, you need to manually *(aack—manually?)* piece the sections together to create one 11 x 17 page. Different printers can accommodate different paper sizes.

18.91 When you print with the "Tile" option and the **Auto overlap __ inches** button checked, PageMaker starts printing at the upper left corner of the publication page, allowing space on the paper for crop marks. Each page is overlapped by the amount you enter in the "Auto overlap" edit box. The overlap makes it possible for you to paste the pieces together precisely (on a light table, paste one page over the other, exactly aligning what is visible on the overlap; trim the excess).

"Aldus print options" specifications —continued

18.92 Manual: The "Manual" button in the "Tile" option causes the page to print very differently than does "Auto." With "Manual" the printer will print *one* sheet of paper, no matter what the page size. The upper left corner of the page will begin wherever the *zero point* (1.43; 1.69–1.71) is located on the screen. It will *literally* begin at that corner, which means a certain portion of the image may not print, as most laser printers cannot print all the way to the edge of the paper. When you set the zero point for manual tiling, be sure to allow space for that non-printing area. Manual tiling ignores any amount that may be entered in the "Auto overlap" edit box.

18.93 Manual tiling is a great way to reprint just certain sections of that larger page size, since with *Auto* tiling you get every section, even if some are blank, whether you want them or not. It's also great for those times when you want to enlarge just a portion of a page, like perhaps a graphic image (18.67–18.69).

18.94 Print blank pages: This is a nice feature. Unless you put a check in this box, PageMaker will not print any blank pages in the publication. "Blank" means *really* blank: master page items count as "something" on the page, as do white, "invisible" boxes or reverse lines.

18.95 Even/odd pages: What a great little addition to PageMaker! This allows you to print on both sides of the laser printed page. First print the **even**-numbered pages. Then take those pages, turn them around, put them back in the printer tray, and print the **odd**-numbered pages. The exact way you place them back into the paper tray depends entirely on your printer. You will probably need to experiment on the first few pages; when you figure it out, write it down so you don't have to figure it out all over again next time. I wish I had done that. Printing odd or even pages prints all blank pages also, whether there is a check in that option or not. You cannot print odd or even pages if either "Thumbnails," "Tile," or "Spot color overlays" is selected.

18.96 Orientation: "Tall" and "Wide" refer to the way the information is printed on the page; "Tall" corresponds to "portrait" mode (taller than it is wide), and "Wide" corresponds to "landscape" mode (wider than it is tall). Many of us think of Wide as "sideways."

Your choice of printing orientation in this dialog box should usually match the orientation you chose in the "Page setup" dialog box. If the choices do not match, the orientation checked in the "Print to" dialog box will take precedence over the page setup.

—continued

"Aldus print options" specifications —*continued*

18.97 Image: You will only have the "Image" choices available if you have first checked the "Spot color overlays" box. You won't often find a need for either "Mirror" or "Invert" when printing to a laser printer; those options are designed for printing to film on an imagesetter according to the specifications of the commercial press that will be reproducing the job.

Printed as a normal image.

18.98 Invert: If you check this box, the printer will print the reverse of what you see on the screen: what is white will be black, and what is black will be white (that's a lot of toner if you're printing to a laser printer). This creates a "negative" image.

Printed as an inverted image.

18.99 Mirror: If you check this box, the page will be printed "backwards," as if you were looking at it in a mirror. If you are ordering output on film to take to your commercial press, the press will ask that the film negs be "right reading emulsion up" or "right reading emulsion down." Every piece of film has two sides; only one side has emulsion on it. Depending on the press, they may need to be able to read the film's image the "right" way (not backwards) while the emulsion side of the film is facing *down*. Or they may need to read it "right" if the emulsion is facing *up*. Whether the film can be read right with the emulsion up or down is directly connected to whether it is also "Inverted" or not. If you don't have a very clear idea of exactly what you need to specify in the "Image" department, call your service bureau. They may prefer to set the specifications themselves, anyway, if you just tell them the specs your commercial press has requested.

Mirrored image.   *Inverted and mirrored.*

etaoin shrdlu *(continued from page 225)*

Like everything else, the newspaper business has changed. It became a business. It used to be "the newspaper game," a term that made us feel better about our ridiculous wages. Who gets paid for having fun except ball-players and maybe some hookers? (Hookers are "turned out" and newspaper people are "broken in" but otherwise there isn't much difference, hence the term presstitute.) In the old days we pounded out the copy with two fingers and hollered "Boy!" to rush this hot stuff to the composing room. Today you yell "Boy!" and a girl arrives along with a member of the union grievance committee. It's silly to holler "Person!" so nobody yells any more.

Gone are the magnificent men on their Linotype machines, gone the galley proofs smelling of fresh ink, gone the paperweights with your name in 90-point type, the gift of a friendly printer. Gone the "Boy!"s of yesterday, gone with the wind, gone with the Winchell, gone with the demon rewrite man with phone cradled to ear and cigaret burning his lips as he pounds out a perfect, tight, non-editable "new lede" (never "lead") on a fast-breaking story. Gone—yes, the very TYPEWRITERS.

When cold type replaced hot lead, the manual typewriter was doomed. The scanner—ours, at least—would "accept" only the IBM Selectric, which doesn't have keys that jam, like a proper typewriter, but a golfball device that runs back and forth like a mouse in a maze. Now, the Selectric is being phased out for VDTs, which is not police shorthand for someone with a social disease plus the shakes. The initials stand for Video Display Terminal.

Although I am generally spineless, I rose off my knees in protest at both the Selectric and the VDT. Old dog, new tricks and all that. Since I do use only two fingers while typing, the Selectric is too much machine for me, and the VDT is either above or below contempt, I forget which. I have thus been allowed to go on using my ancient and beloved Royal manual—metal, not plastic—and living in the past. I edit my copy with an Eagle 314, just as in the old days. I go on writing, and yelling "Boy!" as though it were still 1941. You may have noticed. Where have you gone, etaoin shrdlu? Operator, gimme rewrite! Stop the press—uh, scanner—I gotta story here that'll shake this old town right off its foundations. Boy! Boy? Uh . . .

Typewriter of the '50s

18.100 "Apple print options" dialog box *choose "Print..." from the File menu. Otherwise, just choose "Print..." from the File menu.)*

18.101 When you print using the Apple driver rather than the Aldus driver(18.20–18.28), you get a sequence of three dialog boxes. The actual dialog boxes you see on your screen may look different than the ones shown here, as they depend on the printer you are using.

18.102 Many of the items in these boxes are the same as in the Aldus driver, so many of the references will direct you back to descriptions in that section.

18.103 The first of the three dialog boxes displays the options that Aldus offers for PageMaker. The second dialog box displays the standard Apple page setup for your printer. The third dialog box is specific to your printer.

When you click OK you will get a dialog box for the page setup for your printer. The Apple LaserWriter page setup is shown on the next page.

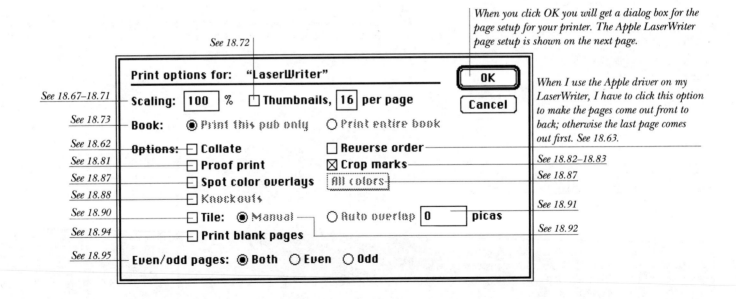

When I use the Apple driver on my LaserWriter, I have to click this option to make the pages come out front to back; otherwise the last page comes out first. See 18.63.

See 18.72

See 18.67–18.71

See 18.73

See 18.62

See 18.81

See 18.87

See 18.88

See 18.90

See 18.94

See 18.95

See 18.82–18.83

See 18.87

See 18.91

See 18.92

Print options for: "LaserWriter"

OK

Cancel

Scaling: 100 %   ☐ **Thumbnails,** 16 **per page**

Book: ● Print this pub only   ○ Print entire book

Options: ☐ **Collate**   ☐ **Reverse order**
☐ **Proof print**   ☒ **Crop marks**
☐ **Spot color overlays**   All colors
☐ **Knockouts**
☐ **Tile:** ● Manual   ○ Auto overlap   0 **picas**
☐ **Print blank pages**

Even/odd pages: ● **Both**   ○ **Even**   ○ **Odd**

The Apple driver print dialog boxes —*continued*

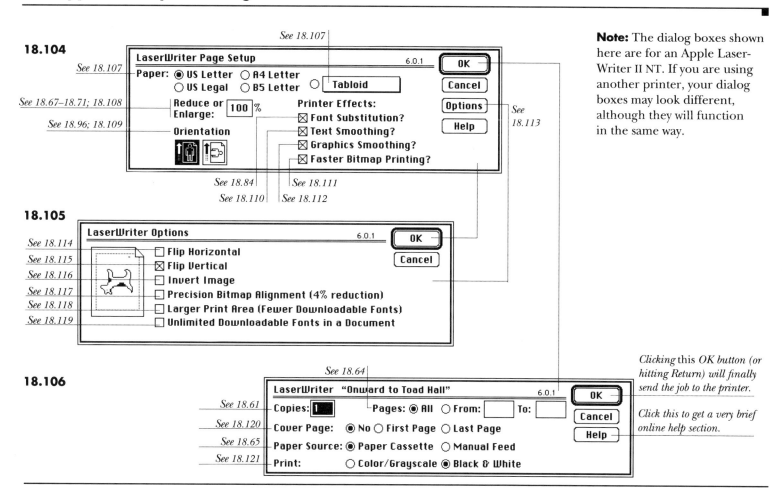

18.104

See 18.107

See 18.107

LaserWriter Page Setup   6.0.1

Paper: ◉ US Letter   ○ A4 Letter
       ○ US Legal   ○ B5 Letter   ○ ▢ Tabloid

See 18.67–18.71; 18.108

Reduce or ▢ 100 %
Enlarge:

See 18.96; 18.109

Orientation

Printer Effects:
☒ Font Substitution?
☒ Text Smoothing?
☒ Graphics Smoothing?
☒ Faster Bitmap Printing?

[OK]
[Cancel]
[Options] *See 18.113*
[Help]

See 18.84   *See 18.111*
See 18.110   *See 18.112*

18.105

See 18.114
See 18.115
See 18.116
See 18.117
See 18.118
See 18.119

LaserWriter Options   6.0.1

☐ Flip Horizontal
☒ Flip Vertical
☐ Invert Image
☐ Precision Bitmap Alignment (4% reduction)
☐ Larger Print Area (Fewer Downloadable Fonts)
☐ Unlimited Downloadable Fonts in a Document

[OK]
[Cancel]

18.106

See 18.64

LaserWriter "Onward to Toad Hall"   6.0.1

See 18.61   Copies: ▮1▮   Pages: ◉ All ○ From: ▢ To: ▢
See 18.120   Cover Page: ◉ No ○ First Page ○ Last Page
See 18.65   Paper Source: ◉ Paper Cassette ○ Manual Feed
See 18.121   Print: ○ Color/Grayscale ◉ Black & White

[OK]
[Cancel]
[Help]

Note: The dialog boxes shown here are for an Apple Laser-Writer II NT. If you are using another printer, your dialog boxes may look different, although they will function in the same way.

Clicking this OK button (or hitting Return) will finally send the job to the printer.

Click this to get a very brief online help section.

The Apple driver print specifications

18.107 Paper: This option is basically the same as the Aldus option. Your choices depend on the paper sizes your printer will support, including any page sizes in the submenu that you may or may not see immediately on your screen (like the one that displays "Tabloid" in the example on page 633).

18.108 Reduce or Enlarge: This option is the same as "Scaling" found in the first dialog box (18.100). Whatever you typed into "Scaling" will automatically appear in this box also. Whatever you type into this box will automatically appear in "Scaling." The most recently entered value is the one that will take precedence.

18.109 Orientation: This option is the same as in the Aldus dialog box, but instead of being named "Tall" or Wide" (18.96) the choices are represented by little pictures.

18.110 Text smoothing: With this box checked, the printer will smooth out the jagged edges of any bitmapped (city-named) fonts you may have accidentally used. This does slow down the printing. See 18.86.

18.111 Graphics smoothing: The printer will smooth out the jagged edges of any bitmapped graphics. This also slows down the printing. See 18.86.

18.112 Faster bitmap printing: This is supposed to make the printer print bit-mapped images faster. If you have trouble printing bitmaps, try turning this off.

18.113 Options: If you click this button, you get the "(Your Printer) Options" dialog box, which may look different than the one shown on the previous page. If you get the same dialog box as the example here, you'll notice as you click in the checkboxes that the little creature* gives you a visual indication of how each option will change the image. The options are cumulative; for instance, you can flip the image vertically and horizontally, then invert it and reduce it four percent.

That creature is Clarus, the official cowdog. He says "Moof."

18.114 Flip Horizontal: This makes the image turn around horizontally, exactly like the "Mirror" option when using the Aldus driver (18.97–18.99). Use it for the same purpose you use "Mirror."

18.115 Flip Vertical: This turns the image upside down, as shown in the example on page 639.

18.116 Invert Image: With this option checked, whatever is black on the screen will print as white, and whatever is white will print as black. See 18.98–18.99 for more details and a purpose.

The Apple "Print options" specifications —*continued*

18.117 Precision Bitmap Alignment:
If you check this option, the printed page will be reduced by four percent. This enhances the appearance of bitmapped graphic images.

18.118 Larger Print Area: With this option checked, the printer can print closer to the edges of the paper. However, it takes memory to do this, so with this checked you cannot store as many downloadable fonts (18.33–18.54) in the printer's memory. You have to decide what your priorities are.

18.119 Unlimited Downloadable Fonts in a Document: See the information on downloadable fonts in 18.43–18.55, especially 18.48–18.49, for an explanation of what this does and why you would or would not want to use it.

18.120 Cover page: If you check **No,** you won't get a cover sheet. If you check **First Page,** then *before* the rest of your publication prints you will get a cover page that labels and names the User, Application, Document, Date, Time, and Printer used. If you check **Last Page,** this cover page will print at the *end* of your publication. It's printed in the very trendy *(that's a joke)* Helvetica font.

18.121 Print: If you are printing color to a color PostScript printer, or if you are printing grayscale images on a monochrome PostScript printer, click the **Color/Grayscale** button. If you click the **Black & White** button, all PostScript printers will produce black-and-white pages. The printing will proceed faster using the "Black & White" option.

On with the dance!
No sleep til morn . . .
chase the glowing hours
with flying feet.
Lord Byron

Illustration by Michael Hawes
for The Tap Dance Studio

Using a service bureau

18.122 A **desktop publishing service bureau** is a new type of service, just invented in the last few years. Isn't it interesting— such dire predictions were made that the computer would put so many people out of work, and instead, an entire new industry was spawned, with jobs for everyone. Why, thousands of people make a living just building booths for all the computer trade shows.

18.123 A service bureau is where you take your publication on a disk (or send it by modem) when you want a higher quality output than your personal laser printer or QuickDraw printer can provide. Service bureaus use **imagesetters** (18.9–18.10) that output your pages onto resin-coated paper at extremely high resolutions. There are some things you should know about taking your job to a service bureau.

18.124 Be nice. Be nice, be friendly. It goes a long way. If you are rude and demanding, or even just plain cold, you can only expect that human nature will respond in kind. If you are pleasant and accommodating, your rush jobs will always be done on time and you will be notified of potential problems before they happen. Besides, it's just more fun to be nice.

18.125 Find a service bureau you like and stick with them. Work with them, ask questions, find out how they operate so you can provide jobs on disk just the way *they* like them so you can get your jobs back just the way *you* like them. A good service bureau is happy to teach you the most efficient, economical, and foolproof way to prepare your documents for remote printing. If you establish a good relationship, you can usually count on the bureau as a technical resource.

18.126 Fill out the job ticket thoroughly. A service bureau usually has you fill out a job ticket for each job you bring in. This ticket asks extremely important information, but to be of any use, it must be complete and precise. Make sure you have the necessary information before you go in:

a When the ticket asks for the fonts you used, *list each and every font, including the vendor's name.* For instance, if you used Goudy from Bitstream as the basis for your publication, list Goudy Regular, as well as Goudy Bold, Goudy Italic, and Goudy Bold Italic, if you used them at all anywhere in the entire publication, and tell them it is the version made by Bitstream. Ask the service bureau if they would like to know the *package number* of the fonts you have used; this may help.

b Write the exact file name of the publication you want printed. Be precise; don't say, "Oh, print the brochure."

c Write the number (amount) of pages you want printed, and their page numbers.

d Write the kind of machine you created the publication on, the System version, and the software version.

e State *clearly* when you need the job returned. Don't write "Tomorrow" or "ASAP." Be specific. And clear it with the service bureau to be sure they can even turn it around for you in the time you need.

f Remember to leave your name and phone number. Always.

18.127 Label the disk. Disks all look the same. It's *critical* that you label the disk with your name, your phone number, the name of the job, the date, etc.

18.128 Give them a clean disk. Make sure you have *only* the publication (and its companion files; 18.129) that you want to print. Don't leave a bunch of unrelated junk on the disk.

Service bureaus —continued

18.129 Include any *companion files.*
Companion files are those external files that are linked (Section 10) to items in the publication. You don't need to include all the text files, as they are stored in the publication (10.15), but bring all TIFF, PICT, MacPaint, and EPS files that you have placed into the pub. You won't really need them all, but they should be there just in case. Put all the files into one folder along with the publication (18.161; 18.165, and label the folder appropriately. Don't worry about PageMaker not being able to find the links—the service bureau will put all the files into one folder on their hard disk. PageMaker can always find the linked files if they are in the same folder as the publication itself.

If your file is really huge (this book, for instance, is over 40 megs, not including the fonts), you may want to take it to the service bureau on a removable cartridge hard disk, rather than on 50 floppies. Check with the service bureau first, of course, to make sure your cartridge is compatible with their machine.

If you are sending the bureau a *PostScript file* (18.134–18.139; 18.162), you will not need to provide the external, linked files.

18.130 Ask if you need to provide the fonts. If the service bureau does not own the fonts you use in the publication, you will need to bring to them the screen fonts (in a suitcase*), as well as the corresponding printer fonts (separate icons; 18.36–18.41). In my Utilities folder I keep a suitcase called "ScreenFontsToGo" in which I load up any necessary fonts. *(Be sure you understand your license agreement with the font vendor.)*

If you are sending the bureau a *PostScript file* (18.134–18.139; 18.162), you will not need to provide any fonts.

*If you don't know how to copy screen fonts into a suitcase, you will find step-by-step directions in The Little Mac Book or in the Macintosh manual. Make a copy of an existing suitcase icon, use the Font/DA Mover to empty it, then copy the fonts you need into it.

18.131 Let them know you're coming.
If the job involves just one or two pages, this step isn't always necessary. But if it is a major job—a manual, a book, a large or complex graphic file, an annual report, etc.—it is thoughtful and often critical to call the service bureau to let them know it will be arriving in a day or two. This helps them schedule their workload and helps ensure you can get your job back when you need it.

18.132 Confirm the price. Get it straight exactly what the costs will be so you won't be surprised and upset when you pick up the job. Many service bureaus charge for downloading fonts or switching files or having to clean up your mistakes, etc. Know what to expect.

Ask what the normal turnaround time is (the time between when you bring the job in and when it is ready for you to pick up). If you need it faster, clarify any rush charges. There may be varying rush charges, depending on how big a rush you're in.

18.133 You can also use a modem. Most service bureaus love it when you send the file over the modem. There are fewer disks floating around; there is less foot traffic and less disruption. Plus it saves you a few trips. To do this, you need to set up an account with the bureau and let a consultant there tell you exactly how to send the file. Generally they prefer you to put all the files into one folder and compress it with a file compression utility. *Give the folder a clearly identifiable name.* The service bureau can even fax you a finished copy for approval and overnight-mail the final job directly to you (or to the commercial press or other destination of your choice).

643

Making a PostScript file (printing to disk)

18.134 Printing your PageMaker publication straight to a printer or imagesetter is not the only way to get output. You can also **print to disk,** called making a **PostScript file.** The publication is changed into a PostScript text file; you or the service bureau can send that file to a PostScript printer, which reads and translates the text into the graphic publication. Many service bureaus *prefer* that you bring your publication as a PostScript file; some even offer substantial discounts when you do. Printing to disk is easy to do.

You can print PostScript to disk in three separate and distinct ways, each used for a particular purpose: Normal, EPS (for one page only), or For Separations.

18.135 When you make a **Normal** Post-Script file (18.162), PageMaker creates a straight-text copy of your publication. The text is in the PostScript language that a PostScript imagesetter can read and translate back into your actual publication. For any one of a number of reasons, your service bureau may want you to provide them with a PostScript file instead of, *or in addition to,* the actual PageMaker publication.

18.136 If you provide the service bureau with a "Normal" PostScript file, you don't need to worry about whether the bureau has all the fonts you included, or whether the links are still connected, or what System file or software version it was created in. All the information to print the entire publication is contained in the PostScript.

18.137 It is critical, though, to set up your print specifications correctly in the dialog boxes before making a "Normal" Postscript file. Make sure the first "Print to" dialog box is set up exactly the way you want it, as well as the "Aldus print options" dialog box (18.79). In the "Printer" option (18.74), choose the printer your service bureau uses (see APDs, 18.11–18.12). The service bureau cannot make any changes, corrections, or additions to the file once it is PostScript— it's like one huge graphic. Check 18.145–18.156 for clarification on the options to check, *but the final word on which options you really need should come from your service bureau.*

18.138 You can print one page at a time to disk as an **EPS** file (18.167). PageMaker creates a straight-text PostScript copy, *plus* a screen version of the image (just like any other EPS graphic; 9.29–9.35); it basically just turns your page into a graphic image. As an EPS graphic file, you can then place it on any publication page just like any other graphic, or you can place it into any other program that reads EPS.

PageMaker-created EPS files, though, are much larger than EPS files created in other programs such as Freehand or Illustrator.

18.139 When you choose to print the file to disk **For separations,** PageMaker creates a PostScript file that is readable by Aldus PrePrint or other separation software. The file is set up specifically for providing four-color separations, which are not covered in this book (see 14.31–14.36 for general information on four-color separations).

18.140 "PostScript print options" dialog box *(from the "Print to" dialog box, click "PostScript...")*

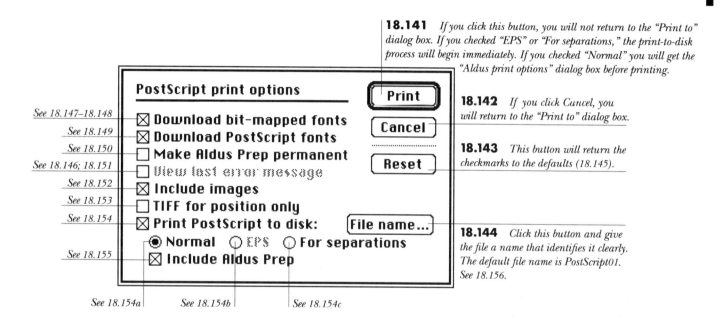

18.141 *If you click this button, you will not return to the "Print to" dialog box. If you checked "EPS" or "For separations," the print-to-disk process will begin immediately. If you checked "Normal" you will get the "Aldus print options" dialog box before printing.*

18.142 *If you click Cancel, you will return to the "Print to" dialog box.*

18.143 *This button will return the checkmarks to the defaults (18.145).*

18.144 *Click this button and give the file a name that identifies it clearly. The default file name is PostScript01. See 18.156.*

See 18.147–18.148
See 18.149
See 18.150
See 18.146; 18.151
See 18.152
See 18.153
See 18.154
See 18.155

See 18.154a *See 18.154b* *See 18.154c*

"PostScript print options" specifications

18.145 The following defaults are checked **on** whenever you print as usual to your personal printer. They are not adding to the publication file size as you print; the information goes into the printer's memory.

- Download bit-mapped fonts
- Download PostScript fonts
- Make Aldus Prep permanent
- Include images

18.146 The following option is available only when printing as usual to your personal printer. It is *not* defaulted on.

- View last error message
  (see 18.151)

18.147 Download bit-mapped fonts: When you are printing to disk, check this option if you have used bitmapped fonts in your publication. This downloading will increase the file size, depending on how many bitmapped fonts you have. Remember, bitmapped fonts are those with city names (with rare exceptions; 18.31–18.32). They look even worse on an imagesetter than they do on a laser printer. The bitmapped fonts are probably in your publication only for special effects, right?

18.148 If you *do not* check this box and you *have* checked the "Substitute fonts" box, then the typical font substitution will go into effect (18.84–18.85).

If you *do not* check this box and you *have not* checked the "Substitute fonts" box, all bitmapped fonts (and any downloadable typefaces without printer fonts; 18.34–18.36) will either be turned into Courier or will be transmogrified in some other equally horrendous fashion.

18.149 Download PostScript fonts: The default is with the checkmark **on,** which tells PageMaker to download the printer fonts as necessary (18.37–18.55), whether you are printing as usual to your own laser printer or if you are printing to disk for a service bureau.

When you are printing to disk, you usually *do* want to download the PostScript fonts, just in case the service bureau does not have the same version from the same vendor of every font you used in the publication.

When I am in a good space, I see obstructions as instructions. When I am in a bad space, even instructions look like obstructions. Norm Howe

"PostScript print options" specifications —*continued*

18.150 Make Aldus Prep permanent:
When printing to your own printer, you want to have this box checked on (which it is by default). It sends Aldus Prep to the printer's memory (18.44).

If you are printing to disk or making an EPS file, it is best to turn this option **off.** Most service bureaus will be mad at you if you stick this in their printer's memory permanently (permanently meaning until the printer is turned off).

18.151 View last error message: This option is designed for debugging printing problems when you are printing directly to the printer (it is not available if you are printing to disk or creating an EPS file). If it is checked on and you have trouble printing, PageMaker will display an error message that "explains" the reason the publication is having trouble; yes, generally explains it in a PostScript language that most mortals don't speak. If you are going to call Tech Support for help, be sure to write down the entire message, including any strange characters you see and including the number displayed in the bottom right corner of the alert box.

18.152 Include images: This option relates to color TIFF or MacPaint images (9.6–9.9, 9.22–9.26). *(Since EPS files [9.29– 9.35] are always stored in the publication anyway, and you cannot assign colors to PICTs [9.14–9.21], this option does not concern those two graphic formats.)*

Turn it **on** if:

- You are printing directly to a color printer.
- You are printing to a black-and-white printer, but you want the color images to print like grayscale files.
- You are printing to disk as Normal.
- You are printing to disk to create color separations for a program that can separate color bitmaps on PageMaker pages.

Turn it **off** if:

- You want to *exclude* TIFFs and MacPaint images because you would rather add them later, either manually or in a prepress program like Aldus PrePrint.

- You are creating an EPS file.
- You are printing to disk to create color separations, but the separation program you are printing through cannot handle color bitmaps.

18.153 TIFF for position only: TIFFS are usually represented on the screen by a low-resolution version, but when the page prints, PageMaker finds the linked file and prints the high-resolution version. If you check this option, the printer will print only the low-resolution screen version, an image used *for position only* to indicate on the page where the final version should be placed. Perhaps you want to place the image manually, or perhaps you want to print this file faster and don't need the high-res version at this point. If it's checked on, you don't need to include the publication's linked TIFF files.

If you are printing to disk for color separations, leave this box **un**checked.

"PostScript print options" specifications —continued

18.154 Print PostScript to disk: Check this box if you are printing to disk to send to a service bureau (18.122–18.139) or other remote printer.

a **Normal:** Click this button to print multiple pages of the publication to disk. The page numbers you have entered in the "Print to" dialog box (From ___ to ___) are the ones that will be printed to disk in this file. The specifications in any other boxes or buttons you have typed into or checked in either the "Print to" or the "Aldus print options" dialog boxes will also be applied to this file. So be careful! The service bureau cannot change any of the specifications you set.

b **EPS:** Click this button to save **one page** of your publication as an EPS graphic file (18.138), which you can later place into any program that accepts the EPS format. The file will contain the usual screen version and printer version.

You will **not** be able to choose the EPS button if you have checked any of the following options in either the "Print to" or the "Aldus print options" dialog boxes:

- Thumbnails
- Spot color overlays
- Tile
- Proof print
- Scaling other than 100%
- More than one page entered in the page range

c **For separations:** Click this button to print-to-disk a file to be sent through a color separation program, such as Aldus PrePrint or Adobe Separator. *This is not for spot color.* If you don't know what four-color separations are, you probably don't need to click this button.

18.155 Include Aldus Prep: You should check this button when printing to disk, just in case the printer does not have the same version your publication used (18.20–18.23).

18.156 File name... Click this button to name the PostScript file you are printing to disk. PageMaker encourages you to identify the file accurately by automatically inserting an extension to the name, appropriate to the file format you chose. That is, if you are making an EPS file, PageMaker automatically includes a ".eps" (pronounced *dot e p s*) at the end of the name; if you are making a file for separations, you'll see a ".sep" (pronounced *dot sep*).

If you want to do this:

18.157 Use Chooser to select a printer

The Chooser window, found in the Apple menu.

Then follow these steps:

- Before you print, choose "Chooser" from the Apple menu (see the note ☞).
- On the left, click on the icon of the printer you want to print to. After you click on a printer icon, the name(s) of the printers of that type will appear on the right.
- On the right, click on the name of the particular printer you want to send your publication through (it may already be selected).
- If you are using a laser printer, or if you are connected to more than one printer, AppleTalk should be Active.
- The edit box "User Name" does not have to have anything in it. But if you type your name there, you will have the great satisfaction of seeing it in lights, er . . . pixels.
- It feels like there should be an OK button in this window, but there isn't. When you click in the close box (upper left), Chooser sends the information to the driver so PageMaker knows to which printer to send the publication.

Shortcuts ▾ Notes ▾ Hints

- You do not need to go to Chooser every time you print. You only need to go there when you print to a certain printer for the first time. After that, the information is stored, even if you turn off the computer and/or the printer. You need never go back to Chooser again until you want to print to a different printer.
- The Chooser will display the printer icons of any printer files (icons) you have in the System folder. If a printer file (icon) is not in the System folder, you cannot print to it.

If you want to do this:	Then follow these steps:	Shortcuts ▼ Notes ▼ Hints

18.158 Print a publication

- Always Save just before you print, as the ever-necessary precaution.
- From the File menu, choose "Print...," *or* press Command P.
  - ☐ If you chose a PostScript printer (18.6–18.9) in Chooser (18.13–18.14; 18.157), you will get the **Aldus driver** "Print to" dialog box (18.56).
  - ☐ If you chose a QuickDraw or other non-PostScript printer (18.7–18.8) in Chooser, you will get the **Apple driver** "Print options for" dialog box (18.100).
- Read through the information appropriate to either driver, then check the buttons and fill in the edit boxes for the results you want.
  - ☐ If you are using the **Aldus driver,** the job will be sent to the printer when you click OK in the "Print to" dialog box.
  - ☐ If you are using the **Apple driver,** you will have to click OK three times before the job is sent to the printer, as there are three successive dialog boxes for entering specifications (18.100; 18.104; 18.106).

- Once you have set up the "Print to" dialog boxes and printed, the information will stay intact—you do not have to redo the specifications each time you print. Just press Command P and hit the Return key (shortcut for OK) to start the process. If you are using the Apple driver, hit the Return key three times.

If you want to do this:

18.159 Print items outside the boundary of the page

This is the 4 x 6 page in PageMaker. Notice the text block handle of "Quote #2" is within the page boundary, but the text itself is on the pasteboard (1.4).

When printed on 8.5 x 11 paper, the text appears outside the 4 x 6 boundary, but within the 8.5 x 11 page.

Registration mark with a white box behind it. The white box needs a line of "None."

Placing the reg mark from the Scrapbook combines all the separate pieces into one graphic.

Then follow these steps:

- As long as at least one handle of the object is placed within the page boundary, the object will print.
- To print **text:** In front of the first character in the text block, hit a couple of Returns to make the text block larger on the top. Place the text block on the page so the top handles touch the page itself, but the rest of the text block hangs into the pasteboard area (1.4). The text block could also hang off either side, in the same manner; use indents (Section 5) to give you space on the sides.
- To print **graphics:** If the graphic has any white space within its boundary, then it is very easy to place an edge of the graphic on the page and hang the image itself on the pasteboard.

    If the graphic is a composite one you created in PageMaker, such as a registration mark (⊕), you can do this:

    ☐ Create the reg mark. Put a white box behind it. Give the white box a line of "None." Select the mark and the box and put them in the Scrapbook as item number one. *Place* the first item in the Scrapbook (9.96), then click on the pointer tool. Hang the edge of the reg mark on the page.

Shortcuts ▾ Notes ▾ Hints

- If the page size you established in the "Page setup" dialog box (from the File menu) *is at least a half-inch less than the paper size you are printing on,* it is possible to print items that are outside the boundary of the smaller page size. This is great for placing automatic page numbers or other notes that you need in order to identify the pages, but that you don't want to appear on the actual, cropped page itself. You can also use this trick to put registration marks on the pages for color registration.

If you want to do this:

18.160 Prepare a publication for do-it-yourself remote printing (printing on a Mac at a copy center, for instance)

Then follow these steps:

- If you have a Mac at home for creating the publication, but you don't have a laser printer, sometimes you must take the pub to someone else's place for printing (*remote* printing).
- Proof your pub on your own machine as carefully as possible. At a copy or service center you will be charged for every page that is printed, whether it has typos or not. Plus you will usually be charged for the time it takes you to fix them.
- Call the copy center to make sure the Mac you will be using has the same version of PageMaker you created your publication with. Also ask which fonts they have installed. If they don't have the fonts you used, you are usually out of luck because copy centers don't like you to install your own fonts on their machines (see the note, though, in the right column).
- Put a blank disk in your drive, then open the publication.
  □ From the File menu, choose "Save as...."
  □ Hold the Option key down; click in the checkbox "Copy linked documents" (see note at right).
  □ Click the "Drive" button (or press Tab) to get to the floppy disk.
  □ Name the publication, click OK.

Shortcuts ▾ Notes ▾ Hints

- Of course, if you have to take your file somewhere else to print, you need to make sure it fits onto a floppy disk.
- **Important tip:** Copy or service centers that have Macs you can rent by the hour sometimes don't keep up on the latest versions of everything, and their stock of fonts is often limited. If you want to bypass their limitations altogether and ensure that your file prints exactly as you set it up, create a PostScript file by printing to disk ("Normal"); see 18.162. Then you can download it into their printer (18.166) and it will print exactly as you prepared it, no matter what they have on their Mac (even if they don't even have PageMaker!).

- If you *Option-check* the "Copy linked documents" box, PageMaker copies all the files that are linked to the publication but *that are not stored within* the publication. This may just be the kern tracks file, or it may be any large graphic that you chose not to store. See 18.165 for more info.

If you want to do this:

Then follow these steps:

Shortcuts ▾ Notes ▾ Hints

18.161 Prepare a publication as a **PageMaker file** for remote printing at a service bureau *(as opposed to preparing it as a PostScript file; 18.162)*

- Before you open the publication, make a new folder on your hard disk (Command N) and give it a very identifiable name.
- Open the publication. Proof it carefully. At a service bureau, you will be charged for every page that is printed, whether it has typos, comes out blank, etc.
- From the File menu, choose "Save as...."
- Locate the new folder you created earlier on your hard disk; double-click on its name so it appears at the top of the list box (16.9).
- Click in the checkbox "Copy linked documents" (10.62). This will copy all the files that are linked to the publication (see the note in the next column**).
- Name the publication, click OK. Quit PageMaker.
- Create a suitcase with the screen fonts you used in the publication (see 18.34–18.36; 18.130). Put the screen font suitcase and the corresponding printer fonts into a folder.
- Copy both the font folder and the publication folder onto a disk. You may need more than one disk to hold all the files; that's okay—you can now take them out of the folders and use as many disks as you need. Just make sure that you include everything.

- Service bureaus don't seem to be listed in the phone books yet under "Service Bureaus." You will probably find them under "Typesetting," "Printing," "Graphic Design," or perhaps, if your phone book is forward-thinking, under "Desktop Publishing."
- Don't worry about links being broken when you copy the linked documents out of their original location. If PageMaker can't find the link in its original spot, she checks the folder that the publication itself is in. When you take your folder to the service bureau, they put the publication and all the companion files you give them into one folder so PageMaker can always connect the links.
** If the service bureau tells you all they want are the files *that are not stored in the publication,* then hold the Option key down while you click the checkbox for "Copy linked documents." The checkbox will become "Copy linked documents for remote printing," and PageMaker will copy into the folder *only* those linked files that do not have a copy stored in the publication (10.15–10.26).

If you want to do this:	**Then follow these steps:**	**Shortcuts ▾ Notes ▾ Hints**

18.162 Prepare a publication as a **PostScript file ("Normal"** or **"For separations")** for remote printing at a service bureau *(as opposed to preparing it as a PageMaker file; 18.161)*

Print to disk:

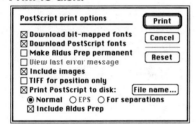

The OK button in this dialog box turns into a Print button when you choose the "Print PostScript to disk" checkbox.

When printing to disk as "Normal," whether you click Cancel or OK in this dialog box, the printing to disk begins.

- Open the publication.
- Make sure you have chosen a PostScript printer in Chooser (18.157; also see right).
  □ With a PostScript printer chosen, PageMaker will use the Aldus driver (18.20–18.28). If you cannot choose a PostScript printer or if you *want* to print to disk using the Apple driver, see 18.163.
- From the File menu, choose "Print...." Set up the specifications *exactly* as if you were going to print as usual.
- Click the "Options..." button and set those specifications also (18.79). Click OK.
- Click on the "PostScript..." button. Set the PostScript specifications appropriately (18.134–18.156).
- Click the "File name..." button, name the file, and click OK.
  □ If you are making a "Normal" file, when you click the "Print" button you get the "Aldus print options" dialog box again. Whether you click Cancel or OK now, PageMaker starts printing to disk.
  □ If you select "EPS" or "For separations," when you click the "Print" button PageMaker will instantly launch into printing the file to disk.

- If you need or want to make a PostScript file (Normal) with the Apple driver, see 18.163.
- You don't have to be *hooked up* to a PostScript printer or even have one in your office or home; you just need to have a PostScript printer icon sitting in your System folder. As long as the icon is in your System folder, you can select it in Chooser and then print to disk.
- PostScript files are very large. This chapter, 42 pages, is normally 1,359K. As a PostScript file it is almost 3 megabytes. Of course, that presents a problem when trying to transport files on disks. A popular item these days is a removable-cartridge hard disk. Check with your service bureau to see if they can accommodate a cartridge, and make sure you get one for yourself that is compatible with theirs.
- Your service bureau may ask you to provide a regular PageMaker version of the publication *in addition to the PostScript file*, just in case there is a simple problem they can fix for you.

If you want to do this:

18.163 Print a PostScript file to disk with the Apple driver

This is the third and final dialog box in the Apple driver print series. It is at this point that you get ready to hold Command F instantly after clicking OK.

> Creating PostScript® file.

You should see this message if you did it right.

Then follow these steps:

- Open the publication.
- From the File menu, choose "Print...," but note the following:
  □ If a PostScript printer has been selected in "Chooser" but you want to use the Apple driver anyway, then hold down the Option key while you choose "Print..." from the File menu.
  □ If a non-PostScript printer has been selected in "Chooser," then PageMaker will automatically use the Apple driver when you choose to print.
- You will get the three Apple dialog boxes, as usual (see 18.100–18.106). Fill in all the specifications, *but don't click OK on the last dialog box yet!*
- On the last dialog box (see left), click OK and then *instantly* press Command F and *hold those two keys down* until you see a little message box that tells you PageMaker is creating a PostScript file.

  If you don't see the message (as shown in the left column), cancel the printing and try again. If it still doesn't work, check the specifications you set; perhaps you clicked an option or entered a value that prevents a PostScript file from being made.

Shortcuts ▾ Notes ▾ Hints

- If you are working under MultiFinder with Background printing turned on, you must first go to Chooser (18.13–18.14) and turn Background printing off.
- You cannot create an EPS file or a separation file with the Apple driver. This technique just prints to disk as "Normal," which you can then take to the service bureau or to the copy center. It comes in handy when you are working on a computer that has no PostScript printer attached, nor even a PostScript printer icon in the System folder.

If you want to do this:	Then follow these steps:	Shortcuts ▾ Notes ▾ Hints

18.164 Copy the publication's kern tracks for remote printing

OR

18.165 Copy only the linked files that are not stored in the publication

- Follow the steps in 18.161 to copy all linked files into the folder, but don't click the "Copy linked documents" checkbox. Make sure there is no X in that checkbox, then hold down the Option key. You will see the phrase change to "Copy linked documents for remote printing." *Now*, while the Option key is held down, click in the checkbox.

  When you click OK PageMaker will copy only the files that are linked to the publication, ***but that are not stored in the publication,*** (which includes the kern track file).

- Sometimes a service bureau may ask you to provide the "kerning tracks" for the publication you want printed. This is the file that PageMaker has stored your kerning values in.
- If you want to copy both the kerning tracks *and* all the linked files for remote printing, you will need to follow 18.161 to "Save as..." and copy the linked files. Then "Save as..." *again* following this technique explained here to put the kern tracks in the same folder.
- If your service bureau needs only the companion files *that are not stored* in the publication (10.15–10.17), then you need to follow only 18.165 (right here), rather than copy every linked file as in 18.161.

18.166 Print a "Normal" PostScript file yourself

Font Downloader   Download

Utilities such as either of these will download your PostScript file to the printer.

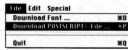

This is the Adobe font downloader menu.

- To print a "Normal" PostScript file yourself, you need a **downloader.** You can use the same downloader you use to download fonts into your printer (18.51). If you have bought PostScript fonts from any vendor, you will find a downloader on the disk.
- Double-click on the downloader, then follow the directions. There will be either a button to click or a menu command to choose to download a PostScript file to the printer.

- You may never need (or want) to print a PostScript file yourself. Then again, you may want to print it to verify your specifications before sending it to the service bureau. Or you may want to take this file and your downloader to a copy center or service center where you can print it to their laser printer yourself.

If you want to do this:

18.167 Create an EPS file of one page

An EPS document icon

ForbiddenSeas.eps

Then follow these steps:

- Follow the steps in 18.162 to print to disk to create a PostScript file. Just make sure that you have specified to print **only one page.** Also make sure you have not checked any of the following options:
  - ☐ Thumbnails
  - ☐ Spot color overlays
  - ☐ Tile
  - ☐ Proof print
  - ☐ Scaling other than 100%
- In the "PostScript print options" dialog box (18.140), click "Print PostScript to disk" and then click the "EPS" button.
- Name the file; click OK.
- When you click the "Print" button, PageMaker instantly launches into the creation of the EPS file.

Shortcuts ▾ Notes ▾ Hints

- If the EPS button is gray after you click "Print PostScript to disk," it indicates there is an option checked somewhere that cannot be included when creating an EPS file.
- Once you have made an EPS file of a PageMaker page, you can then place it on the page just like any other EPS graphic (9.29–9.35; 9.92). The images on page 633 are EPS files of PageMaker pages.

If you want to do this:

Then follow these steps:

Shortcuts ▾ Notes ▾ Hints

18.168 Install another APD

 APD icon, compressed
General.apd

- At the Finder (Desktop), insert Disk 4 of your original PageMaker disks. The window automatically opens and you should see a folder called "APDs."
- Double-click on the "APDs" folder.
- Double-click on the APD icon that you want to add.
- In the resulting dialog box, click "Drive" to get to your hard disk.
- Locate the System folder in the list; double-click on "System folder."
- Double-click on the "Aldus" folder.
- Double-click on the "APDs" folder.
- Click the "Save" button.
- When the procedure is finished, drag the Disk 4 icon to the trash to eject it. The windows will close automatically.

- PageMaker 4.01 includes five more APDs to choose from: Personal LaserWriter NT; HP LaserJet IID, IIP, III, and IIID.
    If you are updating, the new APD files are on Disk 1 of the update disks.

18.169 Find and remove all other versions of Aldus Prep and Laser Prep

- Use Find File to find all copies of Aldus Prep and Laser Prep. See 1.232–1.233 for detailed directions on using Find File. Have the little guy move any extra copies to the Desktop (select the name in the list and press Command M). Then when you close Find File you can trash them all *except one copy of the latest version of each.*

Troubleshooting

18.170 If a job won't print all the way through on your laser printer, it's probably because your printer doesn't have enough memory to deal with your page. Some things that make pages extra complicated are:

- Too many text wraps on a page, or the text wraps are too complex (too many points).

- Too much text has been expanded or condensed with "Set width."

- Too many rotated text blocks, or a rotated text block is too complex (e.g., the text was expanded or condensed before rotating).

- Too many TIFF, EPS, or PICT files.

- One or more TIFF, EPS, or PICT files are too complex.

- Too many downloadable fonts.

- The publication itself is too complex, possibly due to a failure on your part to "Save as..." in order to compress the file size (see 16.4–16.5; 16.25).

18.171 Service bureaus generally don't have as much trouble printing PageMaker publications on their imagesetters because imagesetters have more memory. Even if *you* can't get it to print, it may print just fine at

your service bureau. *Don't always count on it though,* especially if you are under a heavy deadline. If a file is complex, it may take more time to run (and remember that service bureaus do charge extra for long-running files).

18.172 You can try these troubleshooting measures with your laser printer:

- Use "Save as..." to compress the file (16.25). Compressing it makes it less complicated and so sometimes makes the printer happier.

- If you did not compress your TIFFs as you placed them, replace them with compressed versions (9.110).

- Turn the printer off, wait a minute or two, then turn it back on again. This clears out the RAM, which gives you the maximum amount of memory. If you have downloaded fonts into the RAM, you will have to download them again. Try manually downloading fewer fonts next time.

- Try printing with the Apple driver instead of the Aldus driver (18.25).

- In the "Aldus print options" dialog box, check the "Proof print" box. Then if

the job prints okay, you will at least know that the problem is in the graphics.

- Print only a couple of pages at a time. If the problem is with one particular page, the printer will usually print up to that page, then freak out. Try printing just that one particular page alone, then continue printing the rest.

- If the printer gets stuck on one page, then obviously that page has a problem. Try removing one of the graphics, then printing. If the graphics are causing problems, see if there is any way for you to simplify them. If a graphic has heavy cropping (9.104; 9.176), take the image back into the appropriate graphic program and trim off the excess there, rather than cropping it in PageMaker. If a graphic is a TIFF, make sure you compress it as you place it (9.109). (I have had to remove a graphic, print the page, remove everything else on the page, put the graphic back, reprint.)

- If one page is really stuck, try printing that one page to disk (18.162) and then downloading it to print (18.166).

- Try printing the job through someone else's Mac and printer.

TEN WAYS TO DRIVE YOUR SERVICE BUREAU NUTS

1. Always, **always** wait until the last possible moment to bring your work to the imagesetter. Be sure you have an ironclad printer deadline you can tell the service bureau about so if they have trouble outputting your job or something else goes wrong, they can know in their hearts they are ruining your whole production schedule.

2. Complain loudly if they charge you a rush charge and threaten to take your work elsewhere, even though they have bailed you out countless times in the past. This helps to build mutual trust and ensures that they will try **really** hard to please you in the future.

3. Don't bother to call them to let them know you are coming with the rush job—they love surprises like that. Keeps them from becoming bored. Or do call and tell them it's a bona fide life-and-death situation so they'll pull your job and run it ahead of everyone else. Then don't go to pick it up for a week or so.

4. Bring the job in on an unlabeled diskette. The service bureau deals with hundreds of diskettes daily and they love having unidentified ones floating around.

5. Don't bother to fill out the order form completely. Whatever you do, don't put your phone number on it . . . that way if they need to talk to you they can add some adventure to their lives by roaming through the phone book, calling mutual acquaintances, etc., trying to find you. They don't have anything else to do anyway. Don't tell them what fonts you used in your document, either. They love to guess.

6. Put a lot of different files on the diskette you bring in and forget exactly which one it is that you want printed. Write on the order form "I'm not sure what the name of the file I need is, but it's the one that says 'Little Bo Peep' in the lower right-hand corner of page three." Even better, ask if you can just look at the files on the service bureau's computer, just for *one minute.* The operator won't mind interrupting whatever s/he happens to be working on right then so you can figure out the name of the file you need.

7. Don't bother to bring all those companion files and other junk like XPress Data files with you. That way, when the job tries to print and asks for this additional data, the operator can call you on the phone and enjoy a leisurely chat. They don't take enough breaks anyway.

8. Use lots of obscure fonts manufactured by companies that don't understand the rules about fonts. Then "forget" to bring the font with you to the service bureau. Better yet, bring only one part, i.e., the screen (bitmap) part or the printer (outline) part.

9. Don't bother to upgrade your software. So what if you do all your work in ReadySetGo 1.0 with Cricket Draw graphics? The service bureau loves to load up old versions of software so they can print your job.

10. When you send a file by modem, don't bother to compress it. The service bureau's other clients won't mind getting a busy signal for two hours because the modem is busy receiving your file. Also, give the file a name like MXRVB.sit so the operator can identify your job right away. This will get you preferential service for sure.

But seriously, folks . . . most service bureaus will bend over backwards to help you get your job out, whatever it takes. Just remember, as in all your business dealings, a little thoughtfulness and consideration go a long way!

BY JANET BUTCHER
Technical Director, Desktop Composition Center

Containing several clear Matters,
but which flow from the same Fount
as those in the preceding Chapters.

19 ▾ SPECIAL TECHNIQUES

19.1 I have tried, throughout this book, to include any special techniques directly in the section they pertain to. So the first part of this section is just a list of possible special techniques you may be interested in, along with references for where to find their detailed directions in other parts of the book. The second part is a list of techniques that didn't seem to have a proper pigeonhole. If you have any neat tricks, let me know and I'll add them to this section (with due credit, of course).

■ SOMETIMES THE SEAS ARE CALM

■ AND THAT'S WONDERFUL.

■ SOMETIMES THE SEAS ARE NOT CALM

■ AND THAT'S THE WAY IT IS.

RABBI NATHAN SEAGULL

19.2 Techniques in the book

General publication tips

- Begin page numbering with a number other than one: 1.28

- Show the first two pages of a publication as a double-page spread: 1.35

- Change the horizontal ruler measurements: 1.52

- Tricks with page turning and viewing: 1.97–1.116

- View a page at actual size at the exact spot you want: 1.113

- View a page at 200% size at the exact spot you want: 1.114

- Find out what page you are on when there are more than 999 pages: 1.121

- Auto numbering individual pages: 1.142

- Override ruler measurements: 1.221

- Print a publication other than the one that is on the screen: 13.26

- Shortcut to the "Edit color" dialog box: 14.77

- Open a Mac PageMaker 3.0 publication in PageMaker 4.0: 15.38

- Open a PC PageMaker publication in Mac PageMaker: 15.39

- Compress your publication: 16.4–16.5; 16.25

- Reduce the size of a publication: 16.25

- Prevent a laser printer from printing a test page every time you turn it on: 18.4

- Switch to the Apple driver to print: 18.25

- Scale large-sized pages onto letter-sized paper when printing: 18.70-18.71

- Print items that fall outside the boundary of a page: 18.159

Text tips

- Letterspace text across a text block: 1.158; 3.159; 4.164

- Step-and-repeat graphics or text blocks, using power-paste: 1.194-1.195; 9.200

- Turn text into a graphic: 1.205

- Create a confined space to place text into: 1.208; 3.58

- Type numbers with the keypad: 1.222

- Use the keypad as arrow keys: 1.223

- Select text with keyboard: 2.223-2.224; 3.138

- Cut and paste with the keypad: 1.225

- Create a confined space to type text into, or create a text block to override any existing columns: 3.25

- Place stories from another PageMaker publication: 3.59-3.78

- Copy text from another PageMaker 4.0 publication and paste it into this one without leaving this publication: 3.80

- Override auto or manual flow: 3.92

- Cancel a loaded text icon: 3.94

- Combine several separate text blocks into one text block: 3.117

- Separate one text block into several, unconnected text blocks: 3.122

- Add to or delete from the text selection: 3.137

- Create beautiful fractions: 3.171

- Create interesting bullets: 3.172

- Make text or paragraph rules gray (which, when printed in colored ink or toner, will appear to be a tint) Text or rules: 3.174; 14.102; 14.103

- Set a one-em indent for first lines: 3.207

- Break a line of text without getting a new paragraph: 3.230-3.235

Techniques in the book —*continued*

- Create a nicely spaced non-breaking ellipsis: 3.239
- Create non-breaking spaces: 4.107–4.218
- Make the linespacing consistent when there are different points sizes of type in the same paragraph: 4.23–4.26
- Prevent a word from hyphenating: 4.241
- Move the left margin marker independently in the Indents/tabs ruler: 5.30
- Use tab leaders to create forms or fill-in blanks: 5.63
- Create custom leaders: 5.64–5.65
- Copy tab and indent formatting into other contiguous paragraphs: 5.74
- Transform one style sheet definition into another: 7.53
- Find-and-change keyboard formatting: 8.58; 8.61
- Find invisible characters through the Story Editor: 8.61
- Place the table of contents and/or index from a Word file: 15.30
- Place a table from a Word file into PageMaker as a graphic: 15.31

Graphic tips

- Select an object that is underneath another object: 1.172
- Select a line that is under a guide line: 1.173
- Step-and-repeat graphics or text blocks, using power-paste: 1.194–1.195; 9.200
- Turn text into a graphic: 1.205
- Restore a distorted graphic to its original proportions: 1.209; 9.102
- Move a tiny little object: 2.28
- Move or draw objects in perfect alignment with the ruler tick marks: 2.31
- Change the line widths or the fills of more than one line or border at a time: 2.34
- Cancel a loaded text or graphic icon: 3.94
- Step-and-repeat graphics using repeat tabs: 5.60; 9.200
- Make an EPS graphic out of one Page-Maker page: 9.30; 9.117
- Re-size bitmapped graphics and halftoned scans to the printer resolution (to prevent unwanted patterns): 9.103

- Compress TIFFs: 9.109–9.110
- View a grayscale TIFF at high resolution temporarily: 9.115
- Make graphics gray (which, when printed in colored ink or toner, will appear to be a tint): 9.116; 14.104
- Lighten a PICT to a shadow: 9.169
- Adjust the space above and below an inline graphc: 9.201; 9.202
- Center an inline graphic in a text block: 9.203
- Create an inline graphic as the first character in a hanging indent: 9.205
- Turn a text wrap inside out (so text will wrap inside the shape): 11.41
- Access the Apple color wheel: 14.54

If you want to do this: ■	**Then follow these steps:** ■	**Shortcuts ▾ Notes ▾ Hints** ■
19.3 Show the actual fonts in the Font menu	■ Hold down the Option key before you choose "Font" from the Type menu. (If Option doesn't work, try Shift-Option; it depends on your font utility program.)	■ This takes longer to appear than does the normal font menu. After you do it the first time in a publication, successive displays don't take so long.
19.4 Make Zapf Dingbat arrows point to the left, up, or down	All arrows in the font Zapf Dingbats point to the right. To make them point in other directions, simply put them in their own little text blocks, then rotate the text: ■ Type the dingbat in a separate text block. ■ Click once on the **pointer tool;** click once on the text block. ■ From the Element menu, choose "Text rotation...." ■ Click on the direction you want the arrow to point. Click OK.	■ Read 3.180–3.190 for more details regarding rotated text.
19.5 Eliminate *some* master page items from a publication page, but leave others	■ View the page you want to customize. Turn off the master page items (Page menu). ■ Go to the master pages. ■ With the **pointer tool,** Shift-click to select the items you *do* want to display on the publication page. ■ Press Command C (to copy). Press Command Tab to return to the page. ■ Press Command Option V. The master page items will paste onto the page in exactly the same position as they were on the master page.	■ This is in lieu of using opaque boxes to cover up master page items you don't want to show. ■ Command Option V is the power-paste command (1.194–1.195). It pastes any cut or copied items into exactly the same position they were in when they were first cut or copied (provided the same space is visible on the screen).

If you want to do this:	**Then follow these steps:**	**Shortcuts ▾ Notes ▾ Hints**

19.6 Remove a headline from a story and make it span several columns

◀— *Original story. Select the headline and cut it. This may leave an extra line at the top of the body copy that you will have to delete (double-click on the blank line; press the Backspace/Delete key).*

The bounding box will look like this box, with the I-beam at the end of it, until you let go of the mouse. Then the insertion point jumps to the left and the bounding box seems to disappear. But, really, it's still there. Just paste, and the headline will paste into the bounding box, which overrides the columns.

With this first method, the headline is not threaded to the body text.

- With the **text tool,** select the headline.
- Press Command X to cut it (this removes it permanently from the story; if you want it back in, press Command Z immediately to Undo, or you can paste it back in again anytime).
- With the **text tool,** press-and-drag to create a bounding box across the columns.
- Press Command V to paste the headline into that bounding box.

If you want the headline to remain threaded:

- With the **pointer tool,** roll up the entire text block.
- Click once, lightly, on the plus sign in the bottom windowshade loop.
- With the resulting loaded text icon, press-and-drag across the columns, dragging just deep enough to accommodate the headline. Let go at the right edge.
- Click once, lightly, on the arrow sign in the bottom windowshade loop of the headline text block.
- With the loaded text icon, click in the column to pour in the text, as usual. You can also press-and-drag bounding boxes for the columns of text.

- *Threaded* means the text in one text block is connected to the text in another text block. As you edit, the changes can affect all connected, or *threaded,* text blocks (3.99–3.106).
- Read 1.206–1.209 and 3.58 for more details on the text bounding box.

If you want to do this:	**Then follow these steps:**	**Shortcuts ▾ Notes ▾ Hints**

19.7   Adjust line breaks

With money in your pocket,
you are wise and you are
handsome, and you sing well
too.
              Yiddish proverb

With money in your pocket, you
are wise and you are handsome,
and you sing well too.
              Yiddish proverb

In the first text block, the line breaks are awkward, plus there is a widow ("too"). I extended the text block, which wrapped the words into a better arrangement.

With money in your pocket,
you are wise and you are
handsome, and you sing well
too.
              Yiddish proverb

With money in your pocket, you
are wise and you are handsome,
and you sing well too.
              Yiddish proverb

Perhaps it's not possible to extend the text block. In this example, I selected the first couple of lines and tracked it to "Normal." This tightened up the letter spacing just enough to pull the words into a better arrangement.

To uphold the standards of typographic excellence, you really must be conscious of how lines are breaking, not only in headlines, but in body text as well. I touched on this topic in 3.230–3.236. There are several ways to adjust line breaks:

- Rewrite the copy. Sometimes it just takes a word added or deleted several lines back.
- Lengthen or shorten the line length just a hair (by dragging the text block handle in or out a touch).
- If you need to squeeze a few more letters on the line, select the line and set the track to "Normal" (from the Type menu). Or if it's already "Normal" and you need to bump a couple more letters to the next line, then select the line and give it "No track."
- If you need to bump a word down to the next line, you can:
  □ Hit the Tab key before the word to bump it down to the next line. This will not work on justified or right-aligned text.
  □ Press the Spacebar a few times in front of the word to bump it down (okay with justified text).
  □ Position the insertion point just before the word and press Shift-Return (3.230; great with justified text).

—continued

- Be conscious of rag right (left-aligned) body copy lines getting *too* ragged, as when a very short word hangs out above the next line. Usually you can bump the word down to fill in the space and thus smooth out the right edge a little. Notice the second line in this paragraph: you can bump the word *as* down to the next line to fill in the space.

If you want to do this:

Never learn to do anything. If you don't learn, you will always find someone else to do it for you.

Mark Twain

Never learn to do anything. If you don't learn, you will always find someone else to do it for you.

Mark Twain

The word "If" needs to bump down to the next line, as well as the word "to." I bumped "If" down with a Shift Return (line break); I bumped "to" down by attaching it to the word "do" with a hard space. (Then, I noticed that the name "Mark Twain" was hanging out too far, so I put a couple of em spaces after his name [after his name because he is right-aligned] to scoot him over. It's so much fun to be fussy.)

Then follow these steps:

(Each of the above methods will show a visible space when you edit the text, or change the margins, indents, font, size, etc.; see the example to the right.)

☐ You can also try this to adjust those unseemly breaks: Select the space directly *after* the word you want to bump down (press-and-drag over the space, *or* position the insertion point directly after the word and press Shift RightArrow key). After the blank space is selected, press Option Spacebar to create a hard space (4.216). As you edit the text, this won't leave a visible, open space behind (but those two words, now connected with a hard space, will always be seen by the computer as one word).

▪ Sometimes you need to adjust the lines *preceding* the awkward line break, and then the awkward line break will fix itself.

Shortcuts ▾ Notes ▾ Hints

▪ Below is an example of what happens when you adjust the line breaks, and then edit the text or change the margin, etc. I forced a line break with a tab in the following text and then changed the point size; the tab space is visible.

All things are ready
if our minds be so.
King Henry the Fifth

All things are ready   if our minds be so.
King Henry the Fifth

If you want to do this:

Then follow these steps:

Shortcuts ▾ Notes ▾ Hints

19.8 Maintain consistent linespace between two separate text blocks

> Very few things happen at the right time, and the rest do not happen at all. The

Position a ruler guide along the bottom windowshade handles.

Position the top windowshade handles of the next text block along that guide line.

> Very few things happen at the right time, and the rest do not happen at all. The conscientious historian will correct these defects.
> Herodotus 483–425 B.C.

Sometimes you have to separate a text block into more than one part, but you need to align one part directly under the other, with the exact amount of linespace between the two text blocks as there is between the lines of text.

- Separate the two blocks. With the **pointer tool,** click once on the top block.
- Press in the horizontal ruler and bring down a ruler guide. Position it directly along the bottom windowshade handles of the text block.
- With the **pointer tool,** move the lower text block into position under the one above. Position the top windowshade handles of the *lower* text block directly on the guide line. The space between the two text blocks is now exactly one linespace.

Who

knows

where

we're

going,

but

we'll

get

there.

*Keasley Jones
Peachpit Press*

If you want to do this:

Then follow these steps:

Shortcuts ▪ Notes ▪ Hints

19.9 Keep linespacing consistent when an inline graphic has been added

You can do several things.

- One is to remove any excess boundary that may be surrounding the graphic. Just click on it with the cropping tool and crop it away (9.104; 9.176).
- Another thing to do is to *fix* the leading, rather than use Auto leading. Triple-click on the paragraph the graphic is in, then change the leading to anything you like *except Auto* (see 4.12–4.26).
- A simple thing to do is to use Page-Maker's "Align to grid" feature. Select the paragraphs you want to adjust. If the graphic is in a paragraph by itself (such as most of the inline graphics you see in this book in the first column), you only need to select that one graphic.
  □ From the Type menu, choose "Paragraph...."
  □ Click "Rules...."
  □ Click "Options...."
  □ Check the box "Align to grid."
  □ In the "Grid size" edit box, type the leading value used in the rest of the text, or select it from the mini-menu.
  □ Press Option Return to close all the dialog boxes.

- Inline graphics drop in with a boundary around them, and this boundary uses a slug, just like text (4.32–4.33). The slug has its own autoleading, and when you drop the graphic into text it can throw the linespacing off: baselines will not align across columns anymore.
- You may have to adjust the graphic vertically once you have fixed the leading (9.201).
- If your graphic looks fragmented, just redraw the screen (change views, etc.).
- Read 4.89–4.103 about the "Align to grid" feature and what it really does.
- Also see 9.202 for a tip on how to precisely align the space above and below an inline graphic that is in its own paragraph.

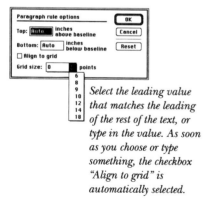

Select the leading value that matches the leading of the rest of the text, or type in the value. As soon as you choose or type something, the checkbox "Align to grid" is automatically selected.

If you want to do this:

19.10 Superscript and kern characters for special effects

The smaller letters are superscripted, (each with different specs) but unkerned.

After kerning.

This is just to show that the type effect is really one text block.

Then follow these steps:

- The example on the left shows two different ways of using superscripts and kerning to create interesting type effects.

  The first word, *Limousine*, has a Typo Upright (Bitstream font) letter *L* at 48 point. The rest of the word is 9-point Walbaum Roman (Adobe font). I selected *imousine* and chose "Type specs..." from the Type menu. I changed "Position" to "Superscript," and then clicked the "Options..." button. I changed the Superscript size to 100% *(you can go up to 200%);* I changed the superscript position to 105% *(you can go up to 500%).*

  Then I set the insertion point between the *L* and the *i* and kerned (pressed Command Delete, repeating the Delete) until the word appeared as you see it.

  The second word, *Service*, has a Typo Upright letter *S* and Walbaum Roman *ervice,* all at 48 point this time. I selected *ervice* and chose "Type specs..." from the Type menu. I changed "Position" to "Superscript," and then clicked the "Options..." button. I changed the Superscript size to 19% (which made it 9 point, like the first word); I changed the superscript position to 41.5%. Then I kerned it.

Shortcuts ▾ Notes ▾ Hints

- This is an expansion on the section about superscript and subscripts. There are lots of fun things to do with this feature. See 3.163–3.172 for more info on super- and subscripts. See 4.165–4.186 for more info on kerning.

If you want to do this:

Then follow these steps:

Shortcuts ▾ Notes ▾ Hints

19.11 Initial caps

Never underestimate
the number of choices
you have.
   Donald K. Lee

The formatted text.

I **N**ever underestimate
the number of choices
you have.
   Donald K. Lee

The leading has been fixed, and the initial cap enlarged.

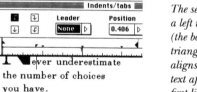

I **N**ever underestimate
the number of choices
you have.
   Donald K. Lee

The setting for a left indent (the bottom triangle). This aligns all the text after the first line.

Never underestimate
the number of choices
you have.
   Donald K. Lee

The initial letter, subscripted. I changed the size, one point at a time, until it sat right on the third baseline.

- This technique uses a subscript letter, (3.163–3.171), fixed leading (4.25–4.26), and indents (5.46–5.52).
- Type the text. Format the text for fonts, sizes, and styles.
- Select the entire paragraph (triple click with the text tool) and *fix* the leading; that is, apply any leading value you want, other than Auto (4.25; 4.54).
- Select the first letter. Change it to the size, or at least the approximate size, you want it to be as an initial cap. Part of it may disappear because it bumps out of the text block. To make it reappear, click on it once with the **pointer tool** and press Command F (to "Bring to front").
- Select the text with the **text tool.** Press Command I to get the Indents/Tabs ruler. Set a left indent to a position to the right of the initial cap (5.71).
- Select the first letter with the **text tool.** Press Command T to get the "Type specs" dialog box. Change "Position" to Subscript.
- Click "Options...." Change the Subscript *size* to 100%. Change the Subscript *position* to a value up to 500%. The higher the value, the lower the number will sit. In the example, the value is 50%. Click OK; OK.
- Adjust the kerning, leading, and indent.

- There are several ways to create initial caps; see 11.40 for another method, using text wrap. The advantage of using a subscripted letter over a text wrap is that with a subscript, the paragraph is still one piece and can be rolled up, edited, or moved easily.
- An initial cap should always have its baseline aligned with another baseline in the text.
- This is just one example. You can use the combination of super- or subscripts, fixed leading, and indents in an incredible variety of ways!
- When a character is bumped out of the text block, it will regularly disappear. You will see it again anytime the screen redraws. In the directions to the left, you redraw the *text block* by bringing it to the front, which is the fastest way to bring back your letter. You can also click in the zoom box (upper right of the window), change views, choose the same view you are looking at—virtually anything that makes the screen draw itself again.

If you want to do this:	Then follow these steps:	Shortcuts ▾ Notes ▾ Hints
19.12 Let go of the text or graphics that are in the loaded text icon without placing them on the page.	■ With any loaded icon (text or graphics), simply click on any tool in the Toolbox, *or* press Command Spacebar.	
19.13 Prevent a word from hyphenating	■ With the **text tool,** click the insertion point directly in front of the first character of the word that you don't want to hyphenate. ■ Press Command Hyphen; this creates a *discretionary hyphen* (4.224) that will prevent the word from hyphenating in this paragraph. You will not *see* the discretionary hyphen. ■ To remove that discretionary hyphen, backspace over it, even though you can't even see it.	■ If you *never* want that word to hyphenate, add it to the user dictionary, specifying no hyphenation (4.243). ■ In PageMaker version 4.01: If you don't want *any* words to ever hyphenate, choose the dictionary "None" for the applicable paragraphs, or default the dictionary "None" (3.210).
19.14 Proportionally re-size a PageMaker-drawn rectangle 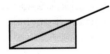 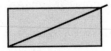	■ Click once on the **diagonal line tool.** ■ Draw a thin line from one corner diagonally across to the other corner, stretching *beyond* the corner if you want to enlarge the rectangle. ■ Click once on the **pointer tool.** ■ Drag the rectangle's corner handle along the diagonal line. As long as you resize along that diagonal line, the rectangle will be in perfect proportion to the original. It's easiest in 400% view. ■ Delete the diagonal line.	■ You've probably tried to proportionally resize a rectangle by holding down the Shift key as you resize, just as you would to a graphic. You discovered that Shift-dragging turns any rectangle into a square. If you did that, I hope you remembered to immediately Command Z to Undo the stretch.

If you want to do this:	**Then follow these steps:**	**Shortcuts ▾ Notes ▾ Hints**
19.15 Start a publication on a left-hand page or on a double-page spread	■ From the file menu, choose "Page setup...." ■ In the "Start page #" edit box, enter an even number. ■ This will, of course, change your automatic page numbers. If you are not going to automatically number the pages, then you have nothing to worry about. If you are going to have PageMaker number the pages, then before you print you will have to go back to the "Page setup" dialog box and change the "Start page #" back to the actual number of the first page.	■ This works great for those times when you have only two pages in your publication and you want to view them together. Unless you use this little trick, they will never display side-by-side on the screen. (Remember, to view pages side-by-side, you must choose "Double-sided" and "Facing pages" in the "Page setup" dialog box; 1.34, 1.35).

19.16 Hang the punctuation

> **"Time is Money, and the way to buy Time is Money."**
> *Chip Swanson*

> **"Time is Money, and the way to buy Time is Money."**
> *Chip Swanson*

I inserted an en space and a thin space in front of the second and third lines. I put two en spaces in front of the fourth line, selected one, and made it one point size smaller. I reduced the size of the quotation marks and the period, kerned the space open a touch between the first quotation mark and the T, and closed up a hair after the period. Yes, I am fussy with my letters. But my house is a mess.

■ It's not possible yet in PageMaker to send text out to the left of the text block, so you must indent everything else. Indent the other lines by either of these methods:

■ Insert hard spaces (ems, ens, or thins; 4.207–4.218) to bump the line over. You can select those hard spaces and reduce or enlarge them increments of a point, if necessary, for perfect alignment.

■ **Or** if the hanging needs to be done on the left and only on the first line, you can set a first-line indent flush left, and set the left indent in just to where the rest of the text should align. (See 5.46–5.52 re: indents.)

■ In large-size text (14-point or above) or in quoted material, always hang the punctuation (*hang* it outside the aligned edge of text, whether on the left or the right). If you don't hang the punctuation, it makes the aligned edge look unaligned.

■ Hanging the punctuation is always the very last thing to do, because if you have to edit the text *after* you've taken care of the punctuation, ya gotta start all over again (unless you use the indent method).

■ Notice in the example I aligned the second and third lines with the *stem* of the T, not the *bar*. That's because in this case the stem was stronger visually.

673

If you want to do this:	**Then follow these steps:**	**Shortcuts ▾ Notes ▾ Hints**

19.17 Use leaders for creating lines that end evenly (when you don't want to, or can't, use paragraph rules)

Hello

My name is _____

My favorite book is _____

I hate _____

When I grow up I want to be _____

The title of my autobiography will be _____

The example above uses the line leader; the example below uses the dots.

Hello

My name is ....

My favorite book is ....

I hate ....

When I grow up I want to be ....

The title of my autobiography will be ....

Section 5 on Indents and Tabs details all the explicit steps for creating tabs with leaders. See 5.32 and 5.63.
- The basic idea is that you set a right-aligned tab at the end of the line, and assign a leader to it.
- Type the text, hit Tab. You probably won't see the leader until you hit a Return.
- Continue typing text and hitting Tabs and Returns. The lines will always end at the same place.
- If you shorten the text block with the text handles, you may need to move the tab over to the left, as well. If you have a 3" text block and you set a tab at 2.5 inches, the tab is defined at 2.5 inches; it is not defined as being .5" from the end of the text block, as paragraph rules are. If you shorten the text block to 2", the tab at 2.5" inches is gone. If you stretch the text block back out to 3", the tab will return.

- The great thing about using leaders is that they are so incredibly easy: You can lengthen or shorten then instantly, you can customize them, you're always assured they'll end neatly, and when you change the point size or the leading, you know the leaders will move right along with the type. Just like paragraph rules. In the example on the left, leaders have an advantage over paragraph rules because they can start wherever the text ends, without having to spec each line. The disadvantage is that you cannot control the point size of the line. You can customize the leader character, though; see 5.63–5.65.

If you want to do this:

19.18 Adjust the height of parentheses, hyphens, quotations marks, etc.

(parentheses) hy-phen

Parentheses and hyphens are designed for use with lowercase letters.

(RAM) (RAM)

Notice in the first RAM how the parentheses hit the top of the caps, but seem to drop too low below the baseline. In the second example, I raised the parentheses a bit.

(707) 570-1564
(707) 570-1564

In the first example, the hyphen seems too low. The parentheses have the same problem around numbers as they do around caps. In the second example, both the hyphen and the parentheses have been raised (and I kerned the hyphen away from the zero).

Then follow these steps:

- After the text has been typed, select a parenthesis or a hyphen (press-and-drag over it, or press Shift Arrow key).
- Press Command T to get the "Type specifications" dialog box.
- In the "Position" mini-menu, choose "Superscript."
- Click the button "Options...."
- Hit the Tab key once to select the "Super/subscript size" edit box. Enter **100.**
- Hit the Tab key once more to select the "Superscript position" edit box. Enter **9.**
- Click OK, click OK; *or* press Option Return to close both dialog boxes.
- This raised the one parenthesis or hyphen. If there are others you want to adjust, you can follow the same procedure for each one, *or* you can copy the adjusted character. Select another character and paste the adjusted one in. (If you paste a left parenthesis where a right parenthesis should go, just select the new one and type the right parenthesis back in; that space, even after you delete the adjusted character, retains the formatting.)
- Unfortunately, you cannot use Find-and-Change to globally search for and replace super- or subscript values. Yet.

Shortcuts ▾ Notes ▾ Hints

- Parentheses and hyphens are designed, by default, to be used with lowercase letters, since that is what they do most often. But when parentheses and hyphens are used with capital letters or with numbers, they appear too low. In Page-Maker 4, you can now adjust the vertical placement of these characters. I know you are so happy. I know those darn things have been bugging you for years and you are so excited that there is finally a solution.
- You may notice that I did not apply this technique throughout this book. When the Find-and-Change dialog box can do this for me, I will redo the entire book.

If you want to do this:

19.19 Print one PageMaker publication while inside another

Then follow these steps:

- From the File menu, choose "Book...."
- If there are any publications listed on the right-hand side, under "Book list," then select and remove them (click on the name, then click the "Remove" button).
- Using the left-hand list box, locate the publication you want to print. Double-click on its name, and it will appear in the right-hand list.
- Click OK.
- From the File menu, choose "Print...."
- Click in the button "Print entire book."
- If you click OK right now, PageMaker will not print the current publication, but will print *only* the publication that is in the Book List. That particular publication will print with the specifications you set here in this dialog box (regardless of page numbers).

  If you want to print the other publication with the type specifications that are stored within it, hold down the Option key while you click OK (the only way to store printing specifications is to print all the way through the document, without canceling or uncompleting in any way).

Shortcuts ▾ Notes ▾ Hints

- If you want to print more than one publication, than transfer the name of more than one publication into the Book List (see 13.6–13.27 for more info on the Book List). PageMaker will print the publications in the order they appear in the List. If you want to renumber the pages in the publication you are about to print, see 13.27 (possible only in PageMaker version 4.01).

If you want to do this:	**Then follow these steps:**	**Shortcuts ▾ Notes ▾ Hints**
19.20 Automatically number the pages, but prevent the front matter (title page, introduction, etc.) from being included in the numbering	■ Often in a publication you have a title page and perhaps some other front matter that you don't want numbered. But then when you automatically number the pages, the *real* first page does not get labeled as page one. To solve that problem simply put the front matter at the *end* of the publication. That is, create the page that you want numbered as page one *on* page one. Create the rest of the pages in their order. At the end of the publication, say pages 14, 15, and 16, create the front matter (the title page, the introduction, etc.). On those end pages, **either:** □ Remove the master page numbers on the current page by choosing "Display master items" from the Page menu. This will remove *all* the master page items on the screen, not just the page numbers (1.135). □ **Or** cover the master page numbers with opaque boxes, drawn with PageMaker's drawing tools (1.136).	

If you want to do this:	**Then follow these steps:**	**Shortcuts ▾ Notes ▾ Hints**
19.21 Keep track of certain information about a publication, such as time spent, client comments, etc.	▪ Simply create a little text block on the pasteboard. Make it a chart, if you like, detailing the time you opened the publication, the time you closed it, the changes you made, etc. Then each time you open and close the publication, fill in the chart to keep a running total of time and current information on the project. To print the chart, just make an extra page at the end of the publication and move the text block onto it. Also see 18.159 for a tip on how to print something off the page.	
19.22 Arrange text in several sets of columns on one page; e.g., in a three-column format across the top two-thirds of the page and a five-column format on the bottom third	▪ Set up your columns guides and place the text for one of the column formats, say three columns. Then change the columns. The text in the first columns will not move. ▪ **Or** you could set up a multiple column format, like six columns, and then drag-place the text into the special column sizes you want. See 1.208 and 3.58 for details on drag-placing.	▪ No, this is not a very elegant trick. But this is the only way to accomplish a multiple column format.

If you want to do this:	Then follow these steps:	Shortcuts · Notes · Hints
19.23 Create text up to 1300 points	▪ Size the type to one-half of the final size you want. For instance, if you want 900-point type, size it to 450. Select the text. ▪ Press Command T to get the type specs. ▪ Change the "Position" to "Superscript." ▪ Click on the "Options…" button. Change the "Superscript size" to 100%. Change the "Superscript position" to 0 (zero). ▪ Click the OK buttons.	▪ Of course, you could change the super-script size to anything from 100% to 200%, instead of always 200%. ▪ See 3.163–3.170 for full details on super- and subscript.
19.24 In PageMaker version 4.01, prevent the last text block from expanding as text is edited	▪ The last text block will expand if it has not been rolled up intentionally. So to prevent the block from expanding, hit an extra return after the last line of text. Then roll up the text block one line.	▪ Sometimes you want the last text block in the story to expand as you edit, sometimes you don't. In version 4.01 you have a choice.
19.25 Apply the same Image Control settings to several TIFFs	▪ Set up a TIFF on the page and apply the Image Control settings you want to recreate. Make a couple copies of it and move them into position. ▪ With the **pointer tool,** click once on one of the copies of the TIFF graphic. ▪ *Place* the new TIFF as usual (9.92), but be sure to first click the button "Replacing entire graphic." The new graphic will replace the selected one, *and* it will drop in with the same Image Control settings and cropped size as the selected graphic. ▪ Repeat the process for the other TIFFs.	▪ This technique will only work with TIFFs that you *place* from the File menu; it will not work with TIFFs that you try to *paste* from the Clipboard.

If you want to do this:	Then follow these steps:	Shortcuts ▾ Notes ▾ Hints
19.26 Recompose all the text in the publication	■ Hold down the Option key and choose "Hyphenation…" from the Type menu. It will take a few minutes. ■ When you get the "Hyphenation" dialog box, just click Cancel. ■ Press Command S to save the publication again or the text will recompose every time you turn a page.	■ If you find that your text has weird spacing problems because you changed fonts or converted the file from another program, or because you opened the publication on someone else's computer, try this global recompose.

19.27 Run a diagnostic on the publication, in addition to recomposing all the text	■ Choose the **pointer tool.**
	■ Hold both the Shift and the Option keys down. From the Type menu, choose "Hyphenation…."
	  □ If you hear **one beep:** PageMaker did not find any problems.
	  □ If you hear **two beeps:** PageMaker found a problem and fixed it.
	  □ If you hear **three beeps:** PageMaker found a problem but could not fix it.
	■ Save your publication again.
		■ This diagnostic sometimes fixes things like bad links or bad styles. If your publication is giving you grief about something or other, start with this diagnostic to see if PageMaker can take care of the problem.

If you want to do this:

19.28 Create paragraph rules that *begin* outside the text block

a

They are ill discoverers Francis Bacon
that think there is no land,
when they can see nothing
but sea.

b

They are ill discoverers Francis Bacon
that think there is no land,
when they can see nothing
but sea.

c

They are ill discoverers Francis Bacon
that think there is no land,
when they can see nothing
but sea.

Then follow these steps:

Really, this is too cool. You can set up paragraph rules that actually begin and end *outside* of the text block.

- Create the rule as usual (see Section 6).
- In the "Paragraph rules" dialog box, set the "Indent" for one side that extends *beyond* the column width or the text (the value for the indent should be a negative number).
- Set the "Indent" for the opposite side as a positive number. It is the positive indent that bumps the negative indent out of the text block. Here's an example:
  - ◻ In **a,** I put a rule in the paragraph *Francis Bacon.* I clicked "Width of text" (I could have used "Width of column" if I chose). The left indent is –8p6; the right indent is 0. So the rule starts at the end of the text (the right indent) and continues 8p6 out to the left of the text (left indent).
  - ◻ In **b,** I set the right indent at 4p5. So the rule *starts* 4p5 from the right, which bumps the right end of the rule over, outside the text block.
  - ◻ In **c,** I set the right indent at 7 picas. So the indent bumps the beginning of the rule over even farther.

Shortcuts ▾ Notes ▾ Hints

- See Section 6 for all the details on creating paragraph rules.
- I used this in a newsletter of PageMaker tips. The far left column had the heads. In the style sheet for the heads, I built a paragraph rule that started a pica-and-a-half outside the headline text block and extended over the next two columns to the right, above the story that belonged to the head. Then, whenever I applied that style, the rule went shooting over the columns right where it belonged.

If you want to do this:	Then follow these steps:	Shortcuts ▾ Notes ▾ Hints

19.29 "Crop" a graphic into an oval or circular shape

On the left is the oval with the thick line enclosing the photograph. On the right, the thick line has been reversed.

- All you need to do is choose the **oval/circle tool** and draw an oval with a thick line, like 12 point.
- With the **pointer tool,** click once on the oval. From the Element menu, go back to the Lines submenu and choose "Reverse." Also from the Element menu, choose a Fill of "None." Then position the shape so that it frames (crops) your graphic.
- If you need more coverage, create the reverse circle and copy it to the Scrapbook. *Place* the image from the Scrapbook (9.96 and 9.107) and then you can resize the oval/circle, resulting in a thicker line.

19.30 Set text flush left and right so it will adjust if the text block changes width

Party at Toad Hall **June 1**

Party at Toad Hall **June 1**

- On the left side of the text block, type the text you want flush left.
- Hit Tab. It doesn't matter where the text goes, as long as there is a tab set somewhere on the line.
- Type the text you want to be flush right.
- With the insertion point still flashing in that line, press Command Shift R (that's the keyboard shortcut for right-aligned text). Now if you resize the text block, the text will adjust to the left and right sides.

A short account intended to allay
the Difficulties and Discouragements
which may attend Users
in the Pursuit of Learning.

20 ▾ HELP!

20.1 This section is a compilation of the most common problems I have seen hundreds upon hundreds of people struggle with in PageMaker as I taught them to use the program. I built many of the answers to these problems into the appropriate sections in this book, but I have also included some of them here so you don't have to go digging through the pages (there are always reference numbers, of course). If you don't find your specific problem here, check the index for information on the most closely-related topic.

20.2 PageMaker provides an online Help file for getting information about every command and various topics. See 20.3 for specific details on accessing the Help file.

The ability to simplify means to eliminate the unnecessary so that the necessary may speak. *—Hans Hoffman*

If:	**Then follow these steps:**	**Shortcuts ▾ Notes ▾ Hints**

20.3 You want to use PageMaker's online Help file

PageMaker's online Help screen

? *The Help cursor*

- From the Windows menu, choose "Help...."
- On the Help screen, click the button "Using Help" for details on exactly how to get the information you need.

- An alternate way to use the Help screen, but to go straight to the information about a command, is to use the **menu-sensitive Help:**
  - Press Command **?** *or* press the Help key on an extended keyboard. This turns your cursor into a question mark.
  - With the **question mark cursor,** choose any item from any menu to get basic information on that command (for commands with submenus, go into the submenu before you let go of the mouse button).
  - If you have the question mark cursor and you don't want any help, just click once on the pointer tool to get your pointer back.

- If you have the Help cursor and you want to get rid of it, either click on the pointer tool *or* press Command Period.

If:	**Then follow these steps:**	**Shortcuts ▾ Notes ▾ Hints**
20.4 You want to reduce the file size of the publication	▪ Use "Save as..." to reduce the file size. See 16.1–16.4 for information on why your files get so large and why "Save as..." reduces them. See 16.25 for the specific steps to actually compress the file. Basically, all you need to do is choose "Save as..." from the File menu, don't change the name of the publication, click OK, and when you are asked if you want to replace the existing file, click Yes.	▪ If you have PageMaker version 4.01 or later, you have the option of automatically compressing the file size every time you save, just as if you went through the "Save as..." procedure. It takes a bit longer, though. See 16.5 for information on this option.
20.5 There is not enough room on the disk to "Save as..." 	Even though "Save as..." makes the file smaller, PageMaker initially must have extra room on the disk to work the changes. If there is no room on the disk, you will have to save onto another disk: ▪ Click Drive *or* press the Tab key to switch disks; you may need to Eject one disk and insert another. ▪ After you "Save as..." onto another disk, you can always replace the larger file with the newer, smaller version later (just copy the smaller one back onto the disk). Even though PageMaker wouldn't let you actually compress the file on the original disk, the smaller file will usually fit on the original disk *after* it has been saved.	

If:	Then follow these steps:	Shortcuts ▾ Notes ▾ Hints

20.6 The OK button is gray when you try to "Save as..."

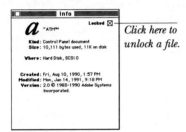

Click here to unlock a file.

The OK button will be gray if you try to save changes to a locked file or if the disk you are saving onto is locked.

To unlock a file so you can save changes:

- Quit PageMaker (if you are working under MultiFinder, just close the publication and return to the Finder).
- Click once on the file that is locked; press Command I to get the Get Info dialog box.
- In the upper right corner, the "Locked" checkbox has a check in it; click in the checkbox to remove the check.
- Close the Get Info box; go back to your publication. Now you can "Save as...."

To unlock a disk so you can save changes:

- In the "Save as..." dialog box, click "Eject" to spit out the disk.
- On the back of the disk is a little hole with a tab that covers or uncovers it. If you can see through the hole, the disk is locked. Slide the tab over the hole to close it.
- Insert the disk back into the drive. Continue saving as usual.

- On high-density disks you will see two holes, one with a tab and one without. The tabbed hole locks the disk; the other hole tells the computer that this disk is high-density.

If:	**Then follow these steps:**	**Shortcuts ▾ Notes ▾ Hints**
20.7 You click the I-beam, but you don't see the insertion point	The insertion point will always jump over to the column edge. Usually the type default is left-aligned, so it jumps to the left edge. If you don't see the insertion point, check these things: ■ Make sure the **text tool** has been chosen. Then click the I-beam once more on the page before you check the rest of these possibilities. ■ Type a couple of words. The screen will usually jump to the text. ■ From the Type menu, check the "Alignment" submenu. If the text is right- or center-aligned, then the insertion point is jumping to the center of the text block or to the right edge. Can you see the right edge or the center? If you can't, change your page view to something smaller. ■ In a small view, such as Fit in Window, you may need to look carefully to see the insertion point flashing. If you are inside the page margins, it will generally flash right on top of the guide lines. If you are outside the page margins, the insertion point may be far over on the right, depending on your alignment and page margins (see note at right).	■ If you have changed the color Paper (on a color monitor) to something other than white, you may find that you cannot see the insertion point. Type a few words and you will find its hiding place. ■ When you click the I-beam within the page margins, PageMaker creates a text block the width of the column (there is always at least one column on the page). The insertion point will place itself in reference to the text block edges, according to the specified alignment. If you click the I-beam outside the page margins, PageMaker automatically sets up a text block that is the width of the space within the margins. That is, if the page is 8.5 x 11, but you specified a one-inch margin left and right, then the width of the space within the margins is 6.5 inches. So any text block outside these page margins will automatically be 6.5 inches. ■ If you click on the pasteboard (1.4) to the left of the page, the text block will bump into the page and stop, in which case the text block *won't* be as wide as the margins. ■ Be sure to read about text blocks and how to control them (3.95–3.122). Especially get the trick about creating bounding boxes: 3.25; 3.58.

If:	Then follow these steps:	Shortcuts ▾ Notes ▾ Hints
20.8 You can see the insertion point, but it is not at the left edge where you really want it	■ The alignment is not left-aligned. From the Type menu, choose "Alignment," then slide out and choose "Align left." ■ If you choose that command while the insertion point is flashing, the alignment will be changed for just that one paragraph of text. ■ If you choose that command while no insertion point is flashing (click once on the text tool, just to make sure), then you will be setting a new alignment *default* (see 3.242–3.247).	■ You could also use the keyboard command, Command Shift L, to change the alignment to "Align left."
20.9 You can't see the guides that you are bringing in	One of two things is probably happening: ■ The guides have been turned off. Check the Options menu; if there is no checkmark next to "Guides," they are turned off. Choose "Guides" again to turn them back on. ■ The guides have all been sent to the back, and thus they can hide behind solid objects. If you want to bring them to the front so you can always see them: □ From the Edit menu, choose "Preferences...." Under "Guides," click the "Front" button. Click OK.	■ If you turned off the guides, or if you sent all the guides to the back because they were irritating you, then you may want to read 1.151–1.157 about layering and getting beneath the layers. If a guide is on top and you want to select something beneath it, hold the Command key down. You can then select the object under the guide (1.173; 1.215).

If:

20.10 You can't unroll a text block, or the text block "exhibits puzzling behavior"

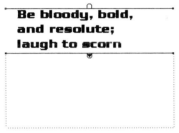

One example of "puzzling behavior" is when you cannot unroll a text block.

Then follow these steps:

- Did you add any **paragraph rules** to the text? What measurement did you enter in the edit boxes for placing the rules above or below the baseline? Did you add any **"paragraph space before or after"**? What measurement did you enter? Go back and check. It is very easy to insert 15 *picas* or *inches,* when you really wanted 15 *points.* If you think you may have added too much space before or after paragraphs or rules, but now you can't unroll the text block to check the paragraph, use the Story Editor (with the text tool, click in the last paragraph you can find, then press Command E).
- **Or** click the insertion point in the last paragraph. Press Command E to get the Story Editor so you can see everything in the story. Do you see any of these **symbols** in the troublesome area: ■ ? These represent inline graphics (9.91). If you see one of these symbols in the paragraph following the last part of the text you are able to get on the screen, that graphic is probably the thing that is causing you trouble. Select it (press-and-drag over it) and hit the Backspace/Delete key to remove it. Press Command E again to get back to your page. Now can you unroll the text block? *—continued*

Shortcuts ▾ Notes ▾ Hints

- See 1.221 for details on how to override the measurement systems in any dialog box (that is, if the measurement spec says "inches," you can temporarily override it by entering values in points, picas, ciceros, millimeters, etc.).
- If you need to select a rolled-up text block you can't see anymore, see 20.11.

- If the inline graphic is causing you trouble, it may be because it is too large. Place or paste the object as an independent graphic first (by choosing the pointer tool before you place or paste). Reduce the size of the graphic, and then cut-and-paste it into the text.

If:	Then follow these steps:	Shortcuts ▾ Notes ▾ Hints
— *"Puzzling behavior" continued*	■ In the Story Editor, click in the paragraph *following* the last one you can see on the screen. Press Command M. Are any of the "Options" checked? Before you uncheck any of the options, make sure you understand what the option is accomplishing; perhaps you want to leave it applied and work with its purpose (see 3.211–3.229 for info on the options, often called "keeps").	■ These paragraph options can really make your text act weird: text blocks won't unroll, they'll hop right off the page, etc.
	■ **If any of these specifications keeps recurring** (like every time you start to type text, the space between the paragraphs gives you trouble), then it means someone *(not you, of course)* has accidentally set an inappropriate default **or** has set the problematic specification in a style sheet.	
	☐ **To fix a style sheet:** Check the style sheet in the problem paragraph. Delete the problem specs.	■ See Section 7 on Style Sheets; see 7.48 for editing a style definition.
	☐ **To change a default:** Click on the **pointer tool.** From the Type menu, slide down to "Style" and choose "No style." Then go into the dialog box that holds the problem specification, and delete the specs.	■ See 1.6–1.16 for general information on defaults. See 3.242–3.247 for information on text defaults.
	■ If the text acts funny when it gets near a graphic image or a line or box, the graphic may have a *text wrap* applied. See 20.21 for a solution.	■ For detailed information on text wrapping, see Section 11.

If:	**Then follow these steps:**	**Shortcuts ▾ Notes ▾ Hints**
20.11 You lost a text block—you rolled it up (or maybe it rolled itself up) and now it has disappeared	■ As long as you didn't hit the Backspace/Delete key to actually *delete* the text block, it is still there. Press Command W to view the page at window size (assuming the lost text block was within that space). ■ Click on the **pointer tool.** ■ Press Command A to select all. Do you see the rolled up windowshade of the lost text block? It will look like this: ■ After you find it, click in any blank area to deselect all the objects. ■ With the **pointer tool,** press-and-drag to create a marquee around the area where you saw this lost block. You may have to do this several times in order to capture it. Remember, you must enclose both ends of the rolled-up text block within the marquee. ■ Once you have the rolled-up text block selected, see if you can unroll it. □ If you can't, press Command E while it is selected. This will open the text block in the Story Editor. Now read 20.10 and see if you have any formatting or inline graphics that are causing problems. ■ If all else fails, Revert to the last time you saved, or mini-Revert to the last mini-save (16.26; 16.27).	■ If you think the lost text block may be on the pasteboard somewhere, then press Command 0 (zero) instead of Command W to view the entire pasteboard. Then follow the rest of the steps. ■ If you don't quite understand how to use the marquee to select objects, see 1.169. ■ Of course, reverting will only help if you saved or mini-saved before this trouble occurred.

If:	Then follow these steps:	Shortcuts ▾ Notes ▾ Hints
20.12 You can't tell what page you are on	■ This will only happen if your pages happen to be numbered beyond 1000; you can't tell if the page is 1234, 4234, etc., because the icons can only fit three numbers in them. See 1.121 for a solution.	
20.13 You can't align objects exactly where you want because they jump around	■ Check the Options menu. □ If "Snap to guides" is on (has a check-mark next to it), then the handles of the objects will jump to any guideline they get close to. In fact, the draw-tool cursor itself will jump to the guidelines. Choose "Snap to guides" again to turn it off. □ If "Snap to rulers" is on, then the handles of the objects *will jump to the tick marks of the rulers*. In fact, the draw-tool cursor itself will jump to the ruler tick marks. You can take advantage of this by customizing your rulers, essentially creating a "snap-on" grid (1.56; 4.89–4.96; 4.99). Choose "Snap to rulers" again to turn the command off.	
20.14 You want to unload the text or graphic that is in the loaded icon, but you don't want to put it on the page	■ Click on any tool in the Toolbox *or* press Command Spacebar. The loaded icon is now gone and you have the tool cursor. ■ **Or** press-and-drag the text or graphic into a small bounding box on the pasteboard (1.208–1.209).	■ Placing the graphic or a small chunk of the text on the pasteboard makes it handy to use later.

If:	Then follow these steps:	Shortcuts ▾ Notes ▾ Hints
20.15 You type, but no text appears on the screen	▪ The most likely cause is that the type is Reverse. With the insertion point still flashing, go up to the Type menu, down to "Type style," and see if "Reverse" has a checkmark next to it. If so, choose "Reverse" again to turn it off; now all text you typc in that text block will be visible. If there is text on the page you still can't see, select it and choose "Reverse" again. *You do need to check to make sure "Reverse" is not a default:* ▫ Click once on the **text tool,** even if it is already selected. Check again to see if "Reverse" has a checkmark next to it. If so, choose it again to turn it off.	▪ See 1.6–1.16 for info on defaults in general; see 3.242–3.247 for info on text defaults. Basically, if there is no text selected and no insertion point flashing, then whatever you choose from the menus will become the new defaults.
20.16 Some reverse text you created is now lost and you want to find it	▪ You'll find detailed directions for solving this problem in 3.148.	
20.17 Every time you type, the text shows up in a font you don't want	▪ Click once on the pointer tool. ▪ From the Type menu, go to the "Font" submenu and choose the font that you do want to show up (as the default).	▪ You need to learn how to control Page-Maker's defaults. See 1.6–1.16 and 3.242–3.247. Check the application defaults as well as the publication defaults.

If:	Then follow these steps:	Shortcuts ▾ Notes ▾ Hints
20.18 You draw a line, but it doesn't show up	■ The Line default is "Reverse." To make the current line show up (if you can still see its handles), go to the Lines submenu and uncheck "Reverse" (select it again). ■ To change the default, click once on the **pointer tool** or either **line tool.** ■ From the Element menu, get the Lines submenu. If there is a checkmark next to "Reverse," choose "Reverse" again to remove the check.	■ See 1.6–1.16 for general info on defaults; see 2.49–2.51 for info on the defaults for the drawing tools.
20.19 You think you created a bunch of reverse lines and you want to get rid of them	■ Click once on the **pointer tool.** ■ Press Command A to select all. Do you see handles with nothing between? Note where the invisible lines are. Click once in a blank area to deselect everything. ■ Go back to where you saw the invisible objects and try to select them (click around, or use the marquee to grab objects within an area; see 1.169). ■ Once you have their handles, hit the Backspace/Delete key to remove them.	■ If there are no other lines or boxes on the page, you can un-reverse the lines without having to deselect everything. "Reverse" from the Lines submenu will not affect text or non-PageMaker-drawn objects.
20.20 Every time you draw a line or a box, it shows up in a line width or a fill you don't want.	■ Learn to control the defaults. See 1.6–1.16 for general info on defaults; see 2.49–2.51 for info on the defaults for the drawing tools.	

If:	**Then follow these steps:**	**Shortcuts ▾ Notes ▾ Hints**
20.21 Everything you draw or paste or place shows up with a text wrap around it *(that is, the text jumps away from every graphic you put on the page)*	■ Someone inadvertently set a text wrap default. To remove the text wrap from the objects on the page, do this to each graphic, one at a time: □ With the **pointer tool,** click once on the graphic. □ From the Element menu, choose "Text wrap...." □ Click on the first icon under "Wrap options": **Wrap option:** . Click OK. ■ To change the default so this doesn't happen again, follow the same steps, just make sure *there is no object selected* before you go to the Element menu (click once on the pointer tool to make sure).	■ If your text is "exhibiting puzzling behavior," also check 20.10.
20.22 The last line of a paragraph has too much linespace above it	■ Choose the **text tool.** ■ Position the I-beam directly after the last character in the paragraph; click to set the insertion point. ■ Hit a Return. This will bump the last line up to match the linespace of the rest of the paragraph. ■ This may give you an extra blank line after the paragraph that you don't want. If so, move the insertion point down to the beginning of the next line of text and hit the Backspace/Delete key.	

If:	Then follow these steps:	Shortcuts ▾ Notes ▾ Hints
20.23 You enlarged a character in a paragraph (like an initial cap), **or** you inserted an inline graphic, and it changed the linespace in a way you don't like	■ The linespace changed because the leading is Autoleading (4.20–4.24). You need to *fix* the leading (4.25–4.26). Fix it *after* the larger character or the graphic has been added to the paragraph, not *before*. ■ With the **text tool,** triple-click in the paragraph. ■ From the Type menu, go down to "Leading," then out to the submenu. Either choose one of the leading values listed, or choose "Other…" and enter your own value. As long as you choose any value other than "Auto," the linespace in the paragraph will be consistent.	■ See 4.12–4.51 for detailed information on leading, both fixed and auto.
20.24 You changed the master page guides, but they didn't change on your publication page	■ On the publication page, go up to the Page menu and choose "Copy master guides." (If that command is gray, it indicates that the page already has the master page guides on it.)	■ If you have added, deleted, or moved any guides on any page, PageMaker leaves your custom ones there and does not switch them to the new master page guides.
20.25 You changed the leading and now the tops of the letters have disappeared	■ This is not really a problem, because the letters will print anyway. But it is disturbing. Anytime the screen redraws (as when you change views or pages, etc.), the letter tops will reappear. I find the simplest thing to do is to click once on the text block with the **pointer tool,** then press Command F (to Bring to Front).	

If:	Then follow these steps:	Shortcuts ▾ Notes ▾ Hints
20.26 You specified paragraph rules that extend beyond the text block, but they don't show up on the screen	▪ Don't worry—they will show up when you print. Things have trouble when they leave the text block; it's like they go into the Twilight Zone. Large inline graphics, long paragraph rules, and text with little leading all freak out, but they do print all right. Reversed text on top of a paragraph rule also disappears, but prints. You can try changing the view; it sometimes makes the rule appear temporarily.	▪ Not being able to see the outer boundaries of a paragraph rule presents only one problem: you cannot tell if the rule reaches to exactly the point you need it to. You will have to print a few proofs to get the length exactly right.
20.27 You specified thick paragraph rules and you have reversed text on top of them. When you insert a tab, the text disappears and won't print.	▪ That's right—it won't.	▪ This is one of those things that Aldus Tech Support calls an "unexplained feature" because they are not allowed to use the B word.
20.28 You want to open a copy of a template, but you can't tell from the list which publications are templates	▪ When you click on a file name in the list box, look at the radio buttons on the bottom right. If the button "Copy" is on, then the selected file is a template.	▪ It's a good idea to label templates as such when you create them so you will always be able to distinguish templates from publications, no matter how you are viewing them.

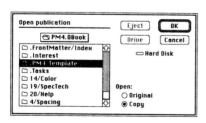

If:

20.29 When you type, the text squishes up

Then follow these steps:

- First of all, check the text block to see where its handles are:
  □ With the **pointer tool,** click once on the text block. Is the text block excessively short? Does the text unsquish when you widen the block? (Press on any corner handle and drag outward.)
- If you lengthen the text block and the text still does not unsquish, check the indents:
  □ With the **text tool,** click once in the line of text. Press Command I to get the Indents/Tabs ruler. If you don't see the large right-indent triangle, scroll the ruler until you do. Is the triangle directly on the dotted line (5.46; 5.49)? If not, press-and-drag the triangle as far to the right as it will go. Click OK.
- If this problem recurs regularly, the problem is a default somewhere, *or* it is embedded in a style sheet. Check the style sheet of the paragraph this is occurring in: with the insertion point in the text that is giving you trouble, check out "Style" in the Type menu; the checked style is the one with the problem. Change the indent in that style sheet. If the style is "No style," the problem is a publication default; with the **pointer tool** selected, change the indent.

Shortcuts ▾ Notes ▾ Hints

- There's a difference between *squished* and *condensed*. *Condensing* type is a conscious act; you can choose to condense type from the "Set width" submenu (3.139; 3.150). *Squishing* is an accident; it indicates something is not right.

Normal: Scarlett Williams
Condensed: Scarlett Williams
Squished: Scarlett Williams

- See 5.68–5.73 for information about indents. See 7.17 and 7.48 for information about editing a style sheet.

If:	Then follow these steps:	Shortcuts ▾ Notes ▾ Hints
20.30 You lengthened the text block to lengthen the line, but the line length didn't change	■ There is probably a right indent set. With the **text tool,** click once in the text. ■ Press Command I to get the Indents/ Tabs ruler. If the right-indent triangle is anywhere but on the dotted line, press-and-drag the triangle as far to the right as it will go. Click OK.	■ See Section 5 for everything you ever wanted to know about indents.
20.31 You want to type numbers with the numeric keypad	■ Press the Caps Lock key down. ■ If the Caps Lock key is not down and the numeric keypad types numbers anyway, see 20.32, below.	■ The number 5 always types a number 5; it never moves the insertion point.
20.32 Sometimes the numeric keypad types numbers and sometimes it moves the insertion point	■ With Caps Lock down, the keypad will always type numbers. With Caps Lock up, the Clear key is in control: ■ Pressing the Clear key on the keypad switches the function back and forth between typing numbers and moving the insertion point. If it is performing the function you don't want, press the Clear key again. Unfortunately, there is no visible sign to indicate which function is currently on; the only way to tell is to press a number on the keypad and see what you get.	■ The number 5 always types a number 5; it never moves the insertion point. ■ See 1.222–1.226 for details on using the keypad to move the insertion point and to select text.

If:	Then follow these steps:	Shortcuts ▾ Notes ▾ Hints
20.33 You press Command Option P to create an automatic page number, but nothing happens	▪ Did you first click with the **text tool** to get a flashing insertion point? ▪ Is Caps Lock down? You cannot make an automatic page number while Caps Lock is down.	
20.34 You pasted or placed a graphic and it is inverted (reversed; black instead of white) *⌐Click on this icon.*	▪ With the **pointer tool,** click on the graphic. ▪ From the Element menu, choose "Image control...." ▪ Click on left-most icon above the image control bars (see left). ▪ Click OK.	▪ If one graphic is selected and the "Image control..." command is gray, then the graphic cannot be reversed. You will have to take it back into a graphic program that can switch it. ▪ See 9.118–9.169 for details on Image Control.
20.35 Everything you place, paste, or draw is automatically tagged with a color	▪ A color has been set as a default for graphics. See 14.84–14.89 for details on how to change the default back to black.	
20.36 A dialog box yells at you because it thinks you have inserted incorrect values, but you don't know which values it's talking about	▪ Check Appendices A1–A8 for views of all the defaults in all the dialog boxes. Then select the edit boxes in the dialog box that is giving you grief, and input the values you see in the appendix. ▪ **Or** you can always just Cancel the dialog box. If you had made some changes you want to keep, you will just have to go back and enter them again.	

If:	Then follow these steps:	Shortcuts ▾ Notes ▾ Hints
20.37 Paragraph rules show up where you don't want them	■ If this problem recurs regularly, the paragraph rule is embedded in a style sheet, **or** there is a default somewhere. ■ With the insertion point in the text that is giving you trouble, look at "Style" in the Type menu; the checked style is the one with the problem. Change the paragraph rules in that style sheet (7.48). ■ If the style is "No style," the problem is a publication default: with the **pointer tool** selected, go into the "Paragraph rules" dialog box and uncheck the rule (6.47).	■ See Section 7 for detailed information about rules.
20.38 You placed or pasted a graphic, but you don't see it anywhere	■ Is the text tool selected? If it is, then you probably pasted the graphic inline somewhere, possibly even on another page. If there is an insertion point flashing, PageMaker will paste or place the graphic *inline* (9.91; 9.170–9.189); the graphic will be pasted right into the text block where that insertion point was. The frightening thing is: *the insertion point can be flashing on another page altogether!* It may be flashing 17 pages away. See 9.198 for a solution to this dilemma. To **prevent** this problem from ever happening, always click once on the **pointer tool** before you paste or place a graphic (unless you *want* an inline graphic).	

If:	**Then follow these steps:**	**Shortcuts ▾ Notes ▾ Hints**

20.39 You accidentally placed a giant-sized graphic in your text (or perhaps you placed the entire Scrapbook) and now your text block won't unroll

- With the **text tool,** click in the last paragraph you see in the text block, then press Command E. If the text block is completely rolled up and all you can see are its handles, press Command E. If you lost the text block altogether and can't even find its handles, see 20.11.
- The Command E will bring you to the Story Editor. You will see the graphic represented by this symbol: ▨ . Select that symbol (press-and-drag over it) and hit the Back-space/Delete key. Press Command W to get back to the layout page.

20.40 When you try to import or place a graphic or text, PageMaker tells you "Unknown file format"

- PageMaker can only import files for which you have installed the proper filter. See 15.6–15.16 for information on the filters you need. See 15.25 for instructions on how to install the proper filter.

If:	**Then follow these steps:**	**Shortcuts ▾ Notes ▾ Hints**
20.41 You can't change the style sheet specifications; PageMaker tells you there is a bad record index	▪ This problem and its solution is explained in detail in Section 7 on Style Sheets: 7.52.	
20.42 In the Story Editor, the "Find" command or the "Change" command is gray	▪ If the command is gray, the dialog box is already open. If you don't see it, the box is hiding behind another window. Use the keyboard commands to bring them forward: Command 8 to bring up the "Find" dialog box; Command 9 to bring up the "Change" dialog box.	
20.43 The Story Editor cannot find something that you know is there **Find what:** [|] **Change to:** [ ] *If there is an underline beneath "Find what," it indicates there are attributes applied to the search.*	▪ The problem may lie in the "Attributes" that are applied. Maybe you didn't even know there were any applied. An underline under "Find what" indicates that PageMaker is looking for text with attributes. To eliminate any attributes in the search, hold down the Option key and click once on the "Attributes" button.	

703

If:	**Then follow these steps:**	**Shortcuts ▾ Notes ▾ Hints**
20.44 You want to change the color of rotated text	▪ You must either unrotate the text or go into the Story Editor with it (triple-click on the rotated text with the **pointer tool**). In either case, select the text with the **text tool** and apply the color (see 14.102 for directions on applying color).	
20.45 PageMaker stops printing because of "LimitCheck"	▪ Some page has more information on it than the printer's memory can deal with. See 18.170–18.172 for details on this problem and how to take care of it.	
20.46 Font names in your menu are gray	• A gray font name means that a particular font has been used somewhere in the publication, but the *screen* font (18.31–18.35) is not installed in the current System. If you use a font utility, you just may have forgotten to open the suitcase that contains that font. If the printer can find the corresponding *printer* font (18.36–18.37) for the missing screen font, it will usually print okay anyway, although it will look awful on the screen. If the font name is gray, you won't be able to choose that font to apply it to any other text.	

Being the Last.
In which this valuable tome
is brought to a happy Conclusion.

APPENDICES

A1.1 Whenever you see an ellipsis (…) after a command in a menu, it means that if you choose that item you will see a dialog box. There is always a Cancel button in every dialog box, so it is quite safe to wander around choosing commands with ellipses because you can rest assured that as long as you click "Cancel" you cannot ruin anything.

A1.2 All of these menus and dialog boxes show the defaults that are built into PageMaker. If you need to reset any defaults in your publication or in the PageMaker application, take a look at the original dialog box here.

Remember, you can reset every one of PageMaker's defaults at once by trashing the default file found in the System folder (1.15).

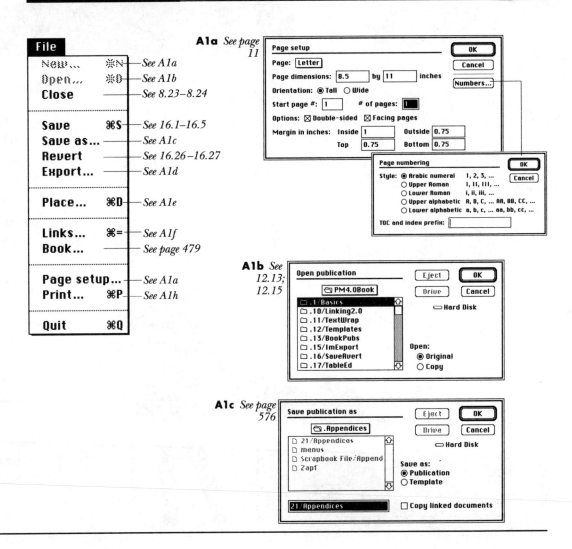

File

New... ⌘N —See A1a
Open... ⌘O —See A1b
Close —See 8.23–8.24

Save ⌘S —See 16.1–16.5
Save as... —See A1c
Revert —See 16.26–16.27
Export... —See A1d

Place... ⌘D —See A1e

Links... ⌘= —See A1f
Book... —See page 479

Page setup... —See A1a
Print... ⌘P —See A1h

Quit ⌘Q

A1a *See page 11*

Page setup
Page: Letter
Page dimensions: 8.5 by 11 inches
Orientation: ● Tall ○ Wide
Start page #: 1   # of pages: 1
Options: ⊠ Double-sided ⊠ Facing pages
Margin in inches: Inside 1   Outside 0.75
Top 0.75   Bottom 0.75
OK   Cancel   Numbers...

Page numbering
Style: ● Arabic numeral   1, 2, 3, …
○ Upper Roman   I, II, III, …
○ Lower Roman   i, ii, iii, …
○ Upper alphabetic   A, B, C, … AA, BB, CC, …
○ Lower alphabetic   a, b, c, … aa, bb, cc, …
TOC and index prefix:
OK   Cancel

A1b *See 12.13; 12.15*

Open publication
� PM4.0Book
📁 .1/Basics
📁 .10/Linking2.0
📁 .11/TextWrap
📁 .12/Templates
📁 .13/BookPubs
📁 .15/ImExport
📁 .16/SaveRvert
📁 .17/TableEd
Eject   Drive   OK   Cancel
⌸ Hard Disk
Open:
● Original
○ Copy

A1c *See page 576*

Save publication as
⌐ .Appendices
📄 21/Appendices
📄 menus
📄 Scrapbook File/Append
📄 Zapf
Eject   Drive   OK   Cancel
⌸ Hard Disk
Save as:
● Publication
○ Template
21/Appendices
☐ Copy linked documents

A1d *See page 571*

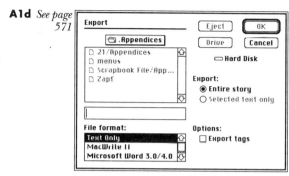

A1e *See page 113*

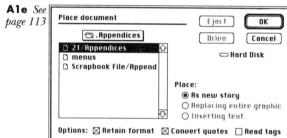

A1f *See page 416*

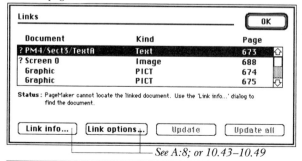

— *See A:8; or 10.43–10.49*

A1h *See page 628*

See page 645

See page 648

See page 632

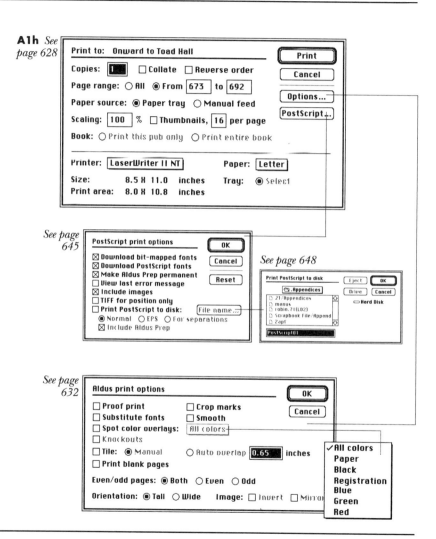

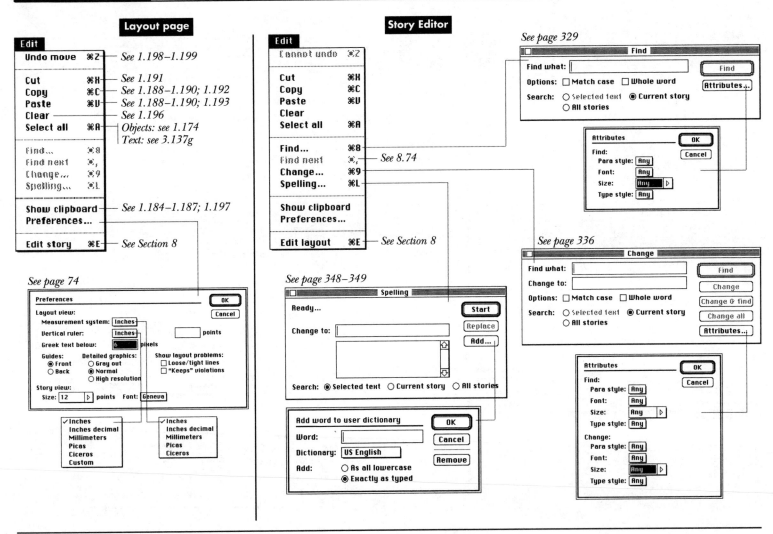

Layout page

Edit

Undo move	⌘Z	— *See 1.198–1.199*
Cut	⌘H	— *See 1.191*
Copy	⌘C	— *See 1.188–1.190; 1.192*
Paste	⌘U	— *See 1.188–1.190; 1.193*
Clear		— *See 1.196*
Select all	⌘A	*Objects: see 1.174* *Text: see 3.137g*
Find...	⌘8	
Find next	⌘;	
Change...	⌘9	
Spelling...	⌘L	
Show clipboard		— *See 1.184–1.187; 1.197*
Preferences...		
Edit story	⌘E	— *See Section 8*

Story Editor

Edit

Cannot undo	⌘Z	
Cut	⌘H	
Copy	⌘C	
Paste	⌘U	
Clear		
Select all	⌘A	
Find...	⌘8	
Find next	⌘;	— *See 8.74*
Change...	⌘9	
Spelling...	⌘L	
Show clipboard		
Preferences...		
Edit layout	⌘E	— *See Section 8*

See page 329

Find

Find what: [ ] [Find]

Options: ☐ Match case   ☐ Whole word   [Attributes...]

Search: ○ Selected text   ● Current story
○ All stories

Attributes   [OK]

Find:
Para style: [Any]   [Cancel]
Font: [Any]
Size: [Any] ▷
Type style: [Any]

See page 336

Change

Find what: [ ]   [Find]
Change to: [ ]   [Change]

Options: ☐ Match case   ☐ Whole word   [Change & find]

Search: ○ Selected text   ● Current story   [Change all]
○ All stories   [Attributes...]

Attributes   [OK]

Find:
Para style: [Any]   [Cancel]
Font: [Any]
Size: [Any] ▷
Type style: [Any]
Change:
Para style: [Any]
Font: [Any]
Size: [Any] ▷
Type style: [Any]

See page 74

Preferences   [OK]

Layout view: [Cancel]
Measurement system: [Inches]
Vertical ruler: [Inches]   [ ] points
Greek text below: [6] pixels
Guides: Detailed graphics: Show layout problems:
● Front   ○ Gray out   ☐ Loose/tight lines
○ Back   ● Normal   ☐ "Keeps" violations
○ High resolution
Story view:
Size: [12] ▷ points   Font: [Geneva]

✓ Inches		✓ Inches
Inches decimal		Inches decimal
Millimeters		Millimeters
Picas		Picas
Ciceros		Ciceros
Custom		

See page 348–349

Spelling

Ready...   [Start]

Change to: [ ]   [Replace]
[Add...]

Search: ● Selected text   ○ Current story   ○ All stories

Add word to user dictionary   [OK]

Word: [ ]   [Cancel]

Dictionary: [US English]   [Remove]

Add: ○ As all lowercase
● Exactly as typed

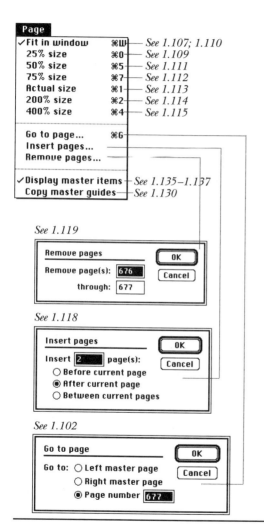

Page
- ✓Fit in window ⌘W ——— *See 1.107; 1.110*
- 25% size ⌘0 ——— *See 1.109*
- 50% size ⌘5 ——— *See 1.111*
- 75% size ⌘7 ——— *See 1.112*
- Actual size ⌘1 ——— *See 1.113*
- 200% size ⌘2 ——— *See 1.114*
- 400% size ⌘4 ——— *See 1.115*

- Go to page... ⌘G
- Insert pages...
- Remove pages...

- ✓Display master items — *See 1.135–1.137*
- Copy master guides — *See 1.130*

See 1.119

Remove pages
- Remove page(s): `676` [OK]
- through: `677` [Cancel]

See 1.118

Insert pages
- Insert `2` page(s): [OK]
  - ○ Before current page [Cancel]
  - ● After current page
  - ○ Between current pages

See 1.102

Go to page
- Go to: ○ Left master page [OK]
  - ○ Right master page [Cancel]
  - ● Page number `677`

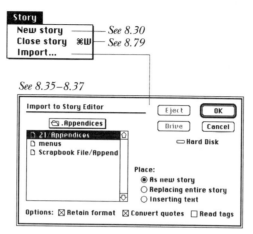

Story
- New story ——— *See 8.30*
- Close story ⌘W ——— *See 8.79*
- Import...

See 8.35–8.37

Import to Story Editor
- [Eject] [OK]
- 📁 .Appendices [Drive] [Cancel]
  - 📄 21/Appendices
  - 📄 menus   ▢ Hard Disk
  - 📄 Scrapbook File/Append

- Place:
  - ● As new story
  - ○ Replacing entire story
  - ○ Inserting text

- Options: ☒ Retain format ☒ Convert quotes ☐ Read tags

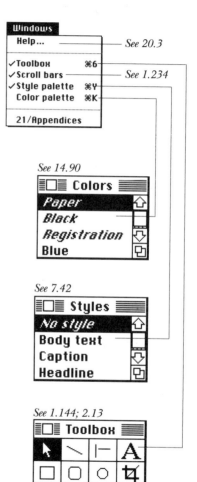

Windows
- Help... ——— *See 20.3*

- ✓Toolbox ⌘6
- ✓Scroll bars ——— *See 1.234*
- ✓Style palette ⌘Y
- Color palette ⌘K

- 21/Appendices

See 14.90

Colors
- *Paper*
- *Black*
- *Registration*
- **Blue**

See 7.42

Styles
- *No style*
- **Body text**
- **Caption**
- **Headline**

See 1.144; 2.13

Toolbox

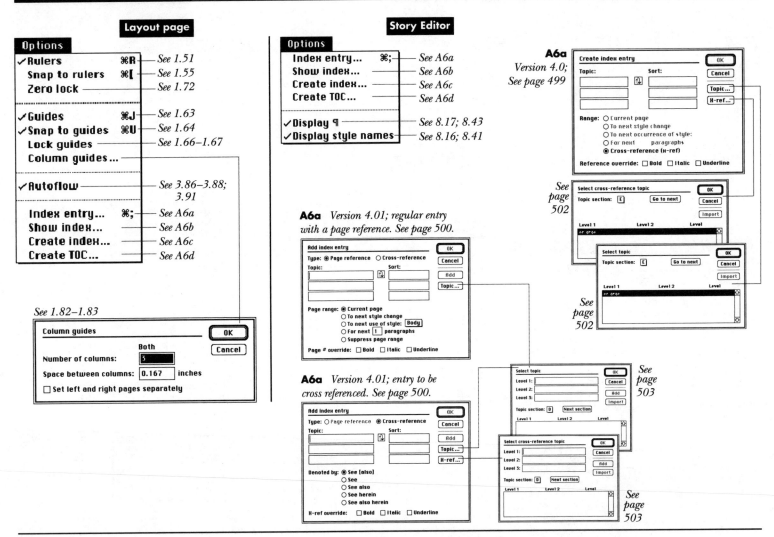

Layout page

Options

✓ **Rulers** ⌘R — *See 1.51*
  Snap to rulers ⌘[— *See 1.55*
  Zero lock — *See 1.72*

✓ **Guides** ⌘J — *See 1.63*
✓ **Snap to guides** ⌘U — *See 1.64*
  Lock guides — *See 1.66–1.67*
  Column guides...

✓ **Autoflow** — *See 3.86–3.88; 3.91*

  Index entry... ⌘; — *See A6a*
  Show index... — *See A6b*
  Create index... — *See A6c*
  Create TOC... — *See A6d*

See 1.82–1.83

Column guides [OK] [Cancel]

Number of columns: 3

Space between columns: 0.167 inches

☐ Set left and right pages separately

Story Editor

Options

  Index entry... ⌘; — *See A6a*
  Show index... — *See A6b*
  Create index... — *See A6c*
  Create TOC... — *See A6d*

✓ **Display ¶** — *See 8.17; 8.43*
✓ **Display style names** — *See 8.16; 8.41*

A6a *Version 4.01; regular entry with a page reference. See page 500.*

Add index entry [OK] [Cancel] [Add] [Topic...]

Type: ⦿ Page reference ◯ Cross-reference
Topic: **Sort:**

Page range: ⦿ Current page
  ◯ To next style change
  ◯ To next use of style: [Body]
  ◯ For next [1] paragraphs
  ◯ Suppress page range
Page # override: ☐ Bold ☐ Italic ☐ Underline

A6a *Version 4.01; entry to be cross referenced. See page 500.*

Add index entry [OK] [Cancel] [Add] [Topic...] [H-ref...]

Type: ◯ Page reference ⦿ Cross-reference
Topic: **Sort:**

Denoted by: ⦿ See [also]
  ◯ See
  ◯ See also
  ◯ See herein
  ◯ See also herein
H-ref override: ☐ Bold ☐ Italic ☐ Underline

A6a *Version 4.0; See page 499.*

Create index entry [OK] [Cancel] [Topic...] [H-ref...]

Topic: **Sort:**

Range: ◯ Current page
  ◯ To next style change
  ◯ To next occurrence of style:
  ◯ For next   paragraphs
  ⦿ Cross-reference (x-ref)

Reference override: ☐ Bold ☐ Italic ☐ Underline

See page 502

Select cross-reference topic [OK] [Cancel] [Import]
Topic section: [E] [Go to next]
Level 1   Level 2   Level

Select topic [OK] [Cancel] [Import]
Topic section: [E] [Go to next]
Level 1   Level 2   Level

See page 502

Select topic [OK] [Cancel] [Add] [Import]
Level 1:
Level 2:
Level 3:
Topic section: [B] [Next section]
Level 1   Level 2   Level

See page 503

Select cross-reference topic [OK] [Cancel] [Add] [Import]
Level 1:
Level 2:
Level 3:
Topic section: [B] [Next section]
Level 1   Level 2   Level

See page 503

A6b *Version 4.0; see page 504*

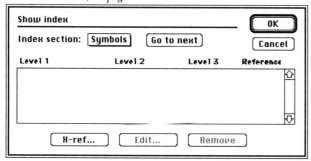

A6b *Version 4.01; see page 504*

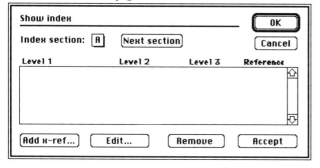

A6c
See page 525

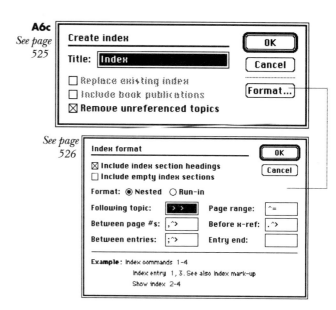

See page 526

A6d
See page 489

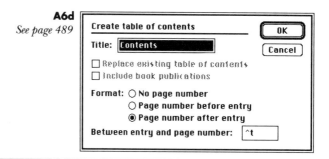

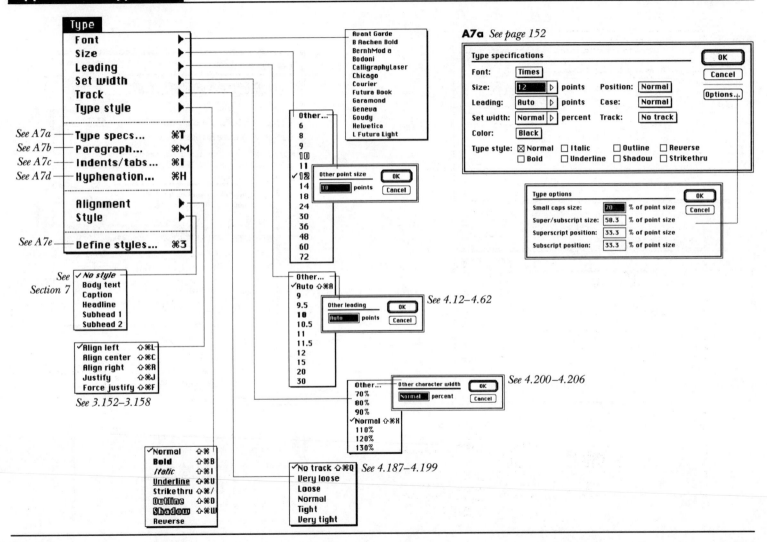

Type

Font ►
Size ►
Leading ►
Set width ►
Track ►
Type style ►

See A7a —— Type specs... ⌘T
See A7b —— Paragraph... ⌘M
See A7c —— Indents/tabs... ⌘I
See A7d —— Hyphenation... ⌘H

Alignment ►
Style ►

See A7e —— Define styles... ⌘3

Avant Garde
B Rachen Bold
BernhMod a
Bodoni
CalligraphyLaser
Chicago
Courier
Futura Book
Garamond
Geneva
Goudy
Helvetica
L Futura Light

Other...
6
8
9
10
11
✓12
14
18
24
30
36
48
60
72

Other point size   OK
10 points   Cancel

See ✓ **No style**
Section 7   Body text
Caption
Headline
Subhead 1
Subhead 2

✓Align left ⇧⌘L
Align center ⇧⌘C
Align right ⇧⌘R
Justify ⇧⌘J
Force justify ⇧⌘F

See 3.152–3.158

Other...
✓Auto ⇧⌘A
9
9.5
10
10.5
11
11.5
12
15
20
30

Other leading   OK
Auto points   Cancel

See 4.12–4.62

Other...
70%
80%
90%
✓Normal ⇧⌘H
110%
120%
130%

Other character width   OK
Normal percent   Cancel

See 4.200–4.206

✓Normal ⇧⌘
Bold ⇧⌘B
Italic ⇧⌘I
Underline ⇧⌘U
Strikethru ⇧⌘/
Outline ⇧⌘D
Shadow ⇧⌘W
Reverse

✓No track ⇧⌘Q   *See 4.187–4.199*
Very loose
Loose
Normal
Tight
Very tight

A7a *See page 152*

Type specifications   OK

Font: Times   Cancel

Size: 12 ▷ points   Position: Normal   Options...

Leading: Auto ▷ points   Case: Normal

Set width: Normal ▷ percent   Track: No track

Color: Black

Type style: ⊠ Normal ☐ Italic ☐ Outline ☐ Reverse
☐ Bold ☐ Underline ☐ Shadow ☐ Strikethru

Type options   OK

Small caps size: 70 % of point size   Cancel

Super/subscript size: 58.3 % of point size

Superscript position: 33.3 % of point size

Subscript position: 33.3 % of point size

A7b *See page 177*

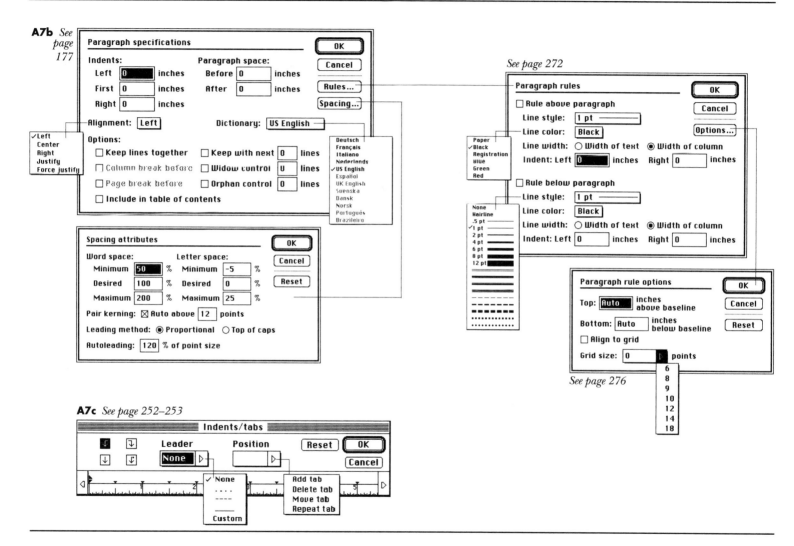

Paragraph specifications

OK

Indents:
Left [0] inches
First [0] inches
Right [0] inches

Paragraph space:
Before [0] inches
After [0] inches

Cancel
Rules...
Spacing...

Alignment: [Left]
Dictionary: [US English]

✓Left
Center
Right
Justify
Force justify

Deutsch
Français
Italiano
Nederlands
✓US English
Español
UK English
Suenska
Dansk
Norsk
Português
Brazileira

Options:
☐ Keep lines together   ☐ Keep with next [0] lines
☐ Column break before   ☐ Widow control [0] lines
☐ Page break before   ☐ Orphan control [0] lines
☐ Include in table of contents

See page 272

Paragraph rules

OK

☐ Rule above paragraph
Line style: [1 pt ————]
Line color: [Black]
Line width: ○ Width of text ● Width of column
Indent: Left [0] inches   Right [0] inches

Cancel
Options...

Paper
✓Black
Registration
Blue
Green
Red

☐ Rule below paragraph
Line style: [1 pt ————]
Line color: [Black]
Line width: ○ Width of text ● Width of column
Indent: Left [0] inches   Right [0] inches

None
Hairline
.5 pt
✓1 pt
2 pt
4 pt
6 pt
8 pt
12 pt

Spacing attributes

OK

Word space:
Minimum [50] %
Desired [100] %
Maximum [200] %

Letter space:
Minimum [-5] %
Desired [0] %
Maximum [25] %

Cancel
Reset

Pair kerning: ☒ Auto above [12] points
Leading method: ● Proportional ○ Top of caps
Autoleading: [120] % of point size

Paragraph rule options

OK

Top: [Auto] inches above baseline
Bottom: [Auto] inches below baseline
☐ Align to grid
Grid size: [0] points

Cancel
Reset

6
8
9
10
12
14
18

See page 276

A7c *See page 252–253*

Indents/tabs

Leader [None ▷]   Position [▷]   Reset   OK
Cancel

✓ None
. . . .
- - - -
————
Custom

Add tab
Delete tab
Move tab
Repeat tab

A7d *See page 239*

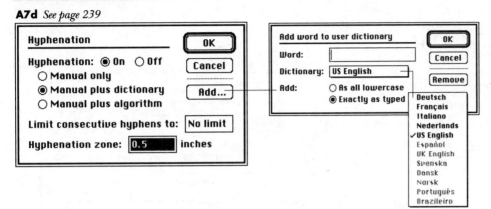

A7e *See page 290*

See page 291

See page 291

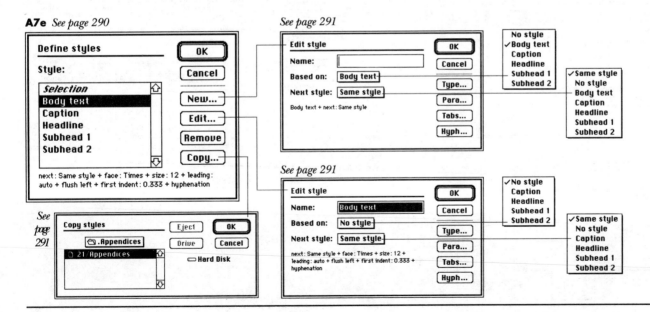

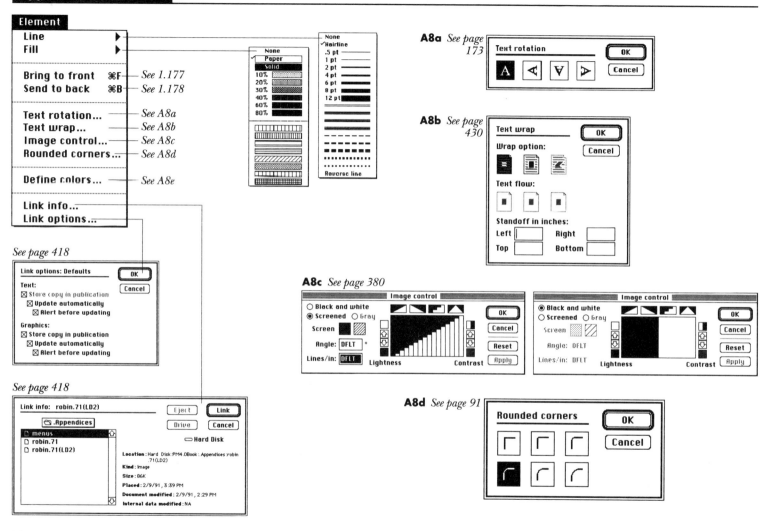

Element
- Line ▶
- Fill ▶

- Bring to front ⌘F — See 1.177
- Send to back ⌘B — See 1.178

- Text rotation... — See A8a
- Text wrap... — See A8b
- Image control... — See A8c
- Rounded corners... — See A8d

- Define colors... — See A8e

- Link info...
- Link options...

None
✓Hairline
.5 pt
1 pt
2 pt
4 pt
6 pt
8 pt
12 pt

None
✓ Paper
Solid
10%
20%
30%
40%
60%
80%

Reverse line

See page 418

Link options: Defaults   OK   Cancel

Text:
☒ Store copy in publication
  ☒ Update automatically
    ☒ Alert before updating

Graphics:
☒ Store copy in publication
  ☒ Update automatically
    ☒ Alert before updating

See page 418

Link info: robin.71(LD2)   Eject   Link   Drive   Cancel

☐ .Appendices   ⊂⊃ Hard Disk
☐ menus
☐ robin.71
☐ robin.71(LD2)

Location: Hard Disk:PM4.0Book::Appendices:robin
.71(LD2)
Kind: Image
Size: 86K
Placed: 2/9/91, 3:39 PM
Document modified: 2/9/91, 2:29 PM
Internal data modified: NA

A8a *See page 173*

Text rotation   OK   Cancel
A ◁ ∀ ▷

A8b *See page 430*

Text wrap   OK   Cancel

Wrap option:

Text flow:

Standoff in inches:
Left ___   Right ___
Top ___   Bottom ___

A8c *See page 380*

Image control   OK   Cancel   Reset   Apply
○ Black and white
◉ Screened   ○ Gray
Screen
Angle: DFLT °
Lines/in: DFLT   Lightness   Contrast

Image control   OK   Cancel   Reset   Apply
◉ Black and white
○ Screened   ○ Gray
Screen
Angle: DFLT
Lines/in: DFLT   Lightness   Contrast

A8d *See page 91*

Rounded corners   OK   Cancel

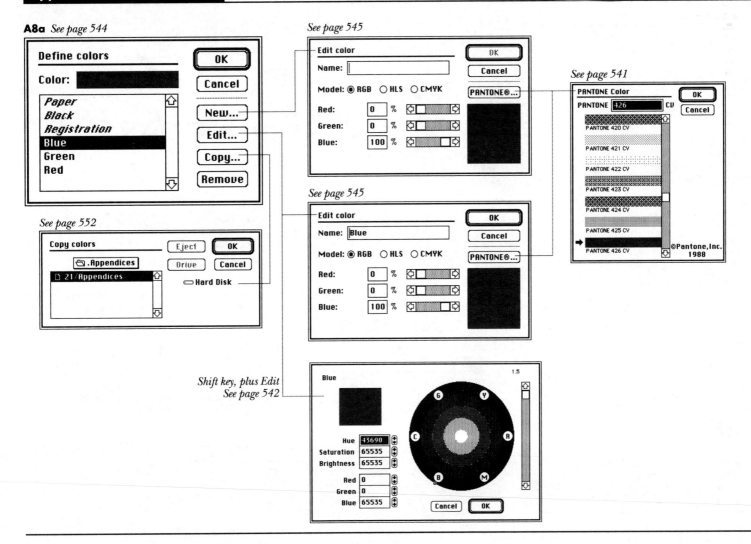

A8a *See page 544*

Define colors

Color:

Paper
Black
Registration
Blue
Green
Red

OK
Cancel
New...
Edit...
Copy...
Remove

See page 552

Copy colors

⊟ .Appendices
▢ 21/Appendices

Eject
Drive
Cancel
OK

▭ Hard Disk

See page 545

Edit color

Name:

Model: ⦿ RGB ○ HLS ○ CMYK

Red: 0   %
Green: 0   %
Blue: 100   %

OK
Cancel
PANTONE®...

See page 545

Edit color

Name: Blue

Model: ⦿ RGB ○ HLS ○ CMYK

Red: 0   %
Green: 0   %
Blue: 100   %

OK
Cancel
PANTONE®...

See page 541

PANTONE Color

PANTONE 426   CV

PANTONE 420 CV
PANTONE 421 CV
PANTONE 422 CV
PANTONE 423 CV
PANTONE 424 CV
PANTONE 425 CV
➡ PANTONE 426 CV

OK
Cancel

©Pantone,Inc.
1988

Shift key, plus Edit
See page 542

Blue   1.5

Hue   43690
Saturation   65535
Brightness   65535

Red   0
Green   0
Blue   65535

G   Y
C   R
B   M

Cancel   OK

Appendix B: Tasks

Section 2 ▾ Drawing Tools

13.136 In version 4.01, create an index entry with no page number reference

13.137 In version 4.0, create an index entry with no page number reference (also see 13.137.)

13.138 Create a secondary (second-level) entry (one method)

13.139 Create a secondary (second-level) entry (another method)

13.140 Create another secondary entry under the same primary topic

13.141 Create a tertiary (third-level) entry (one method)

13.142 Create a tertiary (third-level) entry (another method)

13.143 Create another tertiary entry under the same secondary topic

13.144 Check the Topic List to see what's available

13.145 Import topics

13.146 In version 4.01: Automatically index proper names

13.147 In version 4.01: Automatically capitalize index entries

13.148 Show all the entries before generating the actual index

13.149 Edit entries (especially necessary to amalgamate all primary topics with their respective secondary and tertiary entries)

13.150 In version 4.01: Undo the latest index additions or deletions

13.151 Remove entries from the index

13.152 Remove all page-referenced entries from the entire index (read the warning on the right!)

13.153 Remove all cross-referenced entries from the entire index (read the warning!)

13.154 Remove all cross-referenced entries, as well as all entries with page references, from the entire index (which means eliminating the entire index) (read the warning!)

13.155 Sort an entry by characters different than the entry's original characters

13.156 Sort an entry by several different sets of characters

13.157 Cross-reference an entry

13.158 Cross-reference a secondary or tertiary entry as you create the entry (another method, similar to 13.157)

13.159 Format the cross-reference (or in version 4.01, the page numbers)

13.160 Show all the index entries

13.161 Show the index for just the current publication only

13.162 Get rid of all those useless topics that you don't need anymore in the "Index entry..." Topic and Cross-References Lists

13.184 Create/place the index for the first time (actually put it on the page)

13.185 Update an existing index, replacing the existing one

13.186 Update an existing index, without replacing the existing one

13.187 Search the index for an entry

13.188 Define a prefix for the page numbers in the index (optional)

13.189 Eliminate the entire index (the internal index, not the index that has been placed on the page)

13.190 Eliminate the index in the current publication (the internal index, not the index that has been placed on the page)

Section 14 ▾ Color

14.90 Show or hide the Color palette

14.91 Create/define a new color

14.92 Edit (change) a color in the Color palette

14.93 Change the name of a color

14.94 Use the Apple Color Wheel to edit an existing color

14.95 Use the Pantone Matching System color model

14.96 Change the color "Registration"

14.97 Change the color "Black"

14.98 Change the color "Paper"

14.99 Change the color "Paper" to its original color (white)

14.100 Remove a color from the Color palette

14.101 Copy a Color palette from another publication

14.102 Apply colors to text

14.103 Add colors to paragraph styles

14.104 Apply colors to graphics

14.105 Create a box with a colored border and a fill of a different color

14.106 Change the color of text or graphics

14.107 Print spot colors on separate overlays

14.108 Print spot color overlays with knockouts

14.109 Prepare a file for four-color separations

14.110 Print a color comp on a color printer

14.111 Change the default color for graphics

14.112 Change the default color for text

14.113 Change the defaults back to "Black"

Section 15 ▾ Importing and Exporting

15.24 Check to see which import and export filters are installed

15.25 Install a filter that was not originally installed

15.26 Import a text file into the layout view

15.27 Import a text file into the Story Editor

15.28 Import a graphic

15.29 Import a "Text-only" file

15.30 Import a Microsoft Word 4.0 file, with control over the Table of Contents entries, index entries, character spacing, and "Page break before" setting

15.31 Import a Microsoft Word 4.0 table as a graphic (PICT)

15.32 Import a Microsoft Word 4.0 table as text (tab-delimited)

15.33 Import text files from PCs (except from Microsoft Word; see 15.34)
15.34 Import Microsoft Word text files from PCs
15.35 Import stories from another PageMaker 4.0 publication
15.36 Export a PageMaker story as a text file
15.37 Export graphics

Converting 3.0 Mac or PC to 4.0 Mac

15.38 Convert a Macintosh PageMaker 3.0, 3.01, 3.02, or 3.02CE publication into a PageMaker 4.0 (or 4.01) publication
15.39 Transfer a PC PageMaker publication to Mac PageMaker 4.0

SECTION 16 ▾ SAVING AND REVERTING

16.18 Save a publication
16.19 Save changes to the publication
16.20 Save a template
16.21 Save changes to the template before it has ever been closed
16.22 Open the original template again in order to create and save changes
16.23 Save a copy of the publication or template, with the same name, into a different folder or onto a different disk
16.24 Save a copy (a separate version) of the publication or template, with a different name, into any folder or onto any disk
16.25 Reduce the size of a PageMaker file
16.26 Revert to the last-saved version
16.27 Revert to the last mini-save version
16.28 Close the publication or quit PageMaker without saving changes
16.29 Open a publication that was closed due to a power failure or system malfunction
16.30 Copy linked documents when saving a PageMaker file
16.31 Copy linked documents for remote printing when saving a PageMaker file

SECTION 17 ▾ TABLE EDITOR

17.91 Create a new table
17.92 Open an existing table
17.93 Add rows
17.94 Delete rows
17.95 Add columns
17.96 Delete columns
17.97 Change column width *(and thus change the table size)*
17.98 Change column width, *without changing the size of the adjacent columns (this will also change the table size)*
17.99 Change column width, without changing the table size
17.100 Change row height *(and thus change the table size)*
17.101 Increase the table size without adding more rows or columns
17.102 Decrease the table size
17.103 Group cells
17.104 Ungroup cells
17.105 Type into a cell
17.106 Change the type specs
17.107 Change the alignment of the text within a cell
17.108 Apply shades to a cell or to a range of cells
17.110 Apply borders to a cell or to a range of cells
17.111 Remove existing borders
17.112 Copy or cut just the text from a cell
17.113 Clear just the text from a cell
17.114 Cut or copy the text, shades, and lines from a cell or from a range of cells
17.115 Clear just the text, or just the shades, or just the lines from a cell or from a range of cells
17.116 Change the number format of the numeric values in a cell
17.117 Sum the numeric values from a range of cells

17.118 Import text into an existing table in the Table Editor
17.119 Paste text into the Table Editor
17.120 Define the flow for pasting or importing text
17.121 Export a table as editable text
17.122 Export a table as a graphic (PICT format)
17.123 Save the table as a graphic in the Scrapbook
17.124 In PageMaker, *place* the table as editable text or as a graphic (PICT format)
17.125 In PageMaker, *paste* the table as a graphic
17.126 Remove the white line from around the PICT table, while in PageMaker
17.127 Import a table into PageMaker's Story Editor
17.128 Revise and update the graphic table you placed into the PageMaker publication
17.129 Set the default specifications for the Table Editor application
17.130 Set the default specifications for the open table

SECTION 18 ▾ PRINTING

18.157 Use Chooser to select a printer
18.158 Print a publication
18.159 Print items outside the boundary of the page
18.160 Prepare a publication for do-it-yourself remote printing (printing on a Mac at a copy center, for instance)
18.161 Prepare a publication as a PageMaker file for remote printing at a service bureau (as opposed to preparing it as a PostScript file; 18.162)
18.162 Prepare a publication as a PostScript file ("Normal" or "For separations") for remote printing at a service bureau (as opposed to preparing it as a PageMaker file; 18.161)

—continued

20.27 You specified thick paragraph rules and you have reversed text on top of them; when you insert a tab, the text disappears and won't print

20.28 You want to open a copy of a template, but you can't tell from the list which publications are templates

20.29 When you type, the text squishes up

20.30 You lengthened the text block to lengthen the line, but the line length didn't change

20.31 You want to type numbers with the numeric keypad

20.32 Sometimes the numeric keypad types numbers and sometimes it moves the insertion point

20.33 You press Command Option P to create an automatic page number, but nothing happens

20.34 You pasted or placed a graphic, and it is inverted (reversed; black instead of white)

20.35 Everything you place, paste, or draw is automatically tagged with a color

20.36 A dialog box yells at you because it thinks you have inserted incorrect values, but you don't know which values it's talking about

20.37 Paragraph rules show up where you don't want them

20.38 You placed or pasted a graphic, but you don't see it anywhere

20.39 You accidentally placed a giant-sized graphic in your text (or perhaps you placed the entire Scrapbook) and now your text block won't unroll

20.40 When you try to import or place a graphic or text, PageMaker tells you "Unknown file format"

20.41 You can't change the style sheet specifications; PageMaker tells you there is a bad record index

20.42 In the Story Editor, the "Find" command or the "Change" command is gray

20.43 The Story Editor cannot find something that you know is there

20.44 You want to change the color of rotated text

20.45 PageMaker stops printing because of "LimitCheck"

20.46 There are font names in your menu that are gray

The Aldus PageMaker manual does a pretty good job of walking you through the process of installing PageMaker. For those who hate to read manuals, or who perhaps can't find the manual, here is a brief synopsis. First, a few notes.

- You cannot simply copy the files from the floppy disks onto your hard disk; you **must** go through the installation procedure. The application itself is in two parts on separate disks; once the two parts are on the hard disk, the installer program puts them together.

- If you are making backup copies of your original disks, use the disk-to-disk method to copy (drag the icon of the original disk onto the icon of the copy disk; see *The Little Mac Book* if you don't know how to do a disk-to-disk copy with only one floppy drive). Be sure to name the new disks **exactly** the same, spaces and all, as the disk they were copied from!! Then lock your disks.

- You need System version 6.0.3 or later; Finder version 6.1 or later.

- You need about 7 megs of hard disk space to allow PageMaker to do the installing. If you install all the templates and the tutorial, the entire package will take up about 5 megs of hard disk space. If you

install just the application itself, some import filters and some APDs, PageMaker will take about 3 megs of your hard disk.

- You need at least 1 meg of memory (RAM) to run the program, and Aldus recommends at least 2 megs. I wrote 250 pages of this book in PageMaker 4 on an SE with one meg of RAM. See the following page for a few little tricks for making Page-Maker function best with little RAM.

- If you have at least 2 megs of RAM, you can run PageMaker under MultiFinder. Allocate at least 1.5 megs for it.

- Installing PageMaker 4.0 **does not** replace nor update PageMaker 3.0. The new 4.0 version is installed in a separate folder. If you leave 3.0 on your hard disk, then when you double-click on a 3.0 document, it will open in 3.0. To open a 3.0 document in 4.0, see 15.38.

So, here is a very brief rundown on **how to install PageMaker 4.**

1. Insert Disk 1.

2. The windows will automatically open (if they don't, double-click on the disk icon; then double-click on the folder titled "Utilities"). Double-click on the **Aldus Installer/Utility** icon.

3. You will get a window titled **Aldus Installer Main Window.** You will see some other windows on the screen; read them or ignore them, as you choose.

- In the Main Window, you'll see three checkboxes. You can choose to also install the Templates (see Section 12 for info on templates) and the Tutorial files (containing the files you will need if you want to go through the tutorial lessons in the PageMaker documenta-tion). Leave the boxes checked if you want to install the templates and/or tutorial files; otherwise uncheck them.

- Click **Install.**

4. Now you'll get a dialog box called **Aldus APD installation** that asks you to select the APDs you want to install. An APD is an Aldus Printer Description file (see 18.11–18.12). Hold the Shift key down and click on the name of your printer *and the name of any printer you may ever want to print to,* such as the one your service bureau uses. Also choose "General.apd."

- Click OK.

5. Now you'll get a dialog box called **Aldus filter installation** that asks you to select the filter(s) that you want to install (see 15.6–15.16 for info on filters). I know the list looks intimidating, but if you actually read it you will see it is just a list of word processing programs. **Import** filters allow you to place files created in that program; **export** filters allow you to export Page-Maker text into that program.

- Hold down the Shift key and click on any of the program names that you may want to *import text from* or *export text to*. Also, be sure to select any RTF filters, ASCII and Smart ASCII filters, and the Story Importer filter (which allows you to place stories from other PageMaker publications). If you are going to work with the Tutorial, install the "MS Word 4.0 import" filter.

- Click OK.

6. In a minute you'll get a chance to **personalize your copy of "PageMaker 4.0."** You must type your name, company, and serial number; it is not possible to leave any of those boxes blank. And it is difficult to type in a fake serial number. You must type the serial number exactly as it appears on your license agreement, including any hyphens, spaces, and zeros.

- When you click OK, you will be asked to confirm the data. It had better be right, because you won't be able to change it later.

7. Now you will get the **Install files** dialog box, telling you whether there is enough room on this disk to install the program, and asking where you want PageMaker to put the new folder that will contain the program. If you want the PageMaker folder right there on the hard disk, just click "Install." If you want the PageMaker folder inside another folder, double-click on the folder name in the list before you click "Install."

8. Now the installer will just roll along, putting PageMaker together. When it is finished with Disk 1, the disk will pop out and you will be asked to insert Disk 2. When Disk 2 pops out, insert Disk 3, and so on. A nice little window tells you exactly what is going on while you wait.

When it is all finished, you will have a new folder on your hard disk titled "Aldus PageMaker 4.0." This folder contains the application itself, as well as the Table Editor application, the templates and tutorial files (if you chose to install them), the Help file for providing online Help, and a couple other goodies. If you experience any trouble at all while installing, hang on to the installer files you see in there; they contain information about the installation. If you call Tech Support, they may want to know what the files say.

There will also be a folder inside your System folder titled "Aldus." That folder contains the APDs, the dictionaries, the filters, and a few other odds and ends.

Running PageMaker with 1 meg of RAM:

- "Save as…" regularly to keep the file size as small as possible (16.1–16.5; 16.25).

- Keep your System as small as possible: install only the fonts you use regularly; eliminate any unnecessary Desk Accessories, CDEVs, and INITs.

- Install the minimum number of filters and APDs.

- In the Story Editor, open only one window at a time, and be sure to *close* each window (Command W) before you return to the layout view. Don't edit the style sheet while in the Story Editor.

- Don't cut and paste large amounts at a time. Paste immediately after copying. If you have to cut/copy a large amount, then after you paste, copy a small word twice.

- Don't work faster than the computer can keep up with.

- Set the "Detailed graphics" option to either "Normal" or "Gray out" (1.216). Set the "Greek text below" option to a higher value (1.214).

Appendix D: Entry codes

The chart below provides the entry codes for **invisible characters.** They are indispensable when using the "Find" or the "Change" dialog boxes, or when formatting with the "Index format" dialog box. *These are not for typing regular text.*

To find, change, or enter this character:	Type this:
	The ^ symbol, a caret, is Shift 6.
Spacebar space	*type a space*
Non-breaking space *or type*	Option Spacebar ^S *or* ^s
Non-breaking slash	^/
Non-breaking hyphen	^~
Em space	^M *or* ^m
En space	^>
Thin space	^<
Any kind of blank space	^W *or* ^w
En dash	^=
Em dash	^_ *(Shift hyphen)*
Return	^P *or* ^p
Line break	^N *or* ^n
Tab	^T *or* ^t
Discretionary hyphen	^-
Automatic page number	^# *or* ^3
Index marker	^;
Caret	^^
Inline graphic (in the Story Editor)	Control Q
Wildcard character	^?

Appendix E: Alternate characters

These **alternate characters** can be entered directly into your text. In the Story Editor or in a dialog box, many of these characters will appear to be blank boxes. That's okay—if you are using an outline font (which you should be; 18.29–18.35), you will see the actual characters on your screen and they will print.

Character	Type it this way	What is it?
'	Option]	opening single quote
'	Option Shift]	apostrophe; closing single quote
"	Option [	opening double quote
"	Option Shift [	closing double quote
‹	Option Shift 3	opening single French quote (guillemets)
›	Option Shift 4	closing single French quote (guillemets)
«	Option \ *(notice that's a back slash)*	opening double French quote (guillemets)
»	Option Shift \	closing double French quote (guillemets)
-	Command - *(hyphen)*	discretionary hyphen (4.224–4.226; 4.239–4.241)
-	Command Option - *(hyphen)*	non-wordbreaking hyphen
–	Option - *(hyphen)*	en dash
—	Option Shift - *(hyphen)*	em dash
…	Option ;	ellipsis
®	Option r	registration symbol
©	Option g	copyright symbol
™	Option 2	trademark symbol
•	Option 8	bullet
·	Option Shift 9	raised period (·)
˙	Option h	really raised period (˙), or a dot
°	Option Shift 8	degree symbol
/	Option Shift 1	fraction bar (slash: /; fraction bar: ⁄)
fi	Option Shift 5	ligature for the f-and-i letter combination
fl	Option Shift 6	ligature for the f-and-l letter combination

The font of these three symbols will usually match the font in which you are typing.**

Char.	Type it this way	What is it?
œ	Option q	lowercase oe diphthong, or ligature
Œ	Option Shift q	uppercase OE diphthong, or ligature
æ	Option '	lowercase ae diphthong, or ligature
Æ	Option Shift '	uppercase AE diphthong, or ligature
¶	Option 7	paragraph symbol
§	Option 6	section symbol
†	Option t	dagger
‡	Option Shift 7	double dagger
◊	Option Shift v	diamond, lozenge
¢	Option 4 *(which is the dollar sign)*	U.S. cent
£	Option 3 *(pound sign: #)*	British pound sterling
¥	Option y *(y for yen)*	Japanese yen
¤	Option Shift 2	general currency symbol
¿	Option Shift / *(question mark)*	inverted question mark
¡	Option 1 *(exclamation point)*	inverted exclamation point
ß	Option s	German double s (ss) *or* Beta
ø	Option o	lowercase letter o with slash
Ø	Option Shift o	uppercase letter o with slash
≠	Option =	does-not-equal sign
≈	Option x	approximately-equals sign
≤	Option < *(above the comma)*	less-than-or-equal-to sign
≥	Option > *(above the period)*	greater-than-or-equal-to sign
±	Option Shift =	plus-or-minus sign
÷	Option /	division sign
√	Option v	radical sign; square root
ƒ	Option f	function symbol *or* freeze

Char.	Type it this way	What is it?
∫	Option b	integral symbol
∞	Option 5	infinity symbol
¬	Option l *(the letter el)*	logical NOT, negation symbol
‰	Option Shift e	salinity symbol
ı	Option Shift b	dotless i
ª	Option 9	feminine ordinal indicator
º	Option 0 *(zero)*	masculine ordinal indicator
Δ	Option j	uppercase delta
Σ	Option w	uppercase sigma; summation
Ω	Option z	uppercase omega
Π	Option Shift p	uppercase pi
π	Option p	lowercase pi
μ	Option m	lowercase mu
∂	Option d	lowercase delta
ˆ	Option Shift n	circumflex*
˜	Option Shift m	tilde*
¯	Option Shift , *(comma)*	macron*
˘	Option Shift . *(period)*	breve*
˙	Option h	dot*
˚	Option k	ring*

* *These accent marks cannot be placed above a letter, as can the accent marks on the next page. If you need to place one of these over a character, you can certainly do it by kerning extensively:* ō *(4.165–4.182).*

** *If you need one of these symbols as a serif or a sans serif and you can't get it in your current font, use the font* **Symbol** *and these key combinations:*

serif	sans serif
® Option [	® Option Shift 0 (zero)
© Option Shift [	© Option Shift w
™ Option]	™ Option Shift e

These are the five main **accent marks:**

~	tilde
¨	diaeresis (umlaut)
^	circumflex
´	acute
`	grave

Some of these accent marks you apply in two steps, where the accent is just applied above a regular character. For others, you can press a keyboard combination to get the character with its accent mark attached. The accent marks over capital letters may look a little odd on the screen (sometimes they scrunch the letter and sometimes most of the accent disappears). When you redraw the screen (change view, etc.), the accent marks will re-appear. They print fine.

Tilde	Press	Let go, then press
~	Option n	Spacebar
ã	Option n	a
Ã	Option n	Shift a
ñ	Option n	n
Ñ	Option n	Shift n
õ	Option n	o
Õ	Option n	Shift o

Diaeresis	Press	Let go, then press
¨	Option u	Spacebar
ä	Option u	a
Ä	Option u	Shift a
ë	Option u	e
Ë	Option Shift u	
ï	Option u	i
Ï	Option Shift f	
ö	Option u	o
Ö	Option u	Shift o
ü	Option u	u
Ü	Option u	Shift u
ÿ	Option u	y
Ÿ	Option Shift `	

(` is next to 1, or next to Spacebar; the same key as the regular ~ key)

Circumflex	Press	Let go, then press
^	Option i	Spacebar
â	Option i	a
Â	Option Shift r	
ê	Option i	e
Ê	Option Shift t	
î	Option i	i
Î	Option Shift d	
ô	Option i	o
Ô	Option Shift j	
û	Option i	u
Û	Option Shift z	

Acute	Press	Let go, then press
´	Option e	Spacebar
á	Option e	a
Á	Option e *or* Option Shift y	Shift a
é	Option e	e
É	Option e	Shift e
í	Option e	i
Í	Option e *or* Option Shift s	Shift i
ó	Option e	o
Ó	Option e *or* Option Shift h	Shift o
ú	Option e	u
Ú	Option e *or* Option Shift ;	Shift u

Grave	Press	Let go, then press
`	Option `	Spacebar

(` is next to 1, or next to Spacebar; the same key as the regular ~ key)

à	Option `	a
À	Option `	Shift a
è	Option `	e
È	Option ` *or* Option Shift i	Shift e
ì	Option `	i
Ì	Option ` *or* Option Shift g	Shift i
ò	Option `	o
Ò	Option ` *or* Option Shift l *(letter el)*	Shift o
ù	Option `	u
Ù	Option ` *or* Option Shift x	Shift u

Miscellaneous:	Press:
å	Option a
Å	Option Shift a
ç	Option c
Ç	Option Shift c

	a	b	c	d	e	f	g	h	i	j	k	l	m	n	o	p	q	r	s	t	u	v	w	x	y	z
Zapf																										
Shift																										
Option																										
Opt Shift																										

	`	1	2	3	4	5	6	7	8	9	0	-	=	[	]	\	;	'	,	.	/	spacebar
Zapf																							
Shift																							
Option																							
Option Shift																							

Opt Sh /	①	Opt u Spcbar	①	Opt d	❶	Opt Spcbar	❶	n (outline)	□	(and shadow)	□
Opt 1	②	Opt =	②	Opt w	❷	Opt ` *then* Sh a	❷	l (outline)	○	(and shadow)	○
Opt l	③	Opt Sh '	③	Opt Sh p	❸	Opt n *then* Sh a	❸	t (outline)	▽	(and shadow)	▽
Opt v	④	Opt Sh o	④	Opt p	❹	Opt n *then* Sh o	❹	s (outline)	△	(and shadow)	△
Opt f	⑤	Opt 5	⑤	Opt b	❺	Opt Sh q	❺	u (outline)	◇	(and shadow)	◇
Opt x	⑥	Opt Sh =	⑥	Opt q	❻	Opt q	❻	Opt 6 (outline)	♡	(and shadow)	♡
Opt j	⑦	Opt ,	⑦	Opt 0	❼	Opt -	❼				
Opt \	⑧	Opt .	⑧	Opt z	❽	Opt Sh -	❽	Sh]	"		
Opt Sh \	⑨	Opt y	⑨	Opt '	❾	Opt [	❾	Sh `	"		
Opt ;	⑩	Opt m	⑩	Opt o	❿	Opt Sh [	❿	Sh [	'		
								Sh \	'		

You can't make the outline bold.

Type a dingbat into its own text block; rotate the text (Element menu).

Opt *means press the Option key.* Sh *means press the Shift key.* Spcbar *means press the Spacebar.*

From the Toolbox:

➤ Pointer tool   1.144; 2.12

I Text tool; the I-beam   3.12

+ Lines and shapes;
the crossbar cursor   2.11

⊐ Cropping tool   9.104

Loaded text icons:

▦ Manual flow   3.83; 3.84

▥ Autoflow   3.83; 3.86

▥ Semi-autoflow   3.83; 3.85

▤ Sum icon in
Table Editor   17.117

Loaded graphic icons:

▣ Paint-type (MacPaint)   9.6; 9.92

▨ PICT format   9.14; 9.92

▦ TIFF format   9.22; 9.92

▧ EPS format   9.29; 9.92

▦ Scrapbook file   9.92; 9.96

Text block windowshade loops:

⊓ Very beginning of story   3.100

⊕ Has more text preceding   3.100

⊔ Very end of story   3.101

⊕ Has more text following,
and it is placed on a page   3.102

▽ Has more text following,
but it has not been placed
anywhere   3.102

Stretching and moving text and graphics:

↕ Vertical stretch   2.43; 9.101

↔ Horizontal stretch   2.43; 9.101

↘ Bi-directional stretch   2.43; 9.101

↙ Bi-directional stretch   2.43

⊕ Moving a text block
or an independent
graphic   2.26; 9.98

▤ Moving an inline graphic
vertically on its baseline   9.201

Story Editor:

· Space marker   8.43

¶ Paragraph marker   8.43

→ Tab marker   8.43

↵ Line-break marker
(Shift Return)   8.43

▦ Automatic page number
marker   8.18

▮ Index marker   8.18

▨ Inline graphic marker   8.18

▯ End of story   8.18

▢ Special character that isn't
in the Story Editor font   8.61

Image control

◣ Preset setting: Normal   9.161

◥ Preset setting: Reverse   9.162

◢ Preset setting: Posterized   9.163

◤ Preset setting: Solarized   9.164

Links dialog box:

Blank; element is up-to-date
or is not linked   10.37

? Cannot find the linked
element's external file   10.41

◆ Linked external file has
been modified; internal
file will be updated
automatically   10.39

◇ Linked external file has
been modified; internal file
will **not** be updated
automatically   10.38

△ Both the internal and the
external files have been
modified   10.40

File compression codes:

(P) Moderate compression of
black-and-white or palette-
color TIFFs   9.109

(L) Maximum compression of
black-and-white or palette-
color TIFFs   9.109

(LD) Moderate compression of
grayscale or color TIFFs   9.109

(LD2) Maximum compression of
grayscale or color TIFFs   9.109

(U) Decompressed TIFF   9.109

Style sheet:

+ Style has an override   7.34

* Style is imported   7.35

Menus:

⇧ Shift key

⌘ Command key

Spacebar (blank, as in
Type Style "Normal")

… Dialog box will appear

▶ Submenu will appear

✓ Command is chosen, or "on"

⌊⌋ Grey items indicate command
cannot be used

Miscellaneous

☜ Grabber hand to move page
or to move cropped graphic
within frame   1.117; 9.104

? Menu-sensitive Help   20.3

⌛ Wait a minute or two

RM Right master page
automatic page number
placeholder   1.139a

LM Left master page
automatic page number
placeholder   1.139a

PB Pasteboard automatic page
number placeholder   1.121

Gray or yellow bar over text:
line violates the "Keeps" rules
or desired letter/word
spacing   1.217; 3.213

Gray box instead of
graphic image; set to
"Gray out"   9.112

Selection
marquee   1.169; 1.176;
    9.108

Everything on this page is done with the *text tool* chosen and with text selected or an insertion point flashing.

Select text
(3.123–3.137; also see 3.138)

One word	Double-click
One paragraph	Triple-click
A range of text	Press-and-drag
A large range of text	Click at one end, press Shift, click at the other end
Entire story	Click anywhere in the story, press Command A
With the keypad	See **Numeric keypad**
Deselect text	Click anywhere

Text formatting
(3.123–3.159)

Normal	Command Shift Spacebar
Bold	Command Shift B
Italic	Command Shift I
Outline	Command Shift D
Shadow	Command Shift W
Strikethru	Command Shift /
Underline	Command Shift U
All caps	Command Shift K
Small caps	Command Shift H
Superscript	Command Shift +
Subscript	Command Shift - (hyphen)
Remove kerning	Command Option K
Remove tracking	Command Shift Q
Remove set width	Command Shift X
Apply autoleading	Command Shift A

Paragraph alignment
(3.152–3.158)

Align left	Command Shift L
Align right	Command Shift R
Align center	Command Shift C
Justify	Command Shift J
Force justify	Command Shift F

Kern
(4.165–4.186; with arrow keys: 4.182)

Fine kern closer	Option Delete
Fine kern apart	Option Shift Delete
Coarse kern closer	Command Delete
Coarse kern apart	Command Shift Delete
Remove kerning	Command Option K
Remove tracking	Command Shift Q

Change point size
(3.142)

One point smaller	Command Option Shift <
One point larger	Command Option Shift >
One standard size smaller	Command Shift <
One standard size larger	Command Shift >

Text flow
(3.81–3.94)

Temporarily change Auto to Manual	Command
Temporarily change Manual to Auto	Command
Temporarily change to Semi-Auto	Shift
Interrupt Autoflow	Command Period
Unload the text without placing it	Click on the pointer tool, or press Command Spacebar

Numeric keypad
(1.223–1.225; 3.138)

Use the numeric keypad to move the insertion point. Hold the Shift key down to *select* the text as the insertion point moves. Use the text tool, of course.

With Caps Lock down, you will type numbers. Or you can press Clear (num lock) to use the numbers.

Left one character	4, or LeftArrow
Left one word	Command 4
To beginning of line	7
To beginning of sentence	Command 7
Right one character	6, or RightArrow
Right one word	Command 6
To end of line	1
To end of sentence	Command 1
Up one line	8, or UpArrow
Up one paragraph	Command 8
Up a screen	9, or PageUp key
To top of story	Command 9, or Home key
Down one line	2, or DownArrow
Down one paragraph	Command 2
Down a screen	3, or PageDown key
To bottom of story	Command 3, or End key

Non-breaking spaces
(4.207–4.218)

Em space	Command Shift M
En space	Command Shift N
Thin space	Command Shift T
Fixed space	Option Spacebar
Non-breaking hyphen	Command Option -
Non-breaking slash	Command Option /

All the Graphic shortcuts are done with the *pointer tool* chosen.

Some functions have more than one shortcut; for the sake of clarity, only one is printed here. The Delete key is also known as the Backspace key on some keyboards.

What do I do?

People always ask me what I do and I don't quite know what to say. I've written a few books, but I really wouldn't say I'm a Writer. My background is in graphic design, but I wouldn't call myself a Designer. I do have a particular passion for typography, but no one makes a living being a Typographer. I dance as often as I can, but I'm not really a Dancer. I love to teach, but the college only lets me teach part time so I certainly don't make a living as a Teacher. I suppose I could call myself a Consultant like everyone else, but I do hate to do what everyone else does. I am truly a mother of the three greatest kids in the world, but I've never had the privilege of having Mother as my sole occupation. If I had the option, I would really like to study world literature and live theater and languages. I love to overcome obstacles. I work hard. I throw great parties. I sincerely believe that your attitude is your life.

What do I do? Well, I wear a lot of different hats.

Robin Williams

This book was created entirely
  in PageMaker 3.02, 4.0, and 4.01.

The first half of the book was created
  on an SE with one meg of RAM.
  The second half was created
  on a Mac IIcx with lots of RAM.
  Thank goodness.

Main fonts are ITC Baskerville and Futura,
  both from Adobe. Lots of other fonts
  from LaserMaster, Bitstream, Emigre,
  and Linotype-Hell.

Concept, design, layout, and production
  by Robin. Me.

Pampered out of the Lino by Janet Butcher,
  Desktop Composition Center,
  Petaluma, California.

Beautiful cover design by Gail Johnston.

Order Form

Peachpit Press
2414 Sixth Street ▾ Berkeley ▾ California ▾ 94710
phone: 800.283.9444 or **415.527.8555**
fax: 415.524.9775

	Canned Art: Clip Art for the Macintosh (book only)	29.95	
	Canned Art: Clip Art for the Macintosh (book and disks)	39.95	
	HELP! The Art of Computer Technical Support	19.95	
	Inside PostScript	37.50	
	Learning PostScript: A Visual Approach	22.95	
	The Little Mac Book	12.95	
	The Little System 7 Book	12.95	
	The Macintosh Font Book, 2nd Edition	23.95	
	The Mac is not a typewriter	9.95	
	PageMaker 4: An Easy Desk Reference	29.95	
	The QuarkXPress Book	24.95	
	Real World FreeHand 3	24.95	
	PageMaker 4: Visual QuickStart Guide	12.95	
	TypeStyle: How to Choose and Use Type	24.95	
	Canvas 3.0: The Book	21.95	

California residents only: 7% sales tax.
UPS ground shipping: $4 for first item; $1 each additional.
UPS 2nd day air: $8 for first item, $2 each additional.
Air mail to Canada: $6 first item, $3 each additional.
Air mail overseas: $14 each item

Subtotal	
(CA only) **7% Tax**	
Shipping	
TOTAL	

Name

Company

Address

City

State   Zip

Phone

▽ Check enclosed
▽ Company Purchase Order Number _____
▽ Visa
▽ MasterCard

Credit Card Number

Expiration Date

Your satisfaction is unconditionally guaranteed or your money will be cheerfully refunded!

More from Peachpit Press . . .

CANNED ART: CLIP ART FOR THE MACINTOSH
▼ *Erfert Fenton and Christine Morrissett*

A fully-indexed sample book showing over 15,000 pieces of clip art available from 35 different companies. Includes tear-out coupons for over $1,000 in discounts on commercial clip art. The two optional All Star Sample Disks contain 61 pieces of clip art. *(825 pages)*

HELP! THE ART OF COMPUTER TECHNICAL SUPPORT
▼ *Ralph Wilson*

The first practical guide on the subject of technical support. Explains how to set up and manage a technical support operation. *(260 pages)*

LEARNING POSTSCRIPT: A VISUAL APPROACH
▼ *Ross Smith*

An easy show-and-tell tutorial on the PostScript page description language. *(426 pages)*

THE LITTLE MAC BOOK
▼ *Robin Williams*

A quick and accessible guide to the Macintosh. Includes numerous tips, tricks, and charts of keyboard shortcuts. *(112 pages)*

THE MACINTOSH FONT BOOK, 2ND EDITION
▼ *Erfert Fenton*

Everything you ever wanted to know about buying and using fonts on the Mac. *(360 pages)*

THE MAC IS NOT A TYPEWRITER
▼ *Robin Williams*

Tips and techniques for producing professional-level typography with a computer. *(72 pages)*

PAGEMAKER 4: AN EASY DESK REFERENCE
▼ *Robin Williams*

A reference book that lets you look up how to do specific tasks with PageMaker 4. *(784 pages)*

REAL WORLD FREEHAND 3
▼ *Olav Martin Kvern*

An insider's guide to the latest release of this popular Mac drawing program. *(350 pages)*

PAGEMAKER 4: VISUAL QUICKSTART GUIDE
▼ *Webster & Associates*

Learn the basics of PageMaker 4 with this visually oriented, highly illustrated guide for beginners *(160 pages)*

TYPESTYLE: HOW TO CHOOSE AND USE TYPE ON A PERSONAL COMPUTER
▼ *Daniel Will-Harris*

How to choose laser printer fonts, how to decide which fonts mix well together, etc. Covers not only the mechanics, but also the psychology of type. *(368 pages)*

CANVAS 3.0: THE BOOK
▼ *Deke McClelland*

The first book on this popular and newly enhanced graphics program for the Macintosh. *(300 pages)*

Everything on this page is done with the *text tool* chosen and with text selected or an insertion point flashing.

Select text
(3.123–3.137; also see 3.138)

One word	Double-click
One paragraph	Triple-click
A range of text	Press-and-drag
A large range of text	Click at one end, press Shift, click at the other end
Entire story	Click anywhere in the story, press Command A
With the keypad	See **Numeric keypad**
Deselect text	Click anywhere

Text formatting
(3.123–3.159)

Normal	Command Shift Spacebar
Bold	Command Shift B
Italic	Command Shift I
Outline	Command Shift D
Shadow	Command Shift W
Strikethru	Command Shift /
Underline	Command Shift U
All caps	Command Shift K
Small caps	Command Shift H
Superscript	Command Shift +
Subscript	Command Shift - (hyphen)
Remove kerning	Command Option K
Remove tracking	Command Shift Q
Remove set width	Command Shift X
Apply autoleading	Command Shift A

Paragraph alignment
(3.152–3.158)

Align left	Command Shift L
Align right	Command Shift R
Align center	Command Shift C
Justify	Command Shift J
Force justify	Command Shift F

Kern
(4.165–4.186; with arrow keys: 4.182)

Fine kern closer	Option Delete
Fine kern apart	Option Shift Delete
Coarse kern closer	Command Delete
Coarse kern apart	Command Shift Delete
Remove kerning	Command Option K
Remove tracking	Command Shift Q

Change point size
(3.142)

One point smaller	Command Option Shift <
One point larger	Command Option Shift >
One standard size smaller	Command Shift <
One standard size larger	Command Shift >

Text flow
(3.81–3.94)

Temporarily change Auto to Manual	Command
Temporarily change Manual to Auto	Command
Temporarily change to Semi-Auto	Shift
Interrupt Autoflow	Command Period
Unload the text without placing it	Click on the pointer tool, or press Command Spacebar

Numeric keypad
(1.223–1.225; 3.138)

Use the numeric keypad to move the insertion point. Hold the Shift key down to *select* the text as the insertion point moves. Use the text tool, of course.

With Caps Lock down, you will type numbers. Or you can press Clear (num lock) to use the numbers.

Left one character	4, or LeftArrow
Left one word	Command 4
To beginning of line	7
To beginning of sentence	Command 7
Right one character	6, or RightArrow
Right one word	Command 6
To end of line	1
To end of sentence	Command 1
Up one line	8, or UpArrow
Up one paragraph	Command 8
Up a screen	9, or PageUp key
To top of story	Command 9, or Home key
Down one line	2, or DownArrow
Down one paragraph	Command 2
Down a screen	3, or PageDown key
To bottom of story	Command 3, or End key

Non-breaking spaces
(4.207–4.218)

Em space	Command Shift M
En space	Command Shift N
Thin space	Command Shift T
Fixed space	Option Spacebar
Non-breaking hyphen	Command Option -
Non-breaking slash	Command Option /

Moving to pages (1.97–1.107)

To next page	Command Tab
To previous page	Command Shift Tab
From master page, return to layout page	Command Tab
Jump six page icons	Press Shift, and click on either page icon arrow
Instant scroll to last page icon	Press Command, and click on right page icon arrow
Instant scroll to first page icon	Press Command, and click on left page icon arrow
Go to page... number of page	Command G; enter

Change page view
Use any tool (1.107–1.116)

To Actual Size	Press Command Option, and click on the area to view
To Fit in Window	Command W; or Command Option, click
To 200%	Command Option Shift, and click on the area you want to view
To Mini-View	Press Shift while you choose "Fit in Window" from the menu
To 400%	Command 4
To 25%	Command 0 (zero)
To 50%	Command 5
To 75%	Command 7

Miscellaneous

Select entire story	With the **text tool**, click anywhere in story; press Command A
Select all objects (text blocks and graphics)	With the **pointer tool** selected, press Command A
Cancel out of most dialog boxes	Press Command period
Cancel out of nested dialog boxes	Press Command Option Period
OK out of dialog boxes	Return or Enter
OK out of nested dialog boxes	Option Return
View actual fonts	Press-and-hold Option while choosing "Font"
Edit style sheet	Command-click on style name in Style palette
Edit color style sheet	Command-click on color name in Color palette
Index entry	Command Shift ;
Switch to pointer tool	Command Spacebar
Recompose text	Press Option while choosing "Hyphenation"
Move publication page	Option; press-and-drag
Menu-sensitive Help	Command ?, or Help key
Cancel Help	Command Period, or click in the Toolbox
Power paste	Command Option V
Print with the Apple driver	Press Option while choosing "Print..." from the File menu

All the Graphic shortcuts are done with the *pointer tool* chosen.

Graphics (Section 9)

Select an object under another layer (1.172)	Hold the Command key down; click. Each click will select an object on the next layer deep.
Restrain a PageMaker-drawn line to 45° angles, a rectangle to a square, or an oval to a circle	Hold the Shift key down while drawing a line, a rectangle, or an oval.
Change a PageMaker-drawn rectangle into a square, or an oval into a circle	Hold the Shift key down. Point to a handle; press and count to three.
Straighten a crooked PageMaker-drawn line	Hold the Shift key down; press on a handle.
Resize a graphic proportionally	Hold the Shift key down while dragging a handle.
Resize a bitmapped graphic to fit the resolution of your printer	Hold the Command key while resizing; (see 9.103).
Restore a graphic to its original proportions	Hold the Shift key down. Point to a handle; press and count to three.
Temporarily view a grayscale image at high-res	Hold the Control key anytime you redraw the screen (see 9.115)
Compress a TIFF or a MacPaint graphic as you place it (9.109)	When you are about to place the file, press the Command, Option, and Shift keys before you click OK. Hold the keys to the count of 5.

Some functions have more than one shortcut; for the sake of clarity, only one is printed here. The Delete key is also known as the Backspace key on some keyboards.